www.wadsworth.com

www.wadsworth.com is the World Wide Web site for Wadsworth and is your direct source to dozens of online resources.

At www.wadsworth.com you can find out about supplements, demonstration software, and student resources. You can also send email to many of our authors and preview new publications and exciting new technologies.

www.wadsworth.com
Changing the way the world learns®

Juvenile Justice

Fourth Edition

Kären M. Hess, PhD
Normandale Community College

Robert W. Drowns
Metropolitan State University (late of affiliation)

THOMSON
WADSWORTH

Australia • Canada • Mexico • Singapore
Spain • United Kingdom • United States

THOMSON

★ ™

WADSWORTH

Executive Editor, Criminal Justice: Sabra Horne

Editorial Assistant: Elise Smith

Technology Project Manager: Susan DeVanna

Marketing Manager: Dory Schaeffer

Marketing Assistant: Andrew Keay

Advertising Project Manager: Stacey Purviance

Project Manager, Editorial Production: Matt Ballantyne

Art Director: Vernon Boes

Art Editors: Yvo/Carolyn Deacy

Print/Media Buyer: Karen Hunt

Permissions Editor: Sarah Harkrader

Production Service: Peggy Francomb, Shepherd, Inc.

Photo Researcher: Suzie Wright

Copy Editor: Cindy Blum

Cover Designer: Bill Stanton

Cover Image: Person jumping wall © Allan Davey/Masterfile; Broken store window © F. Hirdes/Masterfile

Compositor: Shepherd, Inc.

Text and Cover Printer: Phoenix Color Corp, Book Tech Park

Printed in the United States of America

1 2 3 4 5 6 7 07 06 05 04 03

For more information about our products, contact us at:
Thomson Learning Academic Resource Center
1-800-423-0563
For permission to use material from this text, contact us by:
Phone: 1-800-730-2214
Fax: 1-800-730-2215
Web: http://www.thomsonrights.com

ExamView® and ExamView Pro® are registered trademarks of FSCreations, Inc. Windows is a registered trademark of the Microsoft Corporation used herein under license. Macintosh and Power Macintosh are registered trademarks of Apple Computer, Inc. Used herein under license.

Library of Congress Control Number: 2003114115

ISBN 0-534-63020-0

Wadsworth/Thomson Learning
10 Davis Drive
Belmont, CA 94002-3098
USA

Asia
Thomson Learning
5 Shenton Way #01-01
UIC Building
Singapore 068808

Australia/New Zealand
Thomson Learning
102 Dodds Street
Southbank, Victoria 3006
Australia

Canada
Nelson
1120 Birchmount Road
Toronto, Ontario M1K 5G4
Canada

Europe/Middle East/Africa
Thomson Learning
High Holborn House
50/51 Bedford Row
London WC1R 4LR
United Kingdom

Brief Contents

Contents

2 The Theories behind the Evolution of the Contemporary Juvenile Justice Process, 42

PART III   The Contemporary Juvenile Justice System

7   The Law Enforcement Response to Abused and Neglected Children and Status Offenders, 208

8   The Law Enforcement Response to Violent Juvenile Offenders, 246

PART IV   21st Century Approaches to Delinquency

Foreword

The juvenile justice system—and there are those who would put quotation marks around "system"—has several specialized components. Each component has long been used to autonomy. Each too often has only superficial knowledge of the other components. And the components seldom work together, even though each may be managing the same problem.

The system should be more than this. Our children are entitled to more. Their lives and their parents' lives are greatly affected by the agencies' responses to their problems. Unfortunately the responses often are unintentionally inconsistent and noncomplimentary.

For the system to improve it must know itself. And that means that each professional within each component must know the functions and functioning of all other professionals in the system as they relate to the delinquency, misconduct and neglect of children. At the least the classic function of each component must be recognized.

- *The police*—must protect the safety of children and the public and investigate the behavioral facts.
- *Welfare and probation services*—must investigate the social facts and provide inpatient and outpatient counseling and supervision of children and their parents.
- *Schools*—must educate children academically and, to a great extent, socially and must ensure peace within their walls.
- *Lawyers*—must stand for their clients, advocating the views of each, whatever they may be.
- *Service providers*—must have treatments that can reunite families and prevent a recurrence of the misconduct that initiated the public's intervention.
- *The court*—must arbitrate and insist on rehabilitative and protective dispositions, and must use force and power within the confines of statutes and the Constitution to ensure due execution of these dispositions.

Each should perform its function knowledgeable of what the others are or may do and of the impact each may have on the others. There needs to be a coordination, a flow, a focus on the child and the family.

Beyond this primary interagency knowledge and respect, there must exist within families—whether the children's own or ones found for them or provided by the streets—solid values, caring and stability. Youths will reflect the values and stability of their families. Therefore the system cannot focus only on the child. It must look at the effective family for its influence on both the causes and the rehabilitation of misconduct, whether it be delinquency, status offenses or inadequate parental care.

Each component must look at the family as it affects its own particular function but, more, it must share its investigation and consider the investigations of others, moving toward a collaborative disposition involving the family that will be the most effective for the children.

And even this is not enough. Each professional working with children must understand children, their behavioral patterns and psychological development, and their changing emotional needs as they mature, seek independence and acquire sexual appetites. They must understand that boys don't become truant just because they don't like school, and that they join gangs because gangs can better satisfy emotional needs that their families have not. Children are not small adults. Legally, they lack the maturity to make important judgments under the stress of changing bodies and with the insistent need for independence.

The juvenile justice system must understand itself and become a system in the true sense of the word, working together toward the common goal of assisting children in trouble and protecting them and the public. The juvenile justice system must know itself. This book can be its primer.

Judge Emeritus Lindsay G. Arthur

Preface

Few social problems arouse public concern more than children who are neglected or abused and juveniles who exhibit antisocial behavior, whether it be minor offenses such as smoking or major crimes such as murder. Any such activities evoke a demand from society for corrective action.

Theories about why juveniles exhibit delinquent behavior and about how to prevent it abound. It is an area charged with emotion. Because of this clear vision is imperative when considering how Americans raise, direct and guide their youths and how they try to make youths' activities conform to social standards, to shape the children's growth and that of the nation.

The causes of problematic youth activity present an intricate puzzle. No easy explanation fits the observed facts. Parents blame social and economic pressures along with lack of cooperation from schools and social services. The school, police, social agencies and the courts blame parents and each other.

What society is willing to call juvenile violations of the law depends in part on what it thinks it can do about the behavior in question. The effectiveness of rehabilitation facilities, social service placements, the family and youth reform depends on their recognized influence on the control of behavior.

Although the rehabilitation of youthful offenders is a worthy goal, society lacks a proven way to accomplish it. Society is always faced with the difficult task of weighing individual liberties against protecting its members from harm.

To focus on only one part of the youth problem without a knowledge of the system in which it is embedded can result in a distorted or misleading interpretation of the juvenile justice system. Not only must the system concern itself with youths who break the law, it must also be responsible for children who are abandoned, neglected or abused—no small responsibility. The latter children are in dire need of protection and help. Yet often they are placed in the same facilities as juvenile delinquents. Further, such children are at much greater risk of becoming delinquents than are children who have not been mistreated.

Juvenile justice is, indeed, a complex topic, and the literature on it is vast. The purpose of this text is to discuss as many key issues as possible. Each section is but a small window into an extensive, complicated area. An understanding of youths, their protection and control must be based on an awareness of youth behavior and the total juvenile justice system.

Organization of the Text

Part I of this text describes the evolution of the juvenile justice system from its historical and philosophical roots (Chapter 1) through its evolution in the United States during the 20th century (Chapter 2). Part II describes the nation's youths, how they grow and develop, the influence of family, school and community (Chapter 3) and the major classifications of youths with whom the juvenile justice system interacts: youths who are neglected, abused, victimized and missing (Chapter 4); those who are status offenders and nonviolent delinquents (Chapter 5) and serious, chronic and violent juvenile offenders (Chapter 6).

Part III takes an up-close look at the contemporary juvenile justice system and its three major components: law enforcement, the juvenile/family court and corrections. The first area of discussion focuses on the law enforcement response to abused/neglected children and status offenders (Chapter 7). Next the law enforcement response to violent offenders, including school shooters and gang members is discussed (Chapter 8). Then the juvenile court and existing alternatives at intake are described (Chapter 9). Next the juvenile court process is discussed from intake to disposition (Chapter 10). This is followed by a look at juvenile corrections (Chapter 11). The section concludes by placing the juvenile justice system within its larger context, the community, and it examines the role of that larger community (Chapter 12). Part IV goes from the theoretical to everyday practices and programs being conducted in the juvenile justice system. It includes current approaches to prevention (Chapter 13) and treatment (Chapter 14). The text concludes with a discussion of the need for rethinking juvenile justice and how it might look and function in the 21st century (Epilogue).

Caring for children in need of protection or correction is a proper concern of society, not just the law enforcement community and others within the juvenile justice system. This concern carries with it the need to be informed, to take into account opposing viewpoints and to keep the principles of justice and fairness in the forefront.

New to This Edition

The fourth edition of *Juvenile Justice* has been completely updated; all sources except "classics" were published between 2000 and 2004—more than 500 new references. All statistics are the most recent available. The text has also been reorganized, condensing the material on child development and greatly expanding the third and fourth parts to focus on the components of the juvenile justice system and exemplary programs in prevention and treatment. Specific changes within each chapter include:

- **Chapter 1 Separate Justice: Philosophical and Historical Roots of the Juvenile Justice System:** Public support for tougher policies directed at juvenile offenders signal a reversal of the judicial due process focus of the previous two decades; crime control period added to the timeline.

- **Chapter 2 The Theories behind the Evolution of the Contemporary Juvenile Justice Process:** Restorative justice is introduced, as are the social disorganization model, the contemporary juvenile justice system structure and process, and a comparison of the juvenile and the criminal justice systems. Diversion is also introduced.

- **Chapter 3 Growth and Development: The First 18 Years:** Combines former Chapters 3 and 4, adding the two major peer influences that can lead to delinquency; how substance abuse correlates with delinquency; how the American Dream may be related to crime; the problem of homelessness for many young people; what family-related risk factors might lead to delinquency; the No Child Left Behind legislation; zero-tolerance policies; and full-service community schools.

- **Chapter 4 Neglected, Abused, Victimized and Missing Children and Youths:** Additions include the three components of child abuse and neglect laws; additional common physical conditions that can be mistaken for physical abuse; illegal child labor; sexual abuse and the Internet; polygamist Tom Green; the abduction of Elizabeth Smart; the minimalist and maximalist positions on ritualistic abuse by satanic cults; Amber Alert; and common warning signs of suicide.

- **Chapter 5 Status Offenders and Nonviolent Delinquents:** The effectiveness of curfew laws and the question of whether they are constitutional; the 2001 Harvard School of Public Health College Alcohol study; the decline in arrests for status offenses; computer delinquents; streaming; the decline in juvenile arrests for property crimes; and risk factors for delinquency by domain and age.

- **Chapter 6 Serious, Chronic and Violent Juvenile Offenders:** Two trajectories for youth violence identified by the surgeon general; when most youth violence begins and ends; the hazards of labeling a youth a psychopath; viewing most youths with conduct disorders as mentally ill; serious child delinquents; predictors of violent behavior; myths about youth violence; the decline in juvenile arrests for violent juvenile crime continues; expanded school crime and violence, including bullying; myths about school shooters; childhood predictors of joining and remaining in a gang; and the juvenile justice perspective versus the public health perspective on juveniles.

- **Chapter 7 The Law Enforcement Response to Abused and Neglected Children and Status Offenders:** Challenges involved in investigating crimes against children and missing children reports; sample protocol for investigating crimes against children; the juvenile holdover; the Virginia model SRO program; and the SHIELD program model.

- **Chapter 8 The Law Enforcement Response to Violent Juvenile Offenders:** Using directed patrol to reduce gun violence; the Boston Gun Project—Operation Ceasefire; four categories of threats; the four-pronged threat assessment approach; controversial measures taken to make schools safer; a three-pronged approach to school security; crisis planning; security technology; proactive lock downs in schools; a key impediment to dealing with youth gangs; effective approaches to gang problems; civil injunctions; and pulling levers.

- **Chapter 9 The Juvenile Court and Alternatives at Intake:** A heavy emphasis on diversion, including specialized courts; possible basis for declaration of wardship; the possible results of an intake hearing; transferring juveniles to criminal court; the most common criteria for participating in drug court; restorative justice in action; the competency issue; and net widening.

- **Chapter 10 The Juvenile Court in Action:** The juvenile court team; four basic types of sentences; blended sentences; graduated sanctions;

respite care; social and legal issues involving juvenile court; confidentiality issues; quality of representation; racism and discrimination; expunging juvenile records; and improving juvenile court.

- **Chapter 11 The Response of Corrections:** Four types of interventions in a comprehensive graduated sanctions system; six performance-based standards for juvenile corrections; immediate and intermediate sanctions; school-based probation; drug testing and probation; alternative schools/education; disproportionate minority confinement; and juveniles sentenced to adult institutions.

- **Chapter 12 The Juvenile Justice System's Reliance on the Broader Community:** Keys to building safe schools and communities; the key elements of a successful career academy; community justice; community prosecution; community courts; community corrections; an in-depth description of the Office of Juvenile Justice and Delinquency Prevention (OJJDP) and its programs; the Internet Crimes against Children Task Force; partnerships between child welfare and juvenile justice services; partnerships with the schools; Project ACHIEVE; and linked strategies.

- **Chapter 13 Approaches to Prevention:** The Blueprints for Violence Prevention initiative; preventing delinquency through improved child protection services and councils; preserving families to prevent delinquency; promoting alternative thinking strategies; bullying prevention programs; numerous prevention programs; after-school programs; a reality-based approach to drug education; substance abuse education for American Indians; and effective and ineffective strategies to reduce gun violence.

- **Chapter 14 Approaches to Treatment:** The two primary characteristics of effective intervention programs; a key to managing delinquency cases in the community; four key elements of a community assessment center; three concerns related to assessment centers; the 8% problem/8% solution; the OJJDP comprehensive strategy for serious, violent and chronic juvenile offenders; multidimensional treatment foster care; functional family therapy; multisystemic therapy; numerous new treatment programs proved effective; treatment for youths with mental illness; treatment for juvenile sex offenders; and resiliency as a treatment approach.

- **Epilogue: Juvenile Justice at the Crossroads—100 Years Later:** Entirely new discussion of issues facing juvenile justice, choices to be made, controversial issues and a look to the future.

How to Use This Book

Juvenile Justice is more than a textbook; it is a planned learning experience. The more actively you participate in it, the better your learning will be. You will learn and remember more if you first familiarize yourself with the total scope of the subject. Read and think about the table of contents; it outlines the many facets of juvenile justice. Then follow these steps for *triple-strength learning* as you study each chapter:

1. Read the objectives at the beginning of the chapter. These are stated as "Do You Know" questions. Assess your current knowledge of each question. Examine any preconceptions you may hold. Glance through the terms presented to see if you can currently define them. Watch for them as you read—in bold print the first time they are defined in the text.

2. Read the chapter, underlining, highlighting or taking notes, whichever is your preferred style.

    a. Pay special attention to all information that is graphically highlighted. For example:

     Juvenile justice currently consists of a "one-pot" jurisdictional approach.

    The key concepts of the chapter are presented this way.

    b. Look up unfamiliar words in the glossary at the back of the book.

3. When you have finished reading a chapter, reread the "Do You Know" questions at the beginning of the chapter to make sure you can give an educated response to each question. If you find yourself stumped by one, find the appropriate section in the chapter and review it. Do the same thing for the "Can You Define" terms.

4. Finally read the discussion questions and be prepared to contribute to a class discussion of the ideas presented in the chapter.

By following these steps, you will learn more information, understand it more fully and remember it longer. It's up to you.

A Note: The material selected to highlight using the triple-strength learning instructional design includes only the chapter's key concepts. While this information is certainly important in that it provides a structural foundation for understanding the topic(s) discussed, do not simply glance over the "Do You Know" highlighted boxes and summaries and expect to master the chapter. You are also responsible for reading and understanding the material that surrounds these basics—the "meat" around the bones so to speak.

Exploring Further

The text also provides an opportunity for you to apply what you have learned or to go into specific areas in greater depth through InfoTrac® College Edition assignments and Internet assignments. Complete these as directed by the text or by your instructor. Be prepared to share your findings with the class.
Good learning!

Ancillaries

To further enhance your study of juvenile justice, several supplements are available:

The Instructor's Resource Manual for this edition has been revised and updated. It includes the following for every chapter in the text: learning objectives, key terms, a detailed chapter outline, a chapter summary, discussion topics/student activities, topically relevant Internet addresses, media resources, and an updated Test Bank. The Test Bank includes multiple choice, true/false, fill-in-the-blank, matching, and essay questions for each chapter.

The **ExamView** computerized testing component allows you to easily edit and import your own questions and graphics, as well as edit and maneuver existing questions and change test layouts. Tests appear on screen just as they will when printed. The ExamView software also allows you to test and grade online.

Acknowledgments

We would like to thank the reviewers of previous editions of *Juvenile Justice* for their constructive suggestions: Kelly J. Asmussen, Peru State College; Steve W. Atchley, Delaware Technical Community College; Jerald C. Burns; Patrick Dunworth; J. Price Foster, University of Louisville; Burt C. Hagerman; Patricia M. Harris; Frederick F. Hawley; James Paul Heuser; Robert Ives; James Jengeleski, Shippensburg University; Peter Kratcoski; Matthew C. Leone; Clarence Augustus Martin; Richard H. Martin, Elgin Community College; and Paul Steele, University of New Mexico.

For this fourth edition we would like to thank these reviewers for their numerous helpful suggestions: David Olson, Loyola University, Chicago; Roger McNally, SUNY Brockport; Dorinda Dowis, Colorado State University; Jennifer Allen, Western Illinois University; and Colleen Clark, Minnesota State University-Mankato.

A heartfelt thank you also to Christine M.H. Orthmann for her hours of research and word processing; and to Sabra Horne, executive editor; Matt Ballatyne, production editor at Wadsworth Publishing; and Peggy Francomb, production editor at Shepherd, Inc. Thanks to these editors for their attention to detail and their support throughout the revision process.

About the Authors

Kären M. Hess, Ph.D. Dr. Hess has written extensively in law enforcement and criminal justice, including these texts for Wadsworth Publishing Company: *Constitutional Law for the Criminal Justice Professional*, 2nd ed.; *Corrections for the 21st Century: Criminal Investigation*, 7th ed.; *Criminal Procedure; Introduction to Law Enforcement and Criminal Justice*, 7th ed.; *Introduction to Private Security*, 5th ed.; *Management and Supervision in Law Enforcement*, 4th ed.; *The Police and the Community: Strategies for the 21st Century*, 3rd ed.; *Police Operations*, 3rd ed.; and *Seeking Employment in Criminal Justice and Related Fields*, 4th ed.

She is also a frequent instructor for report writing workshops and seminars for law enforcement agencies and is a member of the English department at Normandale Community College and President of the Institute for Professional Development. Dr. Hess is a member of the Academy of Criminal Justice Sciences (ACJS), the American Society for Law Enforcement Trainers (ASLET), the International Association of Chiefs of Police (IACP), the National Criminal Justice Association, the National Council of Teachers of English, the National Institute of Justice (NIJ), the Police Executive Research Forum (PERF) and the Textbook and Academic Author's Association (TAA).

Robert W. Drowns, MS (1931–1996). Mr. Drowns was a retired police officer and an instructor at Metropolitan State University (Minnesota). In addition to conducting seminars and workshops on various aspects of juvenile justice, he was a consultant to the Office of Juvenile Justice and Delinquency Prevention (OJJDP).

Separate Justice: Philosophical and Historical Roots of the Juvenile Justice System

Children are our most valuable natural resource.
—Herbert C. Hoover

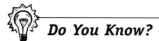

Do You Know?

- What *parens patriae* is and why it is important in juvenile justice?
- What institutions were developed for juveniles in the early nineteenth century?
- When and where the first house of refuge was opened in the United States?
- Who the child savers were and what their philosophy was?
- When and where the first juvenile court was established?
- How the first juvenile courts functioned?
- What functions probation was to serve within the juvenile court system?
- How Progressive Era proponents viewed crime? What model they refined?
- What resulted from the 1909 White House Conference on Youth?
- What act funded federal programs to aid children and families?
- What the Four Ds of juvenile justice refer to?
- What was established by the following key cases: *Kent v. United States, In re Gault, In re Winship, McKeiver v. Pennsylvania, Breed v. Jones, Schall v. Martin*?
- What effect isolating offenders from their normal environment might have?
- What the Uniform Juvenile Court Act provided?
- What the major impact of the 1970 White House Conference on Youth was?
- What the two main goals of the JJDP Act of 1974 were?
- What juvenile delinquency liability should be limited to according to the American Bar Association?

Can You Define?

Bridewell	deterrence	*lex talionis*
child	diversion	medical model
child savers	double jeopardy	minors
common law	due process	net widening
corporal punishment	guardianship	*parens patriae*
custodian	just deserts	PINS
custody	justice	poor laws
decriminalization	justice model	preventive detention
deinstitutionalization	juvenile justice	retaliation
delinquent act	Juvenile Justice and	status offenders
delinquent child	Delinquency	status offense
dependent	Prevention Act	youthful offender
deprived child	of 1974	youth service bureau
deserts	juvenile justice process	

INTRODUCTION

*J*uvenile justice. It is a system that provides a legal setting in which youths can account for their wrongs or receive official protection. It is also a term that necessarily implies distinct and separate treatment between youths and adults in the dispensing of justice. If **justice** is fairness in treatment by the law, why is this separation needed? Is justice not "one size fits all"? And how did this separation arise?

A separate justice system for **youthful offenders** (usually under age 18) is, historically speaking, relatively recent. An understanding of how this system evolved is central to understanding the system as it currently exists and the challenges it faces. It has been said that the historian is a prophet looking backward. History reveals patterns and changes in attitudes toward youths and how they are treated. The emphasis has changed from punishment to protection and back. As one philosophy achieves prominence, problems persist and critics clamor for change. History also reveals mistakes that can be avoided in the future as well as hopes and promises that remain unfulfilled.

This chapter begins with a brief review of social control in early societies and the development of a juvenile justice system in England. This is followed by a look at several distinct periods in the evolution of U.S. juvenile justice, beginning with the Puritan Period and how early colonists built upon the English foundation of juvenile justice to create a system unique to American circumstances. Next the Refuge Period, Juvenile Court Period and Juvenile Rights Period are explored. The fifth stage in the progression of American juvenile justice, the Crime Control Period, brings the discussion current and examines the prevailing philosophies that drive juvenile justice policy and practices today. The timeline in Figure 1.1 provides a guide and illustrates the overlapping influences on juvenile justice at different times in history. The chapter concludes with a discussion of the evolution of child, parent and state relationships and how the juvenile justice system is still evolving.

Social Control in Early Societies

Anthropologists tell us that people have banded together for companionship and protection since the earliest times. As early societies developed, they established rules to maintain social order and protect the safety of their members. Everyone, including its youths, was to conform to society's expectations. Those who broke the rules were severely punished. Most early societies treated all wrongdoings and criminal offenses alike. Children and adults were subject to the same rules and laws. They were tried under the same legal process and, when convicted, suffered the same penalties.

In primitive tribes, the accepted way to deal with members of the tribe who broke the rules was through **retaliation.** Such personal revenge was accepted when victims made their victimizers pay them back. As tribal leaders emerged, they began to help victims by imposing fines and punishments on wrongdoers. If the wrongdoer refused to pay the fine or accept the punishment, that person was declared an *outlaw,* outside the law, and was banished, probably to be eaten by wild animals or killed by the elements. Such social vengeance is the forerunner of our criminal law, taking *public* action against those who do not obey the rules.

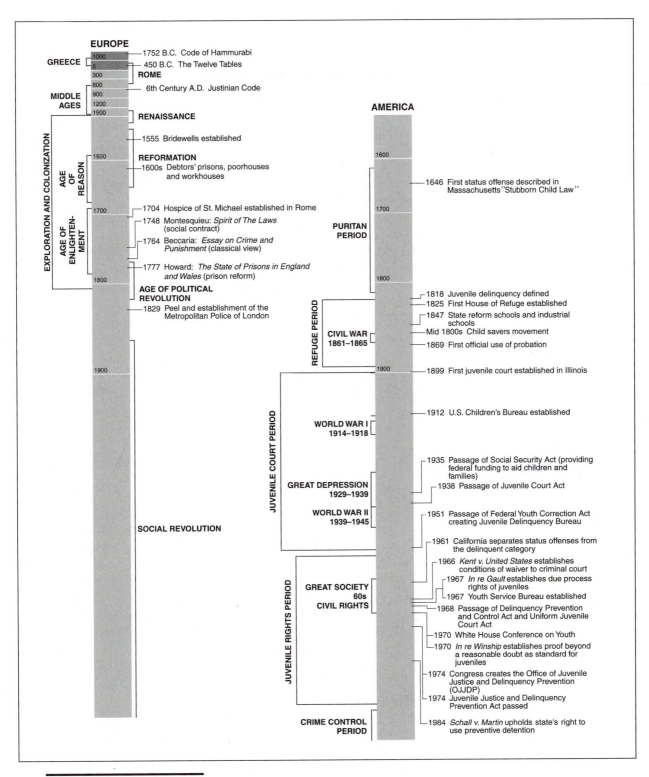

Figure 1.1
**Timeline of Significant
Dates in Juvenile Justice**

Ancient societies also confined wrongdoers, including children, in dungeons, castle towers and even animal cages.

As societies developed writing skills, they began recording their laws. Around 1752 B.C. the Babylonian king Hammurabi set forth rules for his kingdom establishing offenses and punishments. Hammurabi, like all kings in his day, was the supreme lawmaker, enforcer and judge. The Code of Hammurabi is viewed by historians as the first comprehensive description of a system to regulate behavior and at the same time take vengeance on those failing to comply. The Code of Hammurabi's main principle was that the strong shall not injure the weak. It established a social order based on individual rights and is the origin of the legal principle *lex talionis,* that is, an eye for an eye.

In early societies men were the heads of their families, charged with many responsibilities to their wives and children. In such patriarchal societies rebellion against a father, even by adult sons, was not tolerated. Punishment was swift and severe. For example, Item 195 of the Code of Hammurabi states: "If a son strikes his father, one shall cut off his hands" (Kocourek and Wigmore, 1951, p.427).

The father in ancient Roman culture also exercised unlimited authority over his family, being allowed to administer **corporal punishment** (inflict bodily pain) and even sell his children into slavery. One important concept from the Roman civilization that influenced the development of juvenile justice was *patria postestas*—referring to the absolute control fathers had over their children and the children's absolute responsibility to obey. This concept evolved into the doctrine of *parens patriae,* a basic tenet in our juvenile justice system.

Developments in England

Developments in England had a great influence on the juvenile justice system that would later develop in the United States.

The Middle Ages (A.D. 500–1500)

The earliest legal document written in English contained the laws of King Aethelbert (around A.D. 600). These laws made no special allowance for an offender's age. In fact several cases document children as young as 6 being hanged or burned at the stake.

Early in English history, the Church of Rome greatly influenced how children were viewed. Church doctrine stated that children younger than 7 had not yet reached the age of reason and, thus, could not be held liable for sins. English law adopted the same perspective. Under 7 years of age, children were not considered legally able to have the required intent to commit a crime. From ages 7 to 14, it was presumed they did not have such intent, but if evidence proved differently, children could be found guilty of committing crimes. After age 14, individuals were considered adults.

The Feudal Period

The Feudal Period falls near the end of the Middle Ages, covering roughly the ninth to the fifteenth centuries. In thirteenth-century England, **common law** (law of custom and usage) gave kings power of being the "father of his country." The king was perceived as guardian over the person and property of **minors,** who were considered wards of the state and, as such, received special protection.

The Latin phrase meaning "father of the country" is *parens patriae,* a doctrine critical to the evolution of juvenile justice.

 Parens patriae gave a king, through the courts, the right and responsibility to care for children.

Parens patriae was used to justify the state's intervention in the lives of its feudal lords and their children, and it placed juveniles between the civil and the criminal systems. The chancery courts allowed kings to control the wealthier class, and they also enabled the state to act in the best interests of its children. These courts heard issues involving guardianship, for example. The chancery courts did *not* have jurisdiction over children who committed crimes. Such youths were handled within the criminal court system.

The Renaissance

The Middle Ages are generally conceded to have ended with Columbus's discovery of America in 1492. The next two centuries in Europe, the Renaissance, marked the transition from medieval to modern times. The Renaissance was characterized by an emphasis on art and the humanities, as well as a more humanistic approach to criminal justice.

In 1555, London's **Bridewell** Prison became the first institution of its kind to control youthful beggars and vagrants. Based on an underlying theme of achieving discipline, deterrence and rehabilitation through work and severe punishment, Bridewell's goals were "to make [wayward youths] earn their keep, to reform them by compulsory work and discipline, and to deter others from vagrancy and idleness" (Grunhut, 1948, p.15).

The success of Bridewell led Parliament, in 1576, to pass a law calling for Bridewell-type institutions in every county. Modeled after the first prison, the

London's Bridewell was similar to a debtor's prison. It confined both children and adult "vagrants."

© 1995 Stock Montage

Bridewells combined the principles of the workhouse and the poorhouse, as well as the penal institutions' formalities. These Bridewells confined both children and adults who were considered idle and disorderly. Some parents placed their children into these Bridewells believing the emphasis on hard work would benefit the children.

During Elizabeth I's reign, the English passed **poor laws,** which established the appointment of overseers to *indenture* poor and neglected children into servitude. Such children were forced to work for wealthy families who, in turn, trained them in a trade, domestic service or farming. Such involuntary apprenticeships were served until the youths were 21 or older. These Elizabethan poor laws were the model for dealing with poor children for the next 200 years.

In England in 1563, the Statutes of Artificers inaugurated a system of *indenturing* and *apprenticeship* for children over 10 years of age. While the primary aim of the legislation was to ensure an adequate labor supply, the statutes also served to provide and promote an approved method of child care (Zietz, 1969, p.6).

In 1601 England proposed establishing large workhouses for children who could not be supported by their parents. The children would be placed there and "bred up to labor, principles of virtue implanted in them at an early age, and laziness be discouraged . . . and, settled in a way serviceable to the public's good and not bred up in all manners of vice" (Webb and Webb, 1927, p.52). This proposal was finally implemented with the passage of the Gilbert Act of 1782. The act decreed that all poor, aged, sick and those too infirm to work were to be placed in *poorhouses* (almshouses). Under the act, poor infants and children who could not go with their mothers were not placed in the poorhouse but with a "proper person," presumably in a family setting (de Scheveinitz, 1943, pp.20–21).

The Reform Movement

Historians have labeled the eighteenth and nineteenth centuries the Age of Enlightenment. One important milestone in the development of juvenile justice during this time was the founding of the London Philanthropic Society in 1817, one purpose of which was the reformation of juvenile offenders. The Society opened the first English house of refuge for children, a major shift from family-oriented discipline to institutional treatment.

An important reformer was John Howard (1726–1790), sheriff of Bedfordshire and often considered the father of prison reform. Howard undertook a study of England's prisons and traveled to other countries to study their prisons. One institution that greatly impressed Howard was the Hospice (hospital) of San Michele in Rome, commonly referred to as St. Michael.

Built in 1704 by Pope Clement XI, the Hospice was one of the first institutions designed exclusively for youthful offenders. Incorrigible youths under age 20 ate and worked in silence in a large central hall but slept in separate cells. The emphasis was on reading the Bible and hard work. An inscription placed over the door by the pope is still there: "It is insufficient to restrain the wicked by punishment unless you render them virtuous by corrective discipline." The pope said that the facility's purpose was "for the correction and instruction of profligate youth, that they who when idle were injurious, may when taught become useful to the state" (Griffin and Griffin, 1978, p.7).

The Development of Juvenile Justice in the United States

While the English justice system served as the basis for juvenile justice in America, a distinctively American system evolved in response to conditions unique to this country. Juvenile justice in the United States is generally recognized as having progressed through five distinct stages, beginning with the first European settlers to land in the New World, whose philosophies defined and shaped what is now referred to as the Puritan Period.

The Puritan Period (1646–1824)

The American colonists brought with them much of the English criminal justice system, including poor laws and the forced apprenticeship system for poor and neglected children. They also continued the centuries-old philosophy of *patria postestas,* whereby the father was given absolute authority over all family matters and harsh consequences befell children who misbehaved. In fact, early laws prescribed the death penalty for children who disobeyed their parents. The colonial Puritan philosophy regarding juvenile behavior was enacted into law in 1646 when Massachusetts passed the Stubborn Child Law, creating the first **status offense,** which is an act considered illegal for minors only. The law stood unrevised for more than 300 years.

Before 1800, under common law, age was a consideration in juvenile justice. Blackstone (1776, p.23) summarized the law on the responsibility of youths in these words: "Under seven years of age indeed an infant cannot be guilty of a felony; for then a felonious discretion is almost an impossibility in nature; but at eight years old he may be guilty of a felony." He went on to say that under age 14, although by law a youth may be adjudged incapable of discerning right from wrong (*doli incapax*), it appeared to the court and the jury that he *could* discern between good and evil (*doli capax*) (italics in original).

Colonial America handled juveniles much like petty thieves. After a warning, shaming or corporal punishment, the offender would return to the community. If accused of a major criminal act, the juvenile would proceed through the justice system as an adult. Trials and punishment were based on age, and anyone older than 7 was subject to the courts. Jails, the only form of incarceration, were primarily used for detention pending trial.

During this period, the fundamental mode of juvenile control was the family, with the church and other social institutions also expected to handle juvenile delinquents. Until the end of the eighteenth century, the family was also the main economic unit, with family members working together farming or in home-based trades. Children were important contributors to these family-based industries. The privileged classes found apprenticeships for their children so that they could learn marketable skills. The children of the poor, in contrast, often were bound out as indentured servants.

Then came the Industrial Revolution, which began at the end of the eighteenth century and forever changed the face of America. Families left the fields and farms and flocked to the cities to work in the factories. Child labor in these factories, which was used increasingly for the next 20 years, replaced the apprenticeship system. In fact, during this period, children comprised 47 to 55 percent of the cotton mill workforce (Krisberg and Austin, 1993, p.15).

Increasing industrialization, urbanization and immigration had created severe problems for families and their children. The social control once exerted by the family weakened—children in the workforce had to obey the demands of their bosses, often in conflict with the demands of their parents. In addition, poverty was increasing for many families. This combination of poverty and diminished family control set an "ominous stage," with some Americans fearing a growing "dangerous class" and seeking ways to "control the wayward youth who epitomized this threat to social stability" (Krisberg and Austin, p.15).

To counteract the continued breakdown of traditional forms of social control, communities created institutions for children where they could learn good work and study habits, live in a disciplined and healthy environment, and develop "character." During this time, and continuing into the early twentieth century, juveniles were handled by various civil courts and public institutions such as welfare agencies.

Five distinct, yet interrelated, institutions evolved to handle poor, abused, neglected, dependent and delinquent children brought before a court: (1) indenture and apprenticeship, (2) mixed almshouses (poorhouses), (3) private orphanages, (4) public facilities for dependent children and (5) jails.

A **dependent** child is one who needs special care and treatment because the parent, guardian or custodian is unable to provide for his or her physical or mental needs.

The rising concern and social reform that marked the turn of the nineteenth century saw reformers seeking to change laws and public policy as they affected children. During the early 1800s, reform efforts helped lead New York, Pennsylvania and Massachusetts to establish the first halfway houses in America (Keller and Alper, 1970, p.7). Another significant development during this period was an 1818 committee report that identified juvenile delinquency as a major cause of pauperism—the first public recognition of the term *juvenile delinquency.* This link between pauperism, or poverty, and delinquency remained an object of focus in juvenile justice throughout the 1800s and 1900s, receiving increased attention particularly among those who espoused various sociological causes of crime, such as social disorganization theorists and anomie/strain theorists. Indeed, the impact and influence of poverty on delinquency remains a pivotal issue in the field of juvenile justice today.

During 1820 and 1821, a philanthropic entity in New York called the Society for the Prevention of Pauperism conducted an extensive survey of U.S. prisons, the returns of which indicated a prevailing spirit of revenge in the treatment of prisoners. The resulting report criticized the imprisonment of individuals regardless of age or the severity of crime. In 1824, following adoption of the report, the Society reorganized to become the Society for the Reformation of Juvenile Delinquents in the City of New York, the purpose of which was to establish a reformatory. This development signaled a fundamental shift in the underlying philosophy concerning youths and the justice system and moved American juvenile justice into its next evolutionary stage—the Refuge Period.

Highlights of Puritan Period Reform

Philosophy

The consensus was that children were inherently sinful and in need of strict control and/or punishment when necessary. Most nonconforming children were of lower-class parentage; middle-class families protected their children from bad influences by controlling the behavior of less fortunate youths.

Treatment

Misbehaving children were generally controlled by familial punishment. External, community punishment and control were necessary only when the parents failed.

Policies

Communal legal sanctions were guided by the British tradition of common law, allowing children older than 7 to receive public punishment. Children could be punished publicly for several status offenses such as rebelliousness, disobedience and sledding on the Sabbath. Thus, separate systems of justice were set up for children and adults. Institutions created to care for orphaned and neglected children included almshouses and orphanages.

Adapted from materials of the Center for the Assessment of the Juvenile Justice System (Hawkins et al., 1980).

Refuge Period (1824–1899)

During the Refuge Period reformers were instrumental in creating separate institutions for youths such as houses of refuge, reform schools and foster homes. However, as Krisberg and Austin (p.17) note: "From the onset, the special institutions for juveniles housed together delinquent, dependent and neglected children—a practice still observed in most juvenile detention facilities today."

Houses of Refuge

 In 1824 the New York House of Refuge, the first U.S. reformatory, opened to house juvenile delinquents, defined in its charter as "youths convicted of criminal offenses or found in vagrancy."

The House of Refuge was the predecessor of today's training schools. Children were placed there by court order and usually stayed until they reached the age of maturity. The managers of the House believed children's behavior would change through vigilant instruction. Children who misbehaved were punished by losing certain rewarded positions or by whippings. The managers took the position that the public was responsible for disciplining children whose natural parents and guardians refused to do so. The labor of the House was contracted out for a fee to local businesses. Youths were given apprenticeships and training in practical occupations.

A typical day at the house began at sunrise and followed a highly disciplined, regimented routine. Morning prayers were followed by 1½ hours of school and then by work routines until the noon meal. After eating, youths returned to work until 5:00 P.M., at which time they ate, had 1½ hours of school followed by prayers, and then returned to their cells and the rule of silence (Pickett, 1969, p.49). Confinements were lengthy, and escapes were frequent.

Houses of refuge were operated by private philanthropic societies in many of the largest cities of the northeastern states. The authority of the state to send children to such houses of refuge under the doctrine of *parens patriae* was upheld in 1838 in Pennsylvania in *Ex parte Crouse.* In this case a mother claimed that her daughter was incorrigible and had her committed to the Philadelphia House of Refuge. The girl's father sought her release but was denied by the court, which stated:

> The object of the charity is reformation, by training its inhabitants to industry; by imbuing their minds with principles of morality and religion; by furnishing them with means to earn a living; and above all, by separating them from the corrupting influence of improper associates. To this end, may not the natural parents, when unequal to the task of education, or unworthy of it, be superseded by the *parens patriae,* or common guardian of the community?

However, many houses of refuge were prisons with harsh discipline, including severe whippings and solitary confinement. Despite public disapproval of the harsh disciplinary treatment and health hazards, 20 such institutions had opened in the United States by 1860.

Krisberg and Austin (p.16) suggest: "Although early 19th-century philanthropists relied on religion to justify their good works, their primary motivation was protection of their class privileges. Fear of social unrest and chaos dominated

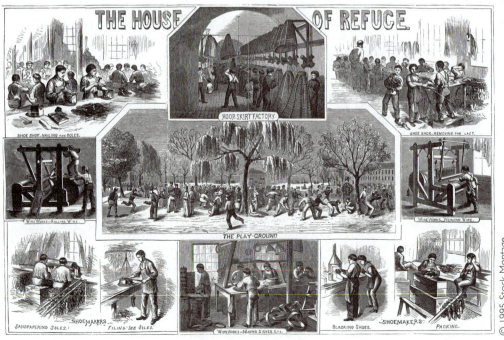

At the New York House of Refuge, children learned various trades and also engaged in physical activities.

their thinking. The rapid growth of a visible impoverished class, coupled with apparent increases in crime, disease and immorality, worried those in power."

From 1859 to 1890 many houses of refuge were replaced by reform schools. In many respects, however, reform schools were indistinguishable from the houses of refuge.

Reform Schools

By the middle of the nineteenth century, the more progressive states began to develop new institutions—*reform schools*—intended to provide discipline in a "homelike" atmosphere where education was emphasized. Although reform schools emphasized formal schooling, they also retained large workshops and the contract system of labor.

Foster Homes

While many states were building reform schools, New York in 1853 emphasized placing neglected and delinquent children in private *foster homes,* frequently located in rural areas. At the time, the city was viewed as a place of crime and bad influences, in contrast with the clean, healthy, crime-free country.

The foster home was to be the family surrogate used in all stages of the **juvenile justice process.** For a variety of reasons this concept faltered. Personality conflicts between foster parents and juvenile clients often caused disruption. Some foster parents were convicted of various abuses and neglect. In addition, the accreditation and monitoring of foster home licenses was inadequate and sometimes was ignored completely.

The Child Savers

Many reforms swept through the United States during the nineteenth century, including the child-saving movement, which began around the middle of the 1800s. The **child savers** believed that children's environments could make them "bad." These wealthy, civic-minded citizens tried to "save" unfortunate children by placing them in houses of refuge and reform schools.

These reformers were shocked that children could be tried in a criminal court like adults and be sentenced to jail with hardened criminals. The reformers believed that society owed more to its children than the guarantee of justice.

 The child savers were reformers whose philosophy was that the child was basically good and was to be treated by the state as a young person with a problem.

The reformers thought that children's contact with the justice system should not be a process of arrest and trial, but should seek answers to what the children are, how they have become what they are, and what society should do in the children's, as well as society's, best interests to save them from wasted lives. The child savers' motivating principles were (Task Force Report, 1976, p.6):

- Children should not be held as accountable as adult transgressors.
- The objective of juvenile justice is to help youngsters, to treat and rehabilitate them rather than punish.

In this engraving from an American newspaper of 1868, a 6 year-old sentenced for vagrancy to the House of Refuge on Blackwell's Island, New York City, pleads unavailingly for mercy for his first offense.

The Bettmann Archive/CORBIS

- Dispositions should be predicated on an analysis of the youth's special circumstances and needs.
- The system should avoid the punitive adversary role and formalized trappings of the adult criminal process.

The child savers were not entirely humanitarian, however; they viewed poor children as a threat to society. These children needed to be reformed to conform, to value hard work and to become contributing members of society. Anthony Platt's (1968, p.176) extensive research on this period led him to write:

> The child savers should in no sense be considered libertarians or humanists:
> 1. Their reforms did not herald a new system of justice but rather expedited traditional policies which had been informally developing during the nineteenth century.
> 2. They implicitly assumed the "natural" dependence of adolescents and created a special court to impose sanctions on premature independence and behavior unbecoming youth.
> 3. Their attitudes toward "delinquent" youth were largely paternalistic and romantic, but their commands were backed up by force.
> 4. They promoted correctional programs requiring longer terms of imprisonment, long hours of labor and militaristic discipline, and the inculcation of middle-class values and lower-class skills.

Other Developments During the Refuge Period

Organizations such as the Young Men's Christian Association (YMCA, 1851) and the Young Women's Christian Association (YWCA, 1861) provided recreation and counseling services to youths to "keep normals normal," thereby preventing delinquency.

Highlights of Refuge Period Reform

In the nineteenth century, children were protected from confinement in jails, prisons and institutions by the opening of houses of refuge. Responsibilities shifted back and forth between the private and public sectors. Chicago, as early as 1861, provided a local commission to hear and determine petty cases of boys from 6 to 17 years old. Between 1878 and 1898 Massachusetts established a statewide system of probation to aid the court in juvenile matters, a method of corrections currently used in every state in the United States.

The same period saw the regulation of child labor, the development of special services for handicapped children and the growth of public education. There was a growing acceptance of public responsibility for the protection and care of children. However, no legal machinery yet existed to handle juveniles who needed special care, protection and treatment as wards of the state rather than as criminals.

Philosophy

Poverty was a crime that could be eliminated by removing children from offending environments and reforming their unacceptable conduct.

Youth problems increased as by-products of rapid urbanization: poverty, immigration and unhealthy environments. Individual treatment and control of juvenile offenders could improve their behavior.

Treatment

Nonconforming children were controlled by external institutions, such as houses of refuge and reformatories created by paternalistic child savers. Public education was used to "Americanize" foreign and lower-class children. Several private organizations were created to assimilate foreign and lower-class youths into American culture. Private groups were organized to rescue children from poor and unfit environments. Locked facilities were built across the nation.

Orphan asylums became popular ways to house and mold the conduct of children left homeless by the Civil War and/or neglected by unfit parents.

Policies

Local and state governments became providers of care and treatment for neglected and delinquent children and expanded their involvement in the lives of these children through the adoption of new educational/assimilation tools (vocational, industrial and manual training schools) for institutionalized and lower-class youths, the passage of immigration restriction laws and the assumption of a stronger role in creating, financing and administering reform institutions.

The costs of building and supervising juvenile institutions were shared by private and public agencies. The *parens patriae* tradition, correctional policies that separated adult and youthful offenders, and indeterminate sentencing for juvenile inmates were adopted. Statutory definitions of juvenile delinquency were expanded to include new status offenses, such as begging, cheating and gambling.

The Civil War (1861–1865) was followed by reconstruction and massive industrialization. Many children were left fatherless by the war, and many families moved to urban areas seeking work. Often children were exploited in sweat-shops or roamed the streets in gangs while their parents worked in factories.

In 1866 the first specialized institution for male juveniles was authorized in Washington, DC. This House of Corrections consisted of several cottages containing some 60 or more beds. In 1869 Massachusetts appointed a State Board of Charities to investigate cases involving children who were tried before the courts.

At this time state reformatories also came into existence, including the New York State Reformatory at Elmira, which opened in 1877.

By the end of the 1800s, reform schools introduced vocational education, military drill and calisthenics into the institutions' regimens. At the same time, some reform schools changed their names to "industrial schools" and later to "training schools," to emphasize the "treatment" aspect of corrections. For example, the Ohio Reform Farm School opened in 1857, later became the Boy's Industrial School, and was renamed again to the Fairfield School for Boys.

Several other significant events occurred during the 1800s that altered the administration of juvenile justice (Griffin and Griffin, p.20):

1870—First use of separate trials for juveniles (Massachusetts)

1877—Separate dockets and records established for juveniles (Massachusetts)

1880—First probation system applicable to juveniles instituted

1898—Segregation of children under 16 awaiting trial (Rhode Island)

1899—First juvenile court established (Illinois)

A juvenile court movement began during the 1890s which provided citizen participation in community-based corrections. This citizen participation through the Parent Teacher Association (PTA), founded in 1897, induced the Cook County (Illinois) Bar Association to write the law establishing a juvenile court in Chicago (Hunt, 1973), the first of its kind in the nation, propelling U.S. juvenile justice into its third evolutionary phase—the Juvenile Court Period.

The Juvenile Court Period (1899–1960)

The Juvenile Court Period was born at the beginning of what is often referred to as the Progressive Era or the Age of Reform—the first quarter of the twentieth century. According to reformers, children were not inherently bad but were made so by society and their environment. Progressives believed that the family was especially influential and that parents were responsible for bringing their children up to be obedient and to work hard. When parents were unable to fulfill such responsibilities, reformers believed in state intervention. Their vision materialized in the shape of the 1899 Juvenile Court Act, which was titled an "Act to Regulate the Treatment and Control of Dependent, Neglected and Delinquent Children."

The 1899 Juvenile Court Act

Passed in Illinois, this act represented the U.S. criminal justice system's first formal recognition that it owed a different duty to children than to adults and that impressionable, presumably salvageable youths should not be mixed in prisons with hardened criminals. The law created a public policy based on the **medical model**—that is, a treatment model—to retard the social and moral decay of the environment, family and youths. An underlying philosophy of the medical model was that delinquency was a preventable condition, and in cases where prevention failed and delinquent behavior occurred, the condition could be treated and cured.

The act created the first juvenile court in the United States and provided social reform and a structured way to restore and control children in trouble. It also provided a way to care for children who needed official protection. According to Breen (2001, p.50):

> "The core belief of the progressive movement of the early 20ᵗʰ century—that government could solve social problems through the application [of] social sciences—drove changes in the treatment of juvenile offenders. . . . The parenting-not-punishing philosophy of the Juvenile Court Period was firmly established in the comprehensive Illinois Juvenile Court Act of 1899. It soon became a model imitated nationwide."

 In 1899 the Illinois legislature passed a law establishing a juvenile court that became the cornerstone for juvenile justice throughout the United States.

Key features of this act included:

- Defining a delinquent as any detainee younger than 16.
- Separating children from adults in institutions.
- Setting special, informal procedural rules for juvenile court.
- Providing for the use of probation officers.
- Prohibiting the detention of children younger than 12 in a jail or police station.

The Juvenile Court Act gave "original jurisdiction in *all* cases coming within the terms of this act," removing those younger than 16 from the jurisdiction of the criminal court and placing them in a paternalistic system that viewed juvenile delinquents as victims of their environments not responsible for their offenses. Rehabilitation and the child's welfare were to be of prime concern. The adjudicative process within the juvenile court was to be special; it was *not* to function as an adult criminal court but more like a social welfare agency. Accordingly, as Schwartz (1989, p.151) notes: "Children who were brought to the attention of the juvenile court were to be helped rather than punished."

 The first juvenile courts were administrative agencies of circuit or district courts. They served a social welfare function, embracing the rehabilitative ideal of reforming children rather than punishing them.

The passage of the Illinois Juvenile Court Act marked the first time that probation and probation officers were formally made *specifically* applicable to juveniles. The act stipulated:

> The court shall have authority to appoint or designate one or more discreet persons of good character to serve as probation officers during the pleasure of the court . . . it shall be the duty of the said probation officer to make such investigation as may be required by the court; to be present in court in order to represent the interests of the child when the case is heard; to furnish to the court

such information and assistance as the judge may require; and to take such charge of any child before and after trial as may be directed by the court.

 Probation, according to the 1899 Illinois Juvenile Court Act, was to have both an investigative and a rehabilitative function.

The juvenile court was the creation of progressive reformers who believed that children were incapable of being fully responsible for antisocial and criminal behavior, that children were malleable and more capable of rehabilitation than adults, and that treatment rather than punishment should be the focus of the juvenile justice system. Social workers served the juvenile court as probation officers and held this same philosophy.

Social workers collected facts about youths' misbehavior, including the history of their families, school performance, church attendance and neighborhood. They made recommendations for disposition to the judges and provided community supervision and casework services to the vast majority of children who were adjudicated by the juvenile courts.

Besides providing for the use of probation officers, the Juvenile Court Act also stipulated that juvenile courts were to have separate records and informal procedures. The adversary function of the criminal court was deemed incompatible with the procedural safeguards of the juvenile court, reflecting the basic doctrine of *parens patriae*. Because children were legally wards of the state, they were perceived to be without constitutional rights. The act was construed liberally so that the care, custody and discipline of children would approximate as nearly as possible that given by individual parents. **Custody** or **guardianship** is a legal status created by court order giving an adult the right and duty to protect, provide food and shelter, train, and discipline a child. To that end, several important parts of a criminal trial, such as the indictment, pleadings and jury, were eliminated. Despite this, juvenile court was initially regarded as far more humane than criminal court. Schwartz (p.150) describes the newly created juvenile court as:

> . . . a special court in which children were denied due process and adversarial proceedings in exchange for informal and confidential hearings and dispositions based on what was felt to be in the "best interests of the child." It was a court in which the distinctions between dependent, neglected and delinquent children were less important than their common need for state supervision in the manner of a wise and devoted parent.

Rieffel (1983, p.3) clarifies this rationalization: "Since both criminal and non-criminal misbehavior were but symptoms of an unhealthy environment, the distinction between them was of minimal significance." However, as Flicker (1990, p.32) contends:

> It could be argued that the most reprehensible feature of the Illinois contribution to juvenile justice is the continued erosion of distinctions between juveniles who commit criminal acts, thereby demonstrating objectively that they are a present threat to community safety, and those who are themselves victims as abused, neglected or dependent children.

Some scholars assert the system was set up to take advantage of children. Disputing the benevolent motives of the founders of the juvenile court, especially in the adjudication procedure, scholars have suggested that the civil liberties and privacy rights of juveniles diminished in the process. They accuse the middle class of promoting the child-saving movement to support its own interests.

Although reformers of the time were optimistic, college-educated people who believed that individualized treatment based on a juvenile's history was critical, they were also concerned with their own futures, as noted by Krisberg and Austin (p.27): "During the Progressive Era, those in positions of economic power feared that the urban masses would destroy the world they had built. . . . From all sectors came demands that new action be taken to preserve social order, and to protect private property and racial privilege."

 The progressives further developed the medical model, viewing crime as a disease to treat and cure by social intervention.

According to Krisberg and Austin (p.27): "The times demanded reform, and before the Progressive Era ended, much of the modern welfare state and the criminal justice system were constructed." Further (p.31): "The thrust of Progressive Era reforms was to found a more perfect control system to restore social stability while guaranteeing the continued hegemony [predominance or authority] of those with wealth and privilege."

Interestingly, an early critique by two prominent progressives of the first juvenile courts in Cook County, Illinois, noted: "Children who do wrong can be found in every social stratum, but those who become wards of the court are the children of the poor" (Breckenridge and Abbott, 1912, pp.42–43). Their findings, which were based on an evaluation of court records dating from 1899 to 1909, confirmed that the juvenile court constituted a powerful means of social control by the dominant class.

Others, however, contend that the development of the juvenile courts and the adjudication function represents neither a great social reform in processing juveniles nor an attempt to diminish juveniles' civil liberties and control them arbitrarily. Rather, it represents another example of the trend toward bureaucracy and an institutionalized compromise between social welfare and the law.

Commonwealth v. Fisher (1905) defended the juvenile court ideal, reminiscent of the holding of the court in the *Crouse* case of 1838:

> To save a child from becoming a criminal, or continuing in a career of crime, to end in maturer years in public punishment and disgrace, the legislatures surely may provide for the salvation of such a child, if its parents or guardians be unwilling or unable to do so, by bringing it into one of the courts of the state without any process at all, for the purpose of subjecting it to the state's guardianship and protection.

Early Efforts at Diversion: The Chicago Boy's Court and Youth Counsel Bureau

Diversion is the official halting of formal juvenile proceedings against a youthful offender and, instead, treating or caring for the youth outside the formal juvenile justice system. In 1914 diversion from juvenile court began in the Chicago Boy's Court, an extralegal form of probation to process and treat young offenders without labeling them as criminals.

The Boy's Court version of diversion used four community service agencies: the Holy Name Society (a Catholic church agency), the Chicago Church Foundation (predominantly Protestant), the Jewish Social Service Bureau and the Colored Big Brothers. The court released juveniles to the supervision and authority of these agencies. After a sufficient time to evaluate each youth's behavior, the agencies reported back to the court. The court took the evaluation and, if satisfactory, the judge officially discharged the individual. No record was made.

Toward the end of the Juvenile Court Period, in the early 1950s, developments in youth diversionary programs included New York City's Youth Counsel Bureau. This bureau was established to handle delinquents who were not deemed sufficiently advanced in their misbehavior to be directed to court and adjudicated. Referrals were made directly to the bureau from police, parents, schools, courts and other agencies. The bureau provided a counseling service and discharged those whose adjustments appeared promising. Again, there was no record to label the youths delinquent.

Federal Government Concern and Involvement

The earliest federal interest in delinquency was demonstrated by the 1909 White House Conference on Youth. Golden (1997, pp.120–121) notes:

> Following the 1909 White House Conference on Dependent Children, in which family preservationists won the debate with the children's rights defenders of the charitable private agencies, the foster care population, ironically, increased. Child welfare's policies supported family preservation, but the practice of child removal advanced by the charity workers continued—to the present day.

 A direct result of the 1909 White House Conference on Youth was the establishment of the U.S. Children's Bureau in 1912.

In addition, in 1912 Congress passed the first child labor laws.

The aftermath of World War I, the Great Depression and World War II occupied much of the federal government's attention during the period from 1920 to 1960 as it sought to help citizens cope with the pressures of the times. However, by 1925 all but two states had juvenile court systems, and the U.S. Children's Bureau and the National Probation Association issued a recommendation for *A Standard Juvenile Court Act* in 1925.

In 1937 a group of concerned juvenile court judges founded the National Council of Juvenile and Family Court Judges. According to Schwartz (p.91): "One of the most significant sources of power and influence over the lives of children and the formulation of youth policy in practically every community is the juvenile court." He notes that over the years, the National Council of Juvenile and Family Court Judges has "established itself as an influential and

Courtesy of The Colorado Historical Society

Judge Benjamin Lindsay presided in juvenile court in Denver, Colorado, from 1900 to 1927. These first juvenile courts were informal proceedings focusing on rehabilitation rather than punishment.

respected organization." He also suggests, however: "In recent years the council's reputation has slipped . . . because the council has become dependent upon and corrupted by the availability of federal funds and has lost sight of its mission." Originally, however, its efforts were focused on the best interests of children, as was the passage of the Social Security Act in 1935.

 Passage of the Social Security Act in 1935 was the beginning of major federal funding for programs to aid children and families.

The National Youth Administration provided work relief and employment for young people ages 16 to 25. Then, in 1936, the Children's Bureau began administering the first federal subsidy program, providing child welfare grants to states for the care of dependent, neglected, exploited, abused and delinquent youths.

The federal government passed the Juvenile Court Act in 1938, adopting many features of the original Illinois act. Within 10 years every state had enacted special laws for handling juveniles. Schmalleger (1993, p.514) contends that the juvenile court movement was based on five identifiable philosophical principles:

1. The belief that the state is the "higher or ultimate parent" of all the children within its borders.

2. The belief that children are worth saving, and the concomitant belief in the worth of nonpunitive procedures designed to save the child.

3. The belief that children should be nurtured. While the nurturing process is underway, they should be protected from the stigmatizing impact of formal adjudicatory procedures.

Highlights of Juvenile Court Period Reform

Policy makers and practitioners differed over the most effective treatment for unacceptable behavior and over who should be responsible for organizing and regulating juvenile justice. Clearly, someone or some agency should be responsible, but at what governmental level—local, state or federal? Specialized rules of juvenile procedure were being set forth by a growing number of judicial bodies.

Also during this period the juvenile court was perceived to be a means for attaining certain social ends. However, a growing belief developed that the juvenile system carried its own stigma that was harmful to juveniles under its jurisdiction. That stigma was applied by procedures that denied due process of law.

By the late 1940s, the gap between the theoretical assistance given to youths in the juvenile court system and the actual punitive practices had become obvious. Legal challenges to the system's informality and lack of safeguards were brought. Many critics asserted that the courts applied legal sanctions and procedures capriciously.

Philosophies

Adolescence was accepted as a unique period of biological and emotional transition from child to adult that required careful control and guidance. Misbehavior by middle-class youths was to be expected and controlled by concerned families, but lower-class youths were to be reformed via public efforts.

Controlling and improving societal rather than individual conditions might decrease the incidence of youthful crime. Children were to be gently led back to conformity, not harshly punished.

Treatment

Children were primarily treated by public efforts guided by new public policies and research. Children in need were handled primarily by juvenile courts.

Policies

The juvenile court system was adopted by every state to adjudicate youths separately from adults, thereby expanding the *parens patriae* precedent. The federal government broadened its role with youths and began providing direction for youth services by sponsoring conferences, stimulating discussions, passing legislation to improve conditions for families and youths during the Depression, passing child-labor legislation, supporting the protection of children's basic constitutional rights and creating the Children's Bureau as the first national child-welfare agency.

4. The belief that justice, to accomplish the goal of reformation, needs to be individualized.

5. The belief that noncriminal procedures give primary consideration to the needs of the child. The denial of due process could be justified in the face of constitutional challenges because the court acted not to punish, but to help.

In the 1940s a number of conferences on children and youths were held, but most of the energy for public support and public programs was directed toward the war and reconstructing families after the war. In 1951 Congress passed the Federal Youth Corrections Act and created a Juvenile Delinquency Bureau (JDB) in the Department of Health, Education and Welfare. The positioning of the

JDB within the Department of Health, Education and Welfare reflects the prevalence of the medical model at this time as well as the emphasis on prevention.

By the end of the Juvenile Court Period, social work and the juvenile justice system movement were flourishing with their combined focus on youths and their families. The movement gradually became more concerned with professionalism in the intake process and correctional supervision. This went unnoticed by outsiders until the early 1960s.

The end of this period also marked the beginning of radical societal changes in the United States that would last the next two decades and extend throughout the fourth developmental phase of our juvenile justice system—the Juvenile Rights Period.

The Juvenile Rights Period (1960–1980)

In the 1960s the American family was undergoing significant changes that directly affected social work and its liaison between the juvenile, the family and the court. Divorces increased, with the result that more children lived in single-parent households. Births to unmarried women increased, and more women entered the labor force. This affected the family structure and prompted a reorganization of social work philosophy and service.

Juvenile crime received increased attention when, in 1960, the United States attorney general reported that delinquency and crime were costing the American public more than $20 million per year. In addition, poor, lower-class delinquents were now joined by youths with middle- and upper-class backgrounds and rural youths.

A significant program, Mobilization for Youth, developed in New York City in 1962 based on the theoretical perspective of Richard Cloward and Lloyd Ohlin, sociologists who believed that delinquency resulted from the disparity that low-income youths perceived between their aspirations and the social, economic and political opportunities available to achieve them. The Mobilization for Youth project encompassed five areas: work training, education, group work and community organizations, services to individuals and families, and training and personnel (Krisberg and Austin, p.43).

President Lyndon Johnson's Great Society initiative of the 1960s, known for its "War on Poverty," advanced causes for families and children, providing federal money to attack poverty, crime and delinquency. Further, the 1960s saw racial tensions at an all-time high with leaders such as Malcolm X and groups such as the Black Muslims and the Black Panthers demanding "power to the people." As noted by Krisberg and Austin (p.44): "The riots of the mid-1960s dramatized the growing gap between people of color in the United States and their more affluent 'benefactors.' "

Civil rights efforts during the 1960s helped broaden concerns for all children, especially those coming under the jurisdiction of juvenile courts. Rieffel (p.3) suggests: "Juvenile law, perhaps more than any other aspect of law, reflects the stumbling and confused nature of our society as its values and goals evolve. So it was in the 1960s, when American society put itself through an extraordinary period of self-examination, that a great many problems were identified in the way we handle juvenile crime."

The Four Ds
of Juvenile Justice

To deal with problems identified within the juvenile justice system, new policies were established regarding four key concepts—deinstitutionalization, diversion, due process and decriminalization. Although it was not until the end of this period when sociologist LaMar Empey (1978) formally described these as the Four Ds of juvenile justice, their implementation in and impact on the juvenile justice system began early in the 1960s.

 The Four Ds of juvenile justice are deinstitutionalization, diversion, due process, and decriminalization.

Throughout this period, the major developments in juvenile justice focused on one or a combination of these key concepts.

For example, **decriminalization**—referring to legislation that makes status offenses, such as smoking and violating curfew, noncriminal acts—was first witnessed in 1961, when California became the first state to separate status offenses from the delinquent category. New York followed suit in 1962, when the revised New York Family Court Act created a new classification for noncriminal misconduct—**PINS,** Person in Need of Supervision. Other states followed suit, adopting such labels as CINS, CHINS (Children in Need of Supervision), MINS (Minors in Need of Supervision), JINS (Juveniles in Need of Supervision) and FINS (Families in Need of Supervision). These new labels were intended to reduce the stigma of being labeled a delinquent. Throughout the juvenile rights period, a broad range of status offenses were decriminalized.

Other policy changes involved the applicability of due process rights to juveniles. Legal challenges to the notion that the juvenile justice system—and the juvenile court in particular—truly was a benign parent, went as far as the U.S. Supreme Court in the 1960s. Society began to demand that children brought before the juvenile court for matters that exposed them to the equivalent of criminal sanctions receive **due process** protection. The due process clause of the U.S. Constitution requires that no person be deprived of life, liberty or property without due process of law. The Supreme Court began protecting juveniles from the court's paternalism. Due process became a clear concern in *Kent v. United States* (1966).

The Kent Decision

Morris Kent, a 16-year-old with a police record, was arrested and charged with housebreaking, robbery and rape. Kent admitted the charges and was held at a juvenile detention facility for almost a week. The judge then transferred jurisdiction of the case to an adult criminal court. Kent received no hearing of any kind.

 The procedural requirements for waiver to criminal court were articulated by the Supreme Court in *Kent v. United States.*

In reviewing the case, the Supreme Court decreed: "As a condition to a valid waiver order, petitioner [Kent] was entitled to a hearing, including access by his counsel to the social records and probation or similar reports which are presumably considered by the court, and to a statement of the reasons for the Juvenile Court's decision."

An appendix to the *Kent* decision contained the following criteria established by the Supreme Court for states to use in deciding whether to transfer juveniles to adult criminal court for trial. The juvenile court was to consider:

- The seriousness of the alleged offense and whether the protection of the community requires waiver.
- Whether the alleged offense was committed in an aggressive, violent, premeditated or willful manner.
- Whether the alleged offense was against persons or against property, greater weight being given to offenses against persons, especially if personal injury resulted.
- The prospective merit of the complaint.
- The desirability of trial and disposition of the offense in one court when the juvenile's associates in the alleged offense are adults who will be charged with crimes in the adult court.
- The sophistication and maturity of the juvenile as determined by a consideration of his or her home, environmental situation, emotional attitude and pattern of living.
- The record and previous history of the juvenile.

The *Kent* decision was a warning to the juvenile justice system that the juvenile court's traditional lack of concern for procedural and evidentiary standards would no longer be tolerated.

The *Gault Decision*

The juvenile court process became a national issue in *In re Gault* (1967). Schwartz (p.99) suggests: "The *Gault* decision is, by far, the single most important event in the history of juvenile justice." This case was instrumental in changing the adjudication process almost completely into a deliberately adversarial process. *In re Gault* concerned a 15-year-old Arizona boy already on probation who was taken into custody at 10:00 A.M. for allegedly making obscene phone calls to a neighbor. No steps were taken to notify his parents. When Mrs. Gault arrived home about 6:00 P.M., she found her son missing. She went to the detention home and was told why he was there and that a hearing would be held the next day. At the hearing, a petition was filed with the juvenile court that made general allegations of "delinquency." No particular facts were stated.

The hearing took place in the judge's chambers. The complaining neighbor was not present, no one was sworn in, no attorney was present and no record of the proceedings was made. Gault admitted to making part of the phone call in question. At the end of the hearing, the judge said he would consider the matter.

Gault was held in the detention home for 2 more days and then released. Another hearing on his delinquency was held 4 days later. That hearing also had no complaining witnesses, sworn testimony, counsel or transcript. The probation officer's referral report listed the charge as lewd phone calls and was filed with the court. The report was not made available to Gault or his parents. At the end of the hearing the judge committed him to the state industrial school until age 21. Gault received a 6-year sentence for an action for which an adult would have received a fine or a 2-month imprisonment. The U.S. Supreme Court overruled Gault's conviction on the grounds that he was deprived of his due process rights.

> The *Gault* decision requires that the due process clause of the Fourteenth Amendment apply to proceedings in state juvenile courts, including the right of notice, the right to counsel, the right against self-incrimination and the right to confront witnesses.

In delivering the Court's opinion, Justice Fortas stated:

Where a person, infant or adult, can be seized by the State, charged and convicted for violating a state criminal law, and then ordered by the State to be confined for six years, I think the Constitution requires that he be tried in accordance with the guarantees of all provisions of the Bill of Rights made applicable to the States by the Fourteenth Amendment. Undoubtedly this would be true of an adult defendant, and it would be a plain denial of equal protection of the laws—an invidious discrimination—to hold that others subject to heavier punishments could, because they are children, be denied these same constitutional safeguards. I consequently agree with the Court that the Arizona law as applied here denied to the parents and their son the right of notice, right to counsel, right against self-incrimination, and right to confront the witnesses against young Gault. Appellants are entitled to these rights, not because "fairness, impartiality and orderliness—in short the essentials of due process"—require them and not because they are "the procedural rules which have been fashioned from the generality of due process," but because they are specifically and unequivocally granted by provisions of the Fifth and Sixth Amendments which the Fourteenth Amendment makes applicable to the States.

Thus, the *Gault* decision provided the standard of due process for juveniles.

The remaining two Ds—deinstitutionalization and diversion—surfaced as focal points for policy change following a harsh examination of the juvenile justice system by the 1967 President's Commission on Law Enforcement and Administration of Justice.

The President's Commission on Law Enforcement and Administration of Justice

In 1967, the President's Commission gave evidence of "disenchantment with the experience of the juvenile court" (President's Commission, 1967, p.17). It criticized lack of due process, law enforcement's poor relationship to youths and the handling of juveniles and the corrections process of confining status offenders and children "in need" to locked facilities. A **status offender** is a juvenile who has commited an act that would not be a crime if commited by an adult, for example, smoking cigarettes.

According to the President's Commission (p.69): "Institutions tend to isolate offenders from society, both physically and psychologically, cutting them off from schools, jobs, families and other supportive influences and increasing the probability that the label of criminal will be indelibly impressed upon them." The commission, therefore, recommended that community-based correctional alternatives to institutionalization, or **deinstitutionalization,** should be considered seriously for juvenile offenders.

At the same time, the U.S. Department of Justice published *The Challenge of Crime in a Free Society* (1967), also questioning the policy of incarceration for nonviolent juvenile offenders. In this document, Harvard professor and criminologist James Q. Wilson expressed his views on two competing philosophies of juvenile crime deterrence (Breen, p.50):

> He first considered the belief that harsh policies might deter juvenile criminal behavior; then he considered the equally plausible argument that juvenile arrests, particularly of first offenders, may actually propel youths to a lifetime of delinquent behavior. Wilson expressed the thoughts of many when he reasoned, one, that arrests may actually give juvenile offenders higher status among their peers, and, two, that the typically light sentencing of juvenile offenders may help breed a contempt for the system among the very juveniles it is designed to assist.

 Isolating offenders from their normal social environment may encourage the development of a delinquent orientation and, thus, further delinquent behavior.

The issues raised by the President's Commission, Wilson and others studying juvenile justice policy and practice indicated a need to integrate rather than isolate offenders. The resulting community-based correctional programs, such as probation, foster care and group homes, represented attempts to respond to these issues by normalizing social contacts, reducing the stigma attached to being institutionalized and providing opportunities for jobs and schooling.

In the early 1970s, Massachusetts undertook what some considered a radical experiment in deinstitutionalization. Jerome Miller, state commissioner of youth services and head of the Massachusetts Department of Youth Services, closed every juvenile institution in the state. As noted by Schmalleger (p.535):

> Deinstitutionalization was accomplished by placing juveniles in foster care, group homes, mental health facilities and other programs. Many were simply sent home. The problems caused by hard-core offenders among the released juveniles, however, soon convinced authorities that complete deinstitutionalization was not a workable solution to the problem of delinquency. The Massachusetts experiment ended as quickly as it began.

Although total deinstitutionalization ended in Massachusetts, hundreds of juveniles were successfully moved into community-based programs. Further, throughout the 1960s and 1970s, deinstitutionalization of status offenders (DSO) was especially recommended on the theoretical basis that labeling a youth as delinquent could become self-fulfilling. This is discussed in Chapter 2.

The President's Commission also strongly endorsed diversion for status offenders and minor delinquent offenses. (Recall that diversion made its first formal appearance in 1914 with the Chicago Boy's Court.) In addition, the commission recommended establishing a national youth service bureau and local or community youth service bureaus to assist the police and courts in diverting youths from the juvenile justice system.

Youth Service Bureaus

In 1967 the President's Commission established a federal **youth service bureau** to coordinate community-centered referral programs. Local youth service bureaus were to divert minor offenders whose behavior was rooted in problems at home, in school or in the community. While a broad range of services and certain mandatory functions were suggested for youth service bureaus, individually tailored work with troublemaking youngsters was a primary goal.

As envisioned by the commission, youth service bureaus were not part of the juvenile justice system. The bureaus would provide necessary services to youths as a substitute for putting them through the juvenile justice process, thus avoiding the stigma of formal court involvement. The three main functions of local youth service bureaus were diversion, resource development and system modification.

Diversion included accepting referrals from the police, courts, schools, parents and other sources, and working with the youths in a voluntary, noncoercive manner through neighborhood-oriented services. *Resource development* included offering leadership at the neighborhood level to provide and develop a variety of youth assistance programs, as well as seeking funding for new projects. *System modification* included seeking to change attitudes and practices that discriminate against troublesome youths and, thereby, contribute to their antisocial behavior. To meet the unique needs of each community, the organization and programming of local youth service bureaus were to remain flexible.

Many youth service bureaus did not survive the federal funding cuts during the Carter and Reagan administrations. Those bureaus that endured have turned their focus to providing employment activities for employable juveniles, particularly during the summer. They have also concentrated on providing health, recreation or educational referrals or services.

Finally, the President's Commission advocated *prevention* as the most promising and important method of dealing with crime, a philosophy embodied in the Uniform Juvenile Court Act of 1968.

The Uniform Juvenile Court Act

In 1968 the historic Delinquency Prevention and Control Act was passed. One provision of this act was to reform the juvenile justice system nationally. Although titled a "court" act, the legislation included provisions that affected law enforcement and corrections, illustrating the interconnectedness of the parts of the system.

 The Uniform Juvenile Court Act provided for the care, protection and development of youths, without the stigma of a criminal label, by a program of treatment, training and rehabilitation in a family environment when possible. It also provided simple judicial and interstate procedures.

The act included the following definitions:

- A **child** is "an individual who is under the age of 18 years or under the age of 21 years who committed an act of delinquency before reaching the age of 18 years."

- A **delinquent act** is "an act designated a crime under the law." It includes local ordinances, but does not include traffic offenses.

- A **delinquent child** is "a child who has committed a delinquent act and is in need of treatment or rehabilitation."

- A **deprived child** is one who "is without proper parental care or control, subsistence, education as required by law, or other care or control necessary for his physical, mental or emotional health, or morals, and the deprivation is not due primarily to the lack of financial means of his parents, guardian or other custodian; or who has been placed for care or adoption in violation of the law; or who has been abandoned by his parents, guardian or other custodian; or is without a parent, guardian or legal custodian."
- A **custodian** is "a person, other than a parent or legal guardian, who stands *in loco parentis* to the child or a person to whom legal custody of the child has been given by order of a court."

The act described probation services, referees, venue and transfer, custody and detention, petitions and summons, hearings, children's rights, disposition, court files and records, and procedures for fingerprinting and photographing children. These areas are described in detail in the chapters dealing with law enforcement and the courts.

Despite the best intentions of this act, a growing body of empirical evidence had cast serious doubt upon the ability of social casework, the linchpin of correctional treatment along with probation and parole, to help rehabilitate youths (Hellum, 1979). And although rehabilitation remained the major premise on which the juvenile justice system rested, research had found that correctional "treatment," especially in institutions, was often unnecessarily punitive and sometimes sadistic. Modern reformers became appalled that noncriminal youths and status offenders could so easily find their way into the same institutions as seriously delinquent youths. This spawned a rapid growth in community-based alternatives to institutionalization, as well as renewed national interest in juvenile justice.

The White House Conference on Youth

The 1970 White House Conference on Youth warned: "Our families and children are in deep trouble. A society that neglects its children and fears its youth cannot care about its future" (*The White House Conference on Youth*, 1972, p.346). The message from the conference was interpreted as a need for special federal assistance to identify the needs of families.

The major impact of the 1970 White House Conference on Youth was that it hit hard at the foundation of the U.S. system for handling youths, including unnecessarily punitive institutions.

Beginning in 1971 a series of federal cases tried to specify minimum environmental conditions for juvenile institutions. By 1972 there was a cooperative effort among federal administrations to focus on programs for *preventing* delinquency and rehabilitating delinquents outside the traditional criminal justice system. According to Breen (p.50): "The need for further research and the need to divert juvenile offenders from the criminal justice system prompted the adoption of the Juvenile Justice and Delinquency Prevention Act of 1974."

The Office of Juvenile Justice and Delinquency Prevention and the Juvenile Justice and Delinquency Prevention Act

In 1974 Congress created the Office of Juvenile Justice and Delinquency Prevention (OJJDP) and placed it in the Department of Justice. Congress also passed the Juvenile Justice and Delinquency Prevention (JJDP) Act by a vote of 329 to 20 in the House and with only one dissenting vote in the Senate. It was signed by a reluctant President Gerald R. Ford. According to Schwartz (p.124): "The Juvenile Justice and Delinquency Prevention Act of 1974 is the most important piece of federal juvenile justice legislation ever enacted." The intent of the act was "to provide a unified rational program to deal with juvenile delinquency prevention and control within the context of the total law."

The landmark JJDP Act required that in order for states to receive federal funds, incarceration and even temporary detention should be used for young people only as a last resort.

 The **Juvenile Justice and Delinquency Prevention Act of 1974** had two key goals: deinstitutionalization of status offenders and separation or removal of juveniles from adult facilities.

The JJDP Act made funds available to states that removed status offenders from prisons and jails and created alternative voluntary services to which status offenders could be diverted. The act was amended in 1976, 1977, 1980 and 1992. According to Decker (1984, pp.37–38), amendments to the JJDP Act in 1977:

- Broadened the functions of State Planning Agency Advisory groups to include the private business sector.
- Involved alternate youth programs and people with special experience in school violence and vandalism programs, including social workers.
- Gave states the opportunity to participate in grant programs for deinstitutionalization.
- Required monitoring of all states with state juvenile detention and correctional facilities to determine their suitability for status offenders.

The 1980 amendment called for the removal of juveniles from adult jails. In 1992, Congress added a disproportionate minority confinement (DMC) mandate requiring that states receiving JJDP Act formula grants provide assurances that they will develop and implement plans to reduce overrepresentation of minorities in the juvenile justice system.

While the JJDP Act promoted the development of diversionary tactics for juvenile offenders through monetary incentives, claiming such practices would benefit both the system and the youths it handled, the policy of diversion soon revealed its drawbacks and was met with some criticism.

Diversion and Net Widening

The juvenile due process requirements from *Kent* and *Gault,* combined with the rising costs of courts and correctional facilities at the end of the 1960s and throughout the 70s, resulted in wider use of community-based alternatives to treat youths before and after adjudication. Young offenders were diverted into remedial education, drug abuse programs, foster homes and out-patient health care and counseling facilities.

However, diversion does not necessarily mean less state social control over juveniles. It has had the negative effect of transferring state power from juvenile courts to police and probation departments. Many youngsters who earlier would have been simply released were instead referred to the new diversionary programs. This phenomenon was called **net widening,** and it was the opposite of diversion's original purpose, which was to lessen the states' power to exercise control over juveniles.

Although efforts to implement diversion programs were encouraged and rewarded, and the use of diversion, in fact, greatly expanded during the past several decades, the number of young people committed to institutions has not decreased appreciably. Instead of weakening state control, the correctional structure has become stronger. One reason: the diversion apparatus has, in many cases, become a prevention apparatus, receiving the bulk of its referrals from parents, schools and welfare agencies, as opposed to the police, intake or the courts. The referrals are, by and large, younger juveniles with minor offenses and without prior records, girls and status offenders.

Not only does diversion widen the net, it also increases the risk of violating rights of due process and fundamental fairness because referrals usually occur *before* adjudication. Thus, it is often never established that referred youngsters are actually guilty of any offense that might make them properly the subjects of conditional placement.

Because diversion is personalized, treatment may be inconsistent from one youth to the next. Diversion is also problematic because it may reflect individual class or social prejudices. It removes juveniles from any penalties with no exposure to the judicial process of the juvenile court. Further, informal diversion is usually unsystematic.

The justifications for diversion lay with labeling theory and differential association theory. While the philosophical, legal, theoretical and practical strengths and weaknesses of diversion have been debated, little research has been done to examine the effectiveness of limiting official intervention in the lives of diverted and nondiverted youths. However, one fact exists: diverted youths tend to remain in the justice system longer than nondiverted youths.

A Return to Due Process Issues: Other Landmark Cases

As in the first half of the Juvenile Rights Period, the 1970s saw a continuation in the flow of cases addressing juveniles' rights and the juvenile court becoming more like the adult court in several important ways. Three landmark cases during the 70s addressed juvenile rights regarding the standard of proof, jury trials and double jeopardy. Whether dealing with status offenders, youths who had committed violent crimes or protecting abused or neglected children, the court no longer had free reign.

The *Winship* Decision: Standard of Proof in Juvenile Proceedings

In re Winship (1970) concerned a 12-year-old New York boy charged with taking $112 from a woman's purse. He was adjudicated a delinquent based on a *preponderance of the evidence* submitted at the juvenile hearing. He was committed to a training school for 18 months, with extension possible until he was 18 years old, a total possible sentence of 6 years. The question raised was whether New York's statute allowing juvenile cases to be decided on the basis of a preponderance of evidence was constitutional.

Gault had already established that due process required fair treatment for juveniles. The Court held that: "The Due Process Clause protects the accused against conviction except upon *proof beyond a reasonable doubt* of every fact necessary to constitute the crime with which he is charged" (italics in original). New York argued that its juvenile proceedings were civil, not criminal; but the Supreme Court said the standard of proof beyond a reasonable doubt not only played a vital role in the criminal justice system, it also ensured a greater degree of safety for the presumption of innocence of those accused of crimes.

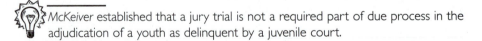 *In re Winship* established proof beyond a reasonable doubt as the standard for juvenile adjudication proceedings, eliminating lesser standards such as a preponderance of the evidence, clear and convincing proof and reasonable proof.

The *McKeiver* Decision: No Right to a Jury Trial

The move toward expanding juveniles' civil rights was slowed by the ruling in *McKeiver v. Pennsylvania* (1971), in which the Court ruled that juveniles do not have the right to a jury trial. This case involved a 16-year-old Pennsylvania boy charged with robbery, larceny and receiving stolen goods, all felonies in Pennsylvania. He was adjudicated a delinquent. The question for the Court to decide was whether the due process clause of the Fourteenth Amendment guaranteeing the right to a jury trial applied to the adjudication of a juvenile court case.

In *McKeiver* the Court held that *Gault* and *Winship* demonstrated concern for the fundamental principle of fairness in justice, with the fact-finding elements of due process necessary and present for this fairness. The Court emphasized in *McKeiver:* "One cannot say that in our legal system the jury is a necessary component of accurate fact finding. There is much to be said for it, to be sure, but we have been content to pursue other ways for determining facts."

McKeiver established that a jury trial is not a required part of due process in the adjudication of a youth as delinquent by a juvenile court.

The Court realized that juvenile courts had not been successful, but it also concluded that juvenile court should not become fully adversarial like the criminal court. Requiring a jury might put an end to "what has been the idealistic prospect of an intimate informal protective proceeding." Requiring jury trials for juvenile courts could also result in delays, as well as in the possibility of public trials.

The *Breed* Decision: Double Jeopardy

Double jeopardy was the issue in *Breed v. Jones* (1975). The Supreme Court ruled that defendants may not be tried twice for the same offense. Breed was 17 when apprehended for committing acts with a deadly weapon. He was adjudicated in a California juvenile court, which found the allegation true. A dispositional hearing determined there were not sufficient facilities "amenable to the care, treatment and training programs available through the facilities of the juvenile court," as required by the statute. Breed was transferred to the criminal court where he was again found guilty. Breed argued that he had been tried twice for the same offense, constituting double jeopardy. The Supreme Court agreed and reversed the conviction.

 A juvenile cannot be adjudicated in juvenile court and then tried for the same offense in an adult criminal court (*Breed v. Jones*, 1975).

Beginning in 1976 the majority of states enacted legislation that made it easier to transfer youths to adult courts, signaling a change in philosophy that would eventually lead juvenile justice into its next (and current) phase—the Crime Control Period—to be discussed shortly.

The Issue of Right to Treatment

Also in the 1970s, two conflicting types of cases emerged: one type tried to establish a "right to treatment," the other to establish the "least restrictive alternative." *Martarella v. Kelley* (1972) established that if juveniles who are judged to be in need of supervision are not provided with adequate treatment, they are deprived of their rights under the Eighth and Fourteenth Amendments. *Morales v. Turman* (1973) ruled that juveniles in a Texas training school have a statutory right to treatment. And, in *Nelson v. Heyne* (1974), the Seventh U.S. Court of Appeals also confirmed juveniles' right to treatment:

> When a state assumes the place of a juvenile's parents, it assumes as well the parental duties, and its treatment of its juveniles should, so far as can be reasonably required, be what proper parental care would provide. . . . Without a program of individual treatment, the result may be that the juvenile will not be rehabilitated, but warehoused.

Although many state courts have established a right to treatment, including minimum standards, the U.S. Supreme Court has not yet declared that juveniles have a constitutional right to treatment.

Decriminalization of Status Offenses

In line with efforts to deinstitutionalize status offenders, the American Bar Association (ABA) Joint Commission on Juvenile Justice Standards voted in 1977 for the elimination of uniquely juvenile offenses, that is, status offenses, such as cigarette smoking or consuming alcohol.

 According to the American Bar Association, juvenile delinquency liability should include only such conduct as would be designated a crime if committed by an adult.

The referral of status offenses to juvenile court has been viewed by many as a waste of court resources. These critics believe that court resources are best used for serious recidivist delinquents.

*Development
of Standards
for Juvenile Justice*

In 1977 a tentative draft of the Institute of Judicial Administration/American Bar Association *Juvenile Justice Standards* was published in 23 volumes. In 1978 the state of Washington began extensive legislative revision of its juvenile justice system based, in part, on these standards. Following implementation of the new legislation it was found that:

- Sentences were considerably more uniform, consistent and proportionate to the seriousness of the offense and the prior criminal record of the youth.

- While the overall severity level of sanctions was reduced during the first two years, there was an increase in the certainty that a sanction of some kind would be imposed.

- There was a marked increase in the use of incarcerative sanctions for the violent and serious/chronic offender, but nonviolent offenders and chronic minor property offenders were less likely to be incarcerated and more apt to be required to pay restitution, do community service or be on probation.

- Compliance with the sentencing guidelines was extremely high; nevertheless, differential handling of minorities and females still existed.

- There was a better record of holding juveniles accountable for their offenses.

- While the new legislation completely eliminated the referral of *status offenses,* it did not eliminate the referral of *status offenders.* Runaways were more likely to be contacted for delinquent acts, for example (Rieffel, pp.36–37, italics in original).

From 1979 to 1980, 20 volumes of these standards received American Bar Association approval. The standards related to the following: adjudication; appeals and collateral review; architecture of facilities; corrections administration; counsel for private parties; court organization and administration; dispositional procedures; dispositions; interim status; the release, control and detention of accused juvenile offenders between arrest and disposition; juvenile delinquency and sanctions; juvenile probation function; intake and predisposition investigative services; juvenile records and information systems; monitoring; planning for juvenile justice; police handling of juvenile problems; pretrial court proceedings; prosecution; rights of minors; transfer between courts; and youth service agencies. A summary and analysis of the project and the standards were released in 1990, reviewing the progress of the application of the standards (Flicker).

In the 1970s the rising fear of youth crime and rebelliousness coincided with a growing disillusionment with the effectiveness of the juvenile justice system. Citizens and lawmakers, amid mounting skepticism of the principles of rehabilitation established by the JJDP Act, began calling for more punitive measures against juvenile offenders, especially those who committed serious or violent

Highlights of Juvenile Rights Period Reform

The combination of serious, stigmatizing results achieved without due process safeguards led the U.S. Supreme Court in the 1960s to impose new requirements in determining when a juvenile could be made a ward of the state.

Since its inception, the juvenile court was guided by a welfare concept. When the U.S. Supreme Court took issue with its procedures, the juvenile court environment moved from a simple family atmosphere to a more adversarial system. The treatment of juveniles changed to a criminal approach, dispensing punishment and placing youths in locked facilities.

Philosophies

Dissent arose among professional child-welfare workers and policymakers about the causes of and treatment for juvenile delinquency. Consensus arose among the public and policymakers that the traditional agents of control—family, police, schools and courts—could not curb the rise of delinquency.

Treatment

The juvenile court system was revised to include due process, deinstitutionalization, decriminalization and diversion programs. Community-based therapy, rather than institutionalization, became the preferred method of treatment.

Policies

The federal executive branch expressed its concern about crime and delinquency by appointing the President's Commission on Law Enforcement and Administration of Justice. Large-scale federal financial and programmatic grants-in-aid were made available to states and localities for delinquency prevention and control programs.

While the Supreme Court questioned the juvenile court on due process procedures, the juvenile court also came under severe criticism because its philosophy of helping all juveniles rather than punishing delinquents led to an indiscriminate mixing of neglected or abused children, status offenders and violent offenders. Public policy has since been developed to separate neglected and abused juveniles from the delinquents, but status offenders have continued to be in contact with violent criminal delinquents.

felonies. The result was a much harsher attitude toward youth crime and a call to "get tough" with youthful lawbreakers, philosophies characteristic of the current crime control period.

The Crime Control Period (1980–Present)

As mainstream attitudes about the response to and treatment of juvenile offenders swung to more punitive measures, the formerly prevailing medical model of viewing unlawful behavior began to shift to what is often called a **justice model.** The issues involved and how they are viewed in each model are summarized in Table 1.1.

According to Schwartz (pp.83–84), the Carter administration (presidential term 1977–1981) was deeply committed to removing juveniles from adult jails, and the Department of Justice recommended a 34 percent increase in fiscal 1981–82 for the OJJDP, to be targeted at juvenile jail removal. However, when Ronald Reagan took office in 1981, his administration significantly reduced this funding level, claiming that the goal of removing children from adult jails had been largely accomplished and that even if not, it was a state and local problem.

Table 1.1
Comparison of the Medical and Justice Models

Issue	Medical Model 1930–1974	Justice Model 1974–Present
Cause of crime	Disease of society or of the individual.	Form of rational adaptation to societal conditions.
Image of offender	Sick; product of socioeconomic or psychological forces beyond control.	Capable of exercising free will, of surviving without resorting to crime.
Object of correction	To cure offender and society; to return both to health; rehabilitation.	Humanely control offender under terms of sentence; offer voluntary treatment.
Agency/institution responsibility	Change offender; reintegrate back into society.	Legally and humanely control offender; adequate care and custody; voluntary treatment; protect society.
Role of treatment and punishment	Voluntary or involuntary treatment as means to change offender. Treatment is mandatory; punishment used to coerce treatment; punishment and treatment viewed as same thing.	Voluntary treatment only; punishment and treatment not the same thing. Punishment is for society's good, treatment is for offender's good.
Object of legal sanctions (sentence)	Determine conditions that are most conducive to rehabilitation of offender.	Determine conditions that are just considering wrong done, best protection for society and deter offender from future crime.
Type of sentence	Indeterminate, flexible; adjust as offender changes.	Fixed sentence (less good time).
Who determines release time?	"Experts" (parole board for adults, institutional staff for juveniles).	Conditions of sentence as interpreted by Presumptive Release Date (PRD) formula.

Source: D. F. Pace, *Community Relations Concepts*, 3rd ed. Copyright © 1993, p.127. Placerville, CA: Copperhouse. Reprinted by permission.

By the 1980s the "best interests" of society had gained ascendency over those of youths. In the 1980s the OJJDP became increasingly conservative. Emphasis shifted to dealing with hard-core, chronic offenders. Also in the 1980s, state and federal concerns tended to center on the problems created by procedural informality and the juvenile court's broad discretion. The adversary system of legal process replaced the sedate environment and process of the "family" court that was directed to consider the "best" interest of the child's health, safety and welfare. The courts returned to a focus on what was right according to the law.

According to Krisberg (1990), the conservative swing added two more Ds to our juvenile justice system: **deterrence** and **just deserts.** *Deterrence* involves the use of punishment to prevent future lawbreaking. It does so in several ways, the most obvious being locking offenders up so that they can do no further harm to society. Incarceration may result in further deterrence by (1) serving as a lesson to the incarcerated person that crime does not pay and (2) sending the same message to the law-abiding public.

Deserts, or *just deserts* as it is often called, is a concept of punishment as a kind of justified revenge—the offending individual gets what is coming. This is the concept of *lex talionis,* or an eye for an eye, expressed in the Code of Hammurabi centuries ago.

In 1982, 214 long-term public institutions in the United States were designated either "strict" or "medium" custody training schools. This number included some original training schools, as well as smaller, high-security institutions built to either replace or augment them. Most schools involved agricultural training, which was thought to be reformative. This training focus required the schools to be located in rural areas. An unanticipated effect of this location policy was to remove the corrections problem from community awareness.

Throughout the 1980s and 1990s, public support increased for tougher policies directed at juvenile offenders, signaling a reversal of the juvenile due process trend of the previous two decades. Breen (p.50) observes:

> This policy shift is evidenced by 49 states that now allow juvenile court prosecutors to waive jurisdiction and transfer cases to adult court. In the opinion of some experts, this authority was given to prosecutors because they traditionally did not have the "soft on crime" attitudes of juvenile court judges. In 26 states, the jurisdictions of juvenile courts now exclude certain violent crimes such as murder, rape and armed robbery. A retreat from the due process revolution of the 1960s is also apparent in *Schall v. Martin.* . . . Here the U.S. Supreme Court, citing the doctrine of *parens patriae,* upheld the constitutionality of New York's law allowing the preventive detention of juveniles.

Schall v. Martin *(1984) and Preventive Detention*

At 11:30 P.M. on December 13, 1977, juvenile Gregory Martin was arrested on charges of robbery, assault and criminal possession of a weapon. Because of the late hour and because he lied about his address, Martin was kept in detention overnight. The next day he was brought before the family court accompanied by his grandmother. The family court judge noted that he had lied to the police about his address, that he was in possession of a loaded weapon and that he appeared to lack supervision at night. In view of these circumstances, the judge ordered Martin detained until trial. New York law authorized such pretrial or **preventive detention** of accused juvenile delinquents if "there is a substantial probability that they will not appear in court on the return date or there is a serious risk that they may before the return date commit an act which if committed by an adult would constitute a crime."

While Martin was in preventive detention, his attorneys filed a habeas corpus petition demanding his release. The petition charged that his detention denied him due process rights under the Fifth and Fourteenth Amendments. The suit was a class action suit on behalf of all youths held in preventive detention in New York. The New York appellate courts upheld Martin's claim, stating that most delinquents are released or placed on probation; therefore, it was unfair to confine them before trial. Indeed, later at trial, Martin was adjudicated a delinquent and sentenced to 2 years of probation.

The prosecution appealed the decision disallowing pretrial detention to the Supreme Court for final judgment. The Supreme Court reversed the decision, establishing the right of juvenile court judges to deny youths pretrial release if they perceived them to be dangerous.

> In *Schall v. Martin* (1984) the Supreme Court upheld the state's right to place juveniles in preventive detention, fulfilling a legitimate state interest of protecting society and juveniles by detaining those who might be dangerous to society or to themselves.

Pretrial detention need not be considered punishment merely because the juvenile is eventually released or put on probation. In *Schall* the Court reiterated its belief in the fundamental fairness doctrine and the doctrine of *parens patriae,* trying to strike a balance between the juvenile's right to freedom pending trial and the right of society to be protected. All 50 states have similar language allowing preventive detention in their juvenile codes.

Schall also established a due process standard for detention hearings. This standard included procedural safeguards, such as a notice, a hearing and a statement of facts given to juveniles before they are placed in detention. The Court further stated that detention based on prediction of future behavior did not violate due process. Many decisions made in the justice system, such as the decision to sentence or grant parole, are based partly on predicting future behavior. These decisions have all been accepted by the Court as legitimate exercises of state power.

Some Effects of Preventive Detention

The effects of preventive detention can be tragic. A 15-year-old California girl arrested for assaulting a police officer hanged herself after 4 days of isolation in a local jail. A 17-year-old boy was taken into custody and detained for owing $73 in unpaid traffic tickets, only to be tortured and beaten to death by his cellmates. In a West Virginia jail a truant was murdered by an adult inmate; in an Ohio jail a teenage girl was raped by a guard. A 15-year-old boy hanged himself in a Kentucky jail where he had been held for only 30 minutes. His offense: arguing with his mother.

The Evolution of Child, Parent and State Relationships

Developments with the evolving juvenile justice system in the United States had a direct effect on the relationships between children and their parents, children and the state and parents and the state. The major developments and influences on these relationships are summarized in Table 1.2. Bear in mind, however, the developments described and neatly categorized in the table are actually fluid, overlapping and ongoing.

Still Evolving

In looking over the development of juvenile justice, it is clear that the system today is considerably different in philosophy and form than that which existed several centuries ago. Be mindful that this history is what paved the way for current "innovations" in policy and practice, such as Balanced and Restorative Jus-

Table 1.2
Juvenile Justice Developments and Their Impact

Periods	Major Developments	Precipitating Influences	Child/State	Parent/State	Parent/Child
Puritan 1646–1824	Massachusetts Stubborn Child Law (1646)	A. Christian view of child as evil B. Economically marginal agrarian society	Law provides: A. Symbolic standard of maturity B. Support for family as economic unit	Parents considered responsible and capable of controlling child	Child considered both property and spiritual responsibility of parents
Refuge 1824–1899	Institutionalization of deviants; New York House of Refuge established (1824) for delinquent and dependent children	A. Enlightenment B. Immigration and industrialization	Child seen as helpless, in need of state intervention	Parents supplanted as state assumes responsibility for correcting deviant socialization	Family considered to be a major cause of juvenile deviancy
Juvenile Court 1899–1960	Establishment of separate legal system for juveniles—Illinois Juvenile Court Act (1899)	A. Reformism and rehabilitative ideology B. Increased immigration, urbanization and large-scale industrialization	Juvenile court institutionalizes legal irresponsibility of child	*Parens patriae* doctrine gives legal foundation for state intervention in family	Further abrogation of parents' rights and responsibilities
Juvenile Rights 1960–1980	Increased "legalization" of juvenile law—*Gault* decision (1966); Juvenile Justice and Delinquency Prevention Act (1974) calls for deinstitutionalization of status offenders	A. Criticism of juvenile justice system on humane grounds B. Civil rights movements by disadvantaged groups	Movement to define and protect rights as well as provide services to children	Reassertion of responsibility of parents and community for welfare and behavior of children	Attention given to children's claims against parents; earlier emancipation of children
Crime Control (1980–present)	Shift from medical (treatment) model to justice model and "get tough" attitude; "best interests" of society gained ascendancy over those of youths; Supreme Court approves of preventive detention for youths—*Schall* decision (1984); emphasis on deterrence and just deserts	A. Increase in violent juvenile crime B. Proliferation of gangs C. Spread of drug use	Adversary system of legal process replaces sedate "family" court process; courts return to a focus on what is right according to the law	Parents in some states are held liable for their child's criminal conduct	Unknown

Source: J. David Hawkins; Paul A. Pastor, Jr.; Michelle Bell; and Sheila Morrison. *Reports of the National Juvenile Justice Assessment Center: A Topology of Cause-Focused Strategies of Delinquency Prevention.* Washington, DC: U. S. Government Printing Office, 1980. Updated by author.

tice (BARJ) clauses, Juvenile Accountability Incentive Block Grants (JAIBG), peer juries, community mediation, the Blueprints for Violence Prevention program, Targeting Community Action Planning (TCAP) and many other programs—initiatives that will be explored in greater detail in later chapters.

Also keep in mind that the philosophies, policies, practices and programs that dominate the field today and are the focus of the remainder of this text, will likely pass, at some point, into the history chapters for future juvenile justice practitioners as the juvenile justice system continues to evolve. Krisberg (p.157) observes: "Although the conservative revolution in juvenile justice was motivated by the concepts of deterrence and deserts, the emergence of a 'get tough' philosophy also produced another 'D' in the world of juvenile justice—disarray." Which direction the system will take in this new century is unclear.

Summary

A separate justice system for youthful offenders (usually under age 18) is, historically speaking, relatively recent. A significant influence on the development of juvenile justice was the English concept of *parens patriae,* which gave kings, through the courts, the right and responsibility to take care of minors. The American colonists brought with them much of the English criminal justice system and its ways to deal with wayward youth. During the Puritan Period (1646–1824), five distinct yet interrelated institutions evolved to handle poor, abused, neglected, dependent and delinquent children brought before a court: (1) indenture and apprenticeship, (2) mixed almshouses (poorhouses), (3) private orphanages, (4) public facilities for dependent children and (5) jails.

The period from 1824 to 1899 is generally referred to as the Refuge Period. In 1824 the New York House of Refuge, the first U.S. reformatory, opened to house juvenile delinquents, defined in its charter as "youths convicted of criminal offenses or found in vagrancy." By the middle of the nineteenth century many states either built reform schools or converted their houses of refuge to reform schools. The middle of the nineteenth century also included the child-saving movement. The child savers were reformers whose philosophy was that the child was basically good and was to be treated by the state as a young person with a problem. They persuaded the 1899 Illinois legislature to pass a law establishing a juvenile court that became the cornerstone for juvenile justice throughout the United States and moved juvenile justice into an era known as the Juvenile Court Period (1899–1960).

The first juvenile courts were administrative agencies of circuit or district courts and served a social service function with the rehabilitative ideal of reforming children rather than punishing them. The passage of the 1899 Illinois Juvenile Court Act marked the first time that probation was formally made *specifically* applicable to juveniles. Probation, according to the act, was to have both an investigative and a rehabilitative function.

The juvenile court was the creation of progressive reformers who believed that treatment rather than punishment should be the focus of the juvenile justice system. During the first quarter of the twentieth century, the progressives further developed the medical model established by the Illinois Juvenile Court Act, approaching crime as a disease that could be treated and cured by social intervention. Federal government concern and involvement also began during this period. A direct result of the 1909 White House Conference on Youth was the establishment of the U.S. Children's Bureau in 1912. Passage of the Social Security Act in 1935 was the beginning of major federal funding for programs to aid children and families.

Radical societal changes began to occur at the beginning of the Juvenile Rights Period (1960–1980). In the 1960s the American family underwent significant changes that directly affected social work and its liaison between the juvenile, the family and the court. To deal with problems identified within the juvenile justice system, new policies were established regarding four key concepts, known as the Four Ds of juvenile justice—deinstitutionalization, diversion, due process and decriminalization.

During the 1960s the concern about the due process rights of youths in juvenile proceedings resulted in several landmark cases. The procedural requirements for waiver to criminal court were articulated by the Supreme Court in *Kent v. United States*. The *Gault* decision required that the due process clause of the Fourteenth Amendment be applied to proceedings in state juvenile courts, including the right of notice, the right to counsel, the right against self-incrimination and the right to confront witnesses.

Deinstitutionalization became a focal point when the 1967 President's Commission on Law Enforcement and Administration of Justice asserted that isolating offenders from their normal social environment may encourage the development of a delinquent orientation and, thus, further delinquent behavior. The resulting community-based correctional programs, such as probation, foster care and group homes, represented attempts to respond to these issues by normalizing social contacts and reducing the stigma attached to being institutionalized. The Uniform Juvenile Court Act (1968) provided for the care, protection and development of youths, without the stigma of a criminal label, by a program of treatment, training and rehabilitation in a family environment when possible. It also provided simple judicial and interstate procedures.

In the 1970s the major impact of the White House Conference on Youth was that it hit hard at the foundation of our system for handling youths, including unnecessarily punitive institutions. The Juvenile Justice and Delinquency Prevention (JJDP) Act of 1974 made federal delinquency prevention funds available to states that removed status offenders from prisons and jails and created alternative voluntary services to which status offenders could be diverted. This act had two key goals: deinstitutionalization of status offenders and separation/removal of juveniles from adult facilities.

The 1970s also saw juveniles' rights being addressed. *In re Winship* established proof beyond a reasonable doubt as the standard for juvenile adjudication proceedings, eliminating lesser standards such as a preponderance of the evidence, clear and convincing proof and reasonable proof. *McKeiver v. Pennsylvania* established that a jury trial is not a required part of due process in the adjudication of a youth as a delinquent by a juvenile court. *Breed v. Jones* established that a juvenile cannot be adjudicated in juvenile court and then tried for the same offense in an adult criminal court (double jeopardy).

By 1977 the American Bar Association endorsed the decriminalization of status offenses, urging that juvenile delinquency liability should include only such conduct as would be designated a crime if committed by an adult.

During the 1980s in *Schall v. Martin* (1984), the Supreme Court upheld the state's right to place juveniles in preventive detention. Preventive detention was perceived as fulfilling a legitimate state interest of protecting society and juveniles by detaining those who might be dangerous to society or to themselves.

Discussion Questions

1. The juvenile justice system has been defined as "justice that applies to children and adolescents with concern for their health, safety and welfare under sociolegal standards and procedures." Is this definition adequate? Why or why not?
2. Under the principle of *parens patriae,* how does the state (or the court) accept the role of "parent"? Are all households administered and managed alike?
3. Who are the present "child savers"? What states, associations and individuals have contributed to the present child-saver philosophy?
4. What do you consider to be the major milestones in the evolution of juvenile justice?
5. Is it possible for one system to effectively and fairly serve both children who need correction and those who need protection?
6. How may diversion result in "widening the net" of juvenile justice processing?
7. What are the rationales on which police diversion of juveniles is based in your community and state?
8. What are the major types of police diversion programs in your area and state?
9. What evidence suggests that diversion programs are effective in reducing juvenile recidivism? What findings, if any, contradict this evidence? Do you know of a diversion program that is working or one that has failed? Why?
10. What are the advantages and disadvantages of diversion?

InfoTrac College Edition Assignments

- Use InfoTrac College Edition to answer the Discussion Questions as appropriate.
- Use the term *parens patriae* as an InfoTrac subject guide to find and review the article, "Remnants of *Parens Patriae* in the Adjudicatory Hearing: Is a Fair Trial Possible in Juvenile Court?" by Joseph B. Sanborn, Jr. What is Sanborn's answer to his own question?
- Use *In re Gault* as an InfoTrac subject guide to find and review "The Common Thread: Diversion in Juvenile Justice," by Franklin E. Zimring. What is Zimring's assessment of today's diversionary juvenile court? Be prepared to share your thoughts with the class.

Internet Assignments

- Go to the OJJDP's Web site (http://ojjdp.ncjrs.org/). Locate the page for the 2002 reauthorization and note when the amended JJDP Act became public law and when it took effect.
- Select either the term *parens patriae* or *lex talionis* as your keywords and conduct an online search for more information about that principle. Be prepared to share your findings with the class.
- Go to www.ncjrs.org to find, read and outline any of the end-of-chapter references with an NCJ number in parenthesis or go to any reference having an online address to find, read and outline an entire article.

References

American Bar Association Joint Commission on Juvenile Justice Standards. Juvenile Justice Section. Washington, DC, no date.

Blackstone, William. *Commentaries on the Laws of England,* Vol. 4. Oxford: Clarendon, 1776.

Breckenridge, Sophoniska P. and Abbott, Edith. *The Delinquent Child and the Home.* New York: Random House, 1912.

Breen, Michael D. "A Renewed Commitment to Juvenile Justice." *The Police Chief,* March 2001, pp.47–52.

Decker, Scott H. *Juvenile Justice Policy.* Beverly Hills, CA: Sage Publications, 1984.

de Scheveinitz, Karl. *England's Road to Social Security.* Philadelphia: University of Pennsylvania, 1943.

Empey, LaMar. *American Delinquency: Its Meaning and Construction.* Homewood, IL: Dorsey, 1978.

Flicker, Barbara Danziger. *Standards for Juvenile Justice: A Summary and Analysis,* 2nd ed. New York: Institute for Judicial Administration, 1990.

Golden, Renny. *Disposable Children: America's Child Welfare System.* Belmont, CA: Wadsworth Publishing Company, 1997.

Griffin, Brenda S. and Griffin, Charles T. *Juvenile Delinquency in Perspective.* New York: Harper & Row, 1978.

Grunhut, Max. *Penal Reform.* New York: Clarendon, 1948.

Hawkins, J. David; Pastor, Paul A., Jr.; Bell, Michelle; and Morrison, Sheila. *Reports of the National Juvenile Justice Assessment Center: A Topology of Cause-Focused Strategies of Delinquency Prevention.* Washington, DC: National Institute for Juvenile Justice and Delinquency Prevention, U.S. Government Printing Office, 1980.

Hellum, F. "Juvenile Justice: The Second Revolution." *Crime and Delinquency,* Vol. 3, No. 25, 1979, pp.299–317.

Hunt, G. Bowdon. "Foreword." In *A Handbook for Volunteers in Juvenile Court,* by Vernon Fox. Special issue of *Juvenile Justice.* February 1973.

Keller, Oliver J. and Alper, Benedict S. *Halfway Houses: Community-Centered Corrections and Treatment.* Lexington, MA: D.C. Heath and Company, 1970.

Kocourek, Albert and Wigmore, John H. *Source of Ancient and Punitive Law, Evolution of Law, Selected Readings on the Origin and Development of Legal Institutions,* Vol. 1. Boston: Little, Brown, 1951.

Krisberg, Barry. "The Evolution of the Juvenile Justice System." Appeared in *The World & I,* April 1990, pp.487–503. Reprinted in *Criminal Justice 92/93,* 16th ed., edited by John J. Sullivan and Joseph L. Victor. Guilford, CT: Dushkin Publishing Group, Inc., 1992, pp.152–159.

Krisberg, Barry and Austin, James F. *Reinventing Juvenile Justice.* Newbury Park, CA: Sage Publications, 1993.

Pickett, Robert. *House of Refuge: Origins of Juvenile Justice in New York State.* Syracuse, NY: Syracuse University Press, 1969.

Platt, Anthony M. *The Child Savers: The Invention of Delinquency.* Chicago: University of Chicago Press, 1968.

The President's Commission on Law Enforcement and Administration of Justice. *The Task Force Report: Juvenile Delinquency and Youth Crime.* Washington, DC: U.S. Government Printing Office, 1967.

Rieffel, Alaire Bretz. *The Juvenile Justice Standards Handbook.* Washington, DC: American Bar Association, 1983.

Schmalleger, Frank. *Criminal Justice Today,* 2nd ed. Englewood Cliffs, NJ: Prentice Hall, 1993.

Schwartz, Ira M. In *Justice for Juveniles: Rethinking the Best Interests of the Child.* Lexington, MA: D.C. Heath and Company, 1989.

Task Force Report on Juvenile Justice and Delinquency Prevention. *Juvenile Justice and Delinquency Prevention.* Washington, DC: U.S. Government Printing Office, 1976.

U.S. Department of Justice. *The Challenge of Crime in a Free Society.* Washington, DC: U.S. Government Printing Office, 1967.

Webb, Sidney and Webb, Beatrice. *English Local Government: English Poor Law History,* Part I. New York: Longmans, Green, 1927.

The White House Conference on Youth. Washington, DC: U.S. Government Printing Office, 1972.

Zietz, Dorothy. *Child Welfare: Services and Perspective.* New York: John Wiley, 1969.

Cases Cited

Breed v. Jones, 421 U.S. 519 (1975)

Commonwealth v. Fisher, 213 Pa. 48, 62 A. 198, 199, 200 (1905)

Ex parte Crouse, 4 Whart. 9 (Pa. 1838)

In re Gault, 387 U.S. 1 (1967)

Kent v. United States, 383 U.S. 541 (1966)

Martarella v. Kelley, 349 F.Supp. 575 (S.D.N.Y. 1972)

McKeiver v. Pennsylvania, 403 U.S. 528 (1971)

Morales v. Turman, 364 F.Supp. 166 (E.D. Tex. 1973)

Nelson v. Heyne, 491 F.2d 352 (7th Cir. 1974)

Schall v. Martin, 467 U.S. 253 (1984)

In re Winship, 397 U.S. 358 (1970)

2

The Theories behind the Evolution of the Contemporary Juvenile Justice Process

The way in which a society treats its children—its young people—says something about the future of that society, its beliefs, and the viability of those beliefs. The way in which a society treats those of its children who break its laws says something about its humanity, its morality, its resilience, and its capacity for self-correction.

—National Center for Juvenile Justice

There are two great injustices that can befall a child. One is to punish him for something he didn't do. The other is to let him get away with doing something he knows is wrong.

—Robert Gardner

Do You Know?

- What types of justice exist?
- How crimes were originally differentiated?
- What two theories exist to explain the purpose of the law?
- What function is served by punishment according to the Durkheimian perspective? The Marxist perspective?
- How the contemporary conservative and liberal approaches to juvenile justice differ?
- What two competing world views have existed over the centuries and the concepts important to each view?
- What proponents of the classical view and those of the positivist view advocate for offenders?
- What theories have been developed to explain the cause of crime and delinquency and the major premises of each?
- Whether any single theory provides a complete explanation?
- What the terminology of the contemporary juvenile justice system emphasizes?
- What the three components of the juvenile justice system are?
- What primary lesson is learned from the funnel effect?

Can You Define?

American Dream	biotic balance	classical world view
anomie	classical view of	concordance
anomie theory	criminality	conflict theory

consensus theory
crime
critical theory
determinism
deterrence
differential association
   theory
distributive justice
diversion
ecological model
ecology
folkways
functionalism theory
funnel effect

incapacitation
labeling theory
mala in se
mala prohibita
mores
natural law
norms
particular justice
phrenology
physiognomy
positivist view of
   criminality
positivist world view
primary deviance

radical theory
restorative justice
retributive justice
secondary deviance
social contract
social disorganization
   theory
social ecology theory
social justice
strain theory
symbiosis
universal justice

INTRODUCTION

Philosophy, theory and history are intertwined—they simultaneously affect and, in turn, are affected by each other. The separation of discussions involving these elements into two chapters is artificial. Therefore, be mindful of information already presented in Chapter 1 while proceeding through this chapter, as these concepts wrap around and support those already covered. It may, at times, appear as if this chapter is backtracking. Indeed, in many cases, the theories discussed in Chapter 2 will have coincided with particular historical events or philosophical eras that prevailed at various times during the evolution of juvenile justice. In other instances, no such specific correlation exists. In either case, the material presented is intended to fill in some of the "why" and "how" gaps left from the first chapter.

As seen in Chapter 1, the juvenile justice system has evolved slowly, influenced by many circumstances. In addition to its historical evolution, the system has deep roots in theories about justice, delinquency, crime and punishment. While the previous chapter focused on historical events with specific relevance to juveniles, this chapter takes a step back to look at broader issues that apply to both youths and adults, such as justice, law and theories of criminality, in an effort to better understand why the paths of juvenile and adult justice diverged.

This chapter begins with a discussion of how justice has been viewed through the ages, the types of laws instituted to achieve justice and contemporary perspectives on punishment. This is followed by an explanation of two competing world views that have influenced the entire criminal justice system, including the juvenile justice system. Next, various theories about the causation of crime and delinquency are explored. These discussions, combined with those from Chapter 1, set the foundation for a look at the juvenile justice system structure and process itself, including a comparison of the contemporary juvenile and criminal justice systems and how cases may enter and flow throughout and between the two systems.

Justice

Centuries ago Aristotle warned that no government could stand that is not founded on justice. As a nation, America is firmly committed to "liberty and justice for all." But is this the reality? And just what is justice?

Aristotle wrote that the *just* is that which is lawful (**universal justice**) and that which is fair and equal (**particular justice**):

> Of particular justice and that which is just in the corresponding sense, one kind is that which is manifested in distributions of honour or money or the other things that fall to be divided among those who have a share in the constitution. . . .
>
> This, then, is what the just is—the proportional; the unjust is what violates the proportion. Hence one term becomes too great, the other too small, as indeed happens in practice; for the man who acts unjustly has too much, and the man who is unjustly treated too little, of what is good (Ross, 1952, pp.378–379).

 Distributive or **social justice** provides an equal share of what is valued in a society to each member of that society. This includes power, prestige and possessions. **Retributive justice** seeks revenge for unlawful behavior.

Distributive justice or social justice is frequently ignored but certainly must be considered in any discussion of justice. Usually, however, the focus is on retributive justice, harkening back to the ancient concept of an eye for an eye (*lex talionis*). When distributive and retributive justice are not differentiated, critics may claim that retributive justice has failed when, in effect, it has no power over the failure.

Merton (1957) views **crime** as being caused by the frustration of people in the lower socio-economic levels within an affluent society that denies them legal access to social status and material goods. He views this denial as not only unjust but also as a root of many social ills, including crime. Merton further suggests that this is especially true of our "underprivileged youth" who need not only groceries in the literal sense, but also "groceries for growing." In discussing justice for juveniles, Springer (1986, p.76) suggests:

> It is beyond the scope of this paper to discuss social justice, what Aristotle called "distributive justice," but it is within its scope to make mention of the sad consequences of our inability to provide a decent social environment for what would appear to be a growing segment of our youthful society.
>
> This is not the place to engage in discourse on the dire ends of poverty, class divisions, urbanization, industrialization, urban blight, unemployment, breakdown of religion, breakdown of the family, and all of the other established criminogenic factors. It is the place, however, to recognize, at least, that the criminal justice system is the least effective means of crime prevention and social control. If we are interested in a relatively crime-free society, we must look elsewhere than the courts.

Krisberg and Austin (1993, p.51), in the conclusion of their discussion of historical approaches to juvenile delinquency, likewise suggest:

> Not surprisingly, juvenile justice reforms have inexorably increased state control over the lives of the poor and their children. The central implication of this historical analysis is that the future of delinquency prevention and control will be determined largely by ways in which the social structure evolves. It is possible that

this future belongs to those who wish to advance social justice on behalf of young people rather than to accommodate the class interests that have dominated this history.

This explanation for the existence of crime is discussed in detail later in this chapter. Another type of justice, restorative justice, has gained momentum and support throughout the juvenile justice field in recent years.

Restorative justice focuses on repairing the harm done to victims and to the community and stresses that offenders must contribute to the repair.

As Karp (2001, p.729) explains: "Fundamentally, restorative approaches are distinguished from retributive and traditional rehabilitation approaches by their focus on sanctions that address the harm caused to victims and communities." Although the concept is actually quite old, it was long overlooked and neglected throughout most of the history of the American justice process. Bazemore and Umbreit (2001, p.1) contend: "Restorative justice suggests that the response to youth crime must strike a balance among the needs of victims, offenders and communities and that each should be actively involved in the justice process to the greatest extent possible." According to Wilson (2001, p.1): "Reconciling the needs of victims and offenders with the needs of the community is the underlying goal of restorative justice. Unlike retributive justice, which is primarily concerned with punishing crime, restorative justice focuses on repairing the injury that crime inflicts." The renewed interest in and focus on restorative justice and using restorative conferencing as a correctional alternative is discussed in Chapter 9.

Justice and the Law

Every society has **norms,** that is, rules or laws governing the actions and interactions of its people. These are usually of two types: folkways and mores. **Folkways** describe how people are expected to dress, eat and show respect for one another. They encourage certain behaviors. **Mores,** in contrast, are the *critical* norms vital to a society's safety and survival. Mores are often referred to as **natural law**—the rules of conduct that are the same everywhere because they are basic to human behavior.

Some behaviors, such as murder and rape, are deemed by any reasonable person to be inherently bad. Natural law states that certain acts are wrong by their very nature, and behavior that disregards the common decency one human owes to another is morally and legally wrong. Each society has a general idea of what constitutes natural law. Our founding fathers identified such principles when they wrote of the "inalienable rights to life, liberty and the pursuit of happiness" and of "truths held to be self-evident."

Acts considered immoral or wrong in themselves, such as murder and rape, are called *mala in se.* Those acts prohibited because they infringe on others' rights, not because they are necessarily considered evil by nature, such as having more than one wife, are called *mala prohibita.*

Crimes were originally differentiated as:

mala in se	*mala prohibita*
wrong in and of itself	a prohibited wrong
origin in mores	origin in folkways
natural law	man-made law
common law	statutory law
stable over time	changes over time

Natural laws may be declared to be criminal acts by man-made laws. Natural laws have remained relatively unchanged over the years, while man-made laws are altered nearly every legislative session.

Purposes of Law

According to sociologist Max Weber, the primary purpose of law is to regulate human interactions—that is, to support social order. Throughout history, law has served many other purposes, including to protect the interests of society, govern behavior, deter antisocial behavior, enforce moral beliefs, support those in power, regulate human interactions, uphold individual rights, identify lawbreakers, punish lawbreakers and seek retribution for wrongdoing.

Two prominent theories about the underlying purpose of law are consensus theory and conflict theory.

Consensus Theory

Consensus theory holds that individuals within a society agree on basic values—on what is inherently right and wrong. Laws express these values.

This theory dates back at least as far as Plato and Aristotle. Deviant acts are deviant because society, in general, feels they are abnormal and unacceptable behavior. Consensus theory was expanded upon by the French historian and philosopher Charles de Montesquieu (1689–1755), a founder of political science. Montesquieu's philosophy centered around the **social contract** theory developed by the 17th century English philosopher Thomas Hobbes, whereby free, independent individuals agree to form a community and give up a portion of their individual freedom to benefit the security of the group.

As discussed in Chapter 1, this social contract applied to minors as well as adults. Youths were expected to obey the rules established by society and to suffer the consequences if they did not. A century later the concept of the social contract was expanded upon by Emile Durkheim.

Punishment and Social Solidarity— The Durkheimian Perspective

Emile Durkheim (1858–1917), a pioneer in sociology, argued that punishment is a moral process to preserve the shared values of a society, that is, its collective conscience. When individuals deviate from this collective conscience, society is outraged and seeks revenge to restore the moral order. Garland (1991, p.123) notes: "Punishment thus transforms a threat to social order into a triumph of social solidarity." Garland (p.127) also notes: "As Durkheim makes clear, an act of punishment is also a sign that authorities are in control, that crime is an aberration, and that the conventions that govern social life retain their force and vitality."

 The Durkheimian perspective sees punishment as revenge and as a way to restore and solidify the social order.

Two key elements of Durkheim's perspective are (1) that the general population is involved in the act of punishing, giving it legitimacy, and (2) it is marked by deeply emotional, passionate reactions to crime. Durkheim (1933, pp.73–80) believed:

- Crime is conduct "universally disapproved of by members of each society."
- "An act is criminal when it offends strong and defined states of the collective conscience."

According to Durkheim, criminal law synthesizes society's essential morality and establishes boundaries that cannot be crossed without threatening the society's very existence. Durkheim (1951 [1897], p.252) developed a concept known as **anomie,** meaning normlessness. Anomie refers to the breakdown of societal norms as a result of society's failure to distinguish between right and wrong.

Although laws usually reflect the majority values of a society, which is important in a democracy, they rarely represent the views of everyone. This may result in conflict.

© 1997 North Wind Pictures

Emile Durkheim (1858–1917) was a French sociologist and author who established the method and theoretical framework of social science.

Conflict Theory

Conflict theory suggests that laws are established to keep the dominant class in power.

The roots of this theory can be found in the writings of Marx and Engels who wrote in the *Manifesto of the Communist Party* (1848):

> The history of all hitherto existing society is the history of class struggles. Freeman and slave, patrician and plebeian, lord and serf, guild-master and journeyman, in a word, oppressor and oppressed stood in constant opposition to one another, carried on an interrupted, now hidden, now open fight, a fight that each time ended in either a revolutionary reconstruction of society at large, or in the common ruin of the contending classes.

Conflict theory shifts the focus from lawbreaking to lawmaking and law enforcing and how they protect the interests and values of the dominant groups within a society. Walker et al. (2000, p.19) suggest:

> Conflict theory explains racial disparities in the administration of justice as products of broader patterns of social, economic, and political inequality in U.S. society. These inequalities are the result of prejudicial attitudes on the part of the white majority and discrimination against minorities in employment, education, housing, and other aspects of society. . . . Conflict theory explains the overrepresentation of racial and ethnic minorities in arrest, prosecution, imprisonment, and capital punishment as both the product of these inequalities and an expression of prejudice against minorities.

Punishment and Class Power— The Marxist Perspective

Rather than viewing punishment as a means of providing social solidarity, Marx (1818–1883) saw punishment as a way to enhance the power of the upper class and an inevitable result of capitalism. Marx referred to the lower class as a "slum proletariat" made up of vagrants, prostitutes and criminals. "In effect, penal policy is taken to be one element within a wider strategy of controlling the poor; punishment should be understood not as a social response to the criminality of individuals but as a mechanism operating in the struggle between social classes" (Garland, p.128).

The Marxist perspective sees punishment as a way to control the lower class and preserve the power of the upper class.

This rationale was doubtless operating throughout the Middle Ages, the Renaissance, the Reformation and into the nineteenth century. Society was divided into a small ruling class, a somewhat larger class of artisans and a vastly larger class of peasants. Intimidation through brutal criminal law was an important form of social control. Flicker (1990, p.38) sees this rationale operating in the development of our juvenile justice system:

> The unfortunate historical fact is that the juvenile justice system . . . began with the right observation and the wrong conclusion. Manifestly, poor people are more likely to beg, steal, and commit certain other crimes related to their social and economic status than affluent people. Although socially unacceptable, crime could

be seen as a response to poverty. It was a way to get money. The preferred solutions—jobs, vocational training, financial assistance for the unemployable—required a constructive community attitude toward the disadvantaged. But a combination of Calvinism, prejudice, and social Darwinism confused cause and effect—idleness, inferiority, and criminality were seen as causing poverty, rather than the reverse. Therefore progressive elements in the community, the social reformers, felt justified in saving impoverished children from the inexorable path of crime by investigating their homes and families, attempting to imbue them with principles of Christian morality, and, if unsuccessful, removing them to a better environment.

Contemporary Perspectives on Justice and Punishment

Today's justice professionals and, in fact, society as a whole have differing attitudes and opinions regarding how the juvenile justice system *should* address the issues of delinquency and punishment. These philosophies are often categorized as either conservative or liberal. The *conservative* attitude is to "get tough," "stop babying these kids" and "get them off the streets." This is reminiscent of the child savers' efforts to "contain" certain children.

 The conservative approach to juvenile justice is "get tough on juveniles"—to punish and imprison them.

The conservative philosophy accepts retribution as a purpose of punishment. The conservative view also supports the use of imprisonment to control crime and antisocial behavior. Rehabilitative programs may be provided during incarceration, but it is imprisonment itself, with its attendant deprivations, that must be primarily relied on to prevent crime, delinquency and recidivism. Correctional treatment is not necessary.

In contrast, the *liberal* attitude toward juvenile justice is "treatment, not punishment" for youths who are antisocial and wayward.

 The liberal approach to juvenile justice stresses treatment and rehabilitation, including community-based programs.

The theoretical roots of these two perspectives can be found in the centuries-old competing world views of who or what is responsible for crime.

Two Competing World Views

Two distinct and opposing views exist as to who or what is responsible for crime—the classical view and the positivist view.

The Classical World View

In the eighteenth century, criminologists began to apply the scientific method to explore the causes of crime. A leader of the classical school was Cesare Beccaria (1738–1794), whose *On Crimes and Punishment* was published in 1764.

 The **classical world view** holds that humans have free will and are responsible for their own actions.

Other important principles of the classical theory, also called the **classical view of criminality,** include the following:

- Individuals have free will. Some choose to commit crime.
- Laws should bring the greatest measure of happiness to the largest number of people.
- Those who break the law should be punished according to penalties established in the law.
- The focus is on crime.

Like Durkheim, Beccaria believed that society functions under a social contract, with individuals giving up certain freedoms to live peacefully together. Classical theorists believed that delinquency was the result of free will. Consequently, they advocated harsh and immediate punishment so offenders would be "unwilling" to commit future crimes.

 Proponents of the classical view advocate punishment for offenders.

Several aspects of the classical view are found in the juvenile justice system. Classical theory suggests that the threat of punishment will lower youths' tendency toward delinquency. If the punishment is severe enough, youths will avoid delinquent activity, a process known as **deterrence.** However, the effectiveness of deterrence is uncertain. Many law violators believe they will never be caught, and if they are, they believe they can "beat the rap." Those who violate the law under the influence of drugs may think they are invincible. Punishment is no threat to them. Juveniles may also resist the threat of punishment because of peer pressure. Being rejected by the gang would be worse than getting caught by the police. Indeed, being arrested and serving time are often seen as rites of passage, endowing a sort of higher status on those who make the journey. Also, many juveniles know the differences between juvenile and adult court and believe they will receive less severe punishment because of their age.

Classical theory also advocates **incapacitation** as a consequence for criminal activity. Institutionalization is intended not to rehabilitate offenders, but to keep them away from law-abiding society. Classical theory holds that criminal offenders should be sanctioned merely because they deserve punishment, and that punishment should be founded on what the offender deserves. Critics say this "just deserts" approach is actually a desire for revenge. Since the first juvenile court in 1899, the juvenile justice system has opposed deserts-based punishment. Incarcerated juveniles were usually given short sentences (1 to 3 years at most) and sent to a nonpunitive, rehabilitation-oriented institution.

 Classical view theorists suggest that deterrence, incapacitation and, in some cases, just deserts punishment is the way to deal with delinquency.

Classical theorists' views conflict with those adhering to the *parens patriae* philosophy, which advocates reform as a more appropriate way to deal with delinquency. During the nineteenth century another view of criminality was developed in reaction to the classical theory.

The Positivist World View   A leader of the positivist world view was Cesare Lombroso (1835–1909), an Italian physician who studied the brains of criminals. Lombroso maintained that criminals were born with a predisposition to crime and needed exceptionally favorable conditions in life to avoid criminal behavior. As the originator of the positivist view of criminality—that is, transferring emphasis from the crime itself to the criminal behavior—Lombroso has been called the father of modern criminology. He firmly believed that criminals were literally born, not made—that the primary cause of crime was biological. He was writing at the same time that Charles Darwin's theory of evolution was becoming widely circulated, and he was probably greatly influenced by Darwin's ideas. Although some of Lombroso's work was later found to be flawed, he started people thinking about causes for criminal behavior other than free will.

 The **positivist world view** holds that humans are shaped by their society and are the product of environmental and cultural influences.

Other important principles of the positivist theory, also called the **positivist view of criminality,** include:

- Individuals' actions are determined not by free will but by biological and cultural factors.
- The purpose of law is to avert revolution and convince the masses to accept the social order.
- The focus is on the criminal.

The positivist-view theorists, who believe delinquent behavior is the result of a youth's biological makeup and life experiences, think treatment should include altering one or more of the factors that contributed to the unlawful behavior.

 Proponents of the positivist view advocate rehabilitation for offenders.

Positivist theorists stress community treatment and rehabilitation rather than incapacitation. For years the *parens patriae* attitude prevailed, with youths shielded from being labeled and punished as criminals.

Building on Lombroso's idea that environmental influences affected criminal behavior, some scholars developed the positivist view of criminality based on the concept of **determinism.** Determinism views human behavior as the product of multiple environmental and cultural influences rather than a single factor.

Throughout the ages societies have embraced one view or the other, with many people taking a middle position but tending toward one view. And these two world views have profoundly affected the various theories about the causes of crime and delinquency that have been set forth over the years.

Causes of Crime and Delinquency: An Overview

Over time, many theories have been developed to explain why people fail to obey society's laws—why do they become criminals? Other theories take the opposite approach and try to explain why people obey the laws—why do they *not* become criminals? As you explore the theories that follow, keep these two questions in mind.

During the first half of the twentieth century, several interpretations of the cause of delinquency gained prominence. The earliest theories explored biological and psychological factors. In fact, physical and psychological examinations of children who were brought before the court were standard orders in the juvenile court process. Judicial disposition often included individual counseling and psychological therapy. In the 1950s, under the influence of therapists such as Carl Rogers, group counseling became common in most juvenile institutions.

Slowly, this approach was replaced with social milieu and environmental explanations for delinquency. Delinquency prevention attempts focused on reorganizing the social environment—both physically, through housing renewal, and socioeconomically, through social welfare. There was a significant philosophical shift of the blame for delinquency from personal to social factors. Consequently, the federal government was increasingly drawn into the process of juvenile delinquency prevention.

 Early efforts to explain crime and delinquency were set forth in the classical theory and the positivist theory. Later theories focused on biological, psychological or sociological causes of crime and delinquency. Most recently, critical theories of the causes of crime and delinquency have been developed.

Biological Theories

Some researchers propose biological explanations for crime. They find that some biological characteristics appear more frequently in criminals than in noncriminals. In other words, they believe there are such things as criminal genes.

 Biological theories include physiognomy, phrenology, body type and heredity studies, including studies of twins and adoptees.

Physiognomy Studies

Physiognomy assigns character traits to physical features, especially facial features. Curran and Renzetti (1994, p.39) note that in the Middle Ages the law specified that if "two people were suspected of having committed the same crime, the uglier one should be regarded as more likely the guilty party." Indeed, people tend to have a mental picture of criminals. Some researchers have pointed out that criminals tend toward large, prominent or crooked noses, abnormal ears, lantern jaws, high cheek bones, higher sex drives, lower intelligence, larger body types, longer arms, larger lips or abnormal amounts of body hair. Researchers search for predominant factors among criminals and compare these factors with their presence or absence in the general population.

Phrenology

Phrenology studies the shape of the skull to predict intelligence and character. This was the approach used by Cesare Lombroso, who believed that at birth criminals are recognizable by certain anomalies. Such anomalies do not cause crime, but they indicate a predisposition to criminal behavior. Techniques used in phrenology are sometimes demonstrated at fairs or shopping malls.

Body Type Theories

Going beyond the study of the skull to predict predisposition to criminality, William Sheldon (1898–1977) theorized that humans can be divided into three distinct body types, or somatotypes, corresponding to three distinct personalities: (1) the endomorphic—soft, fat, easygoing; (2) the mesomorphic—athletic, muscular, aggressive; and (3) the ectomorphic—thin, delicate, shy, introverted.

Heredity Studies

Bohm (1997, pp.39–40) describes studies of twins and of adopted boys that tend to support a biological basis for predisposition to crime. More than a half-century of using this methodology reveals that identical twins are more likely to demonstrate **concordance** (where both twins have criminal records) than are fraternal twins. This supports the heredity link. A problem with the twin studies, however, is the potential confounding of genetic and environmental influences.

The findings from adoption studies reveal that the percentage of adoptees who are criminal is greater when the biological father has a criminal record than when the adoptive father has one. Thus, like the twin studies, the adoption studies presumably demonstrate the influence of heredity but cannot adequately separate it from the influences of the environment.

Other Approaches Supporting Biological Causation Theories

Some biological studies have indicated that chromosomal factors may be responsible for criminal behavior. If this is true, certain people are victims of their own heritage. For example, high testosterone has been associated with aggressive physical and sexual behavior. Testosterone injected into female rats causes them to adopt the male characteristics of aggressive physical and sexual behavior.

Other studies have indicated that high levels of specific chemicals or elements in the body, as well as allergic reactors, contribute to aggression and perhaps criminality. For example, abnormal levels of manganese, zinc, copper or chromium may cause antisocial behavior. Furthermore, some researchers believe that nutritional factors are related to abnormal behavior. Abnormal EEG patterns have also been recorded in some prisoners.

As noted by Donohue (1995, p.1): "The genetics and crime issue is one very hot potato" and results in "a crime–causation hornet's nest."

© Stephen Shames/Polaris

Children's environment can shape their development. Youths growing up in poverty may resort to delinquent acts such as window breaking for entertainment or to more serious delinquent acts to obtain material possessions. Here, a teenager demolishes an apartment after his family was evicted.

He notes (p.12): "Many scientists doubt the existence of a so-called 'crime gene,' adding fuel to the age-old 'nature vs. nurture' debate with respect to crime causation." He concludes:

> Scientists say that low levels of serotonin, a neurotransmitter that helps regulate emotions, may cause people to become violent. Since serotonin deficits have been tied to both genetic defects and environmental factors, serotonin studies may help sociologists and scientists find a common ground in the debate on how to reduce violent crime.

Psychological Theories

Exploring psychological causes of crime has produced a number of explanations, including the following:

- Criminals are morally insane; what they do criminally they do not perceive as wrong.
- Personality is developed in early childhood. Future behavior is determined in early childhood. Subsequent sociological and environmental associations do not change this early behavior development.
- Certain people have personalities so deviant that they have little or no control over their impulses.
- There are criminal families in which succeeding generations gravitate toward criminality.
- Mental and moral degeneration cause crime.

Psychological theories about crime focus on intelligence and psychoanalysis.

Intelligence and Crime

H. H. Goddard (1866–1957) was one of the earliest psychologists to link intelligence and criminality. Goddard believed that criminals are not necessarily biologically inferior, although they might be intellectually inferior. This correlation was again brought to public attention by Hernstein and Murray (1994), who used the bell-shaped normal curve from statistical studies to promote the idea that individuals' intelligence falls within this curve and may also account for criminality.

Psychoanalysis

The psychoanalytic theory of Sigmund Freud (1859–1939) was a popular explanation for human behavior. It stated that personality imbalances had their roots in abnormal emotional and mental development. A person might become fixed at a certain developmental stage or regress to an earlier stage.

Of most importance to the study of criminality is Freud's explanation of problems that arise from fixation at or regression to the phallic stage (3 to 6 years of age). Fixation or regression to this stage may result in sexual assault, rape or prostitution. It may also result in unresolved oedipal or electra conflicts. According to Bohm (p.56):

> Individuals who do not successfully resolve the oedipal or electra complex, and thus do not develop a strong superego capable of controlling the id, were called psychopaths by Freud. (Sociologists call them sociopaths.) Many criminal offenders are presumed to be psychopaths, sociopaths, or antisocial personalities and are characterized by no sense of guilt, no subjective conscience and no sense of right and wrong.

Sociological Theories

Sociology is the study of human social structures and human relationships. People start life as members of families and later learn to live with other work and social groups. Some sociologists believe that criminals are molded by social conditions and the environment in which they develop. Not everyone has the same goals or ways to achieve them. Some people choose to reach goals of financial success and power through illegal acts. To what extent social conditions cause criminal behavior is a subject of much debate.

There are several opinions about the relationship of sociological theories and crime occurrence, including the following:

- Lack of education, poverty-level income, poor housing, slum conditions and conflict within home and family probably increase crime commission. Achievement expectations are low. If all these conditions disappeared, crime would decrease.

- Continual lawbreaking causes an individual to become part of a subculture that advocates crime and violence as a way to achieve goals or solve problems. It operates outside society's rules. Crimes committed within the subculture are rarely reported to police.

- Behavior is learned. There is good and bad, right and wrong behavior. Identical pressures affect criminals and noncriminals alike.

 Sociological theories include ecological models, social disorganization, functionalism, anomie or strain theory, learning theories and social control theories.

The Ecological Model

Ecology is the study of the relationships between organisms and their environment. Findings from ecology were the basis for the **ecological model,** first described by sociologist Robert Park, University of Chicago (1964–1966). Park et al. (1928) compared the growth of a city and its attendant crime problems with growth in nature. They found that cities were environments like those found in nature, governed by the same forces that affect natural ecosystems.

Ecologists explain that the plant life in an area of land goes through several stages of growth. First is an invasion period when a new species of plant attempts to gain a foothold. Next the new plant may take over the area or dominate it. Finally the environment stabilizes, accepting the presence of its new dominant organism. A **biotic balance** occurs when the relations between the different species of plants and their necessary conditions for survival maintain an equilibrium. All the organisms are then able to survive and prosper. Ecologists also describe how two different organisms can live together in a mutually *beneficial* relationship known as **symbiosis.**

Park encouraged his colleagues and students to study the dynamics of urban life using this ecological model to explain many of the conditions that existed and the problems that plagued cities. Communities could be studied in part by analyzing the invasion, domination and succession of different ethnic and racial groups. Problems within the community could perhaps be alleviated by studying the presence or absence of a biotic balance and symbiosis in a neighborhood.

In addition, according to Parks, researchers can demarcate a city based on its outwardly moving growth pattern of concentric zones, with each zone representing a particular form of development and community life. The ecological model stressed that any explanation of criminal behavior cannot be taken out of its social context.

Social Disorganization Theory

Two other Chicago sociologists, Shaw and McKay (1942), applied the ecological model to a study of delinquency. Their area studies involved 25,000 delinquents from the Juvenile Court of Cook County from 1900 to 1933. They, too, found concentric zones within an area, with transitional inner-city zones having the highest crime rates. Their **social ecology theory** suggested that ecological conditions predicted delinquency and that gang membership is a normal response to social conditions.

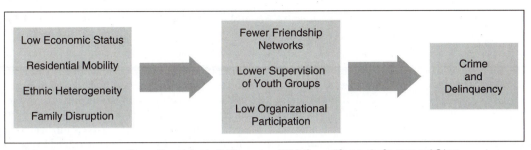

Figure 2.1
Social Disorganization Model

Source: Constructed by R. J. Sampson and W. B. Groves. "Community Structure and Crime: Testing Social-Disorganization Theory." *American Journal of Sociology*, 94, 1989, p.783. Printed in S. Giora Shoham and John Hoffmann. *A Primer in the Sociology of Crime*. New York: Harrow and Heston Publishers, 1991, p.51. Reprinted by permission.

Shaw and McKay's **social disorganization theory** contended that urban areas produced delinquency directly by weakening community controls and generating a subculture of delinquency passed from one generation to the next. Their social disorganization theory was built upon by other sociologists, including Sampson and Groves (1989), who developed the social disorganization model shown in Figure 2.1.

Functionalism

Harvard sociologist Parsons (1902–1979) developed a theory explaining criminal behavior as an integral part of our society. Borrowing from Durkheim, Parsons' **functionalism theory** viewed crime as a necessary part of society. Without crime who would need laws, lawyers, police officers, courts, judges, jails and jailers?

Anomie or Strain Theory

Building on Parsons's theory of functionalism, Robert Merton (1910–2003) saw a basic conflict between cultural goals in the United States and our social structure. Merton (1938) adopted Durkheim's concept of anomie—the breakdown of social norms, individuals dissociating themselves from the collective conscience of the group—as the basis for his theory.

Because most people believe in the **American Dream** (that is, through hard work anyone can become rich), strive for it and fall short, they experience a strain (Merton, 1938). **Anomie** or **strain theory** is explored by Messner and Rosenfeld (1997) in *Crime and the American Dream*. They (p.11) note:

> Our analysis is grounded in the variant of anomie theory associated with the work of the American sociologist Robert K. Merton. Merton combines strategic ideas from Durkheim with insights borrowed from Karl Marx, another founding figure in the social sciences, to produce a provocative and compelling account of the social forces underlying deviant behavior in American society. . . .
>
> Most importantly, we accept Merton's underlying premise that motivations for crime do not result simply from the flaws, failures, or free choices of individuals. A complete explanation of crime ultimately must consider the sociocultural environments in which people are located.

The views of Messner and Rosenfeld are presented in the preface of their text (p.xi):

> The essence of our argument is that the distinctive patterns and levels of crime in the United States are produced by the cultural and structural organizations of American society. American culture is characterized by a strong emphasis on the goal of monetary success and a weak emphasis on the importance of the legitimate means for the pursuit of success. This combination of strong pressures to succeed monetarily and weak restraints on the selection of means is intrinsic to the dominant cultural ethos: the American Dream. The American Dream contributes to crime directly by encouraging people to employ illegal means to achieve goals that are culturally approved. It also exerts an indirect effect on crime through its interconnections with the institutional balance of power in society.
>
> The American Dream promotes and sustains an institutional structure in which one institution—the economy—assumes dominance over all others. The resulting imbalance in the institutional structure diminishes the capacity of other institutions, such as the family, education, and the political system, to curb criminogenic cultural pressures and to impose controls over the behavior of members of society. In these ways, the distinctive cultural commitments of the American Dream and its companion institutional arrangements contribute to high levels of crime.

Cohen (1955) also built upon Merton's work, adapting his anomie/strain theory in an attempt to explain gang delinquency. Cohen replaced Merton's social goals of wealth with acceptance and status. Youths abandoned the middle-class values for their own values—attaining status among their peers. Cohen's study of delinquent subculture, set forth in *Delinquent Boys* (1955), found that delinquency was caused by social and economic limitations, inadequate family support, developmental handicaps and status frustration. The result: short-run hedonism and group autonomy.

Closely related to strain theorists are those who look at the correlation between unemployment and crime. For example, Carlson and Michalowski (1997, pp.210–211) note:

> The proposition that increases in unemployment will generate increases in crime has long been accepted as a basic tenet of the macro sociology of crime and delinquency. A number of otherwise competing models of crime causation such as conflict theory, Marxian theories, social disorganization theories, and strain theory share the assumption that economic distress generated by rises in unemployment will increase crimes against both persons and property.

Another strain theorist is Agnew (1992) who identified three sources of strain: (1) failure to achieve positively valued goals, (2) the removal of positively valued stimuli and (3) the presentation of negative stimuli.

Learning Theories

In the 1930s and 1940s, Sutherland (1883–1950) set forth the proposition that criminal behavior is learned through imitation or modeling. In *Principles of Criminology* (1939) with Cressey, he set forth the principles of differential association. Among their propositions are the following (Sutherland and Cressey, 1974, pp.75–77):

- Criminal behavior is learned in interaction with other persons in a process of communication.

- The principal part of the learning of criminal behavior occurs within intimate personal groups.

- The process of learning criminal behavior by association with criminal and anticriminal patterns involves all the mechanisms involved in any other type of learning.

- A person becomes delinquent because of an excess of definitions favorable to the violation of law over definitions unfavorable to the violation of law. This is the principle of differential association.

Sutherland's **differential association theory** is still an important theory of crime causation. As noted by Bohm (p.99): "Learning theory explains criminal behavior and its prevention with the concepts of positive reinforcement, negative reinforcement, extinction, punishment, and modeling or imitation." Many of these factors were explored thoroughly during the 1960s and 1970s based on the behavior modification studies initiated by B. F. Skinner.

Social Control Theories

An influential contemporary social control theorist is Travis Hirschi, whose text *Causes of Delinquency* (1969) greatly influenced current thinking. Hirschi's social control theory traces delinquency to the bond that individuals maintain with society. Social controls rather than moral values are what maintain law and order. A lack of attachment to parents and school can result in delinquency. Hirschi believed that delinquency resulted from a lack of proper socialization and particularly ineffective child-rearing practices. As Bohm (p.104) suggests: "For Hirschi, proper socialization involves the establishment of a strong moral bond between the juvenile and society. This *bond to society* consists of (1) *attachment* to others, (2) *commitment* to conventional lines of action, (3) *involvement* in conventional activities, and (4) *belief* in the moral order and law."

Critical Theories

As the name suggests, some theorists became disenchanted with the failure of existing theories to satisfactorily explain the causes of crime. **Critical theory** combines the classical free-will and positivist determinism views of crime, suggesting that humans are both self-determined and society-determined. As noted by Bohm (p.110): "Critical theories assume that human beings are the creators of the institutions and structures that ultimately dominate and constrain them."

 Critical theories include labeling theory, conflict theory and radical theory.

Labeling Theory

According to Bohm (p.112), **labeling theory** has its roots in the work of George Herbert Mead (1863–1931), whose ideas can be summarized in three propositions:

- Humans act toward things on the basis of the meanings the things have for them.

- The meaning of things arises out of social interaction.

■ These meanings are handled in, and modified through, an interpretative process people use to deal with things they encounter.

A belief in labeling theory can greatly influence how juveniles are treated by the juvenile justice system.

In labeling theory, it is important to differentiate between primary deviance and secondary deviance. **Primary deviance** is the initial criminal act. **Secondary deviance** is accepting the criminal label and consequently committing other crimes. If a person commits a delinquent act and is labeled a delinquent, this may affect the person's chance to make friends or get a good job. It may also become a self-fulfilling prophecy—that is, the person may accept the label and act accordingly.

Messner and Rosenfeld (p.45) suggest: "The principal contribution of *labeling theory* is to call attention to the interplay between social control and personal identity."

Conflict Theory

Conflict theory has been discussed. To briefly review, as Messner and Rosenfeld (p.45) summarize: "Conflict theories emphasize the political nature of crime production, posing the question of how the norms of particular groups are encoded into law and how, in turn, law is used as a means of domination of certain groups by others." More specifically: "For conflict theorists, the amount of crime in a society is a function of the extent of conflict generated by *stratification, hierarchical relationships, power differentials,* or the ability of some groups to dominate other groups in that society. Crime, in short, is caused by *relative powerlessness*" (Bohm, p.119).

Radical Theory

Bohm (pp.124–125) also describes **radical theory** as a way to explain crime:

Radical criminologists focus their attention on the social arrangements of society, especially on political and economic structures and institutions (the "political economy") of *capitalism*. . . .

Crime is a product of the political economy that, in capitalist societies, encourages an individualistic competition among wealthy people and among poor people and between rich and poor people (the intra- and inter*class* struggle) and the practice of taking advantage of other people (*exploitation*).

Conclusion

Appendix A (Found on the book companion Web site at cj.wadsworth.com/ hess_drowns_jj4e) provides a comprehensive summary of the most prominent theories on the causation of crime and delinquency. As noted by Ohlin (1998, p.143):

One of the most striking developments in juvenile justice over the past 20 years has been the increasing rapidity and the widening scope of change in theories, goals, and knowledge about delinquency and its prevention or control. Many competing biological, psychological, social, and cultural theories of delinquency have emerged in the past two decades, yet none is sufficient to account for the rate and forms of delinquency today.

 No single theory is sufficient to explain why delinquency exists. A reasonable combination of theories must be considered.

Having examined the primary theories and philosophies that have prevailed throughout the evolution of the juvenile justice system, you should better understand the ideologies that led juvenile justice to diverge from the path of adult criminal justice. To conclude, this chapter will look at the structure and process of the contemporary juvenile justice system and its relationship to the criminal justice system. You will then have a framework to see how each of the components within the juvenile justice system relates to each other and how what happens in one component influences what happens in the others.

The Contemporary Juvenile Justice System Structure and Process

The contemporary juvenile justice system parallels the criminal justice system in many ways, but it has important differences that have evolved as the juvenile system changed and adapted to meet the expectations of society and the needs of children and youths.

The Juvenile and Adult Justice Systems Compared

As the juvenile justice system evolved into one separate from the adult system, the terms used were tailored to fit the juvenile system.

 The terminology of the juvenile justice system underscores its emphasis on protecting youths from harmful labels and their stigmatizing effects.

Youths are not *arrested;* they are *taken into custody.* If the allegations against the youth are true, the youth is called a *delinquent* rather than a *criminal.* Youths sentenced to custodial care upon release receive *aftercare* rather than *parole.* Table 2.1 shows other differences in terminology used between the juvenile and adult justice systems.

Although the juvenile justice system is intended to protect youths, even those who commit crimes, provisions have been made to transfer youths into the criminal justice system. According to Griffin (2000):

> All states allow adult criminal prosecution of juveniles under some circumstances. The most common mechanism for transferring juveniles to adult criminal court is the judicial waiver: as of the end of the 1999 legislative sessions, there are 47 states that authorize or require juvenile court judges to waive jurisdiction over individual cases involving minors, so as to allow prosecution in adult criminal courts. Statutes in 15 states give prosecutors discretion to file certain kinds of cases in juvenile or criminal court. And 29 states have laws that exclude certain kinds of cases from the jurisdiction of the juvenile court and require that they be tried in criminal court.

Consider next how cases flow through the juvenile justice system—and sometimes out of it into the criminal justice system.

Caseflow through the Juvenile Justice System

 Like the criminal justice system, the juvenile justice system has three components: law enforcement, the courts and corrections.

Figure 2.2 presents a simplified view of caseflow through the juvenile justice system and illustrates how the juvenile system relates to the criminal justice system.

The flow from law enforcement through the courts to corrections has many places along the way during which **diversion,** the official halting of formal juvenile proceedings and referral of the juvenile to a treatment or care program, may

Table 2.1
The Language of Juvenile and Adult Courts

Juvenile Court Term	Adult Court Term
Adjudication: decision by the judge that a child has committed delinquent acts.	*Conviction of guilt*
Adjudicatory hearing: a hearing to determine whether the allegations of a petition are supported by the evidence beyond a reasonable doubt.	*Trial*
Adjustment: the settling of a matter so that parties agree without official intervention by the court.	*Plea bargaining*
Aftercare: the supervision given to a child for a limited period of time after he or she is released from training school but while he or she is still under the control of the juvenile court.	*Parole*
Commitment: a decision by the judge to send a child to training school.	*Sentence to imprisonment*
Delinquent act: an act that if committed by an adult would be called a crime. The term does not include such ambiguities and noncrimes as being ungovernable, truancy, incorrigibility and disobedience.	*Crime*
Delinquent child: a child who is found to have committed an act that would be considered a crime if committed by an adult.	*Criminal*
Detention: temporary care of an allegedly delinquent child who requires secure custody in physically restricting facilities pending court disposition or execution of a court order.	*Holding in jail*
Dispositional hearing: a hearing held subsequent to the adjudicatory hearing to determine what order of disposition should be made for a child adjudicated as delinquent.	*Sentencing hearing*
Hearing: the presentation of evidence to the juvenile court judge, his or her consideration of it, and his or her decision on disposition of the case.	*Trial*
Juvenile court: the court that has jurisdiction over children who are alleged to be or found to be delinquent. Juvenile delinquency procedures should not be used for neglected children or for those who need supervision.	*Court of record*
Petition: an application for a court order or some other judicial action. Hence, a delinquency petition is an application for the court to act in a matter involving a juvenile apprehended for a delinquent act.	*Accusation or indictment*
Probation: the supervision of a delinquent child after the court hearing but without commitment to training school.	*Probation (with the same meaning as the juvenile court term)*
Residential child care facility: a dwelling other than a detention or shelter care facility that is licensed to provide living accommodations, care, treatment, and maintenance for children and youths. Such facilities include foster homes, group homes, and halfway houses.	*Halfway house*
Shelter: temporary care of a child in physically unrestricting facilities pending court disposition or execution of a court order for placement. Shelter care is used for dependent and neglected children and minors in need of supervision. Separate shelter care facilities are also used for children apprehended for delinquency who need temporary shelter but not secure detention.	*Jail*
Take into custody: the act of the police in securing the physical custody of a child engaged in delinquency. The term is used to avoid the stigma of the word "arrest."	*Arrest*

Souuce: Harold J. Vetter and Leonard Territo *Crime and justice in America. A Human Perspective.* Copyright © 1984 by West Publishing Co. Reprinted by permission of Wadsworth Publishing Co.

occur. Part Three looks at the three components of the juvenile justice system in detail and discusses when and how diversion occurs throughout the process. Notice also the points at which youths may be transferred to the criminal justice system and vice versa.

To Divert or Not?
No problem is more troublesome than the delicate balance between protecting children in a free society and protecting society from criminal behavior. Concern over this issue was evident during the conception and birth of juvenile justice

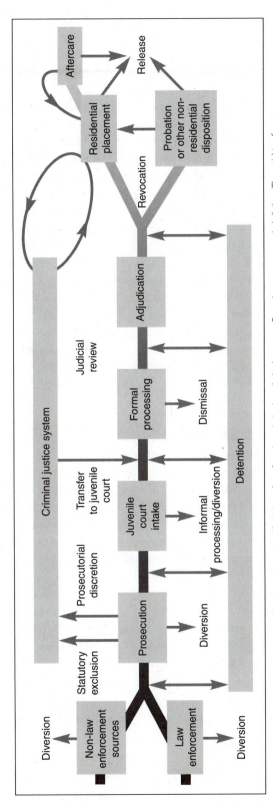

Figure 2.2
Caseflow Diagram

Note: This chart gives a simplified view of caseflow through the juvenile justice system. Procedures vary among jurisdictions. The weights of the lines are not intended to show the actual size of caseloads.

Source: On the Internet: http://ojjdp.ncjrs.org/facts/casehog.html

centuries ago. Indeed, throughout the evolution of the juvenile justice system, society's values and attitudes toward crime and those who commit it have swung back and forth, constantly adjusting to suit how society perceives delinquency.

When viewed against the backdrop of prevailing social sentiment and philosophy regarding crime and punishment, citizens' current attitudes remain pivotal in defining the structure and process of the juvenile justice system. According to the *Sourcebook of Criminal Justice Statistics 2001* (p.139) public sentiment supports the "get tough" trend for youths who commit violent crimes. Fewer than one-fourth (24 percent) thought youths between the ages of 14 and 17 who commit violent crimes should be given more lenient treatment. Sixty-five percent felt they should be treated the same as adults; 1 percent felt they should be treated "tougher." Nine percent responded that it "depends." One percent did not know or refused to answer.

Nonetheless, according to Griffin and Torbet (2002, p.23): "Adolescents really are different from adults, in their bodies and in their minds. It is relatively easy for them to get into trouble. And when they do, it is harder to hold them fully at fault. That's why we have a court that specializes in second chances—for young people who are still learning from their mistakes." In fact, according to Griffin and Torbet (p.33) the second chance may be given before a youth faces the formal juvenile justice process: "Nationally, about a third of all juveniles arrested by police are handled informally within the police department and then released." The decision to divert youths from the juvenile justice process at numerous points along the way results in what is often called the funnel effect.

The Funnel Effect

The **funnel effect** describes how at each point in the system fewer and fewer youths pass through. In the entire justice system, this phenomenon is described by Sickman (2002): "For every 1,000 violent crimes committed, 604 are reported to the police, 286 arrests are made of which 46 involve suspects younger than 18. Twenty-three juvenile court adjudications results. Of these 8 residential placements are ordered and 14 other sanctions imposed, for example, probation, community service, fines and the like."

This same funnel effect in delinquency case processing is illustrated in Figure 2.3. As you study this figure, recall that police officers informally handled one-third of arrested youths, so the funnel actually starts with slightly more than 1,500 arrests. It ends with fewer than one-tenth funneled into corrections.

According to Crowe's classic work in the Serious Habitual Offender Comprehensive Action Program (SHOCAP) (1991, pp.36–37), the funnel effect teaches a number of crucial lessons:

- Schools and police are fundamental to the community control of delinquency.
- School and police officials have more contact with our children than does anyone else, except parents.
- The juvenile justice system is irrelevant to the prevention and diversion of delinquency because the schools and the police are not a significant part of the system. They are at the opening of the "funnel" and have been

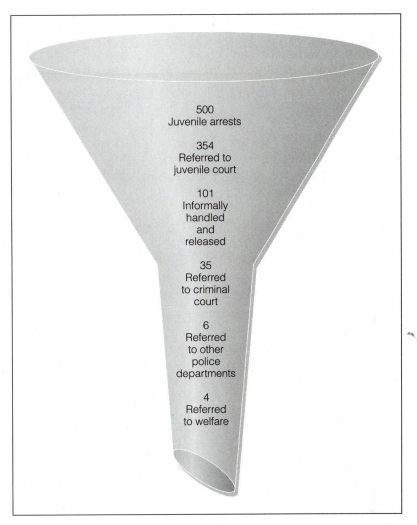

500
Juvenile arrests

354
Referred to
juvenile court

101
Informally
handled
and
released

35
Referred
to criminal
court

6
Referred
to other
police
departments

4
Referred
to welfare

Figure 2.3
**Police Response
to Juvenile Crime**
To understand how police deal
with juvenile crime, picture a
funnel, with the result shown
here. For every 500 juveniles
taken into custody, a little more
than 70 percent are sent to
juvenile court, and a little more
than 20 percent are released.

Source: FBI, *Crime in the United States 2000.* Washington, DC: U.S. Government Printing Office, 2001, p. 273, table 68.

mistakenly excluded from the concept of the community's responsibility
for controlling delinquency.

- The contact and information that *could* be shared between parents, schools
  and police are *key* to the effective functioning of the juvenile justice
  system. They are the filter to the end of the funnel that feeds the legal
  system that has only one purpose—effective control of individuals whom
  the community is unable to control.

 The funnel effect illustrates the crucial role of law enforcement, schools and
parents in the juvenile justice system and process.

*The Justice System
and Community Policing*

In addition to parents, schools and the police, community policing suggests that
collaboration is also needed among the many government agencies and myriad
civic organizations involved directly and indirectly with juveniles.

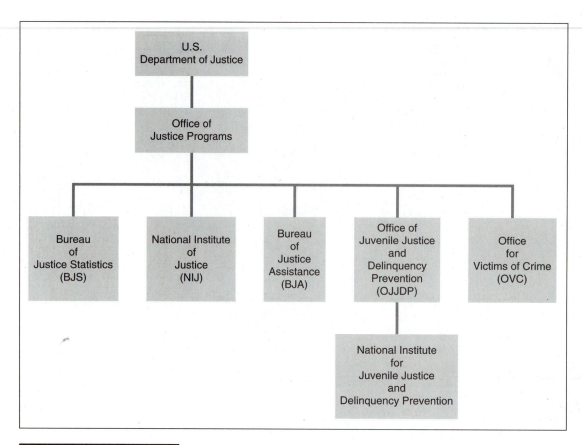

Figure 2.4
**Agencies of the
U.S. Department of
Justice Coordinated by the
Office of Justice Programs**

Most government agencies are under the U.S. Department of Justice through its Office of Justice Programs. The Office of Justice Programs coordinates the activities of these program offices and bureaus: the Bureau of Justice Statistics (BJS), the National Institute of Justice (NIJ), the Bureau of Justice Assistance (BJA), the Office of Juvenile Justice and Delinquency Prevention (OJJDP) and the Office for Victims of Crime (OVC) (see Figure 2.4). These offices often conduct joint efforts and programs.

Restorative justice fits well with the community policing philosophy. As Bazemore and Umbreit (p.1) suggest: "Restorative justice is a framework for juvenile justice reform that seeks to engage victims, offenders and their families, other citizens and community groups both as clients of juvenile justice services and as resources in an effective response to youth crime."

The Complexity of the Juvenile Justice System

As the NCJJ (2002, p.4) notes: "There are not 1, but 51 juvenile justice systems in this country, each with its own history, its own set of laws and policies, and its own unique organizational, administrative and fiscal structures. Even within a

In a North Philadelphia neighborhood that police call "The Land of Oz," children on their way to a game of sandlot football stop to sort through thousands of empty crack vials dropped by a young dealer as he fled from dealers whom he had robbed.

© Eugene Richards/Magnum Photos Inc.

single state, the mandates conceived in the capitol building must be interpreted and implemented by a multitude of local officials, under widely varying conditions, and with widely varying effects. Without a thorough understanding of this background complexity, no broad question of juvenile justice practice or policy can be adequately answered, no legal generalization can be meaningful, and no descriptive statistic can be useful."

In addition to having their own juvenile justice systems, states have begun to de-emphasize traditional confidentiality concerns while emphasizing information sharing. During the early 1990s, states made significant changes in how the juvenile justice system treats information about juvenile offenders, particularly violent juvenile offenders. As juvenile crime became more serious, community protection, the public's right to know and service providers' need to share information displaced the desire to protect minors from the stigma of youthful indiscretions. Legislatures throughout the country have increasingly called for a presumption of open hearings and records, at least for a subset of juvenile offenders.

In addition, pressure has increased to publish the names of young offenders, to lower the minimum age at which youths are under the jurisdiction of the juvenile justice system and to broaden the scope of cases transferable to adult court. As a result, the treatment of youths is becoming more similar to that of adults.

Summary

Distributive or social justice provides an equal share of what is valued in a society to each member of that society. This includes power, prestige and possessions. Retributive justice seeks revenge for unlawful behavior. Restorative justice focuses on repairing the harm done to victims and to the community and stresses that offenders must contribute to the repair. The harm refers to unlawful behaviors or crimes. Unlawful behaviors or crimes were originally differentiated in the following two ways: (1) *mala in se,* an act considered wrong in and of itself based on mores, natural law and common law, and stable over time, or (2) *mala prohibita,* a prohibited wrong, originating in folkways and man-made statutory law and changeable over time.

Two prominent theories as to the underlying purpose of law are consensus theory and conflict theory. Consensus theory contends that individuals within a society agree on basic values, on what is inherently right and wrong. Laws express these values. It includes the Durkheimian perspective, which sees punishment as revenge and a way to restore and solidify the social order.

Conflict theory suggests that laws are established to keep the dominant class in power. It includes the Marxist perspective, which sees punishment as a way to control the lower class and preserve the power of the upper class.

Contemporary views on the treatment of juveniles include the conservative approach—to "get tough on juveniles," to punish and imprison them—and the liberal approach, which stresses treatment and rehabilitation, including community-based programs. These approaches have their roots in two competing world views: the classical view and the positivist view.

The classical world view holds that humans have free will and are responsible for their own actions. Proponents of the classical view advocate punishment for offenders. They suggest that deterrence, incapacitation and, in some cases, "just deserts" punishment is the way to deal with delinquency. The positivist world view holds that humans are shaped by their societies and are the products of environmental and cultural influences. Proponents of the positivist view advocate rehabilitation for offenders.

Early efforts to explain crime and delinquency according to these theories were expanded upon and refined. Later theories focused on biological, psychological or sociological causes of crime and delinquency. Most recently, critical theories of the causes of crime and delinquency have been developed.

Biological theories include physiognomy, phrenology, body type and heredity studies, including studies of twins and adoptees. Psychological theories explaining crime focus on intelligence and psychoanalysis. Sociological theories include ecological models, social disorganization, functionalism, anomie or strain theory, learning theories and social control theories. Critical theories include labeling theory, conflict theory and radical theory. No single theory is sufficient to explain why delinquency exists. A reasonable combination of theories must be considered.

Also of importance are the differences between the adult and the juvenile systems of justice. The terminology of the juvenile justice system underscores its emphasis on protecting youths from harmful labels and their stigmatizing effects. Like the criminal justice system, the juvenile justice system has three components: law enforcement, the courts and corrections. As cases flow through the juvenile justice system, the funnel effect occurs, with diversion reducing the number of youths involved in the formal system at each point in the process. The funnel effect illustrates the crucial role of law enforcement, schools and parents in the juvenile justice system and process.

Discussion Questions

1. Do you take the position of those who hold a classical view or those who hold a positivist view? Do you hold the same view for children as you do for adults?
2. Do you feel that distributive justice is required for the United States to truly provide "liberty and justice for all"?
3. What instances of the Durkheimian or Marxist perspective of punishment can you cite from the historical overview of juvenile justice?
4. Do you support the conservative or liberal approach toward delinquent youths? Which approach is more prevalent in your community? In the United States?
5. Which of the theories of the causation of crime and delinquency seem most logical?
6. Diagram the ecological model as it might look for a major city.
7. How is the labeling theory of importance to parents? Teachers? You?
8. Do you believe you can make the American Dream a reality for yourself? Why or why not?
9. Do you support a separate justice system for juveniles? Why or why not?
10. What are the major differences between the criminal justice system and the juvenile justice system?

InfoTrac College Edition Assignments

- Use InfoTrac College Edition to answer the Discussion Questions as appropriate.
- Select one of the following assignments to complete and share with the class.
  - Use the term *labeling theory* as the subject guide to find "Labeling and Delinquency" by Mike S. Adams et al.
  - Use the term *restorative justice* as the subject guide to find one of the following articles:
    - "Restorative Justice as Strength-Based Accountability" by Robert Ball.
  - "Community-Based Mediation Programs: A Case Study and Comparison" by Russell S. Harrison.
  - "Restorative Justice for Young Offenders and Their Victims" by Anna Seymour and Trudy Gregorie.
  - "Restorative Justice for Offenders: A Return to American Tradition" by Emilio C. Viano.

Internet Assignments

- Go to http://distributive-justice.com/mainpage and click on the icon representing "theory." Enter the "theory" page and familiarize yourself with the seven general theories of distributive justice summarized there. Then find the "games" icon and determine your distributive profile: On the login screen, enter your gender, country and age (red fields); all other information is unnecessary. Share your results with the class and discuss whether one or more profiles predominate the members in your class.
- Using key words *adoption study* and *crime*, select a site of interest to you and review the material presented. Does the literature support a biological cause of criminality? Be prepared to share your findings with the class.
- Go to www.ncjrs.org to find, read and outline any of the end-of-chapter references with an NCJ number in parentheses or go to any reference having an online address to find, read and outline an entire article.

References

Agnew, Robert. "Foundation for a General Strain Theory of Crime and Delinquency." *Criminology,* Vol. 30, 1992, pp.47–87.

Bazemore, Gordon and Umbreit, Mark. *A Comparison of Four Restorative Conferencing Models.* Washington, DC: OJJDP Juvenile Justice Bulletin, February 2001. (NCJ 184738)

Bohm, Robert M. *A Primer on Crime and Delinquency.* Belmont, CA: Wadsworth Publishing Company, 1997.

Carlson, Susan M. and Michalowski, Raymond J. "Crime, Unemployment, and Social Structures of Accumulation: An Inquiry into Historical Contingency." *Justice Quarterly,* June 1997, pp.210–241.

Cohen, Albert K. *Delinquent Boys: The Culture of the Gang.* New York: Free Press, 1955.

Crowe, Timothy D. *Habitual Juvenile Offenders: Guidelines for Citizen Action and Public Response.* Serious Habitual Offender Comprehensive Action Program (SHOCAP). Washington, DC: Office of Juvenile Justice and Delinquency Prevention, October 1991.

Curran, Daniel J. and Renzetti, Claire M. *Theories of Crime.* Boston: Allyn & Bacon, 1994.

Donohue, Stephen. "A Crime-Causation Hornet's Nest." *Law Enforcement News,* December 15, 1995, pp.1, 12.

Durkheim, Emile. *The Division of Labor in Society.* New York: Free Press, 1933.

Durkheim, Emile. *Suicide* (1897). Glencoe, IL: Free Press, 1951.

Flicker, Barbara Danziger. *Standards for Juvenile Justice: A Summary and Analysis,* 2nd ed. New York: Institute for Judicial Administration, 1990.

Garland, David. "Sociological Perspectives on Punishment." In *Crime and Justice: A Review of Research,* Vol. 14, edited by Michael Tonry. Chicago: University of Chicago Press, 1991, pp.115–165.

Griffin, Patrick. "National Overviews." *State Juvenile Justice Profiles.* Pittsburgh, PA: National Center for Juvenile Justice, 2000. Online: http://www.ncjj.org/stateprofiles/

Griffin, Patrick and Torbet, Patricia, editors. *Desktop Guide to Good Juvenile Probation Practice.* Washington, DC: National Center for Juvenile Justice, June 2002.

Hernstein, Richard J. and Murray, Charles. *The Bell Curve: Intelligence and Class Structure in American Life.* New York: Free Press, 1994.

Hirschi, Travis. *Causes of Delinquency.* Berkeley: University of California Press, 1969.

Karp, David R. "Harm and Repair: Observing Restorative Justice in Vermont." *Justice Quarterly,* December 2001, pp.727-757.

Krisberg, Barry and Austin, James F. *Reinventing Juvenile Justice.* Newbury Park, CA: Sage Publications, 1993.

Marx, Karl and Engels, Friedrich. *Manifesto of the Communist Party.* Chicago: Encyclopedia Britannica, Inc., 1848, p.419.

Merton, Robert K. "Social Structure and Anomie." *American Sociological Review,* Vol. 3, 1938, pp.672–682.

Merton, Robert K. *Social Theory and Social Structure,* rev. ed. New York: Free Press, 1957.

Messner, Steven F. and Rosenfeld, Richard. *Crime and the American Dream,* 2nd ed. Belmont, CA: Wadsworth Publishing Company, 1997.

NCJJ Annual Report 2001. Washington, DC: National Center for Juvenile Justice, 2001.

Ohlin, Lloyd E. "The Future of Juvenile Justice Policy and Research." *Crime & Delinquency,* Vol. 44, No. 1, January 1998, pp.143–153.

Park, Robert E.; Burgess, Ernest W.; and McKenzie, Roderick D. *The City.* Chicago: University of Chicago Press, 1928.

Ross, W. D., trans. "Nicomachean Ethics." *Aristotle: II.* Chicago: Encyclopedia Britannica, 1952.

Sampson, R. J. and Groves, W. B. "Community Structure and Crime: Testing Social-Disorganization Theory." *American Journal of Sociology,* Vol. 94, 1989, pp.774–802.

Shaw, Clifford and McKay, H. D. *Juvenile Delinquency and Urban Areas.* Chicago: University of Chicago Press, 1942.

Shoham, S. Giora and Hoffmann, John. *A Primer in the Sociology of Crime.* New York: Harrow and Heston, Publishers, 1991.

Sickmund, Melissa. *Crime Funnels: U.S. Response to Crime.* Pittsburgh, PA: National Center for Juvenile Justice, 2002.

Snarr, Richard W. *Introduction to Corrections,* 2nd ed. Dubuque, IA: Wm. C. Brown Publishers, 1992.

Sourcebook of Criminal Justice Statistics 2001, 29th ed. Washington, DC: Bureau of Justice Statistics, 2002.

Springer, Charles E. *Justice for Juveniles.* Washington, DC: U.S. Department of Justice, Office of Juvenile Justice and Delinquency Prevention, 1986.

Sprott, Jane B. "Understanding Public Opposition to a Separate Youth Justice System." *Crime & Delinquency,* July 1998, pp.399–411.

Sutherland, Edwin H. and Cressey, Donald R. *Principles of Criminology.* Philadelphia: J.B. Lippincott, 1939.

Sutherland, Edwin H. and Cressey, Donald R. *Criminology,* 9th ed. Philadelphia: Lippincott, 1974.

Torbet, Patricia. "States Respond to Violent Juvenile Crime." *National Center for Juvenile Justice in Brief,* Vol. 1, 1997, p.1.

Walker, Samuel; Spohn, Cassia; and DeLone, Miriam. *The Color of Justice: Race, Ethnicity, and Crime in America,* 2nd ed. Belmont, CA: Wadsworth Publishing Company, 2000.

Wilson, John J. "From the Administrator." *A Comparison of Four Restorative Conferencing Models.* Washington, DC: OJJDP Juvenile Justice Bulletin, February 2001. (NCJ 184738)

Helpful Resource

A Primer on Crime and Delinquency Theory, 2nd ed. by Robert M. Bohm. Belmont, CA: Wadsworth Publishing Company, 2001.

Growth and Development:
The First 18 Years

Life affords no greater responsibility, no greater privilege, than the raising of the next generation.

—C. Everett Koop

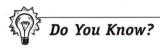

Do You Know?

- At what age most individuals legally become adults?
- What ages are most critical in child development?
- What childhood risk factors for child delinquency and later violent juvenile offending are?
- What danger occurs by labeling a child as deviant?
- What two of the most serious consequences for children who live in poverty are?
- What types of children with special needs may be involved in the juvenile justice system?
- What two major peer influences can lead adolescents to delinquency?
- Whether substance abuse correlates with delinquency?
- What characteristics of a healthy family are?
- What common values might be passed on to children by their parents?
- What family-related risk factors might lead to delinquency?
- What the likely result of succeeding in school is?
- Whose approval is often most important during adolescence?
- How students might respond to failure in school?
- What a school-related early-warning sign of potential delinquency is?
- Whether failure in school and delinquency are linked?
- What have been identified as the biggest problems facing local public schools?
- What rights students have within the school?
- What standard the Supreme Court has set for cases involving students' rights?
- What effect community associations have on child development?
- What community-related risk factors are?

Can You Define?

adolescence
adult supremacy
attention deficit
  hyperactivity
  disorder (ADHD)
behavioral activation
behavioral inhibition
collective efficacy
crack children

EBD
fetal alcohol syndrome
  (FAS)
in loco parentis
labeling
learning disability
Norman Rockwell family

one-pot approach
parental efficacy
radial concept
self-fulfilling prophecy
SRO
thrownaways
zero-tolerance policies

INTRODUCTION

Before examining our contemporary juvenile justice system, it is important to understand those served by this system—our youths. According to *America's Children* (2002, p.iii): "In 2000, there were 70.4 million children under age 18 in the United States, or 26 percent of the population. . . . The racial and ethnic diversity of America's children continues to increase. In 2000, 64 percent of U.S. children were white, non-Hispanic; 15 percent were black, non-Hispanic; 4 percent were Asian/Pacific Islander; and 1 percent were American Indian/Alaska Native. The number of Hispanic children has increased faster than that of any other racial and ethnic group, growing from 9 percent of the child population in 1980 to 16 percent in 2000."

An extreme challenge facing the juvenile justice system is the one-pot approach to youths evident throughout history. The **one-pot approach** lumps children and youths who are abused and neglected, those who commit minor offenses and those who commit vicious, violent crimes into the same judicial "pot."

But their needs and the approaches required to meet those needs are drastically different. The next three chapters discuss the needs of each of these groups. The National Center for Juvenile Justice (*Annual Report 2001*) stresses: "No aspect of national interest is more significant than what happens to young people when they are troubled, particularly those we label as 'abused children,' 'dependent children,' 'neglected children,' 'status offenders' and 'juvenile delinquents.' " Preventing our children and youths from becoming "problems" of the justice system is a logical first step. This chapter focuses on normal patterns of growth and development and special challenges to anticipate.

Growth and development do not occur in isolation. They involve a complex interaction of family, school and community, with the family being the first and most vital influence. As children grow, the school becomes an important influence, be it preschool, kindergarten, public or private school. As youths approach adolescence, the influence of parents and teachers wanes and that of peers becomes stronger. All of this occurs within the broader community within which children live. This **radial concept** of the influences on growth and development is illustrated in Figure 3.1.

This chapter begins with a brief discussion of youths, *parens patarie* and the age at which juvenile courts have jurisdiction as well as the rights our youths ideally enjoy. This is followed by an explanation of how they normally grow and develop. Next the effect of poverty on growth and development is described, followed by a look at children with special needs and those at risk of not developing normally. The chapter then discusses adolescence and the unique challenges and stresses of this developmental stage, including the problems of substance abuse and teenage pregnancy.

The chapter next examines the critical role played by family, school and community in youths' growth and development. It begins with an in-depth look at the importance of the family and at practices such as spanking, at values that might be instilled in our youths, at family-related risk factors and at how the disintegration of the family is affecting the juvenile justice system. The second major influence, the school, has also undergone significant changes and faces

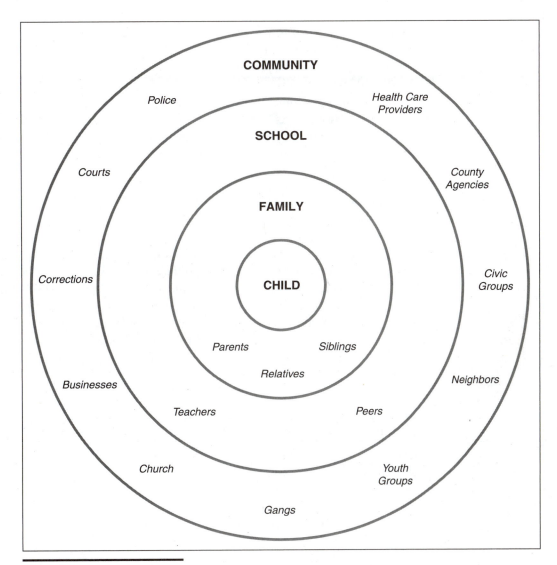

Figure 3.1
**The Radial Influences
on a Child's Growth
and Development**

recurring challenges, including crime and violence and increasing numbers of children entering school not ready to learn. Next the chapter examines common educational practices that might promote failure, how students might react to that failure and what link these have with delinquent behavior. Then steps schools have taken and what more might be done to enhance learning and success are discussed. This is followed by a brief discussion of students' constitutional rights within the school setting. The chapter concludes with a discussion of the third major influence in child development, the community, including the development of full-service community schools in some localities.

Youths, *Parens Patriae* and the Juvenile Court's Jurisdiction

Under the principle of *parens patriae,* the state is to protect its youths. The age at which a child becomes an adult is legally established by each state. The oldest age for original juvenile court jurisdiction in delinquency matters as of the end of the 2002 legislative session is summarized in Table 3.1.

Note the range from 15 to 17 years of age. In previous editions of this text the range was from 16 to 19 with the most common age being 18. This lowering of the oldest age reflects the current tendency to "get tough" on youths in trouble with the law.

 Seventeen is the age most commonly recognized as the beginning of legal adulthood.

Until they "come of age," it is generally understood that youths need special assistance. In fact, more than 30 years ago the Joint Commission on Mental Health of Children (1970, pp.3–4) listed the following children's *rights*—the right to be wanted, to be born healthy, to live in a healthy environment, to satisfaction of basic needs, to continuous loving care, to acquire the intellectual and emotional skills necessary to achieve individual aspirations and to cope effectively, and to receive care and treatment through facilities appropriate to their

Table 3.1
Oldest Age for Original Juvenile Court Jurisdiction in Delinquency Matters

Age 15 (3 states)	Age 16 (10 states)	Age 17 (38 states)	
Connecticut	Georgia	Alabama	Montana
New York	Illinois	Alaska	Nebraska
North Carolina	Louisiana	Arizona	Nevada
	Massachusetts	Arkansas	New Jersey
	Michigan	California	New Mexico
	Missouri	Colorado	North Dakota
	New Hampshire	Delaware	Ohio
	South Carolina	District of Columbia	Oklahoma
	Texas	Florida	Oregon
	Wisconsin	Hawaii	Pennsylvania
		Idaho	Rhode Island
		Indiana	South Dakota
		Iowa	Tennessee
		Kansas	Utah
		Kentucky	Vermont
		Maine	Virginia
		Maryland	Washington
		Minnesota	West Virginia
		Mississippi	Wyoming

Source: © National Center for Juvenile Justice. 2003. "National Overviews."
State Juvenile Justice Profiles, Pittsburgh, PA: National Center for Juvenile Justice.
Online. Available at http://www.ncjj.org/stateprofiles/. Reprinted by permission.

needs that keep them as closely as possible within their normal social settings. Such rights continue to be essential for youths' growth and development.

Child Development— A Brief Overview

The study of child development usually deals with children from birth to adolescence and concerns their physical, intellectual, emotional and social growth as they adjust to the demands of society.

The Critical First Three Years

Child development experts state that the first three years of life lay the foundation for all that follows.

 The period from birth to age three is the most formative time of a child's life.

During this time, with attentive parents or older brothers or sisters, children learn the concept of consequences—rewards and punishments. They also begin to distinguish right from wrong and to develop what is commonly called a *conscience.* Table 3.2 summarizes some of children's basic needs if they are to grow and thrive.

Unfortunately, for many of our nation's children, this is *not* the reality. Their healthy development is hindered by inadequate medical care, poverty, violence and disintegrating families.

Research in molecular biology and neurology shows that what children experience during their first few years affects how many brain cells develop and how many connections are formed between them. Early environmental stimulation increases the number of cells and interconnections. Research also shows that stress early in life may activate hormones that impair learning and memory.

Table 3.2 What Children Need for Healthy Growth and Development

Need	Comments
Choices and challenges	Children need the chance to explore and learn, to stretch to their limits.
Healthy and safe surroundings	Children need to feel secure and protected from harm, supported when confronted with strange or frightening experiences.
Independence	Children need to develop their own personality and self-confidence, to know that others have faith in their ability to do things for themselves.
Love	Children need to be loved—physically and emotionally. They need to feel wanted, appreciated, a part of a family unit. They need hugs.
Direction	Children need to know the rules, their boundaries and what will happen if they overstep these boundaries. They need to know how to interact with others and to get along.
Respect and recognition	Children need to be accepted for who they are and to be praised for their accomplishments.
Encouragement	Children need to be supported and helped to grow and develop.
Nurturing	Children need not only nutritious food, but attention to their mental and emotional growth and development as well.

Wasserman et al. (2003, p.2) contend: "Early antisocial behavior may be the best predictor of later delinquency. . . . In fact, early aggression appears to be the most significant social behavior characteristic to predict delinquent behavior before age 13."

Between the ages of 1 and 3, normal conflicts arise between parents and their children: toilet training, eating certain vegetables, going to bed at a set time, staying within prescribed boundaries and the like. How these conflicts are resolved will establish the pattern for how the child will deal with conflict later in life. Research suggests that the most aggressive age in humans is 2 years old. Unfortunately, many parents, relatives and friends attribute hitting, biting and throwing tantrums to the "terrible twos." But ignoring such behavior or reacting in kind with violence such as spanking or otherwise striking a child can have dire consequences.

The Next 10 Years

Building on the foundation of the first three critical years, children continue to grow and develop physically, mentally and emotionally. During this time they are continuously learning. One of the most critical factors is whether parents allow their children to watch television program containing violence.

Violence on Television and in Video Games

The American Psychological Association ("Violence on Television. . . ," 2003) contends: "Violent programs on television lead to aggressive behavior by children and teenagers who watch those programs." They cite three major effects of seeing violence on television:

1. Children may become less sensitive to the pain and suffering of others.
2. Children may be more fearful of the world around them.
3. Children may be more likely to behave in aggressive or harmful ways toward others.

In addition: "Children who watch the violent shows, even 'just funny' cartoons, were more likely to hit out at their playmates, argue, disobey class rules, leave tasks unfinished and were less willing to wait for things."

The American Academy of Child & Adolescent Psychiatry ("Children and TV Violence," 2003) echoes these findings: "Hundreds of studies of the effects of TV violence on children and teenagers have found that children may become 'immune' to the horror of violence; gradually accept violence as a way to solve problems; imitate the violence they observe on television; and identify with certain characters, victims and/or victimizers."

In addition, as Wright (2003, p.28) notes: "The average seventh-grader spends at least four hours a week playing video games, and about half of those games have violent themes. . . . Psychologists point to decades of research and more than a thousand studies that demonstrate a link between media violence and real aggression." As youths grow and develop, they face other risk factors.

Individual Risk Factors

Wasserman et al. (p.3) identified several individual risk factors for child delinquency and later violent juvenile offending.

 Individual childhood risk factors for child delinquency and later violent juvenile offending include early antisocial behavior, emotional factors such as high behavioral activation and low behavioral inhibition, poor cognitive development, low intelligence and hyperactivity.

Behavioral activation refers to novelty and sensation seeking, impulsivity, hyperactivity and predatory aggression. **Behavioral inhibition** refers to fearfulness, anxiety, timidity and shyness in response to new stimulus or punishment. High levels of behavioral activation and low levels of behavioral inhibition are risk factors for antisocial behavior.

Another consideration is the role that labeling can play in an individual's growth and development.

Labeling and Self-Fulfilling Prophecies

It is human nature to apply labels to *things,* to name them. But when dealing with people, it is important to restrict the **labeling** (naming) to specific *behaviors* rather than to those who exhibit these behaviors. For example, "Hitting is a bad thing" in contrast to "You are a bad child for hitting."

Much has been made of the power of positive thinking. Negative thinking can be just as powerful. People can be talked into believing what or who they are. If children are constantly called stupid, this could retard their intellectual growth.

In a frequently cited research study, psychology majors were given three groups of laboratory rats. They were told in advance how smart each group was. The first set consisted of super-smart rats that would be able to master a maze with no difficulty; therefore, they should have ample rewards along the way and a huge piece of cheese at the end. The second set consisted of rats of average ability that would not be able to make use of the clues along the way; they should have an average amount of cheese at the end. The third group consisted of rats of below-average intelligence that had little hope of finding their way through the maze; a simple picture of some cheese at the end would do.

In a few hours, all the super-smart rats were munching away at the cheese at the end of the maze, some of those with average intelligence had found their way to the end, and the below-average rats were aimlessly milling around in the maze, with none of them yet at the end. Imagine the students' surprise when the professor told them the rats were all of the same intelligence. It was how they were treated, based on how they were labeled, that made the difference.

A similar experiment that used three classes of second-graders has often been cited to illustrate the effects of labeling. The teachers were told that one group was brilliant, one group was of average intelligence, and one group was below average. The "brilliant" group made tremendous gains in learning during a 6-week period; the "average" group made some gains; and the "below-average" group actually lost ground. In reality, all three groups were of the same intelligence, but the teachers treated them differently, expecting large gains from the brilliant group and paying little attention to the below-average group. What they expected is exactly what they got. **Self-fulfilling prophecy** occurs when people live up to the labels they are given.

Consequences of Labeling

Before formalized law enforcement, neighbors watched over neighbors, and if an incident occurred that needed public service, a "hue and cry" was raised. For example, if a neighbor saw a stranger removing a cow, he would pursue the thief yelling, "Stop, thief!" and arouse all the other neighbors to join the chase. If the thief abandoned the animal out of sight of the crowd, and an innocent person stopped to hold the cow and was mistakenly labeled as the thief by the pursuers, he was probably hanged.

The same thing can happen to youths who commit even minor offenses. They may be labeled delinquent and subject to the discipline of the juvenile court. If the court decides to teach such youths a lesson, they can be placed in a locked facility for something as minor as a curfew violation. The youths are not hanged as was the innocent man with the cow, but the consequences can be almost as devastating.

Regardless of social class or environment, children have a strong natural inclination to believe those they respect. What is said to them makes a difference. A 16-year-old boy who appeared in juvenile court was admonished by the judge who called the youth a menace to society. The judge further stated that the boy was the kind of kid who gave good kids a bad name. This insensitive judge did not know that there was a computer error, and the youth was not the ruthless figure he was labeled. The event, however, was so traumatic for the 16-year-old that he wrote in a note, "The judge is right; I am no good." He signed it and then shot himself. It was the third suicide of a youth who appeared before the same judge.

The harmful consequences of negative labeling are stressed here because at some point nearly every child gets into trouble, regardless of social status. It is not just inner-city youths or youths living in poverty who break the rules of society. It is almost *all* youths who do so.

 Labeling theorists state that when a deviant label is attached to people, they become stigmatized and have little chance to be rewarded for conformist behavior. The label becomes a self-fulfilling prophecy.

Fortunately, it is also a fact that most children grow up to be law-abiding, sociable and productive citizens, having developed responsible behavior through the maturation process.

Children playing in an unsafe, abandoned tenement building in New York City's lower east side.

Michael Weisbrot / Stock Boston

Children Living in Poverty

According to Child Health USA 2002, in 2000 about 11 million children younger than 18 lived in families with income below the federal poverty threshold ($17,603 for a family of four). This is a substantial decrease from previous years. Of these children, 55.5 percent lived in homes headed by a single mother. Very young children and black and Hispanic children were particularly vulnerable. Home conditions of economic deprivation or uncertainty can expose children to ills ranging from malnutrition to extreme psychopathology. This country has pockets of squalor found on tenant farms, in migrant camps and in the tenements of large cities. Two possible reasons for this situation are that children do not vote and they do not contribute to political campaigns.

It takes more than economic relief to lift families from a pattern of irresponsibility or depravity. Social agencies in every community know certain families that can be counted on to produce more than their share of school failures, truancy, sexual deviation, alcoholism, disorderliness and disease. They are also all too familiar with the inadequate personalities who become parents of other inadequate personalities in a recurring sequence that led early geneticists to talk about heredity and social incompetence.

It must be remembered, however, that poverty alone cannot be blamed for delinquency. Many children raised in extreme poverty grow up just fine.

 Two of the most serious consequences of poverty for children are homelessness and increased risk of lead poisoning.

Homelessness

According to the 2000 U.S. Census, 170,706 people were homeless. Of this sample, about one-fourth were under age 18 (Smith and Smith, 2001). Holloway (2002/2003, p.89) reports: "Families with children constitute about 40 percent of people who become homeless. . . . Children are the fastest growing segment of the homeless population."

Being homeless places great stress on families and may result in child neglect or abuse. Cauce (2000) reports that in many cases parents physically or sexually abused their children and that more than two-thirds of the children in her sample had mental health problems. In addition, according to Kelly et al. (2000), homeless women with young children were likely to show a high level of depression and disruptive patterns of mother-child interaction. One-half of the homeless children they studied were developmentally delayed, compared with 16 percent of poor but housed children. These findings are confirmed by Koblinsky et al. (2000) who found that homeless students had significantly more behavioral problems in school than did their housed peers. Finally, according to the Institute for Children and Poverty (2001), more than one-fourth of the parents of school-age children reported having problems enrolling their children in school.

Homeless children also experience stress and are likely to exhibit some of the following: restlessness, aggressive behavior, depression, inattentiveness, persistent tiredness and anxiety. In addition to these general tendencies, homeless children often experience constant moving, frequent change of schools and lack of basic resources such as food and clothing. Some homeless youths are entirely on their own, including runaways and **thrownaways** (their family has kicked them out). Difficulties facing such youths are discussed in the next chapter.

Victims of Lead Poisoning

Children who live in poverty are also much more likely than others to be exposed to lead from old paint and old plumbing fixtures and from the lead in household dust. Other sources of lead are old water systems, lead crystal and some imported cans and ceramics. According to *Law Enforcement News* ("Studies Weigh Facets of Juvenile Justice," 2000, p.8): "Early exposure to lead, in the form of paint chips or old paint dust, may have at least as much to do with criminal behavior in adolescents as other, more traditional predictors of delinquency. . . . Research from around the world has found that lead-exposed children show increased impulsiveness, restlessness and aggression."

Babies exposed to low doses of lead before birth often are born underweight and underdeveloped. Even if they overcome these handicaps, when they go to school they face more obstacles such as behavioral problems, low IQ and deficiencies in speech and language. Still other obstacles that hinder growth and development are faced by children with special needs.

Children with Special Needs

The majority of children in our country are "normal," but thousands of children have special needs.

 Children with special needs include those who are emotionally/behaviorally disturbed or have learning disabilities, an attention deficit hyperactivity disorder or behavior problems resulting from prenatal exposure to drugs, including alcohol, or to the human immunodeficiency virus (HIV).

Before looking at children with special needs, consider the caution of Armstrong (2001, p.38): "Diagnostic labels for learning differences hinder educators from celebrating the natural diversity of all students' learning styles." He calls such youths IKSWALs—interesting kids saddled with alienating labels. Teachers, parents and all who interact with children and youths must be aware of the hazards of labeling as discussed previously.

Emotionally/Behaviorally Disturbed Children

One challenging segment of youths are those labeled as emotionally/behaviorally disturbed (**EBD**). These youths usually have one or more of the following behavior patterns: severely aggressive or impulsive behavior; severely withdrawn or anxious behaviors, pervasive unhappiness, depression or wide mood swings; severely disordered thought processes that show up in unusual behavior patterns, atypical communication styles and distorted interpersonal relationships.

Youths with Attention Deficit Hyperactivity Disorder

Attention deficit hyperactivity disorder (ADHD) is a common childhood disruptive behavior disorder. Stern (2001, p.1) reports: "ADHD is the most commonly diagnosed childhood disorder, affecting an estimated 3 to 5 percent of school-age children." ADHD is characterized by heightened motor activity (fidgeting and squirming), a short attention span, distractibility, impulsiveness and lack of self-control.

According to Tannock and Martinussen (2001, p.24): "Contrary to popular belief, research indicates that ADHD is not usually caused by food allergies, excess sugar, too much TV, poor parenting, poor home life or poor schools." They (p.23) note: "Research suggests that about 80 percent of the differences in inattention, hyperactivity and impulsivity between students with and without ADHD can be explained by genetic factors."

Behaviors associated with ADHD can greatly interfere with learning and are usually unnerving for parents, teachers and other adults. Stern notes: "Boys with ADHD are at increased risk for engaging in delinquent and antisocial behavior." Attention deficit hyperactivity disorder is often accompanied by a learning disability.

Youths with Learning Disabilities

Five to 10 million children in the United States experience some form of **learning disability.** The Association for Children with Learning Disabilities (ACLD) describes a learning disabled child in the following way (p.4): "A learning disabled person is an individual who has one or more significant deficits in the essential learning processes."

According to the ACLD (p.3): "The most frequently displayed symptoms are short attention span, poor memory, difficulty following directions, inadequate ability to discriminate between and among letters, numerals, or sounds, poor reading ability, eye-hand coordination problems, difficulties with sequencing, disorganization and numerous other problems." Such children often have discipline problems, are labeled underachievers and are at great risk of becoming dropouts.

Although usually associated with education, the consequences of learning disabilities go well beyond school. Behaviors that may be problematic include responding inappropriately, saying one thing but meaning another, forgetting easily, acting impulsively, demanding immediate gratification and becoming easily frustrated and then engaging in disruptive behavior. Youths with learning disabilities often have experienced failure after failure and lack self-esteem.

Youths Exposed to Drugs, Alcohol or HIV Prenatally

Children exposed to cocaine while in the womb, so-called **crack children,** may exhibit social, emotional and cognitive problems. A closely related problem is **fetal alcohol syndrome (FAS),** now the leading known cause of mental retardation in the western world. According to "Alcohol Effects on a Fetus" (2003): "FAS is present in 1 to 2 of every 1,000 babies in the United States." This source reports that children born with FAS are three times more likely to be born prematurely and that the effects last throughout the child's life. Children with FAS have abnormal facial features, one or more signs of growth retardation and at least one sign of central nervous system abnormality. In addition, a study funded by the National Institute of Alcohol Abuse and Alcoholism found that a woman's heavy, episodic drinking during pregnancy tripled the odds that her child would have drinking problems by age 21 ("Pregnant Women's Alcohol Use Linked to Offsprings' Problems," 2003, p. 5).

Another group of children with special needs are those prenatally exposed to HIV. Such children may experience deficits in both gross and fine motor skills; reduced flexibility and muscle strength; cognitive impairment including decreased intellectual levels, specific learning disabilities, mental retardation, visual/spatial deficits, and decreased alertness; and language delays.

Adolescence

Adolescence refers to the period from age 12 to age 18 or 19. In adolescence, children go through puberty, experiencing hormonal changes. During this time adolescents seek independence but can be very much influenced by their peers. Each generation produces a distinct adolescent subculture with a common language, clothing, music and standards. The result is what is often referred to as a *generation gap.* Figure 3.2 summarizes what occurs as adolescents develop.

Adolescence is often characterized by rapid growth and sexual maturity, self-consciousness, peer pressure and the shift of the primary support system from parents to friends, mood swings, experimentation, re-evaluation of values and a search for identity. Adolescence is no longer typified by the carefree lifestyle of the 1950s, as depicted in the television program *Happy Days,* and this is underscored by the large percentage of high school seniors who report worrying about social problems, as shown in Table 3.3.

Crime and violence have been the primary concerns of high school seniors for decades. However the percent of seniors having this concern has dropped from its all-time high of 92.7 percent in 1995. Concern about drug abuse, hunger and poverty has also declined, as has concern about the chance of nuclear war.

Adolescence is a difficult time of life, not only for youths, but also for their families, schools, neighborhoods and, increasingly, the police. It brings biological, psychological, emotional and social changes, often resulting in stress.

ADOLESCENT DEVELOPMENT—A DEVELOPMENTAL TASKS MODEL

Early Adolescence (10–12 years)

PHYSICAL DEVELOPMENT

Puberty starts (period of rapid growth; bodily changes; fidgets, squirms, has trouble sitting still; requires lots of physical activity). Puberty usually starts two years earlier for girls than boys. Begins to show bodily changes (pubic hair; hair thickens and darkens; testes and breasts enlarge).

COGNITIVE DEVELOPMENT

Inconsistent thoughts as they adjust to an open mind and body. Shifts from immature to mature thinking. Logic and reasoning are discovered. Able to imagine beyond immediate environment. Conversation leads to exchange of ideas. Spends more time talking to parents. It is important to feel that their opinions count. Thoughts lead to feelings of self-consciousness. Girls are more communicative than boys.

EMOTIONAL DEVELOPMENT

Seeks independence, establishes individuality. Wants some control in decisions affecting life. Propensity toward awkwardness, self-consciousness and bouts with low self-esteem. Begins developing mature relationships with siblings. Begins to be self-conscious about appearance. Girls often feel less attractive. Need praise and approval from adults to demonstrate concern and care about their welfare.

SOCIAL DEVELOPMENT

Has a desire to "fit in;" to be well-liked is important. Cliques are formed with others. Wants to be with friends without adult supervision. Feels that peer pressure is constantly present. Begins experimenting with smoking, alcohol and sex. Appreciates conversations that lead to an exchange of ideas to better understand other people's points of view.

Middle Adolescence (13–15 years)

PHYSICAL DEVELOPMENT

Puberty continues (boys begin growth spurts and surpass girls in height and weight by age 15). Acne and body odor are prevalent. Habits are developed that affect lifelong levels of physical fitness. Motor skills increase through physical activity. Clumsiness due to rapid physical development. At-risk habits such as smoking, drinking or drugs are started. Poor eating habits develop. Extremely aware and sensitive to own development and that of peers.

COGNITIVE DEVELOPMENT

Abstract thinking begins. Problem-solving, analytical thinking and writing may be deficient. Learn from doing; expand knowledge; experience through academic activities and performance. Greater separation in school between those who succeed and those who fail. Parents have less influence. Girls may begin failing in school. Decreased evidence of creativity and flexibility. Peer conformity critically important ("belongingness").

EMOTIONAL DEVELOPMENT

Craves freedom. Adept at masking true feelings and state of mind. Neutral responses to feelings of happiness and sadness. Intense desire and need for privacy. Rapid hormonal and body changes often lead to low self-esteem and lack of confidence. Seeks independence from, but still needs structure and limits from, parents and adults. Increased sexual desires and experimentation. Needs praise and approval to show that adults are concerned about their welfare.

SOCIAL DEVELOPMENT

Friendships and romance become increasingly important. Realizes that others have different points of view. Initial perspective-taking critically important to moral reasoning; and that outlook may be influenced by self-interest. Begins to define themselves and develop more concrete self-concept. Shows increased communication and negotiation skills. Experiences increased capacity for meaningful relationships with peers and adults. Explores rights and responsibilities. Wants to hang out with older teens. Same-sex groups socialize together. Parents start to have less influence.

Late Adolescence (16+ years)

PHYSICAL DEVELOPMENT

Boys' growth has doubled since age 12. They are taller and heavier than girls. Appropriate physical tasks have been learned and managed. Appetite has increased. Eating disorders may appear (bulimia and anorexia). Life patterns become consistent.

COGNITIVE DEVELOPMENT

Critical thinking and reasoning skills begin. Want to think out their own decisions. Concerned about the purpose and meaning of life. Can manipulate a number of variables at once. Develop beliefs, values, career choices and an identity. Limited evidence of creativity. Increased peer conformity. New challenges and experiences are required.

EMOTIONAL DEVELOPMENT

Develops a sense of personal identity. Self-esteem continues to develop and improve. Competencies such as decision-making, stress management and coping with problems develop. Thoughts and worries about adult life increase. Friendships are based on mature intimacy, and sharing thoughts and feelings—rather than just hanging out and doing things together. Strong sexual feelings are experienced. Generally, strong ties with the family are maintained with increased need for parental love, care and respect.

SOCIAL DEVELOPMENT

Independence developed and demonstrated. Susceptibility to peer pressure declines; parent-teen conflicts decrease. Cooperation and communication increase. Identity formation experienced through exploration and experimentation. Obsessed about appearance. Want to distinguish themselves from the crowd. Begins forming heterosexual groups and pairs up socially. Strong same-sex friendships continue to exist and strengthen. Has large circle of acquaintances and small circle of friends. After-school work prevalent—usually 15 to 20 hours per week. Is involved with social causes and movements (e.g., local community actions; environmental issues; volunteer work; political awareness).

Source: Barry Glick. "Kids in Adult Correctional Systems." *Corrections Today*, August 1998, p. 97. Reprinted by permission.

Figure 3.2
Adolescent Development

Table 3.3
High School Seniors Reporting That They Worry about Selected Social Problems

**United States
1989–2001**

Question "Of all the problems facing the nation today, how often do you worry about each of the following?"

(Percent responding "sometimes" or "often")

	Class of 1989 (N=2,849)	Class of 1991 (N=2,595)	Class of 1993 (N=2,807)	Class of 1995 (N=2,646)	Class of 1997 (N=2,651)	Class of 1999 (N=2,348)	Class of 2001 (N=2,222)
Crime and violence	86.3%	88.1%	90.8%	90.2%	88.5%	81.8%	81.0%
Drug abuse	79.5	79.5	75.5	72.6	71.1	62.7	61.1
Hunger and poverty	64.1	66.4	71.1	62.3	61.1	54.5	51.3
Chance of nuclear war	52.4	41.5	28.8	20.0	20.4	32.1	23.9
Economic problems	57.6	63.9	71.8	55.7	51.5	44.8	47.0
Pollution	55.9	72.1	72.8	63.6	61.6	49.8	49.6
Race relations	53.6	59.4	75.4	68.9	64.7	55.6	52.6
Energy shortages	27.9	38.2	29.8	17.9	19.4	20.8	31.2
Using open land for housing or Industry	30.8	33.8	32.9	28.9	32.7	27.5	30.6
Population growth	29.6	30.6	38.9	34.9	38.2	31.7	36.7
Urban decay	19.8	21.7	25.3	23.0	22.1	17.2	20.3

Note: These data are from a series of nationwide surveys of high school seniors conducted by the Monitoring the Future project at the University of Michigan's Institute for Social Research from 1975 through 2001. The survey design is a multistage random sample of high school seniors in public and private schools throughout the continental United States. All percentages reported are based on weighted cases; the Ns that are shown in the tables refer to the number of weighted cases.

Response categories were "never," "seldom," "sometimes" and "often." Readers interested in responses to this question for 1975 through 1988 should consult previous editions of SOURCEBOOK. For survey methodology and definitions of terms, see Appendix 6.

Source: *Sourcebook of Criminal Justice Statistics 2001*. Washington, DC: Bureau of Justice Statistics, 2002, p.161.

Juveniles often pretend to be adults in various ways, but becoming emotionally mature, socially accepted adults requires a struggle. From a social standpoint, many never succeed. Adolescents may try to look like adults, talk like adults or take on what they believe to be adult ways, but in general they remain quite immature. At the same time that they imitate adult behavior, juveniles also strive for individuality, independence and freedom, which they believe they can achieve by disassociating themselves from society and their parents. Such a position between imitation and disassociation can generate a great deal of psychological stress.

During adolescence peers become very important. According to Wasserman et al. (p.6): "Two major mechanisms associated with peer factors or influences are association with deviant peers and peer rejection." They (p.7) suggest that the highest degree of deviant peer influence on offending occurs with gang membership.

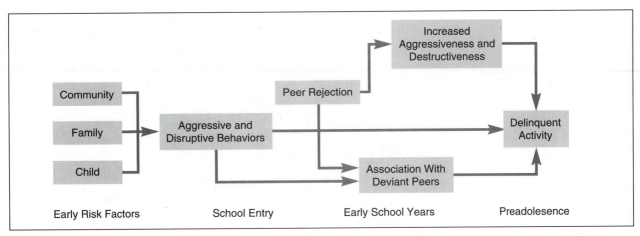

				Increased Aggressiveness and Destructiveness	
Community			Peer Rejection		Delinquent Activity
Family		Aggressive and Disruptive Behaviors			
Child				Association With Deviant Peers	
Early Risk Factors		School Entry		Early School Years	Preadolesence

Figure 3.3
Development of Early Offending Behavior and Peer Influences

Source: J.D. Coie and S. Miller-Johnson. "Peer Factors and Interventions." In *Serious and Violent Juvenile Offenders: Risk Factors and Successful Interventions,* edited by R. Loeber and D.P. Farrington. Thousand Oaks, CA: Sage Publications, Inc., 2001. pp.191–209. Reprinted by permission of Sage Publications, Inc.

 A strong case can be made that during adolescence deviant peers or peer rejection can influence nondelinquent juveniles to become delinquent.

Figure 3.3 illustrates the development of early offending behavior and peer influences.

Life for some adolescents is often lonely and depressing. Parents are involved in demanding careers, travel a lot and leave childcare to paid help or the extended family. They seldom do things as a family. When young people become bored with the happenings around them or with life in general, they often turn to antisocial or unlawful activity or to self-destruction.

The Influence of Early Work Experiences and Delinquency

Staff and Uggen (2003, p.263) note: "Criminologists have long considered the relationship between employment and delinquency." Their own study (p.283) found support for the proposition that several aspects of adult-like work conditions increase adolescent delinquency: "Precocious development and social control theories were especially well supported. Adolescents in more adult-like work setting, with higher social status, wages and autonomy exhibited higher rates of school deviance, alcohol use and arrest. . . . In contrast, work that was more age appropriate and allowed adolescents to balance their work and school roles reduced alcohol use, even when the number of hours worked intensified. . . . Finally, these results are also consistent with hypotheses drawn from power-control theory, showing that autonomous work increases delinquency by expanding adolescents' freedoms and diminishing the social controls to which they are subject." They conclude: "To reduce delinquency, 'good jobs' in adolescence must support rather than displace academic roles and offer genuine opportunities to learn something useful. Such jobs should also provide extensive controls, with circumscribed levels of autonomy, wages and status among peers."

Wu et al. (2003), likewise, found that employment is positively associated with adolescent drug and alcohol use among both males and females. They contend that having a job does not appear to be sufficient; instead, stable employment that reflects a strong commitment or stake in conformity seems to be required. Further evidence of the potential detrimental effect of some jobs is noted by Bellair et al. (2003, p.6): "Our findings suggest that low-wage, service sector employment opportunity directly increases the likelihood of violent delinquency."

Youths Who Abuse Alcohol, Tobacco and Illicit Drugs

Ericson (2001, p.1) reports: "Juveniles are experimenting with drugs, alcohol and tobacco at young ages. . . . The research suggests that significant changes in drug awareness take place between the ages of 12 and 13. Thirteen-year-olds are three times more likely to know how to obtain marijuana or to know someone who uses illicit drugs than are 12-year-olds." He also reports: "By the eighth grade, 52 percent of adolescents have consumed alcohol, 41 percent have smoked cigarettes, and 20 percent have used marijuana. By the twelfth grade, about 80 percent have used alcohol, 63 percent have smoked cigarettes, and 49 percent have used marijuana."

Drug Use Trends (2002, p.3) reports that from 1991 to 2001, use of most major drug types increased among eighth- and tenth-graders. However, after 6 years of increases, eighth-graders' past month marijuana use began to decrease in 1997 and continued to decline through 2001.

Although no single theory can explain the cause of delinquency, one fact *is* clear.

 There is a direct correlation between substance abuse and other forms of delinquency.

Vander-Waal et al. (2001, p.1) report: "For more than two decades, researchers, clinicians and juvenile justice program administrators have known of the link between drug use (including alcohol) and juvenile crime. In many communities, the majority of juveniles entering the system are drug users. Other research indicates that juvenile drug use is related to recurring chronic and violent delinquency that continues well into adulthood."

Youths who persistently abuse illegal substances experience an array of problems including academic difficulties, health-related problems, poor peer relationships and involvement with the juvenile justice system.

Teen Pregnancy

One important change within our culture has been a more open attitude toward sex and at least a tolerance of sexual intimacy outside of marriage. In many instances, marriage is no longer a requirement to live together. The result is a large increase in teenage pregnancy. The United States has the highest rates of teen pregnancy and birth—by far—of any comparable country (National Campaign to Prevent Teen Pregnancy, 2003, p.1). The National Campaign reports:

> Teen pregnancy and birth rates declined steadily during the 1990s. However, despite these declines, four out of ten girls in this country still get pregnant at least once before age 20.

Compared to women who delay childbearing, teen mothers are less likely to complete high school and more likely to end up on welfare. The children of teen mothers are at significantly increased risk of low birth weight and prematurity, mental retardation, poverty, growing up without a father, welfare dependency, poor school performance, insufficient health care, inadequate parenting, and abuse and neglect. U.S. taxpayers shoulder at least $7 billion annually in direct costs and lost tax revenues associated with teen pregnancy and childbearing.

When teenagers become pregnant, not only is their own growth and development affected, the situation into which they bring their newborns often is unsuited for the healthy growth and development of these children. Teenage pregnancy has created an "underclass" of poor young women with small children. These women have no training and limited resources. A large percentage of teen families live in poverty. Even more devastating, however, is strong evidence for the intergenerational transfer of poverty to the children of single-parent families.

For youths who do not turn to crime to achieve monetary success, the American Dream seems impossible. Homes, college education, things formerly taken for granted are now out of reach for millions of Americans. Often the increasing gap in material differences between some youths and their peers becomes intolerable. This may explain why some try to become "somebody" by acting tough, joining a gang, using drugs or running away from home.

A large part of the responsibility for assuring that our youths believe they have a promising future and a stake in our society and avoid offending behaviors rests with the family, the school and the community.

The Influence of Family

In November 1989, the General Assembly of the United Nations adopted several articles outlining the "rights of the child" (United Nations, 1989). The importance of the family was stressed in the preamble to this declaration of rights. The United Nations recognized that:

- The family, as the fundamental group of society and the natural environment for the growth and well-being of all its members and particularly children, should receive the protection and assistance that it needs to fully assume its responsibilities within the community.

- The child, for the full and harmonious development of his or her personality, should grow up in a family environment, in an atmosphere of happiness, love and understanding.

- The child should be fully prepared to live an individual life in society, and be brought up in the spirit of the ideals proclaimed in the Charter of the United Nations, and in particular in the spirit of peace, dignity, tolerance, freedom, equality and solidarity.

These powerful statements convey not only the importance of the family, but also the values that the family is to instill in children as it nurtures them and teaches them to be individuals as well as contributing members of society.

The efforts of skilled and committed judges, legislators, law enforcement officers, health and child care workers, doctors, teachers, attorneys, volunteers

The family is, for most children, the strongest socializing force in their lives. To thrive, children need the love and support of their parents. Here a father helps his daughter with her homework.

and others involved in the lives of deprived children can do little without a rekindled national awareness that the family is the foundation for the protection, care and training of our children. The structure and interaction patterns of the home influence whether children learn social or delinquent behavior.

Alvarado and Kumpfer (2000, p.8) stress: "Because families are the first point of a child's social contact, it is essential that parents understand the critical role they play in their children's development and that they be equipped with the information and skills necessary to raise healthy and well-adapted children. Improving parenting practices and the family environment is the most effective and enduring strategy for combating juvenile delinquency and associated behavioral, social and emotional problems."

In general, the family can have a positive impact on insulating children from antisocial and criminal patterns, providing it can control rewards and effectively maintain positive relationships within itself. Delinquency is highest when family interaction and controls are weak.

The Family as the First Teacher

The family is usually the first teacher and model for behavior and misbehavior. It is the first institution to affect children's behavior and to provide knowledge of and access to society's goals and expectations. However, if the integration process between parents and children is deficient, the children may fail to learn appropriate behaviors.

 In healthy families, self-esteem is high, communication is direct and honest, rules are flexible and reasonable and members' attitudes toward the outside world are trusting and optimistic.

American Child-Rearing Rights and Parenting Practices

Parental efficacy examines how parental support and control are interrelated. According to Wright and Cullen (2001, p.677): "Children in families with high levels of parental efficacy are at lower risk for delinquency throughout their adolescent years. Effective parenting is an important protective factor which can mitigate the impact of risk factors for delinquency such as having delinquent peers."

According to Wasserman et al. (p.5): "Inadequate parenting practices are among the most powerful predictors of early antisocial behavior." They describe three specific parental practices particularly associated with early conduct problems: (1) a high level of parent-child conflict, (2) poor monitoring and (3) a low level of positive involvement. In addition, how parents discipline their children can be positive or negative.

Physically punishing children is generally supported in the United States. The familiar adage, "Spare the rod, and spoil the child," attests to the traditional American view that it is parents' responsibility to teach their children right from wrong. Before children can reason, physical measures may be relied on. The question becomes not so much whether such physical coercion is appropriate, but rather what *degree* of physical coercion is appropriate. When does punishment become abuse? Is a slap on the hand the same as a slap to the face? Is a "paddling" through clothing with a bare hand the same as a beating with a belt on a bare bottom?

Simons et al. (2000, p.47) note: "Several studies with older children have reported a positive relationship between parental use of corporal punishment and child conduct problems." They (p.48) conclude: "Overall, the results [of their research] are consistent with the hypothesis that it is when parents engage in severe forms of corporal punishment, or administer physical discipline in the absence of parental warmth and involvement, that children feel angry and unjustly treated, defy parental authority and engage in antisocial behavior."

Simons et al. (pp.68–69) note: "Most studies of small children report that judicious use of spanking, especially when combined with inductive reasoning, fosters high child compliance and low levels of misbehavior." However, they (p.74) caution: "Our analyses provided little evidence that corporal punishment serves to deter adolescent conduct problems. This suggests that there are no practical justifications for a parent using corporal punishment with an adolescent child. Further, when a parent uses corporal punishment, there is always the danger that he or she will lose control and injure the child. For these reasons, we believe parents should always be discouraged from using corporal methods to discipline adolescent children."

Adult Supremacy

Force and violence toward children, including physical punishment, has been characterized as **adult supremacy.** In this relationship, power is sanctioned by legal rules with the effect being to subordinate one person to the arbitrary authority of another. Adult supremacy subordinates children to the absolute and arbitrary authority of parents. The dangers of adult supremacy were noted almost 100 years ago by Ledlie (1907, p.449):

> The right of control based on family law produces subordination, not a mere obligation. It represents a power over free persons and a power which curtails the freedom of those subject to it, because the person in whom power vests is entitled to exercise it, up to a certain point, in his own interests alone, to exercise it, in a word, as he chooses.

Adults have a legally protected right to bodily integrity, free from assault, but children do not, except in extreme circumstances. Parents are authorized to use force against their children because society believes adults are older and presumably wiser, and because the right to rear one's child as one chooses is held to be fundamental.

Courts give parents wide latitude in disciplining their children so they learn to respect authority. Adult supremacy has its roots in a common law concept of status derived from a feudal order that denied children legal identity and treated them as objects. In the United States until about 1900, the only person in the family who had any legal rights was the father.

Socialization

Children should learn in the home that others have rights that they must respect. They should learn about social and moral values; to be considerate of others' property, possessions and individual selves; to manage their own affairs and to take responsibility for their actions.

It is partly because of the failure of families to teach children basic conformity to social values and standards that children look for alternative groups such as gangs. Children develop their sense of being worthwhile, capable, important and unique from the attention and love given to them by their parents. They can develop a sense of worthlessness, incapability, unimportance and facelessness from a lack of attention and love, or from physical or sexual abuse. The development of social cognition as perceived by psychologists is outlined in Table 3.4.

Note that the development begins during the end of the critical first three years and ends for most children during adolescence. One important aspect of socialization is passing on the values of society.

Values

Values are extremely important in any society. Values reflect the nature of the society, indicate what is most important and describe how people are expected to behave. Throughout the ages societies have embraced certain values, taught these values to their children and punished those who did not adhere to them. When youths do not accept the values of society, conflict is inevitable.

 Common values that might be passed on to children include fairness, honesty, promise-keeping, respect, responsibility and self-control.

Unfortunately, in many families, no values or negative values, such as the use of violence to resolve disputes, are passed on. This may be partially explained by the disintegration of the traditional family.

Family-Related Risk Factors and the Disintegration of the Traditional Family

 The Census Bureau has identified six family-related risk factors: poverty, welfare dependence, absent parents, one-parent families, unwed mothers and parents who have not completed high school.

Unquestionably, the family has undergone great changes over the years. What began as an extended family, with two or three generations of a family living together, gradually became a nuclear family consisting of parents and their chil-

Table 3.4
Development of Social Cognition

	Understanding Self	Understanding Others	Understanding Friends	Understanding Social Roles	Understanding Society
Preoperational Period (About ages 2–7)	Understands concrete attributes. Understands major emotions, but relies on situation.	Understands concrete attributes, including stability of behavior.	One-way assistance (ages 4–9).	Can generalize role (ages 4). Understands person can change role and remain same person.	Feels no need to explain system (ages 5–6).
Concrete Operational Period (About ages 7–12)	Understands personal qualities. Relies on inner feelings as guide to emotions. Understands shame and pride.	Understands personal qualities.	Fairweather cooperation (ages 6–12),	Understands that people can occupy two roles simultaneously.	Understands social functions observed or experienced (ages 7–8). Provides fanciful explanations of distant functions (ages 9–10). Has acquired concrete knowledge of society.
Formal Operational Period (After about age 12)	Capable of complex, flexible, precise description. Understands abstract traits. Establishes identity.	Capable of complex flexible, precise description.	Intimate sharing (ages 9–15).		Can deal with abstract conception of society, government, and politics (by age 15).

Source: Elizabeth Hall, Michael E. Lamb and Marion Perlmutter. *Child Psychology Today.* 2nd ed. New York: Random House, 1986, p.562. Reprinted with permission of the McGraw-Hill Companies.

dren. When the children grew up, they moved out and started their own families. Changes that have occurred in contemporary American society have been more problematic, including more single-parent families, blended families, adoptive families and dysfunctional families. The **Norman Rockwell family**—a working father, a housewife mother and two children of school age—is no longer the norm.

Family Size and Sibling Influence

Wasserman et al. (p.6) state: "The more children in a family, the greater the risk of delinquency. . . . Boys who had four or more siblings by the age of 10 were twice as likely to offend, regardless of the parents' socioeconomic status." They also state: "Compared with teens with lower rates of offending, teens with high rates of offending were more likely to have siblings who also committed delinquent acts at a high rate."

Children Facing Special Challenges

 Children who may face special challenges as they grow and develop are children of immigrants, those whose parents are divorced and those whose mothers or fathers are incarcerated.

Immigrants' Children

Immigrants' children face many problems in addition to language barriers. Families are disrupted when some members emigrate while others are left behind.

Role reversal commonly occurs as children more readily learn English and become translators for their parents, in effect, gaining control over them. Further, native customs and values may differ greatly from what is accepted in the United States. For example, a Southeast Asian family might be investigated for child abuse after health professionals note the skin lesions caused by a traditional coin rubbing treatment. *Coining,* thought to have healing powers, consists of rubbing warm oil and coins across the skin, which sometimes produces long, red bruises. Finally, immigrants may also be subjected to prejudice and discrimination.

Children Whose Parents Are Divorced

A major study of children from one-parent families, conducted by the National Association of Elementary School Principals, found that 30 percent of two-parent elementary school students were ranked as high achievers, compared with only 17 percent of one-parent children. At the other end of the scale, 23 percent of two-parent children were low achievers versus 38 percent of one-parent children. One-parent students had more clinic visits and a higher rate of absence from school. One-parent students were consistently more likely to be late, truant and subject to disciplinary action. One-parent children were found to be more than twice as likely to drop out of school altogether.

Rebellon (2002, p.103) studied 1,725 adolescents and found that: "Divorce/separation early in the life course may be more strongly related to delinquency than prior research implies and that remarriage during adolescence may be strongly associated with status offending." Divorce has a shattering effect on families with young children, particularly if the mother has limited education or job skills.

Children Whose Mothers or Fathers Are Incarcerated

Bilchik et al. (2001, p.108) report: "Nearly 1.5 million children nationwide have at least one parent incarcerated in a state or federal prison. Approximately 600,000 more children have parents who are being held in local jails." They note: "In addition to the trauma of witnessing an arrest and being separated from a parent, children who experience parental incarceration are more likely to develop emotional and behavioral difficulties, including withdrawal, aggression, anxiety and depression. They are also at greater risk for poor academic performance, alcohol and drug abuse, and low self-esteem."

The impact of family relationships on children necessarily has a vital influence on whether children thrive in school and are able to learn the skills they need to succeed in society. Unfortunately, for too many students, the level of success they achieve in school is often hampered by the baggage they bring with them from home—the result of improper socialization, inadequate parenting skills, divorce, poor nutrition, domestic violence, child abuse and neglect.

The Influence of the School

Schools have a responsibility to the students who attend under the principle of *in loco parentis.* The principle of **in loco parentis,** meaning "in place of parents,"

Children who experience success in school are likely to experience success in life; those who experience failure in school are likely to experience failure in life. Here children enjoy learning while using a computer.

gives certain social and legal institutions the authority to act as a parent might in situations requiring discipline or need.

The school is one such institution. A dozen or more years in school has a huge impact on students, not only academically but also socially.

Origins of U.S. Public Schools

After the American Revolution, the leaders of the newly created United States proposed a system of publicly funded schools to educate poor and rich children alike. These early advocates of public schools believed American citizens had a fundamental responsibility to educate all children to become responsible citizens and economically self-sufficient.

The Current Focus of Schools

The United Nations' Convention on the Rights of the Child said of schools that "education should be directed at developing the child's personality and talents, preparing the child for active life as an adult, fostering respect for basic human rights and developing respect for the child's own cultural and national values and those of others" (United Nations, Article 29, p.9). However, many schools tend to stress academic learning over character building, including instilling positive values.

Values and the School

Educators have long felt that the school should be a place where children not only studied academic subjects but were also taught basic values. The values that teachers think are important for children to learn today have changed little over the years. Honesty, responsibility, freedom of speech, courtesy, tolerance and respect for the law are valued. As Kagan (2001, p.51) suggests: "For many students, character and virtues will be acquired in school—or not at all."

Closely related to imparting positive values is the effort to create a true school *community*. Schaps (2003, p.31) suggests: "A growing body of research confirms the benefits of building a sense of community in school. Students in schools with a strong sense of community are more likely to be academically motivated; to act ethically and altruistically; to develop social and emotional competencies; and to avoid a number of problem behaviors, including drug use and violence." Students who feel a sense of community in their schools are more likely to be successful than when such a feeling is absent.

The Importance of Success in School

The No Child Left Behind (NCLB) legislation of 2002 is a sweeping change to the Elementary and Secondary Education Act of 1965. The law changed the federal government's role in K–12 education by asking America's schools to describe their success in terms of what each student accomplishes.

The importance of succeeding in school was emphasized by noted educator William Glasser (1969, p.5) in his classic work *Schools Without Failure:* "I believe that if a child, no matter what his background, can succeed in school, he has an excellent chance for success in life. If he fails at any stage of his educational career—elementary school, junior high, high school, or college—his chances for success in life are greatly diminished." •

Children who succeed in school have a greater probability of succeeding in other areas of their lives.

A serious obstacle to achieving academically is an anti-achievement ethic in many schools. What is perceived as "cool" is skipping school, misbehaving in class, smarting off to teachers and others in authority. What is "uncool" is to get good grades. Teachers describe the "crab bucket syndrome." When one crab tries to climb from a bucket, the others pull it back down. Students are often torn between wanting to be accepted by their peers and wanting to succeed in school. Academic success in many schools assures social ostracism.

Peer approval and acceptance is often more important to adolescents than the approval of parents or teachers.

In addition, consider how much the media have advanced with all their special effects and what teachers now have to compete against. Also consider that several common school practices actually encourage failure.

How Schools Promote Failure

Glasser described five practices that produce failure for students. First is A-B-C-D-F *grading.* Grades are so important they substitute for education itself. Second is *objective testing* usually based on memorizing facts, many of which students see as irrelevant. Closely related to objective testing is *grading on a normal curve.* By definition, in this system, 50 percent of the students must be below average. Fourth is *closed-book exams,* based on the fallacy that knowledge remembered is better than knowledge looked up. In the information age, it is critical that students learn to use references, not to simply memorize often irrelevant facts.

Fifth is *tracking*, grouping students either by ability level or achievement and often labeling the high achieving group the "college-bound" or "college preparatory" group. Such tracking may have all of the negative consequences associated with labeling: stigma, self-fulfilling prophecy and lack of motivation to succeed. In addition, teachers may not have high expectations for lower-track students or expend as much energy on teaching them as they do on high achievers. They also may tend to give lower grades because they do not assign the low achievers as much work and, further, such students do not need good grades because, unlike the high achievers, they are not expected to be college-bound. As Holbrook (2001, p.781) warns: "If children are marked as 'failures' at age 10, again at 14, and again at 16, their motivation will die, and they will spiral downward. They will be robbed of an education and marked forever as failures who have no worth."

What Glasser condemned 30 years ago continues to be standard practice in many schools. The educational practices discussed are not an indictment of the schools but a partial explanation of why so many students fail in school and how this failure affects not only their school performance but also their behavior in other areas.

Student Response to Failure

When students fail to meet the expectations of teachers or parents, they may become involved in delinquent groups of youths who share similar experiences of failure. The group provides the needed outlet for frustration and anger. Some students skip school or drop out completely. Other youths run away. Some seek escape in alcohol and other drugs or attempt suicide.

Students' responses to failure include skipping school, joining gangs, dropping out of school, drinking, doing drugs, performing delinquent acts and even suicide.

Truancy and Dropping Out

Skipping class is something many students do at some point, usually just for a day or two, here and there. The results are often fairly innocuous—perhaps some late homework or a lecture from a parent. When such absences become habitual, however, it becomes a more serious issue.

Baker et al. (2001, p.1) contend: "Truancy, or unexcused absence from school, has been linked to serious delinquent activity in youth and to significant negative behavior and characteristics in adults. As a risk factor for delinquent behavior in youth, truancy has been found to be related to substance abuse, gang activity and involvement in criminal activities such as burglary, auto theft and vandalism."

Truancy is an early warning sign that a youth is headed for potential delinquent activity.

Truancy costs students an education. It costs school districts thousands of dollars in lost federal and state funds based on attendance figures. It costs taxpayers, who must pay higher taxes for law enforcement and welfare costs for dropouts who end up unemployed. Baker et al. (p.2) describe four correlates of truancy:

- *Family factors.* Lack of guidance or parental supervision, domestic violence, poverty, drug or alcohol abuse in the home, lack of awareness of attendance laws and differing attitudes toward education.
- *School factors.* School climate issues—such as school size and attitudes of teachers, other students and administrators—and inflexibility in meeting the diverse cultural and learning styles of students.
- *Economic influences.* Employed students, single-parent homes, high mobility rates, parents with multiple jobs, and lack of affordable transportation and childcare.
- *Student variables.* Drug and alcohol abuse, lack of understanding of attendance laws, lack of social competence, mental health difficulties and poor physical health.

The underlying reasons for dropping out are often more complex than simply not liking school or poor grades. Many children come to school affected by divorce, homelessness and learning disabilities and from homes in which they must become self-sufficient at an early age. Some must deal with crime, drugs and gangs in their neighborhoods; suffer abuse and neglect from adults; or become parents while still children themselves.

The Link between Delinquency and the Schools

 The link between failure in school and delinquency is strong.

Just as the family sometimes fails to provide a nurturing, caring environment or to control children, the school is sometimes nonsupportive and lacking in discipline and control. Wasserman et al. (p.8) report: "A specific school risk factor for delinquency is poor academic performance. . . . Poor academic performance is related to the prevalence, onset, frequency and seriousness of delinquency." In addition, they contend: "Children with weak bonds (low commitment) to school, low educational aspirations and poor motivation are also at risk for general offending."

Problems Facing Schools

The Gallup organization collaborated with Phi Delta Kappa, a professional education organization, in producing "the 35th Annual Phi Delta Kappa/Gallup Poll of the Public's Attitudes Toward the Public Schools." According to the poll (Rose and Gallup, 2003, p.50) the leading problem for the past four years has been lack of financial support (25 percent). Lack of discipline was second at 16 percent; overcrowding was third at 14 percent. In response to why students failed to learn, leading the list was lack of home or parental support (93 percent) followed by lack of student interest (90 percent) and lack of discipline (84 percent) (p.51).

The 35th Gallup Poll of Attitudes toward Public Schools identified lack of discipline as the number two problem in local schools. The leading problem was lack of financial support.

According to past poll results, discipline was the number one problem every year from 1969 to 1985, except 1971. In 1986 the drug problem claimed the number one spot and ranked first among local school problems seven times, tying once with lack of proper financial support. In 1998 drugs dropped to fourth. This poll reflects the public's concern over the lack of discipline in our nation's public schools. This is very likely a contributing factor to the problem of drugs, bullying and crime—other problems facing schools.

 Serious problems facing our schools include substance use, bullying, and crime and violence.

Substance Use in Schools

Finn et al. (2003, p.80) report: "Substance use remains firmly entrenched in teen culture, a sphere in which drinking and drug use are often considered badges of belonging. . . . Although it is difficult to obtain accurate estimates of the pervasiveness of in-school substance use, research indicates that anywhere between 6 and 25 percent of U.S. students have been under the influence of alcohol and marijuana at some point during school hours."

In 1994 Goals 2000 declared that by 2000 every school in the United States would be drugs, alcohol and violence free. However, when the interim report was published in 1995, the use and sales of illicit drugs at school had increased (Duke, 2002). DeVoe et al. (2002) reported that during 2001 5 percent of students grades 9–12 had at least one drink on school property within the past 30 days and that the same percentage had used marijuana on school property in the same time frame. According to the government's *2001 National Household Survey on Drug Abuse,* drug use among adolescents and young adults increased between 2000 and 2001. The survey also found a significant increase in the estimated number of persons age 12 and over needing treatment for drug problems. According to Califano (2001, p.1): "Each year substance use costs our schools at least $41 billion in truancy, special education and disciplinary programs, disruption, teacher turnover and property damage."

Bullying

Cooper and Snell (2003, p.22) note: "In the wake of school shootings and lawsuits brought against schools by victims of bullying, 11 state legislatures— California, Colorado, Georgia, Louisiana, Minnesota, Nevada, New Hampshire, Oklahoma, Oregon, Vermont and Washington—have mandated that schools take active steps to reduce bullying."

According to DeVoe et al., 8 percent of students reported being bullied in 2000. However, research by Olweus (2003, p.13) using a large-scale survey of approximately 11,000 Norwegian students from 54 schools with questions identical to a survey conducted in 1983 found disturbing results: "The percentage of victimized students had increased by approximately 50 percent from 1983, and the percentage of students who were involved (as bullies, victims, or bully-victims) in frequent and serious bullying problems—occurring at least once a week—had increased by approximately 65 percent."

The seriousness of the problem in the United States was supported by a survey conducted for the National Institute of Child Health and Human Development which found that almost one-third of U.S. students in grades 6–10 were directly involved in serious, frequent bullying—10 percent as bullies, 13 percent as victims, and 6 percent as both (Nansel et al., 2001).

Garbarino and deLara (2003, p.21) contend that: "Failing to prevent bullying behavior suggests a lack of understanding of the serious and damaging nature of all forms of bullying for many students. . . . When school personnel do not prevent students from bullying other students, these educators have, in effect, delegated a portion of their authority to the bullies in the system." Preventing bullying is discussed in Chapter 8.

Crime and Violence in the Schools

According to DeVoe et al., important gains have been made in reducing crime and violence in U.S. schools; however the crime problem remains "enormous," with approximately 1.9 million total crimes of violence or theft at schools during 2000. They report that the high of 59 violent victimizations per 1,000 students in 1993 has declined to a low of 26 in 2000. The problems of crime and violence in schools are discussed in Chapter 6.

Schools' Responses

Measures that schools have taken in response to crime and violence include drive-by shooting drills, fencing the campuses, adding metal detectors, conducting locker searches, banning the wearing of overcoats and backpacks that could conceal weapons and adding uniformed and armed security guards or police officers. However, such measures merely treat symptoms rather than focusing on the causes such as teen hopelessness, family breakdown, media violence, the drug culture, demographics and economics.

Zero-tolerance policies mandate predetermined consequences or punishments for specific choices and have become a popular disciplinary choice (Holloway, 2001/2002, p.84). According to the National School Safety Center (2001), nine of ten principals who participated in a survey said that tough discipline, including zero-tolerance policies, were absolutely essential for keeping schools safe even though they result in an increase in suspensions and expulsions. Holloway cautions: "Policies that rely solely on suspending and expelling students do not remedy student misbehavior." A more promising approach is the use of school resource officers.

A school resource officer or **SRO** is "a career law enforcement officer with sworn authority, deployed in community-oriented policing, and assigned by the employing police department or agency to work in collaboration with school and community-based organizations" (Omnibus Crime Control and Safe Streets Act of 1968). Girouard (2001, p.1) explains that this concept evolved during the 1950s in Flint, Michigan, and flourished during the 1960s and 1970s, languished in the 1980s and then gained momentum nationwide in the mid-1990s. According to Atkinson (2001, p.55): "Demand for school resource officers has increased dramatically with heightened public concern about school safety." She (p.57) contends: "Experience has taught that the presence of an SRO has a deterrent effect on illegal and disruptive behavior." In addition, an SRO within a school can also help assure that students' rights are not violated.

Students' Rights within the School

Protecting students' rights within the school is another area of concern to the juvenile justice system. Until the past decade, the landmark case in student rights was *Tinker v. Des Moines Independent Community School District* (1969), which established that students have constitutional rights that must be protected in school.

 Students have full constitutional rights within the school, including freedom of speech as well as the right to be free from illegal search and seizure.

Under *Tinker,* students' rights could not be removed unless exercising them would "substantially interfere with the work of the school or impinge upon the rights of other students." This standard changed in 1985. The current standard is based on three cases: *New Jersey v. T.L.O.* (1985), *Bethel School District #403 v. Fraser* (1986) and *Hazelwood School District v. Kuhlmeier* (1988). In all three cases, students claimed their constitutional rights were violated.

In *New Jersey v. T.L.O.,* a teacher observed two girls, one of whom was T.L.O., smoking cigarettes in a girl's restroom in violation of the school's rules. The girls were accompanied to the school administrator's office, where T.L.O. denied smoking at all. The administrator requested T.L.O.'s purse, inspected it, found cigarettes, marijuana and marijuana paraphernalia. Further examination disclosed money and change amounting to $40.98 and a letter from T.L.O. to a friend asking for her help to sell marijuana in school. The administrator contacted the police, who referred the matter to the juvenile court. The court ruled there was a violation of search and seizure. Upon appeal, the Supreme Court overturned the ruling, saying that schools can make rules for the administration of the school and there was no violation of Fourth Amendment protection. As Ehlenberger (2001/2002, p.31) states: "Student search can be a tool for maintaining safe schools, but school administrators must balance students' individual rights with the school community's need for a safe learning environment."

In *Bethel School District #403 v. Fraser,* a student was suspended from school for three days and had his name removed from a list of candidates for graduation speaker because he used sexually explicit language in his campaign speech. The student brought suit, claiming his First Amendment right to free speech had been violated, but the Court said it was constitutional for a school "to prohibit the use of vulgar and offensive terms in public discourse," and it left the determination of this with the school board.

In *Hazelwood School District v. Kuhlmeier,* a principal prohibited the publication of two pages of a student newspaper because he felt the articles were inappropriate. One article was on student pregnancies written from the point of view of three pregnant students; each gave a positive account of the experience. The other article was on the impact of divorce on students and included comments attributed to specific individuals; the principal considered this to be inappropriate. The Court upheld the prohibition as constitutional.

These three cases set the standard that governs a school's restriction of students' constitutional rights.

 The Court requires only that schools' actions in restricting students' constitutional rights be "reasonably related to legitimate pedagogical concerns."

This standard puts great responsibility on school administrators; it will probably reduce the likelihood that courts will intervene in school-related matters.

Another area involving students' rights is random drug testing of student athletes. At the end of its 1995 session, the Supreme Court upheld the constitutionality of random drug testing for student athletes (*Vernonia School District 47J v. Acton*), stating that such screening does not violate Fourth Amendment protections against unreasonable search and seizure.

The Influence of the Community

The community might be viewed as a series of nested boxes, as shown in Figure 3.4. The community provides the physical environment that shapes its members' health and sense of well-being. It also provides both formal and informal networks including neighbors, school, businesses and a multitude of other groups and organizations.

 The network of community associations is a powerful element of everyday life and a defining factor in childhood development, serving to either help or hinder learning socially acceptable conduct.

Wright and Cullin (p.677) note: "Recently, the concept of 'collective efficacy' has been advanced to understand how communities exert control and provide support to reduce crime. **Collective efficacy** parallels parental efficacy, but is on a much larger scale."

Wasserman et al. (p.8) note: "Numerous risk factors for young children's offending lie within the community domain. . . . Disorganized neighborhoods with few controls may have weak social control networks that allow criminal activity to go unmonitored and even unnoticed. . . . Certain residential areas may support greater opportunities for antisocial learning."

 Community risk factors include disadvantaged or disorganized neighborhoods, a concentration of delinquent peer groups and access to weapons.

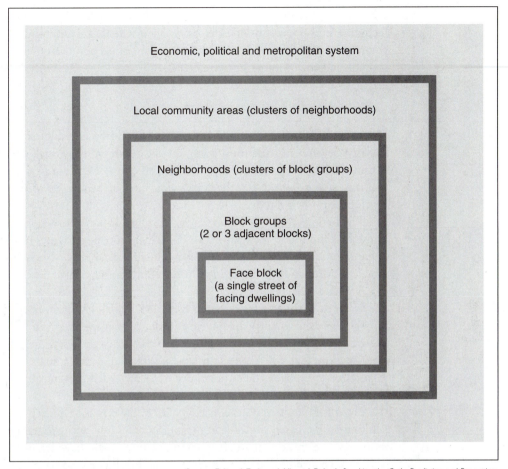

Figure 3.4
**A Community Viewed
as Nested Boxes**

Source: Felton J. Earls and Albert J. Reiss, Jr. *Breaking the Cycle: Predicting and Preventing Crime.* Washington, DC: National Institute of Justice, 1994, p. 10.

Just as building a sense of community in the schools is seen as important, so is building a sense of community within neighborhoods. One way to do so that is gaining in popularity is through full-service community schools.

Full-Service Community Schools

Dryfoos (2002, p.394) explains the features of a full-service community school: "A community school, operating in a public school building, is open to students, families and the community before, during and after school, seven days a week, all year long. It is jointly operated and financed through a partnership between the school system and one or more community agencies. Families, young people, principals, teachers, youth workers, neighborhood residents, college faculty members, college students and businesspeople all work together to design and implement a plan for transforming the school into a child-centered institution."

Full-service community schools address not only students' educational needs, but their mental and physical needs as well. Social workers and counselors are available for students and their families. Health services may be provided, including immunizations and dentistry. Such schools are a natural fit with the community-policing model that has been gaining in popularity within both the juvenile and the criminal justice systems.

Summary

The juvenile justice system exists to serve the children and adolescents of our country. Seventeen is the most common age at which individuals are legally considered adults, no longer under the jurisdiction of the juvenile court. Until that time it is expected that the state will assure the healthy growth and development of its children.

The period from birth to age 3 is the most formative time of a child's life. Individual childhood risk factors for child delinquency and later violent juvenile offending include early antisocial behavior, emotional factors such as high behavioral activation and low behavioral inhibition, poor cognitive development, low intelligence and hyperactivity.

Great care must be taken when using labels with children. Self-fulfilling prophecies occur when people live up to the labels they are given. Children and adolescents in particular incorporate labels as part of their self-images. Labeling theorists state that when a deviant label is attached to individuals, they become stigmatized and have little opportunity to be rewarded for conformist behavior. The label becomes a self-fulfilling prophecy.

Two of the most serious consequences of poverty for children are homelessness and an increased risk of lead poisoning. Children with special needs include those who are emotionally/behaviorally disturbed, who have learning disabilities, who have an attention deficit hyperactivity disorder or who have behavior problems resulting from prenatal exposure to drugs, alcohol or HIV.

A strong case can be made that during adolescence deviant peers or peer rejection can influence nondelinquent juveniles to become delinquent.

The family, the school and the community are powerful influences on children's development. The structure and interaction patterns of the home influence whether children learn socially acceptable or delinquent behavior. In healthy families, self-esteem is high, communication is direct and honest, rules are flexible and reasonable and members' attitudes toward the outside world are trusting and optimistic. Common values that might be passed on to youths include equality, honesty, promise-keeping, respect, responsibility and self-control.

The Census Bureau has identified six family-related risk factors: poverty, welfare dependence, absent parents, one-parent families, unwed mothers and parents who have not completed high school. Children who may face special challenges as they grow and develop are children of immigrants, those whose parents are divorced and those whose mothers or fathers are incarcerated.

The schools also play a vital role in the development of youths. Children who succeed in school have a greater probability of success in other areas of their lives. Peer approval and acceptance often is more important to adolescents than the approval of parents or teachers.

Students' responses to failure may include skipping school, joining gangs, dropping out of school, drinking, doing drugs, performing delinquent acts and even attempting or actually committing suicide. Truancy is an early warning sign that a youth is headed for potential delinquent activity. The link between failure in school and delinquency is strong. The 35th Gallup Poll of Attitudes toward Public Schools identified lack of discipline as the number two problem in local schools. The leading problem was lack of financial support.

If students are to be taught respect for others, their own constitutional rights should be respected within the school. Students do have full constitutional rights, including freedom of speech as well as the right to be free from illegal search and seizure. However, the Supreme Court requires only that schools' actions in restricting students' constitutional rights be "reasonably related to legitimate pedagogical concerns."

The community also plays a pivotal role in the healthy development of youths. Community associations are a powerful element of everyday life and a defining factor in childhood development, serving to either help or hinder the learning of socially acceptable conduct. Community risk factors include disadvantaged or disorganized neighborhoods, a concentration of delinquent peer groups and access to weapons.

Discussion Questions

1. The adult world stresses material and financial gain, social status and winning at any cost. Can children adjust to or understand this attitude? What values should adults communicate to children about these attitudes?

2. What are some common labels for youths used in local high schools—for example, nerd? How can labels hurt youths? How can they be beneficial?

3. Does your community have any ghettos or areas where poverty exists? What are some of visible signs of such conditions?

4. How does your community handle homeless people, particularly youths? Are there special programs for homeless families with children?

5. At what age do people become adults in your state?

6. Is controlled spanking in certain cases justified? Were you spanked as a child?

7. What values should be passed to the next generation?

8. Did you ever skip school when you were young? If you did, do you remember why? Why do youths become truants? Is truancy the responsibility of the school, parents or youths?

9. Do schools contribute to the problem of youths who are disruptive, antisocial, incorrigible and truant? How?

10. Are there neighborhoods in your community where violence seems more tolerated than in others? If so, what factors contribute to this tolerance?

InfoTrac College Edition Assignments

- Use InfoTrac College Edition to help answer the Discussion Questions as appropriate.

- Complete one of the following assignments and be prepared to share your findings with the class.
  - Research any two of the following conditions: attention deficit hyperactivity disorder, EBD, fetal alcohol syndrome, crack children.
  - Read and outline two articles on the school resource officer.
  - Read and outline two articles on zero-tolerance policies. Be prepared to discuss whether you support such policies or not.
  - Outline the characteristics of collective efficacy and parental efficacy.

Internet Assignments

Complete one of the following assignments and share with the class.

■ Go to the No Child Left Behind Web site at http://www.nochildleftbehind.gov/ and outline the four basic reforms called for in the NCLB legislation.

■ Go to www.ojp.usdoj.gov/bjs to find *Indicators of School Crime and Safety, 2002.* Outline the executive summary.

■ Go to www.ncjrs.org to find, read and outline any of the end-of-chapter references with an NCJ number in parentheses or go to any reference having an online address to find, read and outline the entire article.

References

"Alcohol Effects on a Fetus." WebMD with AOL Health, May 8, 2003. http://aolsvc.health.webmd.aol.com/content/healthwise/63/15671

Alvardo, Rose and Kumpfer, Karol. "Strengthening America's Families." *Juvenile Justice,* December 2000, pp.8–17.

America's Children: Key National Indicators of Well-Being 2002. Washington, DC: Federal Interagency Forum on Child and Family Statistics, July 2002.

Armstrong, Thomas. "IKSWAL: Interesting Kids Saddled with Alienating Labels." *Educational Leadership,* November 2001, pp.38–41.

Association for Children with Learning Disabilities. "Taking the First Step to Solving Learning Problems." Pittsburgh, PA: Association for Children with Learning Disabilities, pamphlet, no date.

Atkinson, Anne J. "School Resource Officers: Making Schools Safer and More Effective." *The Police Chief,* March 2001, pp.55–63.

Baker, Myriam L.; Sigmon, Jane Nady; and Nugent, M. Elaine. *Truancy Reduction: Keeping Students in School.* Washington, DC: OJJDP Juvenile Justice Bulletin, September 2001. (NCJ 188974)

Bellair, Paul E.; Roscigno, Vincent J.; and McNulty, Thomas L. "Linking Local Labor Market Opportunity to Violent Adolescent Delinquency." *Journal of Research in Crime and Delinquency,* February 2003, pp. 6–33.

Bilchik, Shay B.; Seymour, Cynthia; and Kreisher, Kristen. "Parents in Prison." *Corrections Today,* December 2001, pp.108–111.

Califano, J. A. *Malignant Neglect: Substance Abuse and America's Schools.* New York: National Center on Addiction and Substance Abuse at Columbia University, 2001.

Cauce, A. "The Characteristics and Mental Health of Homeless Adolescents: Age and Gender Differences." *Journal of Emotional & Behavioral Disorders,* Vol. 8, No.4, 2000, pp.230–239.

Child Health USA 2002. "Children in Poverty." http://www.mchirc.net/HTML/CHUSA02/main_pages/page12.htm

"Children and TV Violence." Washington, DC: American Academy of Child and Adolescent Psychiatry, 2003.

Cooper, Doug and Snell, Jennie L. "Bullying—Not Just a Kid Thing." *Educational Leadership,* March 2003, pp.22–25.

DeVoe, J.F.; Peter, K.; Kaufman, P.; Ruddy, S.A.; Miller, A.K.; Planty, M.; Snyder, T.D.; Duhart, D.T.; and Rand, M.R. *Indicators of School Crime and Safety: 2002.* Washington, DC: U.S. Department of Education and Justice, November 2002. (NCJ 196753) www.ojjdp.usdoj.gov/bjs

Drug Use Trends. Washington, DC: ONDCP Fact Sheet, October 2002. (NCJ 190780)

Dryfoos, Joy. "Full-Service Community Schools: Creating New Institutions." *Phi Delta Kappan,* January 2002, pp.393–399.

Duke, D.L. *Creating Safe Schools for All Children.* Boston: Allyn and Bacon, 2002.

Ehlenberger, Kate R. "The Right to Search Students." *Educational Leadership,* December 2001/January 2002, pp.31–35.

Ericson, Nels. *Substance Abuse: The Nation's Number One Health Problem.* Washington, DC: OJJDP Fact Sheet #17, May 2001. (FS 200117)

Finn, Kristin V.; Willert, H. Jeanette; and Marable, Michele A. "Substance Use in Schools." *Educational Leadership,* March 2003, pp.80–84.

Garbarino, James and deLara, Ellen. "Words Can Hurt Forever." *Educational Leadership,* March 2003, pp.18–21.

Girouard, Cathy. *School Resource Officer Training Program.* Washington, DC: OJJDP Fact Sheet #05, March 2001. (FS 200195)

Glasser, William. *Schools without Failure.* New York: Harper & Row, 1969.

Holbrook, Pixie J. "When Bad Things Happen to Good Children." *Phi Delta Kappan,* June 2001, pp.781–785.

Holloway, John H. "The Dilemma of Zero Tolerance." *Educational Leadership,* December 2001/January 2002, pp.84–85.

Holloway, John H. "Addressing the Needs of Homeless Students." *Educational Leadership,* December 2002/January 2003, pp.89–90.

Institute for Children and Poverty. *Déjà vu: Family Homelessness in New York City.* New York, 2001. www.homesforthehomeless.com

Kagan, Spencer. "Teaching for Character and Community." *Educational Leadership,* October 2001, pp.50–85.

Kelly, J.; Buehlman, K; and Caldwell, K. "Training Personnel to Promote Quality Parent-Child Interaction in Families Who Are Homeless." *Topics in Early Childhood Special Education,* Vol. 20, No. 3, 2000, pp.174–185.

Koblinsky, S.; Gordon, A.; and Anderson, E. "Changes in the Social Skills and Behavior Problems of Homeless Children during the Preschool Years." *Early Education Development,* Vol. 11, No. 3, 2000, pp.321–338.

Ledlie, J. *Sohm's Institute of Roman Law.* 1907. Out of print.

Lemert, Edwin. *Social Pathology.* New York: McGraw-Hill, 1951.

Messner, Steven F. and Rosenfeld, Richard. *Crime and the American Dream,* 3rd ed. Belmont, CA: Wadsworth Publishing Company, 2001.

Moore, Mark. *Drug Trafficking.* Washington, DC: National Institute of Justice, no date.

Nansel, T.R.; Overpeck, M.; Pilla, R.S.; Ruan, W.J.; Simons-Morton, B.; and Scheidt, P. "Bullying Behaviors among U.S. Youth: Prevalence and Associations with Psychosocial Adjustment." *Journal of the American Medical Association,* Vol.285, No.16, 2001, pp.2095–2100.

The National Campaign to Prevent Teen Pregnancy. "Recent Trends in Teen Pregnancy, Sexual Activity and Contraceptive Use." Washington, DC: The National Center to Prevent Teen Pregnancy, February 2003.

National Center for Juvenile Justice, *Annual Report 2001.* Pittsburg, PA: National Center for Juvenile Justice, 2001.

National School Safety Center. *Review of School Safety Research,* 2001. www.nsscl.org/studies/statistics%20resourcespdf.pdf

Olweus, Dan. "A Profile of Bullying at School." *Educational Leadership,* March 2003, pp.12–17.

"Pregnant Women's Alcohol Use Linked to Offsprings' Problems." Washington, DC: *Substance Abuse Letter,* Pace Publications, Vol. 8, No. 15, 2003, p.5.

Rebellon, Cesar J. "Reconsidering the Broken Homes/Delinquency Relationship and Exploring Its Mediating Mechanism(s)." *Criminology,* February 2002, pp.103–136.

Rose, Lowell C. and Gallup, Alec M. "The 35th Annual Phi Delta Kappa/Gallup Poll of the Public's Attitudes toward the Public Schools." *Phi Delta Kappan,* September 2003, pp.41–56.

Schaps, Eric. "Creating a School Community." *Educational Leadership,* March 2003, pp.31–33.

Simons, Ronald L.; Wu, Chyi-In; Lin, Keui-Hsiu; Gordon, Leslie; and Conger, Rand D. "A Cross-Cultural Examination of the Link between Corporal Punishment and Adolescent Antisocial Behavior." *Criminology,* February 2000, pp.47–79.

Smith, A.C. and Smith, D.I. *Emergency and Transitional Shelter Population: 2000, Census 2000 Special Reports.* Washington, DC: U.S. Department of Commerce, 2001. www.census.gov/prod/2001pubs/censr01-2.pdf

Staff, Jeremy and Uggen, Christopher. "The Fruits of Good Work: Early Work Experiences and Adolescent Deviance." *Journal of Research in Crime and Delinquency,* August 2003, pp.263–290.

Stern, Karen R. *A Treatment Study of Children with Attention Deficit Hyperactivity Disorder.* Washington, DC: OJJDP Fact Sheet #20, May 2001. (FS 200120)

"Studies Weigh Facets of Juvenile Justice." *Law Enforcement News,* June 15, 2000, p.8.

Tannock, Rosemary and Martinussen, Rhonda. "Reconceptualizing ADHD." *Educational Leadership,* November 2001, pp.20–25.

2001 National Household Survey on Drug Abuse. Washington, DC: Substance Abuse and Mental Health Services Administration (SAMHSA), September 5, 2002.

United Nations. *Convention on the Rights of the Child.* Adopted by the General Assembly of the United Nations, November 20, 1989.

U.S. Congress, House Committee on Education and Labor. *Hearing Before Subcommittee on Elementary, Secondary, and Vocational Education on H.R. 123.* 96 Congress, 1st Session, April 24, 1979.

Vander-Waal, Curtis J.; McBride, Duane C.; Terry-McElrath, Yvonne M.; and Van Buren, Holly. *Breaking the Juvenile Drug-Crime Cycle: A Guide for Practitioners and Policymakers.* Washington, DC: National Institute of Justice, May 2001. (NCJ 186156)

"Violence on Television—What Do Children Learn? What Can Parents Do?" American Psychological Association. Online: http://www.apa.org/pubinfo/violence.html

Wasserman, Gail A.; Keenan, Kate; Tremblay, Richard E.; Cole, John D.; Herrenkohl, Todd I.; Loeber, Rolf; and Petechuk, David. *Risk and Protective Factors of Child Delinquency.* Washington, DC: Child Delinquency Bulletin Series, April 2003.

Wright, John Paul and Cullen, Francis T. "Parental Control and Support Processes Jointly Influence Children's Behavior." *Criminology,* Vol. 39, No. 3, 2001, p.677.

Wright, Karen. "Guns, Lies and Video." *Discover,* April 2003, pp.28–29.

Wu, Li-Tzy; Schlenger, William E.; and Galvin, Deborah. "The Relationship between Employment and Substance Use among Students Aged 12 to 17." *Journal of Adolescent Health,* Vol. 32, No. 1, 2003, p.5.

Cases Cited

Bethel School District #403 v. Fraser, 478 U.S. 675 (1986).

Hazelwood School District v. Kuhlmeier, 484 U.S. 260 (1988).

New Jersey v. T.L.O., 469 U.S. 325 (1985).

Tinker v. Des Moines Independent Community School District, 393 U.S. 503 (1969).

Vernonia School District 47J v. Acton, _____ U.S. _____, 115 S.Ct. 2386 (1995).

Neglected, Abused, Victimized and Missing Children and Youths

The cycle of abused and neglected children who have become abusing and neglecting parents with their children in turn being abused, neglected, running away, acting out and often ending up before the courts has not been broken.

—Metropolitan Court Judges Committee

Do You Know?

- What risks maltreated children and youths face?
- What often characterizes the homes of neglected children?
- What the three components of child abuse and neglect laws typically are?
- What are thought to be the two leading causes of child abuse?
- What the major cause of death of young children is?
- What the three levels of abuse are?
- Whether child abuse is directly linked to delinquency?
- Which age group has the highest victimization rate?
- What the likely result of violence is for children?
- What six episode types of missing children are identified in the NISMART–2 study?
- What two federal agencies have concurrent jurisdiction for missing and exploited children? What approach each takes toward missing children?
- What the leading cause of youth suicide is? What common warning signs of youth suicide are?

Can You Define?

anticipated strain
caring environment
child abuse
collective abuse
dependency
emotional abuse
extrafamilial sexual abuse
individual abuse

institutional abuse
intrafamilial sexual abuse
maltreatment
maximalist alarmist
    perspective
minimalist skeptical
    perspective
neglect

physical abuse
runaway
seesaw model
thrownaway
vicarious strain

INTRODUCTION

Since 1986 the number of children who are abused, neglected and endangered every year has nearly doubled—to about 1 million today. Emotional and behavior disorders, teen pregnancy, prostitution, substance abuse, and delinquency and criminality are some of the immediate and long-term consequences a child may face because of maltreatment. Each year nearly 1,200 children and youth are killed by caretakers; most of the victims are 5 years old or younger (Delany-Shabazz and Vieth, 2001, p1).

This chapter examines the many ways children are maltreated and victimized. According to Glasscock (2001, p.6): "Millions of children are abused each year." During 2000, 3 million referrals concerning the welfare of approximately 5 million children were made to child protection services (CPS) agencies throughout the United States. Of these, about two-thirds (62 percent) were screened in; one-third (38 percent) were screened out. Almost one-third (32 percent) resulted in a finding that the child was maltreated or at risk of maltreatment. About 879,000 children were found to be victims of child maltreatment. **Maltreatment** includes neglect, medical neglect, physical abuse, sexual abuse and psychological maltreatment (National Child Abuse and Neglect Data System [NCANDS], 2002).

Maltreated youths are at an increased risk for performing poorly in school; displaying symptoms of mental illness; for girls, becoming pregnant; using drugs; and engaging in serious and violent delinquency.

In addition, one of eighteen violent crime victims is younger than 12 (Office of Juvenile Justice and Delinquency Prevention, 2000). Osofsky (2001, p.2) contends: "Juvenile crime and victimization both remain very serious problems. The definition of 'victimization'. . . also includes children's witnessing of and exposure to violence either in their communities or in their homes."

According to Finkelhor and Ormrod (2001c, p.1): "Not only are children the victims of many of the same crimes that victimize adults, they are subject to other crimes, such as child abuse and neglect, that are specific to childhood. The impact of these crimes on young victims can be devastating and the violent or sexual victimization of children can often lead to an intergenerational cycle of violence and abuse."

Research conducted by English et al. (2002, p.1) reaches the same conclusion: "Our findings strongly support the relationship between child abuse and neglect and delinquency, adult criminality and violent criminal behavior. Abused and neglected children are 4.8 times more likely to be arrested as juveniles, 2 times more likely to be arrested as an adult and 3.1 times more likely to be arrested for a violent crime than matched controls." Their findings replicate earlier findings and underscore the devastation that can be caused by maltreatment of children and youths.

This chapter begins with a discussion of child neglect and abuse, including sexual harassment and abuse as well as ritualistic abuse by Satanic cults. This is followed by a discussion of children as victims of crime and violence outside the home. The chapter concludes with a description of some results of victimization, including missing youths who are runaways, thrownaways, abducted and even suicidal.

Defining Child Maltreatment and Rating Its Severity

Maltreatment exists in many forms. Definitions of the various types of maltreatment vary from state and state and even locality to locality. The most common subtypes of child maltreatment and their severity are described in Table 4.1.

The National Clearinghouse on Child Abuse and Neglect Information reports: "In 2001, 3 million referrals concerning the welfare of approximately

Table 4.1
Defining Child Maltreatment and Rating Its Severity

Subtype of Maltreatment	Brief Definition	Examples of Least and Most Severe Cases
Physical Abuse	A caregiver inflicts a physical injury upon a child by other than accidental means.	*Least*—Spanking results in minor bruises on arm. *Most*—Injuries require hospitalization, cause permanent disfigurement or lead to a fatality.
Sexual Abuse	Any sexual contact or attempt at sexual contact that occurs between a caretaker or responsible adult and a child for the purposes of the caretaker's sexual gratification or financial benefit.	*Least*—A child is exposed to pornographic materials. *Most*—A caretaker uses force to make a child engage in sexual relations or prostitution.
Physical Neglect	A caretaker fails to exercise a minimum degree of care in meeting a child's physical needs.	*Least*—Food is not available for regular meals, clothing is too small, child is not kept clean. *Most*—A child suffers from severe malnutrition or severe dehydration due to gross inattention to his or her medical needs.
Lack of Supervision	A caretaker does not take adequate precautions (given a child's particular emotional and developmental needs) to ensure his or her safety in and out of the home.	*Least*—An 8-year-old is left alone for short periods of time (i.e., less than 3 hours) with no immediate source of danger in the environment. *Most*—A child is placed in a life-threatening situation without adequate supervision.
Emotional Maltreatment	Persistent or extreme thwarting of a child's basic emotional needs (such as the need to feel safe and accepted).	*Least*—A caretaker often belittles or ridicules a child. *Most*—A caretaker uses extremely restrictive methods to bind a child or places a child in close confinement such as a closet or trunk for 2 or more hours.
Educational Maltreatment	A caretaker fails to ensure that a child receives adequate education.	*Least*—A caretaker allows a child to miss school up to 15% of the time (when he or she is not ill and there is no family emergency). *Most*—A caretaker does not enroll a child in school or provide any educational instruction.
Moral-Legal Maltreatment	A caretaker exposes or involves a child in illegal or other activities that may foster delinquency or antisocial behavior.	*Least*—A child is permitted to be present for adult activities, such as drunken parties. *Most*—A caretaker causes a child to participate in felonies such as armed robbery.

Source: Adapted from Barnett et al. (1993).

5 million children were made to CPS agencies throughout the United States. Of these, approximately two thirds (67 percent) were screened in" (*Child Maltreatment 2001: Summary of Key Findings,* 2003, p.1). This same report notes that approximately 903,000 children were found to be victims of child maltreatment, giving a victimization rate of 12.4 per 1,000 children.

Children ages birth to 3 years accounted for over one fourth (28 percent) of the victims. Overall, the victimization rate is inversely related to the child's age. More than 80 percent were abused by a parent or parents. According to the report (p.2): "Child fatalities are the most tragic consequence of maltreatment. Approximately 1,300 children died of abuse or neglect during the year 2001, a rate of 1.81 children per 100,000 children."

Neglected Children

Broadly defined, child **neglect** is inattention to the basic needs of a child, including appropriate supervision, adequate clothing and proper nutrition. Often the families from which neglected children come are poor and disorganized. They have no set routine for family activity. The children roam the streets at all hours. They are continually petitioned to juvenile court for loitering and curfew violations. The family unit is often fragmented by death, divorce or the desertion of parents.

Broken homes often deprive children of affection, recognition and a sense of belonging unless a strong parent can overcome these responses and provide direction. If a child's protective shield is shattered, the child may lose respect for moral and ethical standards. The broken home, in and of itself, does not cause delinquency. But it can nullify or even destroy the resources youths need to handle emotional problems constructively. Children from broken homes may suffer serious damage to their personalities. They may develop aggressive attitudes and strike out. They may think that punishment is better than no recognition. Even when marriages are intact, both parents often work. Consequently, many parents spend little time in the home interacting with their children.

Some children are stunted in their emotional growth by being raised in a moral vacuum in which parents ignore them. Even more problematic are parents who do not adhere to moral and ethical standards or who have different values than the dominant moral order; they set poor examples for their children. Such parents cannot ignore the probability that their children may model their actions.

 The homes of neglected children often are disorganized, with parents who ignore the children or who set bad examples for them.

Some parents deliberately refrain from discipline in the mistaken belief that authoritative restrictions inhibit children's self-expression or unbalance their delicate emotional systems. At the other extreme are parents who discipline their children injudiciously, excessively and often, weighing neither transgression nor punishment. Parents' warped ideas, selfish attitudes and twisted values can lead to their children becoming delinquents. Family policies that are inconsistent or that emphasize too much leniency or excessive punishment may result in retaliation directed at society in general.

Children's behavior develops from what they see and understand to be happening around them as discussed in Chapter 3. If children are exposed to excessive drinking, the use of drugs, illicit sex, gambling and related vices by parents or adult role models, they may copy these behaviors.

Neglected children often lack the food, clothing, shelter, medical care, supervision, education, protection or emotional support they need to develop appropriate physical, mental and emotional health. They also may suffer emotional harm through disrespect and denial of self-worth, unreasonable or chronic rejection and failure to receive necessary affection, protection and a sense of family belonging. They may suffer ill health because they are not vaccinated against common childhood illness or are exposed to second-hand smoke or lead. They may even die from preventable accidents.

Another large contributor to neglect is crack cocaine. The Legal Aid Society in New York reports a large increase in cases of child abuse and neglect as the direct result of crack. Even more devastating, however, are the traumatic accidents that maim or kill children. Some of these mishaps result from safety hazards in the home. An estimated 90 percent of permanent childhood injuries could have been prevented by adequate supervision, often the result of a parent being high on drugs or alcohol.

Certainly not all neglect is intentional. It may be the result of parental immaturity or a lack of parenting skills. It may also be the result of a parent's physical, psychological or mental deficiencies. Other parents who neglect their children may do so because they cannot tolerate stress, they cannot adequately express anger or they have no sense of responsibility.

Indicators of Neglect

Among the *physical indicators* of child neglect are frequent hunger, poor hygiene, inappropriate dress, consistent lack of supervision (especially in dangerous activities or for long time periods), unattended physical problems or medical needs and abandonment. The *behavioral indicators* of neglect may include begging, stealing food, extending school days by arriving early or leaving late, constant fatigue, listlessness or falling asleep in school, alcohol or drug abuse, delinquency, stealing and reporting that no one is at home to care for them (Bennett and Hess, 2004, p.288).

Physically or Emotionally Abused Children

The problem of **child abuse** is serious. Such abuse may be physical or emotional. Physical child abuse covers a wide spectrum of behavior. Sometimes, the abuse is discipline carried too far. Controversy exists among child development scholars and parents about where the line between discipline and abuse should be drawn, and many parents who cause physical harm to their children while administering disciplinary measures claim they never *intended* to injure their children. The definition of **physical abuse,** however, leaves less room for interpretation and addresses the issue of intent, stating it is the *nonaccidental,* or intentional, physical injury of a child caused by the child's caretaker.

Injury to a child need not be limited to physical attacks and external wounds. Children may also be damaged through **emotional abuse,** the chronic failure of a child's caretaker to provide affection and support. Emotional abuse includes any treatment that seriously damages a child's emotional development. For example, Charles Manson was raised by an uncle who constantly called him derogatory names and sent him to school dressed in girl's clothing.

Unfortunately the physical and emotional abuse of children is nothing new to humankind. In fact, many times throughout history such abuse was widely and openly practiced.

Historical Roots of Abuse   Throughout history children have been subjected to physical violence. Infants have been killed as a form of birth control, to avoid the dishonor of illegitimacy, as a means of power, as a method of disposing of retarded or deformed children and as a way of protecting financial security.

In ancient Greece a child was the absolute property of the father, and property was divided among the male children. A father could raise the first son and expose subsequent children to the elements. Under Roman law the father had the power of life and death (*patria potestas*) over his children and could kill, mutilate, sell or offer them as a sacrifice.

In the industrial, urban and machine age the exploitation of child labor was common. Children of all ages worked 16 hours a day, usually with irons and chains on their ankles to keep them from running away. They were starved, beaten and dehumanized, and many died from exposure in the workplace, from occupational diseases or from suicide.

Karmen (2001, p.198) notes: "For centuries, parents were permitted to beat their children in the name of imposing discipline. Religious and legal traditions legitimized parental violence toward youngsters as a necessary, even essential, technique of child rearing (unless permanent injury or death resulted; then the problem was labeled 'cruelty to children')."

Before the creation of the first juvenile court in the United States, the Society for the Prevention of Cruelty to Children was formed in 1871 as a result of church workers removing a severely beaten and neglected child from her home under a law that protected animals. The first Child Protection Service was founded in 1875. Fifty years later the Social Security Act authorized public funds for child welfare.

During the 1940s advances in diagnostic X-ray technology allowed physicians to detect patterns of healed fractures in their young patients. In 1946 Dr. John Caffey, a pediatric radiologist, suggested that multiple fractures in the long bones of infants had "traumatic origin," perhaps willfully inflicted by parents. Two decades later Dr. C. H. Kempe and his associates coined the phrase *battered child syndrome* based on clinical evidence of maltreatment. Karmen (p.199) notes: "In the typical case, the victim was younger than 3 years old and suffered traumatic injuries to the head and to limbs; and the caretakers claimed that the wounds were caused by an accident and not a beating." In 1964 individual states began enacting mandatory child abuse laws using Dr. Kempe's definition of a battered child, and by 1966 all 50 states had enacted such legislation.

*Child Abuse
and Neglect Laws*

Laws regarding child abuse and neglect have been passed at both federal and state levels.

 Typically child abuse/neglect laws have three components: (1) criminal definitions and penalties, (2) a mandate to report suspected cases and (3) civil process for removing the child from the abusive or neglectful environment.

Federal Legislation

In 1974 the federal government passed Public Law (PL) 93–247, the Federal Child Abuse Prevention and Treatment Act. It was amended in 1978 under PL 95–266. The law states in part that any of the following elements constitutes a crime:

> The physical or mental injury, sexual abuse or exploitation, negligent treatment, or maltreatment of a child under the age of 18, by a person who is responsible for the child's welfare under circumstances that indicate the child's health or welfare is harmed or threatened.

Nonetheless federal courts have also ruled that parents are free to strike children because "the custody, care and nurture of the child resides first in the parents" (*Prince v. Massachusetts* [1944]). This fundamental right to "nurture" has been supplanted by the U.S. Supreme Court with the "care, custody and management" of one's child (*Santosky v. Kramer* [1982]). This shift from "nurture" to "management" could herald a return to older laws, such as the one expressed in *People v. Green* (1909): "The parent is the sole judge of the necessity for the exercise of disciplinary right and of the nature of the correction to be given." The court need only determine whether "the punishment inflicted went beyond the legitimate exercise of parental authority."

Up to the present, the courts' role has been to decide what, when and to what degree physical punishment steps beyond "the legitimate exercise of parental authority" or what is "excessive punishment." The courts always begin with the presumption that parents have a legal right to use force and violence against their own children. In *Green,* 70 marks from a whipping was held to be excessive and unreasonable, even though the parent claimed he was not criminally liable because there was no permanent injury and he had acted in good faith. But the assumption remained that the parent had an unquestionable right "to administer such reasonable and timely punishment as may be necessary to correct growing faults in young children."

Current laws often protect parents, and convictions for child abuse are difficult to obtain because of circumstantial evidence, the lack of witnesses, the husband-wife privilege and the fact that an adult's testimony often is enough to establish reasonable doubt. All too often the court determines punishment to be reasonable, never reexamining the age-old presumption that hitting children is permissible.

A determination of "reasonableness" was made in *Ingram v. Wright* (1977) regarding the use of physical punishment of children by teachers. The Florida statute specified that the punishment was not to be "degrading or unduly severe."

One student was beaten by 20 strokes with a wooden paddle; another was beaten by 50 strokes.

In 2000 congress passed the Child Abuse Prevention and Enforcement Act making more funds available for child abuse and neglect enforcement and prevention initiatives ("Congress Passes Measures on Child Abuse Enforcement," 2000, p.4).

State Laws

Since the 1960s every state has enacted child abuse and neglect laws. On the whole, states offer a bit more protection to children by statute than does the federal government.

Legal definitions vary from state to state. California, for example, declares it illegal for anyone to willfully cause or permit any child to suffer or for any person to inflict unjustifiable physical or mental suffering on a child or to cause the child to "be placed in such situations that its person or health is endangered" (California Penal Codes, Sec. 273A).

Alaska defines abuse broadly: "The infliction, by other than accidental means, of physical harm upon the body of a child." Other state statutes are much less broad. For example Maryland's statute states that a person is not guilty of child abuse if the defendant's intentions were good, but his or her judgment was bad. The defendant in *Worthen v. State* (1979) admitted he had punished his 2-year-old stepdaughter because she was throwing a temper tantrum, "but sought to explain as not having exceeded the bounds of parental propriety." The jury found him guilty of assault and battery for the multiple contusions about the girl's face, ribs, buttocks and legs, but the appellate court ordered a new trial because the trial court in its jury instructions had omitted the defense of good intentions and also the defense that the stepfather had not exceeded the bounds of parental authority. What is "reasonable" varies from state to state, from one judge or court to another and from jury to jury.

The Causes of Abuse

Parents or caretakers commit most emotional and physical child abuse. The causes of such abuse often center on a cycle of abuse passed from one generation to the next. Other characteristics that correlate to child abuse include low income, social isolation and parental expectations that exceed a child's abilities.

 The two leading causes of child abuse are thought to be violence between husbands and wives and poverty.

Further causes of child abuse include racial discrimination and the desensitization to violence by frequently viewing brutality on television and in the movies.

A **seesaw model** conceptualizes the causes of child abuse, illustrating both functional and nonfunctional families and two critical factors: stress and resources. In the functional family, the resources are available to cope with daily stressors, resulting in a "balanced" family, as illustrated in Figure 4.1.

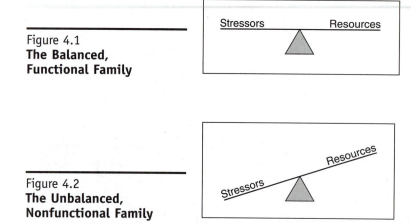

Figure 4.1
The Balanced,
Functional Family

Figure 4.2
The Unbalanced,
Nonfunctional Family

In the nonfunctional family, resources are insufficient to deal with the stresses, and they become overpowering, as illustrated in Figure 4.2. To bring such families into balance, stressors must be removed, or resources to cope with the stressors must be increased—or both.

The American Medical Association (1985, p.797) has identified characteristics of children that increase their risk of being abused: premature birth; birth of a child to adolescent parents; colic, which makes infants difficult to soothe; congenital deficiencies or abnormalities; hospitalization of the newborn resulting in a lack of parental contact; and presence of any condition that interferes with parent-child bonding.

Indicators
of Physical Abuse

Among the *physical indicators* of physical abuse to a child are unexplained bruises or welts, burns, fractures, lacerations and abrasions. Such physical injuries may be in various stages of healing. Among the *behavioral indicators* of physical abuse are children who are wary of adults, apprehensive when other children cry, who show extreme aggressiveness or extreme withdrawal, are frightened of parents or afraid to go home (Bennett and Hess, p.288).

Ennis (2000, p.93) cautions that some common physical conditions have been mistaken for physical abuse: "Hemophiliacs bruise very easily. Mongolian spots, which look similar to bruises, can be found on 95 percent of black children, 81 percent of oriental and Indian children, 70 percent of Hispanic children and 10 percent of white children. Allergic rhinitis (inflammation of the mucous membrane of the nose) can cause black eyes." Also, the condition of osteogenesis imperfecta (OI) can be mistaken for child abuse. This condition is characterized by bones that break easily. According to the Osteogenesis Imperfecta Foundation: "A minor accident may result in a fracture; some fractures may occur while a child is being diapered, lifted or dressed."

Parents' behavior can also provide clues to physical abuse. This can include contradictory explanations for a child's injury; attempts to conceal a child's injury

© Joel Gordon/Joel Gordon Photography

Living in poverty is one of two leading causes of child abuse.

or to protect the identity of the person responsible; the routine use of harsh, unreasonable discipline inappropriate to the child's age or behavior; and poor impulse control (Bennett and Hess, p.376).

Indicators of Emotional Abuse

Physical indicators of emotional abuse may include speech disorders, lags in physical development and a general failure to thrive. *Behavioral indicators* of emotional abuse may include such habit disorders as sucking, biting and rocking back and forth, as well as conduct disorders such as antisocial or destructive behavior. Other possible indicators are sleep disorders, inhibitions in play, obsessions, compulsions, phobias, hypochondria, behavioral extremes and attempted suicide (Bennett and Hess, p.288).

The Seriousness of the Problem

Experts disagree on just how serious the problem of child abuse is. Karmen (p.203) describes two conflicting views: the maximalist alarmist and minimalist skeptical perspectives. The **maximalist alarmist perspective** "contends that the time has come to reject the reluctance of earlier generations to face the facts and to recognize the enormity of the developing crisis. Parents are abusing and neglecting their children in record numbers, and exploitive adolescents, pedophiles (child molesters) and other abusers are preying upon youngsters with impunity." From the **minimalist skeptical perspective** (p.204): "Large numbers of honestly mistaken allegations as well as maliciously false ones are mixed in with true disclosures, making the problem seem worse than it really is."

Abused children often suffer severe physical and emotional damage from family violence, unreasonable corporal punishment, verbal harassment, alcoholic and substance abuse and sexual or other exploitation. Osofsky (p.2) reports that in the United States homicide is one of the leading causes of death for youngsters, with an estimated 2,000 children, most under age 4, murdered by parents or caretakers each year. Of the children in the group 12 and younger, the majority have been previously abused by the person who killed them.

 Child abuse has been identified as the biggest single cause of death of young children.

Finkelhor and Ormrod (2001b, p.2) report: "Overall, the statistics on murders of juveniles in the United States are grim and alarming. Homicide is the only major cause of childhood death that has increased in incidence during the past 30 years. The U.S. [homicide of juveniles] rate is 5 times higher than the rate of the other 25 developed countries combined and nearly double the rate of the country with the next highest rate."

The abuse is sometimes inflicted by those outside the family, but more tragically and commonly it is inflicted by a child's natural parents or members of the immediate family. Finkelhor and Ormrod note: "Most homicides of young children are committed by family members through beatings or suffocation."

Three Levels of Abuse   Thus far, child abuse has been discussed primarily as an act between individuals. In reality, however, three separate levels of abuse exist.

 The three levels of abuse are collective, institutional and individual.

Collective Abuse

Collective abuse is seen in the poverty and other forms of social injustice previously discussed. As has been noted, millions of children live in poverty in the United States. Children eat and drink contaminated food and water. Many are exploited through child pornography. Constant violence blares forth from television sets across the country. Childcare is often grossly inadequate, and the physical punishment of children is widely sanctioned. The collective attitude in America ignores the natural and legal rights of children.

Another form of collective child abuse is that of illegal child labor. Kruse and Mahony (2003) estimate that 148,000 minors are employed illegally in an average week and 290,000 are employed illegally at some point during a year. Total employer cost savings is roughly $155 million per year. Foster and Kramer report that the poorest and most vulnerable children start working before most children start kindergarten, often in exhausting, hazardous jobs ("Secret Child Labor in America").

According to Human Rights Watch World Report 2001 an estimated 250 million children worldwide between ages 5 and 14 worked for a living with 50 million younger than 12 working in hazardous circumstances. One of the most common forms of child labor in both industrialized and developing countries is use of children in agriculture. In the United States, more than

300,000 children worked as hired laborers on commercial farms, often in danger-ous and grueling conditions. These children risked pesticide poisoning, heat ill-nesses, injuries and life-long disabilities.

Human Rights Watch describes the working conditions: "Children working on U.S. farms often worked 12-hour days, sometimes beginning at 3:00 or 4:00 A.M. They reported routine exposure to dangerous pesticides that cause can-cer and brain damage, with short-term symptoms including rashes, headaches, dizziness, nausea and vomiting. Young farm workers became dizzy from laboring in 100°F temperatures without adequate access to drinking water, and were forced to work without access to toilets or hand-washing facilities. . . . An esti-mated 100,000 children suffered agriculture-related injuries during the year."

Institutional Abuse

Institutional abuse of children includes the approved use of force and violence against children in the schools and the neglect and denial of children's due process rights in government institutions. However, the use of corporal punish-ment in schools has been declining; "paddling" has decreased since the early 1980s and has been banned in several states. Like illegal child labor, corporal punishment of children is a worldwide concern as attested to by the launch in April 2001 of the Global Initiative to End All Corporal Punishment of Children.

Individual Abuse

Individual abuse is what is normally thought of when child abuse is discussed. This is one or more people emotionally or physically abusing a child. Individual abuse includes child sexual abuse. A graphic example of such abuse was demon-strated by a Chicago couple who allegedly raped, drugged and fed fried rats and boiled cockroaches to their four children for at least four years.

Child Abuse and the Link with Delinquency Child abuse has been directly linked with delinquency.

When delinquent behavior occurs, it may bring about further abuse, resulting in a vicious cycle and ever-worsening behavior, as illustrated in Figure 4.3.

Children and adolescents who have patterns of delinquency that emanate from the home are imitating the behavior of parents or other family members. In extreme cases, children have been taught how to commit crimes.

Ireland et al. (2002) used official records and longitudinal survey data to find a strong relationship between maltreatment and the behaviors of delin-quency and drug use. They found that childhood-only maltreatment had little impact on negative behavioral outcomes in early and late adolescence. In con-trast, adolescence-only maltreatment and persistent maltreatment from childhood to adolescence were consistently related, in a similar manner, to various types of delinquency and drug use.

Many studies have amplified the link between child abuse and criminal behavior, including the research by English et al. cited at the beginning of this chapter. And many criminal justice professionals on the front lines with juvenile

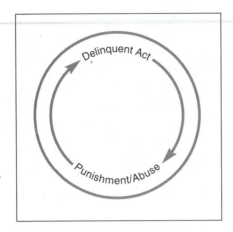

Figure 4.3
The Delinquency/
Abuse Cycle

delinquents believe the war on crime will be won only when the focus shifts from building more prison cells to investing more in children—through early childhood programs such as health care for children and pregnant women, Head Start for infants and toddlers, parenting training for high-risk families, programs aimed at preventing child abuse, recreational programs, after-school programs and mentoring programs.

Sexually Harassed or Abused Children

According to Woods (2002, p.20): "Sexual harassment happens often, occurs right under teachers' noses, can begin in elementary school and upsets both girls and boys. . . . Four out of five students (81 percent) experience some form of sexual harassment. . . . Girls and boys reported that harassment makes them feel embarrassed (53 and 32 percent respectively), self-conscious (44 and 19 percent) and less confident (32 and 16 percent). Harassed students said that they talk less in class and find it hard to pay attention. Not surprisingly, students change their behaviors to avoid harassers, including skipping school (16 percent), dropping out of a particular activity or sport (9 percent) and dropping courses (3 percent). Girls commented that being sexually harassed makes them feel 'dirty—like a piece of trash,' 'terrible,' 'awkward' and 'like a second-class citizen.'"

Sexual harassment is not the only problem some youths experience. Every year roughly 100,000 cases of child sexual abuse are reported. Couple this with experts' estimates that more than 90 percent of child molestations are *not* reported to the criminal justice system and the magnitude of the problem is apparent. Some experts believe that as many as 50 percent of young women have been sexually abused before their eighteenth birthday. However, Jones and Finkelhor (2001, p.1) report: "Data from child protective services (CPS) agencies across the country indicate that the increases [in sexual abuse] of the 1980s were followed by an extensive period of marked declines in the 1990s."

Sexual abuse can be classified as intrafamilial or extrafamilial. **Intrafamilial sexual abuse** is sexual abuse by a parent or other family member. **Extrafamilial sexual abuse** involves a friend or stranger. Babysitters are responsible for a relatively small portion of the reported criminal offenses against children: 4.2 percent of all offenses for children under age 6. Among the reported offenses that babysitters commit, sex crimes outnumber physical assaults nearly two to one (Finkelhor and Ormrod, 2001a, p.2).

A number of lawsuits alleging sexual abuse by clergy have involved large sums of money. An Associated Press article ("Judge OKs $10 Million Settlement in Boston Archdioceses Abuse Lawsuit," 2002, p.A6) noted: "A $ 10 million settlement between the Boston Archdiocese and 86 alleged victims of child-molesting priest John Geoghan won final approval Thursday. . . . The $10 million deal is substantially smaller than settlements in some other major clergy sexual abuse cases. Last week the Diocese of Providence, RI, agreed to pay $13.5 million to settle lawsuits filed by 36 people who said they were sexually abused by 10 priests and a nun over many years."

Another article on the Boston clergy (2003, p.A4) reports: "More than 1,000 people likely were sexually abused by more than 250 clergy and church workers in the Boston archdiocese over 60 years. . . . Church officials supported the needs of offending priests over those of children and did not notify law enforcement or child protection authorities of complaints." According to the Associated Press ("Boston Church Offers to Settle," 2003, p.Al), the Boston Archdiocese is offering $55 million to settle more than 500 cases.

Other prominent cases include Dallas in 1997 where a jury awarded $119.6 million to victims of Diocese of Dallas priest Rudy Kos. The dozens of victims later settled for more than $30 million. Kos was sentenced to life in prison. In 1999 in Palm Beach, Florida, Bishop J. Keith Symons resigned after admitting to molesting five boys. In March 2002, Bishop Anthony O'Connell resigned after admitting to molesting a seminary student. Also in 2002, in Minnesota, St. John's Abbey in Collegeville and the Crosiers in Shoreview acknowledged that a number of monks, priests and brothers had engaged in sexual abuse years ago ("Report: Boston Clergy Abused 1,000," 2003, p.A4).

Indicators of Sexual Abuse

Rarely are the *physical indicators* of sexual abuse seen. Two possible indicators, especially in preteens, are venereal disease and pregnancy.

Among the possible *behavioral indicators* of sexual abuse are being unwilling to change clothes for or to participate in physical education classes; withdrawal, fantasy or infantile behavior; bizarre sexual behavior; sexual sophistication beyond one's age or unusual behavior or knowledge of sex; poor peer relationships; delinquent or runaway behavior; and reports of being sexually assaulted (Bennett and Hess, p.288).

As with physical abuse, the behavior of parents may also provide indicators of sexual abuse. Such behaviors may include jealousy and being overprotective of a child. A parent may hesitate to report a spouse who is sexually abusing their child for fear of destroying the marriage or for fear of retaliation. Intrafamilial sex may be preferred to extramarital sex (Bennett and Hess, p.401).

The Consequences of Being Sexually Abused

Sexual abuse can have many adverse affects on its young victims, including guilt, shame, anxiety, fear, depression, anger, low self-esteem, concerns about secrecy, feelings of helplessness, and an inordinate need to please others (Karmen). In addition, victims of sexual abuse have higher levels of school absenteeism, less participation in extracurricular activities and lower grades.

Research by Siegel and Williams (2003, p.84) found: "Sexual abuse victims were significantly more likely to have been arrested as adults than their matched counterparts even controlling for a childhood history characterized by family problems serious enough to have resulted in a dependency hearing." In this case **dependency** refers to the legal status of children over whom a juvenile court has assumed jurisdiction because the court has found their care to fall short of legal standards of proper care by parents, guardians or custodians.

Sexual Abuse and the Internet

According to Medaris and Girouard (2002, p.1): "Nearly 30 million children and youth go online each year to research homework assignments and to learn about the world they live in." Atkinson-Tovar (2001, p.35) notes: "For criminals seeking children to prey upon, the Web has greatly widened offenders' opportunities, who yesterday combed the country's playgrounds and parks seeking victims but now lurk in chat rooms in cyberspace. The Internet is by far the easiest place for the child sex offender to satisfy his needs."

Parsons (2000, p.25) describes child pornography as a danger on the electronic frontier: "Predators frequently use images depicting the sexual exploitation of children in an attempt to lure children into participating in this type of activity." *Internet Crimes against Children* (2001, p.3) states: "One in five youths received a sexual approach or solicitation over the Internet in the past year. One in four youths had an unwanted exposure in the past year to pictures of naked people or people having sex." This Office of Crime Victims report notes that by 2005 the number of children and teenagers using the Internet will increase to 77 million.

Similar results were obtained from the Youth Internet Safety Survey conducted by the Crimes against Children Research Center and reported by Finkelhor et al. (2001, p.1). The study was based on a national sample of 1,501 youths ages 10 through 17 who used the Internet regularly. It found that almost one in five (19 percent) received an unwanted sexual solicitation in the past year. Five percent received a distressing sexual solicitation (the solicitation made them feel very or extremely upset or afraid). Three percent received an aggressive solicitation involving offline contact or attempts or requests for offline contact.

The Child Protection and Sexual Predator Punishment Act, passed in 1998, imposes tougher penalties for sex crimes against children, particularly those facilitated by the use of the Internet. The act prohibits contacting a minor via the Internet to engage in illegal sexual activity and punishes those who knowingly send obscenity to children.

Cultural Values and Sexual Abuse

Cultural values play a role in determining what constitutes abuse. Some practices regarded as normal and acceptable within one culture may be considered sexual abuse by mainstream society or by those from other cultures. For example in Somalia and other parts of Africa, female circumcision or female genital mutilation (FGM) is a rite of passage performed on infants and young girls. In the United States, however, this practice is considered abuse and is illegal, a situation that causes significant conflict for Somali women who have immigrated to this country.

According to the U.S. Department of Health and Human Resources, an estimated 160,000 girls and women in the U.S. immigrant community have submitted to FGM. Some contend it is hypocritical of the United States to censure another culture for doing to its young girls what America routinely does to its boys.

Another example of how different cultures regard the issue of sexual abuse is seen in the practice of polygamy involving juvenile girls. Within certain areas of the United States, most notably in Utah, polygamy was an acceptable Mormon practice, accompanied by the cultural value that very young girls, some as young as 10, may be forced into arranged marriages. However, as Henetz (2003) reports, the church disavowed polygamy in 1890 and excommunicates those who practice polygamy. Nonetheless, according to Divoky (2002): "An estimated 300,000 families are headed by men with more than one spouse. This is true . . . even though more than a hundred years have passed since the practice was officially banned in exchange for statehood."

Polygamist Tom Green made headlines when he was charged with child rape for having sex with a 13-year-old girl he had married in 1986. Green had five wives and thirty children (Vosepka, 2002). In 2002 the high-profile case of teenager Elizabeth Smart, allegedly kidnapped by Brian David Mitchell, a self-styled prophet, brought the practice of polygamy back to national attention. Mitchell supposedly kidnapped Smart to make her his second wife.

The Issue of Credibility

Because physical indicators of sexual abuse are often not present, allegations of sexual abuse can be difficult to prove. Investigators must also weed out false accusations. Sometimes allegations of child sexual abuse are made in the context of divorce and custody cases. A study of 9,000 families embroiled in contested divorce proceedings found that 1 to 8 percent involved allegations of child sexual abuse. Unfortunately, the warlike atmosphere inherent in divorce often discredits valid claims. Though rare, false allegations of abuse do occur. Another study

Elizabeth Smart (c) and her father (l) applaud as President George W. Bush speaks in the Rose Garden of the White House, April 30, 2003, surrounded by the Smart family and families of other kidnapped children.

© Reuters NewMedia Inc. / CORBIS

revealed that out of 169 cases of alleged child sexual abuse arising in marital relations courts, only 14 percent were deliberate, false allegations." Karmen (pp.205–206) notes:

> When allegations surface during the height of a divorce and tug-of-war over a child, two camps quickly emerge. People on one side argue that since there are no outsiders who witness violations of the incest taboo within the home, these "family secrets" usually are not exposed unless the parents break up. People on the other side contend that baseless allegations are being taken too seriously, and the resulting investigations ruin the lives of innocent parents, usually fathers.
>
> In the mid-1980s, an organization was formed to provide support to adults who insisted they were falsely accused. They nicknamed their predicament the "SAID syndrome": sexual allegations in divorce. Their contention is that in most of these cases, a spiteful mother has pressured her daughter to echo a fictitious story about molestation that never occurred.

Coercing a child to lie about abuse that never occurred is a form of abuse all its own. Unfortunately, many youths become victims of this type of abuse when they are caught in the middle of custody battles. As parents fight to prove they are better equipped to raise the children, they unwittingly inflict a great deal of emotional and psychological damage on the very people they say they are trying to protect.

Ritualistic Abuse by Satanic Cults

During the late 1980s and early 1990s allegations of ritualistic abuse by Satanic cults caused much controversy. As Karmen (pp.210–211) explains:

> The maximalist position was that thousands of people disappeared each year because they were dispatched by secret cults. Believers in the existence of a satanic conspiracy circulated frightening accounts about bizarre "wedding" ceremonies in which covens of witches and devil worshipers chanted, wore costumes, took drugs, sacrificed animals, and even mutilated, tortured, and murdered newborn infants or kidnapped children. . . . The people who came forward and said that they survived ritual abuse were often young women who made these claims after undergoing psychotherapy.
>
> The minimalist position pointed out that the scare developed after bizarre charges about teachers practicing witchcraft at a California preschool generated one of the longest and costliest trials in American history (but no convictions). The minimalist view attributed the panic to sensationalism by the tabloid press and irresponsible talk shows that fed a climate of rumors and fears. . . . Although many people claimed to have witnessed, participated in and survived these devilish ordeals, the skeptical stance concluded that their credibility was as questionable as that of the hundreds of people who swore they had been abducted by aliens from outer space or who said they remembered events from their "past lives" as different people.

Children and Youths as Victims of Crime and Violence

One of the most obvious ways youths are victimized is by becoming a victim of crime. Chapter 3 discussed the victimization that occurs in our nation's schools. Finkelhor and Ormrod (2000) report on juvenile victims of property crimes. One out of every six juveniles ages 12 to 17 has been the victim of a property crime at a rate 40 percent higher than the rate for adults. Property crime victimization rates are particularly high for African-American juveniles and juveniles living in urban areas and the West. By far the most common location for these crimes is the school. The researchers (p.11) conclude: "This type of victimization imposes a substantial burden on the lives and lifestyles of the young. For that reason alone, it deserves increased public policy attention."

 Youths are victims of crime twice as often as those over age 25.

In addition, according to Wordes and Nunez (2002): "Teenagers are at the greatest risk for violent victimization, and this victimization is the 'single greatest factor in predicting criminal behavior' among teens." The pervasiveness of violence in the United States, toward children as well as adults might, in part, be explained by the country's historical reliance upon force and violence in its international relations.

Rennison (2002, pp.6–7) reports: "In general the younger the person, the higher the rate of violent victimization. In 2001 persons ages 12 to 15 and ages 16 to 19 experienced overall violence at similar rates, which were higher than rates of persons in older categories. Beginning with the 20-24 age category, the rate at which persons were victims of overall violent crime declined significantly as the age category increased."

Victimization and Routine Activity Theory

The routine activity theory holds that crime and victimization occur where and when potential offenders, suitable targets and a lack of capable guardians co-exist. Rapp-Paglicci and Wodarski (2000, p.519) conducted a study supporting this theory. They found that a majority of the youthful victims of violent assaults had engaged in risky, delinquent/criminal and or aggressive (RDA) behavior before the victimization, making themselves suitable targets.

Loeber et al. (2001, p.1), likewise, found that among youthful victims are a portion who are more prone to (1) engage in illicit activities that cause conflict (for example, belong to a gang, deal drugs, fence stolen goods), (2) associate with delinquent friends who have poor social and problem-solving skills, (3) victimize other delinquents and (4) have little recourse to legal means of conflict resolution.

Witnessing Violence

Agnew (2002) studied the relationship between experienced, vicarious and anticipated strain. **Vicarious strain** refers to real-life strains experienced by others around the individual; **anticipated strain** refers to the individual's expectation that current strains will continue into the future or that new strains will be experienced. He (p.603) concludes: "Delinquency is related not only to experienced victimization, but also to certain types of anticipated and vicarious physical victimization."

McGee and Baker (2002) studied the impact of violence on problem behavior among adolescents and found a strong association between youths exposed to violence through direct victimization, witnessing violence, and association with delinquent peers and adjustment outcomes, including internalizing (self-rejection, depression) and externalizing (offenses) problem behavior. They also found a link between victimization and avoidance as a coping strategy. They found a greater influence of victimization on offenses, self-rejection and avoidance among men and a stronger influence of victimization on depression among women in the sample (p.74). Kilpatrick et al. (2003, p.1) likewise note: "Most pervasive is victimization by witnessing violence, with approximately 8.8 million youths indicating that they had seen someone else being shot, stabbed, sexually assaulted, physically assaulted or threatened with a weapon." In a sample of youths ages 12 to 17 who reported being victimized, more than half of black, Hispanic and Native American adolescents had witnessed violence in their lifetime (p.4). In addition, Eitle and Turner (2002, p.214) report that recent exposure to violence in the *community* increases the risk for young adult criminal offending.

Domestic Violence

One of the most frequently experienced or observed types of violence is domestic violence. Graves (2002, p.137) states: "Domestic violence has been found to exist in 20 to 40 percent of families of chronically violent adolescents. . . . Child abuse is present in 30 to 70 percent of families in which there is spousal abuse, and the severity of the child abuse generally parallels the severity of the abuse to the spouse." Similar figures are reported in *In Harm's Way: Domestic Violence and Child Maltreatment* (2003): "According to published studies, there is a 30 percent to 60 percent overlap between violence against children and violence against women in the same families. Although the studies on which these ranges are based employ different methodologies (e.g., case record reviews, case studies and national surveys), use different sample sizes and examine different populations, they consistently report a significant level of co-occurrence." This overlap is illustrated in Figure 4.4.

Schechter and Edleson (2000, p.7) report: "Researchers have estimated that 3.3 to 10 million American children annually witness assaults by one parent against another." The results can be devastating as Streit (2001, p.50) notes: "Research shows that children who witness domestic violence experience higher levels of behavioral, social and emotional problems than those who live in a caring environment." A **caring environment** is one in which individuals and institutions protect young people and invest in their ongoing development.

The Cycle of Violence

Violence is learned behavior that often is self-perpetuating. When adults teach children by example that those who are bigger and stronger can use violence to

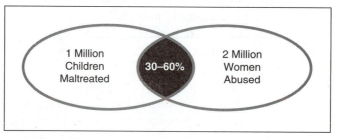

Figure 4.4
Overlap of Child Maltreatment and Domestic Violence

Source: *In Harm's Way: Domestic Violence and Child Maltreatment*. Washington, DC: National Clearinghouse on Child Abuse and Neglect Information, March 2003.
http://calib.com/nccanch/pubs/otherpubs/harmsway.htm

force their wishes on others who are smaller, the lesson is remembered. Children who witness domestic abuse learn that it's ok to hurt the people you care about most and it's ok to use violence to get what you want. In addition, family violence has been directly linked with delinquency, especially violent offenses. This cycle of violence is illustrated in Figure 4.5 and is discussed further in Chapter 6.

Wordes and Nunez also point to a continued and repeated cycle of victimization: "According to researchers, 80 percent of youths reporting victimization were either chronic or multiple victims of violent crimes." Karmen (p.14) describes a cycle of violence in which victims are transformed into victimizers over time:

> A group of picked-upon students may band together to ambush their tormentors; a battered wife may launch a vengeful attack upon her brutal husband; or a physically abused child may grow up to parent his sons in the same excessively punitive way he was raised. A study that tracked the fortunes of about 900 abused

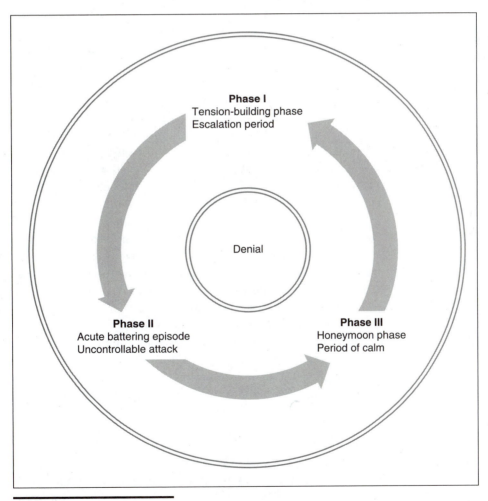

Figure 4.5
The Cycle of Violence

children over a follow-up period that ranged from 15 to 20 years concluded that being victimized substantially increased the odds of future delinquency and criminality.

 Violence often leads to more violence. Children who are abused are more likely to be delinquents and violent themselves.

Menard (2002) studied the short- and long-term consequences of adolescent victimization and concludes (p.14): "Consistent with theory and past research, the findings of the current study show that violent victimization during adolescence has a pervasive effect on problem outcomes in adulthood. It increases the odds of being a perpetrator or victim of violence in adulthood and domestic violence perpetration and victimization. It nearly doubles the odds of problem drug use in adulthood and of ever experiencing PTSD [post-traumatic stress disorder]. It also increases the odds of adult property offending."

Macmillan (2000, p.553) studied the long-term affects of victimization and found: "First, income losses from violent victimization are age-graded, with the greatest costs occurring for victimization experienced in adolescence. Second, criminal violence experienced in adolescence appears to influence later earnings by disrupting processes of educational and occupational attainment. Third, the total costs of criminal violence over the life course for adolescents are considerable in comparison to estimates provided in previous research."

The connection between children's histories of neglect or abuse and subsequent delinquency, crime and other problems has been largely ignored by our juvenile justice and social service systems. This is difficult to understand, given that those who experience violent, abusive childhoods are more likely to become child or spouse abusers than those who have not.

Family violence, abuse and neglect can be found in families of all social and economic backgrounds. Children are lied to and lied about, mutilated, shot, stabbed, burned, beaten, bitten, sodomized, raped and hanged. Figure 4.6 illustrates a model of intrafamily violence, the variables affecting it, individual characteristics of family members, precipitating factors, social variables and the consequences for the child, the family and society.

As Figure 4.6 shows, many familial variables and family member characteristics affect intrafamily violence. Furthermore, conditions in the society within which the family lives also affect familial violence. Such violence may have a multitude of consequences, not only for the child but also for the family and society at large. Among the possible consequences are children who are missing, sometimes for reasons unknown.

Missing and Exploited Children

Another category of victimized youths is children who are missing and exploited, often by choice because of intolerable conditions in the home, including abuse and violence. According to Girouard (2001, p.1): "Since 1982, the National Center for Missing and Exploited Children (NCMEC) has spearheaded the national effort to prevent child abductions and return missing and exploited children to their families."

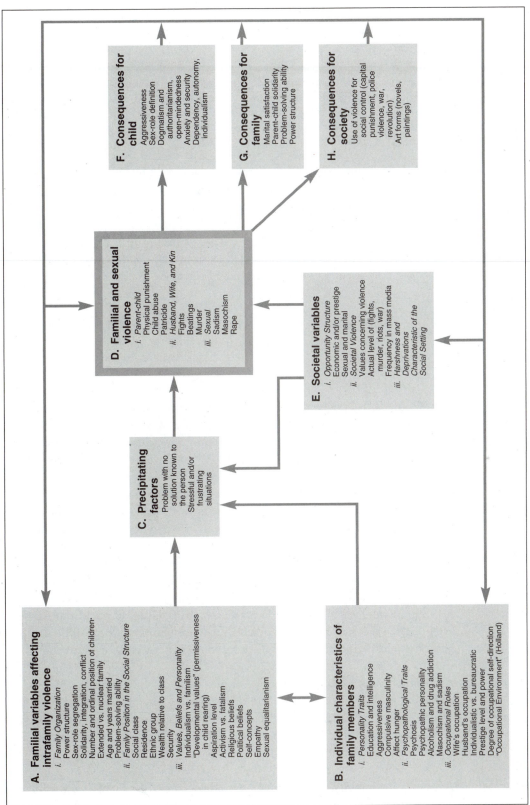

Source: Suzanne K. Steinmetz and Murray A. Straus. *Violence in the Family.* New York: Dodd, Mead, 1974, pp.18–19.

Figure 4.6
**Model of Intrafamily
Violence**

The Missing Children's Act was passed in 1982 and the Missing Children's Assistance Act in 1984. The Missing Children's Assistance Act of 1984 defines a *missing child* as:

> Any individual, less than 18 years of age, whose whereabouts are unknown to such individual's legal custodian—if the circumstances surrounding the disappearance indicate that (the child) may possibly have been removed by another person from the control of his/her legal custodian without the custodian's consent; or the circumstances of the case strongly indicate that (the child) is likely to be abused or sexually exploited.

This act requires the Office of Juvenile Justice and Delinquency Prevention to conduct periodic national incidence studies to determine the actual number of children reported missing and the number of missing children recovered for a given year. This requirement is being met through the National Incidence Studies of Missing, Abducted, Runaway, and Thrownaway Children in America (NISMART). NISMART has completed its second in-depth study of this population and has identified six episode types of missing children.

The six episode types of missing children included in the NISMART–2 study are missing benign explanation; missing involuntary, lost or injured; runaway/thrownaway; nonfamily abduction; stereotypical kidnapping; and family abduction.

NISMART–2 defines a missing child in two ways: those who are missing from their caretakers (caretaker missing) and those who are missing from their caretakers and reported to an agency for help locating them (reported missing). According to NISMART–2 an estimated 1,315,600 were caretaker missing children; 797,500 were reported missing children. Table 4.2 summarizes statistics for these two types of missing children and the episode type involved.

Sedlak et al. (2002, p.10) report: "Only a fraction of 1 percent of the children who were reported missing had not been recovered by the time they entered the NISMART–2 data. Thus, the study shows that, although the number of caretaker missing children is fairly large and a majority come to the attention of law enforcement or missing children's agencies, all but a very small percentage are recovered fairly quickly."

Simons and Willie (2000, p.1) note: "The fact that hundreds of thousands of children leave their homes voluntarily each year compounds the difficulty in accurately classifying a missing child as a runaway or a victim of abduction."

Missing Benign Explanation

A missing benign explanation episode occurs when a child's whereabouts are unknown to the child's caretaker and this causes the caretaker to (1) be alarmed, (2) try to locate the child, and (3) contact the police about the episode for any reason, as long as the child was not lost, injured, abducted, victimized or classified as runaway/thrownaway (Sedlak et al., p.4).

Missing Involuntary, Lost or Injured

A missing involuntary, lost or injured episode occurs when a child's whereabouts are unknown to the child's caretaker and this causes the caretaker to be alarmed

Table 4.2
Reasons Children Became Missing

Episode Type	Estimated Total*	95% Confidence Interval[†]	Percent*	Rate per 1,000 Children in U.S. Population (N = 70,172,700)
		Caretaker Missing Children (n = 1,315,600)		
Nonfamily abduction	33,000[§]	(2,000–64,000)	3[§]	0.47[§]
Family abduction	117,200	(79,000–155,400)	9	1.67
Runaway/thrownaway	628,900	(48,000–776,900)	48	8.96
Missing involuntary, lost, or injured	198,300	(124,800–271,800)	15	2.83
Missing benign explanation	374,700	(289,900–459,500)	28	5.34
		Reported Missing Children (n = 797,500)		
Nonfamily abduction	12,100[§]	(<100–31,000)	2[§]	0.17[§]
Family abduction	56,500	(22,600–90,400)	7	0.81
Runaway/thrownaway	357,600	(238,000–477,200)	45	5.10
Missing involuntary, lost, or injured	61,900	(19,700–104,100)	8	0.88
Missing benign explanation	340,500	(256,000–425,000)	43	4.85

Note: All estimates are rounded to the nearest 100.

*Estimates total more than 1,135,600, and percents total more than 100 because children who had multiple episodes are included in every row that applies to them.

[†]The 95 percent confidence interval indicates that if the study were repeated 100 times 95 of the replications would produce estimates within the ranges noted.

[‡]Nonfamily abduction includes stereotypical kidnapping.

[§]Estimate is based on an extremely small sample of cases; therefore, its precision and confidence interval are unreliable.

Source: Andrea J. Sedlak, David Finkelhor, Healther Hammer and Dana J. Schultz. *National Estimates of Missing Children: An Overview.* Washington, DC: OJJDP, National Incidence Studies of Missing, Abducted. Runaway and Thrownaway Children (NISMART), October 2002, p.6.

for at least one hour and try to locate the child under one of two conditions: (1) the child was trying to get home or make contact with the caretaker but was unable to do so because the child was lost, stranded or injured; or (2) the child was too young to know how to return home or make contact with the caretaker (Sedlak et al., p.4).

Runaway/Thrownaway

"A **runaway** incident occurs when a child leaves home without permission and stays away overnight, or a child 14 years old or younger (or older and mentally incompetent) who is away from home chooses not to return when supposed to and stays away overnight; or a child 15 years old or older who is away from home chooses not to return and stays away two nights" (Sedlak et al., p.4).

When adolescents cannot cope with a relationship in a family, they may perceive their only recourse to be running away. Historically, running away has been considered a behavioral manifestation of psychopathology. In fact, the American Psychiatric Association has classified the "runaway reaction" as a specific disorder.

Running away from home is seen by many youths as a solution to problems at home or school.

© David Woods/CORBIS

Many runaways are insecure, depressed, unhappy and impulsive with low self-esteem. Typical runaways report conflict with parents, alienation from them, rejection and hostile control, lack of warmth, affection and parental support. Running away may compound their problems. Many become streetwise and turn to drugs, crime, prostitution or other illegal activities.

Problems reported by youths seeking services from runaway and homeless youth centers included such family problems as emotional conflict at home, parents who were too strict and physical abuse and neglect. The National Council of Juvenile and Family Court Judges has stated: "We know that many [youths] who are on the streets are there as a result of sound rational choices they have made for their own safety and welfare, such as avoiding physical abuse, sexual abuse, or extreme neglect at home." Other problems reported included parental drug and/or alcohol abuse, mental health problems within the family and domestic violence between the parents.

The two most frequently mentioned personal problems were a poor self-image and depression. Other problems included issues at school such as truancy, poor grades and not getting along with teachers; drug and/or alcohol abuse; and being in trouble with the justice system.

A **thrownaway** incident occurs when a child is asked or told to leave home by a parent or other household adult, no adequate alternative care is arranged for the child by a household adult, and the child is out of the household overnight; or a child who is away from home is prevented from returning home by a parent or other household adult, no adequate alternative care is arranged for the child by a household adult, and the child is out of the household overnight (Sedlak et al., p.4).

According to Slavin (2001, p.9): "The risks runaways [and thrownaways] face are endless. Malnutrition, psychological disorders, HIV infection and other sexually transmitted diseases, unwanted pregnancies, drug and alcohol abuse, robbery, and sexual and physical assaults have all been found in high proportions among these young people. One study found the rates of major depression, conduct disorder, and post-traumatic stress were three times as high among runaway youth as their peers. HIV may be 2 to 10 times as prevalent among runaway and homeless youth than for other adolescents. . . . Life on the streets is a struggle for survival. They may start by panhandling for change, but eventually a runaway will most likely turn to illegal means to survive; many will become involved in prostitution, pornography, drugs, stealing and other crimes."

Nonfamily Abduction

A nonfamily abduction occurs when a nonfamily perpetrator takes a child by the use of physical force or threat of bodily harm or detains a child for at least one hour in an isolated place by the use of physical force or threat of bodily harm without lawful authority or parental permission; or when a child who is younger than 15 years old or is mentally incompetent, without lawful authority or parental permission, is taken or detained by or voluntarily accompanies a nonfamily perpetrator who conceals the child's whereabouts, demands ransom or expresses the intention to keep the child permanently (Sedlak et al., p.4).

Stereotypical Kidnapping

A stereotypical kidnapping occurs when a stranger or slight acquaintance perpetrates a nonfamily abduction in which the child is detained overnight, transported at least 50 miles, held for ransom, abducted with intent to keep the child permanently or killed (Sedlak et al., p.4). Garrett (2002, p.31) contends: "People can install security systems, own a dog, put deadbolts in their homes, but the reality is if someone really wants to take a child, there's little they can do to stop them."

Family Abduction

A family abduction occurs when, in violation of a custody order, a decree or other legitimate custodial rights, a member of the child's family, or someone acting on behalf of a family member, takes or fails to return a child, and the child is concealed or transported out of state with the intent to prevent contact or deprive the caretaker of custodial rights indefinitely or permanently. For a child 15 or older, unless mentally incompetent, there must be evidence that the perpetrator used physical force or threat of bodily harm to take or detain the child (Sedlak et al., p.4).

According to Grasso et al. (2001, p.1): "Abductors may be other family members or their agents (girlfriend, boyfriend, grandparent or even a private investigator), although in most cases the abductor is a child's parent." Sedlak et al. (p.10) note: "Contrary to the common assumption that abduction is a principal reason why children become missing, the NISMART–2 findings indicate that only a small minority of missing children were abducted, and most of these children were abducted by family members (9 percent of all caretaker missing children).

Johnston et al. (2001, pp.2–3) describe six profiles of parents at risk for abducting their children: "(1) when there has been a prior threat of or actual abduction; (2) when a parent suspects or believes abuse has occurred and friends and family members support these concerns; (3) when a parent is paranoid delusional; (4) when a parent is severely sociopathic; (5) when a parent who is a citizen of another country ends a mixed-culture marriage; and (6) when parents feel alienated from the legal system and have family/social support in another community."

In cases of international child abduction by parents even more difficulties are faced. As Chiancone et al. (2001, p.1) note: "A parent who is left behind when a child is abducted to another country faces daunting obstacles to finding and recovering the child."

Responsibility for Investigating Missing and Exploited Children

The primary responsibility for investigating missing and exploited children falls at the local and state levels as will be discussed in Chapter 7, but the federal government is also involved. Two government agencies in particular have responsibilities in the area but come at the problem from very different perspectives.

> The Department of Health and Human Services through its Administration for Children, Youth and Families (ACYF) and the Justice Department through its Office of Juvenile Justice and Delinquency Prevention (OJJDP) have concurrent jurisdiction for missing and exploited children.

Both agencies' authority comes from the 1974 Juvenile Justice and Delinquency Prevention (JJDP) Act, amended in 1978 by the Runaway and Homeless Youth (RHY) Act. The RHY Act took a "social welfare, emergency care" approach to the problem of runaways, playing down law enforcement solutions. This approach is the focus of the ACYF:

> ACYF's approaches to locating, detaining, and returning runaway children do not involve law enforcement or juvenile justice authorities. Instead, they focus on such activities as having shelter staff encourage runaways to contact home; using "runaway switchboards" to exchange messages between runaways and their families; and utilizing mental health programs to provide crisis counseling (and, in some cases, longer term counseling) to assist reunification efforts.

The OJJDP approach is very different, focusing on the challenges that runaways present to law enforcement and the juvenile justice system. It is hampered by the OJJDP's emphasis on deinstitutionalization:

> However well motivated the thinking behind this policy [deinstitutionalization], the fact remains that secure custodial care has often been the only practical, effective means for protecting runaways themselves, and for protecting communities from the problems of juvenile prostitution, drug abuse, theft, and other criminal acts committed by runaway youngsters seeking to support a day-to-day, hand-to-mouth existence.

The ACYF takes a social welfare, emergency care approach to missing children; the OJJDP focuses on the challenges that missing children present to law enforcement and the juvenile justice system.

Clearly, these two approaches are often at odds with each other. Therefore, coordination between the two agencies is vital if the runaway problem is to be effectively addressed.

Youths and Suicide

 The leading cause of youth suicide is untreated depression.

Grayson (2002a) cautions: "Childhood depression is different from the normal 'blues' and everyday emotions that occur as a child develops. An estimated 2.5 percent of children in the United States suffer from depression. Signs and symptoms of depression in children include irritability or anger; continuous feelings of sadness, hopelessness; social withdrawal; increased sensitivity to rejection; changes in appetite—either increased or decreased; changes in sleep—sleeplessness or excessive sleep; vocal outbursts or crying; difficulty concentrating; fatigue and low energy; physical complaints (such as stomachaches, headaches) that do not respond to treatment; feelings of worthlessness or guilt; impaired thinking or concentration; and thoughts of suicide."

Grayson (2002b) notes: "Estimates on how many adolescents experience depression vary from 3 percent to 10 percent. Often depressed teens will display a striking change in their thinking and behavior, lose their motivation or become withdrawn. Major signs of depression in adolescents include sadness, anxiety, or a feeling of hopelessness; loss of interest in food or compulsive overeating that results in rapid weight loss or gain; staying awake at night and sleeping during the day; withdrawal from friends; rebellious behavior, sudden drop in grades or cutting school; complaints of pains including headaches, stomachaches, low back pain or fatigue; use of alcohol or drugs and promiscuous sexual activity; and a preoccupation with death and dying."

According to Grayson (2002b): "Suicide is a serious problem within the teenage population. Adolescent suicide is the second leading cause of death among youth and young adults in the United States. It is estimated that 500,000 teens attempt suicide every year with 5,000 succeeding. These are epidemic proportions." According to the *Sourcebook of Criminal Justice Statistics 2001* (p.243) the number of juveniles attempting to commit suicide has risen from 7.3 percent in 1991 to 8.8 percent in 2001. However, the number of juveniles who have seriously considered suicide has declined from 29.0 percent in 1991 to 19.0 percent in 2001.

 Warning signs of suicide include: threatening to kill one's self; preparing for death, giving away favorite possessions, writing goodbye letters or making a will; expressing a hopelessness for the future and giving up on one's self; and talking as if no one else cares.

Sometimes depression may not be readily apparent. The person may try to cover it up with overactivity, preoccupation with trivia or acting-out behavior, such as delinquency, the use of drugs or sexual promiscuity.

Summary

Approximately 903,000 children were maltreated in 2003. Maltreated youths are at an increased risk for performing poorly in school; displaying symptoms of mental illness; for girls, becoming pregnant; using drugs; and engaging in serious and violent delinquency. Youths are victimized in many ways. Two of the most common types of victimization are neglect and abuse. The homes of neglected children are often disorganized and broken, and neglecting parents ignore their children or set bad examples for them.

Typically child abuse/neglect laws have three components: (1) criminal definitions and penalties, (2) a mandate to report suspected cases and (3) civil processes for removing a child from the abusive or neglectful environment. The two leading causes of child abuse are thought to be violence between husbands and wives and poverty. Child abuse has been identified as the biggest single cause of death of young children. The three levels of abuse are collective, institutional and individual. Child abuse has been directly linked with delinquency.

Youths are also victimized by crime and violence twice as often as those over age 25. Violence often leads to more violence. Children who are abused are more likely to be delinquent and violent themselves. They are also more likely to run away, becoming part of the "missing and exploited children" problem. The six episode types of missing children included in the NISMART–2 study are missing benign explanation; missing involuntary, lost or injured; runaway/thrownaway; nonfamily abduction; stereotypical kidnapping; and family abduction.

The Department of Health and Human Services through ACYF and the Justice Department through OJJDP have concurrent jurisdiction for missing and exploited children. The ACYF takes a social welfare, emergency care approach to missing children; the OJJDP focuses on the challenges that missing children present to law enforcement and the juvenile justice system.

Children and youths who do not receive appropriate assistance may become suicidal. The leading cause of youth suicide is untreated depression. Warning signs of suicide include threatening to kill one's self; preparing for death, giving away favorite possessions, writing goodbye letters or making a will; expressing hopelessness for the future and giving up on one's self; and talking as if no one else cares.

Discussion Questions

1. What causes parents or caretakers of children to abuse them?
2. Do your state laws against child abuse and neglect contain two or more of the following components: nonaccidental physical injury, physical neglect, emotional abuse or neglect, sexual abuse, abandonment?
3. Of all abuses, which has the most lasting effect? Why?
4. How can a society cope with child abuse and strive to control it?
5. What protection does a child have against abuse? Should the courts rescind parental rights in abuse cases?
6. Do courts act in the best interests of children when they allow abused children to remain with the family?
7. What are the strongest predictors of future delinquent or violent behavior?
8. Are the definitions of *child abuse* and *child neglect* the key elements in determining the volume of child abuse cases in various jurisdictions? How is the volume of cases determined?
9. In your area, how are children protected from abuse? Can the system be improved? How?
10. Are the six episode types of missing children identified by NISMART–2 helpful?

InfoTrac College Edition Assignments

- Use InfoTrac College Edition to answer the Discussion Questions as appropriate.
- Select one of the following to read and outline and share with the class:
  - "Childhood Discipline: Challenges for Clinicians and Parents" by J. Barton Banks.
  - "Recidivism at a Shelter for Adolescents: First-Time versus Repeat Runaways" by Amy J. L., Baker et al.
  - "Quit Neglecting Me or I'm Going to Sue You: An Unconventional Look at Child Neglect" by Andrew J. Walker.
  - "Understanding Adolescent Suicide: A Psychosocial Interpretation of Development and Contextual Factors" by Pedro R. Portes et al.

- "Suicide in Teenagers: Assessment, Management and Prevention" by Alan J. Zametkin et al.
- "Adolescent Suicide Attempts: Risks and Protectors" by Iris Wagman Borowsky et al.
- "Amber Alert Debuts with Successful Rescue of Kidnapped Girls" by John Woolfolk.
- "Protecting Children on the Electronic Frontier" by Matt Parsons.
- "Runaway or Abduction? Assessment Tools for the First Responder" by Andre B. Simmons and Jeannine Willie.

Internet Assignments

Select one of the following assignments to complete.

- Go to www.ojjdp.ncjrs.org and find one of the NCJ publications listed in the references for this chapter.
- Research one of the following key words or phrases: *child prostitution, parental abduction, child labor.*

- Go to the site of one of the following references listed for this chapter: Foster and Kramer; Hentz; Human Rights Watch; Internet Crimes against Children; Kruse and Mahony; or National Child Abuse and Neglect Data Systems. Outline the material and be prepared to share it with the class.

References

Agnew, Robert. "Experienced, Vicarious, and Anticipated Strain: An Exploratory Study on Physical Victimization and Delinquency." *Justice Quarterly,* December 2002, pp.603–632.

American Medical Association. "AMA Diagnostic and Treatment Guidelines Concerning Child Abuse and Neglect." *Journal of the American Medical Association,* Vol. 254, No. 6, 1985, pp. 796–800.

Atkinson-Tovar, Lynn. "Smart Parents, Safe Kids." *Law and Order,* April 2001, pp.35–37.

Bennett, Wayne M. and Hess, Karen M. *Criminal Investigation,* 7th ed. Belmont, CA: Wadsworth Publishing Company, 2004.

"Boston Church Offers to Settle: Archdiocese Would Give Plaintiffs $55 Million." Associated Press as reported in the (Minneapolis/St. Paul) *Star Tribune,* August 9, 2003, pp.A1, A12.

Chiancone, Janet; Girdner, Linda; and Hoff, Patricia. *Issues in Resolving Cases of International Child Abduction by Parents.* Washington, DC: OJJDP Juvenile Justice Bulletin, December 2001. (NCJ 190105)

Child Maltreatment 2001: Summary of Key Findings. Washington, DC: National Clearinghouse on Child Abuse and Neglect Information, April 2003. Online: www.calib.com/nccanch/prevmnth

"Congress Passes Measures on Child Abuse Enforcement." *Criminal Justice Newsletter,* February 18, 2000, p.4.

Delany-Shabazz, Robin V. and Vieth, Victor. *The National Center for Prosecution of Child Abuse.* Washington, DC: OJJDP Fact Sheet #33, April 2001. (FS 200133)

Divoky, Diane. "Utah Women to Highlight Hazards of Polygamy." *Wenews,* January 8, 2002. http://www.polygamyinfo.com/plygmedia%201wenews.htm

Eitle, David and Turner, R. Jay. "Exposure to Community Violence and Young Adult Crime: The Effects of Witnessing Violence, Traumatic Victimization, and Other Stressful Life Events." *Journal of Research in Crime and Delinquency,* May 2002, pp.214–237.

English, Diana J.; Widom, Cathy Spatz; and Brandford, Carol. *Childhood Victimization and Delinquency, Adult Criminality, and Violent Criminal Behavior: A Replication and Extension.* Washington, DC: National Institute of Justice, February 1, 2002. (NCJ 192291)

Ennis, Charles. "Twelve Clues that Could Save a Child." *Law and Order,* June 2000, pp.92–95.

Finkelhor, David; Mitchell, Kimberly; and Wolak, Janis. *Highlights of the Youth Internet Safety Survey."* Washington, DC: OJJDP Fact Sheet #04, March 2001. (FS 200104)

Finkelhor, David and Ormrod, Richard. *Juvenile Victims of Property Crimes.* Washington, DC: OJJDP Juvenile Justice Bulletin, December 2000. (NCJ 1844740)

Finkelhor, David and Ormrod, Richard. *Crimes against Children by Babysitters.* Washington, DC: OJJDP Juvenile Justice Bulletin, September 2001a. (NCJ 189102)

Finkelhor, David and Ormrod, Richard. *Homicides of Children and Youth.* Washington, DC: OJJDP Juvenile Justice Bulletin, October 2001b. (NCJ 187239)

Finkelhor, David and Ormrod, Richard. *Offenders Incarcerated for Crimes against Juveniles.* Washington, DC: OJJDP Juvenile Justice Bulletin, December 2001c. (NCJ 191028)

Foster, David and Kramer, Farrell. *Secret Child Labor in America.* http://hometown.aol.com/inunrnei/labor.html

Garrett, Ronnie. "Protecting Our Children." *Law Enforcement Technology,* October 2002, pp.28–33.

Girouard, Cathy. *The National Center for Missing and Exploited Children.* Washington, DC: OJJDP Fact Sheet #28, July 2001. (FS 200128)

Glasscock, Bruce D. "The Child Protection Summit: Exploring Innovative Partnerships." *The Police Chief,* August 2001, p.6.

Grasso, Kathi L.; Sedlak, Andrea J.; Chiancone, Janet L.; Gragg, Frances; Schultz, Dana; and Ryan, Joseph F. *The Criminal Justice System's Response to Parental Abduction.* Washington, DC: OJJDP Juvenile Justice Bulletin, December 2001. (NCJ 186160)

Graves, Alexander J. "Child Abuse and Domestic Violence." *Law and Order,* July 2002, pp.137–142.

Grayson, Charlotte E., editor. *Depression in Children.* The Cleveland Clinic Department of Psychiatry and Psychology, 2002a. http://aolsvc.health.webmd.aol.com

Grayson Charlotte E., editor. *Teens and Depression.* The Cleveland Clinic Department of Psychiatry and Psychology, 2002b. http://aolsvc.health.webmd.aol.com

Henetz, Patty. "Smart Case Highlights Utah Polygamy." Associated Press, March 16, 2003. http://www.polygamyinfo.complygmedia%2003%2033ap.htm

Human Rights Watch World Report 2001: Children's Rights— Child Labor. http://www.hrw.org/wr2k1/children/child5.html

In Harm's Way: Domestic Violence and Child Maltreatment. Washington, DC: National Clearinghouse on Child Abuse and Neglect Information, March 2003.

Internet Crimes against Children. Washington, DC: OVC Bulletin, May 2001. (NCJ 184931) www.ncjrs.org

Ireland, Timothy O.; Smith, Carolyn A.; and Thornberry, Terence P. "Developmental Issues in the Impact of Child Maltreatment on Later Delinquency and Drug Use." *Criminology,* Vol. 40, No. 2, 2002, pp.359–380.

Johnston, Janet R.; Sagatun-Edwards, Inger; Blomquist, Martha-Elin; and Girdner, Linda K. *Early Identification of Risk Factors for Parental Abduction.* Washington, DC: OJJDP Juvenile Justice Bulletin, March 2001. (NCJ 185026)

Jones, Lisa and Finkelhor, David. *The Decline in Child Sexual Abuse Cases.* Washington, DC: OJJDP Juvenile Justice Bulletin, January 2001. (NCJ 184741)

"Judge OKs $10 Million Settlement in Boston Archdiocese Abuse Lawsuit." Associated Press, as reported in the (Minneapolis/St. Paul) *Star Tribune,* September 20, 2002, p.A6.

Karmen, Andrew. *Crime Victims: An Introduction to Victimology,* 4th ed. Belmont, CA: Wadsworth Publishing Company, 2001.

Kilpatrick, Dean G.; Saunders, Benjamin E.; and Smith, Daniel W. *Youth Victimization: Prevalence and Implications.* Washington, DC: National Institute of Justice, April 2003. (NCJ 194972)

Kruse, Douglas and Mahony, Douglas. *Illegal Child Labor in the United States: Prevalence and Characteristics.* April 2003. http://netec.mcc.ac.uk/WoPEc/data/Papers/nbrnberwo6479.html

Loeber, Rolf; Kalb, Larry; and Huizinga, David. *Juvenile Delinquency and Serious Injury Victimization.* Washington, DC: OJJDP Juvenile Justice Bulletin, August 2001. (NCJ 188676)

Macmillan, Ross. "Adolescent Victimization and Income Deficits in Adulthood: Rethinking the Costs of Criminal Violence from a Life-Course Perspective." *Criminology,* May 2000, pp.553–588.

McGee, Zina T. and Baker, Spencer R. "Impact of Violence on Problem Behavior among Adolescents." *Journal of Contemporary Criminal Justice,* February 2002, pp.74–93.

Medaris, Michael and Girouard, Cathy. *Protecting Children in Cyberspace: The ICAC Task Force Program.* Washington, DC: OJJDP Juvenile Justice Bulletin, January 2002. (NCJ 191213)

Menard, Scott. *Short- and Long-Term Consequences of Adolescent Victimization.* Washington, DC: OJJDP Youth Violence Research Bulletin, February 2002. (NCJ 191210)

National Child Abuse and Neglect Data System (NCANDS). *Summary of Key Findings from Calendar Year 2000,* April 2002. http://www.calib.com/nccanch/pubs/factsheets/canstats.cfm

Office of Juvenile Justice and Delinquency Prevention. *Children as Victims.* Washington, DC: OJJDP Juvenile Justice Bulletin, 2000.

Osofsky, Joy D. *Addressing Youth Victimization.* Washington, DC: Coordinating Council on Juvenile Justice and Delinquency Prevention Action Plan Update, October 2001.

Osteogenesis Imperfecta Foundation. *OI Issues: Child Abuse.* http://www.oif.org/tier2/childabuse.htm

Parsons, Matt. "Protecting Children on the Electronic Frontier: A Law Enforcement Challenge." *FBI Law Enforcement Bulletin,* October 2000, pp.22–26.

Rapp-Paglicci, Lisa A. and Wodarski, John S. "Study Supports Routine Activities Theory of Crime." *Deviant Behavior: An Interdisciplinary Journal,* Vol. 21, No. 5, 2000, p.519.

Rennison, Callie. *Criminal Victimization 2001: Changes 2000-01 with Trends 1993-2001.* Washington, DC: Bureau of Justice Statistics National Crime Victimization Survey, September 2002. (NCJ 194610)

"Report: Boston Clergy Abused 1,000." *Washington Post* as reported in the (Minneapolis/St. Paul) *Star Tribune,* July 24, 2003, p.A4.

Schechter, Susan and Edleson, Jeffrey L. *Domestic Violence & Children: Creating a Public Response.* Open Society Institute, 2000.

Sedlak, Andrea J.; Finkelhor, David; Hammer, Heather; and Schultz, Dana J. *National Estimates of Missing Children: An Overview.* Washington, DC: Office of Juvenile Justice and Delinquency Prevention, October 2002.

Siegel, Jane A. and Williams, Linda M. "The Relationship between Child Sexual Abuse and Female Delinquency and Crime: A Prospective Study." *Journal of Research in Crime and Delinquency,* February 2003, pp.71–94.

Simmons, Andre B. and Willie, Jeannine. "Runaway or Abduction? Assessment Tools for the First Responder." *FBI Law Enforcement Bulletin,* November 2000, pp.1–7.

Slavin, Peter. "Life on the Run, Life on the Streets." *Children's Voice,* July 2001, pp.8–14.

Sourcebook of Criminal Justice Statistics 2001. Washington, DC: Bureau of Justice Statistics, 2001. (NCJ 165361) http://www.albany.edu/sourcebook

Streit, Corinne. "Preventing Child Abuse in Your Community." *Law Enforcement Technology,* October 2001, pp.50–55.

Vosepka, Rich. "Judge: Tom Green Can Be Charged with Child Rape." Associated Press, January 10, 2002. http://www.polygamyinfo.com/plygmedia%2002%204ap.htm

Woods, Jacqueline. "Hostile Hallways." *Educational Leadership,* December 2001/January 2002, pp.20–23.

Wordes, Madeline and Nunez, Michell. *Our Vulnerable Teenagers: Their Victimization, Its Consequences, and Directions for Prevention and Intervention.* Washington, DC: National Council on Crime and Delinquency and the National Center for Victims of Crime, May 2002. http://www.ncvc.org/teens

Cases Cited

Ingram v. Wright, 430 U.S. 651 (1977).

People v. Green, 155 Mich. 524, 532, 119 N.W. 1087 (1909).

Prince v. Massachusetts, 321 U.S. 158 (1944).

Santosky v. Kramer, 455 U.S. 745 (1982).

Worthen v. State, 42 Md.App. 20, 399 A.2d 272 (1979)

Status Offenders and Nonviolent Delinquents

The Cold War was over before they were 10. They think the stock market goes nowhere but up. They know all about sex, but also about AIDS. Their schools have computers in the classroom, but metal detectors by the front door. They wear studs in their tongues and pagers on their belts. They are the class of 2000, more than 3 million young Americans now starting their senior year in high school.

—David Foster

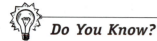

Do You Know?

- How researchers measure the nature and extent of youthful offenses?
- How prevalent delinquency is according to self-reports?
- What acts are classified as status offenses in most states?
- Whether arrests for status offenses have increased?
- Which delinquency offenses result in the highest number of juvenile arrests?
- Whether juvenile arrests for property crimes have increased?
- The major theories of the causes of juvenile delinquency and the main thesis of each?
- What a major characteristic of juvenile delinquency is?
- What three developmental pathways have been identified and the behaviors associated with each?

Can You Define?

acting out	broken-window theory	Index crimes
anomie	dark figure of crime	rave
at-risk youths	delinquent	streaming
binge drinking	developmental pathways	Uniform Crime Report

INTRODUCTION

Some actions discussed in Chapter 4, such as running away from home, not only place youngsters at risk of being victimized, they also violate the law and, therefore, put the youngsters at risk of being arrested. In addition, according to Wooden and Blazak (2001, p.217), today's "Generation Why?" is experiencing **anomie**—a state of normlessness produced by rapid change described by Durkheim in his 1897 suicide study: "The crucible of this anomie is the family. Parents, too busy or too self-involved to bond with their children, are letting their kids drift. Five million kids under the age of 13 are 'latchkey children,' left unattended after school each day. Half of teenagers in the United States have divorced parents, and 64 percent live in homes in which both parents work outside the home. A Temple University study conducted by Lawrence Steinberg found high rates of parent noninvolvement with their teens. Of the 20,000 teens studied, about 30 percent of their parents were unable to describe how the youth spent their time or who their friends were."

This chapter looks at the sources of information about the ways in which youths break the law as well as the range of offenses committed by juveniles. This range goes from minor status offenses, such as smoking cigarettes, to major violent crimes, such as rape and murder, discussed in the next chapter. Next status offenses are described, including running away, truancy, curfew violations and early substance use. This is followed by a discussion of juvenile delinquents and property crimes, including vandalism, burglary, arson, larceny/theft and motor vehicle theft. The arrest figures are from the Uniform Crime Reports throughout those discussions. The chapter then discusses other problems including disorderly youths in public places and computer delinquency.

The chapter next presents a brief review of theories about the causes of delinquency, followed by a discussion of developmental pathways. The chapter concludes with a review of risk factors associated with delinquency.

Measuring the Number of Juvenile Offenses Committed

Just how serious is the problem of youths breaking the law in the United States?

Official Data

 Researchers use three methods to measure the nature and extent of unlawful acts by juveniles: official data, self-report data and victim surveys.

Official data is information and statistics collected by the police, courts and corrections agencies on the local, regional and national levels. One widely used official source of delinquency statistics is the FBI's Uniform Crime Report, an annual collection of data from more than 15,000 police agencies.

The **Uniform Crime Report** (UCR) divides crimes into Part I and Part II. Part I, also called **Index crimes,** includes the eight major crimes: homicide and non-negligent manslaughter, forcible rape, robbery, aggravated assault, burglary, larceny, arson and motor vehicle theft.

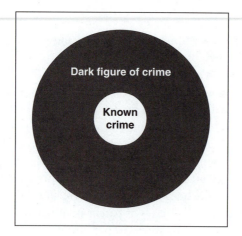

Figure 5.1
The Dark (Unknown) Figure of Crime vs. Known Crime

The UCR's statistics on number of crimes reported and number of arrests illustrate the extent of the delinquency problem. The statistics must be interpreted cautiously, however. The data represent only youths who have been arrested. Many are never caught. It has been estimated that 80 to 90 percent of children in the United States younger than 18 commit some offense for which they could be arrested, but only about 3 percent are. In addition, multiple arrests of the same youth for different crimes are counted separately. The total number of arrests does not equal the number of youths who have been arrested because chronic offenders have multiple arrests.

Other sources of official statistics are the Bureau of Justice Statistics (BJS), the Office of Juvenile Justice and Delinquency Prevention (OJJDP) and the National Institute of Justice (NIJ).

Official statistics have several problems, such as how the data are collected, variations in interpretation and police bias in arrest decisions. In addition, it is well known that of all crime committed by youths and adults, only a fraction comes to the attention of law enforcement agencies. The unknown fraction of crime is called the **dark figure of crime,** as shown in Figure 5.1. Official statistics also do not provide information about the personality, attitudes and behavior of delinquents. This comes from self-reports.

Self-Reports

Self-report studies let youths personally reveal information about their violations of the law. Self-report formats include one-to-one interviews, surveys and anonymous questionnaires. If truancy, alcohol consumption, smoking marijuana or cigarettes and petty theft are included in self-report scales, delinquency appears almost universal.

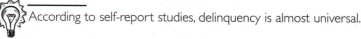

According to self-report studies, delinquency is almost universal.

The University of Michigan's Institute for Social Research (ISR) has conducted surveys of thousands of high school seniors regarding delinquent activities, the self-reported results of which appear in Figure 5.2.

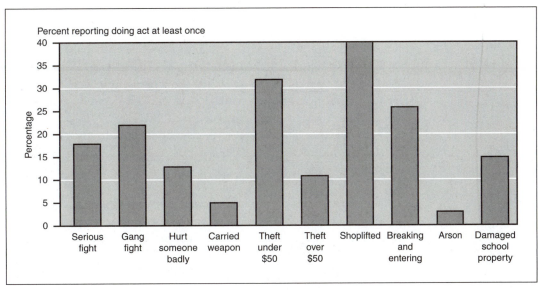

Percent reporting doing act at least once

Figure 5.2
Self-Reported Delinquent Acts

Source: Institute for Social Research. *Monitoring the Future,* 1994. Ann Arbor, MI: ISR, 1995.

Victimization Data

A third source of information about the extent of the delinquency problem is victimization data. The U.S. Department of Justice's Bureau of Justice Statistics, working with the U.S. Census Bureau, conducts annual house-to-house surveys of crime victims. The National Crime Victimization Survey (NCVS) involves twice-yearly interviews with about 50,000 people age 12 and older to gather information about crimes, including those not reported to police.

Status Offenders

Status offenses are based solely on the offender's age and are unique to juveniles. The age limit for status offenses ranges from 16 to 19, but in most states it is 17. Anyone above the legal age who engages in the same behaviors would not be committing an offense.

 Status offenses include actions such running away, habitual truancy, violating curfew and early substance use, including alcohol.

Running Away

The runaway problem was discussed in Chapter 4. However running away is a status offense in most communities, so the juvenile justice system has jurisdiction in the matter and can act "in the best interest of the child." In 2000 an estimated 142,000 youths were arrested for running away, an 18 percent decrease since 1991. Fifty-nine percent of the incidents involved females and 39 percent involved juveniles under age 15. In 2001 91,168 youths were arrested for running away, a significantly lower number. A problem closely related to running away is truancy.

Truancy

Truancy has been labeled as one of the top 10 problems in our schools, with absentee rates as high as 30 percent in some cities. Truancy is the most frequent offense for those under age 15, probably because after that age those who would be truant have simply dropped out of school. The adverse effects of skipping school include falling behind in classes and a resultant loss of self-esteem. Chronic truancy can be detrimental to students' chances of promotion and graduation and to their employment potential.

Among identified causes of truancy are boredom, irrelevant courses, suspensions and bad relationships with teachers. Peers are a strong influence. In one study more than 80 percent of truants said their friends skipped school.

Curfew Violations

One of the most common status offenses is curfew violation. As Ward, Jr. (2000, p.17) explains: "For over a century, American communities have imposed juvenile curfews to help maintain order and reduce crimes committed by youths." McDowall et al. (2000, p.76) note: "Between 1990 and 1995, 60 percent of the 200 largest American cities enacted a new curfew statute or revised an existing one."

The effectiveness of curfew laws is controversial. A press release headline by the National League of Cities (2001, p.1) reports: "Cities Say Curfews Help Reduce Gang Activity and Violent Crime." According to this news release: "The overwhelming majority of cities with curfews say the curfews are effective in improving safety in several areas: combating juvenile crime (effectiveness reported by 97 percent of respondents), fighting truancy (96 percent of respondents), making streets safer (95 percent of respondents) and reducing gang violence (98 percent of respondents).

However, McDowall et al. (pp.88–89) contend: "Our analysis provides, at best, extremely weak support for the hypothesis that curfews reduce juvenile crime rates. Of the offense and victimization measures, only burglary, larceny and simple assault arrests significantly decreased after cities adopted curfew statutes. . . . Any influence of the curfews appeared only for revised statutes, however, and new laws were ineffective in reducing offending or victimization."

In addition, some parents and organizations such as the American Civil Liberties Union have taken curfew ordinances to court, claiming that they violate students' and parents' constitutional rights. It is claimed that curfews are age discrimination in its purest form and that curfews undermine parental authority, are ineffective and punish law-abiding teenagers. In October of 1998 a U.S. Fourth Circuit Court of Appeals held in *Schleifer v. Charlottesville* that Charlottesville, Virginia's curfew was not a violation of the child's or the parents' rights. This case was appealed all the way to the Supreme Court, which in 1999 denied the request to review the case.

In 2000 154,700 juveniles were arrested for curfew and loitering violations, an increase of 81 percent from 1991. Twenty-eight percent of curfew arrests involved juveniles under age 15, and 31 percent involved females. In 2001 100,701 youths were arrested for curfew and loitering violations, also significantly lower than the previous year.

Table 5.1
Students Reporting Use of Alcohol and Drugs by Grade Level of Respondent and Frequency of Use, 2000–2001

	Grades 6 to 8 (N=37,653)		Grades 9 to 12 (N=38,151)		12th grade (N=8,138)	
	Annual use[a]	Monthly use[b]	Annual use[a]	Monthly use[b]	Annual use[a]	Monthly use[b]
Any alcohol	36.5%	11.0%	67.5%	37.0%	74.6%	46.4%
Beer	24.5	7.9	54.5	30.9	62.4	40.1
Wine coolers	27.4	7.7	50.6	22.3	54.4	25.3
Liquor	17.3	6.0	52.8	28.7	62.5	37.0
Any illicit drugs	13.7	7.0	35.3	22.5	41.4	26.6
Marijuana	9.3	5.3	32.3	20.5	39.0	24.2
Cocaine[c]	2.1	1.2	5.5	3.0	7.9	4.2
Inhalants	5.4	2.1	5.6	2.7	5.6	3.1
Hallucinogens[d]	2.2	1.3	7.9	3.9	11.3	5.3
Heroin	1.6	1.0	3.2	2.1	4.4	2.8
Steroids	2.6	1.3	3.5	2.2	4.0	2.7

[a]Used one or more times in the past year.

[b]Used once a month or more in the past year.

[c]Includes crack.

[d]Includes LSD and PCP.

Source: PRIDE Surveys. "2000–01 National Summary, Grades 6 through 12." Bowling Green, KY: PRIDE Surveys, 2001. (Mimeographed.) p.9,10. Table adapted by SOURCEBOOK staff.

Early Substance Use

The most frequent offense for those 16 and older is liquor violations. Table 5.1 summarizes students reporting use of alcohol and drugs.

Beer held a slight edge over liquor for monthly use, and marijuana was clearly the most popular illicit drug. According to Geier (2003, p.100): "It is estimated that in the United States there are over 10 million people between the ages of 12 and 20 who drink on a regular basis. . . . The total costs in the nation are near $53 billion." Glasscock (2001, p.7) reports: "In 2000 the use of ecstasy by 12th graders rose 46 percent."

The National Center for Juvenile Justice (Griffin and Torbet, 2002, p.109) cautions: "Drug users between the ages of 12 and 17 are more than 5 times as likely to shoplift, steal or vandalize property as non-users in that age range, 9 times as likely to steal cars or commit armed robbery, and 19 times as likely to break and enter or burglarize." White et al. (2002, p.131) also studied the proximal effects of alcohol and drug use on adolescent illegal activity. Four years of longitudinal data from the Pittsburgh Youth Study revealed that participants reported commiting offenses against persons more often than general theft under the influence of alcohol or drugs.

Ericson (2001, p.1) cites the findings of a report: *Substance Abuse: The Nation's Number One Health Problem*: "By the eighth grade, 52 percent of adolescents have consumed alcohol, 41 percent have smoked cigarettes, and 20 percent have used marijuana. By the 12th grade, about 80 percent have used alcohol, 63 percent have smoked cigarettes, and 49 percent have used marijuana. . . . Young adults (ages 18–25) are most likely to engage in heavy use of alcohol, drugs and tobacco than all other age groups."

Cleo Photography/Photo Edit

The American Bar Association supports decriminalizing status offenses such as smoking cigarettes.

Wechsler et al. (2002, p.203) report on the 2001 Harvard School of Public Health College Alcohol Study, which surveyed students at 119 four-year colleges in 38 states that had participated in the study in 1993, 1997 and 1999. More than 10,000 students participated. Responses from the four survey years were compared regarding heavy episodic alcohol use or **binge drinking.** Binge drinkers were defined as men who had five or more (or women who had four or more) drinks in a row at least once in the two weeks before they completed the survey questionnaire. Frequent binge drinkers had consumed these amounts at least three times in the previous two weeks.

In 2001 approximately 2 in 5 (44.4 percent) college students reported binge drinking, a rate almost identical to rates in the previous three surveys (p.203). The researchers (p.210) found that problems related to alcohol use among students who drank alcohol during the past 30 days remained steady or increased slightly over the eight years of the study, as shown in Table 5.2.

More than one-fourth of the respondents missed a class, did something they regretted, forgot where they were or what they did and drove after drinking in

Table 5.2
**Alcohol-Related Problems
among Students Who
Drank Alcohol,
1993,1997,
1999 and 2001**

| Alcohol-related problem | Prevalence in % | | | | Change over time | | Test for linear time trend p |
| | 1993[a] | 1997[b] | 1999[c] | 2001[d] | 2001 vs 1993 | | |
					OR	95% CI	
Miss a class	26.9	31.1	29.9	29.5	1.14	1.06, 1.23***	<.0001
Get behind in school work	20.5	24.1	24.1	21.6	1.07	0.99, 1.16	.0004
Do something you regret	32.1	37.0	36.1	35.0	1.13	1.06, 1.21***	<.0001
Forget where you were or what you did	24.7	27.4	27.1	26.8	1.12	1.03, 1.21**	.0005
Argue with friends	19.6	24.0	22.5	22.9	1.22	1.13, 1.31***	<.0001
Engage in unplanned sexual activities	19.2	23.3	21.6	21.3	1.14	1.06, 1.24***	.0002
Not use protection when you had sex	9.8	11.2	10.3	10.4	1.07	0.97, 1.19	.1840
Damage property	9.3	11.7	10.8	10.7	1.16	1.04, 1.30**	.0031
Get into trouble with the campus or local police	4.6	6.4	5.8	6.5	1.43	1.25, 1.65***	<.0001
Get hurt or injured	9.3	12.0	12.4	12.8	1.42	1.29, 1.57***	<.0001
Require medical treatment for an overdose	0.5	0.6	0.6	0.8	1.76	1.07, 2.91*	.0334
Drove after drinking	26.6	29.5	28.8	29.0	1.12	1.04, 1.21**	.0010
Have ≥ 5 different alcohol-related problems	16.6	20.8	19.9	20.3	1.28	1.27, 1.39***	<.0001

Note: Analysis limited to only those who drank alcohol in the past year. % is the prevalence of those who had the problem one or more times since the beginning of the school year. OR = odds ratio; CI = confidence interval.

[a]n = 12,708. [b]n = 11,506. [c]n = 10,825. [d]n = 8,783.

*p <.05; **p <.01; ***p <.001.

Source: Wechsler et al. "Trends in College Binge Drinking during a Period of Increased Prevention Efforts." *Journal of American College Health,* p.210, March 2002.

Reprinted with permission of the Helen Dwight Reid Educational Foundation. Published by Heldref Publications, 1319 Eighteenth St., NW, Washington, DC 20036-1802. Copyright © 2002.

each of the four years studied. And this is despite concerted efforts to curb the drinking on college campuses following the findings of the first Harvard study. To date it appears that the numerous interventions have had little impact on the problem.

An extensive three-year investigation by the Task Force on College Drinking, commissioned by the National Institute on Alcohol Abuse and Alcoholism (NIAAA) (*Changing the Culture of Campus Drinking,* 2002, p.1) found: "Drinking on college campuses is more pervasive and destructive than many people realize." The Task Force reported: "Alcohol consumption is linked to at least 1,400 student deaths and 500,000 unintentional injuries annually." In addition: "Alcohol consumption by college students is associated with drinking and driving, diminished academic performance, and medical and legal problems. Nondrinking students, as well as members of the surrounding community, also may experience alcohol-related consequences, such as increased rates of crime, traffic crashes, rapes and assaults, and property damage."

White et al. (2002, p.131) report on four years of longitudinal data analyzed for 506 male adolescents: "Participants reported committing offenses against persons more often than general theft under the influence of alcohol or drugs. Aggressive acts were more often related to self-reported acute alcohol use than to marijuana use. Those who reported committing illegal acts under the influence reported committing offenses with other people and being arrested more often than those who did not. Offenses under the influence were more prevalent among heavier alcohol and drug users, more serious offenders, more impulsive youth, and youth with more deviant peers."

One problem associated with alcohol and drugs is the **rave,** an all-night party generally with loud techno music, dancing, drinking and doing drugs. Ecstasy or MDMA is the drug of choice at raves, but LSD is making a comeback and is often used in combination with Ecstasy. Johnson (2001, p.186) reports: "The number one cause of deaths for persons attending raves is not drug overdoses, but DUI related traffic crashes."

In 2000 an estimated 203,900 juveniles were arrested for drug abuse violations, an increase of 145 percent from 1991. An estimated 159,400 juveniles were arrested for liquor law violations, an increase of 20 percent from 1991; 21,700 were arrested for drunkenness, a decrease of 3 percent from 1991; and 21,000 were arrested for driving under the influence, an increase of 14 percent from 1991.

In 2001 an estimated 139,238 juveniles were arrested for drug abuse violations, 92,326 for liquor law violations, 13,397 for drunkenness and 13,971 for driving under the influence, all significant *decreases* from the previous year.

The Decline in Arrests for Status Offenses

Arrests for the status offenses of running away, habitual truancy, violating curfew and early substance use including alcohol all declined significantly from 2000 to 2001.

Other Problem Behaviors

Two areas also of concern to the juvenile justice system are disorderly youths in public places and computer delinquents.

Disorderly Youths in Public Places

Disorderly youths may be engaged in status offenses as just discussed. Scott (2001, pp.1–2) cites these additional disorder and youth-related problems: graffiti, intimidation by youth gangs, loud car stereos, open-air drug dealing, panhandling, rave parties, reckless bicycle riding and skateboarding, shoplifting, street cruising, truancy, underage drinking and vandalism. He (p.5) notes that such problem behaviors most commonly occur at shopping malls, at plazas in business districts, at video arcades, in public parks, on school grounds, in apartment complex common areas, at public libraries and at convenience stores and fast-food restaurants.

Scott (p.3) suggests: "Whether the conduct is deemed disorderly depends on many factors, including the youths' specific objectionable behavior, the youths' ages, the complainants' tolerance levels, the community norms, and the specific times and places where the problem occurs."

A strikingly different problem is posed by youths who sit alone and use their computers to commit offenses.

The Computer Delinquent

Bowker (2000, p.7) cites several examples of juveniles pleading guilty to using computers to trespass by hacking into others' computer systems, to counterfeiting money on a home computer, to trafficking in child pornography on the Internet and to stealing passwords from Internet providers. He estimates that during 2002 45 million youths used the Internet. Juveniles can easily commit a five-figure high-tech embezzlement. They can disrupt traffic signals, floodgates and power grids. They can also cause expensive systems to crash, resulting in large capital outlays to restore them. In addition, there are jurisdictional concerns as juvenile hackers can cross state and even international borders.

Scott (p.9) explains: "Persons involved in computer crimes acquire their interest and skills at an early age. They are introduced to computers in school, and their usual 'career path' starts with illegally copying computer programs. Serious offenders then get into a progression of computer crimes including telecommunications fraud (making free long distance calls), unauthorized access to other computers (hacking for fun and profit) and credit card fraud (obtaining cash advances, purchasing equipment through computers)."

A Key Issue

Should the term *juvenile delinquency* encompass both those youths who commit status offenses and those who commit nonviolent crimes? Incorporating crimes and status offenses is a key issue in juvenile justice.

Juvenile Delinquents

A juvenile **delinquent** is a youth who commits an act that would be a crime were it to be committed by an adult. The term is intended to avoid stigmatizing youths as criminals. The term *delinquent* should not be applied to status offenders. Table 5.3 summarizes high school seniors' self-reported involvement in certain delinquent activities. The adult equivalent is given in parentheses. The most frequently engaged in delinquent behavior by self-report is shoplifting.

Profile of Delinquency

No single type of personality is associated with delinquency. However, some characteristics are common among delinquents. Those who become delinquent are more likely to be socially assertive, defiant, ambivalent about authority, resentful, hostile, suspicious, destructive, impulsive and lacking in self-control. They typically are doing poorly in school, skip classes often or have dropped out altogether.

Wolfgang's classic long-term study of delinquents in Philadelphia found that 6 to 8 percent of male juveniles were responsible for more than 60 percent of the serious juvenile offenses. His studies also showed that by the third arrest, a delinquent was almost guaranteed a life of crime.

The profile of delinquency has changed in the past decade to include more female delinquents. According to the National Center for Juvenile Justice (*Frequently Asked Questions,* 2003, p.1): "Between 1980 and 2000, juvenile arrest rates increased proportionately more for females than for males, especially for violent crimes."

Table 5.3
High School Seniors Reporting Involvement in Selected Delinquent Activities in Past 12 Months United States, 1989–2001

Delinquent activity	Class of 1989 (N=2,879)	Class of 1992 (N=2,690)	Class of 1995 (N=2,656)	Class of 1998 (N=2,656)	Class of 2001 (N=2,218)
Shoplifting Taken something from a store without paying for it?					
Not at all	70.8%	69.6%	70.1%	70.3%	69.4%
Once	12.8	12.6	12.0	12.5	12.0
Twice	5.4	6.7	6.0	6.5	6.4
3 or 4 times	4.1	5.2	5.5	4.1	5.4
5 or more times	6.9	5.9	6.4	6.4	6.8
Auto theft Taken a car that didn't belong to someone in your family without permission of the owner?					
Not at all	94.6	94.0	95.2	95.2	93.3
Once	3.0	3.1	2.7	2.7	3.3
Twice	1.1	1.4	1.0	0.9	1.2
3 or 4 times	0.5	0.7	0.6	0.6	0.8
5 or more times	0.9	0.9	0.6	0.7	0.9
Taken part of a car without permission of the owner?					
Not at all	93.2	93.9	94.9	94.9	95.3
Once	3.8	3.2	2.6	2.5	2.0
Twice	1.3	1.2	1.2	1.2	1.2
3 or 4 times	0.9	1.0	0.6	0.6	0.5
5 or more times	0.8	0.8	0.7	0.8	1.0
Trespass Gone into some house or building when you weren't supposed to be there?					
Not at all	74.4	74.0	76.5	75.4	75.7
Once	11.9	12.1	10.9	10.6	12.4
Twice	7.1	6.9	6.1	6.5	6.1
3 or 4 times	3.4	3.9	3.1	3.6	2.7
5 or more times	3.2	3.2	3.3	3.9	3.1

(continued)

Juvenile Arrest Statistics and Delinquency Rates

According to Snyder (2002, p.10): "Juvenile arrests disproportionately involved minorities." In 2000 16 percent of the juvenile population was black; however black youths accounted for 41 percent of motor vehicle theft arrests, 28 percent of drug abuse violation arrests, 26 percent of the larceny-theft arrests and 25 percent of the curfew and loitering arrests. Table 5.4 shows the total number of juvenile arrests in 2000 compared with previous years. Property crimes continue to head the list.

 The most frequent delinquency offenses are property crimes, with larceny-theft being the most common.

Table 5.3 (continued)

Delinquent activity	Class of 1989 (N=2,879)	Class of 1992 (N=2,690)	Class of 1995 (N=2,656)	Class of 1998 (N=2,656)	Class of 2001 (N=2,218)
Arson					
Set fire to someone's property on purpose?					
Not at all	97.5	97.2	97.5	97.1	96.9
Once	1.5	1.6	1.5	1.1	1.6
Twice	0.4	0.4	0.4	0.8	0.5
3 or 4 times	0.2	0.4	0.3	0.2	0.3
5 or more times	0.4	0.4	0.4	0.8	0.7
Vandalism					
Damaged school property on purpose?					
Not at all	86.8	85.3	86.0	85.7	86.0
Once	6.3	7.9	6.5	7.5	6.7
Twice	3.1	3.5	3.2	2.6	3.7
3 or 4 times	1.7	1.2	2.6	2.0	2.0
5 or more times	2.2	2.1	1.7	2.3	1.7
Damaged property at work on purpose?					
Not at all	93.6	94.0	93.8	92.7	92.7
Once	2.9	2.7	3.3	3.3	3.3
Twice	1.7	1.3	1.2	1.6	2.1
3 or 4 times	1.0	1.0	0.7	0.9	0.5
5 or more times	0.9	1.0	1.0	1.6	1.4
Been arrested and taken to a police station?					
Not at all	X	X	91.0	89.8	92.0
Once	X	X	5.9	6.9	4.7
Twice	X	X	1.6	1.5	1.7
3 or 4 times	X	X	0.7	0.6	0.8
5 or more times	X	X	0.7	1.2	0.8

Source: Lloyd D. Johnston, Jerald G. Bachman, and Patrick M. O'Malley, *Monitoring the Future 1989*, pp.103–105; *1991*, pp.106–109; *1993*, pp.107–110; *1995*, pp.106–110 (Ann Arbor, MI: Institute for Social Research, University of Michigan); Jerald G. Bachman, Lloyd D. Johnston, and Patrick M. O'Malley, *Monitoring the Future 1990*, pp.106–109; *1992*, pp.106–109; *1994*, pp.106–109 (Ann Arbor, MI: Institute for Social Research, University of Michigan); and data provided by the Monitoring the Future Project, Survey Research Center, Lloyd D. Johnston, Jerald G. Bachman, and Patrick M. O'Malley, principal investigators. Table adapted by SOURCEBOOK staff p.227.

    While these figures may seem alarmingly high, they actually represent a *decrease* in juvenile arrests. According to the most recent available FBI statistics (*Crime in the United States, 2001*), the number of juveniles arrested in 2001 for Index offenses went down for the fourth straight year. As MacLellan (2001, p.16) notes: "This [decline] is even more significant considering that the number of youths in this country grew 8 percent from 1993 to 1999."

    Delinquency rates tend to increase dramatically as age increases, peaking in the mid-teens. Arrest data show that the intensity of criminal behavior slackens after the teens and continues to decline with age. Table 5.5 summarizes the arrest data for 2001 by age.

Table 5.4
Number of Juvenile Arrests in 2000—2.4 Million (5% below 1999 and 15% below 1996)

Most serious offense	2000 Estimated number of juvenile arrests	Percent of total juvenile arrests		Percent change		
		Female	Under age 15	1991–2000	1996–2000	1999–2000
Total	2,369,400	28%	32%	3%	-15%	-5%
Crime Index total	617,600	28	38	-28	-27	-5
Violent Crime Index	98,900	18	33	-17	-23	-4
Murder and non-negligent manslaughter	1,200	11	13	-65	-55	-13
Forcible rape	4,500	1	39	-26	-17	-5
Robbery	26,800	9	27	-29	-38	-5
Aggravated assault	66,300	23	36	-7	-14	-4
Property Crime Index	518,800	30	39	-30	-28	-5
Burglary	95,800	12	39	-38	-30	-5
Larceny-theft	363,500	37	40	-24	-27	-6
Motor vehicle theft	50,800	17	26	-51	-34	-3
Arson	8,700	12	65	-7	-17	-7
NonIndex						
Other assaults	236,800	31	43	37	-1	0
Forgery and counterfeiting	6,400	34	12	-20	-24	-7
Fraud	10,700	32	18	-3	-15	-5
Embezzlement	2,000	47	6	132	48	11
Stolen property (buying, receiving, possessing)	27,700	16	29	-40	-33	-1
Vandalism	114,100	12	44	-21	-19	-4
Weapons (carrying, possessing)	37,600	10	33	-26	-28	-10
Prostitution and commercialized vice	1,300	55	13	-13	-4	-3
Sex offense (except forcible rape and prostitution)	17,400	7	52	-4	8	5
Drug abuse violations	203,900	15	17	145	-4	0
Gambling	1,500	4	18	-27	-30	-22
Offenses against the family and children	9,400	37	38	92	-8	2
Driving under the influence	21,000	17	3	14	13	-3
Liquor law violations	159,400	31	10	20	4	-6
Drunkenness	21,700	20	13	-3	-19	-3
Disorderly conduct	165,700	28	38	33	-9	-8
Vagrancy	3,000	23	28	-33	-7	27
All other offenses (except traffic)	414,200	26	28	35	-5	-5
Suspicion	1,200	22	23	-76	-53	-29
Curfew and loitering	154,700	31	28	81	-16	-11
Runaways	142,000	59	39	-18	-29	-6

Note: Detail may not add to totals because of rounding.

Data source: *Crime in the United States 2000.* Washington, DC: U.S. Government Printing Office, 2001, tables 29, 32, 34, 36, 38 and 40. Arrest estimates were developed by the National Center for Juvenile Justice.

Table 5.5
Arrests by Age, 2001
(9,511 agencies: 2001 estimated population 192,580,262)

Offense charged	Total all ages	Ages under 15	Ages under 18	Ages 18 and over	Under 10	10–12	13–14	15	16	17	18	19	20	21
TOTAL	9,324,953	498,986	1,558,496	7,766,457	22,966	119,245	356,775	300,890	365,291	393,329	456,715	469,414	443,163	401,775
Percent distribution[1]	100.0	5.4	16.7	83.3	0.2	1.3	3.8	3.2	3.9	4.2	4.9	5.0	4.8	4.3
Murder and non-negligent manslaughter	9,426	114	957	8,469	6	9	99	134	254	455	582	643	618	587
Forcible rape	18,576	1,180	3,119	15,457	34	323	823	509	662	768	885	879	836	774
Robbery	76,667	4,354	18,111	58,556	95	920	3,339	3,515	4,746	5,496	6,336	5,835	4,745	4,151
Aggravated assault	329,722	16,498	44,815	284,907	878	4,524	11,096	8,215	9,646	10,456	12,083	12,745	12,737	13,634
Burglary	198,883	23,287	61,623	137,260	1,390	6,344	15,553	11,631	13,066	13,639	14,725	12,370	10,029	8,278
Larceny-theft	806,093	92,317	238,605	567,488	3,859	25,384	63,074	44,914	50,469	50,905	49,976	41,258	33,503	28,024
Motor vehicle theft	102,607	8,425	33,563	69,044	68	1,036	7,321	8,007	8,892	8,239	7,679	6,648	5,231	4,613
Arson	12,763	4,048	6,313	6,450	677	1,439	1,932	905	757	603	555	404	338	339
Violent crime[2]	434,391	22,146	67,002	367,389	1,013	5,776	15,357	12,373	15,308	17,175	19,886	20,102	18,936	19,146
Percent distribution[1]	100.0	5.1	15.4	84.6	0.2	1.3	3.5	2.8	3.5	4.0	4.6	4.6	4.4	4.4
Property crime[3]	1,120,346	128,077	340,104	780,242	5,994	34,203	87,880	65,457	73,184	73,386	72,935	60,680	49,101	41,254
Percent distribution[1]	100.0	11.4	30.4	69.6	0.5	3.1	7.8	5.8	6.5	6.6	6.5	5.4	4.4	3.7
Crime Index Total[4]	1,554,737	150,223	407,106	1,147,631	7,007	39,979	103,237	77,830	88,492	90,561	92,821	80,782	68,037	60,400
Percent distribution[1]	100.0	9.7	26.2	73.8	0.5	2.6	6.6	5.0	5.7	5.8	6.0	5.2	4.4	3.9
Other assaults	898,298	70,642	163,142	735,156	3,348	20,436	46,858	30,260	31,942	30,298	29,736	30,578	31,115	33,400
Forgery and counterfeiting	77,692	422	3,975	73,717	22	81	319	525	1,117	1,911	3,457	4,234	4,235	3,953
Fraud	211,177	958	5,830	205,347	54	173	731	880	1,558	2,434	5,460	7,802	9,193	9,271
Embezzlement	13,836	83	1,258	12,578	1	16	66	86	380	709	945	993	851	803
Stolen property: buying, receiving, possessing	84,047	4,982	18,467	65,580	135	1,008	3,839	3,630	4,637	5,218	6,155	5,469	4,842	4,207
Vandalism	184,972	31,597	71,962	113,010	2,921	9,608	19,068	12,391	14,202	13,772	12,067	10,022	8,073	7,636
Weapons: carrying, possessing, etc.	114,325	8,691	25,861	88,464	479	2,203	6,009	4,721	5,763	6,686	7,711	7,182	6,319	6,113
Prostitution and commercialized vice	58,638	155	1,034	57,604	4	16	135	152	263	464	1,244	1,646	1,689	1,780
Sex offenses (except forcible rape and prostitution)	62,997	6,625	12,381	50,616	428	2,010	4,187	2,016	1,833	1,907	2,166	2,168	2,048	1,979

Table 5.5—(continued)

Offense charged	Total all ages	Ages under 15	Ages under 18	Ages 18 and over	Under 10	10–12	13–14	15	16	17	18	19	20	21
Drug abuse violations	1,091,240	24,061	139,238	952,002	297	2,976	20,788	24,956	38,401	51,820	71,912	70,475	64,907	57,536
Gambling	7,769	129	1,000	6,769	2	11	116	191	266	414	441	465	450	418
Offenses against the family and children	93,909	2,296	6,286	87,623	253	592	1,451	1,245	1,443	1,302	1,887	2,070	2,463	2,876
Driving under the influence	946,694	629	13,397	933,297	381	28	220	613	3,425	8,730	21,508	28,753	32,661	42,911
Liquor laws	408,203	8,879	92,326	315,877	174	643	8,062	14,209	27,162	42,076	65,734	69,163	56,822	12,174
Drunkenness	423,561	1,805	13,971	409,590	128	152	1,525	2,081	3,493	6,592	12,321	13,707	13,765	18,283
Disorderly conduct	425,751	47,043	117,635	308,116	1,463	12,240	33,340	23,932	23,891	22,769	21,063	19,478	18,253	20,349
Vagrancy	19,509	394	1,607	17,902	9	81	304	307	424	482	925	781	678	660
All other offenses (except traffic)	2,453,100	76,546	269,317	2,183,783	4,083	16,011	56,452	53,524	65,657	73,590	99,055	113,533	116,653	116,926
Suspicion	2,629	277	834	1,795	20	51	206	194	215	148	107	113	109	100
Curfew and loitering law violations	100,701	28,245	100,701	—	570	5,020	22,655	22,910	28,394	21,152	—	—	—	—
Runaways	91,168	34,304	91,168	—	1,187	5,910	27,207	24,237	22,333	10,294	—	—	—	—

[1]Because of rounding, the percentage may not add to total.

[2]Violent crimes are offenses of murder, forcible rape, robbery and aggravated assault.

[3]Property crimes are offenses of burglary, larceny-theft, motor vehicle theft and arson.

[4] Includes arson.

Source: FBI Uniform Crime Reports 2001, p.244.

Vandalism

Vandalism is usually a mischievous, destructive act done to get attention, to get revenge or to vent hostility. Philip Zimbardo, a Stanford psychologist, reported in 1969 on some experiments that tested human behavior and vandalism. He arranged to have two comparable automobiles without license plates parked with their hoods up on a street in the Bronx, New York, and on a street in Palo Alto, California. The car in the Bronx was attacked by "vandals" within 10 minutes of its "abandonment."

The first people to arrive at the Bronx car were a family—father, mother and young son—who removed the radiator and battery. Within 24 hours virtually everything of value had been removed. Then random destruction began. Windows were smashed, parts torn off, upholstery ripped. Children began to use the car as a playground. Most of the adult "vandals" were well-dressed, clean-cut whites.

The car in Palo Alto sat untouched for more than a week. Then Zimbardo smashed part of it with a sledgehammer. Soon passersby were joining in. Within a few hours, the car had been turned upside down and utterly destroyed. Again, the "vandals" appeared to be primarily white adults. Commenting on this research in their classic work describing the **broken-window theory,** Wilson and Kelling (1982, pp.29–38) state:

> Untended property becomes fair game for people out for fun or plunder, and even for people who ordinarily would not dream of doing such things and who probably consider themselves law-abiding. Because of the nature of community life in the Bronx—its anonymity, the frequency with which cars are abandoned and things are stolen or broken, the past experience of "no one caring"— vandalism begins much more quickly than it does in staid Palo Alto, where people have come to believe that private possessions are cared for, and that mischievous behavior is costly. But vandalism can occur anywhere once communal barriers— the sense of mutual regard and the obligations of civility—are lowered by actions that seem to signal that "no one cares."

This vandalized car in the South Bronx depicts graphically the broken-window theory: "Untended property becomes fair game for people out for fun or plunder." If it appears that no one cares—if broken windows go unfixed—vandalism and crime will flourish.

© Farnsworth/The Image Works

Rowdy children sometimes send messages of personal problems by vandalism. Destructive behavior can occur because children lack ways of communicating a need for help. Graffiti and tagging are prevalent forms of vandalism in many areas. In 2000 114,400 juveniles were arrested for vandalism, a 21 percent decrease since 1991. In 2001 71,962 juveniles were arrested for vandalism, a significant decrease.

Burglary

Burglary is usually committed for quick financial gain, often to support a drug habit. It is the most accessible route to money for unemployed juveniles. In 2000 the juvenile arrest rate for burglary was approximately 440 per 100,000 juveniles ages 10 to 17. According to Snyder (p.7): "Unlike the juvenile arrest rates for any of the other Index offenses, the rate for burglary declined consistently and substantially between 1980 and 2000. Over this period, the burglary arrest rate was cut by nearly two-thirds (63%)." In 2000 95,800 juveniles were arrested for burglary, a 38 percent decrease from 1991. In 2001 61,623 juveniles were arrested for burglary, yet another significant decrease.

Arson

Arson, like vandalism, sends a message through a delinquent act. For many children setting fires is a symbolic act, often a symptom of underlying emotional or physical stress. Children who do not abandon normal childhood experiments with fire often are crying for help, using fire as an expression of their stress, anxiety and anger. What turns these troubled youths into repeat fire setters is positive reinforcement for their incendiary activities. Fire setting provides a sense of power and control. Juvenile fire setters often take out their hostility on school property.

Snyder (p.7) notes: "With the exception of running away from home and curfew and loitering law violations (crimes for which only juveniles can be arrested), arson is the offense with the greatest proportion of juvenile arrests. In the 1980s an annual average of 415 of all arson arrests involved juveniles. In the 1990s the percentage grew to 50 percent. In 2000 it was 53 percent." In 2000 8,700 juveniles were arrested for arson, a 7 percent decrease from 1991. Sixty-five percent of those arrested for arson were under age 15. In 2001 6,313 juveniles were arrested for arson, another significant decrease. However, juveniles accounted for almost half (49 percent) of all arrests for arson. In addition, almost two-thirds (64 percent) of those arrested were under age 15.

Larceny-Theft

As mentioned, larceny-theft is the most frequent offense for which juveniles are arrested. Shoplifting accounts for much of the larceny-theft figures. As Wooden and Blazak (p.32) note: " 'Boosting' store items allows girls to be as criminal as boys. They describe the phenomenon of **streaming,** where bands of juveniles race through store aisles, grabbing what they can and then tearing out of the stores before they could be apprehended."

In 2000 363,500 juveniles were arrested for larceny-theft, a 24 percent decrease from 1991. Thirty-seven percent of those arrested were female. In 2001 238,605 juveniles were arrested for larceny-theft, a significant decrease.

Shoplifting is a common form of delinquent behavior. Some youths shoplift because they have no money to purchase wanted items. Others shoplift for the thrill of it.

Motor Vehicle Theft

In 2000 50,800 juveniles were arrested for motor vehicle theft, a decrease of 51 percent from 1991. One-fourth (26 percent) of those arrested were under age 15; 17 percent were female. According to Snyder (p.7): "After the 1990 peak, the juvenile arrest rate for motor vehicle theft declined both consistently and substantially, so that by 2000 the rate was just 10 percent above its lowest level of 1983 and 54 percent below its 1990 peak."

In 2001 33,563 juveniles were arrested for motor vehicle theft, yet another significant decrease.

The Decline in Arrests of Juveniles for Property Crimes

 Arrests for vandalism, burglary, arson, larceny-theft and motor vehicle theft declined from 2000 to 2001.

A Brief Recap of the Causes of Delinquency

Delinquency is a focal point for the juvenile justice system. More energy and effort are spent by those within the system on delinquency than on any other responsibility. The United States generates more aftercare programs than any other country. But delinquency, its causes and effects are usually examined *after the fact,* with research on preventing delinquency getting little attention, which leaves the question: What leads youths to become delinquent?

Do children often grow up to be like their parents because they have inherited something from them or because of the way their parents have raised them? This question is especially relevant for children who become delinquents. Many researchers have tried to answer the question "Why do youths become delinquent?" The vast array of theories that have resulted range from the very conservative to what some may consider outlandish. Modern research on the causes of crime and delinquency centers on such areas as biology, sociology and psychology.

Theories about the causes of juvenile delinquency include biological, behavioral, sociological and psychological theories.

The following theories provide a base to understand juvenile behavior and related offenses. They were discussed in greater depth in Chapter 2.

Biological Theories

Biological theorists contend that criminals are born, not made. The classic studies of Lombroso (1913) and Garofalo (1915) support a hereditary, genetic causation for deviant behavior. Some researchers believe that a genetic mishap may cause one member of a family to deviate from the norm. For example, Richard Speck, who murdered eight Chicago nurses, showed an unusual genetic structure—he had one extra male chromosome. Speck is not the only convicted criminal to display such a genetic abnormality.

Modern biological theorists possess scientific rigor, and they look to biochemical relationships, endocrine imbalances, chromosomal complements, brain wave activity and other biological determinants of behavior. Violence and aggression have been associated with the presence or absence of certain chemicals in the brain. The fact that biological explanations are supported by research cannot be ignored when looking at the causes of delinquent and antisocial behavior.

Behavioral Theories

A counter position to biological theory is behavioral theory, which contends that criminals are made, not born. Behavioral theorists argue that people become who they are because of their life experiences.

As children grow and develop, they learn from their families the rules that govern their conduct. Any wrongdoing or mischief reflects what was learned and manipulated for whatever gain might be desired, without taking into account the risk or punishment that might result. If children who misbehave are corrected by their parents, they are likely to conform to society's expectations; if they are not corrected, they are likely to ignore society's rules.

Sociological Theories

Sociological theorists take the behavioral position one step further. Socialization provides children with accepted behavior repertoires and endows them with the basic values of their social milieu. During the socialization process, children may also learn antisocial values, if such values are important in their social and cultural environments. In such instances socialization actually contributes to delinquent behavior.

Although delinquency often begins when children first enter school, its most serious manifestations usually occur in adolescence. Most youths at one time or another test the limits, shoplift, steal from their mother's purse or engage in similar petty thefts. Such behavior is usually outgrown without intervention from the juvenile justice system if the parents administer appropriate discipline. Unfortunately not all youths outgrow these tendencies to misbehave.

The Gluecks also favor a sociological causation for delinquency. Their extensive studies of delinquent boys enabled them to create a *predictive index*. The accuracy of this index was tested in the 1950s, and of 220 predictions, 209 were accurate. The social factors in their index included how children were disciplined and supervised, how much affection was shown in the home and family cohesiveness. In a classic work, *Unraveling Juvenile Delinquency*, the Gluecks (1950) reported that 85 percent of the delinquents released from a Massachusetts correctional institution were from families in which other members were delinquent.

The research was conducted in the late 1940s and early 1950s, when families were less fragmented than families are now. In 45 percent of the delinquent cases, the mother of the offender had a criminal record; in 66 percent the father had a criminal record.

Psychological Approaches

Many delinquent youths have to deal with poor home lives and destructive relationships. Such an environment can lead to a disturbed personality structure marked by negative, antisocial behavior. While many delinquents do not show significant psychological disturbances, enough do suffer from problems to allow psychological factors to be considered in the theory of delinquency.

Adolescence is normally a time of inner tensions, excessive energy and ambiguity. It is a time when the individual is neither child nor adult. Youths still have childish needs and a desire for dependency, though they have adult expectations imposed by themselves or others. If the emotional foundation is weak, the result can be catastrophic.

 A major characteristic of juvenile delinquents is that they act out their inner conflicts.

In **acting out,** youths freely express their impulses, particularly hostile ones. Acting out is the free, deliberate, often malicious indulgence of impulse, which often leads to aggression as well as other manifestations of delinquency, such as vandalism and cruelty to animals. Acting out essentially reflects an absence of self-control and a desire for immediate gratification.

Such a lack of self-control may result from an early history of severe parental rejection or deprivation, or from witnessing or being the victim of severe physical abuse and violence. As noted by Widom and Maxfield (2001, p.1): "Being abused or neglected as a child increased the likelihood of arrest as a juvenile by 59 percent, as an adult by 28 percent, and for a violent crime by 30 percent." Children strike back against a world they perceive as hostile. Acting out may also give adolescents a sense of importance, a way to overcome feelings of inadequacy and inferiority.

Adolescents who act out come from all socioeconomic levels and are not psychopathic according to conventional classifications. They may have a clear sense of conscience and be capable of strong feelings of loyalty to a gang. But their impulses are stronger than their consciences. The acting out may be a form of defense against feelings of anxiety produced by an awareness of guilt.

Other Factors

Several factors commonly cited as contributing directly to delinquency include poverty, unemployment, the breakdown of religion, the breakdown of the family, effects of the media (TV, movies, music) and peer pressure. Other factors contributing to the risk of a youth becoming delinquent include:

- Divorce.
- Alcohol- and/or drug-abusing parent(s).
- Two-income households with diminished supervision of children.
- Family criminal history.
- Transient patterns—frequent family moves or shuffling between relatives.
- Special education needs or attention deficit disorder (ADD).

All the theories ask the same basic question: "Are delinquents made or born?" The answer is both. Delinquency is caused by a *combination* of predisposing genetic traits influenced by social circumstances and life experiences. As explained by Wilson (1983, p.86):

> We now have available an impressive number of studies that, taken together, support the following view: Some combination of constitutional traits and early family experiences account for more of the variation among young persons in their serious criminality than any other factors, and serious misconduct that appears relatively early in life tends to persist into adulthood. What happens on the street corner, in the school, or in the job market can still make a difference, but it will not be as influential as what has gone before.

Earlier research also stressed the importance of early delinquency and of paying attention to problem behaviors.

Developmental Pathways

Longitudinal research from the Pittsburgh Youth Study, a component of the OJJDP's Program of Research on the Causes and Correlates of Delinquency, has revealed that the development of disruptive and delinquent behavior in boys typically occurs in an orderly, progressive manner known as **developmental pathways.** Kelley et al. (1997b, p.2) have documented "three developmental pathways that display progressively more serious problem behaviors among boys in three conceptually similar domains: authority conflict (defiance and running away), covert actions (lying and stealing), and overt actions (aggression and violent behavior)." As these researchers explain (1997b, p.2): "A pathway is identified when a group of individuals experience a behavioral development that is distinct from the behavioral development of other groups of individuals. In a developmental pathway, stages of behavior unfold over time in an orderly fashion." The behaviors exhibited in these pathways are illustrated in Figure 5.3.

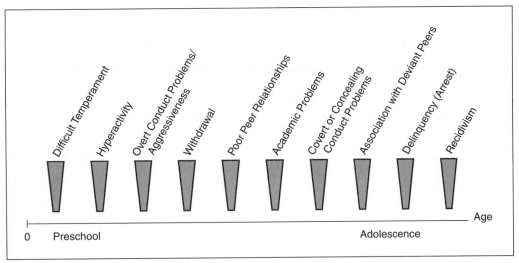

Figure 5.3
Approximate Ordering of the Different Manifestations of Disruptive and Antisocial Behaviors in Childhood and Adolescence

Source: Barbara Tatem Kelley et al. *Development Pathways in Boys' Disruptive and Delinquent Behavior.* Washington, DC: OJJDP Juvenile Justice Bulletin, December 1997, p.4. (NCJ 165692)

Kelley et al. (p.4) have identified an approximate ordering of the different manifestations of disruptive and antisocial behaviors (Figure 5.4).

Conduct such as stubborn behavior "tended to occur earliest at median age 9, with a wide range of onset—the 25th percentile at age 3 and the 75th percentile at age 13. This was followed by minor covert acts, such as lying and shoplifting, at median age 10. Defiance, which involves doing tasks in one's own way, refusing to follow directions and disobeying, emerged next at median age 11. Aggressive behaviors, such as bullying and annoying others, followed at age 12, along with property damage, such as vandalism and fire setting. More seriously aggressive acts, such as physical fighting and violence, came last at median age of 13" (Kelley et al., p.6).

- The *authority conflict path* includes stubbornness, doing things one's own way, refusing to do things and disobedience. It may culminate in authority avoidance by staying out late, truancy and/or running away.

- The *covert behavior path* includes lying, shoplifting, setting fires, damaging property, joyriding, pick pocketing, stealing from cars, fencing stolen goods, writing illegal checks and using illegal credit cards. It may culminate in serious delinquency such as stealing a car, selling drugs and/or breaking and entering.

- The *overt behavior* path includes annoying others, bullying and fighting. It may culminate in violence, including attacking someone, strong-arming and/or forcing sex.

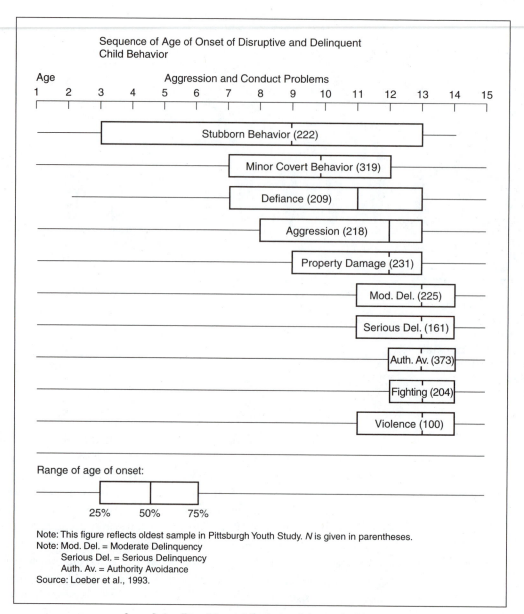

Figure 5.4
**Sequence of Age of
Onset of Disruptive and
Delinquent Child Behavior**

Source: Barbara Tatem Kelley et al. *Development Pathways in Boys' Disruptive and Delinquent Behavior.* Washington, DC: OJJDP Juvenile Justice Bulletin, December 1997, p.8. (NCJ 165692)

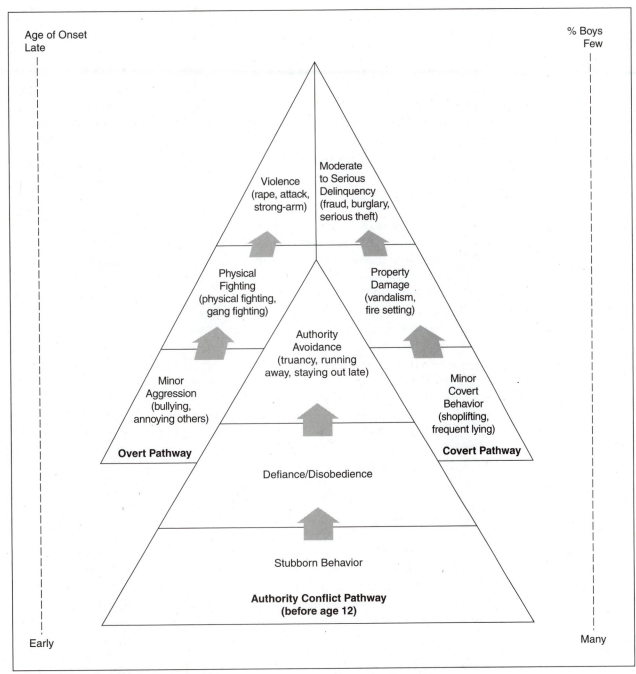

Figure 5.5
**Three Pathways to Boys'
Disruptive Behavior
and Delinquency**

Source: Barbara Tatem Kelley et al. *Development Pathways in Boys' Disruptive and Delinquent Behavior.* Washington, DC: OJJDP Juvenile Justice Bulletin, December 1997, p.9. (NCJ 165692)

As indicated, a difficult temperament is generally the earliest problem noted in infants, with hyperactivity becoming more apparent once a child begins to walk, and so on. Figure 5.5 shows how these problem behaviors can be sequenced into three distinct pathways to delinquency.

Kelley et al. (p.4) see "children's failures to master developmental tasks and to acquire other prosocial skills reflected in these tasks as breeding grounds for the development of disruptive and delinquent behavior. Therefore, many youths who eventually become seriously and chronically delinquent somewhere during childhood and adolescence probably missed opportunities to learn one or more key prosocial behaviors."

At-Risk Behaviors and Circumstances

Many of the status offenses are also a means to identify **at-risk youths.** At-risk behaviors include habitual truancy, incorrigibility, gang activity, drug abuse, alcoholism, promiscuity, criminal activity, tattooing or self-mutilating behaviors, vandalism, and possession and use of weapons.

Shader (2002, p.1) notes: "Researchers have concluded that there is no single path to delinquency and note that the presence of several risk factors often increases a youth's chance of offending. Studies also point to the interaction of risk factors, the multiplicative effect when several risk factors are present, and how certain protective factors may work to offset risk factors." Table 5.6 summarizes these risk factors and protective factors that might offset them.

Recall from the previous chapter that youths who are victims of other youths are often themselves delinquents. According to Loeber et al. (2001, p.1): "Delinquency and victimization are often intertwined and mutually stimulate each other." They note that many victims are prone to engage in illegal activities, associate with delinquents, victimize other delinquents and avoid legal recourse to resolve conflicts.

Summary

Researchers use three methods to measure the nature and extent of unlawful acts by juveniles: official data, self-report data and victim surveys. According to self-report studies, delinquency is almost universal. One reason is that status offenses are often included as acts of delinquency. Status offenses include actions such as running away, habitual truancy, violating curfew and early substance use including alcohol. Arrests for the status offenses of running away, habitual truancy, violating curfew and early substance use including alcohol all declined significantly from 2000 to 2001.

The most frequent delinquency offenses are property crimes, with larceny-theft being the most common. Arrests for vandalism, burglary, arson, larceny-theft and motor vehicle theft also declined from 2000 to 2001.

Theories of the causes of juvenile delinquency include biological, behavioral, sociological and psychological theories. A major characteristic of juvenile delinquents is that they act out their inner conflicts.

Three pathways to boys' disruptive behavior and delinquency have been identified. The *authority conflict path* includes stubbornness, doing things one's

Table 5.6
Risk and Protective Factors, by Domain

Domain	Risk Factor		Protective Factor*
	Early Onset (ages 6–11)	Late Onset (ages 12–14)	
Individual	General offenses Substance use Being male Aggression** Hyperactivity Problem (antisocial) behavior Exposure to television violence Medical, physical problems Low IQ Antisocial attitudes, beliefs Dishonesty**	General offenses Restlessness Difficulty concentrating** Risk taking Aggression** Being male Physical violence Antisocial attitudes, beliefs Crimes against persons Problem (antisocial) behavior Low IQ Substance use	Intolerant attitude toward deviance High IQ Being female Positive social orientation Perceived sanctions for transgressions
Family	Low socioeconomic status/poverty Antisocial parents Poor parent-child relationship Harsh, lax or inconsistent discipline Broken home Separation from parents Other conditions Abusive parents Neglect	Poor parent-child relationship Harsh or lax discipline Poor monitoring, supervision Low parental involvement Antisocial parents Broken home Low socioeconomic status/poverty Abusive parents Family conflict**	Warm, supportive relationships with parents or other adults Parents' positive evaluation of peers Parental monitoring
School	Poor attitude, performance	Poor attitude, performance Academic failure	Commitment to school Recognition for involvement in conventional activities
Peer group	Weak social ties Antisocial peers	Weak social ties Antisocial, delinquent peers Gang membership	Friends who engage in conventional behavior
Community		Neighborhood crime, drugs Neighborhood disorganization	

*Age of onset not known.

**Males only.

Adapted from Office of the Surgeon General, 2001.

Source: Michael Shader. *Risk Factors for Delinquency: An Overview*, online article, 2002.

own way, refusing to do things and disobedience. It may culminate in authority avoidance by staying out late, truancy and/or running away. The *covert behavior path* includes lying, shoplifting, setting fires, damaging property, joyriding, pick pocketing, stealing from cars, fencing stolen goods, writing illegal checks and using illegal credit cards. It may culminate in serious delinquency such as stealing a car, selling drugs and/or breaking and entering. The *overt behavior path* includes annoying others, bullying and fighting. It may culminate in violence, including attacking someone, strong-arming and/or forcing sex.

Discussion Questions

1. What are the most common status offenses in your community?
2. Were you ever stopped (or arrested) for a status offense when you were a juvenile? Do you know anyone who was? How did you feel?
3. Do other countries have status offenses?
4. Do you believe status offenders should be treated the same as youths involved in serious, violent crimes?
5. Is human development fixed more by biological inheritance or by life experiences?
6. Should the term *juvenile delinquency* encompass both those youths who commit status offenses and those who commit nonviolent crimes? Violent crimes?
7. How do you account for the decrease in arrests for status offenses? For property crimes?
8. To what do you attribute the racial disparity in youths arrested?
9. Do you think the developmental pathways have validity?
10. Do you think status offenses should be decriminalized?

InfoTrac College Edition Assignments

- Use InfoTrac College Edition to help answer the Discussion Questions as appropriate.
- Complete one of the following assignments and be prepared to share what you learn with the class.:
  - "The Advent of the Computer Delinquent" by Arthur L. Bowker.
  - "The Failure of Higher Education to Reduce the Binge Drinking Rate" by Taris Glassman.
  - "Development Pathways from Child Maltreatment to Peer Rejection" by Kerry E. Bolger and Charlotte J. Patterson.
  - "Successful Programs for At-Risk Youths" by Everett et. al.

Internet Assignments

Select one of the following assignments to complete.

- Go to www.ojjdp.ncjrs.org and find one of the NCJ publications listed in the references for this chapter.
- Go to the FBI Web site at www.FBI and update the arrest statistics in this chapter.

- Search the Internet to select an article relating to a concept discussed in this chapter using one of the following key words or phrases: *anomie (Durkheim's), binge drinking (Harvard study), broken window theory, dark figure of crime, developmental pathways.*

References

Bowker, Arthur L. "The Advent of the Computer Delinquent." *FBI Law Enforcement Bulletin,* December 2000, pp.7–11.

Changing the Culture of Campus Drinking. Bethesda, MD: National Institute on Alcohol Abuse and Alcoholism: Alcohol Alert, October 2002.

Cities Say Curfews Help Reduce Gang Activity and Violent Crime. Washington, DC: National League of Cities News Fax, October 25, 2001.

Crime in the United States 2000. Washington, DC: U.S. Department of Justice, Federal Bureau of Investigation, November 2001. (NCJ 167578)

Crime in the United States 2001. Washington, DC: U.S. Department of Justice, Federal Bureau of Investigation, November 2002.

Ericson, Nels. *Substance Abuse: The Nation's Number One Health Problem.* Washington, DC: OJJDP Fact Sheet #17, May 2001. (FS 200117)

Geier, Michael. "Party Patrol: A New Approach to Underage Drinking Enforcement." *Law and Order,* March 2003, pp.96–103.

Glasscock, Bruce D. "The Global Menace of Drugs." *The Police Chief,* June 2001, p.7.

Glueck, Sheldon and Glueck, Eleanor. *Unraveling Juvenile Delinquency.* Cambridge, MA: Harvard University Press, 1950.

Griffin, Patrick and Torbet, Patricia (eds.) *Desktop Guide to Good Juvenile Probation Practice.* Washington, DC: National Center for Juvenile Justice, June 2002.

Johnson, Matt. "Successful Rave Operations." *Law and Order,* October 2001, pp.184–188.

Kelley, Barbara Tatem; Loeber, Rolf; Keenan, Kate; and DeLamatre, Mary. *Developmental Pathways in Boys' Disruptive and Delinquent Behavior.* Washington, DC: OJJDP Juvenile Justice Bulletin, December 1997. (NCJ 165692)

Loeber, Rolf; Kalb, Larry; and Huizinga, David. *Juvenile Delinquency and Serious Injury Victimization.* Washington, DC: OJJDP Juvenile Justice Bulletin, August 2001. (NCJ 188676)

MacLellan, Thomas M. "Declining Juvenile Crime Rates: An Opportunity to Reduce Future Juvenile Violence." *The Associate,* March/April 2001, pp.16–19.

McDowall, David; Loftin, Colin; and Wiersema, Brian. "The Impact of Youth Curfew Laws on Juvenile Crime Rates." *Crime & Delinquency,* January 2000, pp.76–91.

National Center for Juvenile Justice. *Frequently Asked Questions,* February 2003.

Shader, Michael. *Risk Factors for Delinquency: An Overview,* online article, 2002. http://ojjdp.ncjrs.org/ccd/pubsrfd.html

Scott, Michael S. *Disorderly Youth in Public Places.* Washington, DC: Office of Community Oriented Policing Services: Problem-Oriented Guides for Police Series, No. 6, September 2001.

Snyder, Howard N. *Juvenile Arrests 2000.* Washington, DC: OJJDP, Juvenile Justice Bulletin, November 2002. (NCJ 191729)

Ward, J. Richard, Jr. "Implementing Juvenile Curfew Programs." *FBI Law Enforcement Bulletin,* March 2000, pp.15–18.

Wechsler, Henry; Lee, Jae Eun; Kuo, Meichun; Seibring, Mark; Nelson, Toben F.; and Lee, Hang. "Trends in College Binge Drinking during a Period of Increased Prevention Efforts: Findings from 4 Harvard School of Public Health College Alcohol Study Surveys: 1992-2001." *Journal of American College Health,* March 2002, pp.203–217.

White, Helene Raskin; Tice, Peter C.; Loeber, Rolf; and Strouthamer-Loeber, Magda. "Illegal Acts Committed by Adolescents under the Influence of Alcohol and Drugs." *Journal of Research in Crime and Delinquency,* May 2002, pp.131–152.

Widom, Cathy S. and Maxfield, Michael G. *An Update on the "Cycle of Violence."* Washington, DC: National Institute of Justice Research in Brief, February 2001. (NCJ 184894)

Wilson, James Q. "Thinking about Crime." *The Atlantic Monthly,* September 1983, p.86.

Wilson, James Q. and Kelling, George L. "The Police and Neighborhood Safety: Broken Windows." *The Atlantic Monthly,* March 1982, pp. 29–38.

Wooden, Wayne S. and Blazak, Randy. *Renegade Kids, Suburban Outlaws: From Youth Culture to Delinquency.* Belmont, CA: Wadsworth Publishing Company, 2001.

Helpful Resource

Chesney-Lind, Meda and Shelden, Randall G. *Girls, Delinquency and Juvenile Justice,* 2nd ed. Belmont, CA: Wadsworth Publishing Company, 1998.

CHAPTER

6

Serious, Chronic and Violent Juvenile Offenders

The greatest future predictor of violent behavior is a previous history of violence. Without systematic and effective intervention, early aggression commonly will escalate into later violence and broaden into other antisocial behavior.

—American Psychological Association Commission on Violence and Youth

Do You Know?

- What two general trajectories for youth violence are identified by the surgeon general?
- When most youth violence begins and ends?
- What some predictors of youth violence are?
- What the hazards of labeling a youth a psychopath are?
- How most youths with conduct disorders should be viewed by the juvenile justice system and the public?
- How youths who carry guns for protection differ from those who have guns for sport?
- What offenses are included in the FBI's Violent Crime Index?
- Approximately what percent of juveniles ages 10 to 17 were arrested for a violent crime in 2000?
- Whether juvenile arrests for a Violent Crime Index offense have increased or decreased from 2000 to 2001?
- What some explanations for the change in juvenile arrests for a Violent Crime Index offense are?
- Whether school crime and violence are increasing or decreasing?
- What the most serious consequences of bullying are?
- How common it is for a school shooter to provide a warning of the impending violence?
- How street gangs acquire their power?
- What activities gangs participate in?
- What basic functions are served by youth gangs?
- What are some causes of gangs?
- How contemporary gangs can be classified?
- How public health and juvenile justice view violence?

Can You Define?

antisocial personality disorder
bullying
chronic juvenile offender
conduct disorder
contagion

corporate gang
crew
deviance
expressive violence
gang
hedonistic gang

instrumental gang
instrumental violence
predatory gang
psychopathic behavior
psychopaths
scavenger gang

166

serious child delinquent   sociopathic behavior   turf
serious juvenile offender   street gang   violent juvenile offender
socialized delinquency   territorial gang   youth gang

INTRODUCTION

"A decade ago, Americans faced frightening predictions about an approaching storm of juvenile violence. Popular terms from the early 1990s, such as 'juvenile super predator,' 'coming blood bath,' and 'crime time bombs,' suggested the nation was heading toward an unavoidable collision with a growing generation of violent youth" (Butts and Travis, 2002, p.2). Butts and Travis note that the United States did experience sharply growing rates of juvenile violence during the 1980s and early 1990s, and had those trends continued, it would have caused a "national crisis." *Youth Violence: A Report of the Surgeon General* (2001, p.1) notes:

> Youth violence is a high-visibility, high-priority concern in every sector of U.S. society. No community, whether affluent or poor, urban, suburban or rural, is immune from its devastating effects. . . . Since 1993, when the epidemic peaked, youth violence has declined significantly nationwide, as signaled by downward trends in arrest records, victimization data and hospital emergency room records. But the problem has not been resolved.
>
> Another key indicator of violence—youths' confidential reports about their violent behavior—reveals no change since 1993 in the proportion of young people who have committed physically injurious and potentially lethal acts. . . . Arrest records give only a partial picture of youth violence. For every youth arrested in any given year in the late 1990s, at least 10 were engaged in some form of violent behavior that could have seriously injured or killed another person.

This report (p.8) concludes: "In the aggregate, the best available evidence from multiple sources indicates that youth violence is an ongoing national problem, albeit one that is largely hidden from public view." According to the Children's Safety Network (2000), violence perpetrated by youths cost the United States the following:

$ 5,902,605,000	medical
24,408,716,000	lost work and other
127,948,639,000	quality of life
30,311,314,000	monetary
158,259,953,000	comprehensive

This chapter returns to the widespread problem of violence in our society and the effect it has on our youths. The chapter begins with definitions of importance and descriptions of chronic juvenile offenders and violent juvenile offenders. Next is a discussion of myths about youth violence and of antisocial personality disorders. This is followed by a look at the influence of guns on the youth violence problem. Then the chapter addresses youths' involvement in violent crimes, in school violence and in gang violence. This is followed by a brief look at the difference between the public health and the juvenile justice perspective on violence. The chapter concludes with an example of factors underlying violent behavior and a discussion of the role of the media in the public's attitudes toward youth violence.

Definitions

The serious, chronic and/or violent juvenile offenders are often transferred out of the juvenile justice system to the criminal justice system. However, it is still important for all individuals involved with juveniles to understand this population.

- A **serious juvenile offender** has been convicted of a Part I offense as defined by the FBI Uniform Crime Reports, excluding auto theft, petty theft/larceny or distribution of a controlled dangerous substance.
- A **serious child delinquent** is between the ages of 7 and 12 and has committed one or more homicides, aggravated assaults, robberies, rapes or serious arsons.
- A **chronic juvenile offender** has a record of five or more separate charges of delinquency, regardless of the offenses' gravity.
- A **violent juvenile offender** has been convicted of a violent Part I offense, one against a person rather than property, and who has a prior adjudication of such an offense, or a youth who has been convicted of murder.

Most serious offenders are also chronic or violent offenders, and some are both chronic and violent as illustrated in Figure 6.1.

Serious or chronic offenders are typically from low-income families, are rated troublesome by teachers and peers between the ages of 8 and 10, have poor school performance by age 10, are adjudicated a delinquent before age 13 and have a sibling convicted of a crime.

Chronic Juvenile Offenders

Kempf-Leonard et al. (2001, p.454) suggest: "The term *chronic* usually incorporates two dimensions: frequency of offending and the length of time over which offending persists." Their review of chronic offender studies led to several conclusions: "First, the proportions of chronic offenders vary considerably from study to study (from 7 percent to 25 percent). Second, the amount of crime accounted for by chronic offenders varies by ethnicity: nonwhite male chronic offenders account for a greater proportion of official serious delinquency. Third, there are large gender differences: chronic offending is lower in females than in males."

Jones et al. (2001, p.480) are among the researchers who have attempted to identify first-time offenders who are most likely to become chronic juvenile offenders. They call this population "the 8 percent problem." Krohn et al. (2001, p.68) found that early-onset offenders (age 10 and younger) have more serious and more violent offender careers in adolescence and young adult years. Burns et al. (2003, p.1) came to a similar conclusion, but set the age two years higher: "Compared with juveniles who start offending in adolescence, child delinquents (age 12 and younger) are two to three times more likely to become tomorrow's serious and violent offenders." The serious child delinquent is discussed shortly.

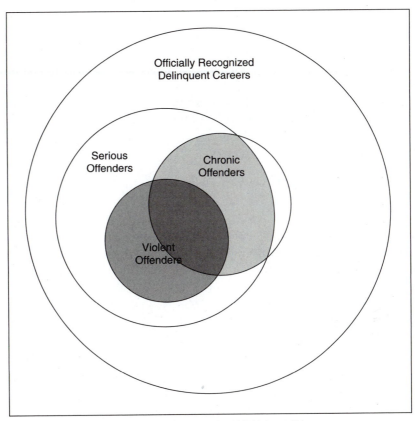

Figure 6.1
The Overlap of Serious, Chronic and Violent Offenders

Source: Melissa Sickmund et al. *Juvenile Offenders and Victims: 1997 Update on Violence.*
Office of Juvenile Justice and Delinquency Prevention, August 1997, p.25. (NCJ 165703)

Risk Factors

Cottle et al. (2001, p.367) identified several risk factors for juvenile recidivism: "The most powerful predictors of recidivism were demographic factors (males and juveniles of low socio-economic status were at higher risk) and offense history (earlier contact with the law, greater numbers of prior arrests/commitments, and more serious prior crimes)." They also identified family and social variables as risk factors for reoffending: "Juveniles who had been physically or sexually abused, were raised in a single-parent family, had a higher number of out-of-home placements, or had experienced significant family problems were at higher risk of recidivism. Juveniles who did not use their leisure time effectively and juveniles with delinquent peers were also at higher risk. A history of special education classes was a risk factor for recidivism, but school attendance and academic achievement were not significant predictors. . . . The strongest predictors of recidivism were age at first commitment, age at first contact with law enforcement and a history of nonsevere pathology."

Violent Juvenile Offenders

Youth Violence: A Report of the Surgeon General (p.4) identifies two general onset trajectories for youth violence.

The two general onset trajectories for youth violence are *early*, in which violence begins before puberty, and *late*, in which violence begins in adolescence.

According to this report: "Youths who become violent before about age 13 generally commit more crimes, and more serious crimes, for a longer time. These young people exhibit a pattern of escalating violence through childhood, and they sometimes continue their violence into adulthood."

The report also notes that surveys consistently find about 30 to 40 percent of male youths and 15 to 30 percent of female youths report having committed a serious violent offense by age 17. Serious violence is part of a lifestyle that includes drugs, guns, precocious sex and other risky behaviors.

 Most youth violence begins in adolescence and ends with the transition into adulthood.

Serious Child Delinquents

A key finding of the Office of Juvenile Justice and Delinquency Prevention (OJJDP) Study Group on Serious and Violent Offenders—that most chronic juvenile offenders begin their delinquency careers before age 12 and some as early as age 10—led OJJDP in 1998 to establish its Study Group on Very Young Offenders (*OJJDP Research 2000,* 2001, p.3). This study group found that for very young offenders, the most important risk factors are likely individual (e.g., birth complications, hyperactivity and impulsivity) or family related (e.g., parental substance abuse and poor childrearing practices).

Snyder et al. (2003) report on the most recent findings of this study group. They (p.1) note: "An increasing number of very young offenders, those between the ages of 7 and 12, are becoming involved with the juvenile justice system. According to the latest statistics, children younger than 13 are involved in almost 1 in 10 juvenile arrests. . . . Compared with juveniles who become delinquent in adolescence, very young delinquents are at greater risk of becoming serious, violent and chronic offenders. They are also more likely than older delinquents to continue their delinquency for extended periods of time." They also suggest, however: "The good news is that prevention and intervention efforts focused on very young offenders could yield significant benefits."

This same conclusion is reached in *Youth Violence: A Report of the Surgeon General* (p.6): "The most important conclusion of this report is that youth violence is not an intractable problem. We now have the knowledge and tools needed to reduce or even prevent much of the most serious youth violence." Efforts to prevent violence are discussed throughout the remainder of this text.

Violent Adolescent Females

Girls have traditionally entered the juvenile justice system through their involvement in status offenses. Violence by adolescent girls is often the result of a combination of victimization, substance abuse, economic conditions and dysfunctional family systems. Researchers have linked the violence perpetuated against females to the increased involvement of females in violent crime, that is, females are becoming perpetrators in response to their own victimization. Such research supports the theory that violence perpetuates violence.

According to research by Chesney-Lind and Paramore (2001, p.142): "More recently girls represent a growing proportion of juveniles arrested for serious offenses." They suggest, however, that increases in female delinquency may reflect relabeling of behaviors. For example, they contend that increases in female robbery arrests may be accounted for by changes in policy, crime reporting patterns and redefining schoolyard thefts as robberies. *Female Offenders* (2003, p.1) reports that between 1980 and 2000, juvenile arrest rates increased proportionately more for females than for males, especially for violent crimes.

Predictors of Youth Violence

Corbitt (2000, p.18) contends: "Several factors—such as child abuse, a difficult home life and exposure to crime—can predict certain types of future behavior. Although these factors may adversely affect juvenile behavior, serious and violent juvenile offenders tend to develop behavior problems—such as aggression, dishonesty, property offenses and conflict with authority figures—from childhood to adolescence."

 Predictors of youth violence include exposure to violence, early aggressive behavior, early delinquency and animal abuse.

According to Kracke (2001, p.1): "Children who experience violence, either as victims or as witnesses, are at increased risk of becoming violent themselves. These children begin committing crimes at younger ages, commit nearly twice as many offenses as nonabused children and are arrested more frequently than nonabused children." Shaffer and Ruback (2002, p.1) also suggest: "Violent victimization is indeed a warning signal for future violent offending among juveniles." They also found that violent victimization and violent offending share many of the same risk factors including previous violent victimization and offending, drug and alcohol use, and depression."

Recall that Loeber et al. (2001, p.1) also note that juvenile victims are often involved in delinquency: "These victims are prone to engage in illegal activities, associate with delinquents, victimize other delinquents and avoid legal recourse in resolving conflicts." They (p.5) identified several risk factors for victimization in Pittsburgh and Denver, including participating in gang or group fights, carrying a weapon, committing serious assault, selling drugs and associating with delinquent peers.

Embry (2001, p.97) notes another predictor: "Early aggressive and disruptive behaviors in preschool or primary grades have been established as predictors of serious violent offending a decade later." Likewise, as Burns et al. (p.1) report: "Compared with juveniles who start offending in adolescence, child delinquents (age 12 and younger) are two to three times more likely to become tomorrow's serious and violent offenders."

Yet another predictor for violence is animal abuse. According to Ascione (2001, p.3): "Animal abuse and interpersonal violence toward humans share common characteristics: both types of victims are living creatures, have a capacity for experiencing pain and distress, can display physical signs of the pain and distress (with which humans could empathize) and may die as a result of inflicted injuries." He reports on several studies establishing the relation between childhood histories of animal abuse and later violent offending. He (p.1) suggests that one of the most well-documented examples is Luke Woodham, who, in the April before his October 1997 murder of his mother and two schoolmates, tortured and killed his pet dog. Ascione (pp.4–5) describes the role of animal abuse as a possible symptom of conduct disorder, a condition discussed later in the chapter.

Other predictors of violence are described by the American Psychological Association (no date, p.6): "Social forces such as prejudice, economic inequality and attitudes toward violence in the mainstream American culture interact with the influences of early childhood to foster the expression of violence." The Association describes several developmental experiences that violent youths frequently share (p.21):

> Youths at greatest risk of becoming extremely aggressive and violent tend to share common experiences that appear to place them on a "trajectory toward violence." These youths tend to have experienced weak bonding to caretakers in infancy and ineffective parenting techniques, including lack of supervision, inconsistent discipline, highly punitive or abusive treatment, and failure to reinforce positive, pro-social behavior. These developmental deficits, in turn, appear to lead to poor peer relations and high levels of aggressiveness.
>
> Additionally, these youths have learned attitudes accepting aggressive behavior as normative and as an effective way to solve interpersonal problems. Aggressive children tend to be rejected by their more conforming peers and do poorly in school, including having a history of problems such as poor school attendance and numerous suspensions. These children often band together with others like themselves, forming deviant peer groups that reinforce antisocial behaviors. The more such children are exposed to violence in their homes, in their neighborhoods and in the media, the greater their risk for aggressive and violent behaviors.

 Other predictors of violent behavior include ineffective parenting and lack of supervision, accepting aggressive behavior as normal, having problems in school and banding together with other aggressive peers.

Myths about Youth Violence

When considering youth violence, the tendency is to overgeneralize about research results. The surgeon general's report (pp.5–6) presents and debunks several myths about youth violence:

- Most future offenders can be identified in early childhood.
- Child abuse and neglect inevitably lead to violent behavior later in life.
- African-American and Hispanic youths are more likely to become involved in violence than other racial or ethnic groups.
- A new, violent breed of young superpredators threatens the United States.
- Getting tough with juvenile offenders by trying them in adult criminal courts reduces the likelihood that they will commit more crimes.
- Nothing works with respect to treating or preventing violent behavior.
- Most violent youths will end up being arrested for a violent crime.

Another area in which fact and fiction are sometimes confused is in discussions of juvenile antisocial personality disorders.

Antisocial Personality Disorders

The American Psychiatric Association has defined **antisocial personality disorder** as a disorder that exists in individuals age 18 or older who show evidence of a conduct disorder before age 15 as well as a pattern of irresponsible and antisocial behavior since age 15. It occurs in about 3 percent of American males and fewer than 1 percent of American females. Table 6.1 lists the behaviors indicative of conduct disorders and irresponsible, antisocial behavior.

The Association asserts: "In early adolescence these people characteristically use tobacco, alcohol and other drugs and engage in voluntary sexual intercourse unusually early for their peer group. . . . Almost invariably there is a markedly impaired capacity to sustain lasting, close, warm and responsible relationships with family, friends or sexual partners." The Association lists the following predisposing factors: attention deficit hyperactivity disorder and conduct disorder during prepuberty, absence of consistent parental discipline, abuse as a child, removal from the home and growing up without parental figures of both sexes. Violent youths are sometimes characterized as exhibiting personality disorders such as psychopathic or sociopathic behavior.

Psychopathic/Sociopathic Behavior

Personality disorders have been studied by psychiatrists and psychologists. Two distinct types of personality disorders are often described. **Psychopathic** or **sociopathic behavior** refers to chronic asocial behavior rooted in severe deficiencies in developing a conscience. Failure to develop feelings of guilt is usually attributed to the absence or neglect of a strong identification with stable parental figures or to having parents who have problems with social values. Failure to develop a conscience begins with the use or exploitation of children by parents. The children are encouraged to carry out the parents' own forbidden impulses and wishes. This encourages children in their own antisocial behavior. Such patterns of behavior usually originate with an overly dominant mother and a child who believes in acting out maternal wishes. Psychopaths are remarkable for emotional blandness, particularly about actions that profoundly shock normal people.

Psychopaths are virtually lacking in conscience. They do not know right from wrong. They may, however, profess to recognize and speak smoothly about devotion to accepted values, and they can be charming in casual personal contacts. Psychopaths often make glib promises and resolutions. Meanwhile, they may be stealing from the person or company they work for, or from the person they are talking to at a particular time. They are profoundly egocentric and never see their own responsibility for anything that goes wrong. Although most psychopaths have normal intelligence, their thinking is essentially superficial. Despite an ability to learn, they do not profit by the lessons of their own experience, so their behavior is out of step with what they abstractly know. In fact they not only seem indifferent to the consequences for other people of what they do, but they do not seem concerned about the almost certain unfortunate consequences for themselves.

According to Hare (2003): "The psychopath is one of the most fascinating and distressing problems of human experience. . . . A psychopath can have high verbal intelligence, but they typically lack 'emotional intelligence.' " Hare has developed "The Hare Psychopathy Checklist-Revised" containing the most highly researched and recognized characteristics of psychopathic personality. This

Table 6.1
Antisocial Personality Disorder

A. Current age at least 18.

B. Evidence of conduct disorder with onset before age 15, as indicated by a history of *three* or more of the following:
   (1) was often truant
   (2) ran away from home overnight at least twice while living in parental or parental surrogate home (or once without returning)
   (3) often initiated physical fights
   (4) used a weapon in more than one fight
   (5) forced someone into sexual activity with him or her
   (6) was physically cruel to animals
   (7) was physically cruel to other people
   (8) deliberately destroyed others' property (other than by fire-setting)
   (9) deliberately engaged in fire-setting
   (10) often lied (other than to avoid physical or sexual abuse)
   (11) has stolen without confrontation of a victim on more than one occasion (including forgery)
   (12) has stolen with confrontation of a victim (e.g., mugging, purse-snatching, extortion, armed robbery)

C. A pattern of irresponsible and antisocial behavior since the age of 15, as indicated by at least *four* of the following:
   (1) is unable to sustain consistent work behavior, as indicated by any of the following (including similar behavior in academic setting if the person is a student):
       (a) significant unemployment for six months or more within five years
       (b) repeated absences from work unexplained by illness in self or family
       (c) abandonment of several jobs without realistic plans for others
   (2) fails to conform to social norms with respect to lawful behavior, as indicated by repeatedly performing antisocial acts that are grounds for arrest (whether arrested or not), e.g., destroying property, harassing others, stealing, pursuing an illegal occupation
   (3) is irritable and aggressive, as indicated by repeated physical fights or assaults (not required by one's job or to defend someone or oneself), including spouse- or child-beating
   (4) repeatedly fails to honor financial obligations, as indicated by defaulting on debts or failing to provide child support or support for other dependents on a regular basis
   (5) fails to plan ahead, or is impulsive, as indicated by one or both of the following:
       (a) traveling from place to place without a prearranged job or clear goal for the period of travel or clear idea about when the travel will terminate
       (b) lack of a fixed address for a month or more
   (6) has no regard for the truth, as indicated by repeated lying, use of aliases, or conning others for personal profit or pleasure
   (7) is reckless regarding his or her own or others' personal safety, as indicated by driving while intoxicated or recurrent speeding
   (8) if a parent or guardian lacks ability to function as a responsible parent, as indicated by one or more of the following:
       (a) malnutrition of child
       (b) child's illness resulting from lack of minimal hygiene
       (c) failure to obtain medical care for a seriously ill child
       (d) child's dependence on neighbors or nonresident relatives for food or shelter
       (e) failure to arrange for a caretaker for young child when parent is away from home
       (f) repeated squandering, on personal items, of money required for household necessities
   (9) has never sustained a totally monogamous relationship for more than one year
   (10) lacks remorse (feels justified in having hurt, mistreated or stolen from another)

D. Occurrence of antisocial behavior not exclusively during the course of schizophrenia or manic episodes

Source: American Psychiatric Association. *Diagnostic and Statistical Manual of Mental Disorders*, 4th ed. (Copyright 1994 American Psychiatric Association), pp.344–346. Reprinted with permission.

checklist and other information about the psychopathic personality can be found on his Web site www.hare.org

Steinberg (2002, p.37) sums up the psychopathic personality: "Psychopathy is a type of personality disorder defined chiefly by a combination of antisocial behavior, callousness and emotional detachment." He (p.43) contends: "Today's sense of urgency over the need to determine which offenders are genuine psychopaths has its origins in the now infamously wrong prediction about the coming wave of superpredators."

Steinberg (p.36) points out: "There are many reasons to sound a note of caution within the juvenile and criminal justice systems about the potential overuse of psychopathy as a diagnostic label when applied to juveniles. Juveniles who are branded as psychopaths are more likely to be viewed as incorrigible, less likely to receive rehabilitative dispositions, and, if it is an option, more likely to be transferred to the criminal justice system to be tried as adults and face the possibility of adult sanctions, including incarceration in adult jails and prisons."

Labeling a youth as a psychopath reduces the youth's likelihood of receiving rehabilitation and increases the youth's likelihood of being transferred to the criminal justice system and treated as an adult.

Another, perhaps less stigmatizing way to view violent youth is to describe them as having a conduct disorder.

Conduct Disorders

The term *conduct disorder* appears often in discussions about youths' problems. **Conduct disorder** is a politically correct term describing the anger exploding among violent teenagers. The American Psychiatric Association states that this disorder is characterized by prolonged antisocial behavior and can range from truancy to fistfights.

According to Focus Adolescent Services: "Conduct disorder is the most serious psychiatric disorder in childhood and adolescence. Those with this disorder have great difficulty following rules and behaving in a socially acceptable way. They are often viewed by other children, adults and social agencies as 'bad' or delinquent, rather than mentally ill."

Most youths with conduct disorders should be viewed as mentally ill rather than as delinquent.

Focus Adolescent Services reports that children or adolescents with conduct disorder may exhibit some of the following behaviors:

- Aggression to people and animals (including bullying, fighting, robbing, forcing someone into sexual activity and abusing animals)
- Destruction of property
- Deceitfulness, lying or stealing
- Serious violations of rules (violating curfew, running away, being truant)

Youngsters with conduct disorders are likely to have ongoing problems if they and their families do not receive early and comprehensive *treatment*. Treatment is discussed in Chapter 13.

According to Burns et al. (pp.4–5): "Conduct disorder is characterized by externalizing behaviors as opposed to internalizing behaviors. It is not surprising, then, that this disorder is found more often among juveniles referred to the juvenile justice system than in the general population. In one review of nine studies, the prevalence rates of conduct disorder for juveniles in the juvenile justice system ranged from 10 to 90 percent, and rates were higher for incarcerated juveniles than for those residing in the community."

Many people believe juvenile violence will be an unavoidable part of life in American society unless significant changes are made in how such youths are identified *before* they become seriously delinquent. Reasons for the increase in the seriousness of the offenses and the decrease in the age of the offenders range from the problems of increasing gang activity and drug use in the elementary schools to the heightened level of violence in society in general and to increasing stress on families, especially in economically deprived areas. One primary reason for the rise in teen violence is the ready availability of handguns.

Guns and Juveniles

According to Holtz (2003, p.90): "Statistics show that every year more than 30,000 people—more than 4,000 of whom are children—die as a result of gunshot wounds." In announcing a program to develop comprehensive gun violence reduction programs, President Bush said: "In America today, a teenager is more likely to die from a gunshot than from all natural causes of death combined."

Child Health USA 2002 reports: "Results from the 2001 Youth Risk Behavior Survey reveal that 17.4 percent of students had carried a weapon, such as a gun, knife or club. On one or more days in the last 30 days nearly 6 percent had carried a gun. Boys (29.3 percent) were significantly more likely to carry a weapon than girls (6.2 percent). The percent of high school students who carry weapons had decreased significantly since 1991 but has remained level since 1997."

Lizotte and Sheppard (2001, p.1) report: "Although many adolescents own and use guns for legitimate, legal sporting activities, other youths report that they own and carry guns for protection or for the purpose of committing a crime." Table 6.2 describes the percentage of boys involved in delinquency by gun ownership status.

Table 6.2
Percentage of Boys Involved in Delinquency by Gun Ownership Status

Type of Delinquency	Gun Ownership Status (%)		
	No Gun Owned (n = 548)	Gun Owned for Sport (n = 27)	Gun Owned for Protection (n = 40)
Gun carrying	3.2	11.1	70.0
Gun crime	1.3	3.7	30.0
Street crime	14.8	18.5	67.5
Gang membership	7.2	11.1	55.0
Drug selling	3.5	7.4	32.5

Source: Alan Lizotte and David Sheppard. *Gun Use by Male Juveniles: Research and Prevention*. Washington, DC: OJJDP Juvenile Justice Bulletin, July 2001, p.2. (NCJ 188992)

Concerned parents pick up their children after a student was shot, but not killed when he was dropped off for school at Benjamin Tasker Middle School.

Boys who own guns for protection are significantly and substantially more likely to be involved in delinquent behavior than either those who do not own guns or those who own guns for sport.

Lizotte and Sheppard (p.2) found that: "A protection owner was 6 times more likely than a sport owner to carry a gun. Further, protection owners were 8 times more likely than sport owners to commit a gun crime, 3.5 times more likely to commit a street crime, nearly 5 times more likely to be in a gang and 4.5 times more likely to sell drugs—all statistically significant differences." In many cases youths obtain weapons not by buying them but as gifts from parents or other relatives.

Many think it is wholly inappropriate for parents or legal guardians to supply children with weapons and that such adults should be held liable, under parental-responsibility laws, for any crimes youths commit with those weapons. Unfortunately, parental-responsibility law is a gray area. Child access prevention (CAP) laws may also hold adults accountable when youths are allowed access to guns. Such charges are harder to dismiss than parental-responsibility laws. Unlike parent-responsibility laws, CAP laws draw a direct causal relationship between adults and the crimes committed by juveniles. If a parent possesses a firearm and fails to keep the firearm away from their children, it is easier to connect that to a criminal act by the child using the firearm. Florida passed the first CAP law in 1989, and 14 other states have enacted similar legislation. If you look at the figures and the rise in youth violence, one of the spikes is youth committing homicides against youth. The only comparable spike that matches it is youths in possession of guns.

Violent Juvenile Crime

 The FBI's Violent Crime Index includes murder and nonnegligent manslaughter, forcible rape, robbery and aggravated assault.

America's Children: Key National Indicators of Well-Being 2002 (2002, p.iv) reports: "Since 1993, the violent crime offending rate for youths ages 12 to 17 has decreased by 67 percent from 52 violent crimes per 1,000 youth in 1993 to 17 per 1,000 youths in 2000." According to Snyder (2002, p.1): "Arrests of juveniles accounted for 12 percent of all violent crimes cleared by arrest in 2000—specifically 5 percent of murders, 12 percent of forcible rapes, 16 percent of robberies and 12 percent of aggravated assaults." Table 6.3 summarizes the number of juvenile arrests during 2000 for Violent Crime Index Offenses.

Using data from the Uniform Crime Reports, Snyder (p.4) reports: "Juvenile arrests for violence in 2000 were the lowest since 1988." Table 6.4 shows the percent change in arrests from 1991 to 2000 for both juveniles and adults.

Table 6.3
Number of Juvenile Arrests in 2000 for Violent Crime Index Offenses

The number of juvenile arrests in 2000—2.4 million—was 5 percent below the 1999 level and 15 percent below the 1996 level

| Most Serious Offense | 2000 Estimated Number of Juvenile Arrests | Percent of Total Juvenile Arrests | | Percent Change | | |
		Female	Under Age 15	1991–2000	1996–2000	1999–2000
Total	2,369,400	28%	32%	3%	-15%	-5%
Crime Index total	617,600	28	38	-28	-27	-5
Violent Crime Index	98,900	18	33	-17	-23	-4
Murder and nonnegligent manslaughter	1,200	11	13	-65	-55	-13
Forcible rape	4,500	1	39	-26	-17	-5
Robbery	26,800	9	27	-29	-38	-5
Aggravated assault	66,300	23	36	-7	-14	-4

In 2000, there were an estimated 1,200 juvenile arrests for murder. Between 1996 and 2000, juvenile arrests for murder fell 55 percent.

Females accounted for 23 percent of juvenile arrests for aggravated assault and 31 percent of juvenile arrests for other assaults (i.e., simple assaults and intimidations) in 2000. Females were involved in 59 percent of all arrests for running away from home and 31 percent of arrests for curfew and loitering law violations.

Note: Detail may not add to totals because of rounding.

Source: *Crime in the United States 2000.* Washington, DC: U.S. Government Printing Office, 2001. Arrest estimates were developed by the National Center for Juvenile Justice.

Table 6.4
Percent Change in Arrests 1991–2000

Most Serious Offense	Juvenile	Adult
Violent Crime Index	-17%	-10%
Murder	-65	-37
Forcible rape	-26	-30
Robbery	-29	-32
Aggravated assault	-7	-1

Source: *Crime in the United States 2000.*

Snyder (p.4) notes: "There were 309 arrests for Violent Crime Index offenses for every 100,000 youths between 10 and 17 years of age. If each of these arrests involved a different juvenile (which is unlikely), then no more than 1 in every 320 persons ages 10 through 17 was arrested for a Violent Crime Index offense in 2000."

 About one-third of 1 percent of juveniles ages 10 to 17 were arrested for violent crimes in 2000. The decline in arrests for violent juvenile crime continued in 2001.

Table 6.5 shows this decline and how the arrests divide by age.

Murder

The murder rate in 2000 was the lowest since 1965. In 2000 an estimated 1,200 juveniles were arrested for murder. In 2001 this figure dropped to 957, about one-tenth of the total number of murders. This was a 65 percent decrease from 1991.

Snyder (p.6) notes that the juvenile arrest rate for murder peaked in 1993 when about 3,800 people under age 18 were arrested for murder. In the 7 years before the peak, the juvenile arrest rate for murder more than doubled. In the 7 years following the peak, the juvenile arrest murder rate fell 74 percent, dropping to the lowest level in more than two decades and erasing all earlier growth.

Ousey and Augustine (2001) studied the relationship between juvenile firearm homicide rates, concentrated disadvantage, racial inequality and the juvenile illicit drug market activity. They found partial support for the concentrated disadvantage and the juvenile drug market explanations, but, contrary to expectations, these relationships were significant only in models for white juveniles.

Forcible Rape

According to Snyder (p.6) the juvenile arrest rate for forcible rape did not vary as much as the rates for the other violent crimes from 1980 to 2000. The rate increased 44 percent between 1980 and 1991 and then fell. By 2000 it was 13 percent less than the 1980 rate, at its lowest level in at least two decades.

In 2000 an estimated 4,500 juveniles were arrested for forcible rape, a decrease of 26 percent from 1991. Females constituted 1 percent of those arrested; youths under age 15 constituted 39 percent. In 2001 an estimated 3,119 youths were arrested for forcible rape.

Table 6.5
Arrests by Age, 2001

Offense charged	Total all ages	Ages under 15	Ages under 18	Ages 18 and over	Under 10	10–12	13–14	15	16	17	18	19	20	21
TOTAL	9,324,953	498,986	1,558,496	7,766,457	22,966	119,245	356,775	300,890	365,291	393,329	456,715	469,414	443,163	401,775
Percent distribution[1]	100.0	5.4	16.7	83.3	0.2	1.3	3.8	3.2	3.9	4.2	4.9	5.0	4.8	4.3
Murder and non-negligent manslaughter	9,426	114	957	8,469	6	9	99	134	254	455	582	643	618	587
Forcible rape	18,576	1,180	3,119	15,457	34	323	823	509	662	768	885	879	836	774
Robbery	76,667	4,354	18,111	58,556	95	920	3,339	3,515	4,746	5,496	6,336	5,835	4,745	4,151
Aggravated assault	329,722	16,498	44,815	284,907	878	4,524	11,096	8,215	9,646	10,456	12,083	12,745	12,737	13,634
Burglary	198,883	23,287	61,623	137,260	1,390	6,344	15,553	11,631	13,066	13,639	14,725	12,370	10,029	8,278
Larceny-theft	806,093	92,317	238,605	567,488	3,859	25,384	63,074	44,914	50,469	50,905	49,976	41,258	33,503	28,024
Motor vehicle theft	102,607	8,425	33,563	69,044	68	1,036	7,321	8,007	8,892	8,239	7,679	6,648	5,231	4,613
Arson	12,763	4,048	6,313	6,450	677	1,439	1,932	905	757	603	555	404	338	339
Violent crime[2]	434,391	22,146	67,002	367,389	1,013	5,776	15,357	12,373	15,308	17,175	19,886	20,102	18,936	19,146
Percent distribution[1]	100.0	5.1	15.4	84.6	0.2	1.3	3.5	2.8	3.5	4.0	4.6	4.6	4.4	4.4
Property crime[3]	1,120,346	128,077	340,104	780,242	5,994	34,203	87,880	65,457	73,184	73,386	72,935	60,680	49,101	41,254
Percent distribution[1]	100.0	11.4	30.4	69.6	0.5	3.1	7.8	5.8	6.5	6.6	6.5	5.4	4.4	3.7
Crime Index Total[4]	1,554,737	150,223	407,106	1,147,631	7,007	39,979	103,237	77,830	88,492	90,561	92,821	80,782	68,037	60,400
Percent distribution[1]	100.0	9.7	26.2	73.8	0.5	2.6	6.6	5.0	5.7	5.8	6.0	5.2	4.4	3.9
Other assaults	898,298	70,642	163,142	735,156	3,348	20,436	46,858	30,260	31,942	30,298	29,736	30,578	31,115	33,400
Forgery and counterfeiting	77,692	422	3,975	73,717	22	81	319	525	1,117	1,911	3,457	4,234	4,235	3,953
Fraud	211,177	958	5,830	205,347	54	173	731	880	1,558	2,434	5,460	7,802	9,193	9,271
Embezzlement	13,836	83	1,258	12,578	1	16	66	86	380	709	945	993	851	803
Stolen property: buying receiving, possessing	84,047	4,982	18,467	65,580	135	1,008	3,839	3,630	4,637	5,218	6,155	5,469	4,842	4,207
Vandalism	184,972	31,597	71,962	113,010	2,921	9,608	19,068	12,391	14,202	13,772	12,067	10,022	8,073	7,636
Weapons: carrying, possessing, etc.	114,325	8,691	25,861	88,464	479	2,203	6,009	4,721	5,763	6,686	7,711	7,182	6,319	6,113
Prostitution and commercialized vice	58,638	155	1,034	57,604	4	16	135	152	263	464	1,244	1,646	1,689	1,780
Sex offenses (except forcible rape and prostitution)	62,997	6,625	12,381	50,616	428	2,010	4,187	2,016	1,833	1,907	2,166	2,168	2,048	1,979

Table 6.5—(continued)

Offense charged	Total all ages	Ages under 15	Ages under 18	Ages 18 and over	Under 10	10–12	13–14	15	16	17	18	19	20	21
Drug abuse violations	1,091,240	24,061	139,238	952,002	297	2,976	20,788	24,956	38,401	51,820	71,912	70,475	64,907	57,536
Gambling	7,769	129	1,000	6,769	2	11	116	191	266	414	441	465	450	418
Offenses against the family and children	93,909	2,296	6,286	87,623	253	592	1,451	1,245	1,443	1,302	1,887	2,070	2,463	2,876
Driving under the influence	946,694	629	13,397	933,297	381	28	220	613	3,425	8,730	21,508	28,753	32,661	42,911
Liquor laws	408,203	8,879	92,326	315,877	174	643	8,062	14,209	27,162	42,076	65,734	69,163	56,822	12,174
Drunkenness	423,561	1,805	13,971	409,590	128	152	1,525	2,081	3,493	6,592	12,321	13,707	13,765	18,283
Disorderly conduct	425,751	47,043	117,635	308,116	1,463	12,240	33,340	23,932	23,891	22,769	21,063	19,478	18,253	20,349
Vagrancy	19,509	394	1,607	17,902	9	81	304	307	424	482	925	781	678	660
All other offenses (except traffic)	2,453,100	76,546	269,317	2,183,783	4,083	16,011	56,452	53,524	65,657	73,590	99,055	113,533	116,653	116,926
Suspicion	2,629	277	834	1,795	20	51	206	194	215	148	107	113	109	100
Curfew and loitering law violations	100,701	28,245	100,701	—	570	5,020	22,655	22,910	28,394	21,152	—	—	—	—
Runaways	91,168	34,304	91,168	—	1,187	5,910	27,207	24,237	22,333	10,294	—	—	—	—

[1]Because of rounding, the percentage may not add to total.

[2]Violent crimes are offenses of murder, forcible rape, robbery and aggravated assault.

[3]Property crimes are offenses of burglary, larceny-theft, motor vehicle theft and arson.

[4] Includes arson.

(9,511 agencies; 2001 estimated population 192,580,262)

Source: Crime in the United States. Washington, DC: Federal Bureau of Investigation, 2002, p.244.

Zolondek et al. (2001) studied self-reported characteristics of juvenile sex offenders and concluded that offenders often began sexual **deviance*** at a young age, had committed multiple sex offenses and had committed other delinquent acts. The victims were usually younger children the offenders had known. In most cases, offenders did not resort to physical force in committing their offenses.

Righthand and Welch (2001) conducted a review of the professional literature on juveniles who have sexually offended. They (p.xi) caution: "The scope of the problem [of sexual abuse] may be underestimated because juvenile sex offenders known to the system may represent only a small proportion of juveniles who have committed such offenses. Studies of adult sex offenders suggest another dimension of the problem: many of these offenders began their sexually abusive behavior in their youth."

Robbery

The juvenile arrest rate for robbery declined during much of the 1980s, falling 30 percent between 1980 and 1988. The rate increased 70 percent between the low year of 1988 and the peak years of 1994 and 1995. Between these years and 2000, the juvenile robbery arrest rate declined 57 percent, its lowest level in two decades (Snyder, p.6).

In 2000 an estimated 26,800 juveniles were arrested for robbery, a decrease of 29 percent. In 2001 an estimated 18,110 juveniles were arrested for robbery.

Aggravated Assault

Unlike the juvenile arrest rate trends for murder and robbery, the decline in the juvenile arrest rate for aggravated assault between 1994 and 2000 did not erase the increase that began in the mid-1980s. Although the juvenile aggravated assault arrest rate fell 30 percent between 1994 and 2000, the 2000 rate was still 42 percent more than the 1980 level. Among the four Violent Crime Index offenses, only aggravated assault had a juvenile arrest rate in 2000 that was not at its lowest level in two decades (Snyder, p.6).

In 2000 an estimated 66,300 juveniles were arrested for aggravated assault, a 7 percent decrease since 1991. In 2001 44,815 juveniles were arrested for aggravated assault.

The Decline in Juvenile Arrests for Violent Index Crimes

Butts (2000, p.1) notes: "The year thought to be the beginning of the crime decline varies depending on which data elements are used to measure violent crime." He uses the peak year of violent crime as 1995 when the national number of arrests for Violent Crime Index offenses reached a high point of nearly 800,000. Snyder places the peak year for juvenile crime as 1994. Lynch (2002, p.1), likewise, cites 1994 as the peak year for juvenile crime.

Regardless of the year used, criminologists have proposed several reasons for the sudden decline.

 Explanations for the decline in violent crime include a strong economy, changing demographics, changes in the market for illegal drugs and the use of firearms, expanded imprisonment, policing innovations and a growing cultural intolerance for violent behavior (Blumstein and Wallman, 2000).

---

*Behavior that departs from the social norm.

The statistics supporting the decline in violent crime are all from the FBI's Uniform Crime Reports (UCR), figures that reflect offenses reported to the police. As Lynch (p.3) points out: "A large, nonrandom portion of offending behavior is not reported to the police." In addition to looking for trends using the FBI's data, Lynch also studied the results of the National Crime Victimization Survey (NCVS). He (p.16) concludes: "This examination of offending using NCVS data confirms the general picture of offending derived from UCR arrest data."

School Crime and Violence

While incidents of school violence are to be taken seriously and have received much media attention recently, such publicity has also generated a widespread but baseless fear that today's schools are teeming with violent youths. In fact, in *Indicators of School Crime and Safety: 2001* Kaufman et al. (2001, p.iii) report: "National indicators affirm that the levels of crime in school have continued to decline, that acts that promote fear and detract from learning are decreasing, and that students feel more safe in school than they did a few years ago."

 Like violent crime, school crime and violence are decreasing.

And that trend continued into 2002. In *Indicators of School Crime and Safety: 2002* Devoe et al. (2002, p.v) report:

> In 2000 students ages 12 through 18 were victims of about 1.9 million total crimes of violence or theft at school. In that same year, students in this age range were victims of about 128,000 serious violent crimes at school (i.e., rape, sexual assault, robbery and aggravated assault). There were also 47 school-associated violent deaths in the United States between July 1, 1998, and June 30, 1999, including 38 homicides, 33 of which involved school-aged children.
>
> The total nonfatal victimization rate for students ages 12 through 18 generally declined between 1992 and 2000 from 144 per 1,000 students in 1992 to 72 per 1,000 students in 2000. . . .
>
> However, the prevalence of other problem behavior at school has increased. For example, in 2001, 8 percent of students reported that they had been bullied at school in the last six months, up from 4 percent in 1999.
>
> Students also seem to feel more secure at school now than just a few years ago. The percentage of students ages 12 through 18 who reported avoiding one or more places at school for their own safety decreased from 9 percent in 1995 to 5 percent in 1999 and 2001 (p.vi).
>
> Between 1993 and 2001, the percentage of students in grades 9 through 12 who reported carrying a weapon such as a gun, knife or club on school property within the previous 30 days declined from 12 percent to 6 percent (p.ix).

For many people the words "school violence" bring to mind images of weapon-wielding youths. Hoang (2001, pp.18–19), however, states: "The definition of school violence, an unacceptable social behavior ranging from aggression to violence that threatens or harms others, goes beyond highly publicized incidents of mass bloodshed to include acts such as bullying, threats and extortion."

Bullying

Some parents, other adults and even students tend to dismiss schoolyard bullying as a rite of passage, a simple cycle of the big kids picking on the little kids, who in turn grow up to be the big kids who pick on the little kids, and so on. However, the U.S. Department of Education asserts that **bullying** is more than just big versus small: "Bullying involves intentional, repeated hurtful acts, words or other behavior. There is a real or perceived power imbalance between bully and victim" (Peterson, 2001, p.18). They note bullying may be:

- Physical—hitting, kicking, spitting, pushing, punching, poking, hair-pulling, biting.
- Verbal—name-calling, taunting, gossip, malicious teasing, making threats.
- Psychological/Emotional—rejection, humiliation, ostracism, intimidation, extortion, spreading rumors, manipulating social relationships, berating personal characteristics such as perceived sexual orientation.
- Sexual—harassment and actual abuse.

Sampson (2002, p.2) notes: "Bullying has two key components: *repeated harmful acts* and an *imbalance of power.* It involves repeated physical, verbal or psychological attacks or intimidation directed against a victim who cannot properly defend him- or herself because of size or strength, or because the victim is outnumbered or less psychologically resilient."

Research has shown an estimated 1.6 million children in grades 6 through 10 in the United States are bullied at least once a week, and 1.7 million children bully others as often (Ericson, 2001, p.1). Bullying is a serious concern because of its far-reaching and long-lasting impact. Ericson (p.1) contends: "Bullying can affect the social environment of a school, creating a climate of fear among students, inhibiting their ability to learn, and leading to other antisocial behavior . . . such as vandalism, shoplifting, skipping or dropping out of school, fighting, and the use of drugs and alcohol."

If the bullying is intense enough, it may even cause the victim to commit suicide. As one social work professor says: "Suicide is bullying's quiet little secret. It's one kid at a time, so it doesn't catch our attention" (Piazza, 2001, p.68).

The effects of bullying can also lead its victims to turn their anger and frustration outward. Consider the following excerpt from a 15-year-old boy's journal:

> I hate being laughed at. But they won't laugh after they're scraping parts of their parents, sisters, brothers and friends from the wall of my hate.

These are the words of Kip Kinkel, who later killed his parents and then went on a shooting spree at his high school in Springfield, Oregon, killing two students and wounding two dozen more. Kinkel was not the only juvenile to take out frustrations through school violence.

Wooden and Blazak (2001, p.45) suggest other consequences of bullying: "Victims tend to have chronic physical and psychological problems, including low self-esteem, depression and the tendency to become chronic victims. Their problems can reach into adulthood, leading to fearfulness and schizophrenia."

The most serious consequences of bullying are chronic physical and psychological problems, suicide and school shootings.

School Shootings

Small and Tetrick (2001, p.3) note: "Crime and violence in schools are a matter of significant public concern, particularly after the spate of tragic school shootings in recent years." School shootings have occurred throughout the United States, from Alaska to Florida, from Pennsylvania to California as shown in Table 6.6.

Despite the geographic spread, a common thread seems to pull a majority of these events together: "Many of the recent shooters have felt put upon at school. Even the Secret Service worries about bullying. A study run by its National

Table 6.6
Summary of School Shootings in the United States, February 1996 to March 2001

Date	Location and Estimated Population	Number Killed	Number Wounded	Shooter(s)
February 2, 1996	Moses Lake, WA (16,300)	2 students, 1 teacher	1	Barry Loukaitis, 14
February 19, 1997	Bethel, AK (6,500)	1 student, principal	2	Evan Ramsey, 16
October 1, 1997	Pearl, MS (23,600)	2 students	7	Luke Woodham, 16
December 1, 1997	West Paducah, KY (25,800)	3 students	5	Michael Carneal, 14
December 15, 1997	Stamps, AR (2,400)	0	2	Colt Todd, 14
March 24, 1998	Jonesboro, AR (52,500)	4 students, 1 teacher	10	Mitchell Johnson, 13 Andrew Golden, 11
April 24, 1998	Edinboro, PA (6,800)	1 teacher	2 students	Andrew Wurst, 14
May 19, 1998	Fayetteville, TN (7,500)	1	0	Jacob Davis, 18
May 21, 1998	Springfield, OR (50,700)	2 students	22	Kip Kinkel, 15
June 15, 1998	Richmond, VA (199,300)	0	1 teacher, 1 guidance counselor	Male, 14
April 20, 1999	Littleton, CO (41,300)	14 students (including 2 shooters), 1 teacher	23	Eric Harris, 18 Dylan Klebold, 17
May 20, 1999	Conyers, GA (8,500)	0	6	Thomas Solomon, 15
November 19, 1999	Deming, NM (14,900)	1 student	0	Victor Cordova, Jr., 12
December 6, 1999	Fort Gibson, OK (3,800)	0	4 students	Seth Trickey, 13
February 29, 2000	Mt Morris, MI (3,100)	1 (6-year-old)	0	Male, 6
May 26, 2000	Lake Worth, FL (29,000)	1 teacher	0	Nathaniel Brazil, 13
March 5, 2001	Santee, CA (53,900)	2	13	Charles Williams, 15
March 7, 2001	Williamsport, PA (29,900)	0	1	Elizabeth Bush, 14
March 22, 2001	El Cajon, CA (90,200)	0	5	
September 24, 2003	Cold Spring, MN (3,000)	2 students	0	Jason McLaughlin, 15

Source: Adapted from Borgna Brunner, editor. *The Time Almanac,* 2002, p.362.

Population data from the U.S. Bureau of the Census

Threat Assessment Center found that in about two-thirds of 37 school shootings over the last 25 years, the attackers felt 'persecuted, bullied, threatened, attacked or injured' " (Peterson, p.17).

In a study of school shootings, the FBI's National Center for the Analysis of Violent Crime (NCAVC) found: "In general, people do not switch instantly from nonviolence to violence. Nonviolent people do not 'snap' or decide on the spur of the moment to meet a problem by using violence. Instead, the path toward violence is an evolutionary one, with signposts along the way (O'Toole, 2000, p.7). Often a student lets out his feelings through clues in the weeks and months before a violent act. O'Toole (p.16) notes: "These clues can take the form of subtle threats, boasts, innuendos, predictions or ultimatums. They may be spoken or conveyed in stories, diary entries, essays, poems, letters, songs, drawings, doodles, tattoos or videos." As Wattendorf (2002, p.11) asserts: "In 75 percent of the 37 shooting incidents studied, school shooters disclosed their plans in advance to classmates."

Prinz (2000, p.24), likewise, observes: "It is rare that youths who initiate school violence have no history of problem behavior of any kind."

 School shootings almost never occur without warning.

Myths about School Shooters

O'Toole (p.4) cites the following widespread but wrong or unverified impressions of school shooters:

- School violence is an epidemic.
- All school shooters are alike.
- The school shooter is always a loner.
- School shootings are exclusively revenge motivated.
- Easy access to weapons is the most significant risk factor.
- Unusual or aberrant behaviors, interests and hobbies are hallmarks of the student destined to become violent.

As Lawrence (2000, p.1) notes: "Violence in schools attracts widespread media coverage. Hundreds of newspaper and television stories have been done on incidents of school violence, in spite of the fact that school violence has *not* been increasing, and the fact that the number of youth killed or injured per day by other means far outnumbers those killed or injured in school." Responding to the problem of school shootings as well as general crime and violence in the schools is discussed in Chapter 8.

Sometimes crime and violence in the schools is made worse by the presence of gangs. Gang violence also spills into the streets.

Gang Violence

Gang activity, when viewed from a juvenile justice perspective, is a study in violent crime. A perpetual cycle of violence by gang rivalries can date back many years. Gang members often do not know why they came to be rivals.

Hill et al. (2001, p.1) assert: "Gang members engage in more delinquent behavior than their peers who are not in gangs. . . . Other studies also show that gang members are more likely to commit violent crimes and property crimes and use drugs. They are more than twice as likely to carry guns."

> Street gangs acquire their power in the community through violent behavior.

Shelden et al. (2001, p.110) note that part of the violence is due to the fact that "gangs often attract young men who, frankly, enjoy violence." The ready availability of guns, "especially the high-powered, semiautomatic weapons have profoundly altered the balance of power on the streets."

According to Miller (2001, p.iii): "The last quarter of the 20th Century was marked by significant growth in youth gang problems across the United States. In the 1970s, less than half the states reported youth gang problems, but by the late 1990s, every state and the District of Columbia reported youth gang activity. In the same period, the number of cities reporting youth gang problems mushroomed nearly tenfold—from fewer than 300 in the 1970s to more than 2,500 in 1998."

The 2000 National Youth Gang Survey (Egley and Mehala, 2002, p.1) reported 24,500 gangs with about 772,500 gang members active in 3,330 jurisdictions. The 2001 National Youth Gang Survey (Egley and Major, 2003, p.1) found an estimated 3,000 jurisdictions across the United States experiencing gang activity. Just as violent juvenile crime and school crime and violence have been declining, so has the number of gangs.

Howell et al. (2002, p.2) report that gangs tend to form later in less populated jurisdictions. They note: "Compared with gangs in earlier onset jurisdictions, gangs in later onset jurisdictions tended to have younger members, a slightly larger proportion of female members and a much larger proportion of Caucasian and African-American members." Moore and Hagerdorn (2001, p.5) contend: "In general, female gang members commit fewer violent crimes than male gang members and are more inclined to property crimes and status offenses." They (p.3) also found: "There is one aspect of female gang life that does not seem to be changing—the gang as a refuge for young women who have been victimized at home."

Definitions

Everyone has a general definition of gang. But in the context of juvenile justice, it is important that terms associated with gangs are clear and understood. In the context of juvenile justice, a **gang** is an ongoing group of people that have a common name or common identifying sign or symbol, form an allegiance for a common purpose and engage in unlawful or criminal activity.

A **street gang** is a group of individuals who meet over time, have identifiable leadership, claim control over a specific territory in the community and engage in criminal behavior. Street gangs engage in criminal activity either individually or collectively. They create an atmosphere of fear and intimidation in a community. The **youth gang** is a subset of the street gang.

An important distinction must be made between youth gangs and delinquent groups. Research has shown that gang members engage in significantly more criminal behavior than members of delinquent groups; they have higher rates of police contact, more arrests and more drug-related offenses.

Illegal Activity

The primary characteristic distinguishing gangs from lawful groups is illegal activity. Gang members commit a full range of street crimes, although the most distinctive form of gang offense is gang fighting, in which two or more gangs engage in violent combat. Occasionally, innocent bystanders are caught in the crossfire, yet as Shelden et al. (p.128) note: "The major victims of gang violence are other gang members. Innocent bystanders are rarely the victims, despite claims of law enforcement and other officials to the contrary."

 Gang activity ranges from property crimes to violent crimes against persons and includes graffiti painting, vandalism, arson, student extortion, teacher intimidation, drug dealing, rape, stabbings and shootings.

Often gang members have minimal financial or worldly assets. Their most important possession becomes their reputation. A "hard look" or minor insult directed at a gang member by a rival gang member must be avenged, an attitude that results in the bloodbaths often seen on urban streets. In fact, a gang's reputation is often enhanced by engaging in vicious, violent crimes.

Drive-by shootings receive much media attention, particularly when stray bullets hit an innocent child or adult. Sometimes the shooters hit their mark and realize after the fact that it was a case of mistaken identity. Curry et al. (2001, p.1) report that the overall number of youth gang homicides in U.S. cities declined during the 1990s. They also report that Los Angeles and Chicago stand out among cities with the highest rates of gang homicide.

Thornberry and Burch (1997) report on a study to determine what portion of delinquency in American society is attributable to gang members. Among the findings (p.2) were that gang membership made up 30 percent of the youth population, yet 65 percent of the delinquent acts were committed by gang members: "The data . . . indicate that gang members' delinquencies are not proportionate to their representation in the larger population." Furthermore: "The disproportionate contribution of gang members to delinquency is greater for the more serious crimes." The general results of the study are presented in Figure 6.2. Table 6.7 compares gang and nongang criminal behavior.

Statistically significant differences at the .001 level occur for auto theft, assault rivals, assault own members, drive-by shootings, guns and knives in school, concealed weapons, drug sales and drug theft.

Causes of Gangs and Why Youths Join Them

Two separate yet very related questions are: (1) What causes gangs? and (2) Why do youths continue to join gangs? Myriad studies have identified causes for gangs and what attracts youths to join them. Rowell (2000, p.35) suggests: "Gangs grow because the gang provides kids with basic human needs. These include the need for security, love, friendship, acceptance, food, shelter, discipline, belonging, status, respect, identification, power and money."

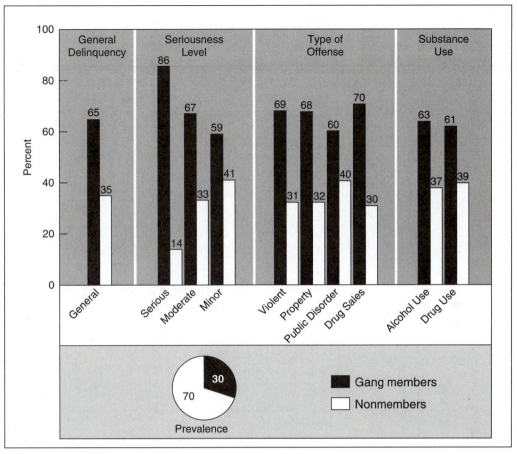

Figure 6.2
Percent of Delinquent Acts Attributable to Gang Members and Prevalence of Gang Membership

Source: Terence P. Thornberry and James H. Burch II. *Gang Members and Delinquent Behavior.* Washington, DC: OJJDP Juvenile Justice Bulletin, June 1997, p.3.

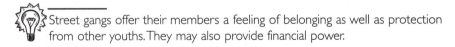 Street gangs offer their members a feeling of belonging as well as protection from other youths. They may also provide financial power.

Allender (2001, p.4) contends: "Young people normally seek gang involvement for some combination of the following five reasons: (1) structure, (2) nurturing, (3) sense of belonging, (4) economic opportunity and (5) excitement." Table 6.8 summarizes the prevailing theories about why gangs exist.

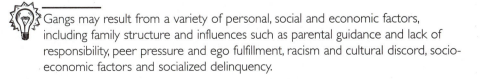 Gangs may result from a variety of personal, social and economic factors, including family structure and influences such as parental guidance and lack of responsibility, peer pressure and ego fulfillment, racism and cultural discord, socioeconomic factors and socialized delinquency.

Table. 6.7
**Comparison of Gang
and Nongang Criminal
Behavior (Cleveland)**

Crime(p[1])	Gang N = 47	Nongang N = 49
Auto Theft (***)	44.7%	4.1%
Assault Rivals (***)	72.3	16.3
Assault Own Members (*)	30.4	10.2
Assault Police (n.s.)	10.6	14.3
Assault Teachers (n.s.)	14.9	18.4
Assault Students (n.s.)	51.1	34.7
Mug People (n.s.)	10.6	4.1
Assault in Streets (*)	29.8	10.2
Theft-Other (***)	51.1	14.3
Intim/Assault Vict/Wit (***)	34.0	0.0
Intim/Assault Shoppers (*)	23.4	6.1
Drive-by Shooting (***)	40.4	2.0
Homicide (**)	15.2	0.0
Sell Stolen Goods (*)	29.8	10.2
Guns in School (***)	40.4	10.2
Knives in School (***)	38.3	4.2
Concealed Weapons (***)	78.7	22.4
Drug Use (**)	27.7	4.1
Drug Sales (School) (n.s.)	19.1	8.2
Drug Sales (Other) (***)	61.7	16.7
Drug Theft (***)	21.3	0.0
Bribe Police (n.s.)	10.6	2.0
Burglary (Unoccupied) (*)	8.5	0.0
Burglary (Occupied) (n.s.)	2.1	2.0
Shoplifting (n.s. [0.58])	30.4	14.3
Check Forgery (n.s.)	2.1	0.0
Credit Card Theft (n.s.)	6.4	0.0
Arson (*)	8.5	0.0
Kidnapping (n.s.)	4.3	0.0
Sexual Assault/Molest (n.s.)	2.1	0.0
Rape (n.s.)	2.1	0.0
Robbery (*)	17.0	2.0

Level of statistical significance: *p<.05, **p<.01, ***p<.001; n.s. = no significant
difference.

Source: Ronald C. Huff. *Comparing the Criminal Behavior of Youth Gangs and At-
Risk Youths.* National Institute of Justice Research in Brief, October 1998, p.4.
(NCJ 172851)

Table 6.8
Theories of Why Gangs Exist

Theory/Creator or Major Proponent	Premise
Social Disorganization Theory/Thrasher	Industrialization, urbanization and immigration break down institutional, community-based controls in certain areas. Local institutions in these areas (schools, families, churches) are too weak to give the people living there a sense of community. Consequently, within such environments, conventional values are replaced by a subculture of criminal values and traditions that persist over time, regardless of who moves into or out of the area.
Strain Theory/Merton	The lack of integration between culturally defined goals (professional success, wealth and status) and the legitimate, institutionalized means of achieving these goals imposes a strain on people, who may, as a result, react with deviant criminal behavior. Thus, people at an economic disadvantage are motivated to engage in illegitimate activities (perhaps because of the unavailability of jobs, lack of job skills, education and other factors).
Cultural-Deviance (Subcultural) Theory/Cohen	Working-class youth are ill-prepared for participation in middle-class institutions and thus become frustrated. This situation leads to reaction formation, which, in turn, fosters the development of a delinquent (gang) subculture, in which the values of middle-class society are turned upside down. These values enable youth to gain status and improved financial standing through non-utilitarian, malicious, negative behavior.
Social Learning Theory/Sutherland	Youth become delinquent through association with other delinquents and also through contact with social values, beliefs and attitudes that support criminal/delinquent behavior.
Social Bond (Control) Theory/Hirschi	Youths drift into gangs because of the limbo-like nature of adolescence—being suspended between childhood and adulthood, having greater expectations placed on them than when they were children, yet lacking the rights and privileges of adults. Proper socialization is essential at this critical juncture, which effectively "bonds" youth to society. What keeps people in check and away from deviant behavior is the social bond to society, especially the internalized norms of society.
Social Development Theory	Integrates social learning theory with control/bonding theory. The major cause of delinquency is a lack of bonding to family, school and prosocial peer groups coupled with the reinforcement of delinquent behavior. Looks at 17 risk factors (societal/cultural and individual/interpersonal) present before the onset of delinquency to determine whether, and to what extent one is likely to become involved in persistent delinquent activity.
Labeling Perspective	Youths who are simply hanging out together may be referred to as a gang often enough that they come to feel as if they are a gang.
Critical/Marxist Perspectives	The capitalist political and economic system produces inequality. Those oppressed by capitalism engage in various types of crimes related to accommodation and resistance (predatory crime, personal crime) in an attempt to adapt to their disadvantaged positions and to resist the problems created by capitalist institutions.

Source: Adapted from Randall G. Shelden et al. *Youth Gangs in American Society*. Belmont, CA: Wadsworth Publishing Company, 1997, pp. 28–49. Reprinted by permission.

These combined factors may be pictured as spokes in a wheel. The more spokes, the stronger the wheel. The gang itself is the hub of the wheel, supporting the rest.

Family Structure

Probably the most important factor in the formation of a gang member is family structure. Shelden et al. (pp.203–204) state:

> Nearly every criminologist agrees that the family is probably the most critical factor related to crime and delinquency. In fact, for over 50 years research has shown that three or four family-related factors best distinguish the habitual delinquent from the rest of his or her peers. These factors include the affection of the parents toward the child (the lower the level of affection, the higher the rate of delinquency), the kind of discipline the parents use (those who use consistently harsh and physical discipline will produce the most habitual and violent delinquent), the prolonged absence of one or both parents (those from single-parent households are more likely to become delinquent), and the degree of supervision provided by the parents (the lesser the amount of supervision, the higher the rate of delinquency).

Chapter 3 discussed the importance of families in developing children's feelings of belonging and self-worth. If youths do not get this support at home or at school, they will seek it elsewhere. The largest draw a gang has for its young members is a sense of belonging, of importance, of family.

Investigators have found certain common threads running through most families that have hard-core gang members. A family containing gang members is quite often a racial minority on some form of government assistance. It often lacks a male authority figure. If a male authority figure is present, he may be a criminal or drug addict, therefore representing a negative role model. Typically, adult family members lack more than an elementary school education. Children live with minimal adult supervision.

When a child first encounters law enforcement authorities, the dominant figure (usually the mother) makes excuses for the child, normally in the form of accusations against society. Thus children are taught early that they are not responsible for their actions and are shown how to transfer blame to society.

A second common type of family structure is one that may have two strong family leaders in a mother and father. Usually graduates from gangs themselves, they see little wrong with their children belonging to gangs. This attitude serves to perpetuate the traditional gang culture.

A third common family structure involves immigrant groups and parents who do not speak English. The children tend to adapt rapidly to the American way of life and, en route, lose respect for their parents and the traditions of their native culture. They quickly become experts at manipulating their parents, and the parents lose all control. This family structure is often seen with Asian gang members. It is important to recognize that many of these family structures overlap.

Peer Pressure and Ego Fulfillment

A natural part of adolescence is a shift from seeking the approval and acceptance of parents and teachers to seeking the approval and acceptance of one's peers.

Youths in Brooklyn, New York, play with toy guns as a prelude to becoming gang members when real guns will replace these toys.

When a child's family has never been a true source of approval or acceptance, as is the case with many gang-members-to-be, the need for acceptance by peers is that much stronger. Consequently, the lure of the gang may be nearly irresistible, and the transition into gang life may occur more readily for these youths.

For some youths the prestige and recognition that come with gang affiliation fulfill an egotistic need that they cannot achieve through other, more mainstream, associations. They may see themselves as rebels, and the sense of danger and adventure inherent in gang activity satisfies a need to take risks. In fact biochemical research has shown that certain people thrive on the adrenaline rush that accompanies fear and risk-taking, and some researchers postulate that youths who are drawn to gangs may have a biological/chemical makeup that drives them to seek dangerous liaisons.

Racism and Cultural Discord

Racism played an early and important role in the formation of street gangs in California. Racism often results in a particular group banding together, lending support to one another and excluding all other groups, sometimes even seeking to harm members of other groups. Although racism is most often associated with white people showing prejudice against nonwhites, in reality racism refers to the belief that one's own ethnic group is superior to all others. Walker et al. (2000, p.54) clarify the role of racism in gang formation: "Most gangs are racially and ethnically homogenous. . . . Although violent conflicts do occur between and within ethnic gangs, violence is seldom the reason for gang formation. Racism as a societal phenomenon that creates oppressive conditions can contribute to gang formation. However, individual racism explains very little in terms of the formation of gangs or the decision to join gangs." They also mention neo-Nazi, or skinhead, gangs as a notable exception, with gang formation almost exclusively a function of individual racism.

© Katherine McGlynn

Socioeconomic Pressure

To some members, the gang is all about money and power and a chance to get out of the ghetto. Youth who do not have legitimate options for buying fancy clothes or cars may see gangs, crime and selling drugs as attractive alternatives. Such a perspective is supported by both the strain and cultural-deviance theories described previously in Table 6.8.

In a pioneering work on gangs—*The Gang: A Study of 1,313 Gangs in Chicago* (1927)—Thrasher concluded that gangs resulted from a breakdown in social controls, particularly among newly arriving immigrants who settled in Chicago's ganglands. Gangs created a social order where none existed. This can be a partial explanation for why so many Asian gangs are currently forming across the country.

Socialized Delinquency

Socialized delinquency is common among lower-class children who have been frustrated or hurt by a predominantly middle-class society. To youths socialized delinquency is not delinquency at all. It is delinquency only in terms of middle-class standards. When individuals behave in ways sanctioned by their culture— the gang—they feel no guilt for their unlawful activities. The gang, in effect, becomes a surrogate family. Within this family, violence toward others is common. One reason for this is that gang members were often neglected or abused as children. Other factors can also help predict who might become a gang member. Table 6.9 summarizes the risk factors for youth gang membership.

Precursors of Gang Membership

Hill et al. (p.1) stress: "Understanding what predicts gang membership is vital for preventing youths from joining gangs." Table 6.10 presents risk factors for gang membership.

Types of Gangs

 Contemporary gangs may be classified as scavenger, territorial or corporate.

Scavenger Gangs

Members of a **scavenger gang** often have no common bond beyond their impulsive behavior and the need to belong. Leadership changes weekly, even daily sometimes. They are urban survivors who prey on the weak of the inner city. Their crimes are usually petty, senseless and spontaneous. They often commit acts of violence just for fun. They have no particular goals, no purpose and no substantial camaraderies. Generally scavenger gang members are characteristically low achievers and illiterates with short attention spans. They are prone to violent, erratic behavior, and most come from the lower class and the underclass.

Territorial Gangs

A **territorial gang** or **crew** designates something or someplace as belonging exclusively to the gang. The traditional designation of a gang's territory is better known as **turf.**

Table 6.9
Risk Factors for Youth Gang Membership

Domain	Risk Factors
Community	Social disorganization, including poverty and residential mobility
	Organized lower-class communities
	Underclass communities
	Presence of gangs in the neighborhood
	Availability of drugs in the neighborhood
	Availability of firearms
	Barriers to and lack of social and economic opportunities
	Lack of social capital
	Cultural norms supporting gang behavior
	Feeling unsafe in neighborhood: high crime
	Conflict with social control institutions
Family	Family disorganization, including broken homes and parental drug/alcohol abuse
	Troubled families, including incest, family violence and drug addiction
	Family members in a gang
	Lack of adult male role models
	Lack of parental role models
	Low socio-economic status
	Extreme economic deprivation, family management problems, parents with violent attitudes, sibling antisocial behavior
School	Academic failure
	Low educational aspirations, especially among females
	Negative labeling by teachers
	Trouble at school
	Few teacher role models
	Educational frustration
	Low commitment to school, low school attachment high levels of antisocial behavior in school, low achievement test scores and identification as being learning disabled
Peer group	High commitment to delinquent peers
	Low commitment to positive peers
	Street socialization
	Gang members in classroom
	Friends who use drugs or who are gang members
	Friends who are drug distributors
	Interaction with delinquent peers
Individual	Prior delinquency
	Deviant attitudes
	Street smartness: toughness
	Defiant and individualistic character
	Fatalistic view of the world
	Aggression
	Proclivity for excitement and trouble
	Locuro (acting in a daring, courageous and especially crazy fashion in the face of adversity)
	Higher levels of normlessness in the context of family, peer group and school
	Social disabilities
	Illegal gun ownership
	Early or precocious sexual activity, especially among females
	Alcohol and drug use
	Drug trafficking
	Desire for group rewards, such as status, identity, self-esteem, companionship and protection
	Problem behaviors, hyperactivity, externalizing behaviors, drinking, lack of refusal skills and early sexual activity
	Victimization

Source: James C. Howell. *Youth Gangs Overview.* Washington, DC: Office of Juvenile Justice and Delinquency Prevention, August 1998, pp.6–7. (NCJ 167249)

Table 6.10
Childhood Predictors of Joining and Remaining in a Gang

Risk Factor	Odds Ratio*	Risk Factor	Odds Ratio*
Neighborhood		**Individual**	
Availability of marijuana	3.6	Low religious service attendance	ns‡
Neighborhood youth in trouble	3.0	Early marijuana use	3.7
Low neighborhood attachment	1.5	Early violence§	3.1 (2.4)
Family		Antisocial beliefs	2.0
Family structure†		Early drinking	1.6
One parent only	2.4	Externalizing behaviors§	2.6 (2,6)
One parent plus other adults	3.0	Poor refusal skills	1.8
Parental attitudes favoring violence	2.3		
Low bonding with parents	ns‡	

*Odds of joining a gang between the ages of 13 and 18 for youth who scored in the worst quartile on each factor at ages 10 to 12 (fifth and sixth grades), compared with all other youth in the sample. For example, the odds ratio for "availability of marijuana" is 3.6. This means that youth from neighborhoods where marijuana was most available were 3.6 times more likely to join a gang, compared with other youth.

†Compared with two-parent households.

‡ns = not a significant predictor.

§These factors also distinguished sustained gang membership (more than 1 year) from transient membership (1 year or less). For each factor, the number in parentheses indicates the odds of being a sustained gang member (compared with the odds of being a transient member) for youth at risk on that factor.

Source: Karl G. Hill; Christina Lui and J. David Hawkins. *Early Precursors of Gang Membership: A Study of Seattle Youth.* Washington, DC: OJJDP Juvenile Justice Bulletin, December 2001, p.4.

Low household income	2.1
Sibling antisocial behavior	1.9
Poor family management	1.7
School	
Learning disabled	3.6
Low academic achievement	3.1
Low school attachment	2.0
Low school commitment	1.8
Low academic aspirations	1.6
Peer group	
Association with friends who engage in problem behaviors§	2.0 (2.3)

Once scavenger gangs get serious about organizing, they become territorial gangs. At this stage the gang defines itself and someone assumes leadership. Gangs defend their turf to protect their particular business. Mobility through financial power has greatly enhanced the traditional definition of territory and turf. Prior to the windfall of illegal drug profits, the concept of *territory* was confined to the immediate neighborhood. However, today, with the power of organized crime, technology and increased financial leverage, a gang's territory can be intrastate, interstate or even international.

Organized/Corporate Gangs

These well-organized groups are characterized by having very strong leaders or managers. The primary focus of a **corporate gang** is participation in illegal moneymaking operations. Discipline is akin to that of the military, and goals resemble those of Fortune 500 corporations.

RICO (Racketeer Influenced and Corrupt Organization Act) was an important measure of the Organized Crime Control Act passed in 1970. The act was designed to limit the activity of organized crime by defining racketeering to include conspiring to use racketeering as a means of making income, collecting loans or conducting business. Although aimed at organized crime, RICO statutes can also be applied to the illegal activities of gangs.

Gangs may also be classified as hedonistic, instrumental or predatory.

A **hedonistic gang** focuses on having a good time, usually by smoking pot, drinking beer and sometimes engaging in minor property crimes.

An **instrumental gang,** in contrast, focuses on money, committing property crimes for economic reasons rather than for the thrill. Although some may sell drugs, this is not their primary activity. Members may also smoke pot and drink beer. This categorization fits well with the distinction between instrumental violence and expressive violence. **Instrumental violence** uses violence as a way to obtain material possessions. It is a juvenile justice issue. **Expressive violence,** in contrast, is a way to vent emotions. Violence is simply a way of life and always has been.

A **predatory gang** commits more violent crimes against persons, including robberies and street muggings. These gangs are likely to use hard drugs such as crack cocaine, which contributes to their volatile, aggressive behavior.

Gang Structure—Leadership and Organization

Compared with other types of law-violating youth groups, gangs usually have a more formalized structure. Varying levels of involvement can be found in most gangs. Most gangs contain leaders, hard-core members, regular members and fringe members or wannabes.

Gang leadership tends to be better defined and more clearly identifiable than leadership in other types of delinquent groups. The leaders are usually the oldest members of the gang and have extensive criminal records. They may surround themselves with hard-core members, giving orders and expecting unquestioned obedience. The hard-core members usually commit the crimes and are the most violent. Some have had to earn the right to become true gang members through some sort of initiation.

On the fringes of most gangs are youths who aspire to become gang members, called *wannabes.* They dress and talk like the hard-core members, but they have not yet been formally accepted into the gang. Walker (2003) contends that the term wannabe should not be used: "By overlooking the fact that these youths have adopted a gang name, use gang signs and symbols and commit crimes, these youths are "Gonnabes." Their progression from high-risk youth to hard-core gang member is illustrated in Table 6.11.

Another group of youths could be described as "potentials" or "could be's." Figure 6.3 shows one typical gang organization.

Associational Patterns

Compared with other types of law-violating youth groups, gangs tend to have closer relational bonds and more continuous affiliation between members. Gangs usually adopt specific criteria for membership eligibility, and many gangs employ initiation rituals, often involving one or more criminal acts, as a prerequisite to membership. Gang members also demonstrate associational patterns and bonds through certain identifying characteristics such as their names, symbols and communication styles.

Ages	Risk Indicators
Table 6.11 **The Development and Path of a High-Risk Youth**	
8	Youth plays outdoors a lot and is difficult to bring into the house.
9	Youth gets into mischief and neighborhood disputes.
10	Youth has first contact with police for petty thefts, vandalism, fire-setting and animal abuse.
11	Youth engages in malicious and mischievous play; enters into delinquent networking (gang) activity; engages in stealing and destroying property.
12	Youth develops conflict with societal norms and values, resulting in further peer and older youth criminal networking activity; experiments with drugs and alcohol; bullies younger children; is truant and unruly.
13–14	Youth's gang identity emerges as a result of community's failure to integrate youth into adult law-abiding society, commits residential burglaries and bicycle thefts; deals with stolen property; becomes runner for drug entrepreneur.
15–16	Youth's behavior characterized by loyalty to the gang; gang becomes family and provides education and experience. Youth commits burglaries and other thefts to finance drugs and alcohol; sells drugs; engages in auto theft and fraud. Youth's high truancy results in underachieving, leading to school dropout; becomes a social thrownaway; comes to the attention of the police.
16–17	Gang member: Youth, because of behavior; becomes institutionalized for violent acts; murder, rape, assault; is heavy drug and alcohol user. Gang nonmember or loner: Youth is highly socially dysfunctional; turns on family to vent frustration over inability to be socially stable; considers and may fulfill self-destruction.
18–20	Gang member: Youth goes from delinquent to more criminal associates; is intravenous drug abuser; commits crimes to satisfy addiction; is highly volatile; commits crimes against women and, if married, abuses spouse and children. Gang nonmember: Youth, if no criminal record or a gang dropout and from a highly dysfunctional family, has tendency to commit violent acts against women and children.

Gang Recruitment

Transforming a youth into a gang member involves slow assimilation. Once youths reach an age at which they can prove themselves to peer leaders within the gang, they may perform some sort of rite of passage or ceremony called "turning," "quoting" or "jumping in." Or they may be "courted in," simply accepted into the gang without having to prove themselves in any particular way.

According to Shelden et al. (p.69): "Most youth are informally socialized into the gang subculture from a very early age so that they do not so much join a gang, but rather evolve into the gang naturally. Actually turning or being jumped is little more than a rite of passage."

Gang Myths

This chapter has contained many generalizations about gangs and gang members from many sources. A fitting conclusion is to consider the following myths about gangs:**

- **Myth**—*The majority of street gang members are juveniles.*
  Fact—Juveniles, those who are 18 years or younger, actually compose a minority of gang membership.

- **Myth**—*All street gangs are turf-oriented.*
  Fact—Some gangs may not claim any specific turf, while other gangs may operate in multiple locations or even in very unsuspecting small cities.

**Courtesy of Lorne Kramer, Chief of Police, Colorado Springs, Colorado.

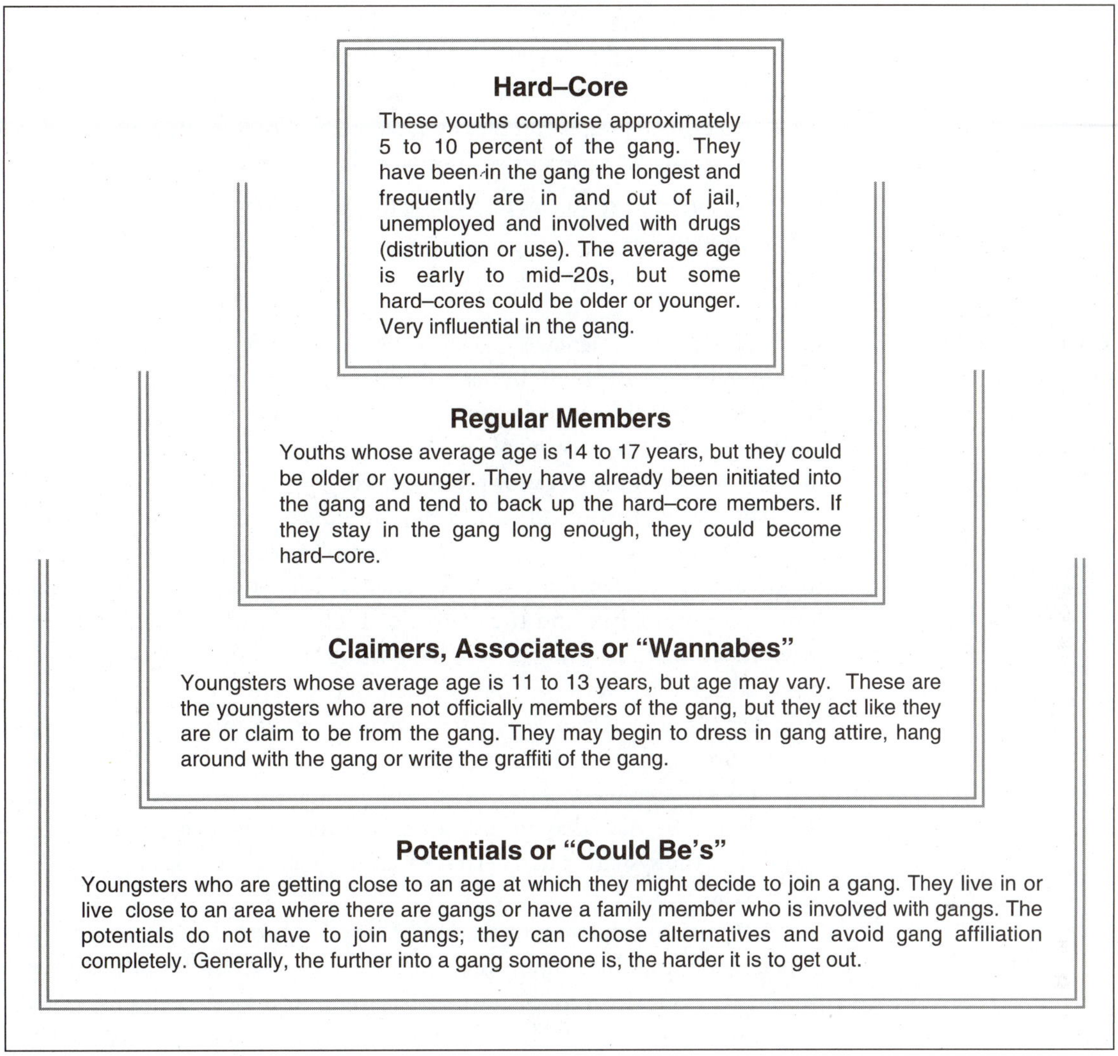

Hard–Core

These youths comprise approximately 5 to 10 percent of the gang. They have been in the gang the longest and frequently are in and out of jail, unemployed and involved with drugs (distribution or use). The average age is early to mid–20s, but some hard–cores could be older or younger. Very influential in the gang.

Regular Members

Youths whose average age is 14 to 17 years, but they could be older or younger. They have already been initiated into the gang and tend to back up the hard–core members. If they stay in the gang long enough, they could become hard–core.

Claimers, Associates or "Wannabes"

Youngsters whose average age is 11 to 13 years, but age may vary. These are the youngsters who are not officially members of the gang, but they act like they are or claim to be from the gang. They may begin to dress in gang attire, hang around with the gang or write the graffiti of the gang.

Potentials or "Could Be's"

Youngsters who are getting close to an age at which they might decide to join a gang. They live in or live close to an area where there are gangs or have a family member who is involved with gangs. The potentials do not have to join gangs; they can choose alternatives and avoid gang affiliation completely. Generally, the further into a gang someone is, the harder it is to get out.

Figure 6.3
Gang Organizational Chart

- **Myth**—*Gang weapons usually consist of chains, knives and tire irons.*
  Fact—Perhaps brass knuckles, knives and chains were the key weapons in the gangs of yesteryear, but today Uzis, AK-47s and semiautomatic firepower are the weapons of choice.

- **Myth**—*All gangs have one leader and are tightly structured.*
  Fact—Most gangs are loosely knit groups and likely will have several leaders. If one member is killed, other potential gang leaders seem to be waiting in the wings.

- **Myth**—*One way to cure gang membership is by locking the gang member away.*
  Fact—Incarceration and rehabilitation of hard-core gang members has not proven to be effective. Changing criminal behavior patterns is difficult. Prisons often serve as command centers and institutions of higher learning

for ongoing gang-related crime. Often prisoners are forced to take sides with one group or another simply for protection.

- **Myth**—*Gangs are a law enforcement problem.*
  Fact—Gangs are a problem for everyone. Communities need to develop system-wide programs to effectively address the gang problem in their areas.

Programs and strategies to address the gang problem are discussed in Chapters 8 through 13.

The Public Health Model and the Juvenile Justice Perspective

One approach to violence is to view it not just as a problem to be dealt with by the juvenile justice system, but as a threat to our national health. When violence is viewed in this way, it makes sense to adopt the approach used in our public health system. A basic principle of the public health response to problems is to focus resources on the areas of greatest need.

Another contribution from the public health model is the metaphor of **contagion** as a way to explain the spread of violence. Acts of violence tend to spread rapidly within high-risk areas or hot spots and within groups. Some criminologists find the source of high rates of violence in a subculture of violence that encourages people—young males in particular—to use physical force to command respect and settle conflicts. Others view violence as spreading through cycles of revenge and retaliation among perpetrators and victims.

This explanation of the rapid spread of violence as a kind of retaliation or self-help can be viewed as an indication that those who engage in violence have no faith in the system. They perceive that justice is not to be obtained through the system.

A barrier to implementing a public health approach is the distinct and opposing philosophical traditions of the two approaches. From the juvenile justice perspective, the most important fact about the social reality of violence in our society is that those who perpetrate violence are criminal offenders. The juvenile justice system has its roots in the adult criminal justice system, which is part of the classical tradition that conceives of human action as a product of rational and moral choice. Public health is rooted in positivist conceptions of human behavior as "caused" by external forces that, in principle, are subject to modification.

 The juvenile justice perspective on juvenile violence is that it is the result of youths' free choice and is to be punished as criminal. The public health perspective is that youths are victims of social forces and they are to be treated.

How these conflicting philosophies translate into programming for the prevention and treatment of delinquency is discussed in Section Four. Before leaving the discussion of violent offenders, consider a matrix for organizing risk factors for violent behavior that pulls several of the findings reported in this chapter together.

Analyzing and Organizing Risk Factors for Violent Behavior

Table 6.12 presents a matrix for organizing risk factors for violent behavior.

Two illustrations show how violence resulted in the death of a child and then how the matrix helps to explain what happened. The first illustration involved Dave, Evelyn and their 10-month-old son Jason. Evelyn had just turned 20 when Jason was born, and Dave had just lost his job. The family was struggling, and Dave became moody and argumentative. During some of the arguments over money, Dave would slap Evelyn, but always begged forgiveness. He also began to resent Jason. Evelyn, hoping to help the situation, went back to work as a waitress. Her first day back at work Dave "hit bottom," overwhelmed by feelings of humiliation and rejection with his new role as babysitter. Jason's crying made it worse. And nothing Dave did could stop the crying. When Jason wet on Dave, Dave lost control, filled the bathtub with scalding water and held

Table 6.12
Matrix for Organizing Risk Factors for Violent Behavior

Units of Observation and Explanation	Proximity to Violent Events and Their Consequences		
	Predisposing	Situational	Activating
Social Macrosocial	Concentration of poverty Opportunity structures Decline of social capital Oppositional cultures Sex role socialization	Physical structure Routine activities Access: weapons, emergency medical services	Catalytic social-event
Microsocial	Community organizations Illegal markets Gangs Family disorganization Preexisting structures	Proximity of responsible monitors Participants' social relationships Bystanders' activities Temporary communication impairments Weapons: carrying, displaying	Participants' communication exchange
Individual Psychosocial	Temperament Learned social responses Perceptions of rewards/penalties for violence Premeditation Violent deviant sexual preferences Social, communication skills Self-identification in social hierarchy	Accumulated emotion Alcohol/drug consumption Sexual arousal	Impulse Opportunity recognition
Biological	Neurobehavioral* "traits" Genetically mediated traits Chronic use of psychoactive substances or exposure to neurotoxins	Transient neurobehavioral* "states" Acute effects of psychoactive substances	Sensory signal processing errors

*Includes neuroanatomical, neurophysiological, neurochemical and neuroendocrine. "Traits" describe capacity as determined by status at birth, trauma and aging processes such as puberty. "States" describe temporary conditions associated with emotions, external stressors, etc.

Source: Jeffrey A. Roth. *Understanding and preventing Violence*. National Institute of Justice. Research in Brief. Washington, DC: February 1994, p.7. Adapted from Albert Reiss, Jr., and Jeff A. Roth eds., *Understanding and Preventing Violence*. Washington, DC: National Academy Press, 1993, p. 297. Reprinted by permission

Jason in the tub by his arm and leg, causing third-degree burns over 35 percent of his body, according to the medical examiner's report.

The second illustration involves a beer bash in a tough blue-collar suburb involving two friends, Andy and Bob, who had begun drinking heavily as teenagers. In this tough town, Bob was known as one of the toughest, almost always winning his fights. He had recently lost his job for missing work and had spent time in jail after a bar brawl. At this particular beer bash, Bob began making passes at Andy's sister, who resisted the passes and finally slapped him. Several partygoers began laughing at Bob. Andy, wanting to protect his sister, came at Bob. As they began to fight, Andy's older brother told them to "take it outside," which they did. The crowd followed, cheering them on. Bob got a tire iron out of his car's trunk and knocked Andy out, then proceeded to get in his car and drive over him two times. Andy died in the hospital four hours later from massive internal injuries. These two examples demonstrate the risk factors in operation, as shown in Table 6.13.

Table 6.13
Examples of Possible Risk Factors in Two Murders

Units of Observation and Explanation	Proximity to Violent Events and Their Consequences		
	Predisposing	Situational	Activating
Social Macrosocial	1. Low neighborhood social interaction.	1. No child care providers in neighborhood.	
	2. Neighborhood culture values fighting, drinking, sexual prowess.	2. No local emergency medical services.	
Microsocial	1. Dave began hitting Evelyn months ago.	1. Baby cries. Dave unable to cope.	1. Baby wets Dave.
	2. Widespread expectations of wild drinking parties at Andy's house.	2. Charlene humiliates Bob by resisting his advances.	2. Older brother says "take it outside", crowd goes outside to watch and cheer.
Individual Psychosocial	1. Dave has low self-esteem.	1. Dave humiliated by Evelyn's new job, his own lack of parenting skills.	
	2. Bob develops adolescent pattern of drinking and violent behavior.	2. Threats to Andy's family status, Bob's personal status.	
Biological	2. Possible familial traits of alcoholism and antisocial behavior in Bob's family.	2. Andy, Bob and bystanders under alcohol influence.	
	Murder 1: 10-month-old baby scalded to death by father; no witnesses.	Murder 2: 20-year-old male beaten and intentionally run over by automobile; many witnesses.	

Source: Jeffrey A. Roth. *Understanding and Preventing Violence*. Washington, DC: National Institute of Justice Research in Brief, February 1994, p. 8. Adapted from Albert Reiss, Jr. and Jeff A. Roth, eds., *Understanding and Preventing Violence*. Washington, DC: National Academy Press, 1993, p.297. Reprinted by permission.

Violence and the Media

The influence of violence in the media is often blamed for the amount of violence in society. The American Psychological Association Commission on Violence and Youth takes a stronger position, stating (p.33): "Children's exposure to violence in the mass media, particularly at young ages, can have harmful lifelong consequences." The Commission noted: "Aggressive habits learned early in life are the foundation for later behavior. . . . A longitudinal study of boys found a significant relation between exposure to television violence at 8 years of age and antisocial acts—including serious, violent criminal offenses and spouse abuse— 22 years later."

The media also greatly affects how the public views juvenile violence. Paradoxically, the relative infrequency of juvenile violent crime increases its newsworthiness and leads to frequent appearance in crime news. Says Lawrence (p.1): "Crime news thus takes the rare crime event and turns it into the common crime image." Concurring, Dorfman and Schiraldi (2001, p.6) contend: "Relatively few youth are arrested each year for violent crimes, yet the message from the news is that this is a common occurrence. . . . Violence stories made up 25 percent of all youth coverage, when only three young people in 100 perpetrated or became victims of violence."

Summary

The two general onset trajectories for youth violence are early, in which violence begins before puberty, and late, in which violence begins in adolescence. Most youth violence begins in adolescence and ends with the transition into adulthood. Predictors of youth violence include exposure to violence, early aggressive behavior, early delinquency and animal abuse. Other predictors of violent behavior include ineffective parenting and lack of supervision, accepting aggressive behavior as normal, having problems in school and banding together with others like themselves.

Some delinquency is rooted in psychopathic behavior. However, labeling a youth as a psychopath reduces the youth's likelihood of receiving rehabilitation and increases the youth's likelihood of being transferred to the criminal justice system and treated as an adult. Most youths with conduct disorders should be viewed as mentally ill rather than as delinquent.

The ready availability of guns is partially responsible for youth violence. Boys who owned guns for protection were significantly and substantially more likely to be involved in delinquent behavior than either those who did not own guns or those who owned guns for sport.

The FBI's Violent Crime Index includes murder and nonnegligent manslaughter, forcible rape, robbery and aggravated assault. About one-third of 1 percent of juveniles ages 10 to 17 were arrested for a violent crime in 2000. The decline in arrests for violent juvenile crime continued in 2001. Explanations for the decline in violent crime include a strong economy, changing demographics, changes in the market for illegal drugs and the use of firearms, expanded imprisonment, policing innovations and a growing cultural intolerance for violent behavior.

Like violent crime, school crime and violence are decreasing. The most serious consequences of bullying are chronic physical and psychological problems, suicide and school shootings. School shootings almost never occur without warning.

Yet another challenge facing the juvenile justice system is gangs. Street gangs acquire their power in the community through their violent behavior. Gang activity ranges from property crimes to violent crimes against persons and includes graffiti painting, vandalism, arson, student extortion, teacher intimidation, drug dealing, rape, stabbings and shootings. Street gangs offer their members a feeling of belonging as well as protection from other youths. They may also provide financial power. Gangs may result from a variety of personal, social and economic factors, including family structure and influences such as parental guidance and lack of responsibility, peer pressure and ego fulfillment, racism and cultural discord, socioeconomic factors and socialized delinquency.

Contemporary gangs may be classified as scavenger, territorial or corporate. They may also be classified as hedonistic, instrumental or predatory. The juvenile justice perspective on juvenile violence is that it is the result of youths' free choice and is to be punished as criminal. The public health perspective is that youths are victims of social forces and they are to be treated.

Discussion Questions

1. Have there been any instances of youths involved in serious, violent crimes in your community during the past year?
2. When you think of serious, violent crime, what comes to mind?
3. Should parents and guardians be held legally responsible when a juvenile commits a violent crime? Why or why not?
4. For serious, violent crimes, such as armed robbery and murder, should the age of the offender be an issue?
5. Why do you think violent juvenile crime is declining?
6. Did you experience bullying when you were growing up? If so, describe it and how it made you feel.
7. Are there gangs in your community? If so, what problems do they cause?
8. Have you seen any movies or TV programs about gangs? How are gang activities depicted?
9. What do you think are the main reasons people join gangs?
10. How does a youth gang member differ from other juveniles?

InfoTrac College Edition Assignments

- Use InfoTrac College Edition to answer the Discussion Questions as appropriate.
- Read and outline one of the following articles and be prepared to share your findings with the class:
  - "Violent Crimes among Juveniles: Behavioral Aspects" by William Andrew Corbitt.
  - "Gangs in Middle America: Are They a Threat?" by David M. Allender.
  - "Addressing School Violence: Prevention, Planning and Practice" by Francis Q. Hoang.

Internet Assignments

Complete one of the following assignments and be prepared to share your findings with the class.

- Go to the National Institute of Justice Web site to find and read any of the NCJ publications listed in the references for this chapter.

- Go to any Web site listed for references listed in this chapter and outline the material: Child Health USA, Children's Safety Network, Hare, Youth Violence.

- Go to CourtTV.com and select Court TV's Crime Library and find *The Young Rampage Killer* to read and outline.

- Go to the National Gang Crime Research Center at http://www.ngcrc.com and outline their resources on gangs.

- Go to the Gangs Or Us Web site at http://www.gangsorus.com and outline their resources on gangs.

- Go to http://www.surgeongeneral.gov to read and outline the surgeon general's report on youth violence.

References

Allender, David M. "Gangs in Middle America: Are They a Threat?" *FBI Law Enforcement Bulletin,* December 2001, pp.1–9.

American Psychological Association. *Violence & Youth: Psychology's Response,* Vol. 1. Summary Report of the American Psychological Association Commission on Violence and Youth, no date.

America's Children: Key National Indicators of Well-Being 2002. Washington, DC: Federal Interagency Forum on Child and Family Statistics, July 2002.

Ascione, Frank R. *Animal Abuse and Youth Violence.* Washington, DC: OJJDP Juvenile Justice Bulletin, September 2001. (NCJ 188677)

Blumstein, Alfred and Wallman, Joel (Editors). *The Crime Drop in America.* New York: Cambridge University Press, 2000.

Burns, Barbara J.; Howell, James C.; Wiig, Janet K.; Augimeri, Leena K.; Welsh, Brendan C.; Loeber, Rolf; and Petechuk, David. *Treatment, Services and Intervention Programs for Child Delinquents.* Washington, DC: Child Delinquency Bulletin Series, March 2003.

Butts, Jeffrey A. *Youth Crime Drop.* Washington, DC: Urban Institute, December 2000.

Butts, Jeffrey and Travis, Jeremy. *The Rise and Fall of American Youth Violence: 1980 to 2000.* Washington, DC: Urban Institute Justice Policy Center, March 2002.

Chesney-Lind, Meda and Paramore, Vickie V. "Are Girls Getting More Violent?" *Journal of Contemporary Criminal Justice,* May 2001, pp.142–166.

Child Health USA 2002. "Violence." http://www.mchire.net/HTML/CHUSA-02

Children's Safety Network Economics and Insurance Resource Center, National Public Services Research Institute, Landover, MD, 2000. http://www.csneirc.org/csneirc/pubs/can/us-can.htm

Corbitt, William Andrew. "Violent Crimes among Juveniles." *FBI Law Enforcement Bulletin,* June 2000, pp.18–21.

Cottle, Cindy C.; Lee, Ria J.; and Heilbrun, Kirk. "Identifying Risk Factors for Juvenile Recidivism in Juveniles: A Meta-Analysis." *Criminal Justice and Behavior,* Vol. 28, No. 3, 2001, p.367.

Crime in the United States 2000. Washington, DC: U.S. Department of Justice, Federal Bureau of Investigation, 2001.

Curry, G. David; Maxson, Cheryl L.; and Howell, James C. *Youth Gang Homicides in the 1990s.* Washington, DC: OJJDP Fact Sheet #03, March 2001. (FS 200103)

DeVoe, Jill F.; Ruddy, Sally A.; Miller, Amanda K.; Planty, Mike; Peter, Katharin; Kaufman, Phillip; Duhard, Detis T.; and Rand, Michael R. *Indicators of School Crime and Safety: 2002.* Washington, DC: U.S. Departments of Education and Justice, November 2002. (NCJ 196753)

Dorfman, Lori and Schiraldi, Vincent. *Off Balance: Youth, Race & Crime in the News.* Berkeley Media Studies Group and the Justice Policy Institute, April 2001.

Egley, Arlen, Jr. and Major, Aline K. *Highlights of the 2001 National Youth Gang Survey.* Washington, DC: OJJDP Fact Sheet #01, April 2003. (FS 200301)

Egley, Arlen, Jr. and Mehala, Arjunan. *Highlights of the 2000 National Youth Gang Survey.* Washington, DC: OJJDP Fact Sheet #04, February 2002. (FS 200204)

Embry, Dennis D. "More Violent Young Offenders?" *Corrections Today,* December 2001, pp.96–153.

Ericson, Nels. *Addressing the Problem of Juvenile Bullying.* Washington, DC: OJJDP Fact Sheet #27, June 2001. (FS 200127)

Female Offenders. Washington, DC: National Center for Juvenile Justice, February 18, 2003. http://brendan.ncjfcj.unr.edu/homepage/ncjj/ncjj2/faq/femaleoffenders.htm

Focus Adolescent Services. *Conduct Disorder.* http://www.focusas.com/ConductDisorders.html

Hare, Robert D. *Without Conscience Web site,* 2003. www.hare.org

Hill, Karl G.; Lui, Christina; and Hawkins, J. David. *Early Precursors of Gang Membership: A Study of Seattle Youth.* Washington, DC: OJJDP Juvenile Justice Bulletin, December 2001. (NCJ 190106)

Hoang, Francis Q. "Addressing School Violence: Prevention, Planning and Practice." *FBI Law Enforcement Bulletin,* August 2001, pp.18–23.

Holtz, Larry. "New Jersey Fosters Smart Gun Development." *Law Enforcement Technology,* May 2003, p.90.

Howell, James C.; Egley, Arlen, Jr.; and Gleason, Debra K. *Modern-Day Youth Gangs.* Washington, DC: OJJDP Juvenile Justice Bulletin, June 2002. (NCJ 191524)

Jones, Peter R.; Harris, Philip W.; Fader, Jamie; and Grubstein, Lori. "Identifying Chronic Juvenile Offenders." *Justice Quarterly,* September 2001, pp.479–507.

Kaufman, Phillip; Chen, Xianglei; Choy, Susan P.; Peter, Katharin; Ruddy, Sally A.; Miller, Amanda K.; Fleury, Jill K.; Chandler, Kathryn A.; Planty, Michael G.; and Rand, Michael R. *Indicators of School Crime and Safety: 2001.* Washington, DC: Bureau of Justice Statistics and National Center for Education Statistics, October 2001. (NCJ 190075)

Kempf-Leonard, Kimberly; Tracy, Paul E.; and Howell, James C. "Serious, Violent and Chronic Juvenile Offenders: The Relationship of Delinquency Career Types to Adult Criminality." *Justice Quarterly,* September 2001, pp.449–478.

Kracke, Kristen. *Children's Exposure to Violence: The Safe Start Initiative.* Washington, DC: OJJDP Fact Sheet #13, April 2001. (FS 200113)

Krohn, M.D.; Thornberry, T.P.; Rivera, C.; and LeBlanc, M. "Later Delinquency Careers." In *Child Delinquents: Development, Intervention and Service Needs,* edited by R. Loeber and D.P. Farrington. Thousand Oaks, CA: Sage, 2001, pp.67–94.

Lawrence, Richard. "School Violence, the Media and the ACJS." *ACJS Today,* May/June 2000, pp.1, 4–7.

Lizotte, Alan and Sheppard, David. *Gun Use by Male Juveniles: Research and Prevention.* Washington, DC: OJJDP Juvenile Justice Bulletin, July 2001. (NCJ 188992)

Loeber, Rolf; Kalb, Larry; and Huizinga, David. *Juvenile Delinquency and Serious Injury Victimization.* Washington, DC: OJJDP Juvenile Justice Bulletin, August 2001. (NCJ 188676)

Lynch, James P. *Trends in Juvenile Violent Offending: An Analysis of Victim Survey Data.* Washington, DC: OJJDP Juvenile Justice Bulletin, October 2002. (NCJ 191052)

Miller, Walter B. *The Growth of Youth Gang Problems in the United States: 1970–1998.* Washington, DC: Office of Juvenile Justice and Delinquency Prevention, April 2001. (NCJ 181868)

Moore, Joan and Hagerdorn, John. *Female Gangs: A Focus on Research.* Washington, DC: OJJDP Juvenile Justice Bulletin, March 2001. (NCJ 186159)

OJJDP Research 2000. Washington, DC: OJJDP Report, May 2001. (NCJ 186732)

O'Toole, Mary Ellen. *The School Shooter: A Threat Assessment Perspective.* Washington, DC: Federal Bureau of Investigation, 2000.

Ousey, Graham C. and Augustine, Michelle Campbell. "Young Guns: Examining Alternative Explanations of Juvenile Firearm Homicide Rates." *Criminology,* Vol. 39, No. 4, 2001, pp.933–968.

Peterson, Karen S. *USA Today,* April 10, 2001.

Piazza, Peter. "Scourge of the Schoolyard." *Security Management,* November 2001, pp.68–73.

Prinz, Ron. "Research-Based Prevention of School Violence and Youth Antisocial Behavior: A Developmental and Educational Perspective." *Preventing School Violence: Plenary Papers of the 1999 Conference on Criminal Justice Research and Evaluation—Enhancing Policy and Practice through Research,* Vol. 2. Washington, DC: U.S. Department of Justice, May 2000, pp.23–36. (NCJ 180972)

Righthand, Sue and Welch, Carlann. *Juveniles Who Have Sexually Offended: A Review of the Professional Literature.* Washington, DC: Office of Juvenile Justice and Delinquency Prevention, March 2001. (NCJ 184739)

Rowell, James D. "Kids' Needs and the Attraction of Gangs." *Police,* June 2000, p.35.

Sampson, Rana. *Bullying in Schools.* Washington, DC: Office of Community Oriented Policing Services, Problem-Oriented Guides for Police Series No. 12, March 22, 2002.

Shaffer, Jennifer N. and Ruback, R. Barry. *Violent Victimization as a Risk Factor for Violent Offending among Juveniles.* Washington, DC: OJJDP Juvenile Justice Bulletin, December 2002. (NCJ 195737)

Shelden, Randall G.; Tracy, Sharon K.; and Brown, William B. *Youth Gangs in American Society,* 2nd ed. Belmont, CA: Wadsworth Publishing Company, 2001.

Small, Margaret and Terrick, Kellie Dressler. "School Violence: An Overview." *Juvenile Justice,* June 2001, pp.3–12.

Snyder, Howard N. *Juvenile Arrests 2000.* Washington, DC: OJJDP Juvenile Justice Bulletin, November 2002. (NCJ 191729)

Snyder, Howard N.; Espiritu, Rachele C.; Huizinga, David; Loeber, Rolf; and Petechuk, David. *Prevalence and Development of Child Delinquency.* Washington, DC: OJJDP Child Delinquency Bulletin Series, March 2003. (NCJ 193411)

Steinberg, Laurence. "The Juvenile Psychopath: Fads, Fictions and Facts." *Perspectives on Crime and Justice: 2000–2001 Lecture Series.* Washington, DC: National Institute of Justice, March 2002. (NCJ 187100)

Thornberry, Terence P. and Burch, James H., II. *Gang Members and Delinquent Behavior.* Washington, DC: OJJDP Juvenile Justice Bulletin, June 1997. (NCJ 165154)

Thrasher, Frederic M. *The Gang: A Study of 1,313 Gangs in Chicago.* Chicago: University of Chicago Press, 1927.

Walker, Robert. Gangs Or Us Web site 2003. http://www. gangsorus.com/law.html

Walker, Samuel; Spohn, Cassia; and DeLone, Miriam. *The Color of Justice: Race, Ethnicity, and Crime in America,* 2nd ed.. Belmont, CA: Wadsworth Publishing Company, 2000.

Wattendorf, George E. "School Threat Decisions Demonstrate Support for Early Action." *The Police Chief,* March 2002, pp.11–12.

Wooden, Wayne S. and Blazak, Randy. *Renegade Kids, Suburban Outlaws: From Youth Culture to Delinquency.* Belmont, CA: Wadsworth Publishing Company, 2001.

Youth Violence: A Report of the Surgeon General, 2002. http://www.surgeongeneral.gov

Helpful Resource

Zolondek, Stacey C.; Abel, Gene G.; Northey, William F., Jr.; and Jordan, Alan. "The Self-Reported Behaviors of Juvenile Sexual Offenders." *Journal of Interpersonal Violence,* Vol. 16, No. 1, 2001, p.73.

The Law Enforcement Response to Abused and Neglected Children and Status Offenders

Children spend up to 25 percent of their waking
hours in school. It has been estimated that
18 percent of their time is spent with their peers—
other children. Another 18 percent of their waking
hours may be spent in front of the television. Police
are the only other significant parental type, albeit
surrogate, in contact with our children.

—Timothy D. Crowe

Do You Know?

- What primary responsibility officers assigned a child abuse or neglect case have?
- What challenges are involved in investigating crimes against children?
- What challenges are involved in investigating a missing child report?
- What factors affect how police officers respond to status offenders?
- Whether the police have discretionary power when dealing with juveniles?
- What action police usually take when confronting juveniles?
- What the fundamental nature of the juvenile justice system is?
- What the majority of police dispositions involve?
- What predelinquent indicator often goes unnoticed?
- What seems to be the most visible indicator of a future victim or offender?
- How prevention methods have changed over the years and why?
- What greatly influences youths' attitudes toward law and law enforcement?
- What shift in policing philosophy affects how law enforcement deals with youths?

Can You Define?

Amber Alert
arrest
beyond a reasonable
    doubt
community policing
community relations
detention

intake
petition
police-school liaison
    program
school resource officer
    (SRO)

station adjustment
street justice
taking into custody
temporary custody
    without hearing
window of opportunity

INTRODUCTION

Juvenile justice, as already discussed, is basically concerned with three distinct groups of youths: those who are victims of abuse and/or neglect, those who commit status offenses and those who commit serious crimes. Law enforcement is commonly the first contact young victims and victimizers have with the juvenile justice system, serving as the gatekeeper to the rest of the system. The police are charged with protecting youths, both victims and offenders, and dealing fairly with them. Questions of what is in the best interest of the youth must be balanced with what is best for the community. Also, the crime-fighting philosophy must be balanced with the service ideal.

The chapter first discusses the police response to children and youths who are abused and neglected, missing or abducted. Next it discusses the police response to status offenders. The discussion includes the various dispositions police officers can make when dealing with youths and police discretion. Then the law enforcement portion of the juvenile justice system is examined from the time of **taking into custody (arrest),** to detention, to intake and, finally, to prosecution. The issue of the overrepresentation of minorities being processed by the system is then discussed. This is followed by a look at how law enforcement interacts with the various types of status offenders including those who violate curfew, loiter, are truant, are disorderly, run away, drink alcoholic beverages under age or use drugs.

Next the chapter reviews delinquency prevention strategies undertaken by law enforcement, including the importance of school resource officers (SROs). The chapter ends with a look at how law enforcement is changing and the challenges that the changes present.

Neglected and Abused Children

Finkelhor and Ormrod (2001, p.1) contend: "A substantial portion of child abuse cases are investigated and adjudicated by the criminal justice system." Nationwide more than 1 million children are neglected or abused each year. Bennett and Hess (2004, p.280) note:

> Law enforcement agencies are charged with investigating all crimes, but their responsibility is especially great where crimes against children are involved. Children need the protection of the law to a greater degree than other members of society because they are so vulnerable, especially if the offense is committed by one or both parents. Even after the offense is committed, the child may still be in danger of further victimization.

In most states, action must be taken on a report within a specified time, frequently three days. If in the judgment of the person receiving the report it is necessary to remove the child from present custody, this is discussed with the responsible agency, such as the welfare department or the juvenile court. If the situation is deemed life-threatening, the police may temporarily remove the child.

The primary responsibility of police officers assigned to child neglect or abuse cases is the immediate protection of the child.

Under welfare regulations and codes, an officer may take a child into temporary custody without a warrant if there is an emergency or if the officer has reason to believe that leaving the child in the present situation would subject the child to further abuse or harm. **Temporary custody without hearing** usually means for 48 hours. Conditions that would justify placing a child in protective custody include:

- Maltreatment in the home that might cause the child permanent physical or emotional damage.
- A parent's refusal to provide needed medical or psychiatric care for a child.
- The child is physically or mentally incapable of self-protection.
- The home's physical environment poses an immediate threat.
- The parents cannot or will not provide for the child's basic needs.
- The parents abandon the child.

Among the service providers mandated to report incidents of suspected child abuse or neglect are childcare providers, clergy, educators, hospital administrators, nurses, physicians, psychologists and those in the social services. No matter who receives the report or whether the child must be removed from the situation, it is the responsibility of the law enforcement agency to investigate the charge.

Challenges to Investigation

Many prosecutors at all levels of the judiciary perceive crimes against children as among the most difficult to prosecute and obtain convictions. Therefore, officers interviewing child witnesses and victims should have specialized training not only to convict the guilty but also to protect the innocent. Regardless of whether crimes against children are handled by generalists or specialists within the department, certain challenges are unique to these investigations.

 Challenges in investigating crimes against children include the need to protect the child from further harm, the possibility of parental involvement, the difficulty of interviewing children, credibility concerns and the need to collaborate with other agencies.

Consultation with local welfare authorities is sometimes needed before asking the court for a hearing to remove a child from the parents' custody or for protective custody in an authorized facility because police rarely have such facilities. As soon as possible the child should be taken to the nearest welfare facility or to a foster home, as stipulated by the juvenile court. The parents or legal guardians of the child must be notified as soon as possible.

Sample Protocol

The following excerpt from the Boulder City (Nevada) Police Department's protocol for investigating reports of sexual and physical abuse of children is typical. (Reprinted by permission.)

It is the policy to *team* investigate all abuse allegations.

When a report comes in, a juvenile officer is immediately assigned all abuse cases. This officer is responsible for maintaining a 72-hour time frame. Contact is made as soon as possible.

The investigative process includes the following:

- The investigator contacts Nevada Welfare, and together they contact the victim at a location where the victim can be interviewed briefly, and not in the presence of the alleged perpetrator of the crime.
- During the initial interview the juvenile officer tries to determine if the report is a substantiated abuse, unsubstantiated or unfounded.
- If the report is substantiated, the juvenile officer or Nevada State Welfare remove the child from the home and book the child into protective custody. If the juvenile officer and Nevada State Welfare investigator determine the child is not in danger of *any* abuse, the child can be allowed to remain in his/her home environment.
- If the report is unsubstantiated, the child is left in the home.
- If the report is unfounded, the reason for the false report is also investigated to identify other problems.
- If the case is substantiated abuse, the victim is housed at Child Haven, and there is a detention hearing at 9:00 A.M. the following working day.

An in-depth interview is conducted with the victim by the juvenile officer and the Nevada State Welfare investigator. Several aids are used, depending on the child's age and mental abilities: structured and unstructured play therapy, picture drawings and use of anatomical dolls.

The juvenile officer also contacts the accused person and interviews him/her about the specific allegations, makes a report or statement relevant to the interview and makes these reports available to Nevada State Welfare and/or Clark County Juvenile Court. Nevada State Welfare is encouraged to attend these interviews, and a team approach is used during this phase of the investigation also.

The juvenile officer also interviews other people, including witnesses or victims—anyone who might have information about the case. The officer prepares an affidavit and presents the case to the district attorney's office to determine whether the case is suitable for prosecution. If so, a complaint is issued, and a warrant or summons is issued for the accused. Once a warrant is obtained, the investigating officer locates and arrests or causes the accused person to be arrested.

Evidence

All the officer's observations pertaining to the physical and emotional condition of the victim must be recorded in detail. Evidence in child neglect or abuse cases includes the surroundings, the home conditions, clothing, bruises or other body injuries, the medical examination report and other observations. Photographs may be the best way to document child abuse and neglect where it is necessary to show injury to the child or the conditions of the home environment. Pictures should be taken immediately because children's injuries heal quickly and home conditions can be changed rapidly.

Improving the Law Enforcement Response to Child Abuse/Neglect

Delany-Shabazz and Vieth (2001, p.1) suggest:

> The growing number and complexity of child abuse cases and abusers' increasing sophistication (e.g., use of the Internet to seduce children) severely challenge those who work to address these crimes. Small, rural communities, in particular, face serious difficulties in responding to abuse cases because these communities often possess limited resources and their prosecutors and investigators cannot specialize in child abuse. Even in communities with greater resources, the task of protecting children can be daunting: in many cases there is little, if any, physical evidence of abuse and the primary witness is usually a child, who the defendant's lawyers may claim has been easily manipulated by the prosecution. The rate of burnout and staff turnover among investigators and prosecutors working on these cases is high. Often, the most difficult cases are given to new or ill-prepared prosecutors.

Law enforcement agencies should consider a variety of ways to improve their responses to child abuse, including:

- A written, agency-wide child abuse policy
- Written interagency protocols and interagency teams to handle child abuse investigations
- Immediate telephone notification of the police by protective service agency workers regarding all sexual abuse cases and all cases of serious physical injury or danger
- Initial interviews conducted jointly with child protective agency workers, especially in sexual abuse cases
- Patrol officers trained in the identification of abuse
- Child abuse specialists, skilled as investigators and comfortable interviewing young children
- Child-friendly interview settings
- Limited and selective use of videotaping and anatomical dolls by properly trained individuals

The National Center for Prosecution of Child Abuse in Alexandria, Virginia, has several training classes, including "Equal Justice: Investigation and Prosecution of Child Abuse," its core course. The center also provides professional development and guidance to investigators and prosecutors. Its Web site is www.ndaa-apri.org.

Missing Children: Runaway or Abducted?

Simons and Willie (2000, p.1) note: "When a child simply vanishes, no clear indicators may exist to suggest a voluntary or an involuntary disappearance. When responding police officers navigate through a situation with no witnesses, obvious crime scene, nor clues to what happened, they might find it difficult to distinguish an abducted child from a runaway initially." They (p.2) explain: "The fact that hundreds of thousands of children leave their homes voluntarily each year compounds the difficulty in accurately classifying a missing child as a runaway or a victim of abduction."

They also stress: "No other criminal investigation is as time-sensitive as this type of case, where the very life of the victim often may depend on the swift and effective mobilization of investigative resources." According to Domash (2002, p.53): "The vast majority (74 percent) of abducted children who are murdered are dead within three hours."

 A special challenge in cases where a child is reported missing is determining whether the child has run away (a status offense) or been abducted.

Simons and Willie (p.3) present guidelines to clarify procedures for categorizing the missing child case:

- *The parental interview:* separation of parents, family members and reporting parties during interviews
- *Victimology:* examination of the missing child's family dynamics, comfort zones, and school and peer group associates
- *Scene assessment:* assessment of the child's residence for evidence, or lack of, predeparture preparation
- *Resources:* evaluation of resources available to the child that would enable or inhibit a voluntary departure
- *Time factors:* consideration of the amount of time that has passed since the child was last seen

If it is determined that the child has been abducted, law enforcement officers should know that the most frequent type of abduction is parental abduction.

Parental Abductions

Lord et al. (2001, p.3) report: "Research and investigative experience have shown that family abductions, motivated by domestic discord and custody disputes, overwhelmingly represent the most frequent type of child abduction." According to Johnston et al. (2001, p.2): "Unwed, married, separated or divorced parents and parents who have sole or joint custody or visitation or no custody rights can commit parental abduction by violating the rights of the other parent."

Grasso et al. (2001, p.12) note: "Parental abduction can be a form of serious child maltreatment and is a crime in all 50 states and the District of Columbia." They (p.10) suggest that police departments: "Develop and implement written policies and procedures addressing the handling of parental abduction cases."

Johnston et al. identify factors that predict parental abduction. In some instances one parent, usually the mother, believes, correctly or incorrectly, that the other parent is physically or sexually abusing or neglecting the child. The risk of abduction increases if the parents making the allegations of child abuse were themselves victims of abuse or neglect as children. The risk also increases if the suspecting parent has a network of family members, friends or an "underground network" of supporters who help the abducting parent obtain a new identity and find a new home.

Resources Available

One valuable resource in missing children cases is the Missing and Exploited Children's Program, described by Girouard (2001b). This program provides direct services through the National Center for Missing and Exploited Children (NCMEC), the Association of Missing and Exploited Children's Organizations (AMECO) and Project H.O.P.E. It also provides training and technical assistance to law enforcement, and it conducts research.

Girouard (2001c, p.1) also describes the National Center for Missing and Exploited Children (NCMEC): "Since 1984, NCMEC has received more than 1.5 million calls from around the world. The 24-hour hotline (800-THE-LOST), with 23 incoming lines, can handle phone calls in more than 140 languages. Once a call is received, photos and reports of missing children can be forwarded immediately to appropriate law enforcement agencies, nonprofit organizations and state missing children clearinghouses."

The NCMEC provides two services to law enforcement agencies investigating missing children cases. The first is an age progression program that creates photographs of a child that approximate what the child would look like at the present time. The greatest age difference they have created is from age 6 to age 31. The second service is called Project KidCare, provided in collaboration with Polaroid Corporation. This service consists of an educational packet and a high-quality photo in a form that NCMEC and law enforcement consider ideal.

Jezycki (2000, p.19) explains the Team H.O.P.E. project (Help Offering Parents Empowerment): "Established in 1998, Team H.O.P.E. helps families of missing children handle the day-to-day issues of coping with holidays, birthdays and disappearance anniversaries; caring for family members; keeping marriages together; and working with the media and law enforcement. Team H.O.P.E. links victim parents with experienced and trained parent volunteers who have gone through the experience of having a missing child. Because they speak from first-hand experience, these volunteers provide compassion, counsel and support in ways no other community agency can."

Another valuable resource is the **Amber Alert** program. Amber Alert plans are voluntary partnerships between law enforcement agencies and public broadcasters to notify the public when a child has been abducted. According to Rasmussen (2002, p.43): "The Amber Plan was created in the Dallas-Fort Worth region after the murder of Amber Hagerman, a 9-year-old girl who was abducted from her home. . . . Amber Alert is an early-warning network that law enforcement can use to quickly convey key information to the general public via television and radio soon after a child has been abducted." It is not intended to be a federal program.

Krainik (2002, p.84) describes three criteria that should be met before an alert is sent: "(1) law enforcement should confirm that a child 17 or under has been abducted; (2) law enforcement should believe that the circumstances surrounding the abduction indicate that the child is in danger of serious bodily harm or death; and (3) there is enough descriptive evidence about the child, abductor or vehicle to believe an immediate broadcast alert will help."

Although law enforcement is responsible for investigating cases of child abuse/neglect and missing children, much more of their time is involved in responding to status offenders.

Police Dispositions of Status Offenders

Police dispositions range from taking no action to referring status offenders to social service agencies or to the juvenile court. The police alternatives are guided by the community, the local juvenile justice system and individual officer discretion.

 In the disposition of status offenders, how police resolve matters often depends on the officers' discretion, the specific incident and the backup available.

Whether the police actually arrest a juvenile usually depends on several factors, the most important being the seriousness of the offense. Other factors affecting the decision include character, age, gender, race, prior record, family situation and the youth's attitude.

The decision may also be influenced by public opinion, the media, available referral agencies and the officer's experience. Officers' actions usually reflect community interests. For example, conflict may occur between the public's demand for order and a group of young people wanting to "hang around." How police respond to such hanging around is influenced by the officer's attitude and the standards of the neighborhood or community, rather than rules of the state. Each neighborhood or community and the officer's own feelings dictate how the police perform in such matters.

Some localities may handle a delinquent act very differently from others. For example, police investigating an auto theft in the suburbs and finding a youth responsible will often simply send the youth home for parental discipline. The youth will receive a notice of when to appear in court. In contrast, urban juveniles—especially minority youths—caught stealing an automobile are often detained in a locked facility. Sometimes, however, urban youths are at an advantage. What rural law enforcement officers may perceive as criminal behavior is often viewed as a prank by that officer's urban counterpart. Clearly, justice for juveniles is not a neatly structured, impartial decision-making process by which the rule of law always prevails and each person is treated fairly and impartially.

Sometimes police may "roust" and "hassle" youths who engage in undesirable social conduct, but they probably will not report the incident; in this case, street justice is the police disposition. **Street justice** occurs when police decide to deal with a status offense in their own way—usually by ignoring it.

Police Discretion and the Initial Contact

Between 80 and 90 percent of youths commit some offense for which they could be arrested, yet only about 3 percent of them are. This is in large part because they do not get caught. Further, those who are caught usually have engaged in some minor status offense that can be better handled by counseling and releasing in many instances. Although the "counsel and dismiss" alternative may be criticized as being soft on juveniles, this approach is often all that is needed to turn a youth around.

Police officers have considerable discretionary power when dealing with juveniles.

Law enforcement officers have a range of alternatives to take:

- Release the child, with or without a warning, but without making an official record or taking further action.
- Release the child, but write up a brief contact or field report to juvenile authorities, describing the contact.
- Release the child, but file a more formal report referring the matter to a juvenile bureau or an intake unit for possible action.
- Turn the youth over to juvenile authorities immediately.
- Refer the case directly to the court through the district or county attorney.

In some instances youths engaging in delinquent acts are simply counseled. In other instances they are returned to their families, who are expected to deal with their child's deviant behavior. Sometimes they are referred to social services agencies for help. And sometimes they are charged and processed by the juvenile justice system.

The most common procedure is to release the child, with or without a warning, but without making an official record or taking further action.

Figure 7.1 illustrates the flow of the juvenile justice system.

Parents, schools and the police are the main sources for the referral of youths into the juvenile justice system. Of these three sources, the police are, by far, the most common source of referrals.

In a few jurisdictions, if the child is not released without official record, he or she is automatically turned over to the juvenile authorities, who make all further decisions in the matter. If the child is referred to court, another decision is whether police personnel should release or detain the child. Officers try to dispose of juvenile cases in a way that considers the best interests of both the juvenile and the community.

Taken into Custody

Police contact with children may result either from a complaint received or from observing questionable behavior. In their initial contact with juveniles, the police are indirectly guided by the language of the Juvenile Court Act, which states that juveniles are "taken into custody," not arrested. This is interpreted to mean the police's role is to salvage and rehabilitate youth, a role indirectly sanctioned by many judges who encourage settling disputes and complaints without referral to the court.

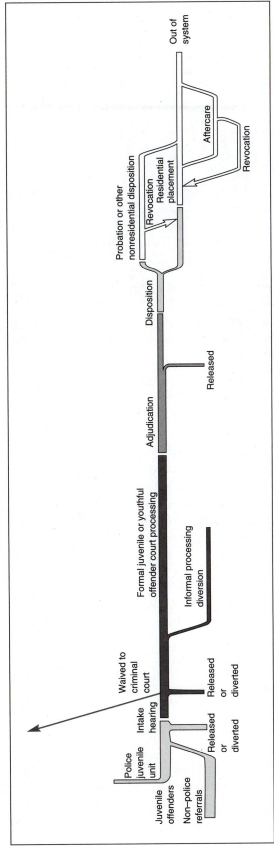

Figure 7.1
Progression through the Juvenile Justice System

Source: Adapted from *The Challenge of Crime in a Free Society*. President's Commission on Law Enforcement and Administration of Justice, 1967. This revision, a result of the Symposium on the 30th Anniversary of the President's Commission, was prepared by the Bureau of Justice Statistics in 1997. *What Is the Sequence of Events through the Criminal Justice System?* Washington, DC: Bureau of Justice Statistics, January 1998 (Chart). (NIJ 67894)

Positive face-to-face contacts between police officers and children can help promote the idea of the police officer as a friend and helper.

When a juvenile is taken into custody, this is technically not considered an arrest. The law enforcement process for arrest is modified in most jurisdictions when juveniles are apprehended. Police officers should be concerned about the mental health of juveniles. They should be good listeners and try to discover the problem or the reason for the juveniles' behavior. It is paramount in administering juvenile justice that youths be protected by all sociolegal requirements.

 The fundamental nature of the juvenile justice system is rehabilitative rather than punitive.

Most states' juvenile justice systems reflect this basic rehabilitative philosophy. In addition the Supreme Court has emphasized the full constitutional rights of persons under legal age. The protection, critical to the juvenile offender, is twofold:

1. At no point in any criminal investigation may the rights of the juvenile be infringed upon.

2. A crime by a juvenile must be proven beyond a reasonable doubt, and all subsequent efforts by a state should be directed toward correlating and eliminating the cause of the crime rather than punishing the individual for having committed it. **Beyond a reasonable doubt** is less than absolute certainty, but more than high probability.

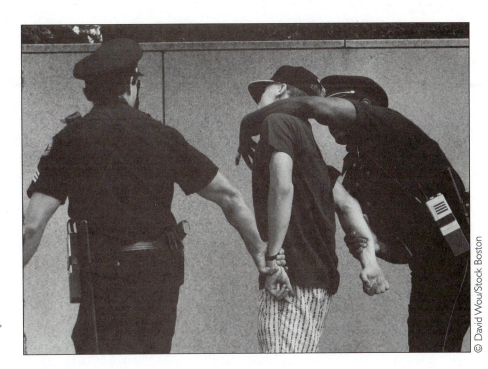

Youths are not arrested; they are "taken into custody." Here a 15-year-old is taken into custody for trying to start a riot in Dallas, Texas. Because he is a minor, he was turned over to his parents.

© David Wou/Stock Boston

Juveniles must be treated with consideration to build their respect for authority. Officers must be firm but fair, and they must show genuine interest. They must try to understand the juveniles' reasoning. In handling juveniles, if officers resort to vulgarity or profanity, lose their tempers, display prejudicial behavior or label juveniles as "liars" or "no good," this is counterproductive. Such actions are often followed by further disruptive conduct by the juvenile or by a lack of cooperation in any attempt to divert juvenile conduct.

If a youth is detained, the officers must remember that juveniles have the same constitutional rights as adults, including the right to remain silent, the right to counsel, the right to know the specific charge and the right to confront witnesses. Given the *parens patriae* philosophy underlying the juvenile justice system, it might be expected that the police would exercise extra care in dealing with youths.

Of the juvenile offenders taken into custody in 2001, almost three-fourths (72.4 percent) were referred to juvenile court jurisdiction. Slightly fewer than one-fifth (19 percent) were handled within the department and released—called **station adjustment.** Figure 7.2 shows the police dispositions of juvenile offenders taken into custody in 2001. Table 7.1 shows the disposition by agency/population.

One problem of referral for juvenile authorities and the court, especially in a metropolitan area, is that it may be difficult to determine by appearance alone if a person is a juvenile. Youths may lie about or try to manipulate their age for practical reasons. For example, a youth detained on a status offense may claim to be over the age limit and, consequently, *not* an offender. Or youths taken into custody for minor offenses such as disorderly conduct or prostitution often claim

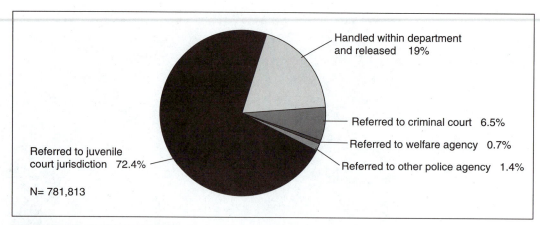

Figure 7.2
Police Dispositions of Juvenile Offenders Taken into Custody, 2001

Source: *Crime in the United States 2001*. Washington, DC: FBI Uniform Crime Reports, 2001, p.291.

to be over the age limit, reasoning that if treated as adults they will simply be forced to spend a night in jail, hear a lecture by a judge and accept whatever penalty is disposed. If they identify themselves as juveniles, their detention usually is extended, and interference with their freedom and liberty may well be more substantial.

In small towns and in rural areas, the procedure for the pre-referral process is to release the youths to their custodians, allowing the custodians to dispense justice and relieve the workload of the court.

The Juvenile Holdover

An Implementation Guide for Juvenile Holdover Programs (2001) cites the following scenario:

It was early Saturday morning. David, a 15-year-old who lives in a small town with a population of about 1,500, was driving his father's car and was stopped by the only police officer on duty. The headlights on David's car were not turned on and he was driving erratically. The officer suspected that David had been drinking. When tested with the officer's preliminary breath tester, David blew a 0.07. His blood alcohol content (BAC) was below the legal level of 0.08 for driving under the influence (DUI) in this state, but it is a zero-tolerance jurisdiction, meaning that the presence of any alcohol in the system of a 15-year-old was a violation.

In addition, David did not have a valid driver's license and he was out after curfew. He was cited for all three violations, the car was secured, and a tow was ordered. David, now seated in the rear of the squad car, told the officer that he had been at a party and acknowledged that he had been drinking beer. David revealed that he had been drinking a lot lately. He stated that his parents were out of town for the weekend and could not be reached by phone. He was to be alone at home until late Sunday night and had no other relatives living in this community.

The officer had no on-duty backup and there were five more hours left on his shift. There was no safe place to drop David off, and department policy prohibited having the youth ride in the squad car for the remainder of the shift. The nearest emergency shelter facility for youths would be a three-hour round trip. Driving

Table 7.1
Police Disposition of Juvenile Offenders Taken into Custody, 2001
[2001 estimated population]

Population group	Total[1]	Handled within department and released	Referred to juvenile court jurisdiction	Referred to welfare agency	Referred to other police agency	Referred to criminal or adult court
TOTAL AGENCIES: 5,813 agencies; population 122,154,066						
Number	781,813	148,238	566,187	5,073	10,568	51,117
Percent[2]	100.0	19.0	72.4	0.7	1.4	6.5
TOTAL CITIES: 4,277 cities; population 86,590,978						
Number	647,492	127,271	467,652	4,539	9,218	38,812
Percent[2]	100.0	19.7	72.2	0.7	1.4	6.0
GROUP I						
36 cities, 250,000 and over; population 20,512,259						
Number	139,394	33,419	98,890	300	2,960	3,825
Percent[2]	100.0	24.0	70.9	0.2	2.1	2.7
GROUP II						
91 cities, 100,000 to 249,999; population 13,416,737						
Number	90,048	14,617	69,992	1,195	1,114	3,130
Percent[2]	100.0	16.2	77.7	1.3	1.2	3.5
GROUP III						
228 cities, 50,000 to 99,999; population 15,529,044						
Number	115,891	25,762	82,359	465	2,040	5,265
Percent[2]	100.0	22.2	71.1	0.4	1.8	4.5
GROUP IV						
390 cities, 25,000 to 49,999; population 13,674,258						
Number	97,443	17,230	71,819	1,210	1,448	5,736
Percent[2]	100.0	17.7	73.7	1.2	1.5	5.9
GROUP V						
848 cities, 10,000 to 24,999; population 13,584,903						
Number	107,935	18,260	77,809	770	815	10,281
Percent[2]	100.0	16.9	72.1	0.7	0.8	9.5
GROUP VI						
2,684 cities, under 10,000; population 9,873,777						
Number	96,781	17,983	66,783	599	841	10,575
Percent[2]	100.0	18.6	69.0	0.6	0.9	10.9
SUBURBAN COUNTIES						
604 agencies; population 23,751,585						
Number	95,266	15,566	70,747	716	944	7,293
Percent[2]	100.0	16.3	74.3	0.8	1.0	7.7
RURAL COUNTIES						
932 agencies; population 11,811,503						
Number	39,055	5,401	27,788	448	406	5,012
Percent[2]	100.0	13.8	71.2	1.1	1.0	12.8
SUBURBAN AREA[3]						
3,176 agencies; population 59,110,616						
Number	330,939	64,357	234,090	2,065	2,937	27,490
Percent[2]	100.0	19.4	70.7	0.6	0.9	8.3

[1] Includes all offenses except traffic and neglect cases.

[2] Because of rounding, the percentages may not add to total.

[3] Suburban area includes law enforcement agencies in cities with less than 50,000 inhabitants and county law enforcement agencies that are within a Metropolitan Statistical Area. Suburban area excludes all metropolitan agencies associated with a central city. The agencies associated with suburban areas will also appear in other groups within this table.

there would take up most of the time left on the officer's shift. The only option was to return to police headquarters and wait with David until morning. Then, arrangements could be made to locate his parents or to find a place for David to stay for the rest of the weekend. It was Friday night and because of one juvenile who was drinking alcohol and driving while impaired police coverage was not available for the community for the rest of the night.

As Bolton (2002, p.105) suggests: "Without clear guidance, officers who encounter a juvenile offender may sense a management directive to look the other way whenever police action could create a juvenile holdover problem."

The *Implementation Guide* (p.1) notes: "When viewed from a national perspective, juvenile holdover programs are multifaceted. In general, however, they are short-term, temporary holding programs for youths that can be located in either a secure, nonsecure or a combination secure/nonsecure setting." The guide (pp.7–8) describes the key elements of a successful holdover program. It is an easily accessible, short-term alternative integrated into a network of services for youths. It has a trained staff and is able to respond to a youth's immediate needs, able to provide comfortable facilities with minimum services for an overnight stay and is able to respond to and de-escalate the immediate situation if necessary (crisis intervention). It has screening and assessment capacity and referral expertise. It is also able to coordinate post-release services to the youth and family and able to evaluate its effectiveness. In some instances, law enforcement officers may determine that the most appropriate disposition is detention.

Detention

Detention is the period during which a youth is taken into custody by police and probation before a petition is filed. Detention is governed by two requirements of the JJDP Act: (1) removing all juveniles from adult jails and lockups and (2) separating juvenile and adult offenders. The act states:

> Provide that juveniles alleged to be or found to be delinquent and youths within the purview of paragraph (12) (i.e., status offenders and nonoffenders) shall not be detained or confined in any institution in which they have regular contact with adult persons incarcerated because they have been convicted of a crime or are awaiting trial on criminal charges.

In addition state laws and department policies may affect who is detained and under what conditions. Most state statutes governing the detention of juveniles are quite general. Among the criteria used by states are:

- For the juvenile's or society's protection
- Lack of parental care available
- To ensure a juvenile's presence at a juvenile court hearing
- The seriousness of the offense and the juvenile's record

Release vs. Detention

Juvenile court statutes often require that once children have been taken into custody, they may be released only to their parents, guardians or custodians. Where such a law exists, a decision to detain automatically follows if the parents,

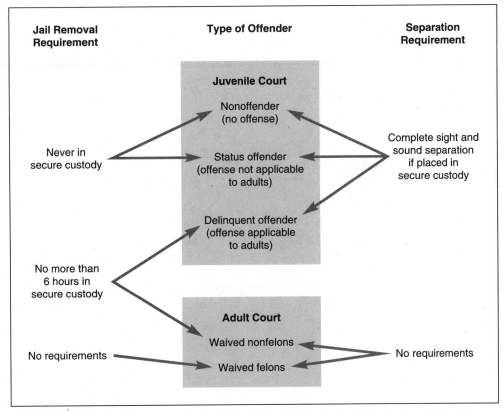

Jail Removal Requirement	Type of Offender	Separation Requirement

Juvenile Court

Nonoffender (no offense)

Never in secure custody → Status offender (offense not applicable to adults)

Delinquent offender (offense applicable to adults)

Complete sight and sound separation if placed in secure custody

No more than 6 hours in secure custody

Adult Court

Waived nonfelons

No requirements → Waived felons ← No requirements

Figure 7.3
Federal Jail Removal and Separation Requirements for Juveniles

Source: Timothy D. Crowe. *Habitual Juvenile Offenders: Guidelines for Citizen Action and Public Responses.* Serious Habitual Offender Comprehensive Action Program (SHOCAP). Washington, DC: Office of Juvenile Justice and Delinquency Prevention, October 1991, p.21.

guardians or custodians cannot be found. The child is placed in detention and must be referred to court. Thus the police are removed from the referral process.

In most states police may take a child into custody for the child's own protection until appropriate placement can be made. Standards to guide police personnel in the decision whether to release or detain may be formally prepared in written instructions by police administrators and court authorities. In some states *mandatory referral* to juvenile authorities or even directly to court may be required for all crimes of violence, felonies and serious misdemeanors. Similarly all juveniles on parole or probation may be referred. Some jurisdictions refer if the juvenile has had previous contact with the police. Figure 7.3 summarizes the federal jail removal and separation requirements for juveniles.

During detention, police have a **window of opportunity** to be an agency for change for youngsters. Drug testing can be used diagnostically to identify high-risk youths before they become established in the cycle of illicit drug use and crime. Such youths can be put into drug-treatment programs, hopefully averting the drug-crime-drug cycle. Other windows of opportunity are discussed throughout the remainder of the text.

Intake

Intake is the stage at which someone must decide whether a referral merits a petition, that is, whether the matter described in the complaint against the juvenile should become the subject of formal court action. The intake officer decides whether a case should move ahead for court processing. This officer may release the juvenile to the parents with a warning or reprimand. Or the officer may release youths on the condition that they enroll in a community diversion program or be placed on probation and be under the supervision of a juvenile court officer.

The intake process of the juvenile justice system requires the development of employee screening practices, certification standards and caseload guidelines. Caseworkers should be certified to practice on the basis of education, training and experience.

According to Griffin and Torbet (2002, p.34): "Intake may be the most crucial case processing point in the juvenile justice system because so much follows from that decision. Intake authority is entrusted to prosecutors in some jurisdictions—either in all cases or in those involving allegations of serious crimes—and to juvenile court intake or juvenile probation departments in others. The Guide suggests that intake officers must ask two basic questions:

1. From a review of the complaint and the evidence, is it clear that the complaint against the juvenile is *legally sufficient*? If not, the case should be dismissed.

2. If so, does a background investigation of legal and social factors—including interviews with the juvenile as well as parents, victims and others—indicate that the case *ought not to be diverted* from formal processing?

Youths released at intake with no further processing should be followed up after any referral to a community agency by either the police or the intake unit. Such follow-up promotes closer cooperation between the agencies involved.

If the intake officer determines that the case should move ahead for court processing, the officer will recommend that a **petition** (charge) be filed and will refer the case to the juvenile court prosecutor. In addition, if a petition is recommended, the intake officer determines whether the youth should be detained pending further court action or be released to the custody of the parents pending the hearing. When juveniles are detained, this decision is reviewed by a judge or court administrator at a detention hearing.

Prosecution

When the prosecutor receives the recommendation for petition by the intake officer, at least three options are available: dismiss the case, file the petition or determine that the charges are so serious that the case should be heard in adult court, waiving jurisdiction. If a petition is filed, this begins the formal adjudication process. Based on police reports, the county attorney may refer a juvenile to the screening unit of the juvenile court.

Circumstances may vary depending on the age and experience of the officer making the disposition. This exercise of individual authority may be repeated by court personnel, probation officers and correction workers.

Overrepresentation Issues

From arrest through sentencing and incarceration, disproportionate minority representation and differential treatment are sometimes evident along the entire juvenile justice system continuum. Snyder (2002, p.10) flatly states: "Juvenile arrests disproportionately involve minorities." Walker et al. (2000, p.167) note: "Researchers recently have begun to examine the juvenile justice system for evidence of racial discrimination. Noting that the juvenile system, with its philosophy of *parens patriae,* is more discretionary and less formal than the adult system, researchers have suggested that there is greater potential for racial discrimination in the processing of juveniles than in the processing of adults." They conclude: "There is compelling evidence that racial minorities are overrepresented in the juvenile justice system."

Pope and Snyder (2003, p.1) report: "Although a broad array of research over the past half century has explored the degree to which race impacts the juvenile justice system, the results are mixed. Some studies have found evidence of racial bias, while others have found that race is not significant." Their (p.6) own conclusion: "Overall, the NIBRS [National Incident Based Reporting System] data offer no evidence to support the hypothesis that police are more likely to arrest nonwhite juvenile offenders than white juvenile offenders once other incident attributes are taken into consideration."

In November 2002 changes were made to the Juvenile Justice and Delinquency Prevention Act (JJDPA). One important change, titled "Disproportionate Minority Confinement (DMC)" requires states to address prevention efforts and systemic efforts to reduce the disproportionate representation of minorities that come in contact with the juvenile justice system (Child Welfare League of America).

Status Offenders

 The majority of police dispositions involve status offenses.

In making dispositions on juvenile matters, the police have found that the parents are often so absorbed with their own desires and problems that they have little time to consider their children's needs. They tend to rely on church, school or civic groups to guide their children. They often pursue a policy of appeasement in the home rather than maintaining family discipline. In effect these parents want society to be their babysitters. The increasing reliance on community services and the parental emphasis on individual rights rather than responsibilities in the training and education of their children has, to a large extent, weakened the family and contributed to the growing delinquency problem, as was discussed in Chapter 3. Partly as a result of this lack of parental guidance, law enforcement agencies are faced with the constant problem of taking youths into custody on relatively minor charges such as curfew violations and loitering.

Curfew Violations and Loitering

When youths' behavior is such that the community wants them off the streets at night, a curfew is established for the public good, as discussed in Chapter 5. Recall that McDowall et al. (2000, p.88) found "at best, extremely weak support for the hypothesis that curfews reduce juvenile crime rates."

The 1990s' popularity of curfews as a response to youth crime is simply the most recent revival of a delinquency control measure that has waxed and waned across urban America several times during the past century.

When youths hang around corners, walkways, alleys, streets and places of business without any purpose, their loitering must be controlled for the safety and security of the public. Both curfew violations and loitering can be offenses for those under legal age. (Loitering is also an adult offense in some states.) Cruising and hanging out or loitering are frequent activities of juveniles.

Curfew ordinances must demonstrate a compelling state interest and be narrow in interpretation to meet constitutional standards. For example:

> The curfew applies to youths under age 17 between 11 p.m. and 6 a.m. Sunday through Thursday and between midnight and 6 a.m. Friday and Saturday. Exemptions include juveniles accompanied by an adult, traveling to or from work, responding to an emergency, married or attending a supervised activity.

Curfews may face resistance from police officers, who see them as babysitting detail and an infringement on crime fighting efforts. Further, many agencies lack adequate personnel to enforce curfew laws. If an officer picks up a child and transports him or her to the station, waits for a parent and does the necessary paperwork, it could take several hours. Taking a street officer off the beat, even for an hour, requires shifting units to cover the officer's beat. Nonetheless, many officers see curfews as a way to curtail youth crime.

Ward, Jr. (2000, p.16) stresses: "A juvenile curfew can succeed only if authorities enforce it in a consistent, fair and uniform manner." He also suggests: "Communities should implement comprehensive curfew programs that change the punitive nature of the curfew into an intervention process that can attack the primary causes of juvenile delinquency and victimization." These programs should include such strategies as:

- Creating a dedicated curfew center or using recreation centers and churches to house curfew violators.
- Staffing these centers with social service professionals and community volunteers.
- Offering referrals to social service providers and counseling classes for juvenile violators and their families.
- Establishing procedures—such as fines, counseling or community service—for repeat offenders.
- Developing recreation, employment, antidrug and antigang programs.
- Providing hot lines for follow-up services and intervention.

In some instances daytime curfews have been implemented to curb truancy.

Truants

Recall from Chapter 3 the vital role of the school in preparing children for productive adult lives and developing their respect for human rights and national values through education. When children skip school habitually, they miss some very valuable lessons, not only academically but socially. They also tend to engage in delinquent or criminal activity while on these unsanctioned leaves. For these reasons truancy is a major problem in many school districts. Antitruancy ordinances enacted in some cities have met with varied success.

Santoro (2001, p.34) describes the Monrovia, California, antitruancy ordinance as "one giant step toward keeping kids in school and out of trouble." Santoro (p.37) notes: "In Monrovia, city officials believe the daytime curfew/antitruancy ordinance, amended in 1999 to provide exceptions to the regulations, has resulted in a 'win-win-win' situation. Parents are happy because their kids are in school instead of running the streets during school hours. School officials are pleased in part because improved attendance has increased the amount of average-daily-attendance (ADA) money the school district receives from the state. And the Monrovia police are delighted because there has been a significant reduction in daytime crime, which they see as a direct result of the curfew/truancy program.

Berger and Wind (2000, p.16) describe another approach to the truancy problem used by the North Miami Beach PET Project: Police Eliminating Truancy. This project assigns two officers to patrol community hot spots during regular school hours. If the officers encounter youths under age 16 with no legitimate reason to be out of school, the officers take them to the Truancy Evaluation Center (TEC):

> Located in an off-campus classroom, TEC shares space with the Department's Alternate to Suspension Program (ASP). Like its new counterpart, ASP aims to get juveniles off the street. Its intensive learning environment and disciplined approach have helped a number of students rededicate themselves to school. . . .
>
> After the counselor evaluates the students, one of three things may happen. If students have no history of truancy, PET officers take them back to school. Suspended students take part in ASP, and about 50 percent successfully complete the program and return to school without incident. Students who seem to be making truancy a habit usually meet with their parents and the counselor to discuss possible solutions to the problem.

In North Miami Beach, Part I crimes all decreased. The department's crime analyst tracked and mapped these crimes, many of which occurred during school hours. The TEC survey revealed that 20 percent of truants admitted to committing crimes while they were skipping school.

Crisp and Vancil (2001, p.40) describe a situation where the Zero Tolerance For Truancy program in Greer, South Carolina, was resulting in numerous student suspensions. Many youths were not playing hooky but were suspended from school: "The suspensions created problems for law enforcement. Most suspended students had little or no daytime supervision. When they were removed from the structured environment of the school, they were spending their days roaming the streets. Left to their own devices, some engaged in criminal behavior, driving juvenile crime statistics upwards or were themselves victims of crime."

The Greer police chief recognized that officers seldom have contact with youths in middle school unless the youths were in trouble. He also realized that positive intervention could be difficult if not impossible after adversarial encounters, and he wanted to reach these at-risk youths before they entered the juvenile justice system. The solution was the Middle School Suspension Camp, also known as Boot Camp:

> The Middle School Suspension Camp places suspended students in an intensive five-day program operated on school grounds by sworn police officers who serve as camp directors. The camp offers students one-on-one assistance with schoolwork, instruction on life skills such as conflict resolution and physical fitness training. In return, students perform community service projects around the school. There is no corporal punishment. Students who successfully complete suspension camp have the suspension removed from their school record. . . .
>
> The first students enrolled in the suspension camp in November 1997. Since then the program's success has exceeded even the police department's expectations by contributing to sharp declines in the number of middle school suspensions and juvenile crimes.

Closely related to the truancy problem is the problem of disorderly youths in public places.

Disorderly Youths in Public Places

Scott (2001, pp.13–14) describes three general approaches to addressing problems of disorderly youths in public places:

1. A *pure control* approach views the youths as offenders whose conduct is to be controlled and prohibited coercively.

2. A *developmental* approach views youths more neutrally and adopts methods that, in addition to controlling misconduct, seek to improve the youths' general welfare.

3. An *accommodation* approach balances the youths' needs and desires against the complainants' needs and desires.

Scott (p.14) notes that police response to youth disorder might use all three approaches by (1) establishing and enforcing rules of conduct for youths, (2) creating alternative legitimate places and activities for youths and (3) modifying public places to discourage disorderly behavior. Scott (p.24) contends: "Merely increasing uniformed police officers' presence around locations where youths gather is expensive, inefficient and usually ineffective." In some instances among youths who are behaving disorderly, a runaway will be discovered.

Runaways

The police are interested in runaways because of public concern for youths' safety and welfare, not because they have committed crimes. Youthful runaway behavior often is a precursor of future delinquent behavior and is usually—in most law enforcement agencies—the least investigated status offense.

Technically runaways are individuals under the statutory age of an adult who leave home without authorized consent and are reported to the police as missing. The object of a police search is to locate such youths and return them to their families. Generally no police investigation, social service inquiry or school inquiry is conducted to determine why these children left home, why they were truant because of this absence or why they continue to run away.

Running away is a predelinquent indicator, but its value often is not recognized by parents, police, schools, social agencies or the courts.

If this danger signal is ignored, society loses another battle in controlling antisocial behavior or criminal activity. Runaways may become violent, or they may turn to robbery, burglary, drug abuse and prostitution to meet their needs.

Because children run away for many reasons, police must be sensitive in their treatment of runaways. Police must treat runaways differently to account for their age, gender, family social order, paternal makeup (original, adopted or foster) or who represents control.

When the police take an initial complaint report on a runaway, the responsible adults seldom can give a reason for the youths leaving home. In middle-class families, with few exceptions, parents do not know why their child left home. They firmly believe their son or daughter was the victim of something evil, was under the influence of neighborhood children or that the fault lies with the school system.

Police experience has shown, without too much inquiry, that these so-called sinister happenings seldom occur. They are a screen to the real problem. In most instances police do not investigate why a child left home, nor do court services personnel, unless the matter is disposed of in juvenile court and requires a final disposition of aftercare. This may be the result of priorities in personnel allocation, a lack of court support or a lack of support from state agencies.

If police dispositions are to be effective, the family must recognize the early signs of maladjustment in children. Running away is the most visible indicator of a possible future victim (assaulted, murdered) or involvement in criminal activity to support individual needs (prostitution, pornography, burglary, theft, robbery).

In its early stages, running away can often be corrected by cooperative law enforcement policies and parents. The parents must constantly be informed of the consequences of running away and advised about available assistance. Police officers can take a professional approach in their associations with children and youths who commit minor offenses by being available and helping to meet their needs. Officers know that children and youths want the opportunity to talk openly and freely about themselves and their lives to someone who will listen without judging and who will be interested in them as individuals rather than as problems to be solved or disposed of in some manner.

Another challenge facing law enforcement is dealing with underage drinking.

Underage Drinking

As with curfews, some officers see underage drinking as a low priority because of the perceived legal obstacles in processing juveniles; unpleasant, tedious paperwork; special detention procedures required for minors; lack of juvenile detention facilities or centers already above capacity; lack of significant punishment for underage drinking; and personal disagreements regarding underage drinking laws, particularly as they apply to people ages 18 to 20. Despite the objections officers may have, serious and valid reasons exist for making the enforcement of underage drinking laws a higher priority.

Scialdone (2001, p.61) describes a program to reduce underage drinking in Fontana, California: "DRY2K is a comprehensive program designed to help and encourage minors to remain alcohol-free in the new millennium." The program uses five distinct strategies to address the problem (pp.61–62):

- Minor Decoy Program—uses underage minors to conduct compliance checks on liquor-licensed stores, targeting availability of alcohol to minors.
- Shoulder Tap Program—places minors outside a store to ask customers to buy them beer, targeting adults who furnish alcohol to minors.
- Cops in Shops Program—places officers posing as clerks inside licensed locations to look for alcohol violations.
- LEAD Program—offers free training for owners and employees of stores with liquor licenses.
- Educational Program—45-minute multimedia interactive program takes students on an emotional roller coaster entertaining and educating with cartoon characters.

Geier (2003) describes the party patrol as the approach to underage drinking enforcement used in Albuquerque, New Mexico: "In addition to such offenses by minors as possession and consumption of alcohol, the Party Patrol officers enforce ordinances designed to deal with noise violations and premise liability." Officers have a planned, coordinated approach to handling party calls involving a "wolf pack response." They respond as a group, surrounding the target home and blocking off potential exit routes to ensure that no one drives from the scene after drinking alcohol. They thoroughly investigate and check the sobriety of all those in attendance. In addition to acting on tips about parties with alcohol involved, the Party Patrol also periodically checks parks, arroyos, parking lots and other hangouts where alcohol may be consumed.

Geier (p.103) reports: "The results of this underage drinking enforcement program have been remarkable. In a three-month period, officers issued 190 traffic citations and 1,284 misdemeanor citations. The unit responded to 174 actual party calls and wrote over 380 police reports."

Kurz (2001, pp.68–73) describes the Durham (New Hampshire) Alcohol Enforcement Initiative using problem-oriented community policing. Durham implemented four initiatives. The first initiative was physical arrest for alcohol violations. According to an attorney hired by the University of New Hampsire to represent charged students, being placed in handcuffs, transported to a holding facility and being booked made her clients take the alcohol issue much more seriously.

The second initiative was parental notification. Police were at a disadvantage in this college town because many students' parents lived miles away, limiting discussing the situation. Instead the parents of each minor arrested were sent a letter stating that the student had been arrested and charged with a criminal offense.

The third initiative was an Adopt-A-Cop Program where each fraternity and sorority was offered the chance to adopt a police officer in the role of mentor and advisor.

The final initiative was developing a Seacoast Alcohol Task Force to focus on initiatives such as compliance checks of businesses that sold alcohol, high visibility patrols during community festivals and plainsclothes surveillance of businesses suspected of selling to underage youths.

In conjunction with the Harvard study of binge drinking on college campuses, a survey at Louisiana State University was taken regarding alcohol policies at LSU (*LSU Campus-Community Coalition for Change*). Support or strong support was indicated for making alcohol rules clearer (94 percent), offering alcohol-free dorms (89 percent) and providing more alcohol-free recreational and cultural opportunities such as movies, dances, sports and lectures (86 percent).

The National Institute on Alcohol Abuse and Alcoholism (NIAAA)(*Alcohol Alert*, 2002, pp.2–3) studied various strategies for preventing alcohol-related problems on college campuses. It reports: "Strong evidence supports the effectiveness of the following strategies: (1) simultaneously addressing alcohol-related attitudes and behaviors (e.g., refuting false beliefs about alcohol's effects while teaching students how to cope with stress without resorting to alcohol); (2) using survey data to counter students' misperceptions about their fellow students' drinking practices and attitudes toward excessive drinking; and (3) increasing students' motivation to change their drinking habits.

The NIAAA also reports on strategies that have proved successful in populations similar to those found on college campuses: (1) increasing enforcement of minimum legal drinking age laws; (2) implementing, enforcing and publicizing other laws to reduce alcohol-impaired driving; (3) increasing the prices or taxes on alcoholic beverages; and (4) instituting policies and training for servers of alcoholic beverages to prevent sales to underage or intoxicated patrons. A closely related problem is that of youths using drugs.

Juveniles and Drug Use

Probably the best known drug prevention program is the Drug Abuse Resistance Education (DARE) Program developed in 1983 by the Los Angeles Police Department and the Los Angeles Unified School District. This program targets elementary school children offering a highly structured, intensive fifth- and sixth-grade curriculum taught by uniformed law enforcement officers.

Over the years many proponents and critics of the DARE program have surfaced, with numerous arguments presented to support the differing views. According to Schennum (2001, p.103): "Today DARE is taught in more than 80 percent of all U.S. school districts, benefiting over 26 million students. DARE is an excellent program to assist parents and society as a whole in the fight against the influences of drugs, alcohol and tobacco on children and young adults."

However, in the late 1990s DARE came under fire: "More than a decade of research studies have pointed to the program's failure to live up to supporters' claims. Federal education officials, who distribute about $500 million in drug prevention grants each year, said last year that they would no longer allow schools to spend money from the Office of Safe and Drug Free Schools on

The Drug Abuse Resistance Education (DARE) program is designed to teach elementary-age schoolchildren to say "No" to drugs. Experienced police officers teach the classroom sessions and act as facilitators. Although highly popular, the effectiveness of the program has been challenged.

DARE because it did not consider the program to be scientifically proven" ("Truth, DARE & Consequences," 2001, p.1).

A study by the University of Illinois tracked 1,800 students over six years and found that by the end of high school any impact of the program had worn off. According to Brown (2001, p.760): "DARE has been the subject of 30 other studies over the past several years and all of them have arrived at the same conclusion—any effect that the program has in deterring drug use disappears by the time students are seniors in high school." Many DARE opponents within the law enforcement community are hesitant to publicly criticize the program because their chiefs and sheriffs have invested significant time, money and political capital into it. As noted by Zernike (2001, p.A16): "DARE organizers have long dismissed criticism of the program's approach as flawed or the work of groups that favor decriminalization of drug use. But the body of research had grown to the point that the organization could no longer ignore it." In response, the curriculum was revised and will be tested in 80 high schools and 176 middle schools across the nation ("Drug Abuse Resistance Education. . .," 2001, p.2). One key change in the new version is that police officers are used more as facilitators and less as instructors.

Despite the many criticisms of DARE, Merrill et al. (2002, p.81) contend: "DARE represents the single largest prevention effort directed at reducing the use of drugs and other harmful substances among school-age children in the United States. DARE programs exist in all states and include 15,000 DARE officers working in about 8,400 schools in 1,800 school districts."

The National DARE Parent Program

A new addition to the DARE program is the DARE Parent Program (DPP), created to stimulate interest from the community and to motivate families to actively participate in preventing substance abuse. The program consists of a series of meetings at which parents learn about the DARE program their children are participating in, as well as how to recognize signs of drug use, how to use local program resources and how to communicate effectively with their children.

Whether a law enforcement agency is dealing with truants, underage drinking or drug use, efforts might be enhanced through mentoring programs.

Police as Mentors to Troubled Youths

Police who are committed to a mentoring relationship have an enormous impact on youths who are at risk of becoming chronic offenders. Carefully selected and trained police personnel can be the conduit for restoring youthful lives to productive relationships with families, schools and the community.

Mentoring is especially effective in dealing with troubled youths at risk of becoming juvenile offenders because it strikes directly at the individual's alienated condition. The youth's isolation and sense of meaninglessness is often dissolved over time through a long-term relationship characterized by respect. The youth's sense of powerlessness is eroded through a relationship with someone who helps to clarify their choices and who empowers them to make responsible decisions.

Police mentoring is the most effective means available for optimizing meaningful contact between society and alienated youth. As a youth begins to bond with a mentor, a new world view crystallizes, opening up a new range of perceived choices that reflects the values of the mentor and the community. Mentoring remains the best hope for reclaiming our troubled youths, our families, communities and society as a whole. To a large extent, the success or failure of the juvenile justice system depends on its effectiveness in handling youthful offenders—ensuring that for the vast majority of juvenile offenders their first brush with the law is the last.

Sanchez (2002, p.60) notes that police departments throughout the country are embracing mentoring. He suggests: "Researchers have identified three vitally important areas to the success of any mentoring program: screening, orientation and training, and support and supervision. Research also indicates that a young person who meets regularly with a mentor is 52 percent less likely to skip a day of school, 46 percent less likely to start using drugs, 33 percent less likely to engage in violent behavior, and 27 percent less likely to start drinking."

The Juvenile Mentoring Program (JUMP) of the OJJDP supports one-to-one mentoring projects for youths at risk of failing in school, dropping out of school or becoming involved in delinquent behavior, including gang activity and substance abuse. The OJJDP defines mentoring as a one-to-one supportive relationship between a responsible adult 18 or older (mentor) and an at-risk juvenile (mentee), which takes place on a regular basis, one to two hours per week for an average of at least one year.

The three principal program goals for JUMP are (1) to reduce juvenile delinquency and gang participation by at-risk youths, (2) to improve academic performance of at-risk youths and (3) to reduce the school dropout rate for at-risk youths.

Prevention Strategies

Common sense suggests that it is prudent to prevent youths from becoming victims or victimizers. Among the many preventive strategies available, one that costs nothing is fair and just treatment of juveniles during all contacts, whether the juvenile is a victim, a status offender, a delinquent or a gang member. Peace officers can serve as role models for personal responsibility and accountability and expect the same from the youths with whom they come in contact.

Other preventive efforts commonly engaged in by police departments include educational programs, recreation programs, crime prevention programs and diversion programs. Effective delinquency prevention programs conducted by law enforcement agencies reflect public policy and public attitudes. They often result from a reaction to a specific incident rather than from long-range preventive goals.

Early Efforts at Delinquency Prevention

When law enforcement first formally recognized the importance of actively promoting positive community relations, the approach selected was the best one possible under the existing conditions. More than 50 years ago in an effort to "get the boys off the streets" and control gang activity, the New York police started the Police Athletic League (PAL). Youngsters, mostly males, were given instruction in boxing (for Golden Glove competition), basketball and baseball. Police sponsored athletic games and tournaments.

Law enforcement also promoted programs about subjects of interest to children and their parents, including a variety of safety programs: bicycle, auto, household (poisons and related household hazards), guns and outdoor water.

Initially law enforcement sought to build a positive image rather than to develop constructive, lasting delinquency prevention programs.

Many law enforcement agencies continue to provide one-time and seasonal programs designed to address a particular problem rather than carefully planned, long-range programs.

Evolution of Prevention Programs

During the 1930s and 1940s, aside from PAL, law enforcement directed its energies toward school safety patrol programs. These programs were started with the assistance of civic and community groups for pedestrian safety. When conditions changed in the 1950s and 1960s, and mass busing of children to schools became the norm, the programs began to dissipate.

Delinquency prevention programs promoted by the police often focused on matters common to children and of concern to parents, with no eye to the future. For example in the 1960s cough medicine containing codeine, a morphine derivative, was being sold faster than druggists could stock the shelves. When law enforcement and parents became aware that such over-the-counter drugs could be purchased without a prescription and that children of all ages were buying them, prevention programs pushed to stop future purchases. Eventually legislation restricted the purchases of such cough medicines.

Police-School Liaison Programs to School Resource Officers (SROs)

A much publicized delinquency prevention plan was developed in 1958 in Flint, Michigan, with the cooperation of school authorities, parents, social agencies, juvenile court officials, businesses and the police department. The foundation for the **police-school liaison program** established a workable relationship with the public school system. This program gradually evolved into what is today the **school resource officer (SRO)** program.

Part Q of Title I of the Omnibus Crime Control and Safe Streets Act of 1968 defines the SRO as "a career law enforcement officer, with sworn authority, deployed in community-oriented policing, and assigned by the employing police department or agency to work in collaboration with school and community-based organizations." Over 30 years later, according to Lavarello (2000, p.6): "School-based policing programs are now one of the, if not THE, fastest growing areas of law enforcement." Miller (2001, p.166) reports: "About 73 percent of police departments with 100 or more sworn employees have SROs on their payrolls."

Girouard (2001a, p.1) notes: "The school resource officer concept offers an approach to improving school security and alleviating community fears." This view is shared by Atkinson (2001, p.55) who contends: "As public safety specialists, SROs contribute daily to the safety and security of the schools in which they work."

School resource officers do not enforce school regulations, which are left to the school superintendent and staff. Instead the officers work with students, parents and school authorities to apply preventive techniques to problems created by antisocial youths who have not or will not conform to the community's laws and ordinances.

The techniques used by school resource officers involve counseling children and their parents, referring them to social agencies to treat the root problems, referring them to drug and alcohol abuse agencies and being in daily contact in the school to check their progress. Often school resource officers deal with predelinquent and early delinquent youths with whom law enforcement would not have been involved under traditional programs.

The Flint SRO Program

The goals of the Flint school resource officer program are (1) to reduce crime incidents involving school-age youths, (2) to improve the attitudes of school-age youths and the police toward one another and (3) to suppress by law enforcement any and all illegal threats that endanger the child's educational environment.

In the Flint program, the resource officers' home base is the middle or senior high school because such schools are centralized and accessible. Also the bulk of investigations and contacts with juveniles are at this level. Officers become acquainted with the building directors at the various schools and reassure them that they are available should they be needed. They check the club activities at the schools and periodically appear at various club affairs to become familiar with their rules and procedures. At the same time, they check for any loitering in and around the schools during these events and take steps to correct any matters that conflict with city ordinances. As a rule school personnel supervise the social events. The officers do not become involved in matters pertaining to school policy, but they are available to give advice and help.

SROs frequently patrol the elementary school areas until school starts in the morning, and also during the noon hour and after school. They watch for any suspicious people or automobiles and for infractions of safety rules regarding routes to and from school. They also check the middle school areas for anyone loitering around the building or grounds trying to pick up students in the area. Appendix B (located on the book companion Web site at cj.wadsworth.com/hess_drowns_jj4e) provides a detailed job description for an SRO.

Many aspects of the school resource officer program benefit students, the school and the community. The communication developed between the law enforcement agencies and school personnel provides information to guide young people. Respect for law enforcement agencies is built up in the minds of the youths. The SRO becomes their friend. The effective preventive work of the school resource officer program may be a considerable part of the answer to the problem of juvenile antisocial behavior.

Trump (2002) reports on the results of the largest survey of school resource officers conducted by the National Association of School Resource Officers (NASRO). On a scale of 1 to 5, with 5 being excellent, SROs reported strong positive relationships with school administrators (4.40), students (4.39), school support staff (4.36) and teachers (4.27). Two-thirds of the 689 respondents indicated they have prevented a faculty or staff member from being assaulted by a student or someone else on campus. More than 90 percent said that they prevent 1 to 25 violent acts on campus every year, and most reported preventing 11 or more per year. Most SROs said their principal role was preventive and that they participated in a range of activities to that end, including one-on-one counseling with students, crisis preparedness planning, security audits and truancy prevention. More than 97 percent of SROs carry firearms, and almost all favored being armed.

Lavarello (2001, p.12) reports: "The National Association of School Resource Officers (NASRO) has experienced tremendous growth since its incorporation in 1989. With over 6,000 members in North America, NASRO continues to serve as the premier training organization for school-based law enforcement officers."

Goals of School Resource Officer Programs

The goals of the school resource officer program fall into two general categories: preventing juvenile delinquency and improving community relations.

Preventing Delinquency

In seeking to prevent delinquency, officers focus on both preventive actions and the official investigation of criminal activity, apprehension and court referral.

School resource officers (SROs) are a visible reminder of the need for law and order. They stress positive interactions with students who do not misbehave as well as dealing with those who are delinquent.

© Tom Carter/Photo Edit

Officers assigned to schools approach delinquency prevention through a variety of activities:

- *Act as instructors* for various school groups and classes.
- *Act as counselors* to students, separately or with school personnel.
- *Maintain contacts with parents or guardians* of students who exhibit antisocial behavior.
- *Make public appearances.*
- *Maintain files* of information on students contacted.
- *Investigate complaints of criminal activity* occurring within the school complex and the surrounding area.
- *Maintain close contact with other police agencies.*

Weiss and Davis (2002, p.99) describe how campus K9s are used in Pinellas County, Florida, to sniff out drugs and weapons: "These random checks make students less likely to bring drugs and weapons onto school grounds. The K9s are allowed to make these random checks because of the strong support of the school administration and because of the county's Code of Student Conduct, a document each parent and child must sign at the beginning of the school year."

Improving Community Relations

The second general goal of SRO programs focuses on **community relations,** projecting and maintaining an image of the police as serving the community, rather than simply enforcing laws. Enhancing community relations is accomplished in several ways.

Public appearances are a key technique. Officers speak and present films or slide programs to many types of groups, such as PTAs, service groups, church fellowships, civic gatherings, youth clubs and civil rights groups. There usually is an interplay of ideas at such gatherings, and the officers sell the idea of community service.

Another focus is *parent contacts.* Behavioral problems are often apparent in the school before they develop into more serious delinquent activity. Officers in the school know about such problems and can contact parents. They can work together with the parents to avoid any progression into serious delinquent behavior. Most parents take an interest in their children. This dissipates the age-old contest of parent versus school in the control of children. Likewise, it affects parents' attitudes toward others in authority disciplining their children.

Possibly the most effective community relations technique at officers' disposal is *individual contact.* Officers have contact with many young people at every age level. In projecting an image of the "good guys," they influence the attitudes not only of those students counseled, but also of their friends and families. Many popular myths about laws and law enforcement officers are dispelled through this type of interaction.

Another important area is *liaison work with other interested agencies,* including juvenile courts, social agencies, mental health agencies, other schools and private organizations. Officers gain operational knowledge of each and learn to coordinate their efforts with these other agencies to better treat children.

Displaying interest indicates to these agencies that police are concerned with more than simply apprehension and detention in dealing with delinquency. Undoubtedly teachers have a definite effect on their students' attitudes. Officers who help teachers with problem students improve teachers' image of the police. This, along with personally knowing a police officer, does much in long-range police-community relations and, as any preventive program must be, this preventive program is long range.

Finally, *recreational participation* is a type of interaction with youths that breaks down many walls of resentment. Officers who participate in organized athletics with youngsters build a rapport that is carried over into their other contacts with those youths.

The Virginia Model SRO Program

Schuiteman (2000, p.75) describes guidelines for adopting the Virginia Model SRO Program:

- That SRO programs reflect a community-oriented policing philosophy
- That all persons hired as SROs be certified, sworn law enforcement officers
- That all officers hired have community experience that demonstrates their interest and ability to work with youths, school personnel and the public to solve problems
- That SROs perform multiple roles, including those of law enforcer, instructor of law-related education classes, criminal justice liaison, role model and crime prevention specialist
- That SROs complete a 40-hour, DCJS-sponsored SRO Basic School
- That SROs be assigned to a single, specified secondary school (although assignment to two schools is permitted if the schools are in close physical proximity)

The SHIELD Program

The Strategic Home Intervention and Early Leadership Development (SHIELD) program of the Westminster Police Department in Orange County, California, is described by Wyrick (2000). This program capitalizes on contacts made by law enforcement officers to identify youths at risk of delinquency and refer them to appropriate community services. Figure 7.4 illustrates the SHIELD Program model.

The Importance of Teachers in Delinquency Prevention Programs

Because most delinquency prevention programs are based in schools or, at least, focus on school-age populations, it is critical that teachers be included in any delinquency prevention programs. Teachers are of vital importance to the success of any delinquency prevention program. Teachers from all grade levels might be taken on police ride-alongs so they can see the consequences for those who drop out of or fail in school.

Other Programs

Other well-known programs found throughout the country include the Officer Friendly program and the police dog McGruff ("Taking a bite out of crime") program. The McGruff program goes beyond delinquency prevention and seeks to help youths contribute positively to the community. Sometimes the McGruff crime dog also promotes safety. For example at Halloween, many police departments distribute trick or treat bags to children. These bags feature McGruff and list some tips for a safe Halloween.

Explorer Posts also are popular. These groups are an advanced unit of the Boy Scouts of America; they include high school students ages 14 to 18. Explorers wear uniforms similar to those of law enforcement officers and are taught several skills used in law enforcement, such as firearms safety, first aid, fingerprinting and the like.

Another successful police-community prevention effort is that of the Rochester (New York) Police Department. Rochester's Teens on Patrol (TOP) program uses youths to patrol the city's parks and recreational areas during the summer. Each season about 100 youths are hired to keep order in the parks. At the same time, they learn about police work. Many TOP participants have gone on to become police officers.

The Officer on the Street and Youths' Attitudes

The importance of the officer on the street cannot be overlooked. Every law enforcement officer, no matter at what level, has an opportunity to be a positive influence on youths. Ultimately youths' perceptions about the law and law enforcement will be based on one-on-one interactions with law enforcement officers.

 Youths' attitudes toward law and law enforcement are tremendously influenced by personal contacts with law enforcement officers. Positive interactions are critical to delinquency prevention.

Positive interactions, however, may not come automatically or easily, particularly within certain segments of the population. Juveniles' attitudes toward the

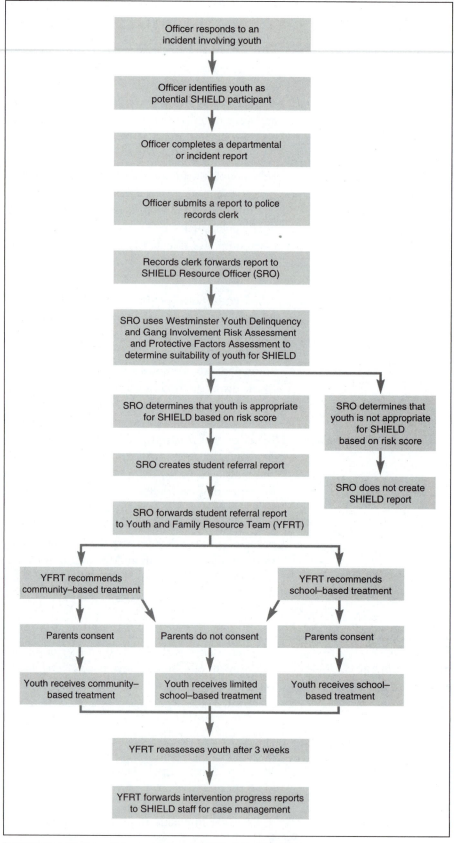

Figure 7.4
The SHIELD Program Model

Source: Phalen A. Wyrick. *Law Enforcement Referral of At-Risk Youth: The SHIELD Program.*
Washington, DC: OJJDP Juvenile Justice Bulletin, November 2000, p.4. (NCJ 184579)

police do not develop simply as a function of actual contacts with the police. Minority youths often express more negative views of the police than whites.

Coordination of Efforts and Community Policing

The need for cooperative efforts when dealing with juveniles has been stressed in preceding chapters. Law enforcement must draw upon the expertise of psychologists, psychiatrists and social workers. They also need the assistance of parents, schools, churches, community organizations and businesses. Such collaboration is at the heart of community policing. The thrust of the **community policing** philosophy is toward proactive, problem-oriented policing, seeking causes to crime and allocating resources to attack those causes through partnerships.

Traditionally law enforcement has been *separate* from the community and *reactive,* responding to incidents as they occur. During the past few years, however, the emphasis has shifted to viewing law enforcement—indeed, the entire juvenile justice system—as part of the community, reliant upon collaborative efforts to deal with our nation's youths.

 The shift to a community-policing philosophy directly affects law enforcement as well as the juvenile courts and corrections.

Police officers need to be aware of the referral resources available in the community, including not only the names of the resource agencies but also addresses, phone numbers and contact persons. Among the possible referral resources for the juvenile justice system are the following:

- Child welfare and child protection services
- Church youth programs
- Crisis centers
- Detox centers
- Drop-in centers or shelters for youths
- Guardian *ad litem* programs
- Human services councils
- Juvenile probation services
- School resources, including chemical dependency counselors, general counselors, nurses, school psychologists and social workers
- Support groups such as AlAnon, Emotions Anonymous and Suicide Help Line
- Victim/witness services
- YMCA or YWCA programs
- Youth Service Bureaus

Ideally police officers would serve on community boards and task forces that promote services for youths.

Responding to a Changing Society

Policing today is at a critical point. People of different races, cultures and languages are coming into closer contact with each other, and enormous demands are being made on people's understanding and tolerance. There are widening class divisions, more broken families and homelessness, a growing anger on the part of the disadvantaged and a rise in violence. These are the signs of a society in transition, but they are also the seeds of social unrest. Like migration, social disorder is cyclical. What happens in the present can be a reenactment of past social conflict that pitted different races and generations against each other.

Policing also is cyclical. To be prepared for the future requires a strategic plan that anticipates changes likely to occur. The police must be in partnership with the community. Policing must be proactive, identifying local crime and disorder problems. Problem-oriented policing means getting at root causes, analyzing the needs of the community and recognizing those factors that endanger the physical, mental and moral well-being of citizens. But making the transition from a reactive, incident-driven style of policing to a more proactive, problem-directed style of community-oriented policing requires a comprehensive strategy directed to officers on the street, who intervene one-on-one in efforts to make the community safe.

To identify and solve problems, the police must be able to associate with the youths of a community, especially those who misbehave and are on the brink of criminal activity. Officers in the community understand its "trouble areas" and the environmental factors that have contributed to the personalities and behaviors of young offenders.

Summary

The primary responsibility of police officers assigned to child neglect or abuse cases is the immediate protection of the child. Challenges in investigating crimes against children include the need to protect the child from further harm, the possibility of parental involvement, the difficulty of interviewing children, credibility concerns and the need to collaborate with other agencies. A special challenge in cases where a child is reported missing is determining whether the child has run away (a status offense) or has been abducted.

Law enforcement is the initial contact in the juvenile justice system. In the disposition of status offenders, how police resolve matters often depends on the officers' discretion, the specific offense and the backup available. Police officers have considerable discretionary power when dealing with juveniles. The most common procedure is to release the child, with or without a warning, but without making an official record or taking further action. The fundamental nature of the juvenile justice system is rehabilitative rather than punitive.

The majority of police dispositions involve status offenders. Running away is a predelinquent indicator, but its value often is not recognized by parents, police, schools, social agencies or the courts. If police dispositions are to be effective, the family must recognize the early signs of maladjustment. Running away is the most visible indicator of possible victimization (assault, murder) or involvement in criminal activity to support individual needs (prostitution, pornography, burglary, theft, robbery).

Initially law enforcement sought to build a positive image rather than develop constructive, lasting delinquency prevention programs. Youths' attitudes toward law and law enforcement are tremendously influenced by personal contacts with law enforcement officers. Positive interactions are crucial to any delinquency prevention attempts. The shift to a community policing philosophy directly affects law enforcement as well as the juvenile courts and corrections.

Discussion Questions

1. How are referrals to juvenile court handled in your state? Do police contribute the greatest percentage of referrals?
2. Do you believe police should make unofficial referrals, such as to community service agencies? What problems would police face when referring youths to community service agencies?
3. Do the police display a helping attitude toward youths when they make their referrals?
4. Do you believe the social standing, race and age of juveniles influence the referral procedure?
5. Should status offenses be decriminalized?
6. Which do you think is more effective, street justice by police or processing juveniles through the court system? Why?
7. Should the police be in the schools as a crime prevention method? Why or why not?

8. What police delinquency prevention programs are available in your area? Do they work? Why or why not?
9. Joe, a 13-year-old white male, has been apprehended by a police officer for stealing a bicycle. Joe took the bicycle from the school grounds shortly after a program at the school by the police on "Bicycle Theft Prevention." Joe admits to taking the bicycle, but says he only intended to "go for a ride" and was going to return the bicycle later that day. Joe has no prior police contacts that the officer is aware of. The bicycle has been missing for only an hour and is unharmed. What should the officer do in handling the incident? Do you think the bicycle theft prevention program is worthwhile? Why or why not?
10. Do you have any personal experiences with delinquency prevention programs and police?

InfoTrac College Edition Assignments

- Use InfoTrac College Edition to answer the Discussion Questions as appropriate.
- Read and outline one of the following articles and be prepared to share your outline with the class:
  - "Arrest My Kid" by Anne-Marie Cusac
  - "Police Eliminating Truancy: A PET Project" by William B. Berger and Susan Wind
  - "Investigating Potential Child Abduction Cases: A Developmental Perspective" by Wayne D. Lord, Monique G. Boudreaux and Kenneth V. Lanning
  - "Runaway or Abduction? Assessment Tools for the First Responder" by Andre B. Simons and Jeannine Willie

  - "Implementing Juvenile Curfew Programs" by Richard J. Ward, Jr.
- Go to the Web site of one of the following reference for this chapter: Child Welfare League of America or Delany-Shabazz et al. Outline the material and be prepared to share it with the class.
- Use the key word *truancy* to find either "Tackling Truancy" (no author) or "Tackling Truancy, Tackling Underachievement and Tackling Crime" by Lewis.

Internet Assignments

Complete one of the following assignments and be prepared to share your findings with the class.

■ Go to the OJJDP Web site to find and locate one of the NCJ sources listed in the references for this chapter.

■ Search the Internet to select an article relating to a concept discussed in this chapter using one of the following key words or phrases: *Amber Alert, community policing, community relations, detention, school resource officer, street justice.*

■ Go to any reference having an online address to find, read and outline the entire article.

References

Alcohol Alert. Bethesda, MD: National Institute on Alcohol Abuse and Alcoholism, October 2002.

Atkinson, Anne J. "School Resource Officers: Making Schools Safer and More Effective." *The Police Chief,* March 2001, pp.55–63.

Bennett, Wayne and Hess, Kären M. *Criminal Investigation,* 7th ed. Belmont, CA: Wadsworth Publishing Company, 2004.

Berger, William B. and Wind, Susan. "Police Eliminating Truancy: A PET Project." *FBI Law Enforcement Bulletin,* February 2000, pp.16–19.

Bolton, Joel. "Community Solutions to Juvenile Holdover Problems." *The Police Chief,* February 2002, p.105.

Brown, Cynthia. "DARE Officials Responding to Critics, Come Up with New Program." *American Police Beat,* April 2001, p.76.

Child Welfare League of America. *Summary of Juvenile Justice Provisions in 21st Century Department of Justice Appropriations Act (P.L. 107–273).* http://www.cwla.org/advocacy/jjpnjja.htm

Crisp, H. Dean and Vancil, Jolene. "Back to School: Suspension Camp Puts Students to Work while Reducing Juvenile Crime." *The Police Chief,* March 2001, pp.40–44.

Delany-Shabazz, Robin V. and Vieth, Victor. *The National Center for Prosecution of Child Abuse.* Washington, DC: OJJDP Fact Sheet #33, August 2001. (FS 200133) Web site: www.ndaa.apri.org/apri/NCPCA/Index.html

Domash, Shelly Feuer. "Protecting the Innocent." *Police,* October 2002, pp.52–56.

"Drug Abuse Resistance Education Plans Test of a New Curriculum." *Criminal Justice Newsletter,* February 26, 2001, pp.2–3.

Finkelhor, David and Ormrod, Richard. *Child Abuse Reported to the Police.* Washington, DC: OJJDP Juvenile Justice Bulletin, May 2001. (NCJ 187238)

Geier, Michael. "Party Patrol: A New Approach to Underage Drinking Enforcement." *Law and Order,* March 2003, pp.96–103.

Girouard, Cathy. *School Resource Officer Training Program.* Washington, DC: OJJDP Fact Sheet #05, March 2001a. (FS 200105)

Girouard, Cathy. *The Missing and Exploited Children's Program (Update).* Washington, DC: OJJDP Fact Sheet #16, May 2001b. (FS 200116)

Girouard, Cathy. *The National Center for Missing and Exploited Children.* Washington, DC: OJJDP Fact Sheet #28, July 2001c. (FS 200128)

Grasso, Kathi L.; Sedlak, Andrea J.; Chiancone, Janet L.; Gragg, Frances; Schultz, Dana; and Ryan, Joseph F. *The Criminal Justice System's Responses to Parental Abduction.* Washington, DC: OJJDP Juvenile Justice Bulletin, December 2001. (NCJ 186160)

Griffin, Patrick and Torbet, Patrick (eds.). *Desktop Guide to Good Juvenile Probation Practice.* Washington, DC: National Center for Juvenile Justice, June 2002.

An Implementation Guide for Juvenile Holdover Programs. National Highway Traffic Safety Administration, the Office of Juvenile Justice and Delinquency Prevention and the American Probation and Parole Association, June 2001. (DOT HS 809260)

Jezycki, Michelle. "Team H.O.P.E.: Help Offering Parents Empowerment." *Juvenile Justice,* December 2000, pp.19–24.

Johnston, Janet R.; Sagatun-Edwards, Inger; Blomquist, Martha-Elin; and Girdner, Linda K. *Early Identification of Risk Factors for Parental Abduction.* Washington, DC: OJJDP Juvenile Justice Bulletin, March 2001. (NCJ 185026)

Krainik, Peggy Wilkins. "Amber Alert: America's Missing: Broadcast Emergency Response." *Law and Order,* December 2002, pp.84–85.

Kurz, David L. "The Durham Alcohol Enforcement Initiative: Problem Oriented Community Policing in a University Setting." *The Police Chief,* October 2001, pp.66–73.

Lavarello, Curtis. "School Based Policing." *The Law Enforcement Trainer,* November/December 2000, pp.6–7.

Lavarello, Curtis. "Managing One of Law Enforcement's Fastest Growing Areas: School-Based Policing." *The Associate,* March/April 2001, pp.12–13.

Lord, Wayne D.; Boudreaux, Monique G.; and Lanning, Kenneth V. "Investigating Potential Child Abduction Cases: A Developmental Perspective." *FBI Law Enforcement Bulletin,* April 2001, pp.1–10.

LSU Campus-Community Coalition for Change. May 2003.

McDowall, David; Loftin, Colin; and Wiersema, Brian. "The Impact of Youth Curfew Laws on Juvenile Crime Rates." *Crime & Delinquency,* January 2000, pp.76–91.

Merrill, Jeffrey; Dilascio, Tracey; and Pinsky, Ilana. "Law Enforcement and Drug Prevention: A Profile of the DARE Officer." *The Police Chief,* August 2002, pp.81–88.

Miller, Christa. "The Small-Town School Resource Officer: Prudent Investment or Prohibitive Cost?" *Law Enforcement Technology,* October 2001, pp.166–174.

Pope, Carl E. and Snyder, Howard N. *Race as a Factor in Juvenile Arrests.* Washington, DC: OJJDP Juvenile Justice Bulletin, April 2003. (NCJ 189180)

Rasmussen, Janell L. "Amber Alert: Working to Curb Child Abductions." *Minnesota Police Chief,* Summer 2002, pp.43–49.

Sanchez, Tom. "Cops Mentoring Kids." *The Police Chief,* June 2002, p.60.

Santoro, Joseph A. "Monrovia's Anti-Truancy Ordinance: One Giant Step toward Keeping Kids in School and Out of Trouble." *The Police Chief,* March 2001, pp.34–39.

Schennum, Tim. "Unfair Rap for DARE." *Law and Order,* August 2001, pp.103–104.

Schuiteman, John G. "Early Returns Positive for Virginia's Model SRO Program." *The Police Chief,* November 2000, pp.74–77.

Scialdone, Frank J. "DRY2K: A Program to Reduce Underage Drinking." *The Police Chief,* October 2001, pp.57–64.

Scott, Michael S. *Disorderly Youth in Public Places.* Washington, DC: Office of Community Oriented Policing Services Problem-Oriented Guides for Police Series No. 6, September 2001.

Simons, Andre B. and Willie, Jeannine. "Runaway or Abduction? Assessment Tools for the First Responder." *FBI Law Enforcement Bulletin,* November 2000, pp.1–7.

Snyder, Howard N. *Juvenile Arrests 2000.* Washington, DC: OJJDP Juvenile Justice Bulletin, November 2002. (NCJ 191729)

Trump, Kenneth S. *2002 NASRO School Resource Officer Summary.* National Association of School Resource Officers, September 2002.

"Truth, DARE & Consequences." *Law Enforcement News,* February 28, 2001, pp.1, 10.

Walker, Samuel; Spohn, Cassia; and DeLone, Miriam. *The Color of Justice,* 2nd ed. Belmont, CA: Wadsworth Publishing Company, 2000.

Ward, J. Richard, Jr. "Implementing Juvenile Curfew Programs." *FBI Law Enforcement Bulletin,* March 2000, pp.15–18.

Weiss, Jim and Davis, Mickey. "How Campus K9s Are Keeping Students Safe." *Law and Order,* September 2002, pp.98–100.

Wyrick, Phelan A. *Law Enforcement Referral of At-Risk Youth: The SHIELD Program.* Washington, DC: OJJDP Juvenile Justice Bulletin, November 2000. (NCJ 184579)

Zernike, Kate. "Criticized as Ineffective, DARE Program to Change Strategy for Drug Prevention." *New York Times,* as reprinted in the (Minneapolis/St. Paul) *Star Tribune,* February 16, 2001, p.A16.

The Law Enforcement Response to Violent Juvenile Offenders

Street gangs prey upon their neighborhood much like a malignant growth which continues to spread through its host until only a wasted shell remains.

—Los Angeles White Paper

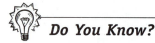

Do You Know?

- What type of patrol has the best chance of reducing gun violence?
- What four categories of threats exist?
- What the four-pronged threat assessment approach is?
- What three-pronged approach to an effective response to school violence is?
- What controversial measures have been taken to make schools safer?
- What the first step in dealing with a gang problem usually is?
- What might indicate gang activity?
- How gang members may be identified?
- How gang members communicate?
- What purpose is served by graffiti?
- What a key impediment to dealing with youth gangs is?
- How gang problems might be dealt with?
- What approaches to gang problems are being used? Which are most effective?
- At what age youths are at greatest risk for becoming a gang member?

Can You Define?

civil injunction	horizontal prosecution	representing
conditional threat	indirect threat	SHOCAP
direct threat	lock down	tagging
geographic integrity	moniker	veiled threat
graffiti	pulling levers	vertical prosecution

INTRODUCTION

Chapter 6 described the type of violent offenders the juvenile justice system must respond to: those with guns, those who commit violent crimes, those who initiate crime and violence in the schools and gangs.

While reading this chapter, keep in mind that because the police have a monopoly on the *legitimate* use of force, they have the authority to impose themselves on conflicts as agents of social control. Therefore, police-violent youth encounters are *always* potentially coercive relationships. This is a particularly important contextual variable when considering the role of the police in controlling violent encounters. The dangers implicit in this for both the police and the citizens involved are thoroughly documented in research on violence.

This chapter begins by describing the problem of guns and youths and some approaches law enforcement has used to address it. Next the challenge of youths who commit violent crimes is described. This is followed by a look at crime and violence in our schools. The chapter concludes with a discussion of the gang problem and various strategies to deal with it, including prosecution.

Guns and Youths

"This is no time for complacency. The epidemic of lethal violence that swept the United States from 1983 to 1993 was fueled in large part by easy access to weapons, notably firearms. If the sizeable number of youths still involved in violence today begin carrying and using weapons as they did a decade ago, this country may see a resurgence of the lethal violence that characterized the violence epidemic" (*Youth Violence: A Report of the Surgeon General,* 2001).

Harlow (2001, p.4) reports that more than a third (35.5 percent) of those who possessed a firearm when arrested were 20 or younger at the state level and almost one fourth (23.0 percent) at the federal level. Lizotte et al. (2000) studied factors related to gun-carrying among young people and found that gang membership and drug use affect gun-carrying when youths are younger, while high incidence of drug selling, peer gun ownership and drug use affect gun-carrying as youths get older. Such information can be helpful as law enforcement plans its approaches to the problem.

Many states have passed legislation on minors' possession of guns based on age and offender status, as shown in Table 8.1.

The Boston Gun Project, Operation Ceasefire

Lizotte and Sheppard (2001, p.6) report on the widely publicized Boston Gun initiative that demonstrated the value of problem-solving planning to reduce gun violence: "The strategies developed in Boston included gun use reduction tactics employing new gun-tracing technologies to interrupt the flow of illegal firearms to youths and a deterrence approach to inform juveniles of the severe criminal consequences they would face if caught with an illegal firearm. As a result of these and other strategies initiated by the city, youth firearm-related homicides dropped 75 percent during 1990-1998."

Braga et al. (2001a, p.195) also describe how the Boston Gun Project, Operation Ceasefire, represented an innovative partnership between researchers and practitioners to assess the city's youth homicide problem and implement an

Table 8.1
Minors: Restrictions Based on Age or Juvenile Offender Status, June 30, 2001

Jurisdiction	Minimum age: unrestricted possession and purchase[a]		Juvenile offenders restricted[b]	
	Handgun	Long gun	Handgun	Long gun
Federal	21	18	—	—
Alabama	18	—	—	—
Alaska	16	16	X	—
Arizona	18	18	X	X
Arkansas	18	18	—	—
California	21	18	X	X
Colorado	18	18	X	X
Connecticut	21	18	X	X
Delaware	21	18	X	X
Florida	18	18	X	X
Georgia	18	—	X	—
Hawaii	21	18	X	X
Idaho	18	18	—	—
Illinois	21	21	X	X
Indiana	18	18	X	—
Iowa	21	18	—	—
Kansas	18	—	X	X
Kentucky	18	—	X	X
Louisiana	18	—	—	—
Maine	16	16	X	X
Maryland	21	18	X	—
Massachusetts	21	18	X	X
Michigan	18	18	—	—
Minnesota	18	18	X	X
Mississippi	18	18	—	—
Missouri	21	18	—	—
Montana	14	14	—	—
Nebraska	21	—	—	—
Nevada	18	18	—	—
New Hampshire	18	—	—	—
New Jersey	21	18	X	X
New Mexico	19	—	—	—
New York	21	16	—	—
North Carolina	18	—	—	—
North Dakota	18	—	—	—
Ohio	21	18	X	X
Oklahoma	18	18	X	X
Oregon	18	18	X	X
Pennsylvania	18	18	X	X
Rhode Island	21	18	—	—
South Carolina	21	—	—	—
South Dakota	18	—	—	—
Tennessee	18	18	—	—
Texas	18	18	—	—
Utah	18	18	X	—
Vermont	16	16	—	—
Virginia	18	18	X	X
Washington	21	18	X	—
West Virginia	18	18	—	—
Wisconsin	18	18	X	X
Wyoming	—	—	—	—

[a] No restrictions on purchase or possession by or transfer to persons over this age.
[b] See state summaries for details of restrictions on purchase and possession.

Source: *Survey of State Procedures Related to Firearm Sales, Midyear 2001.*
April 2002. (NCJ 192065)

intervention designed to have a substantial near-term impact on the problem. These researchers' impact evaluation found: "The Ceasefire intervention was associated with significant reductions in youth homicide victimization, shots-fired calls for service and gun assault incidents in Boston." Specifically (Braga et al., 2001b, p.58): "The Ceasefire intervention was associated with statistically significant reductions in all time series, including a 63 percent decrease in the monthly number of youth homicides in Boston, a 32 percent decrease in the monthly number of citywide shots-fired calls, a 25 percent decrease in the monthly number of citywide all-age gun assault incidents, and a 44 percent decrease in the monthly number of District B-2 youth gun assault incidents."

Details about Operation Ceasefire are given by Kennedy et al. (2001) as they describe the technique of **pulling levers** used by the Boston Police Department to stop the violence perpetrated by the Vamp Hill Kings. The Kings were invited to a forum where the master of ceremonies addressed them:

> "This isn't a sting; everybody's going to be home for dinner, we just wanted you to know a few things. And this is nothing personal either; this is how we're going to be dealing with violence in the future, and you just happened to be first. So go home and tell your friends about what you hear today."
>
> The forum was dramatic. In essence, the Working Group's message to the Kings was that they and their activities were known, and although the group could not stop every instance of offending, violence would no longer be tolerated. . . .
>
> Many gang members in the audience smiled and scoffed. They stopped when the Assistant U.S. Attorney assigned to the group spoke:
>
> "This kind of street crime used to be a local matter. Not any more. The Attorney General cares more about youth violence than almost anything else. . . . We can bring in the DEA, we can bring in the FBI, we can bring in the ATF; we can prosecute you federally, which means you go to Lompoc, not stateside, and there's no parole in the federal system any more. You serve your time.
>
> The room became more silent when the panel turned to Freddie Cardoze, who was featured on his own flyer used as a handout. (Figure 8.1).

In addition to involving other agencies, the pulling levers strategy involves arresting targeted gang members for the slightest infraction, even jaywalking.

Directed Patrol

Another approach to reducing gun violence is directed patrol. Sherman et al. (1995) report on a study conducted in the early 1990s. Kansas City police officers, trained to search for illegal guns, increased traffic enforcement in a police beat with high levels of violent crime. Their efforts led to increased seizures of illegal firearms, which in turn were associated with a significant decrease in gun-related crime in the targeted area. The beat experienced a 65 percent increase in firearm seizures and an approximately 50 percent decrease in the incidence of gun-related crime.

The Indianapolis Police Department's Directed Patrol Project experienced similar success, as described by McGarrel et al. (2002, p.3): "The results of the Indianapolis directed patrol program are consistent with a growing body of research that shows that when police identify a specific problem and focus their attention on it, they can reduce crime and violence. As in the Kansas City gun intervention project, directed police patrol led to sizable reductions in gun crime. Additionally, it did not shift crime to surrounding areas or harm

---

FREDDIE CARDOZA

PROBLEM: VIOLENT GANG MEMBER

"Given his extensive criminal record,
if there was a Federal law against
jaywalking we'd indict him for that."

—Don Stern, US Attorney

SOLUTION: ARMED CAREER
CRIMINAL CONVICTION

Arrested with one bullet
Sentence: 19 years, 7 months
No possibility of parole

ADDRESS:

OTISVILLE FEDERAL
CORRECTIONAL INSTITUTE

Maximum Security Facility, New York

Figure 8.1
**Cardoza Flyer Created
by the Gun Project
Working Group**

police-community relations." McGarrel et al. (p.17) conclude: "The results of this study indicate that directed patrol, using a *targeted* rather than a *broad* general deterrence strategy can have a significant effect on violent crime."

 Directed patrol rather than general patrol can have a significant effect on violent crime.

*Youth Firearms
Violence Initiative*

Another approach was the Youth Firearms Violence Initiative (YFVI) launched in 1995 by the U.S. Department of Justice's Office of Community Oriented Policing Services. COPS provided up to $1 million to police departments in 10 cities to fund interventions directed at combating the rise of youth firearms violence (Baltimore, Maryland; Birmingham, Alabama; Bridgeport, Connecticut; Cleveland, Ohio; Inglewood, California; Milwaukee, Wisconsin; Richmond, Virginia; Salinas, California; San Antonio, Texas; and Seattle, Washington).

Among the key findings of this initiative, according to Dunworth (2000, pp.1–2) were:

- A dedicated unit may exert a greater effect on gun-related crime than a unit that applies traditional tactics and uses patrol officers on a rotating basis.
- When employed as part of YFVI, traditional enforcement tactics did not produce significant changes in firearms violence levels.
- Cooperating with other law enforcement agencies and community organizations and representatives was a key factor in effective implementation of firearms violence control and prevention strategies.
- Proactive arrest policies focused on gun-related offenses were shown to have a consistent measurable association with subsequent gun-related crime.
- Most of the participating departments returned to traditional policing approaches when federal funding ended.

Table 8.2 summarizes the strategies and tactics used at five of the sites. It is of interest that only Baltimore implemented school-based activities.

Project Safe Neighborhoods

Yet another gun reduction initiative is Project Safe Neighborhoods, a nationwide commitment to reduce gun crime by networking existing local programs that target gun crime and providing those programs with additional tools necessary to be successful. The goal is to take a hard line against gun criminals through every available means to create safer neighborhoods. Project Safe Neighborhoods seeks to achieve heightened coordination among federal, state and local law enforcement, with an emphasis on tactical intelligence gathering, more aggressive prosecutions and enhanced accountability through performance measures. The Project Safe Neighborhoods Web site is www.psn.gov. It is anticipated that a reduction in youths carrying firearms would also result in a reduction in violent juvenile crime.

Violent Juvenile Crime

Butts and Travis (2002, p.10) suggest:

Clearly, something happened to cause the increase in violent youth crime seen during the 1980s and early 1990s, and just as clearly, other factors combined to bring down violent crime after 1994. Such rapid changes in violent behavior argue against the hypothesis of demographic inevitability that led some researchers to predict a violent crime wave in the late 1990s. Rather, crime trends over the past two decades suggest that changes in violent crime may be associated with fluctuation in unemployment and economic distress, the nexus between violent drug markets and firearms, and general levels of community disorder and the quality of everyday life for children, youths and families.

Perhaps the key question for future policy and research is whether a particular combination of social forces sets off each wave of juvenile violence. In a volatile social environment, researchers should routinely monitor community conditions as well as the attitudes and expressed norms of young people to understand better what behaviors are considered inappropriate and unacceptable within the youth population. A research program to detect "tipping points" in these conditions and attitudes may help communities anticipate and avoid the next sudden increase in youth violence.

Table 8.2
Police Department Strategies and Tactics of the Youth Firearms Violence Initiative (YFVI)

Site	Total Budget and Configuration	Street-Based Activities	School-Based Activities	Community-Based Activities	GIS*/Crime Analysis
Baltimore	$999,906 • Cherry Hill: 9 officers • Park Heights: 15 officers	• Juvenile Violent Crime Flex Team: surveillance, intelligence gathering and targeted enforcement • Curfew Enforcement Team: focused on chronically truant students	• In Park Heights, two city police officers worked with middle and high schools • Supported the Magnet School for Law Enforcement, a criminal justice curriculum for high school students • Three officers implemented the Straight Talk About Risk (STAR) Program	• Community resource centers (Kobans) in schools provided a police presence and liaison with community groups • Curfew enforcement officers provided information, counseling and housing to truant students and families	• Department had GIS capability prior to YFVI
Cleveland	$685,342 • 27 officers, 2 sergeants	• Residential Area Policing Program (RAPP) Houses in neighborhoods with high violence, staffed around the clock for 90 days	None	• RAPP House officers coordinated cleanup and youth activities • RAPP House used for neighborhood meetings	• Department had GIS capability prior to YFVI
Inglewood	$787,201 • Strategy Against Gang Environments (SAGE) Gang Enforcement Task Force: 1 sergeant, 6 officers • Strengthened the Street Terrorist Enforcement and Prevention (STEP) Task Force: 6 officers, 1 probation officer, 1 district attorney	• SAGE program: civil remedies against gang members; task force focused on weapons violations • STEP: act with criminal sanctions against street gangs and a task force that conducted street enforcement • Probation officer targeted gang members on probation	None	• Rites-of-Passage Mentoring Program used police officers, firefighters and community leaders to teach youths civic values, self-esteem and conflict mediation • Gun and Weapons Buy-Back Program • KIDSAFE campaign taught parents about the dangers of handgun use and possession • Media and poster campaign addressed youth firearm violence prevention	• Juvenile records computerized for YFVI • Internally developed a GIS system (with minimal YFVI funding)
Salinas	$999,524 • Violence Suppression Unit (VSU): 1 lieutenant, 2 sergeants, 16 officers	• VSU: dedicated to work full time on suppressing youth handgun violence • Crime tip hotline • Intensified efforts to locate firearms and track down their origins	None	None	• An outside contractor implemented ArcView/ArcInfo system
San Antonio	$999,963 • Rotation: 9 officers deployed nightly	• Weapons Recovery and Tracking Team • Street Crime Arrest Team	None	None	• Research the youth firearm violence problem • Computer linkup with trauma centers throughout the city

* Geographic information systems.

Source: Terence Dunworth. *National Evaluation of the Youth Firearms Violence Initiative.* Washington, DC: National Institute of Justice Research in Brief, November 2000, p.5. (NCJ 184482)

Senna et al. (2003, p.396) also express concern about future trends: "Though the juvenile violent crime rate has recently declined, the future is uncertain. Some experts believe that a surge of violence will occur as the children of baby boomers enter their 'prime crime' years. Some experts predict that juvenile arrests for violent crime will double by the year 2010."

It is well documented that a large number of crimes are committed by a small number of repeat offenders. Often these recidivists are also violent. In the 1990s the Office of Juvenile Justice and Delinquency Prevention instituted a Serious Habitual Offender Comprehensive Action Program (**SHOCAP**) aimed at youth violence. Most recommendations of this program are still applicable today for violent offenders.

The recommendations for *detention* are to establish a policy of separate and secure holding of all designated habitual offenders, to provide a special close custody classification for all designated violent offenders to protect staff and other correctional clients, and monitor and record all activities and transactions of these offenders.

The recommendations at *intake* are mandatory holding of all identified violent offenders brought in on new charges, immediate notification of the prosecutor of the intake, and special follow-up and records preparation for the detention hearings.

The recommendations for *prosecution* of violent offenders are to file a petition (charges) with the court based on the highest provable offense, resist any pretrial release, seek a guilty plea on all offenses charged and vertically prosecute all cases (assign only one deputy district attorney to each case). Other recommendations include providing an immediate response to police and detention officials upon notification of the arrest, participating in interagency working groups and on individual case management teams, and sharing appropriate information with the crime analyst or official designated to develop and maintain profiles on violent offenders. A formal policy of seeking the maximum penalty for each conviction or adjudication should be established.

Fingerprinting and Photographing Juveniles

Children and youths involved in juvenile justice system proceedings may be fingerprinted or photographed under specific conditions. Section 56 of the Uniform Juvenile Court Act specifies that law enforcement officers may take and file fingerprints of children 14 and older who are involved in the crimes of murder, non-negligent manslaughter, forcible rape, robbery, aggravated assault, burglary, housebreaking, purse snatching and automobile theft. Children's fingerprint files should be kept separate from adult files and should be kept locally—not sent to a central state or federal depository unless in the interest of national security. The fingerprints should be removed from the file and destroyed if the child is adjudicated not to be delinquent or if the child reaches age 21 and has not committed a criminal offense after age 16. If latent fingerprints are found during an offense and law enforcement officers have probable cause to believe they are the prints of a particular child, they may fingerprint the child, regardless of age or the offense. If the comparison of the latent and inked prints is negative, the fingerprint card is to be immediately destroyed.

Section 56 also specifies that, without a judge's consent, children should not be photographed after being taken into custody unless the case is transferred to another court for prosecution.

*A Comprehensive
Approach*

All too often chronic, serious violent juvenile offenders "fall through the cracks" of the juvenile justice system because efforts are not coordinated. In response to rising numbers of habitually violent youths, the Colorado Springs Police Department instituted a Serious Habitual Offender/Directed Intervention (SHO/DI) Program aimed at this group of juvenile offenders. The program had three goals:

- To develop trust and cooperation between agencies serving juveniles
- To identify and overcome real and perceived legal obstacles to cooperative efforts
- To build a credible interagency information process to identify and track habitual juvenile offenders

The ultimate goal was to *incapacitate* repeat offenders, whether through detention, incarceration, probation or other means. One important component of the program was a court order signed by a juvenile judge allowing the police department to share information with other agencies in the juvenile justice system. Another important outcome of the program was a change in how the juvenile portion of the justice system was viewed. Traditionally juvenile matters received low priority. "Kiddy Court" was not taken seriously, and beginning lawyers were assigned to prosecute juveniles. This practice was changed with the institution of the SHO/DI Program.

SHOCAP, introduced earlier in the chapter, recommended the following action steps for the *management* of violent offenders:

- Develop special crime analysis and violent offender files.
- Coordinate interagency activities and services for designated violent offenders.
- Prepare profiles of violent offenders.
- Conduct instantaneous radio checks of a juvenile's prior police contacts for patrol officers.
- Use field interrogation cards or juvenile citations to document reprimands and non-arrest situations.
- Institute directed patrol assignments to increase field contacts, assist in community control of probationers and follow up on habitual truancy cases.
- Provide daily transmittal of all field interrogation or juvenile citation cards to probation authorities.
- Supply regularly updated lists of designated violent offenders to all police officers.

The juvenile justice system must recognize that some youthful offenders are simply criminals who happen to be young. Every experienced law enforcement officer has dealt with criminally hardened 13- or 14-year-olds. Although this group represents only a small fraction of our youths, they commit a large percentage of all violent crimes. Public safety demands that law enforcement recognize and respond to this criminal element. The challenge for the juvenile justice system is to identify this group of hard-core offenders and to treat them as adults, including providing for the use of juvenile offense records in adult sentencing. It is this group of hard-core offenders who often are responsible for the crime and violence found in the nation's schools and for the violence perpetrated by gangs.

School Crime and Violence

Many youths are demonstrating an increased capacity for violence, which has crept into the schools and made students fearful of victimization by their classmates. Metal detectors, surveillance cameras and drug- and weapons-detector dogs are a growing presence on school campuses nationwide. When the final bell rings and the class day is over, the violence carries over to extracurricular activities and athletic fields, where students often are taught to compete and win at all costs. Aggression is rewarded and even modeled by the parents who, in front of their own children, shamelessly hurl more than words at coaches, umps and parents of the opposing team. Sometimes the competitive spirit turns deadly, as was seen at a Boston skating rink in July 2000 when one hockey dad killed another in a dispute over rough play during a practice of their sons' teams.

Chapter 6 looked at some of the problems in schools. Several states have passed laws requiring school officials to report certain types of offenses to local police. Illinois school principals, for example, must report acts of intimidation and attacks on school personnel in addition to other crimes committed by students. In many states failure to report violent incidents to a law enforcement agency is a criminal offense—usually a misdemeanor (*Reporting School Violence,* 2002, p.3).

Pollack and Sundermann (2001, p.13) contend: "More than anything else, the school shootings of recent years have taught us that school safety is not about any one method of control: metal detectors, surveillance systems, or swift punishment. . . . We now understand that safe schools require broad-based efforts on the part of the entire community, including educators, students, parents, law enforcement agencies, businesses and faith-based organizations."

As noted earlier, educators are commonly the ones who detect and report incidents of suspected child abuse or family violence. Educators may also, however, be first-hand witnesses to and, on occasion, victims of violence, as the aggression experienced at home by some children finds its way onto school grounds. A variety of elements may lead police in a certain jurisdiction to respond to incidents of school violence, as Welsh et al. (2000, p.252) report: "Community or neighborhood factors frequently associated with school misbehavior and delinquency include high population density, high residential mobility, high poverty rate, availability of weapons and drugs, and a high rate of adult involvement in crime."

Bullying

As noted in Chapter 6, some victims of bullying suffer such humiliation and loss of self-esteem they become violent toward themselves. According to Piazza (2001, p.68), estimates based on suicide statistics released by the Centers for Disease Control and Prevention place the number of suicides by children under age 19 that are bully-related, or "bullycides," in the triple digits.

Playgrounds are a common location for bullying to occur. They should be carefully supervised.

Ericson (2001, p.2) suggests that students be surveyed anonymously to determine the nature and prevalence of a school's bullying problem, increase supervision of students during breaks and conduct school-wide assemblies to discuss the issue. Rules against bullying should also be strictly enforced.

Sampson (2002, pp.19–23) recommends using a multifaceted, comprehensive "whole-school" approach, including increasing student reporting of bullying; developing activities in less-supervised areas; reducing the time students spend less supervised; staggering recess, lunch and class-release times; monitoring areas where bullying can be expected (e.g., lavatories); assigning bullies to a particular location or to particular chores during release times; and posting classroom signs prohibiting bullying and listing the consequences for it.

Sampson (pp.23–24) notes responses with limited effectiveness: training students in conflict resolution and peer mediation, adopting a zero-tolerance policy, providing group therapy for bullies and encouraging victims to simply stand up to bullies.

School Shooters

Following traditional law enforcement protocol, many have tried profiling the shooters and victims involved in school violence, searching for a pattern that may help predict or prevent similar events in the future. Reporting on the Santana High School shootings in Santee, California, Maran (2001) states: "The shooter is a boy again—this time he's 15, a freshman—and once again, he's a kid who got picked on at school all the time. . . . He [fits] the increasingly familiar profile of the school-yard gunman—a white teenage boy, a misfit, in a large suburban high school."

Pedersen (2002, p.33) adds: "A convincing commonality in the history of perpetrators of school violence is their propensity to animal cruelty. Inquiries into such behaviors should not be overlooked, nor evidence of such behavior minimalized." Turner (2000, p.28) notes the Humane Society of the United States considers animal cruelty one link in the chain of family violence, further observing: "The FBI has used the correlation between childhood animal abuse and adult violence for years in profiling serial killers."

O'Toole (2000, p.1), recall, warned against relying on profiles or checklists of danger signs to identify the next youth likely to bring lethal violence to a school, stating simply: "Those things do not exist." As noted in Chapter 6, school violence almost never occurs without warning.

Early Warning Signs

Although use of profiles and checklists is strongly discouraged, early warning signs of violent behavior have been recognized which, when presented in combination, might aid in identifying and referring children who may need help. Among these are low tolerance for frustration, poor coping skills, signs of depression, alienation, lack of empathy, an exaggerated sense of entitlement, an attitude of superiority, anger management problems, intolerance, lack of trust, rigid and opinionated, and negative role models (O'Toole, pp.18–21).

Threat Assessment

O'Toole (p.5) notes: "All threats are NOT created equal." Some herald a clear and present danger; others represent little danger.

 Threats may be classified as direct, indirect, veiled or conditional.

A **direct threat** identifies a specific act against a specific target and is delivered in a straightforward manner, clearly and explicitly; for example, "I am going to put a bomb in a locker." An **indirect threat** is vague and ambiguous; for example, "If I wanted to, I could blow up this school." A **veiled threat** strongly implies but does not explicitly threaten violence; for example, "We would be better off if this school were destroyed." A **conditional threat** warns that a violent act will occur unless certain demands are met; for example, "If you don't pay me $100,000, I will blow up this school."

O'Toole (pp.10–24) describes a four-pronged assessment approach to determine the likelihood of a student becoming a school shooter based on the "totality of the circumstances" known about a student.

 The four-pronged threat assessment approach examines the student's personality, family dynamics, school dynamics and the student's role in those dynamics, and social dynamics.

This model provides a framework to evaluate a student to determine whether he or she has the motivation, means and intent to carry out a threat.

The Law Enforcement Response

As the nature of school violence has changed over the years, so too has law enforcement's response to such incidents. According to Sanders (2001, p.100):

> The tragic shootings in Littleton, CO, changed the entire landscape of police tactics and training. . . . Gone are the days when the first police officers at the scene of an active shooter were expected merely to contain the scene and call SWAT. . . .
>
> Large and small agencies are accepting they must be adequately prepared at the patrol level to handle such time-critical, mega-violent incidents as school shootings. Hard experience has proven these events are not a strictly urban problem, nor can they wait for a traditional SWAT response. Patrol staffs and tactical teams nationwide are expanding their traditional roles, blurring the lines somewhat in a trend toward training and equipping officers at all levels to quickly and decisively put an end to such incidents.

The crime prevention unit of the San Jose (California) Police Department has developed the Safe Alternatives and Violence Education (SAVE) program in response to a 70 percent increase in crimes involving weapons on school campuses. This one-day, six-hour class is taught primarily by police officers during which the realities of violence as well as the consequences of and responsibilities for bad choices are discussed. Students referred to the program have been caught with knives (60 percent), replica/BB guns (11 percent) and real guns (2 percent). Of all student participants, 84 percent do not commit new violations of any kind, including truancy, for one year. After six years, 78 percent remained violation free ("Short-Term Youth Violence Prevention Program Claims Long-Term Success," 2000, pp.12–13).

Another trend, particularly among smaller departments, is toward more cross-training and pooling of resources. A comprehensive, step-by-step discussion of police response to school violence is beyond the scope of this text; however, several publications focus entirely on this subject. A particularly useful document addressing school violence is published by the International Association of Chiefs of Police (IACP). It is based on the input of more than 500 experts and 15 focus groups with a diverse range of disciplines. The *Guide for Preventing and Responding to School Violence* is available online at www.theiacp.org

In Search of Safer Schools

According to Sheley (2000, p.48), the most common measure taken to reduce school violence has been automatic suspensions for weapons violations. The problem with school suspensions has been discussed. Other common measures include revising disciplinary codes, designating schools as drug-free zones and conducting conflict resolution and mediation programs.

Paynter (2000, p.72) suggests a three-pronged approach to enhance school security and respond to incidents of school violence.

 An effective three-pronged approach to school security encompasses crisis planning, security technology and school/law enforcement/community partnerships.

Crisis Planning

Every agency and institution affected or involved during an episode of school violence must decide in advance how they plan to respond, knowing that no two situations will be exactly the same and even the best-laid plans will require on-the-spot, last-minute adjustments. For police, the first step is generally to obtain blueprints or floor plans and to conduct walk-throughs of local schools. Law enforcement should know the layouts of every school in its jurisdiction. Pedersen (p.32) adds: "Most experts agree that all schools should have a violence prevention plan available for law enforcement officers; one that identifies access points, dark hallways and architectural considerations that will affect physical safety."

Some departments stage mock disasters to test their emergency preparedness for acts of school violence and to identify areas that need improving. Such drills frequently highlight the importance of collaboration and communication with other agencies for an effective response. Referring to mock disaster exercises in Hampton, Virginia, Minetti and Caplan (2000, p.12) state: "The drills gauged the response capabilities of all the department's systems and units. They also illustrated the department's ability to work with fire departments and other police departments. SWAT teams, hostage negotiators, role players and emergency fire and medical personnel joined uniformed officers to try to diffuse situations that in real life could be violent or fatal."

Rosenbarger (2001, p.30) describes a similar exercise in another jurisdiction: "The Benton County, IN, Sheriff's Department's mock shooting at the county's sprawling rural high school involved: tactical teams from four different sheriff's departments; patrol officers from more than a dozen police and sheriff's departments; negotiators from the state police; EMS from three locations; emergency management, paramedics and a moulage team from the regional medical center; electronic and print media from three counties; and a MedEvac helicopter." He (p.36) concludes: "The overall lesson from this training is the same lesson that happens so frequently. Teams cannot train for just one piece of the police response to an emergency and expect the pieces to all fit together seamlessly during the real emergency. At some point, every aspect of the response, from the patrol response to the tactical response, to the command response to the EMS and MedEvac response, must be brought together for a realistic test."

Law enforcement in San Diego County has the dubious distinction of having responded to two high school shootings just 17 days apart, both in March 2001. They credit much of their success in resolving the incidents to the regional communications system (RCS), a network that "provided us with the interoperability we needed to talk with all of the agencies dispatched to the call and coordinate their work at the scene" (Zoll and Munro, 2001, p.55).

Schools must also necessarily participate in crisis planning. Most, if not all, schools have preparedness plans for emergencies such as fires, tornados, hurricanes or earthquakes. Many, however, have neglected to devise a response plan for school violence, thus remaining unsecure and unprepared for such crises. Some school systems in the United States have adopted a lock-down procedure as a standard response to the threat of an active shooter. Schmitt (2000, p.139) explains: "Some plans are simple, some so complex they require a notebook to hold them, but most stressed that, if word reaches the classrooms that a shooter is loose in the building, teachers should turn out their lights, lock their doors (if possible) and have their students hide while waiting for the SWAT team that will rescue them."

Schmitt also notes that, while this response is the current norm in schools across the country, some officers completely disagree with it. For example, two officers in suburban Chicago are teaching schools in their area a much simpler response plan: Get out of the building. NOW. As one of the officers asserts: "School shootings are not SWAT operations. Standard critical response tactics don't apply here. By the time SWAT arrives on the scene, the damage has already been done" (Schmitt, p.139). These officers (p.140) recommend the following action plan: (1) Leave the kill zone. If you can't, then (2) Find a safe room. If there isn't one, then, as a last resort, (3) Lock down.

Security Technology

A second prong in the effort to achieve safer schools involves implementing security technology, such as weapons screening programs, entry control systems and video cameras. According to Dorn (2001, p.32):

> Currently, students who carry weapons to school are caught only on very rare occasions. Based on student surveys, [a] conservative estimate is that students carry guns to school 18 million times each year. Less than 4,000 student gun expulsions are reported to the United States Department of Education each year. Even after factoring for underreporting, it's estimated that only one gun is recovered for every 4,500 times that a gun is carried to school. For knives and other types of weapons, the rate of carry is even higher, and the recovery rates are lower.

Paynter (p.76) states: "Metal detectors, either handheld or portal types, efficiently detect the presence of firearms, knives, razor blades, etc. But these systems present their share of problems. . . . In many cases, walk-through metal detectors are simply not practical, as most schools have multiple entrances and exits." Furthermore: "[While] the technology itself is very cheap, . . . the manpower it takes to [use] it well is expensive. These systems really are for less than 10 percent of the schools in the country" (p.76).

Recognizing that a significant proportion of school violence is perpetrated by those who neither attend nor work at the school, many districts are implementing entry control systems, such as photo ID cards, to make it easier to spot outsiders. In addition: "Issuing every visitor a self-expiring pass also limits access. These badges use a 'disappearing' ink that erases within 24 hours, preventing an individual from using the same pass to enter the school at a later date" (Paynter, p.76).

Video cameras are also being installed as a way to curb school violence. Most cameras are not actively monitored but, rather, tape on a continuous loop and are reviewed only when an incident is reported. When a high school in Washington State became beset by bullying problems, the school put the issue under the microscope and gathered as much data as they could. According to Smith-LaBombard (2001, p.10): "Through police incident reports and student surveys, I identified the lunchroom as the center of bullying and harassment. [The] school resource officer had to spend a disproportionate amount of time in the lunchroom to keep a lid on aggression. Students most often mentioned the lunchroom when they talked of feeling unsafe in school." She (p.9) also reports that incidents of bullying, harassment and intimidation decreased, in part, as a result of surveillance video cameras being placed in the lunchroom.

While many other schools have found positive benefits in using video cameras and other security devices, Paynter (p.79) stresses: "Technology and planning cannot replace personnel. . . . Schools should not become overly dependent on security technology and dehumanize the school environment. . . . These technologies work most efficiently and effectively when schools appropriately balance human resources and technology resources."

Partnerships

In cannot be emphasized enough that, as with so many other areas of police operations, partnerships are a vital component in an effective response to school violence. As Dorn (p.31) states bluntly: "A school without a law enforcement partnership is as outdated as a school without electricity." While partnerships to address the issue of school violence can take many forms and involve numerous entities, one of the most effective approaches has been to station officers directly on school campuses as school resource officers (SROs), as discussed in Chapter 7.

School Resource Officers (SROs)

Dorn (p.31) suggests: "While every school does not require a full time SRO, every school should have an effective collaboration with law enforcement." Demand for SROs has increased dramatically, which can be understood by looking at the School Safety Pyramid developed by the Center for the Prevention of School Violence. Illustrated in Figure 8.2, the pyramid reflects the importance of the community policing concept in school safety.

The community sits at the pyramid's base because the school environment often mirrors what's happening in the community. Community problems can disrupt the school environment and contribute to crime and violence in that environment. The school resource officer rests on the pyramid's next level because the SRO is an integral connection between the school and the community.

While SROs have traditionally served to educate students about topics such as pedestrian safety and the dangers of substance abuse, Scott (2001, p.69) notes: "More recently the role of the school liaison program has changed as local law enforcement agencies are attempting to defuse potentially violent student situations in light of shootings at high schools across the country in recent years." He adds: "They have realized the need to impact children at an earlier age to help stop a potential problem down the road. The real goal is to keep kids out of the prison system and help them to establish a variety of values early on."

Schuiteman (2000, p.77) asserts: "SROs are also gaining acceptance as players in school disciplinary processes and are increasing the usage of school and community resources for resolving conflict, aiding victims, and reducing the destructive impulses of at-risk youths. . . . School staff members strongly endorse the presence of SROs, and SROs report success in reducing violence, preventing conflict, and improving school security."

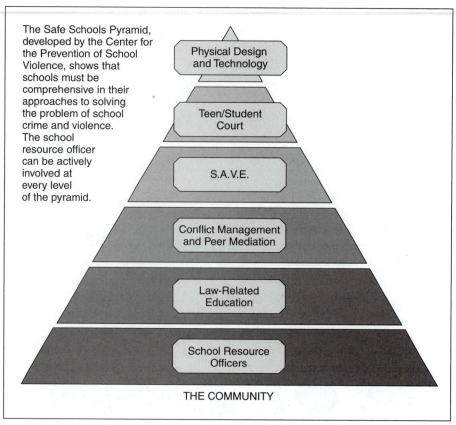

The Safe Schools Pyramid, developed by the Center for the Prevention of School Violence, shows that schools must be comprehensive in their approaches to solving the problem of school crime and violence. The school resource officer can be actively involved at every level of the pyramid.

Physical Design and Technology

Teen/Student Court

S.A.V.E.

Conflict Management and Peer Mediation

Law-Related Education

School Resource Officers

THE COMMUNITY

Figure 8.2
The Safe Schools Pyramid

Source: Ronnie L. Paynter. "Policing the Schools." *Law Enforcement Technology*, October 1999, p.35. Reprinted by permission of the Center for the Prevention of School Violence.

Challenge U is another law enforcement effort to encourage positive student behavior. As Dyer (2000, p.32) explains: "Oxnard [California] police officers can offer this choice [Challenge U] to students who engage in fighting, smoking, graffiti, truancy and similar behaviors." Challenge U has three parts: 6 hours of afternoon school instruction in dealing with antisocial behavior, 8 hours of weekend community service and an 8-hour hike. As the name implies, Challenge U challenges students with behavior problems to enter into agreements to conduct themselves in a positive way and to accept responsibility for abiding to the agreement.

San Bernardino County, California, has developed its own three-pronged approach to school safety through Operation CleanSWEEP (Success with Education/Enforcement Partnership), a triple partnership between the office of the superintendent of schools, the sheriff's department and the court system. Using juvenile citations, security assessment and special projects, this triumvirate tackled the problem of school crime and violence perpetrated by youths who previously had received neither genuine punishment nor rehabilitative guidance. As Penrod (2001, p.21) explains:

Operation CleanSWEEP is a system that, among many different efforts, places students into *other* programs—programs designed to stymie their unacceptable behavior. For many teenagers, this program represents their first encounter with the concept of personal accountability, and it intends to have them feel the sting of a collective societal reprimand for their actions. At the same time, CleanSWEEP seeks to avoid criminalizing offending students (no permanent criminal record exists for cited students). Moreover, by keeping offenders in the classroom, the program avoids disrupting their education and also helps the school not lose attendance funding due to suspended or expelled students.

He (p.22) concludes: "School resource officers have reported that as offenders have gone through the court system and told other students about their experiences, students have begun to realize that the consequences for personal misbehavior are becoming unavoidable. All in all, Operation CleanSWEEP has had a tremendous impact. Not only have measurably fewer fights and acts of disruption and defiance occurred on participating school campuses but educators and students alike feel safer in their learning environment."

Other Efforts to Prevent School Violence

Some schools have supplemented their violence prevention efforts with programs, policies and procedures aimed at problematic student behavior. Intervention and behavior modification programs have proved successful in some jurisdictions. For example, a high school once plagued by bullying, harassment and intimidation resolved such issues through a multi-faceted effort involving:

- Increased staff presence in identified problem areas, such as the lunchroom.
- Mandatory participation in Harassment Awareness Training class for student harassers.
- A Big Brothers/Big Sisters mentoring program that paired high school and middle school students to help prevent bullying among freshmen.
- Workshops that brought together student athletes (identified as the group primarily involved in bullying), victimized students, school staff, victim services advocates and police officers. Parents, counselors and other community members concerned about violence issues also were allowed to attend (Smith-LaBombard, p.9).

Most such policies and procedures focus on the possession of weapons and other contraband on school property. And while it seems to make good sense that schools, in fulfilling their duty to maintain a safe learning environment, should restrict what students are allowed to carry on campus, policies and procedures aimed at achieving the goal of safety are not without controversy.

 Some schools have adopted controversial measures such as zero-tolerance policies or school security procedures known as lock downs.

Zero-Tolerance Policies

Holloway (2001/2002, p.84) notes: "Zero-tolerance policies, those school policies that mandate predetermined consequences or punishments for specific offenses, have become a popular disciplinary choice. A recent government study found more than three-quarters of all schools reported having such policies."

Criticism of these policies is expressed by Heck (2001, p.9), who cautions: "Schools across the nation have adopted zero-tolerance policies hoping that they will lessen the chances that a violent incident will occur. However, while such policies might prove useful in some situations, school administrators must use them with discretion and common sense; otherwise, a net-widening effect may result, which can place additional strain on students, teachers, parents, law enforcement, and the juvenile justice system." Consider, for example the following case from Ft. Myers, Florida:

> A high school honor student who will graduate next week was sent to jail and will miss the ceremony because a kitchen knife was found in her car. [According to a report,] school officials saw the knife on the floor of the passenger's side of [her] car while she was in the school. [The girl], 18, spent Monday in jail on a felony charge of possession of a weapon on school property. . . .
>
> "They're taking away my memories," [she] said, as she walked out of the Lee County Jail . . . after posting $2,500 bail. "I'm so angry. I won't get to graduate with my friends because of a stupid kitchen knife." The knife, which has a 5-inch blade, had been left in the car after [she] moved some possessions over the weekend, she said. Her family claims the arrest is a case of political correctness run amok. But [the] principal said, "A weapon is a weapon is a weapon" ("Florida Honor Student . . .," 2001, p.A13).

Another controversial effort aimed at preventing school violence is the planned but unannounced lock down.

Proactive Lock Downs

Some schools use a **lock down** not as a reactive response to a crisis, but rather as a proactive step to avoid a crisis. Guy (2001, p.7) describes how these efforts aim to deter school violence:

> Students in McMinn County, Tennessee, have one more reason against mixing drugs, guns, and school. They know that at any time they will face a surprise lock down. Then the school hallways will not be filled with students and teachers, but with police dogs and SWAT teams.
>
> During a lock down, high school students are detained in classrooms while police and dogs scour the campus, searching for contraband or any danger to a safe educational environment. It is a new, controversial approach to keeping schools safe. So far, the results are positive.

Numerous legal issues must be considered when planning such a lock down, and collaboration with the district attorney's office is required with this approach. While part of the lock down team searches the campus for contraband, another part meets with students to discuss what is occurring (Guy, p.8):

> In the classrooms, officers explain about "amnesty time," which allows students to turn over illegal narcotics, unlawful prescription medications, inhalants, knives, or firearms in their possession without fear of prosecution. Students are also given the opportunity to list such items in their cars and lockers. To provide some degree of anonymity, teachers and officers leave the classrooms for several minutes while students put their lists and illegal items in an amnesty box.

While some criticize such lock downs as being frightening or intimidating to students, and some students complain they feel threatened when their day is interrupted by the police, this approach has, thus far, not been challenged in court or before school boards (Guy, p.8). Furthermore, beyond curbing the possession of drugs and weapons in the public schools, these lock downs emphasize "the essential partnership between law enforcement and the school system. They provide the community with tangible evidence that government agencies are cooperating to prevent drug abuse and violence in schools and to provide a safe educational environment for students and teachers" (Guy, p.8).

Although proactive lock downs may be effective in locating and securing weapons that might be used in incidents of school violence, they are employed very infrequently in very few schools. Zero-tolerance policies fall dangerously short in their effectiveness if students believe any prohibited items they bring to school will go unnoticed. In fact, many weapons are discovered only after they have been used in a violent episode. Metal detectors, again, are used relatively infrequently, especially in smaller schools and in smaller communities, despite statistics showing these jurisdictions also are vulnerable to fatal school violence.

So even though these efforts are seen as luxuries for schools able to afford the fiscal and human resources needed to implement them, they cannot be relied on alone and are no substitute for the power of partnerships between students, teachers, officers, parents and other members of a community. Indeed: "While metal detectors and security guards can spot guns in book bags, adults and students must work together to deal with bullying, teasing, and harassment before they escalate to one more Columbine" ("Bullying, Teasing . . .," 2000, p.5). Dorn (p.31) adds: "The problem of weapons violence in our schools is complex. No single strategy will show lasting success. If used as stand-alone solutions, school resource officer programs (SROs), metal detectors, peer mediation programs and bullying programs will fail to produce a truly safe school environment. When a wide range of protective measures are integrated into a comprehensive strategy, dramatic improvement can result. This strategy should involve a community-based approach tailored to fit the needs and resources of the community."

Community Policing and School Violence

Besides police personnel, other participants vital in a community's effort to address school violence include parent group leaders, such as PTA officers; business leaders; violence prevention group representatives; youth workers and volunteers; family resource center staff; recreational and cultural organizations staff; mental health and child welfare personnel; physicians and nurses; media representatives; other criminal justice professionals, such as lawyers, judges and probation officers; clergy and other representatives from the faith community; and local officials, such as school board members.

The South Euclid School Bullying Project

The South Euclid School Bullying Project* is a 2001 Herman Goldstein Award winner for excellence in problem-oriented policing. It used the SARA problem-solving model to address the problem of bullying in the school.

---

*Source: Adapted from "The South Euclid School Bullying Project." In *Excellence in Problem-Oriented Policing: The 2001 Herman Goldstein Award Winners.* Washington, DC: National Institute of Justice, Community Oriented Policing Services and the Police Executive Research Forum, 2001, pp.55–62.

Scanning. Unchecked disorderly behavior of students in South Euclid, Ohio, led the school resource officer (SRO) to review school data regarding referrals to the principal's office. He found that the high school reported thousands of referrals a year for bullying, and the junior high school had recently experienced a 30 percent increase in referrals for bullying. Police data showed that juvenile complaints about disturbances, bullying and assaults after school hours had increased 90 percent in the past 10 years.

Analysis. All junior high and high school students were surveyed. Interviews and focus groups were also conducted with students—identified as victims or offenders—teachers and guidance counselors. Finally, the South Euclid Police Department purchased a Geographic Information System to complete crime and incident mapping of hotspots within the schools. The main findings pointed to four main areas of concern: the environmental design of school areas, teachers' knowledge and response to the problem, parents' attitudes and responses, and students' perspectives and behaviors.

Environmental Design Findings

- Locations in the school with less supervision or denser population (primarily the hallways, cafeteria and gymnasium) were more likely to have higher rates of bullying.

- Students avoided certain places at school because of fear of being bullied (for example, students avoid hallways near lockers of students who are not their friends or who are not in their classes).

- Race and ethnicity was not a primary factor in bullying.

- A vast majority of students reported witnessing bullying or being bullied in the classroom during class.

Teacher Issues

- Although bullying occurred frequently, teachers and students infrequently intervened.

- When students were asked what would happen if they told a teacher about an incident of bullying, more than 30 percent said "nothing."

- In interviews, students said they wouldn't tell teachers about bullying incidents because they were afraid of further retaliation, they expected the teacher to "do nothing," or were afraid the teacher wouldn't believe or support them, especially if the bully was popular or well liked by the teacher.

Parent Issues

- Students who reported being physically disciplined at home were more likely to report that they had been bullied.

- More than one-third of parents who had talked to their children about bullying had instructed them to fight back. Students said they would not tell a parent if they are bullied because they believed their parents would overreact.

Student Issues

- Students who reported that they engaged in bullying typically perceived their own behavior as playful or a normal part of growing up. They said that everyone gets picked on but some "don't know how to take it," "take things too seriously," or "just don't know how to fight back."
- Victims of bullying did not perceive this behavior as fun or normal.
- Victims viewed bullies as popular.
- Only 23 percent of students were likely to tell their parents they were a victim of bullying.
- Students were more likely to seek adult help for someone else who was bullied than for themselves.
- Students with lower grade point averages were significantly more likely to physically hurt someone else.
- Students who were secure in a peer group were more likely to intervene in bullying and less fearful of retaliation.
- Students suggested that involvement in school activities helped them to form a niche where they felt safe, supported and free from victimization.

Response. The SRO, collaborating with a social worker and university researchers, coordinated a Response Planning Team to respond to each of the areas identified in the analysis. Environmental changes involved modifying the school bell times and increasing teacher supervision of hotspot areas. Counselors and social workers conducted teacher training courses in conflict resolution and bullying prevention. Parent education included mailings with information about bullying, an explanation of the new school policy, and discussion about what they could do at home to address the problems. Finally, student education focused on classroom discussions with homeroom teachers and students, and assemblies conducted by the SRO. The Ohio Department of Education also contributed by opening a new training center for at-risk students to provide a nontraditional setting for specialized help.

Assessment. The results from the various responses were dramatic. School suspensions decreased 40 percent. Bullying incidents dropped 60 percent in the hallways and 80 percent in the gym area. Follow-up surveys indicated positive attitudinal changes among students about bullying and more students felt confident teachers would take action. The overall results suggested that the school environments were not only safer, but that early intervention was helping at-risk students succeed in school.

In this project Crime Prevention through Environmental Design (CPTED)-style modifications were paired with better teacher supervision of hotspots. Role-playing training for teachers in conflict resolution was paired with anti-bullying education for students and parents. Combining physical prevention with social and managerial prevention strategies is called "2nd Generation CPTED." It represents the most advanced form of crime prevention.

Many schools are also experiencing problems with gangs.

Law Enforcement's Response to Gangs

Shelden et al. (2001, p.243) note: "It has been argued that law enforcement represents society's first line of defense against crime. Consequently, law enforcement is the first segment of the [juvenile] justice system that responds to the youth gang dilemma." Although gangs are of concern to law enforcement, it should be recognized that not all gangs engage in violence and certainly not all violent youths belong to gangs.

The Importance of Definitions

Langston (2003, p.7) stresses: "A key issue in combating youth gangs is providing a uniform definition for them, distinguishing them from troublesome youth groups and adult criminal organizations." Esbensen et al. (2001a, p.105) comment: "Obviously, the definition used greatly affects the perceived magnitude of the gang problem. By restricting gang membership status to gangs that are involved in delinquent activity and have some level of organization, we reduce the size of the gang problem substantially."

Recognizing a Gang Problem

Many communities are blind to local gang activity. Domash (2000, p.30) stresses: "The first step in dealing with gangs is the acknowledgement of their presence in the community." According to Fraser (2001, p.11): "The presence of gangs can be seen everywhere. Gang members do not represent an invisible empire; they thrive on attention and recognition, constantly seeking ways to make their presence felt. They go unseen only when law enforcement personnel, as well as educators and parents, fail to recognize the signs of gang activity. Such failure to recognize or acknowledge the existence of gang activity, whether willingly or through the lack of gang identification training, dramatically increases a gang's ability to thrive and develop a power base."

 The first step in dealing with a gang problem is to recognize it.

Indicators of Gang Activity

The telltale signs of gang activity will show up in a variety of ways.

 Indicators of gang activity include graffiti, intimidation assaults, open sale of drugs, drive-by shootings and murders.

Table 8.3 shows the criteria used by some departments for identifying gangs. Once a department determines that a gang problem exists, the next step is to identify the gang members.

Identifying Gang Members

Gang members take pride in belonging to their specific gangs and will make their membership known in various ways. Many gang members have a street name, called a **moniker.** Often more than one gang member has the same moniker. The color and type of clothing can also indicate gang membership. For example, Bloods are identified by red or green colors. Crips are associated with blue or purple bandanas or scarves. However, as Howell (2000, p.27) cautions:

Table 8.3
Criteria for Defining Gangs

Criteria Used	Large Cities* (Percent)	Smaller Cities* (Percent)
Use of Symbols	93	100
Violent Behavior	81	84
Group Organization	81	88
Territory	74	88
Leadership	59	78
Recurrent Interaction	56	60

* Of the cities surveyed, 70 (89 percent) of the large cities and 25
(58 percent) of the smaller cities indicated the criteria used to define gangs.

Source: G. David Curry et al. *Gang Crime and Law Enforcement Recordkeeping.*
Washington, DC: National Institute of Justice Research in Brief, August 1994,
p.7. Data from NIJ Gang Survey.

"Determining a particular individual's gang involvement is as difficult as identifying true youth gangs."

One of the most common ways to identify gang members is through self-nomination. Esbensen et al. (2001b) report: "Traditional self-nomination techniques for identifying gang members appear to be valid." Gang affiliation might also be verified in the following ways: body tattoos of gang symbols, jewelry or apparel associated with gangs, written communications such as doodling on notebooks, hand-signing, vocabulary and use of monikers, group photos that include known gang members, known gang associates and reliable informants.

Other signs that an individual may be involved in a gang include abrupt changes in personality and behavior, newly acquired and unexplained money or, conversely, requests to borrow money, and "hanging around" behavior.

 Gang members may be identified by their names, symbols (including clothing and tattoos) and communication styles, including sign language and graffiti.

Gang Names   Gang names vary from colorful and imaginative to straightforward. They commonly refer to localities, rebellion, animals, royalty and religion. Localities are typically streets (for example, the Seventeenth Streeters), cities or towns (the Center City Boys), neighborhoods (the Westsiders) and housing projects (the Tiburon Courts). Names denoting rebellion, revolution or lawlessness include the Gangsters, Outlaws, Hustlers, Savages, Warlords and Assassins. Common animal names include the Tigers, Cougars, Panthers, Cobras, Ravens and Eagles. Royal titles include the Kings, Emperors, Lords, Imperials, Knights, Dukes and even Royals. Religious names include the Popes and Disciples. Gangs may also be designated by the leader's name such as "Garcia's Boys." Often, a locality is coupled with another category, for example, the South Side Savages.

Gang Symbols   Gangs use symbols or logos to identify themselves. Often these symbols are taken from professional or college sports teams (for example, the Latin Kings use the L.A. Kings logo as an identifying symbol), religion and the occult (crosses and pentagrams and other universally recognized symbols, including the Playboy bunny).

Clothing   It is important for gang members to reinforce their sense of belonging by adopting a gang style of dress. As noted by Wrobleski and Hess (2003, p.279): "Gang symbols are common. Clothing, in particular, can distinguish a particular gang. Sometimes 'colors' are used to distinguish a gang. Gang members also use jerseys, T-shirts and jackets with emblems."

Representing also signifies gang allegiance. Representing is a manner of dressing that uses an imaginary line drawn vertically through the body. Anything to the left of the line is representing left, anything to the right is representing right: for example, a hat cocked to the right, right pant leg rolled up and a cloth or bandana tied around the right arm.

Other important symbols may include certain hairstyles, gold jewelry in gang symbols and certain cars. The following list itemizes some identifying symbols of some better-known gangs:

- *Black Gangster Disciples* wear blue and black colors, represent to the right and have as symbols a six-point star, flaming heart and crossed pitchfork.
- *Vice Lords* wear red and black colors, represent to the left and have as symbols a five-point star, a circle surrounded by fire, a half-crescent moon, a pyramid, top hat, cane, white gloves and martini glass.
- *Latin Kings* wear gold and black colors, represent to the left and have as a symbol a three- or five-point star.
- *Asian gangs* usually wear no colors and show no representation. They are often deadly and violent.
- *Skinheads* wear black boots and leather jackets and have as a symbol the swastika. Their heads are shaved or very nearly bald.

Tattoos   Some gangs, particularly outlaw motorcycle gangs and Hispanic gangs, use tattoos as a method of communication and identification. The traditional Hispanic gang uses tattoos extensively, usually visible on arms, hands or shoulders. By contrast, black gang members are not enthusiastic about using tattoos to identify their members. Branding, however, is becoming somewhat popular among black and Asian gangs.

Gang Communication Styles   Street gangs communicate primarily through their actions. Youth gangs need and seek recognition, not only from their community, but also from rival gangs. A variety of verbal and nonverbal gang communication is ever-present. Clothing, tattoos and symbols can be powerful and effective communication tools. Other avenues of gang communication include slang, hand signals and graffiti.

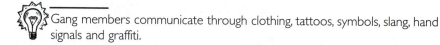

Gang members communicate through clothing, tattoos, symbols, slang, hand signals and graffiti.

Hand Signals   Another method of gang communication is that of flashing gang signs or hand signals. The purpose of these hand signals is to identify the user with a specific gang. Hand signs communicate allegiance or opposition to

A gang member makes the hand signal of a pitch fork representing the Folk Nation.

another group. Most hand signs duplicate or modify signing used by the deaf and hearing impaired. Figure 8.3 shows some ways various gangs identify themselves with hand signs.

Graffiti   Certainly the most observable gang communication is wall writings or graffiti, an important part of the Hispanic and black gang traditions. It proclaims to the world the status of the gang, delineates the boundaries of their turf and offers a challenge to rivals. Graffiti may show opposition for rival gangs by displaying a rival gang's symbols upside down, backwards or crossed out—a serious insult to the rival.

Graffiti is a method of communication commonly used to mark a street gang's turf.

Police can gain much valuable information from gang graffiti. For instance, one may be able to determine which gang is in control of a specific area by noting the frequency of the unchallenged graffiti. Throwing a *placa* on a wall

The signs shown on these pages are an important part of the sign language of the gangs. The letters and numbers represent affiliation with the particular gang. It is important and advisable not to imitate any of the signs being shown. To do so could represent affiliation or identification with a specific gang and could lead to unfortunate consequences.

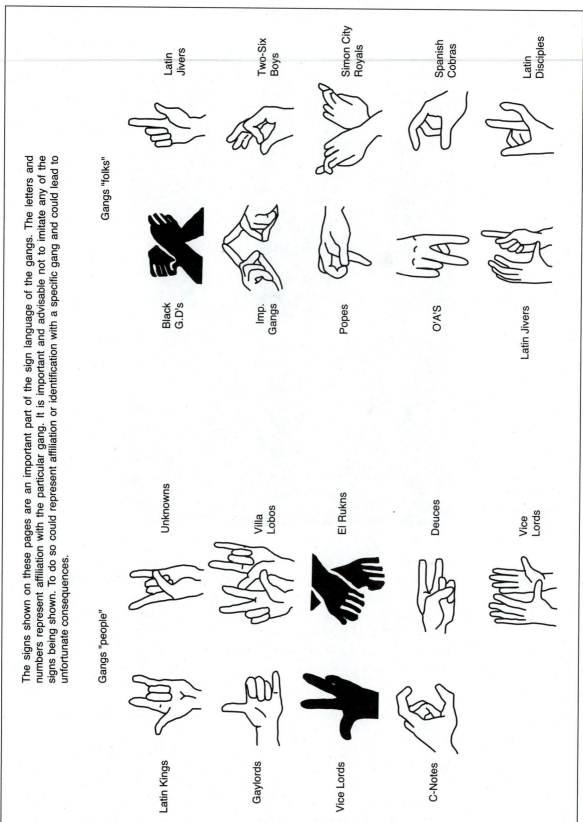

Figure 8.3
Gang Signs

Source: "Gang Awareness," City of Chicago, Department of Human Services, The Youth Development Services Division, in cooperation with the Gang Crime Unit of the Chicago Police Department and the Chicago Crime Commission, no date, pages 4–5. Reprinted by permission.

© Sven Martson/The Image Works

Graffiti has been called the "newspaper of the street" for gangs. Often abbreviations such as R.I.P. (rest in peace) are found as in the upper left corner of this graffiti.

corresponds to claiming a territory. Writing left unchanged reaffirms the gang's control. As one moves away from the center or core area of a gang's power and territory, more rival graffiti and cross-outs are observed. Graffiti can also insult rival gangs, warn of impending death, list fallen comrades or show gang alliances.

The black and Hispanic styles of wall writings differ vastly. Black gang graffiti lacks the flair and attention to detail evidenced by Hispanic gang graffiti. Much of the black gang wall writing is loaded with profanity and expressions not found in Hispanic graffiti.

Gang symbols in the form of graffiti usually appear throughout the turf and define boundaries. Such graffiti usually includes the gang name and the writer's name. It may also assert the gang's power by such words as *rifa,* meaning "to rule," or *P/V* meaning "por vida" (for life). In other words, the gang rules this neighborhood for life. The number 13 has traditionally meant that the writer used marijuana, but now it also can mean that the gang is from Southern California. Figure 8.4 depicts some of the symbols the Vice Lords use in their graffiti.

Another type of graffiti, called **tagging,** mimics gang graffiti, but often those doing the tagging are not members of gangs or involved in criminal activity (other than vandalism). According to Shelden et al. (p.52): "Such graffiti is not done to mark turf. Rather it is a way these mostly white middle-class youths call attention to themselves." Examples of tagging are shown in Figure 8.5. Differences between tagging and gang graffiti are listed in Table 8.4.

In some instances taggers band together into a crew. Sometimes the tagging becomes very serious and may even turn deadly. Regardless of the method of communication, gang messages are clear. Gang members are telling the world that their gangs or barrios are number one, the best. They also are expressing their commitment to the turf and gang.

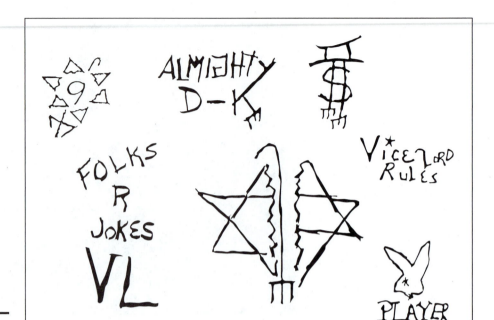

Figure 8.4
Typical Graffiti

Typical Vice Lord markings documented in Minneapolis, Minnesota. Bear in mind that these markings are often personalized and may appear in various combinations. Watch for repeated code and image patterns.

Domain Identification

Youth gangs characteristically claim identification with and control over specific domains—geographic locations, facilities or enterprises. The best-known manifestation of gang domain identification is the "turf" phenomenon. Gangs establish turf, territorial boundaries, within which they operate and which they protect at all costs from invasion by rival gangs. Solidarity and neighborhood cohesiveness are intense. In fact, the query, "Where are you from?" is the challenge of the street. An inappropriate response may bring a severe beating or even death.

Law enforcement officers should guard against misinterpreting what appears to be gang activity. For example, in one jurisdiction a new gang sign was showing up in suburban school yards, a line about 3 feet off the ground, usually painted in white on a brick wall where there were no windows. About 20 yards away from the wall is another white stripe painted on the ground. Several officers reported seeing such lines. But upon investigation it turned out to be a strike zone. Youths would throw a tennis ball against the wall, and it acted as their backstop. Officers who set out to find signs of gang activity may turn an innocent marking into the symbol of some new gang.

Gangs in Schools

Schools are a prime recruiting ground for gangs. They are also a market for illicit drugs and for extorting money from other students. Often gangs will stake out certain areas of a school as their turf. They may engage in vandalism, arson and graffiti painting, stabbings and shootings between rival gangs, as well as student extortion and teacher intimidation.

Fort Worth, Texas

Deciphered, the writing reads, "southside home girls."

Denver, Colorado

From left to right the first three tags deciphered reveal the following letters/words: "MIR," "Vestige," and "Orion." The fourth's obscurity makes uninitiated deciphering impossible.

Fort Worth, Texas

Deciphered the tag says, "Spicer."

San Marcos, Texas

Deciphered the tag says, "hi-tek."

San Antonio, Texas

The tags make uninitiated deciphering only guesswork.

Figure 8.5
Examples of Tagging

Source: Daniel D. Gross and Timothy D. Gross. "Tagging: Changing Visual Patterns and the Rhetorical Implications of a New Form of Graffiti." *Et cetera*, Fall, 1993, pp.259–262. Reprinted from *ETC: A Review of General Semantics*, Fall 1993, with permission of the International Society for General Semantics.

Table 8.4
Differences between Tagger and Gang Graffiti

Tagger Graffiti	Gang Graffiti
Communication secondary, if present at all	Intent made to communicate
Artistic effort a major consideration	Artistic effort secondary, if present at all
Territorial claims infrequent	Territorial claims prominent
Explicit threats rare	Explicit threats made
Explicit boasts about tagger common	Explicit boasts made about gang
Pictures and symbols dominant, letters and numbers secondary	Letters, numbers and symbols dominant
Police intelligence value limited	Intelligence to police provided

Source: *Addressing Community Gang Problems: A Practical Guide*. Washington, DC: Bureau of Justice Assistance, May 1998, p.37. (NCJ 164273)

Indications of gangs operating in a school include groups of students congregating by race and naming their group to solidify their identity, the number of violent, racially based incidents is increasing, as is the rate of absenteeism and crimes in the community being committed by truants. Other indicators include graffiti and crossed-out graffiti visible on or near the school, colors worn symbolically by various groups who also use hand signals, and unique symbols on T-shirts or in jewelry.

 A key impediment to dealing with youth gang members is the inability to share information, since the records of juveniles are often sealed.

Gangs and Drugs

It is well known that many gang members abuse certain drugs, such as alcohol, marijuana, phencyclidine (PCP) and cocaine. It is also well known that many gangs deal in drugs. According to Shelden et al. (p.116): "There is little question that drug usage and violent crime are closely related. What is still in doubt, however, is the relationship between drugs (both usage and sales) and gangs. Research on this issue has produced conflicting findings."

As Sgt. Jackson of the Los Angeles Police Department observes: "How can you tell a kid who's making $500 a week guarding a rock house that he really ought to be in school or that he ought to be getting up at 4 a.m. every day to ride his bicycle around the neighborhood to deliver the morning papers?"

The consensus among the most experienced gang researchers is that the typical street gang lacks the skills needed to organize and manage a successful drug trafficking operation. However, other gang researchers contend that gangs are rational organizations with established leadership structures, roles, rules and the kind of control over members that would allow them to organize and manage drug operations. Table 8.5 identifies some common differences between street gangs and drug gangs.

Table 8.5
Common Differences between Street Gangs and Drug Gangs

Characteristic	Street Gangs	Drug Gangs
Crime focus	Versatile ("cafeteria-style")	Drug business exclusively
Structure	Larger organizations	Smaller organizations
Level of cohesion	Less cohesive	More cohesive
Leadership	Looser	More centralized
Roles	Ill-defined	Market-defined
Nature of loyalty	Code of loyalty	Requirement of loyalty
Territories	Residential	Sales market
Degree of drug selling	Members may sell	Members do sell
Rivalries	Intergang	Competition controlled
Age of members	Younger on average, but wider age range	Older on average, but narrower age range

Source: From The American Street Gang by Malcolm Klein, © 1995 by Oxford University Press, Inc. Used by permission of Oxford University Press, Inc.

It is generally agreed that gangs organize along one of two basic lines: violence-oriented gangs who exist to fight or entrepreneurially focused gangs structured to make money. Among those gangs for whom drug trafficking is a primary activity, however, violence may accompany their entrepreneurial activities.

Investigating Gangs' Illegal Activities

The same procedures used in investigating any other kind of illegal activity apply to investigating gangs' illegal activities. Information and evidence must support the elements of specific offenses and link gang members to those offenses.

Howell (p.53) stresses: "Long-term proactive investigations of entire gangs are more effective than short-term reactive investigations of individual gang members." It is often difficult to obtain information about a gang's illegal activities because the gang members stick together and will intimidate the people living and working within their turf. Businesspeople and residents alike are usually fearful of telling the police anything, believing the gang will cause them great harm if they do.

If a neighborhood canvass is conducted and information is received, it is important that the canvass not stop at that point. This would implicate the house or business at which the canvass was terminated as the source of information. In addition, more information might be available from a source not yet contacted during the canvass.

Crime scenes that involve gangs are unique. Often the crime scene is part of a chain of events. When a gang assault occurs, for example, often a chase precedes the assault, considerably widening the crime scene. If vehicles are involved, the assault is probably by a rival gang. If no vehicles appear to have been involved, the suspects are probably local, perhaps even members of the same gang as the victim. This frequently occurs when narcotics, girlfriends or family disputes are involved. Evidence obtained in gang investigations is processed in the same way as evidence related to any other crime.

Obtaining and Recording Information

According to Howell (p.53): "Each city's gang program should be supported by a gang information system that provides sound and current crime incident data that can be linked to gang members and used to enhance police and other agency interventions."

An effective records system is critical in dealing with any gang problem. Information is an essential tool for law enforcement and should include the following: type of gang (street, motorcycle, etc.), ethnic composition, number of active and associate members, territory, hideouts, types of crimes usually committed and method of operation, leadership and members known to be violent.

Katz et al. (2000, p.413) studied the usefulness of gang intelligence systems and conclude: "Gang lists may be more helpful to the police than first believed." Table 8.6 shows the methods used to gather information on gangs.

Methods used by more than half the surveyed agencies were internal contacts with patrol officers and detectives, internal departmental records and computerized files, review of offense reports, interviews with gang members and information obtained from other police departments.

Table 8.6
Methods Used for Gathering Information on Gangs, Ranked by "Often Used" Category

	Never Used	Sometimes Used	Often Used
Internal contacts with patrol officers and detectives	1	22	64
Internal departmental records and computerized files	4	22	62
Review of offense reports	2	25	60
Interviews with gang members	5	26	56
Obtain information from other local police agencies	1	35	51
Surveillance activities	6	37	44
Use of unpaid informants	2	44	42
Obtain information from other criminal justice agencies	3	43	42
Obtain information from other governmental agencies	3	47	37
Provision of information by schools	2	50	35
Reports from state agencies	11	63	14
Use of paid informants	28	46	13
Reports from federal agencies	16	62	9
Obtain information from private organizations	27	51	9
Infiltration of police officers into gangs or related groups	75	11	2

Source: James W. Stevens. "Youth Gangs' Dimensions." *The Encyclopedia of Police Science*, 2nd ed., edited by William G. Bailey, New York: Garland, 1995, p.832. Reprinted by permission.

The National Crime Information Center soon will be capturing information on gangs and terrorist groups in a specific computer file. The OJJDP suggests several ways for law enforcement to combat the gang problem, including the following.

To combat a gang problem:

- Gather information.
- Do not tolerate graffiti.
- Target hard-core gang leaders.
- Consolidate major gang-control functions.

The Bureau of Justice Assistance (BJA) has awarded the Police Executive Research Forum (PERF) a grant to develop a prototype model of the Comprehensive Gang Initiative Program. This model is based on the following principles: adaptability, flexibility and a multifaceted approach. The model calls for a variety of government and private agencies to work with police and community members to simultaneously address the many factors that create and sustain gang problems. The model has the following key components:

- A focus on harmful behaviors
- Continuous diagnosis of problems

- Coordination of groups or agencies in their response
- Monitoring performance
- Evaluation of impact
- Adaptation to change

Educational Approaches to the Gang Problem

The Gang Resistance Education and Training (GREAT) program was developed by the Bureau of Alcohol, Tobacco and Firearms, the Federal Law Enforcement Training Center and the Phoenix (Arizona) Police Department. This program, similar to the DARE program, helps students say no, but in this case to gangs. The audience is older; GREAT focuses on seventh-graders. Students are taught to set goals, resolve conflicts nonviolently, resist peer pressures and understand the negative impact gangs can have on their lives and on their community.

Research on the effectiveness of this program by Esbensen et al. (2001b) concluded: "Over time GREAT students exhibited more pro-social attitudinal changes than did non-GREAT students. However, there were no significant differences in the behavioral outcomes of gang membership, delinquency and drug use." Based on these modest positive results, the authors conclude that law enforcement officers can be effective deliverers of prevention curricula in schools.

Law enforcement should view street gangs as criminal organizations and capitalize on laws against organized crime, for example, money-laundering and asset forfeiture laws help in efforts to arrest and prosecute gang members and thereby weaken the street gang structure.

Prevention Efforts

Most law enforcement efforts are aimed primarily at crime control: gathering information; developing information systems; making arrests; and sharing information with others in the law enforcement community. Increasingly, they also include prevention activities:

- Participating in community awareness campaigns (e.g., developing public service announcements and poster campaigns)
- Contacting parents of peripheral gang members (through the mail or during personal visits) to alert them that their children are involved with a gang
- Sponsoring gang hotlines to gather information and facilitate a quick response to gang-related issues
- Organizing athletic events with teams of law enforcement officers and gang members
- Establishing working relationships with local social service agencies
- Making presentations about gangs to schools and community groups as a combined effort at prevention and information gathering
- Sponsoring school-based gang and drug prevention programs (e.g., DARE)
- Serving as a referral for jobs and other community services

Table 8.7
Law Enforcement Strategies and Perceived Effectiveness*

Strategy	Used (Percent)	Judged Effective If Used (Percent)
Some or a lot of use		
Targeting entry points	14	17
Gang laws	40	19
Selected violations	76	42
Out-of-state information exchange	53	16
In-state information exchange	90	17
In-city information exchange	55	18
Federal agency operational coordination	40	16
State agency operational coordination	50	13
Local agency operational coordination	78	16
Community collaboration	64	54
Any use		
Street sweeps	40	62
Other suppression tactics	44	63
Crime prevention activities	15	56

*Percentage of cities n = 211. The number of cities responding to each question varied slightly.

Source: James C. Howell. *Youth Gang Programs and Strategies.* Washington, DC: OJJDP, August 2000, p.46. (NCJ 171154)

Efforts to Address Existing Gang Problems

 Four approaches are being used to deal with gang problems: (1) suppression or law-enforcement efforts, (2) social intervention, (3) opportunities provision and (4) community organization.

According to Howell (p.55): "The most effective program model will likely prove to be a combination of prevention, intervention and suppression strategies." He notes: "Law enforcement agents view suppression tactics (e.g., street sweeps, intensified surveillance, hot spot targeting and caravanning), crime prevention activities and community collaboration—in that order—as most effective in preventing and controlling gang crime."

Suppression

Table 8.7 shows the law enforcement strategies being used, with what frequency and with what perceived effectiveness when used. Although in-state information exchange was the most-used strategy, it was also among those judged least effective. Street sweeps and other suppression tactics were used by fewer than half the departments, but their effectiveness was judged high.

One measure being used is the **civil injunction.** "Civil gang injunctions (CGI)," according to Maxson et al. (2003, p.239), "are a legal tool for addressing the hold that entrenched gangs have on urban neighborhoods. . . . CGIs are spatially based, neighborhood-level interventions intended to disrupt a gang's routine activities." They (pp.245–246) describe how the injunction mechanism functions:

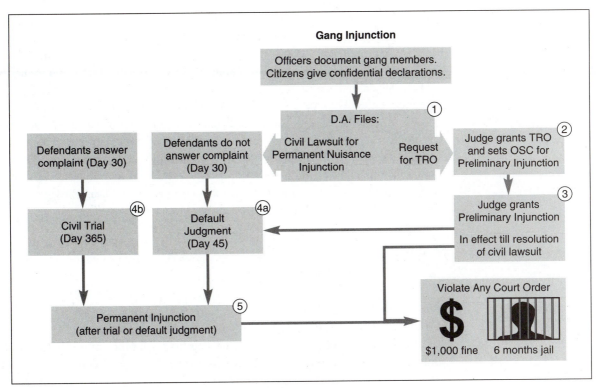

Used by permission of San Diego Deputy District Attorney Susan Mazza.

Figure 8.6
The Gang Injunction Process

The process used to obtain CGIs varies somewhat from jurisdiction to jurisdiction. The procedure commonly used in Southern California involves gathering evidence to support the claim that gang members create a public nuisance in a specified community and then applying to a civil court to require these individuals to refrain from continuing nuisance behavior. After the injunction is issued and targeted individuals are notified, they can be arrested for violating the conditions and prosecuted in either civil or criminal court. . . .

According to prosecutors, the primary goal is usually to obtain a preliminary injunction with or without a temporary restraining order (TRO). The preliminary injunction is anticipated to have an immediate impact on the targeted gang's activities and stays in effect until the resolution of the lawsuit. If the defendants do not file an answer to the lawsuit, the injunction becomes permanent by default.

Figure 8.6 illustrates the gang injunction process.

Gang suppression efforts in Dallas, Texas, through saturation patrol and aggressive curfew and truancy enforcement are described by Fritsch et al. (2003). They (p.279) conclude: "This study found, consistent with previous research, that undirected saturation patrol has little impact on reducing crime. In short, simply adding more police officers without direction is not very effective. Unfortunately, this conclusion is typically overgeneralized to mean that policing and patrol does not work. Fortunately, research does show that directed patrol (whether directed toward offenders, places, victims or offenses) is effective in varying degrees. This research provides support for the latter statement because the aggressive enforcement of truancy and curfew laws was shown to be effective in reducing gang-related violence in certain areas."

Decker and Curry (2003) describe suppression efforts undertaken in St. Louis, Missouri. The city's Anti-Gang Initiative (AGI) had three components: (1) curfew enforcement, (2) gun enforcement and (3) surveillance and enforcement activities. They state: "It is clear that in St. Louis the AGI was more effective in the specialized unit (Gang Intelligence) than in routine patrol." In addition St. Louis implemented SafeFutures, a federal programmatic response to increases in juvenile violence focusing on providing opportunities to at-risk youths. Decker and Curry (p.212) conclude: "The experience in St. Louis with the suppression emphasis (AGI) and the social opportunities approach (SafeFutures) suggests that neither program can successfully address youth violence by itself."

 The most successful gang intervention strategies combine suppression efforts with providing social opportunities.

Gang Units

As early as the 1970s, the Los Angeles Police Department saw the need for specialized units to deal with the gang problem. Their first such program was called Community Resources Against Street Hoodlums (CRASH). CRASH consisted of several specially trained units of patrol officers and detectives organized on a bureau or area level. CRASH put tremendous pressure on the Los Angeles gangs and resulted in many gang members being arrested. In 1988 the department instituted another program to focus specifically on the problem of narcotics and black street gangs. This program was called Gang-Related Active Trafficker Suppression (GRATS).

Many departments have established gang units, which use a combination of prevention, suppression and intervention. The suppression component, according to Valdez (2000, p.54), involves a collaborative effort between police, probation and prosecution, targeting the most active gang members and gang leaders. The intervention component includes giving gang members the chance to finish high school or obtain a GED, to have tattoos removed, to obtain gainful employment and legal assistance. The prevention component includes conflict resolution skills and peer counseling. The full-service gang unit is illustrated in Figure 8.7.

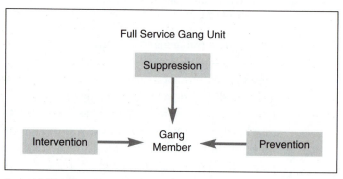

Figure 8.7
Full-Service Gang Unit

Source: Al Valdez. "Putting Full-Service Gang Units to Work." *Police*, July 2000, p.54. Reprinted by permission.

According to Katz (2001, p.37), among agencies with 100 or more sworn officers, 56 percent of municipal police departments had special gang units, as did 50 percent of all sheriff's departments, 43 percent of all county police agencies and 20 percent of all state law enforcement agencies. These numbers give an estimate of about 360 police gang units currently in operation in the United States. Webb and Katz (2003, p.17) note that the rise and growth of police gang units parallels the shift or attempted shift toward community policing.

The anti-gang initiative in Detroit had as one core component a new unit within the Special Crimes Section (SCS) as described by Bynum and Varano (2003). Another important core component was to establish **geographic integrity,** that is, to concentrate intervention efforts in an identified section of the city. Previous efforts had been city-wide and generally ineffective. The primary strategy of this initiative was *aggressive policing.* Bynum and Varano (p.234) report: "Over the period of the intervention and operation of the AGI project, there was a considerable decline in gun crimes in the target precincts, whereas the number of such offenses rose in the comparison precinct. . . . There is a strong indication that these aggressive policing tactics contributed significantly to this meaningful reduction."

Graffiti Removal

An important part of suppression is graffiti removal. Piraino (2002, p.23) contends: "Graffiti vandalism is a quality of life issue. Globally, graffiti has an estimated annual cost of $30 billion." The first step is to document the vandalism in a police report, including photographs. According to Piraino (p.24): "The most important step is the removal of the graffiti. The graffiti should be removed as soon as possible (within 24 hours). This is important because if the graffiti is left up it will appear that the community does not care."

Problem-Solving Approaches to Gangs

Boston's Gun Project's Operation Ceasefire was introduced earlier in this chapter. According to McDevitt et al. (2003, p.73): "Operation Ceasefire was a problem-solving initiative designed to address a very specific problem arising from a very specific group." They caution: "Although the tactics of Operation Ceasefire were appropriate to control violence among traditional gangs, they may not be as effective in dealing with the emerging gang problems."

Boston used problem-solving to attack the problem of gang-related youth homicides, with an average of 44 people under age 25 being murdered annually, of which 60 percent were gang-related. In addition, 15 percent of the city's junior high school students said they had stayed home from school within the past month because they were afraid ("Boston Program. . .," 2001, pp.5–7). Their program, Operation Ceasefire, began with the creation of the Youth Violence Strike Force (YVSF).

This strike force reviewed what had been done in the past and found one program mentioned over and over: the Wendover Street operation. In that operation police disrupted gang violence by cracking down on any type of criminal activity and by telling gang members that the crackdown would continue until the violence stopped. The YVSF decided to take the pulling levers approach, telling gang members: "We're here because of the shooting. We're not going to leave until it stops. And until it does, nobody is going to so much as jaywalk, nor make any money, nor have any fun. The plan involved pulling every legal lever the police could, which was not difficult as many gang members were on probation, selling drugs or otherwise chronically offending."

McGarrel and Chermak (2003) describe how Indianapolis, Indiana, used the model developed by Operation Ceasefire to address the problem of gang and drug-related violence using multiagency problem solving. To this end, law enforcement and city officials formed the Indianapolis Violence Reduction Partnership (IVRP). Their first step was to analyze homicide data to determine patterns. Next they developed a strategic plan consisting of two basic strategies: (1) tightening the criminal justice system to concentrate on violent chronic offenders and (2) lever pulling. Table 8.8 presents the key interventions of the IVRP.

Tita et al. (2003) describe how problem-solving, including pulling levers was also successfully used in a Los Angeles barrio. This project focused on preventing people from becoming violent and in their response portion of the SARA model developed a "carrot," noting: "Nothing stops a bullet like a job" (p.122). They (p.126) also stress: "Good knowledge of what is driving local crime problems is vital to developing appropriate interventions."

Thurman and Mueller (2003) describe The Mountlake Terrace (Washington) Neutral Zone AmeriCorps Program, a late-night juvenile crime prevention program that has been found to be "an effective alternative to traditional law enforcement crackdowns and curfews to regulate gang activity" (p.171). The NeutralZone incorporates several important elements, including social intervention (midnight basketball; keeping youths engaged and off the streets; community organization; and provision of opportunities such as job preparation and career skills).

The other strategies, social intervention, opportunities provision and community organization are discussed under community policing efforts directed at gang problems. Before looking at community policing efforts, however, consider several of the recommendations made in *Youth Gang Programs and Strategies* (Howell, pp.53–54):

- Both denial of gang problems and overreaction to them are detrimental to the development of effective community responses to gangs.

- Community responses to gangs must begin with a thorough assessment of the specific characteristics of the gangs themselves, crimes they commit, other problems they present and localities they affect.

- Because gang problems vary from one community to another, police, courts, corrections and community agencies often need assistance from gang experts in assessing their gang problem(s) and in developing appropriate and measured responses.

- Programs are needed to break the cycle of gang members moving from communities to detention to corrections and prisons and back into communities.

Table 8.8
**Key Interventions
of IVRP**

Problem (Target)	Strategic Intervention	Nature of Intervention	Gang/Group Focus?
Young men with extensive criminal records	Chronic violent offender program (VIPER)	System tightening—increase arrest and prosecution of most serious and chronic violent offenders	Not initially; over time began to focus on chronic violent offenders involved in groups/gangs
	Probation, parole, law enforcement field teams; U.S. marshal warrant service	System tightening—increase accountability	
	Lever-pulling meetings	Warn high-risk offenders to increase perception of sanctions for violence and link to legitimate services and opportunities	
	Faith-based groups intervening with youth	Increase legitimate opportunities; discourage participation in drug and violent activity	Street outreach, including former gang members in prevention efforts
	Covert investigations of drug-selling gangs	Gang suppression	Yes
Use of firearms in violent crime	Joint firearms unit	System tightening—increase prosecution of offenders using firearms and illegal possession	No
Areas with high levels of violent crime	Directed police patrol	Focused deterrence in these areas	No
	Probation, parole, law enforcement field teams; U.S. marshal warrant service	System tightening—increase accountability	Over time began to include group/gang members as a response to violent incidents
	Weed and seed	Increased police presence and community involvement in high-crime neighborhoods	Indirectly through prevention efforts aimed at youth

Source: Edmund F. McGarrell and Steven Chermak. "Problem Solving to Reduce Gang and Drug-Related Violence in Indianapolis." In *Policing Gangs and Youth Violence* by Scott H. Decker. Belmont, CA: Wadsworth Publishing Company, 2003, p.87. Reprinted by permission.

- Jurisdictions can control and reduce gang problems by targeting serious, violent and chronic juvenile offenders who may not necessarily be known gang members.
- Preventing children and adolescents from joining gangs may be the most cost-effective solution, but little is known about how to do this. Providing alternatives for potential or current gang members appears to hold promise, particularly if gang conflicts are mediated at the same time.

Most of these recommendations rely on the cooperation of several agencies in addition to law enforcement. A total community effort is needed to ensure success. Table 8.9 summarizes major gang program evaluations from 1994 to 1999.

Table 8.9
Selected Gang Program Evaluations 1994–99

Program	Study	Design	Type of Intervention	Results
Youth Gang Drug Prevention Program (Administration on Children, Youth and Families)*	Cohen et al., 1994	Quasi-experimental treatment and control comparison (multiple sites)	Prevention—discouraging adolescents from joining gangs; community mobilization	Little or no effect on gang involvement; some delinquency reduction
Aggression Replacement Training (Brooklyn)	Goldstein and Glick, 1994; Goldstein, Glick and Gibbs, 1998	Quasi-experimental treatment and control comparison	Skills training, anger control and moral education	Preliminary results positive with members of 10 gangs
Tri-Agency Resource Gang Enforcement Team (TARGET) (Orange County, CA)	Kent and Smith, 1995; Kent et al., 2000	Quasi-experimental	Suppression—targeting gang members for prosecution, supervision and incarceration	Successfully targeted hard-core gang members and showed serious crime reduction
The Neutral Zone (State of Washington)	Thurman et al., 1996	Direct observation, focus group and crime statistics	Prevention and alternatives to gang involvement	Some positive results (but see Fritsch, Caeti and Taylor, 1999:26)
Montreal Preventive Treatment Program	Tremblay et al., 1996	Longitudinal study from kindergarten; random assignment	Prevention via skills development (in pro-social skills and self-development)	Reduced delinquency, drug use, and gang involvement
Little Village Gang Violence Reduction Program (Chicago)	Spergel and Grossman, 1997; Spergel, Grossman and Wa, 1998	Quasi-experimental community comparison	Social intervention and suppression	Positive results; best results with combined approach
Youth Gang Drug Intervention and Prevention Program for Female Adolescents* (Pueblo, CO; Boston, MA; and Seattle, WA)	Curry, Williams and Koenemann, 1997	Quasi-experimental	Prevention and social intervention	Pueblo program showed positive results with culture-based programs for Mexican American females
Gang Resistance Education and Training Program (G.R.E.A.T.)	Winfree, Esbensen and Osgood, 1996; Esbensen and Osgood, 1997, 1999	Quasi-experimental treatment and control comparison (multiple sites)	Prevention—discouraging adolescents from joining gangs	Modest reductions in gang affiliation and delinquency
Gang Resistance Education and Training Program (G.R.E.A.T.)	Palumbo and Ferguson, 1995	Quasi-experimental and use of a focus group (multiple sites, different from G.R.E.A.T. sites above)	Prevention—discouraging adolescents from joining gangs	Small effects on attitudes and gang resistance
Operation Cul-De-Sac (Los Angeles)	Lasley, 1998	Quasi-experimental; before, during, and after comparisons with control area	Suppression—using traffic barriers to block gang mobility	Gang homicides and assaults appeared to be reduced
Antigang Initiative (Dallas)	Fritsch, Caeti and Taylor, 1999	Quasi-experimental; compared target and control areas	Suppression—using saturation patrol, curfew and truancy enforcement	Aggressive curfew and truancy enforcement appeared to be effective

* These programs are not described in the main body of the Summary. Adapted from Loeber and Farrington, 1998.

Source: James C. Howell. *Youth Gang Programs and Strategies*. Washington, DC: Office of Juvenile Justice and Delinquence Prevention, August 2000, p.4. (NCJ 171154)

Gangs and Community Policing

Howell (p.54) stresses the importance of the community in approaching the gang problem:

> Police should not be expected to assume sole responsibility for youth gang problems. Broad-based community collaboration is essential for long-term success. Communities that begin with suppression as their main response generally discover later that cooperation and collaboration between public and private community agencies and citizens are necessary for an effective solution. Considerable advantage accrues from involving the entire community from the onset, beginning with a comprehensive and systematic assessment of the presumed youth gang problem. Key community leaders must mobilize the resources of the entire community, guided by a consensus on definitions, program targets and interrelated strategies. Comprehensive programs that incorporate prevention, intervention and enforcement components are most likely to be effective.

Allender (2001, p.7) also contends: "The gang problem is not an exclusive law enforcement problem, nor can police deal with it in a vacuum." He notes: "Society must provide young people with meaningful alternatives that will draw them away from the gang lifestyle. These alternatives should vary and include educational programs, social interaction, recreational activities and employment opportunities. Obviously, the provision of these services will take cooperation among families, local schools, government-funded social services, area businesses, religious organizations and other neighborhood resources."

Responding to gangs requires a systematic, comprehensive and collaborative approach that incorporates prevention, intervention and suppression strategies. While each strategy has a specific vision and a pressing mandate, the greatest hope is on the side of prevention, for only by keeping children from joining gangs in the first place will the rising tide of terror and violence that gangs represent be halted.

When to Start?

Hill et al. (2001, p.2) report: "Youth were at risk of joining every year, but the risk rose most sharply at age 15—the age at which most students make the transition to high school."

The age at which youths are at most risk for joining a gang is 15.

Hill et al. (p.4) point out that although the peak age for joining a gang is 15, this does not mean that prevention efforts should be aimed at 14-year-olds. Rather they should target the risk factors (identified in Chapter 6) during the late elementary grades. In addition, they should target youths exposed to multiple risk factors and address all facets of youths' lives.

Prosecution

In addition to efforts to suppress, intervene and prevent gang activity, the juvenile justice system needs to aggressively prosecute gang members who engage in criminal activity. However, as Shelden et al. (p.263) note: "Prosecutors—key agents of the state—have a tremendous amount of discretionary power and can be quite political in dealing with gang members. As elected officials, prosecutors have a political agenda driven by a combination of public perceptions and fears (which can be and have been manipulated by a zealous media) and self-interest (getting reelected or running for higher office.)"

Bynum and Varano (p.227) note: "Today, many prosecutors' offices, especially in larger jurisdictions, have adopted vertical prosecution strategies to handle gang-related crimes." They explain: "**Vertical prosecution** can be defined as one assistant prosecutor or small group of assistant prosecutors handling one criminal complaint from start to finish through the entire court process. In contrast, **horizontal prosecution** is an organizational structure strategy whereby individual assistant prosecutors or a small group of assistant prosecutors are responsible for certain phases of the adjudication of criminal complaints."

Summary

Youths and guns, violent crime, crime and violence in our schools and gangs pose significant challenges to law enforcement. Research shows that directed patrol rather than general patrol can have a significant effect on violent crime.

When dealing with school violence it is important to recognize the threats that might be present. Threats may be direct, indirect, veiled or conditional. The four-pronged threat assessment approach examines the student's personality, family dynamics, school dynamics and the student's role in those dynamics, and social dynamics. An effective three-pronged approach to school security encompasses crisis planning, security technology and school/law enforcement/community partnerships. Some schools have adopted controversial measures such as zero-tolerance policies or school security procedures known as lock downs. Often violence in schools is due to the presence of gangs.

The first step in dealing with a gang problem is to recognize it. Indicators of gang activity include graffiti, intimidation assaults, open sale of drugs, drive-by shootings and murders. Gang members may be identified by their names, symbols (including clothing and tattoos) and communication styles, including sign language and graffiti. Gang members communicate through clothing, tattoos, symbols, hand signals and graffiti. Graffiti is a method of communication commonly used to mark a street gang's turf. A key impediment to dealing with youth gang members is the inability to share information because the records of juveniles are often sealed. To combat a gang problem, law enforcement should gather information, not tolerate graffiti, target hard-core gang leaders and consolidate major gang-control functions. The age at which youths are at most risk for joining a gain is 15.

Discussion Questions

1. Have there been any instances of students carrying weapons to schools in your area? If so, what happened to them?
2. Find your state in Table 8.1 to see what restrictions are placed on minors owning firearms. Does your state have more or fewer restrictions than the majority of other states?
3. How does your local law enforcement agency interact with schools to deal with youth crime and violence?
4. Is there a gang problem in schools in your area? How do you know whether there is or isn't?
5. How strong do you believe the link is between drugs, violence and gang membership?

6. Should convicted youth gang members be treated like other juvenile delinquents, including status offenders?

7. What might influence you to become a gang member? To not become a gang member?

8. Do you believe the juvenile justice system should support gang summits that claim to be working toward peaceful, lawful ways to improve the situation of gang members?

9. How much, if any, do gangs today differ from those of the 1960s and 1970s?

10. Do you think the gang problem will increase or decrease?

InfoTrac College Edition Assignments

- Use InfoTrac College Edition to help answer the Discussion Questions as appropriate.

- Read and outline one of the following articles:
  ○ "Safe Streets Task Force: Cooperation Gets Results" by David M. Allender
  ○ "Addressing the Need for a Uniform Definition of Gang-Involved Crime" by Mike Langston

  ○ "The Violence of Hmong Gangs and the Crime of Rape" by Richard Straka
  ○ "The School Shooter: One Community's Experience" by William P. Heck
  ○ "Operation CleanSWEEP: The School Safety Program that Earned an A+" by Gary S. Penrod

Internet Assignments

Complete one of the following assignments and be prepared to share your findings with the class:

- Go to the National Gang Youth Center Web site at http://www.ngyc.com and select one document to review and outline.

- Go to the National Gang Crime Research Center Web site at http://www.ngcrc.com and either summarize what services this center provides or click on *gang profiles* and select one profile to outline.

- Go to Web site http://ojp.usdoj.gov/nij and read and outline the report *Reducing Gun Violence: The Boston Gun Project's Operation Ceasefire.*

- Go to www.ncjrs.org to find, read and outline any of the end-of-chapter references with an NCJ number in parenthesis or go to any reference having an online address to find, read and outline the entire article.

References

Allender, David M. "Gangs in Middle America: Are They a Threat?" *FBI Law Enforcement Bulletin,* December 2001, pp.1–9.

"Boston Program Said to Show Problem-Solving Policing Works." *Criminal Justice Newsletter,* December 13, 2001, pp.5–7.

Braga, Anthony A.; Kennedy, David M.; Piehl, Anne M.; and Waring, Elin J. "Measuring the Impact of Operation Ceasefire." *Reducing Gun Violence: The Boston Gun Project's Operation Ceasefire,* September 2001a. (NCJ 188741)

Braga, Anthony A.; Kennedy, David M.; Waring, Elin J.; and Piehl, Anne Morrison. "Problem-Oriented Policing, Deterrence and Youth Violence: An Evaluation of Boston's Operation Ceasefire." *Journal of Research in Crime and Delinquency,* August 2001b, pp.195–225.

"Bullying, Teasing, and Harassment in School." *American Association of University Women in Action,* Summer 2001, pp.1, 5.

Butts, Jeffrey and Travis, Jeremy. *The Rise and Fall of American Youth Violence: 1980 to 2000.* Washington, DC: Urban Institute Justice Policy Center, Research Report, March 2002.

Bynum, Timothy S. and Varano, Sean P. "The Anti-Gang Initiative in Detroit: An Aggressive Enforcement Approach to Gangs." In *Policing Gangs and Youth Violence* by Scott H. Decker, Belmont, CA: Wadsworth Publishing Company, 2003, pp.214–238.

Decker, Scott H. *Policing Gangs and Youth Violence.* Belmont, CA: Wadsworth Publishing Company, 2003.

Decker, Scott H. and Curry, G. David. "Suppression without Prevention, Prevention without Suppression: Gang Intervention in St. Louis." In *Policing Gangs and Youth Violence* by Scott H. Decker, Belmont, CA: Wadsworth Publishing Company, 2003, pp.189–213.

Domash, Shelly Feuer. "Youth Gangs in America: A National Problem Evading Easy Solutions." *Police,* June 2000, pp.22–30.

Dorn, Michael. "Preventing School Weapons Assaults: The Nuts and Bolts of Stopping the Violence before It Happens." *Police,* May 2001, pp.30–35.

Dunworth, Terence. *National Evaluation of the Youth Firearms Violence Initiative.* Washington, DC: National Institute of Justice Research in Brief, November 2000. (NCJ 184482)

Dyer, Karl. "Oxnard Police Programs Encourage Positive Teen Behavior." *The Police Chief,* April 2000, p.32.

Ericson, Nels. *Addressing the Problem of Juvenile Bullying.* Washington, DC: OJJDP Fact Sheet #27, June 2001.

Esbensen, Finn-Aage; Winfree, L. Thomas, Jr.; He, Ni; and Taylor, Terrance J. "Youth Gangs and Definitional Issues: When Is a Gang a Gang, and Why Does It Matter?" *Crime and Delinquency,* January 2001a, pp.105–130.

Esbensen, Finn-Aage; Osgood, D. Wayne; Taylor, Terrance J.; Peterson, Dana; and Frend, Adrieene. "How Great is G.R.E.A.T.? Results from a Longitudinal Quasi-Experimental Design." *Criminology and Public Policy,* November 2001b, pp.87–118.

"Florida Honor Student Tripped Up by Zero-Tolerance Policy." Associated Press, as reported in the (Minneapolis/St. Paul) *Star Tribune,* May 24, 2001, p.A13.

Fraser, William J. "Getting the Drop on Street Gangs and Terrorists." *Law Enforcement News,* November 30, 2001, pp.11, 14.

Fritsch, Eric J.; Caeti, Tory J.; and Taylor, Robert W. "Gang Suppression through Saturation Patrol and Aggressive Curfew and Truancy Enforcement: A Quasi-Experimental Test of the Dallas Anti-Gang Initiative." In *Policing Gangs and Youth Violence* by Scott H. Decker, Belmont, CA: Wadsworth Publishing Company, 2003, pp.267–284.

Guy, Joe D. "Lock Down." *Community Links,* September 2001, pp.7–8.

Harlow, Caroline Wolf. *Firearm Use by Offenders.* Washington, DC: Bureau of Justice Statistics Special Report, November 2001. (NCJ 189369)

Heck, William P. "The School Shooter: One Community's Experience." *FBI Law Enforcement Bulletin,* September 2001, pp.9–13.

Hill, Karl G.; Lui, Christina; and Hawkins, J. David. *Early Precursors of Gang Membership: A Study of Seattle Youth.* Washington, DC: OJJDP Juvenile Justice Bulletin, December 2001. (NCJ 190106)

Holloway, John H. "The Dilemma of Zero Tolerance." *Educational Leadership,* December 2001/January 2002, pp.84–85.

Howell, James C. *Youth Gang Programs and Strategies.* Washington, DC: Office of Juvenile Justice and Delinquency Prevention, August 2000. (NCJ 171154)

Katz, Charles M. "The Establishment of a Police Gang Unit: An Examination of Organizational and Environmental Factors." *Criminology,* February 2001, pp.37–74.

Katz, Charles M.; Webb, Vincent J.; and Schaefer, David R. "The Validity of Police Gang Intelligence Lists: Examining Differences in Delinquency between Documented Gang Members and Nondocumented Delinquent Youth." *Police Quarterly,* December 2000, pp.413–437.

Kennedy, David M.; Braga, Anthony A.; and Piehl, Anne M. "Developing and Implementing Operation Ceasefire." *Reducing Gun Violence: The Boston Gun Project's Operation Ceasefire,* September 2001. (NCJ 188741)

Langston, Mike. "Addressing the Need for a Uniform Definition of Gang-Involved Crime." *FBI Law Enforcement Bulletin,* February 2003, pp.7–11.

Lizotte, Alan J. and Sheppard, David. *Gun Use by Male Juveniles: Research and Prevention.* Washington, DC: OJJDP Juvenile Justice Bulletin, July 2001. (NCJ 188992)

Lizotte, Alan J.; Krohn, Marvin D.; Howell, James C.; Tobin, Kimberly; and Howard, Gregory. "Factors Influencing Gun Carrying among Young Urban Males over the Adolescent-Young Adult Life Course." *Criminology,* Vol. 38, No. 3, 2000, p.811.

Maran, Meredith. "Deadly Ambivalence." March 6, 2001. http://www.salon.com/news/feature/2001/03/06/misfit/print.html

Maxon, Cheryl L.; Hennigan, Karen; and Sloane, David C. "For the Sake of the Neighborhood?" Civil Gang Injunctions as a Gang Intervention Tool in Southern California." In *Policing Gangs and Youth Violence* by Scott H. Decker, Belmont, CA: Wadsworth Publishing Company, 2003, pp.239–266.

McDevitt, Jack; Braga, Anthony A.; Nurge, Dana; and Buerger, Michael. "Boston's Youth Violence Prevention Program: A Comprehensive Community-Wide Approach." In *Policing Gangs and Youth Violence* by Scott H. Decker, Belmont, CA: Wadsworth Publishing Company, 2003, pp.53–76.

McGarrell, Edmund F. and Chermak, Steven. "Problem Solving to Reduce Gang and Drug-Related Violence in Indianapolis." In *Policing Gangs and Youth Violence* by Scott H. Decker, Belmont, CA: Wadsworth Publishing Company, 2003, pp.77–101.

McGarrell, Edmund F.; Chermak, Steven; and Weiss, Alexander. *Reducing Gun Violence: Evaluation of the Indianapolis Police Department's Directed Patrol Project.* Washington, DC: National Institute of Justice, November 2002. (NCJ 188740)

Minetti, P.G. and Caplan, Kelli. "School Mock Disaster Exercises." *The Police Chief,* April 2000, pp.12–19.

O'Toole, Mary Ellen. *The School Shooter: A Threat Assessment Perspective.* Washington, DC: Federal Bureau of

Investigation, 2000.
www.fbi.gov/publications/school/school2.pdf

Paynter, Ronnie L. "Back-to-School Security." *Law Enforcement Technology,* September 2000, pp.72–79.

Pedersen, Dorothy. "Student Threats: Benign or Malignant?" *Law Enforcement Technology,* January 2002, pp.30–33.

Penrod, Gary S. "Operation CleanSWEEP: The School Safety Program that Earned an A+." *FBI Law Enforcement Bulletin,* October 2001, pp.20–23.

Piazza, Peter. "Scourge of the Schoolyard." *Security Management,* November 2001, pp.68–73.

Piraino, Anthony. "The Northwest Block Watch Coalition: Winning the War on Graffiti." *Law and Order,* April 2002, pp.22–26.

Pollack, Ira and Sundermann, Carlos. "Creating Safe Schools: A Comprehensive Approach." *Juvenile Justice,* June 2001, pp.13–20.

Reporting School Violence. Washington, DC: Office for Victims of Crime Legal Series Bulletin #2, January 2002. (NCJ 189191)

Rosenbarger, Matt. "Multi-Jurisdictional Mock School Shooting." *Law and Order,* December 2001, pp.30–36.

Sampson, Rana. *Bullying in Schools.* Washington, DC: Office of Community Oriented Policing Services Problem-Oriented Guides for Police Series, No.12, March 2002.

Sanders, John R. "A Model Approach to School Violence." *Law and Order,* August 2001, pp.100–101.

Schmitt, Sheila. "Unlocking the Lockdown Mentality." *Law and Order,* June 2000, pp.139–144.

Schuiteman, John G. "Early Returns Positive for Virginia's Model SRO Program." *The Police Chief,* November 2000, pp.74–77.

Scott, Mike. "School Liaison." *Law and Order,* September 2001, pp.68–70.

Shelden, Randall G.; Tracy, Sharon K.; and Brown, William B. *Youth Gangs in American Society,* 2nd ed. Belmont, CA: Wadsworth Publishing Company, 2001.

Sheley, Joseph F. "Controlling Violence: What Schools Are Doing." *Preventing School Violence.* Washington, DC: NIJ Research Forum, May 2000. (NCJ 180972)

Sherman, Lawrence W.; Shaw, J.W.; and Rogan, D.P. *The Kansas City Gun Experiment.* Washington, DC: National Institute of Justice Research in Brief, 1995. (NCJ 150855)

"Short-Term Youth Violence Prevention Program Claims Long-Term Success." *NCJA Justice Bulletin,* June 2000, pp.12–13.

Siegel, Larry J.; Welsh, Brandon C.; and Senna, Joseph J. *Juvenile Delinquency: Theory, Practice and Law,* 8th ed. Belmont, CA: Wadsworth Publishing Company, 2003.

Smith-LaBombard, Halley. "Bullies Find No Refuge in Oak Harbor." *Community Links,* September 2001, pp.9–10.

Tita, George; Riley, K. Jack; and Greenwood, Peter. "From Boston to Boyle Heights: The Process and Prospects of a 'Pulling Levers' Strategy in a Los Angeles Barrio." In *Policing Gangs and Youth Violence* by Scott H. Decker, Belmont, CA: Wadsworth Publishing Company, 2003, pp.102–130.

Thurman, Qunit C. and Mueller, David G. "Beyond Curfews and Crackdowns: An Overview of the Mountlake Terrace Neutral Zone—Americorps Program." In *Policing Gangs and Youth Violence* by Scott H. Decker, Belmont, CA: Wadsworth Publishing Company, 2003, pp.167–187.

Turner, Nancy. "Animal Abuse and the Link to Domestic Violence." *The Police Chief,* June 2000, pp.28–30.

Valdez, Al. "Put Full-Service Gang Units to Work." *Police,* July 2000, pp.54–55.

Webb, Vincent J. and Katz, Charles M. "Policing Gangs in an Era of Community Policing." In *Policing Gangs and Youth Violence* by Scott H. Decker, Belmont, CA: Wadsworth Publishing Company, 2003, pp.17–49.

Welsh, Wayne N.; Stokes, Robert; and Greene, Jack R. "A Macro-Level Model of School Disorder." *Journal of Research in Crime and Delinquency,* August 2000, pp.243–283.

Wrobleski, Henry M. and Hess, Kären M. *Introduction to Law Enforcement and Criminal Justice,* 7th ed. Belmont, CA: Wadsworth Publishing Company, 2003.

Youth Violence: A Report of the Surgeon General. Washington, DC, 2001.

Zoll, Tom and Munro, Curt. "Regional Communications System Plays Vital Role in Resolving Two High School Shootings." *The Police Chief,* November 2001, pp.55–59.

Useful Resource

Wooden, Wayne S. and Blazak, Randy. *Renegade Kids, Suburban Outlaws: From Youth Culture to Delinquency.* Belmont, CA: Wadsworth Publishing Company, 2001.

The Juvenile Court and Alternatives at Intake

"The first idea that should be grasped concerning the juvenile court is that it came into the world to prevent children from being treated as criminals."

—Miriam Van Waters

Do You Know?

- Whether the juvenile court is primarily civil or criminal?
- What most state courts' purpose statement contains?
- What three classifications of children are under juvenile court jurisdiction?
- What two factors determine whether the juvenile court has jurisdiction?
- What the possible bases for the declaration of wardship are?
- What the three types of juvenile courts are?
- What two actions juvenile courts may take on behalf of children in need?
- What two kinds of intervention for abused children are available?
- What the possible results of an intake hearing might be?
- How juveniles may be transferred to criminal court?
- Who can certify a juvenile as an adult?
- What a major concern when transferring a juvenile to criminal court is?
- What forms diversion from juvenile court may take?
- What the two most common criteria for participating in drug court are?
- Who is eligible to participate in juvenile gun court?
- What the four models of restorative justice are?
- What the three main components of restorative justice are?

Can You Define?

adjudicated	concurrent jurisdiction	juvenile court
adjudication	deep end strategy	net widening
admit	detention hearing	public defender
certification	diversion	reverse certification
civil law	family courts	therapeutic intervention
coercive intervention	intake unit	venue
competence	jurisdiction	waiver
competent	justice model	

INTRODUCTION

In the United States, justice for juveniles is administered by a separate system with its own juvenile court. The **juvenile court** has jurisdiction over minors alleged to be delinquent, status offenders, dependents or in need of decisions by the court. The juvenile justice court system enforces and administers a blend of civil and criminal law, but theoretically the system is a civil system. **Civil law** refers to all law that is not criminal, for example contract law. A civil system was adopted by early juvenile courts to avoid inflicting the stigma of a criminal conviction on youths processed by the courts.

 The juvenile justice system is basically a civil system.

Juvenile court generally is bound more by the rules of the court, than statutes. And at no point in history have challenges been greater for the juvenile court.

This chapter examines the basic philosophy of the juvenile court, its jurisdiction, the types of juvenile courts and the characteristics exhibited in most such courts. This is followed by a discussion of court actions for neglected and abused children. Next an overview of the juvenile court process focuses on custody and detention and the intake process and alternatives it presents. Then the option of transferring a juvenile to criminal court is described, including exclusion, concurrent jurisdiction, waiver and certification as well as the issue of juveniles and capital punishment.

The next major topic is diversion from juvenile court. This may be accomplished by referral to specialized courts such as teen courts, drug courts and gun courts. Youths also may be diverted through four forms of restorative justice: victim-offender mediation, community reparative boards, family group conferencing and circle sentencing. The chapter concludes with a brief look at net widening.

Basic Philosophy of Juvenile Court

A philosophy underlying the juvenile court is that of *parens patriae*, a concept previously discussed. The aim of the first juvenile court was to offer youths and adolescent offenders individualized justice and treatment rather than punishment. According to the National Center for Juvenile Justice (*National Overviews*) there is considerable variation in the way the states define the purposes of their juvenile courts—not just in their assumptions and underlying philosophies, but also in the approaches they take to the task. Many juvenile court purpose clauses have been substantially and repeatedly amended over the years, reflecting philosophical or rhetorical shifts and changes in emphasis in the states' overall approaches to juvenile delinquency. As of the end of the 2002 legislative session, most state juvenile court purpose clauses fell into one or more of five thematic categories.

Most state juvenile court purpose statements contain (1) balanced and restorative justice (BARJ) clauses; (2) Standard Juvenile Court Act clauses; (3) legislative guide clauses; (4) clauses that emphasize punishment, deterrence, accountability and/or public safety clauses; or (5) clauses with traditional child welfare emphasis.

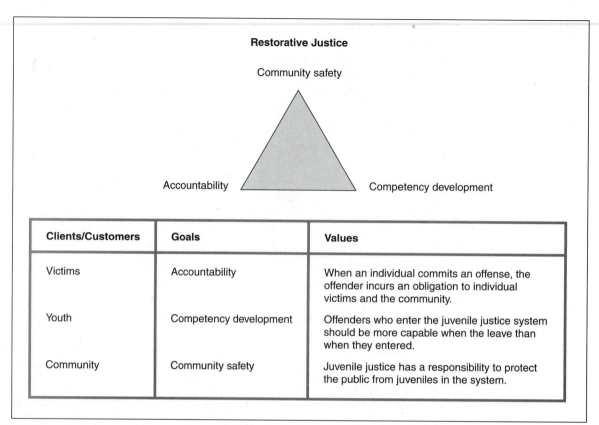

Figure 9.1
The Balanced Approach

Source: *Guide for Implementing the Balanced and Restorative Justice Model.* Washington, DC: Office of Juvenile Justice and Delinquency Prevention, December 1998, p.6.

Balanced and Restorative Justice (BARJ) Clauses

At least 16 state purpose clauses incorporate the language of the balanced and restorative justice (BARJ) movement, which advocates that juvenile courts give balanced attention to three primary interests: public safety, individual accountability to victims and the community, and the development in offenders of those skills necessary to live law-abiding and productive lives, as shown in Figure 9.1.

Standard Juvenile Court Act Clauses

Nine states have purpose clauses modeled after the Standard Juvenile Court Act, first issued in 1925 and revised many times. The declared purpose of the Standard Act is that "each child coming within the jurisdiction of the court shall receive . . . the care, guidance and control that will conduce to his welfare and the best interest of the state, and that when he is removed from the control of his parents the court shall secure for him care as nearly as possible equivalent to that which they should have given him." At least seven other states retain some trace of the Standard Act formula.

Legislative Guide Clauses

Six states use all or most of a more elaborate, multi-part purpose clause contained in the Legislative Guide for Drafting Family and Juvenile Court Acts, a publication issued by the Children's Bureau in the late 1960s. This guide states four purposes: (1) "to provide for the care, protection and wholesome mental and physical development of children" involved with the juvenile court; (2) "to remove from children committing delinquent acts the consequences of criminal behavior and to substitute therefore a program of supervision, care and rehabilitation"; (3) to remove a child from the home "only when necessary for his welfare or in the interests of public safety"; and (4) to assure all parties "their constitutional and other legal rights." In addition, at least six more states retain recognizable vestiges of the guide's language.

Clauses Emphasizing Punishment, Deterrence, Accountability and/or Public Safety

At least six states' purpose clauses can be loosely characterized as "tough" in that they stress community protection, offender accountability, crime reduction through deterrence or outright punishment, either predominantly or exclusively. This is often a matter of interpretation. Texas and Wyoming, for example, have largely adopted the multi-purpose language of the Legislative Guide but have inserted two extra items—the "protection of the public and public safety" and the promotion of "the concept of punishment for criminal acts"—at the head of the list.

Clauses with Traditional Child Welfare Emphasis

At least four states, including the District of Columbia, have statutory language emphasizing the promotion of the welfare and best interests of the juvenile as the sole or primary purpose of the juvenile court system. For example, one state says only that accused juveniles should be "treated, not as criminals, but as children in need of aid, encouragement and guidance." Another declares that it intends to institute "all reasonable means and methods that can be established by a humane and enlightened state, solicitous of the welfare of its children, for the prevention of delinquency and for the care and rehabilitation of juvenile delinquents.

The Justice Model vs. the Welfare Model

Traditionally, juvenile courts followed the welfare model with its underlying *parens patriae* philosophy that focuses on the "best interests of the child," as discussed in Chapter 1. As states experienced the wave of increasing juvenile violence during the late 1950s and early 1960s, many responded by viewing juveniles not as having problems, but as being problems. These states called for a **justice model** whereby youths would be held accountable and, in some instances, punished.

This position is contrary to the social welfare philosophy of the traditional juvenile court. But it is not necessarily contrary to the way that juvenile court judges have traditionally handled delinquent cases. Treating and caring for youthful criminals, rather than punishing them, is too contrary to our experience and too counterintuitive to be accepted by judges or the general public. A philosophy that denies moral guilt and punishment and views criminals as innocent, hapless victims of bad social environments may be written into law, but this does not mean that it will be followed in practice. Law violators, young and old, should be punished for their crimes. Children understand punishment, and they understand fairness.

Jurisdiction of the Juvenile Court

The **jurisdiction** of the juvenile court refers to the types of cases it is empowered to hear. In almost every state, the juvenile court's jurisdiction extends to three classifications of children: (1) those who are neglected, dependent or abused because those charged with their custody and control mistreat them or fail to provide proper care; (2) those who are incorrigible, ungovernable or status offenders and (3) those who violate laws, ordinances and codes classified as penal or criminal.

 The jurisdiction of the juvenile court includes children who are in poverty, neglected or abused; who are unruly or commit status offenses and who are charged with committing serious crimes.

The juvenile court system has been criticized for its "one-pot" jurisdictional approach, in which deprived children, status offenders and youths who commit serious crimes are put into the same "pot." Historically, all three kinds of children were thought to be the products or victims of bad family and social environments. As a result, it was thought, they should be subject, as wards of the court, to the same kind of solicitous, helpful care. The common declaration of status was that of wardship.

The importance of differentiating between criminal and noncriminal conduct committed by juveniles and the limitation on the state's power under *parens patriae* was established more than 100 years ago in *People ex rel. O'Connell v. Turner* (1870). In this case Daniel O'Connell was committed to the Chicago Reform School by an Illinois law that permitted the confinement of "misfortunate youngsters." The Illinois Supreme Court's decision was that the state's power of *parens patriae* could not exceed that of the parents except to punish crime. The court ordered Daniel to be released from the reform school.

Factors Determining Jurisdiction

In most states two factors determine the jurisdiction of the court.

 Jurisdiction of the juvenile court is determined by the offender's age and conduct.

The limit for the exercise of the juvenile court's jurisdiction is determined by establishing a maximum *age* below which children are deemed subject to the improvement process of the court, as discussed in Chapter 3. A "child" is generally defined as a person under the maximum age that establishes the court's jurisdiction. Age 17 is accepted in two-thirds of the states and in the District of Columbia (see Table 3.1, p.74). Many states have lowered their juvenile court age cap in response to acts of violence committed by children younger than the established jurisdictional age. For example a bill was passed in Texas to reduce from 14 to 10 the age at which youths can be tried in adult criminal court. The bill was motivated by the school shooting in Jonesboro, Arkansas, in which four students and a teacher were killed by two boys, ages 11 and 13.

Fifteen states have established a minimum age below which the court does not have jurisdiction as shown in Table 9.1.

Table 9.1
Lowest Age for Original Juvenile Court Jurisdiction in Delinquency Matters as of the End of the 2002 Legislative Session
(Updated: February 4, 2003)

Age 6	Age 7	Age 8	Age 10	
North Carolina	Maryland	Arizona	Arkansas	Pennsylvania
	Massachusetts		Colorado	South Dakota
	New York		Kansas	Texas
			Louisiana	Vermont
			Minnesota	Wisconsin
			Mississippi	

No Specified Lowest Age				
Alabama	Georgia	Maine	New Jersey	South Carolina
Alaska	Hawaii	Michigan	New Mexico	Tennessee
California	Idaho	Missouri	N. Dakota	Utah
Connecticut	Illinois	Montana	Ohio	Virginia
Delaware	Indiana	Nebraska	Oklahoma	Washington
DC	Iowa	Nevada	Oregon	West Virginia
Florida	Kentucky	N. Hampshire	Rhode Island	Wyoming

© 2002 National Center for Juvenile Justice

Source: National Center for Juvenile Justice. "National Overviews." *State Juvenile Justice Profiles*. Pittsburgh, PA: NCJJ. 2003. Online. http://www.ncjj.org/stateprofiles/. Reprinted by permission.

The issue of jurisdiction and age was first questioned in 1905 by the Pennsylvania Supreme Court. Frank Fisher was **adjudicated** (judged) a delinquent in the Philadelphia Juvenile Court. On appeal his lawyer challenged the constitutionality of the legislation establishing the court, urging in particular that Fisher was denied due process in the manner in which he was taken into custody and that he was denied his constitutional right to a jury trial for a felony. The Pennsylvania Supreme Court upheld a lower court's sanction. The court found that due process, or lack of it, simply was not at issue, since its guarantee applied only to criminal cases. The state could, on the other hand, place a child within its protection without any process at all if it saw fit to do so. Recall that in *Commonwealth v. Fisher* (1905) the court stated: "To save a child . . . the legislature surely may provide for the salvation of such a child . . . by bringing it into the courts of the state without any process at all, for the purpose of subjecting it to the state's guardianship and protection." The court further stated:

> The natural parent needs no process to temporarily deprive his child of its liberty by confining it to his own home, to save it and to shield it from the consequences of persistence in a career of waywardness; nor is the state, when compelled as *parens patriae,* to take the place of the father for the same purpose, required to adopt any process as a means of placing its hands upon a child to lead it into one of its courts.

Similarly, the court argued, a jury trial could hardly be necessary to determine whether a child deserved to be saved. In addition to the jurisdictional age, *conduct* determines the juvenile court's jurisdiction. Although the definition of delinquency varies from state to state, the violation of a state law or local ordinance (an act that would be a crime if committed by an adult) is the main category. Youths who violate federal laws or laws from other states, who are wayward, incorrigible or habitually truant, who commit status offenses or who associate with immoral people are all considered delinquent and subject to juvenile court jurisdiction.

Other Cases within Juvenile Court Jurisdiction

In addition to having jurisdiction over children who are in need of protection, who commit status offenses or who commit serious crimes, some juvenile courts have authority to handle other issues, such as adoptions, matters of paternity and guardianship.

The court's jurisdiction is further extended by provisions in many states that it may exercise its authority over adults in certain cases involving children. Thus in many states the juvenile court may require a parent to contribute to child support, or it may charge and try adults with contributing to the delinquency, neglect, abuse or dependency of a child.

The state is the "higher or ultimate parent" of all children within its borders. The child's own parents' rights are always subject to state control when in the court's opinion the best interests of the child demand it. If the state has to intervene in the case of any child, it exercises its power of guardianship over the child and provides him or her with the protection, care and guidance needed.

Although the substantive justice system for juveniles is administered by a specialized court, a great deal of variation exists in juvenile law between different jurisdictions. Before a court with juvenile jurisdiction may declare a youth a ward of the state, it must be convinced that a basis for that wardship exists.

 The possible bases for a declaration of wardship include demonstrating that the child is abused or neglected, or has committed a status offense or a criminal act.

Offenses Excluded from Juvenile Court Jurisdiction

Not all offenses committed by young people are within juvenile court jurisdiction. There are no firm assurances that a case will be heard in the juvenile court. The juvenile judge is given discretion to waive jurisdiction in a case and to transfer it to a criminal court if the circumstances and conduct dictate, as will be discussed later.

In some states delinquency is not exclusively within the scope of the juvenile court. Jurisdiction in juvenile court may be concurrent with criminal court jurisdiction—that is, it happens at the same time or may occur in either. Often this **concurrent jurisdiction** is limited by law to cases being handled by either court. Furthermore, certain offenses, such as murder, manslaughter or rape, may be entirely excluded from juvenile court jurisdiction. In states with such laws, children charged with these offenses are automatically tried in criminal court. Several states have excluded specified offenses from juvenile court jurisdiction. Colorado statutes, for example, state:

Juvenile court does not have jurisdiction over: children 14 or older charged with crimes of violence classified as Class 1 felonies; children 16 or older who within the previous two years have been adjudicated delinquent for commission of a felony and are now charged with a Class 2 or Class 3 felony or any nonclassified felony punishable by death or life imprisonment.

Several other states exclude youths who have had previous problems with the law.

Venue and Transfer

The geographic location of a trial, called its **venue,** is established by constitutional or statutory provisions. Usually proceedings take place in the county where the juvenile lives. If a proceeding involving a juvenile begins in a different county, the court may ask that the proceedings be transferred to the county where the juvenile lives. Likewise transfer can be made if the child's residence changes before proceedings begin.

Types of Juvenile Courts

The term *juvenile court* is somewhat of a misnomer. Only in isolated cases have completely separate courts for juveniles been established. Where they have been, it has been primarily in larger cities. Boston, for example, has a specialized court for handling juvenile matters, but its jurisdiction is less than citywide. Elsewhere throughout the country, juvenile court jurisdiction resides in a variety of courts: municipal, county, district, superior or probate. Some are multiple-judge courts; others are served by a single judge.

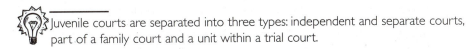

Juvenile courts are separated into three types: independent and separate courts, part of a family court and a unit within a trial court.

Independent and separate courts are those whose administration is entirely divorced from that of other courts. Such courts are found in Connecticut, Rhode Island and Utah. Many separate and independent courts are presided over by judges from other courts, however, so their separateness and independence is more in name than in reality. A second type of organization has juvenile court as part of *family court.* In addition to such matters as child custody and support, family courts often have jurisdiction over matters concerning delinquency, status offenses and child-victim cases. The third typical organization has juvenile court as a unit of the *trial court.*

Characteristics of the Juvenile Court

Just as the terminology used in the juvenile justice system differs from that used in the adult system (see Table 2.1, p.62), several characteristic features of the systems also differ, as summarized in Table 9.2.

The juvenile court has had an uneven development and has manifested a great diversity in its methods and procedures. However as early as 1920, Evelina

Table 9.2
Comparison of Juvenile Court and Adult Criminal Court

Characteristic Feature	Juvenile Court	Adult Court
Purpose	Protect/treat	Punish
Jurisdiction	Based mainly on age	Based on offense
Responsible noncriminal acts	Yes (status offense)	No
Court proceedings	Less formal/private	Formal/Public
Proceedings considered to be criminal	No	Yes
Release of identifying information to press	No	Yes
Parental involvement	Usually possible	No
Release to parental custody	Frequently	Occasionally
Plea bargaining	Less frequently, open admission of guilt more common	Frequently
Right to jury trial	No(*McKeiver* case)	Yes
Right to treatment	Yes	No
Sealing/expungement of record	Usually possible	No

Source: Richard W. Snarr. *Introduction to Corrections,* 2nd ed. Dubuque, IA:
Wm. C. Brown Communications, Inc., 1992, p.311. All rights reserved.
Reprinted by permission of the McGraw-Hill Companies.

Belden of the United States Children's Bureau listed the following as the essential characteristics of the juvenile court:

- Separate hearings for children's cases
- Informal or chancery procedure
- Regular probation service
- Separate detention of children
- Special court and probation records
- Provisions for mental and physical examinations

Unfortunately many juvenile courts lack these characteristics. Critics argue that such courts cannot claim to be juvenile courts.

In the United States, juvenile courts vary from one jurisdiction to another, manifesting all stages of the system's complex development. Its philosophy, structure and functions are still evolving. Rarely is the court distinct and highly specialized. In rural counties, juvenile court is largely rudimentary. Usually it is part of a court with more jurisdiction. In Minnesota, for example, it is a part of the probate court. Judges hold sessions for juveniles at irregular intervals or when the hearings can be held in clusters. Since there is great diversity, no simple description of U.S. juvenile courts can be given.

Court Action for Neglected and Abused Children

Two distinct kinds of court action may result for neglected or abused children.

 Court action on behalf of neglected and abused children may be noncriminal or criminal.

Court action on behalf of neglected, abused or dependent children is *non-criminal*. It seeks to identify whether the child is in danger and, if so, what is needed for the child's protection. The parents may lose custody of the child, be required to pay child support or be ordered to make adjustments in care, custody and control. This type of action does not permit punitive sanctions against the parents, however.

A second option is *criminal* prosecution of the parents on charges that they have committed a harmful act against the child or have failed to discharge their responsibility, thus placing the child in active danger. This action does not involve the status of the child. The scope of the court's position in these referrals is based on the juvenile court's responsibility for the child's welfare under the philosophy of *in loco parentis*.

Referrals carry the same weight as a court process and are subject to rules of law and procedure to protect children. Referrals include the information that court personnel need to proceed in a directed course, such as diversion or channeling to the proper authority.

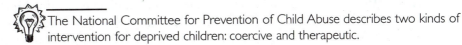

The National Committee for Prevention of Child Abuse describes two kinds of intervention for deprived children: coercive and therapeutic.

Coercive intervention is out-of-home placement, detainment or mandated therapy or counseling. **Therapeutic intervention** is a recommendation of an appropriate treatment program.

Coercive intervention should be used with children only when necessary, either to protect society or to impose an effective treatment plan for the children. Policy recommendations include the following:

- *Therapeutic intervention for all abused children who come to the attention of the court exhibiting problem behavior, regardless of the disposition of the case.* The present drift toward stricter delinquency statutes in some states, in which community protection is foremost and the best interest of the child standard is secondary, is based on an erroneous assumption. Protection of the community and rehabilitation of the child are not conflicting goals. Among this group of abused children are two subgroups in particular in need of attention: the child exhibiting violent behavior and the sexually abused child.

- *Specific and different treatment within the correctional system of the young person who was abused.* Much of our nation's delinquent population is in a debilitated condition—physically (neurologically), developmentally and psychologically. . . . We know, for instance, that treatment for the abused child will have to take place over a long term. We know that corporal punishment, physical coercion and violent or belittling language are inappropriate therapeutic tools; they add institutional abuse to the existing familial abuse.

- *Early intervention.* The optimal point of intervention with an abused delinquent would be before the abuse occurred. The earliest treatment intervention we can offer the young abused child would be aimed at keeping him from becoming a delinquent as a later reaction to the earlier abuse. The next opportunity for early intervention occurs when the young person comes to the attention of the court, before he becomes delinquent. Youths who enter the court as minors in need of supervision could be recognized as the abused children they often are and helped in such a way as to preclude further delinquent activity.

- *Attractive, benign, broad-based intervention styles and services.* Services are needed that do not identify the clients as abusive, abused or delinquent. Efforts to strengthen families, particularly the development and provision of services that could be called parent education, are recommended.

If neglected and abused children are referred to juvenile court, these recommendations should be kept in mind.

An Overview of the Juvenile Court Process

Changes in the juvenile court interrelate with such factors as industrialization, urbanization, population shifts, the use of natural resources, the rapid development of technology and the acceleration of transportation and communication. All have influenced the family and neighborhood, forcing communities to find new or additional sources of social control. This has given considerable impetus to taking a broader look at the juvenile court process, another version of which is illustrated in Figure 9.2.

Custody, detention and intake have been discussed in the context of law enforcement, as have the four possible outcomes of the intake hearing. Briefly review these portions of the juvenile process in the context of the juvenile court.

Custody and Detention

Juveniles typically enter the court system through some sort of contact with the police. Children can be taken into custody by court order, under the laws of arrest or by a law enforcement officer if there are reasonable grounds to believe that the child is suffering from illness or injury, is in immediate danger from his surroundings or that the child has run away. The Uniform Juvenile Court Act (UJCA) of 1968 notes: "The taking of a child into custody is not an arrest, except for the purpose of determining its validity under the constitution of this state or of the United States." Section 14 of the UJCA deals with the detention of children:

> A child taken into custody shall not be detained or placed in shelter care prior to the hearing on the petition unless his detention or care is required to protect the person or property of others or of the child or because the child may abscond or be removed from the jurisdiction of the court or because he has no parent, guardian, or custodian or other person able to provide supervision and care for him and return him to the court when required, or an order for his detention or shelter care has been made by the court pursuant to this Act.

The National Juvenile Detention Association provides the following definition: "Juvenile detention is the temporary and safe custody of juveniles who are accused of conduct subject to the jurisdiction of the court who require a

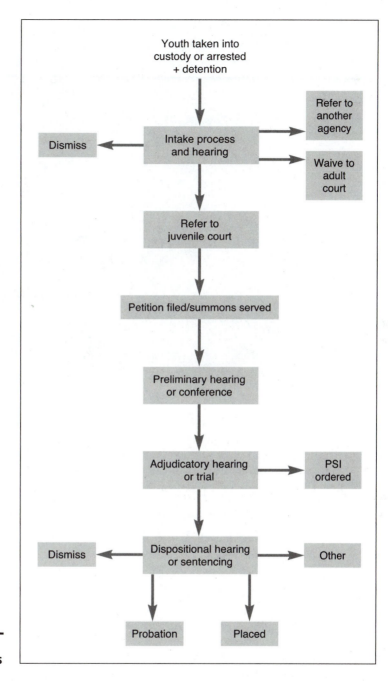

Figure 9.2
The Juvenile Court Process

restricted environment for their own or the community's protection while pending legal action" (*OJJDP Guide,* 1997, p.33).

After children are taken into custody they should either be released to their parents, guardians or custodians; brought before the court; or delivered to a detention or shelter care facility, or to a medical facility if needed. This is to be done "with all reasonable speed and without first taking the child elsewhere." The parent, guardian or custodian and the court must promptly be given a

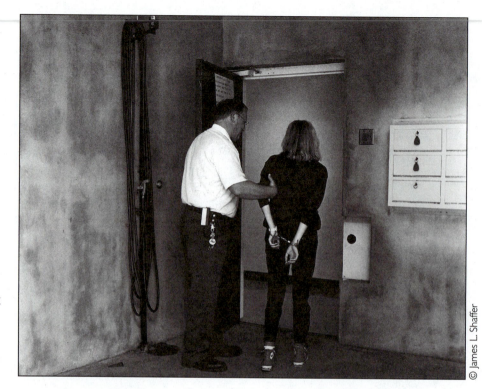

Officers on the street have great discretion, especially when dealing with juveniles. They may take a juvenile into custody, as shown here, or they may simply give them a warning, often referred to as street justice.

© James L. Shaffer

written notice stating the reason the child was taken into custody. The UJCA provides in Section 16 that a delinquent can be detained only in:

- A licensed foster home or a home approved by the court
- A facility operated by a licensed child welfare agency
- A detention home or center for delinquent children that is under the direction or supervision of the court or other public authority or of a private agency approved by the court
- Any other suitable place or facility, designated or operated by the court

The final catchall clause in this provision of the UJCA weakens the act's effectiveness.

Section 16 further specifies that delinquents may be kept in a jail or other adult detention facility only if the preceding are not available, the detention is in a room separate from adults and it appears that public safety and protection reasonably require detention. The act requires that the person in charge of a jail inform the court immediately if a person under age 18 is received at the jail. The act further stipulates that deprived or unruly children "shall not be detained in a jail or other facility intended or used for the detention of adults charged with criminal offenses or of children alleged to be delinquent." The intent of this section is to protect children from the harm of exposing them to criminals and the "degrading effect of jails, lockups and the like."

Section 17 states that if a child is brought before the court or delivered to a detention or shelter care facility, an investigation must be made immediately as to whether detention is needed. If the child is not released, a petition must be filed promptly with the court. In addition an informal **detention hearing** should be held within 72 hours to determine whether detention is required. A written notice of the time, place and purpose of the hearing is given to the child and, if possible, to the parents or guardians. Before the hearing begins, the court must inform the people involved of their right to counsel—court-appointed if they cannot afford to pay private counsel—and of the child's right to remain silent during the hearing.

Intake

As discussed in Chapter 7, intake is the initial phase of the juvenile court process. In most jurisdictions the offender is referred immediately to juvenile authorities or to an intake unit. The **intake unit** is the office that receives referrals to the juvenile court and decides the action to be taken. At the intake stage of the referral, an intake officer decides to adjust, settle or terminate the matter. The intake officer also makes referrals to other interests out of concern for the health, welfare and safety of the child. This process in most states is called the intake hearing. The purpose of these proceedings is not to adjudicate the affirmation (guilty) or denial (not guilty) of juveniles in the matter, but to determine whether the matter requires the court's attention. The intake unit serves in an advisory capacity.

Another important function of the intake hearing is to provide an authoritarian setting in which a severe lecture or counsel may be administered to the youth so as to avoid future difficulties. Beyond a lecture several other options are available to intake officers: write a reprimand, divert to another social agency, direct to the district/county attorney's office for a petition or dismiss the matter.

Intake cases are screened in the referral process by an officer appointed by the juvenile court. This officer is usually a probation officer or designated court personnel, not a lawyer. In matters handled by intake, the biggest disparity from state to state is in how abused, neglected and dependent children are helped.

Alternatives at Intake for Alleged Youthful Offenders

As noted in Figure 9.2, the intake hearing may lead to several outcomes, including dismissal of the case or referral to another agency.

 The intake hearing may result in dismissal, transfer to adult court, diversion or referral to juvenile court for **adjudication** (judging).

Transfer to Criminal Court

 Juveniles may be transferred to criminal court through statutory exclusion provisions, through concurrent jurisdiction, through a waiver or through certification.

During the mid-1990s, 46 states passed legislation making it easier to transfer juvenile offenders to adult court. According to Puzzanchera (2001, p.1): "All states have mechanisms to handle juveniles in criminal court." He cautions: "Simply putting young offenders in the adult justice system does not reduce crime. Studies of juveniles tried as adults are even more likely to commit new crimes than those who are judged in juvenile courts." According to Sickmund (2003, p.24): "Of every 1,000 delinquency cases handled in 1998, five were waived to criminal court." Table 9.3 summarizes the mechanisms states use to transfer juveniles to criminal court.

Exclusion and Concurrent Jurisdiction

These two methods of transferring juveniles to criminal court have been briefly introduced. A common way juveniles are transferred to criminal court is through statutory exclusion provisions, as discussed earlier. Such provisions currently exist in 28 states. Some states have mandatory adult court requirements for 14-, 15- and 16-year-olds for certain serious, violent offenses. According to Butts (2003): "Prosecution of these [violent] juveniles is increasingly controlled by automatic, legislated sentencing that lets politicians, not judges, decide who should be incarcerated, who should be tried and punished as an adult, and who should be sent to a juvenile program for intensive supervision."

Torbet et al. (2000) describe how a major reform in Wisconsin related to the exclusion of all people 17 and older, making them no longer under the jurisdiction of the juvenile court. The reform went into effect in January 1996, and since that time nearly everyone agrees that the adult criminal corrections system held 17-year-olds accountable, although some argue that it came at the expense of those 17-year-olds committing less serious offenses, which the system is ill-equipped to handle. The reform made Wisconsin more congruent with neighboring states, but the reform did not shift resources as easily to the younger population as was planned. According to the OJJDP's *Research 2000,* (2001, pp.11–12):

> Exclusion laws are not necessarily having their intended effect. . . . Although transfer provisions are often adopted to address a perceived problem of increasing juvenile violence, the studies in Florida and Pennsylvania show that it is unclear whether broader transfer provisions actually result in increased use of transfer. The Florida data, for example, indicate that the state's 1994 reforms did not result in the transfer of more juveniles to criminal court. The Pennsylvania study of exclusions similarly showed that only those juveniles who would have ended up in criminal court anyway remained there. The Pennsylvania exclusions study also revealed a considerable time lag in prosecuting juveniles in criminal court. Thus, while the sanction ultimately imposed was similar to the sanction a youth would have received in the juvenile system, the criminal system expended greater resources to prosecute the case and detain the juvenile prior to sentencing.

Concurrent jurisdiction, also previously discussed, allows the prosecutor to make the determination regarding where a given case in heard. This is currently used in15 states.

Waiver

The juvenile court may waive jurisdiction and transfer a case to criminal court (**waiver**). The judicial waiver allows judges (usually juvenile court judges) to make an individual determination about whether a juvenile meeting statutory criteria should be tried in juvenile or criminal court. The waiver may be discretionary,

Table 9.3
Mechanisms Used to Transfer Juveniles to Adult Court

Most States Have Multiple Ways to Impose Adult Sanctions on Juveniles
Statutes at the End of the 1999 Legislative Session

State	Judicial Waiver — Discretionary	Judicial Waiver — Presumptive	Judicial Waiver — Mandatory	Concurrent Jurisdiction	Statutory Exclusion	Reverse Waiver	Once an Adult, Always an Adult	Blended Sentencing
Total States	46	16	15	15	29	24	34	22
Alabama	■				■		■	
Alaska	■	■			■			■
Arizona	■	■		■		■	■	
Arkansas	■			■		■		■
California	■	■			■		■	■
Colorado	■	■		■		■		■
Connecticut			■			■		
Delaware	■		■		■		■	
Dist. of Columbia	■	■		■			■	
Florida	■			■	■		■	■
Georgia	■		■	■	■			
Hawaii	■						■	
Idaho	■				■		■	■
Illinois	■	■	■		■		■	■
Indiana	■		■		■		■	
Iowa	■				■	■	■	■
Kansas	■	■					■	■
Kentucky	■		■			■		
Louisiana	■		■	■	■			
Maine	■	■					■	
Maryland	■				■	■	■	
Massachusetts				■				■
Michigan	■			■			■	■
Minnesota	■	■					■	■
Mississippi	■				■		■	
Missouri	■						■	
Montana	■			■	■	■		
Nebraska				■		■		
Nevada	■	■			■	■	■	
New Hampshire	■	■					■	
New Jersey	■	■	■					
New Mexico					■			■
New York					■	■		
North Carolina	■		■				■	
North Dakota	■	■	■				■	
Ohio	■		■				■	
Oklahoma	■			■	■	■	■	■
Oregon	■				■		■	
Pennsylvania	■	■			■		■	
Rhode Island	■	■	■				■	■
South Carolina	■		■		■	■	■	■
South Dakota	■				■		■	
Tennessee	■					■	■	
Texas	■						■	■
Utah	■	■			■		■	
Vermont	■		■	■	■		■	■
Virginia	■			■		■	■	
Washington	■				■			
West Virginia			■					■
Wisconsin	■				■	■	■	
Wyoming	■			■		■		

■ In states with a combination of provisions for transferring juveniles to criminal court, the exclusion, mandatory waiver or concurrent jurisdiction provisions generally target the oldest juveniles and/or those charged with the most serious offenses, while those charged with relatively less serious offenses and/or younger juveniles may be eligible for discretionary waiver.

Source: Melissa Sickmund. *Juveniles in Court.* Washington, DC: Juvenile Offenders and Victims National Report Series Bulletin, June 2003, p.6.

Table 9.4
Characteristics of Waived Cases Changed between 1989 and 1998

	1989	1994	1998
Total Cases Waived	8,000	12,100	8,100
Most Serious Offense			
Persons	28%	43%	30%
Property	48	37	40
Drug	16	11	15
Public order	7	8	8
Gender			
Male	95%	95%	93%
Female	5	5	7
Age at Time of Referral			
Under 16	11%	13%	13%
16 or older	89	87	87
Race/ethnicity			
White	49%	51%	55%
Black	50	45	42
Other	2	4	3
Predisposition Detention			
Detained	59%	56%	50%
Not detained	41	44	50

Note: Detail may not equal 100% due to rounding.

Source: Charles M. Puzzanchera. *Delinquency Cases Waived to Criminal Court, 1989–1998*. Washington, DC: OJJDP Fact Sheet #35, September 2001. p.2. (FS 200135)

presumptive or mandatory. In some states the waiver decision is up to the prosecutor. Snyder et al. (2000) note: "Juvenile court judges largely concur with prosecutors as to which juveniles should be transferred to criminal court." Snyder et al. studied use of the waiver and found drastic increases in its use over 10 years. Although juvenile arrests for violent crimes increased 32 percent, use of judicial waivers increased 84 percent. The prosecuting attorney may make the decisions in other major crime situations.

Puzzanchera notes: "For every 1,000 formally handled delinquency cases, eight were waived to criminal court." Table 9.4 describes the characteristics of waived cases and the changes between 1989 and 1998.

When waiver occurs certain procedural guidelines apply. For example no statements made by the child before the transfer may be used against him or her in the criminal proceedings after the transfer. Figure 9.3 depicts the youngest age that a juvenile can be transferred to criminal court.

Certification

Another possibility is that the court may decree that a juvenile should be certified as an adult (**certification**). Certification is of paramount importance, since it may result in far more severe consequences to the juvenile than would have occurred had the youth remained under juvenile court jurisdiction.

While transfer to criminal court is not too frequent, when it does occur, juveniles go through the same procedures and have the same constitutional rights as adults tried in a criminal court. Recall from Chapter 1 that the procedural

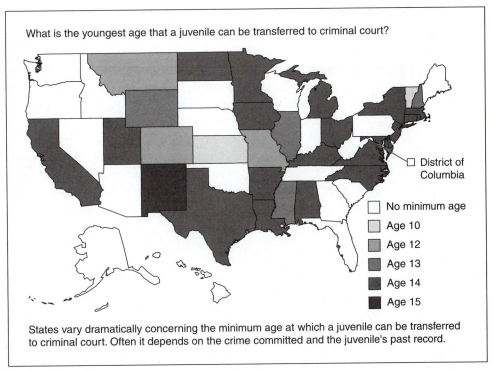

What is the youngest age that a juvenile can be transferred to criminal court?

District of Columbia

☐ No minimum age
◻ Age 10
◻ Age 12
◻ Age 13
◻ Age 14
◻ Age 15

States vary dramatically concerning the minimum age at which a juvenile can be transferred to criminal court. Often it depends on the crime committed and the juvenile's past record.

Figure 9.3
Youngest Age a Juvenile Can Be Transferred to Criminal Court

Source: Elizabeth A. Klug. "Geographical Disparities among Trying and Sentencing Juveniles." *Corrections Today,* December 2001, p.106. Reprinted by permission.

requirements for waiver to criminal court were articulated by the Supreme Court in *Kent v. United States.*

Jurisdictions may consider the child's age, alleged offense or a combination of other factors when determining whether a juvenile is fit for transfer to adult court. The procedures differ from state to state.

 In some states the court makes the decision to certify a juvenile as an adult. In other states this is done by the prosecutor.

To decide whether a minor should be tried as an adult, the court's decision is guided by five criteria: (1) the minor's criminal sophistication, (2) whether the minor can be rehabilitated before the juvenile court's jurisdiction's expires, (3) the minor's previous delinquent history, (4) the success of the court's previous attempts to rehabilitate the minor and (5) the gravity of the alleged offense.

Mendal (2000, p.39) cautions: "Rather than waiving as many youths as possible to adult court (or ending the juvenile court jurisdiction altogether), it seems much more practical and beneficial to ensure that most youthful offenders are treated as juveniles and direct our attention toward improving the services provided for them."

The Issue of Competency

Grisso et al. (2003, p.3) note: "It is well established that a criminal proceeding meets the constitutional requirements of due process only when the defendant is competent to stand trial, which includes capacities to assist counsel and to understand the nature of the proceeding sufficiently to participate in it and make decisions about rights afforded all defendants."

The concept of **competence** greatly influences how the legal system deals with children. Adults are presumed **competent,** that is fit or qualified to understand right from wrong. Children (i.e., minors) are presumed incompetent under the law in virtually all contexts. While children may be "heard" on behalf of themselves or may be treated as adults in a variety of circumstances, these situations are generally preceded by a qualifying process, incorporated in some specific statutory or common law exception. The statute may be specific as to whether a juvenile offender is to be tried as an adult. Under law a person's competence is conceptualized as a specific functional ability. The word *competent* is usually followed by the phrase "to . . . " rather than presented as a general attribute of a person. An adult who is deemed incompetent to stand trial for a specific offense may still be presumed competent to function as a custodial parent or to manage financial affairs. For the adult, specific incompetence must be proved case by case.

Conversely minors are presumed incompetent for most purposes, without any concern for whether they have the capacity to make required decisions in a practical sense. Juveniles who are deemed legally competent for one purpose are often considered generally incompetent in other decision-making contexts. For example a juvenile offender who has been found competent to waive rights and who has even been bound over for trial as an adult would still be considered generally incompetent to consent to medical treatment or make contracts.

In general, there has been little recognition that youths in criminal court may be incompetent due to developmental immaturity (Redding and Frost, 2002). In addition, until now, little meaningful data have been available regarding the capacities of adolescents relevant for adjudicative competence (Grisso, 2000). However, basic research on cognitive and psychosocial development suggests that some youths will manifest deficits in legally relevant abilities similar to deficits seen in adults with mental disability, but for reasons of immaturity rather than mental disorder (Grisso and Schwartz, 2000).

Grisso et al. (p.29) report: "Our results indicate that juveniles age 15 and younger are significantly more likely than older adolescents and young adults to be impaired in ways that compromise their ability to serve as competent defendants in a criminal proceeding." They also note: "Because a greater proportion of youths in the juvenile justice system than in the community are of below-average intelligence, the risk for incompetence to stand trial is therefore even greater among adolescents who are in the justice system than it is among adolescents in the community." Of particular concern to the justice system is their finding (p.30) regarding authority figures: "Adolescents are more likely than young adults to make choices that reflect a propensity to comply with authority figures, such as confessing to the police rather than remaining silent or accepting a prosecutor's offer of a plea agreement." Based on their findings, they (p.33) contend: "When youths are charged directly in criminal court, the proper mechanism might be a requirement that an evaluation and determination of competence to stand trial would automatically precede the adjudication."

> A major concern when transferring a juvenile to criminal court is that the juvenile may not be competent to stand trial there.

Reverse Certification

In some states the criminal court has exclusive jurisdiction over juveniles who commit specified serious crimes, such as murder, but the court may transfer the case to juvenile court by a process known as **reverse certification.** For example New York statutes specify that juvenile court jurisdiction:

> Excludes children 13 or older charged with second degree murder and children 14 or older charged with second degree murder, felony murder, kidnapping in the first degree, arson in the first or second degree, assault in the first degree, manslaughter in the first degree, rape in the first degree, sodomy in the first degree, aggravated sexual abuse, burglary in the first or second degree, robbery in the first or second degree, attempted murder, or attempted kidnapping in the first degree, unless such case is transferred to the juvenile court from the criminal court.

The decision to transfer a juvenile to criminal court is especially critical when the offense committed might carry the death penalty.

Juveniles and Capital Punishment

"The United States is currently the only nation in the world (since 1977) known to have executed inmates who committed crimes when they were younger than 18" (Manning and Rhoden-Trader, 2000, p.22). *Juveniles and the Death Penalty* (2000) reports that currently 23 of the 38 states that authorize the death penalty permit the execution of offenders who committed capital offenses before their eighteenth birthday. This report also notes that 2 to 3 percent of death sentences are imposed for juvenile crimes. Table 9.5 provides information on executions of juvenile offenders from 1973 through 2000. Table 9.6 provides the minimum age authorized for capital punishment in 2001.

At year-end 2001, of the 3,311 prisoners under sentence of death, 77 (2.3 percent) were 17 or younger at the time of their arrest, but none were under sentence of death on December 31, 2001 (Snell and Maruschak, 2002, p.9).

On June 26, 1989, the Supreme Court ruled that the death penalty for 16- and 17-year-olds is not necessarily "cruel and unusual punishment" and that juveniles may be executed. The decision whether to apply the death penalty to juveniles is now in the hands of the individual states (*Stanford v. Kentucky* and *Wilkins v. Missouri*). In 2002, the U.S. Supreme Court declined to hear a case challenging the constitutionality of imposing the death penalty against a man who committed murder at age 17 ("Supreme Court Declines Case on Juvenile

Table 9.5
Executions of Juvenile Offenders, January 1, 1973, through June 30, 2000

Name	Date of Execution	State	Race	Age at Time of Offense	Age at Time of Execution
Charles Rumbaugh	9/11/1985	Texas	White	17	28
J. Terry Roach	1/10/1986	S. Carolina	White	17	25
Jay Pinkerton	5/15/1986	Texas	White	17	24
Dalton Prejean	5/18/1990	Louisiana	Black	17	30
Johnny Garrett	2/11/1992	Texas	White	17	28
Curtis Harris	7/1/1993	Texas	Black	17	31
Frederick Lashley	7/28/1993	Missouri	Black	17	29
Ruben Cantu	8/24/1993	Texas	Latino	17	26
Chris Burger	12/7/1993	Georgia	White	17	33
Joseph John Cannon	4/22/1998	Texas	White	17	38
Robert A. Carter	5/18/1998	Texas	Black	17	34
Dwayne A. Wright	10/14/1998	Virginia	Black	17	26
Sean R. Sellars	2/4/1999	Oklahoma	White	16	29
Christopher Thomas	1/10/2000	Virginia	White	17	26
Steve E. Roach	1/19/2000	Virginia	White	17	23
Glen C. McGinnis	1/25/2000	Texas	Black	17	27
Gary L. Graham	6/22/2000	Texas	Black	17	36

Source: *Juveniles and the Death Penalty.* Washington, DC: Coordinating Council on Juvenile Justice and Delinquency Prevention, November 2000, no page. (NCJ 184748)

Death Penalty," 2002, p.2). Four of the justices sharply dissented. The case, *In re Kevin Niegle Stanford,* involved a Kentucky man sentenced to death in 1982 for abducting, sexually assaulting and shooting to death a woman when he was 17 years old. Stanford asked the court to reconsider the issue in light of its ruling earlier in *Atkins v. Virginia* (2002) in which the Court struck down the death penalty against mentally retarded persons. It was Stanford's case in 1989 in which the Court held capital punishment not to be "cruel and unusual punishment."

Moon et al. (2000, p.664) studied the extent to which the public in Tennessee supported the juvenile capital punishment. They found: "A majority of respondents favored juvenile capital punishment, often for young offenders. As an alternative to juvenile capital punishment, nearly two-thirds of the sample favored life in prison without the possibility of parole (LWOP); four-fifths favored a life sentence with work and restitution requirements (LWOP + W/R). Although the public is willing to execute juveniles who commit first-degree murder, they prefer alternative sentencing options that avoid putting youths to death."

According to the UJCA, if during a criminal proceeding it is learned that the defendant is younger than 18 or was younger than 18 at the time the offense occurred, the case may be transferred back to juvenile court. Waiver to criminal court is usually in keeping with a "get tough" philosophy. At the opposite extreme, some form of diversion is usually in keeping with the "best interests of the child" and *parens patriae* philosophy.

Table 9.6
Minimum Age Authorized for Capital Punishment, 2001

Age 16 or less	Age 17	Age 18	None specified
Alabama (16)	Georgia	California	Arizona
Arkansas (14)[a]	New Hampshire	Colorado	Idaho
Delaware (16)	North Carolina[b]	Connecticut[c]	Louisiana
Florida (16)	Texas	Federal system	Montana[d]
Indiana (16)		Illinois	Pennsylvania
Kentucky (16)		Kansas	South Carolina
Mississippi (16)[e]		Maryland	South Dakota[f]
Missouri (16)		Nebraska	
Nevada (16)		New Jersey	
Oklahoma (16)		New Mexico	
Utah (14)		New York	
Virginia (14)[g]		Ohio	
Wyoming (16)		Oregon	
		Tennessee	
		Washington	

Note: Reporting by states reflects interpretations by state attorney generals' offices and may differ from previously reported ages.

[a]See Ark. Code Ann. 9-27-31 8(c)(2)(Supp. 2001)

[b]Age required is 17 unless the murderer was incarcerated for murder when a subsequent murder occurred; then the age may be 14.

[c]See Conn. Gen. Stat. 53a-46a(g)(1).

[d]Montana law specifies that offenders tried under the capital sexual assault statute be 18 or older. Age may be a mitigating factor for other capital crimes.

[e]The minimum age defined by statute is 13, but the effective age is 16 based on interpretation of U.S. Supreme Court decisions by the Mississippi Supreme Court.

[f]Juveniles may be transferred to adult court. Age can be a mitigating factor.

[g]The minimum age for transfer to adult court by statute is 14, but the effective age is 16 based on interpretation of U.S. Supreme Court decisions by the State attorney general's office.

Source: Tracy L. Snell and Laura M. Maruschak. *Capital Punishment 2001*. Washington, DC: Bureau of Justice Statistics Bulletin, December 2002, p.5. (NCJ 197020)

Diversion from Juvenile Court

Zimring (2000, p.12) reminds us: "In 1899, a criminal justice system that removed youths from community settings and thrust them into lock-ups and jails was seen as a principal threat to adolescent development in normal society. . . . Growing up is the one certain cure for most juvenile crime." The juvenile court was established to prevent children from being treated as criminals. This is the same rationale in the 21st century that considers **diversion** from the juvenile court as a viable option for some youths.

Potter and Kakar (2002, p.20) contend: "One of the main purposes of juvenile diversion programs has been to divert youths from their early encounters with the juvenile justice system." Table 9.7 contains the legal variables involved in the diversion decision-making process.

The differences between the two groups is interesting. Prior record was the only legal variable that was very important to both groups. Table 9.8 presents the extra-legal variables influencing the diversion decision-making process.

County attorneys found the child's attitude toward the offense and toward treatment as more important than did court-designated workers. Neither indicated that the local political environment was very important.

Table 9.7
Test of Significance for Differences in Juvenile Court Practitioners' Perceptions on the Effects of Legal Variables: Prior Record, Severity of Crime, Severity of Injury/ Damage and Premeditated Action

	County Attorneys (n = 48)		Court-Designated Workers (n = 52)		
	%	f	%	f	Chi-Square
Prior record[a]					
Important			3.8	2	4.31
Somewhat important	10.4	5	9.6	5	
Very important	89.6	43	88.3	45	
Severity of crime					
Not important	2.0	1	13.4	7	7.08*
Important	12.5	6	23.0	12	
Somewhat important	14.5	7	15.3	8	
Very important	70.8	34	48.0	25	
Severity of injury/damage					
Not important	2.0	1	9.6	5	5.81
Important	10.4	5	23.0	12	
Somewhat important	20.8	10	15.3	8	
Very important	66.6	32	51.9	27	
Premeditated action					
Not important	2.0	1	21.1	11	16.84**
Important	6.2	3	13.4	7	
Somewhat important	16.6	8	26.9	14	
Very important	75.0	36	38.4	20	

a. The specific question asked was: "How important is prior record in making diversion decision? Not important, important, somewhat important or very important?"

*$p < .05$. **$p < .001$.

Source: Roberto Hugh Potter and Suman Kakar. "The Diversion Decision-Making Process from the Juvenile Court Practitioners' Perspective." *Journal of Contemporary Criminal Justice*, February 2002, p.31. Reprinted by permission of Sage Publications, Inc.

Griffin and Torbet (2002, p.49) suggest: "Diversion from formal juvenile court processing serves a number of important purposes: avoiding stigma, involving the community and the victim, reducing burdens on the court system and exercising wise restraint."

Specialized Courts

 Diversion from juvenile court may take the form of referral to a specialized court such as teen court, drug court or gun court.

Teen Court

An innovative alternative to the traditional juvenile court is the teen court, also called peer or youth court. Butts et al. (2002, p.1) explain: "Teen courts (or youth courts) are specialized diversion programs for young offenders. The typical youth referred to teen court is 14 to 16 years old, in trouble with the police for the first time and probably charged with vandalism, stealing or some other non-violent offense. . . . Teen courts operate much like juvenile courts except that fewer adults are involved in the process." They (p.2) report: "Growing from a handful of programs in the 1970s, there may be more than 800 teen court pro-

Table 9.8
Test of Significance for Differences in Juvenile Court Practitioners' Perceptions on the Effects of Extra-Legal Variables: Child's Appearance, Child's Attitude toward Offense and Treatment and Local Political Environment

	County Attorneys (n = 48)		Court-Designated Workers (n = 52)		
	%	f	%	f	Chi-Square
Child's appearance[a]					3.97
Not important	58.3	28	67.3	35	
Important	27.0	13	15.3	8	
Somewhat important	14.5	7	9.6	5	
Very important			7.6	4	
Child's attitude toward offense[b]					21.41**
Not important	4.1	2	13.4	8	
Important	12.5	6	40.3	21	
Somewhat important	16.6	8	11.5	6	
Very important	66.6	32	32.6	17	
Child's attitude toward treatment[c]					16.74**
Not important			13.4	8	
Important	14.5	7	32.6	17	
Somewhat important	22.9	11	5.7	3	
Very important	58.3	28	46.1	24	
Local political environment[d]					2.74
Not important	81.2	39	82.6	43	
Important	8.3	4	7.6	4	
Somewhat important	10.4	5	4.0	2	
Very important			7.6	3	

a. The specific question asked was: "How important is the child's appearance in making diversion decision? Not important, important, somewhat important or very important?"

b. The specific question asked was: "How important is the child's attitude toward offense in making diversion decision? Not important, important, somewhat important or very important?"

c. The specific question asked was: "How important is the child's attitude toward treatment in making diversion decision? Not important, important, somewhat important or very important?"

d. The specific question asked was: "How important is the local political environment in making diversion decision? Not important, important, somewhat important or very important?"

Source: Roberto Hugh Potter and Suman Kakar. "The Diversion Decision-Making Process from the Juvenile Court Practitioners' Perspective." *Journal of Contemporary Criminal Justice,* February 2002, p.32. Reprinted by permission of Sage Publications, Inc.

grams now in operation across the country. These courts handle a large and growing caseload." Figure 9.4 shows the points at which juvenile offenders can be diverted to teen court.

Butts and Buck (2000, p.6) note: "Thirteen percent of teen courts are authorized to hold trials. Eighty percent have paid program directors. Thirty-nine percent accept only first-time offenders, and 73 percent operate throughout the year."

Peterson and Elmendorf (2001, p.58) report that cases that may be handled in youth court include shoplifting/theft, alcohol possession, criminal mischief, vandalism/property damage, possession of small amounts of marijuana, traffic offenses, disorderly conduct and other offenses deemed appropriate. Participation is voluntary.

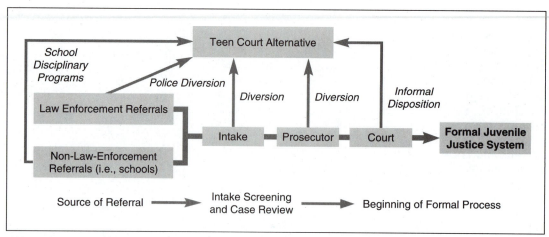

Source: The Urban Institute. Evaluation of Teen Courts Project.
Reprinted by permission.

Figure 9.4
Points at Which Juvenile Offenders Can Be Diverted to Teen Court

Table 9.9
Courtroom Models Used by U.S. Teen and Youth Courts

	Adult Judge Model	Youth Judge Model	Tribunal Model	Peer Jury Model
Who performs the role of judge in the courtroom?	Adult	Youth	3 Youth	Adult (sometimes no judge)
Are teen attorneys included in the process?	Yes	Yes	Yes	No
What is the role of the teen jury during court?	Listen to attorney presentations, recommend sentence to judge	Listen to attorney presentations, recommend sentence to judge	Usually no jury	Question defendant, recommend or order sentence

Source: Jeffrey A. Butts et al. *The Impact of Teen Court on Young Offenders.*
Washington, DC: Urban Institute Justice Policy Center, April 2002, p.7.
Reprinted by permission.

The courtroom models used in teen courts are generally divided into four types: adult judge, youth judge, youth tribunal and peer jury. Table 9.9 presents courtroom models used by teen and youth courts in the United States. The typical teen court process is shown in Figure 9.5.

Teen courts provide an effective intervention in jurisdictions where the enforcement of misdemeanor charges is given low priority due to heavy caseloads of more serious offenses. Furthermore: "Most teen courts require defendants to plead guilty prior to participation in the program; however, a small number of these courts are structured to determine guilt or innocence." Figure 9.6 illustrates sanctions imposed by teen courts.

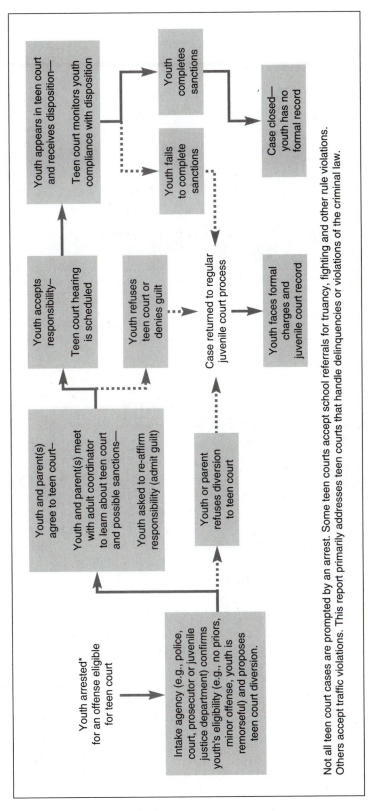

The following boxes and flow appear in the figure:

Youth arrested* for an offense eligible for teen court

Intake agency (e.g., police, prosecutor or juvenile justice department) confirms youth's eligibility (e.g., no priors, minor offense, youth is remorseful) and proposes teen court diversion.

Youth and parent(s) agree to teen court—

Youth and parent(s) meet with adult coordinator to learn about teen court and possible sanctions—

Youth asked to re-affirm responsibility (admit guilt)

Youth accepts responsibility—

Teen court hearing is scheduled

Youth refuses teen court or denies guilt

Youth or parent refuses diversion to teen court

Youth appears in teen court and receives disposition—

Teen court monitors youth compliance with disposition

Youth completes sanctions

Youth fails to complete sanctions

Case closed—youth has no formal record

Case returned to regular juvenile court process

Youth faces formal charges and juvenile court record

Not all teen court cases are prompted by an arrest. Some teen courts accept school referrals for truancy, fighting and other rule violations. Others accept traffic violations. This report primarily addresses teen courts that handle delinquencies or violations of the criminal law.

Source: Jeffrey A. Butts et al. *The Impact of Teen Court on Young Offenders.* Washington, DC: Urban Institute Justice Policy Center, April 2002, p.5. Reprinted by permission.

Figure 9.5
Typical Teen Court Process

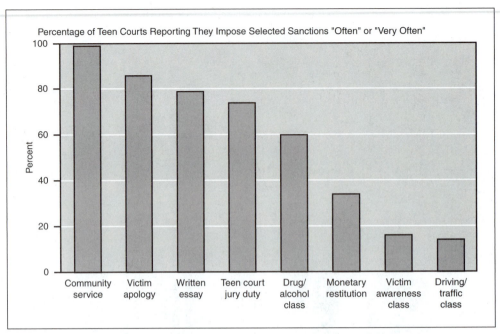

Source: Jeffrey A. Butts and Janeen Buck. *Teen Courts: A Focus on Research.* Washington, DC: OJJDP Juvenile Justice Research Bulletin, October 2000, p.6.

Figure 9.6
Sanctions Imposed
by Teen Courts

Research by Harrison et al. (2001) found that teen courts have an intuitive appeal. Proponents of the courts believe it delivers benefits such as holding teens accountable; instilling respect for the judicial system (law-related education); and promoting restorative justice. Critics argue that teen courts promote net widening by targeting the least serious juvenile court referrals, which would otherwise receive minimal dispositions. (The problem of net widening is discussed later in the chapter.) Most significantly, youths who completed teen court had significantly lower recidivism rates (23 percent) than youths who were referred to but did not complete the program (32 percent).

Juvenile Drug Courts

During the past century juvenile courts have struggled with increasingly complex and difficult caseloads and diminishing resources. One approach to the crowded court dockets is the drug court. A typical juvenile drug court offers delinquents who meet certain eligibility criteria the option of participating in the drug court rather than in a traditional case processing.

 The two most common criteria for participating in a drug court are having a substance abuse problem and not having committed a violent offense.

The juvenile and his or her parents must participate in an intensive treatment regimen in addition to receiving sanctions ranging from community service to short-term detention. As Cooper (2001, p.1) explains:

> Juvenile drug courts are intensive treatment programs that provide specialized services for drug-involved youths and their families. Cases are assigned to a juvenile drug court docket based on criteria set by local officials to carry out the goals of the drug court program.
>
> Juvenile drug courts provide (1) intensive and continuous judicial supervision over delinquency and status offense cases that involve substance-abusing juveniles and (2) coordinated and supervised delivery of an array of support services necessary to address the problems that contribute to juvenile involvement in the justice system. Service areas include substance abuse treatment, mental health, primary care, family and education. Since 1995, more than 140 juvenile drug courts have been established in the United States, and more than 125 are currently being planned.

Cooper (p.7) describes the goals of most juvenile drug courts:

- Provide immediate intervention, treatment and structure in the lives of juveniles using drugs through the ongoing, active oversight and monitoring by the drug court judge.

- Improve juveniles' level of functioning in their environment, address problems that may be contributing to their use of drugs and develop/strengthen their ability to lead crime- and drug-free lives.

- Provide juveniles with skills that will aid them in leading productive substance-free and crime-free lives, including skills relating to their educational development, sense of self-worth and capacity to develop positive relationships in the community.

- Strengthen the families of drug-involved youths by improving the capacity of families to provide structure and guidance to their children.

Juvenile Drug Courts: Strategies in Practice (2003) lists 16 strategies that can be used in a juvenile drug court, summarized in Table 9.10. Participants who successfully complete a drug court program may be rewarded by dismissed charges, shortened sentences or reduced penalties. According to Cooper (p.13): "Measured by indicators such as recidivism, drug use and educational achievement, juvenile drug courts appear to hold significant promise."

Juvenile Gun Courts

Sheppard and Kelly (2002, p.1) provide background: "Although gun-related juvenile crime has decreased over the past few years, gun violence involving youths nevertheless remains at unacceptably high levels. Throughout the nation, juvenile and **family courts** [courts with broad jurisdiction over family matters] have been criticized for not providing appropriate sanctions and program services for young offenders involved in gun crimes." In response, some states have

Table 9.10
The Strategies Used in Juvenile Drug Courts

1. **Collaborative Planning**—Engage all stakeholders in creating an interdisciplinary, coordinated and systemic approach to working with youth and their families.

2. **Teamwork**—Develop and maintain an interdisciplinary, nonadversarial work team.

3. **Clearly Defined Target Population and Eligibility Criteria**—Define a target population and eligibility criteria that are aligned with the program's goals and objectives.

4. **Judicial Involvement and Supervision**—Schedule frequent judicial reviews and be sensitive to the effect that court proceedings can have on youth and their families.

5. **Monitoring and Evaluation**—Establish a system for program monitoring and evaluation to maintain quality of service, assess program impact and contribute to knowledge in the field.

6. **Commnunity Partnerships**—Build partnerships with community organizations to expand the range of opportunities available to youth and their families.

7. **Comprehensive Treatment Planning**—Tailor interventions to the complex and varied needs of youth and their families.

8. **Developmentally Appropriate Services**—Tailor treatment to the developmental needs of adolescents.

9. **Gender-Appropriate Services**—Design treatment to address the unique needs of each gender.

10. **Cultural Competence**—Create policies and procedures that are responsive to cultural differences and train personnel to be culturally competent.

11. **Focus on Strengths**—Maintain a focus on the strengths of youth and their families during program planning and in every interaction between the court and those it serves.

12. **Family Engagement**—Recognize and engage the family as a valued partner in all components of the program.

13. **Educational Linkages**—Coordinate with the school system to ensure that each participant enrolls in and attends an educational program that is appropriate to his or her needs.

14. **Drug Testing**—Design drug testing to be frequent, random and observed. Document testing policies and procedures in writing.

15. **Goal-Oriented Incentives and Sanctions**—Respond to compliance and noncompliance with incentives and sanctions that are designed to reinforce or modify the behavior of youth and their families.

16. **Confidentiality**—Establish a confidentiality policy and procedures that guard the privacy of the youth while allowing the drug court team to access key information.

Source: *Juvenile Drug Courts: Strategies in Practice.* Washington, DC: Bureau of Justice Assistance, March 2003, p.10. (NCJ 197866)

instituted juvenile gun courts and targeted interventions that expose youths charged with gun offenses to the ramifications of such acts.

According to Sheppard and Kelly (p.2): "The juvenile gun court, another type of speciality court, intervenes with youths who have committed gun offenses that have not resulted in serious physical injury. Most juvenile gun courts are short-term programs that augment rather than replace normal juvenile court proceedings. . . . Other juvenile courts do replace normal juvenile court proceedings."

The principal elements in a juvenile gun court are (Sheppard and Kelly, p.3):

- Early intervention—in many jurisdictions, before resolution of the court proceedings.
- Short-term (often a single 2- to 4-hour session), intensive programming.
- An intensive educational focus.
- The inclusion of a wide range of court personnel and law enforcement officials—judges, probation officers, prosecutors, defense counsel and police—working together with community members.

A major goal is to effectively deliver to juveniles the message that gun violence hurts victims, families and entire communities; guns cannot protect juveniles; being involved in gun violence will negatively affect their entire lives; there are adults who can and will help them find nonviolent ways to solve problems. As Sheppard and Kelly (p.8) note: "Before the gun court was implemented, police officers usually did not arrest youths for gun possession; they released the youth to a parent without filing any charges. Now that the court is in place, however, police can arrest youths for all gun-related offenses."

 First-time, nonviolent gun offenders age 17 and younger are sometimes eligible to participate in juvenile gun court programs.

In addition to specialized courts, diversion can also be provided through various models of restorative justice, often through some form of conferencing.

Forms of Restorative Justice

 Four models of restorative justice may also be a means of diversion: victim-offender mediation, community reparative boards, family group conferencing and circle sentencing.

The concept of balanced and restorative justice was introduced earlier in the chapter. As Bazemore and Umbreit (2001, p.1) explain: "Restorative justice is a framework for juvenile justice reform that seeks to engage victims, offenders and their families, other citizens and community groups both as clients of juvenile justice services and as resources in an effective response to youth crime. . . . Reconciling the needs of victims and offenders with the needs of the community is the underlying goal of restorative justice. Unlike retributive justice, which is primarily concerned with punishing crime, restorative justice focuses on repairing the injury that crime inflicts."

 The three main components of restorative justice are the offender, the victim and the community, including juvenile justice professionals.

Figure 9.7 illustrates the three main components of restorative justice.

Figure 9.7
Restorative Justice

Source: *Balanced and Restorative Justice Project: Program Summary.* Washington, DC: Office of Juvenile Justice and Delinquency Prevention. No date or page. (NCJ 149727)

In the balanced and restorative justice format offenders, victims, community members and juvenile justice professions have new roles as they seek to sanction offenders through accountability, rehabilitate them through competency development and enhance community safety. These new roles are briefly summarized in Table 9.11.

Victim-Offender Mediation

Victim-offender mediation originated in the mid-1970s. Eligibility varies, but it is primarily used with first-time property offenders. Referrals are made by the court, the police and other entities. A mediator, victim and offender meet in a neutral setting such as a church or community center. Parents also may be involved. The primary outcome sought is to allow the victim to relay the impact of the crime to the offender, expressing feelings and needs while at the same time the offender has increased awareness of the harm of the offense, gains empathy with the victim and agrees on a reparative plan. Bazemore and Umbreit (p.9) provide the following example:

> The victim was a middle-aged woman. The offender, a 14-year-old neighbor of the victim, had broken into the victim's home and stolen a VCR. The mediation session took place in the basement of the victim's church.
>
> In the presence of a mediator, the victim and offender talked for two hours. At times, their conversation was heated and emotional. When they finished, the mediator felt that they had heard each other's stories and learned something important about the impact of the crime and about each other.
>
> The participants agreed that the offender would pay $200 in restitution to cover the cost of damages to the victim's home resulting from the break-in and would also reimburse the victim for the cost of the stolen VCR (estimated at $150). They also worked out a payment schedule.
>
> During the session, the offender made several apologies to the victim and agreed to complete community service hours working in a food bank sponsored by the victim's church. The victim said that she felt less angry and fearful after learning more about the offender and the details of the crime.

Community Reparative Boards

Reparative boards typically consist of a small group of citizens who have received intensive training and who then conduct public, face-to-face meetings with offenders ordered by the court to participate in the process. The target group is nonviolent offenders assigned to the board. During the board meeting, board members discuss with the offender the offense and its negative consequences. The board then develops a set of proposed sanctions that they discuss with the offender. The board also monitors compliance and submits a compliance report to the court. Bazemore and Umbreit (p.4) provide the following example of a community reparative board session:

> The reparative board convened to consider the case of a 17-year-old who had been caught driving with an open can of beer in his father's pickup truck. The youth had been sentenced by a judge to reparative probation, and it was the board's responsibility to decide what form the probation should take. For about 30 minutes, the citizen members of the board asked the youth several simple, straightforward questions. The board members then went to another room to deliberate on an appropriate sanction for the youth. The youth awaited the board's

Table 9.11
New Roles in the Balanced and Restorative Justice Model

	Sanctioning through Accountability	Rehabilitation through Competency Development	Enhancement of Community Safety
Juvenile Offender	Must accept responsibility for behavior and actively work to restore loss to victims (if victims wish) and the community and face victims or victim representatives (if victims wish) and community members	Actively participates as a resource in service roles that improve quality of life in the community and provide new experiences, skills and self-esteem as a productive resource for positive action	Becomes involved in constructive competency building and restorative activities in a balanced program while under adult supervision, develops internal controls and new peer and organizational commitments, and helps others escape offending patterns of behavior
Victim	Actively participates in all stages of the restorative process (if victim wishes and is able), documents psychological and financial impact of crime, participates in mediation voluntarily and helps determine sanctions for juvenile offender	Provides input into the rehabilitative process, suggests community service options for juvenile offenders and participates in victim panels or victim-awareness training for staff and juvenile offenders (if victim wishes)	Provides input regarding continuing safety concerns, fear and needed controls on juvenile offenders and encourages protective support for other victims
Community Member	Participates as volunteer mediator/facilitator and community panel member, develops community service and compensated work opportunities for juvenile offenders with reparative obligations and assists victims and supports juvenile offenders in completing obligations	Develops new opportunities for youth to make productive contributions, build competency and establish a sense of belonging	Provides guardianship of juvenile offenders, mentoring and input to juvenile justice systems regarding safety concerns; addresses underlying community problems that contribute to delinquency; and provides "natural surveillance"
Juvenile Justice Professional	Facilitates mediation, ensures that restoration occurs (by providing ways for juvenile offenders to earn funds for restitution), develops creative/restorative community service options, engages community members in the process and educates community on its role	Develops new roles for young offenders that allow them to practice and demonstrate competency, assesses and builds on youth and community strengths and develops community partnerships	Develops range of incentives and consequences to ensure juvenile offender compliance with supervision objectives, assists school and family in their efforts to control and maintain juvenile offenders in the community and develops prevention capacity of local organizations

Adapted from Bazemore and Washington. "Charting the Future for the Juvenile Justice System: Reinventing Mission and Management. *Spectrum*." *The Journal of State Government*, 1995, pp. 51–66.

Source: *Guide for Implementing the Balanced and Restorative Justice Model.* Washington, DC: Office of Juvenile Justice and Delinquency Prevention, December 1998, p.41.

decision nervously, because he did not know whether to expect something tougher or much easier than regular probation.

When the board returned, the chairperson explained the four conditions of the offender's probation contract: (1) begin work to pay off his traffic tickets, (2) complete a state police defensive driving course, (3) undergo an alcohol assessment and (4) write a three-page paper on how alcohol had negatively affected his life. The youth signed the contract, and the chairperson adjourned the meeting.

Family Group Conferencing

Family group conferencing originated in New Zealand. Referrals are usually by police and school officials. Family group conferencing involves those most affected by a youth's crime, usually the victim, offender and family, friends and key supporters of the victim and offender. These individuals are brought together by a trained facilitator to discuss how they and others have been harmed by the offense and how that harm might be repaired. Such conferences typically take place in a social welfare office, school, community building or police facility. The primary outcomes sought are to clarify the facts of a case and to denounce crime while affirming and supporting the offender and restoring the victim's loss. Bazemore and Umbreit (p.5) provide the following example of a family group conferencing session:

> A family conferencing group convened in a local school to consider a case in which a student had injured a teacher and broken the teacher's glasses in an altercation. Group members included the offender, his mother and grandfather, the victim, the police officer who made the arrest and about 10 other interested parties, including two of the offender's teachers and two friends of the victim.
>
> The conferencing process began with comments by the offender, his mother and grandfather, the victim and the arresting officer. Each spoke about the offense and its impact. The youth justice coordinator next asked for input from the other group members and then asked all participants what they thought the offender should do to pay back the victim and the community for the damage caused by his crime. In the remaining 30 minutes of the hour-long conference, the group suggested that the offender should make restitution to the victim for his medical expenses and the cost of new glasses and that the offender should also perform community service work on the school grounds.

McGarrell (2001, p.1) contends that restorative justice conferences are an appropriate diversion option for young offenders, noting: "Youths who become involved in the juvenile justice system at an early age are significantly more likely to continue offending than their older counterparts." He (p.3) suggests the following criteria for eligibility: (1) be no older than 14 years of age, (2) be a first-time offender (i.e., have no prior adjudications), (3) have committed a nonserious, nonviolent offense, (4) have no pending charges and (5) **admit** responsibility for the offense—this is equivalent to pleading guilty in criminal court. The most common offense in McGarrell study was shoplifting, followed by battery and theft.

McGarrell (p.9) reports: "The data indicate reasonably high levels of satisfaction among participants in both conferences and other court-ordered diversion program (i.e., control group programs). . . . The interview data suggest that the conference approach makes a positive difference for victims. When compared with victims participating in other diversion programs, victims in the conference program were more satisfied with how their cases were handled and much more likely to recommend the program to a friend. . . . The conference approach also appears to make a difference for parents and youths. . . . Youths who attended conferences were significantly less likely than youths who attended other diversion programs to be rearrested during the 6 months after the incident that initially brought them to the attention of the court."

Circle Sentencing

Circle sentencing is a modernized version of the traditional sanctioning and healing practices of aboriginal peoples in Canada and American Indians in the United States. According to Bazemore and Umbreit (p.6): "Circle sentencing is a holistic reintegrative strategy designed not only to address the criminal and delinquent behavior of offenders but also to consider the needs of victims, families and communities." The circle usually includes victims, offenders, family and friends of both, justice and social service personnel and interested community residents.

The target group is offenders who admit guilt and express willingness to change. The primary outcomes sought are to increase community strength and capacity to resolve disputes and prevent crime; develop reparative and rehabilitative plans; address victim concerns and public safety issues; assign victim and offender support group responsibilities and identify resources. Bazemore and Umbreit (p.7) provide the following example of a circle sentencing session:

> The victim was a middle-aged man whose parked car had been badly damaged when the offender, a 16-year-old, crashed into it while joyriding in another vehicle. The offender had also damaged a police vehicle.
>
> In the circle, the victim talked about the emotional shock of seeing what had happened to his car and his costs to repair it (he was uninsured). Then, an elder leader of the First Nations community where the circle sentencing session was being held (and an uncle of the offender) expressed his disappointment and anger with the boy. The elder observed that this incident, along with several prior offenses by the boy, had brought shame to his family. The elder also noted that in the old days, the boy would have been required to pay the victim's family substantial compensation as a result of such behavior. After the elder finished, a feather (the "talking piece") is passed to the next person in the circle, a young man who spoke about the contributions the offender had made to the community, the kindness he had shown toward elders and his willingness to help others with home repairs.
>
> Having heard all this, the judge asked the Crown Council (Canadian prosecutor) and the **public defender,** [lawyer who works for the defense of indigent offenders] who were also sitting in the circle to make statements and then asked if anyone else in the circle wanted to speak. The Royal Canadian Mounted Police officer, whose vehicle had also been damaged, then took the feather and spoke on the offender's behalf. The officer proposed to the judge that in lieu of statutorily required jail time for the offense, the offender be allowed to meet with him on a regular basis for counseling and community service. After asking the victim and the prosecutor if either had any objections, the judge accepted this proposal. The judge also ordered restitution to the victim and asked the young adult who had spoken on the offender's behalf to serve as a mentor for the offender.

Table 9.12
**Restorative Community
Justice: Least- to Most-
Restorative Impacts**

Least-Restorative Impact	Most-Restorative Impact
Entire focus is on determining the amount of financial restitution to be paid, with no opportunity to talk directly about the full impact of the crime on the victim and the community, and also on the offender.	Primary focus is on providing an opportunity for victims and offenders to talk directly to each other, to allow victims to describe the impact of the crime on their lives and receive answers to questions, and to allow offenders to appreciate the human impact of their behavior and take responsibility for making things right.
No separate preparation meetings with the victim and offender prior to bringing the parties together.	Separate preparation meetings with the victim and offender, with emphasis on listening to how the crime has affected them, identifying needs and answering questions about the mediation process.
Victims not given choice of meeting place (where they would feel most comfortable) or participants; given only written notice to appear for mediation session at preset time, with no preparation.	Victims continually given choices throughout the process: where to meet, whom they would like to be present, etc.
Mediator or facilitator describes offense and offender then speaks, with the victim simply asking a few questions or responding to questions from the mediator.	Victims given choice to speak first and encouraged to describe offense and participate actively.
Highly directive styles of mediation or facilitation, with the mediator talking most of the time, little if any direct dialog between the involved parties.	Nondirective style of mediation or facilitation with minimal mediator interference, and use of a humanistic or transformative mediation model.
Low tolerance for moments of silence or expression of feelings.	High tolerance for silence, expression of feelings and discussion of the full impact of the crime.
Voluntary for victim but required of offender regardless of whether he or she takes responsibility.	Voluntary for victim and offender.
Settlement-driven and very brief (10–15 minutes).	Dialog-driven and typically lasts about an hour (or longer).
Paid attorneys or other professionals serve as mediators.	Trained community volunteers serve as mediators or facilitators, along with agency staff.

Source: Gordon Bazemore and Mark Umbreit. *A Comparison of Four Restorative Conferencing Models.* Washington, DC: OJJDP Juvenile Justice Bulletin, February 2001, p.16.

Considerations When Using a Restorative Justice Approach

Bazemore and Umbreit studied the four models of restorative justice just discussed and found that each model had strengths and weakness. Their conclusion is that different approaches will work best in certain situations. They looked at strategies within each model and determined which approaches had the least restorative impact and which had the most restorative impact, as shown in Table 9.12.

In addition to the findings of Bazemore and Umbriet, Griffin and Torbet (p.51) recommend that when using diversion programs such as just discussed, the programs will be more successful if they have a participatory rather than an adjudicatory focus. The differences between these two approaches are summarized in Table 9.13.

Griffin and Torbet (p.97) suggest that success is also more likely using a strength-based approach as opposed to a problem-centered approach. The features of these two approaches are summarized in Table 9.14.

Although diversion is a highly touted approach for nonviolent first-time juvenile offenders, critics caution that diversion can result in net widening.

Table 9.13
Types of Alternative Dispute Resolution Programs

Adjudicatory	Participatory
Intent is to assert a moral or legal message and impose a solution	Intent is to preserve and enhance ongoing relationships
Facilitator/panel makes and imposes all decisions	Parties arrive at mutually acceptable agreement with aid of facilitator
Facilitator/panel assesses facts and culpability in determining appropriate remedy	Less fact-finding; parties define issues, engage in search for solutions
Focus is on the immediate conflict and the issues raised in the complaint	Focus is on-going relationships among neighbors, family members, etc.
Teaches accountability for offenses	Teaches conflict-resolution and problem-solving techniques
The more formal the process and the more serious the problem presented, the more formal the resulting agreement	The more participatory and inclusive the process, the less formal the resulting agreement

Adapted from National Council of Juvenile and Family Court Judges, *Court-Appointed Alternative Dispute Resolution: A Better Way to Resolve Minor Delinquency, Status Offense and Abuse/Neglect Cases.* (1989) NOJFCJ: Reno, NV.

Source: Patrick Griffin and Patricia Torbet, editors. *Desktop Guide to Good Juvenile Probation Practice.* Pittsburgh, PA: National Center for Juvenile Justice, June 2002, p.51. Reprinted by permission.

Table 9.14
Problem-Centered Approach vs. Strength-Based Approach

Problem-centered Approach	Strength-based Approach
Approaches clients with attention to their failure, dysfunction and deficits with an eye to fixing their flaws.	Approaches clients with a greater concern for their strengths, competencies and possibilities, seeking not only to fix what is wrong but to nurture what is best.
Assumes an "expert" role in naming the client's problems and then instructing clients how to fix them.	Assumes clients to be competent and "expert" on their life and situation. Helps clients discover how strengths and resources can be applied to negotiate third-party concerns and mandates while also furthering their wants and concerns as well.
Sanction-focused: client "takes the punishment" without taking responsibility or earning redemption.	Incentive-focused: holds youth accountable while furthering their pro-social interests, skills or passions.
Route to solution: fix the problem.	Route to solution: strengthen connection to clients' competencies, past successes, positive interests and wants.
Goals are obedience and compliance.	Initial goals are obedience and compliance; final goals are behavior change and growth.
No direct strategies are used for building motivation. Relies on coercion and "pushing from without."	Employs specific principles and strategies for building client motivation to change. Uses sanctions to stabilize out-of-control behavior but works to raise motivation that comes from within.
Court has non-negotiable mandates, and probation officer determines both the goals and the means for reaching those goals.	Court has non-negotiable mandates but beyond these, clients are partners in the process of setting personalized goals. Probation officer helps them focus on what they want to change, maintains the focus and works to increase positive options.

Source: Patrick Griffin and Patricia Torbet, editors. *Desktop Guide to Good Juvenile Probation Practice.* Pittsburgh, PA: National Center for Juvenile Justice, 2002, p.97. Reprinted by permission.

Net Widening

Jamison (no date, p.1) explains that **net widening** refers to involving youths in a diversion program who without such opportunities probably would not be involved in any type of intervention. He notes: "The process results in diversion of resources from youths most in need of intervention to youths who may require no intervention. This process depletes the system's resources and impairs its ability to properly intervene with appropriate youths. Instead of improving public safety, these early intervention and prevention strategies promote net widening by shifting resources from youths most in need to youths least in need."

Jamison (p.4) contends: "For the past 40 years criminal justice research repeatedly shows that almost 70 percent of youths who are arrested once are never arrested again. In other words, by doing nothing the state can achieve a 70 percent success rate—meaning no subsequent arrests—with first-time offenders. . . By reducing net widening, research shows that systems can improve their effectiveness and better promote public safety. To shorten the net and improve public safety, juvenile justice systems and affiliated community-based agencies need to adopt a deep end strategy." A **deep end strategy** would target youths with the highest likelihood of continuing their delinquent careers without comprehensive interventions. Jamison suggests: "The current favored approach of intervention with first-time offenders is counter to this strategy and a likely waste of the system's limited resources."

Summary

The juvenile justice system is basically a civil system. Most state juvenile court purpose statements contain (1) balanced and restorative justice (BARJ) clauses; (2) Standard Juvenile Court Act clauses; (3) legislative guide clauses; (4) clauses that emphasize punishment, deterrence, accountability and/or public safety clauses; or (5) clauses with traditional child welfare emphasis. Juvenile court jurisdiction includes children who are in poverty, neglected or abused, who are unruly or commit status offenses and who are charged with committing serious crimes. This jurisdiction is determined by the offender's age and conduct. The possible bases for a declaration of wardship include demonstrating that the child is abused or neglected or has committed a status offense or a criminal act.

Throughout their history juvenile courts have been separated into three types: designated courts, independent and separate courts, and coordinated courts. Court action on behalf of neglected, abused or dependent children may be noncriminal or criminal. The National Committee for Prevention of Child Abuse describes two kinds of intervention for deprived children: coercive and therapeutic.

The intake hearing may result in dismissal, transfer to adult court, diversion or referral to juvenile court for adjudication. Juveniles may be transferred to criminal court through statutory exclusion provisions, concurrent jurisdiction, waiver or certification. In some states the court makes the decision to certify a juvenile as an adult. In other states this is done by the prosecutor. A major concern when transferring a juvenile to criminal court is that the juvenile may not be competent to stand trial there.

Diversion from juvenile court may take the form of referral to a specialized court such as teen court, drug court or gun court. The two most common criteria for participating in a drug court are having a substance abuse problem and not having committed a violent crime. First-time, nonviolent gun offenders 17 and younger are sometimes eligible to participate in juvenile gun court programs. Four models of restorative justice may also be a means of diversion: victim-offender mediation, community reparative boards, family group conferencing and circle sentencing. The three main components of restorative justice are the offender, victim and community, including juvenile justice professionals.

Discussion Questions

1. Should the juvenile court have two separate courts for civil and criminal matters?
2. Should there be a separate justice system for juveniles, or should all juveniles be dealt with in the adult system?
3. What is the purpose statement of the juvenile court in your area?
4. What criteria are used in decisions to waive juvenile court jurisdiction?
5. Who can certify a juvenile as an adult in your state?

6. Should juveniles be subject to the death penalty?
7. Do you think most juveniles are competent to stand trial in criminal court?
8. Is diversion being too soft on youths who commit status offenses?
9. Is restorative justice compatible with the juvenile justice system?
10. What form of restorative justice do you find most appealing?

InfoTrac College Edition Assignments

- Use InfoTrac College Edition to answer the Discussion Questions as appropriate.
- Read and outline one of the following:
  - ○ "The Common Thread: Diversion in Juvenile Justice" by Franklin E. Zimring

  - ○ "Restorative Justice for Victims and Offenders: A Return to Tradition" by Emilio C. Viano
  - ○ "Balanced and Restorative Justice and Educational Programming for Youth at Risk" by Donald DeVore and Kevin Gentilcore

Internet Assignments

Complete one of the following assignments and be prepared to share your findings with the class:

- Research one of the following key words or phrases: *civil law, concurrent jurisdiction, detention hearing, family court, justice model, juvenile court, net widening, restitution.*
- Go to http://ojjdp.ncjrs.org/pubs;court.html#184748 to find and outline *Juveniles and the Death Penalty.*

- Go to http://www.ojp.usdoj.gov/depo.familydrug and read and outline *Juvenile and Family Drug Courts: Profile of Program Characteristics and Implementation Issues* (NCJ 171142)
- Find and outline "Juveniles Facing Criminal Sanctions: Three States that Changed the Rules."
- Go to www.ncjrs.org to find, read and outline any of the end-of-chapter references with NCJ number in parentheses or go to any reference having an outline address to find, read and outline the entire article.

References

Balanced and Restorative Justice: Program Summary. Washington, DC: Office of Juvenile Justice and Delinquency Prevention. No date. (NCJ 149727)

Bazemore, Gordon and Umbreit, Mark. *A Comparison of Four Restorative Conferencing Models.* Washington, DC: OJJDP Juvenile Justice Bulletin, February 2001. (NCJ 184738)

Butts, Jeffrey A. "Juvenile Justice Deadly Distraction." *San Francisco Chronicle,* January 12, 2003.

Butts, Jeffrey A. and Buck, Janeen. *Teen Courts: A Focus on Research.* Washington, DC: OJJDP Research Bulletin, October 2000. (NCJ 183472)

Butts, Jeffrey A.; Buck, Janeen; and Coggeshall, Mark B. *The Impact of Teen Court on Young Offenders.* Washington, DC: OJJDP Urban Institute Research Report, April 2002. http://www.urban.org

Cooper, Caroline S. *Juvenile Drug Court Programs.* JAIBG Bulletin, May 2001. (NIJ 184774)

Griffin, Patrick and Torbet, Patricia (eds.) *Desktop Guide to Good Juvenile Probation Practice.* Pittsburgh, PA: National Center for Juvenile Justice, June 2002.

Grisso, T. "What We Know about Youths' Capacities as Trial Defendants." In *Youth on Trial: A Developmental Perspective on Juvenile Justice,* edited by T. Grisso and R. Schwartz. Chicago, IL: University of Chicago Press, 2000, pp.139–171.

Grisso, T. and Schwartz, R. (eds.) *Youth on Trial: A Developmental Perspective on Juvenile Justice.* Chicago, IL: University of Chicago Press, 2000.

Grisso, Thomas; Steinberg, Laurence; Woolard, Jennifer; Cauffman, Elizabeth; Scott, Elizabeth; Graham, Sandra; Lexcen, Fran; Reppucci, N. Dickon; and Schwartz, Robert. "Juveniles' Competence to Stand Trial: A Comparison of Adolescents' and Adults' Capacities as Trial Defendants." In press *Law and Human Behavior.* Online: www.mac-adoldev-juvjustice.org

Harrison, Paige; Maupin, James R.; and Mays, G. Larry. "Teen Court: An Examination of Processes and Outcomes." *Crime & Delinquency,* April 2001, pp.243–264.

Jamison, Ross. *Widening the Net in Juvenile Justice and the Dangers of Prevention and Early Intervention.* San Francisco, CA: Center on Juvenile and Criminal Justice, no date. http://207.158.206.242/pubs/net/netwid.html

Juvenile Drug Courts: Strategies in Practice. Washington, DC: Bureau of Justice Assistance, March 2003. (NCJ 197866)

Juveniles and the Death Penalty. Washington, DC: Coordinating Council on Juvenile Justice and Delinquency Prevention, November 2000. (NCJ 184748)

Manning, Will and Rhoden-Trader, Jacqueline. "Rethinking the Death Penalty." *Corrections Today,* October 2000, pp.22–25.

McGarrell, Edmund F. *Restorative Justice Conferences as an Early Response to Young Offenders.* Washington, DC: OJJDP Juvenile Justice Bulletin, August 2001. (NCJ 187769)

Mendel, Richard A. *Less Hype More Help: Reducing Juvenile Crime: What Works—and What Doesn't.* Washington, DC: American Youth Policy Forum, 2000.

Moon, Melissa M.; Wright, John Paul; Cullen, Francis T.; and Pealer, Jennifer A. "Putting Kids to Death: Specifying Public Support for Juvenile Capital Punishment." *Justice Quarterly,* December 2000, pp.663–684.

National Center for Juvenile Justice. "National Overviews." *State Juvenile Justice Profiles.* Pittsburgh, PA: National Center for Juvenile Justice. Online http://www.ncjj.org/stateprofiles/

OJJDP. *Research 2000.* Washington, DC: Office of Juvenile Justice and Delinquency Prevention, 2001. (NCJ 186732)

Peterson, Scott B. and Elmendorf, Michael J., II. "Youth Courts: A National Youth Justice Movement." *Corrections Today,* December 2001, pp.54–113.

Potter, Roberto Hugh and Kakar, Suman. "The Diversion Decision-Making Process from the Juvenile Court Practitioners' Perspective." *Journal of Contemporary Criminal Justice,* February 2002, pp.20–36.

Puzzanchera, Charles M. *Delinquency Cases Waived to Criminal Court, 1989–1998.* Washington, DC: OJJDP Fact Sheet #35, September 2001. (FS 200135)

Redding, R. and Frost, L. "Adjudicative Competence in the Modern Juvenile Court." *Virginia Journal of Social Policy and the Law,* Vol.9, 2002, pp.353–410.

Sheppard, David and Kelly, Patricia. *Juvenile Gun Courts: Promoting Accountability and Providing Treatment.* JAIBG Bulletin, May 2002. (NCJ 187078)

Sickmund, Melissa. *Juveniles in Court.* Washington, DC: Juvenile Offenders and Victims National Report Series Bulletin, June 2003. (NCJ 195420)

Snell, Tracy L. and Maruschak, Laura M. *Capital Punishment 2001.* Washington, DC: Bureau of Justice Statistics, December 2002. (NCJ 197020)

Snyder, Howard N.; Sickmund, Melissa; and Poe-Yamagata, Eileen. *Juvenile Transfers to Criminal Court in the 1990s: Lessons Learned from Four Studies.* Washington, DC: Office of Juvenile Justice and Delinquency Prevention, 2000.

"Supreme Court Declines Case on Juvenile Death Penalty." *Criminal Justice Newsletter,* October 20, 2002, pp.2–3.

Torbet, P.; Griffin, P.; Hurst, H., Jr.; and MacKenzie, I.R. *Juveniles Facing Criminal Sanctions: Three States that Changed the Rules.* Washington, DC: Office of Juvenile Justice and Delinquency Prevention, 2000. (NCJ 181203)

Zimring, Franklin E. "The Common Thread: Diversion in Juvenile Justice." *California Law Review,* December 2000, Vol. 88, No. 6, p.2477.

Cases Cited

Commonwealth v. Fisher, 213 Pa. 48, 62 A. 198, 199, 200 (1905).

In re Kevin Niegle Stanford, U.S. 1, 19–21, 26–28, 87 S.Ct. 1428, 1439–1440, 1442–1444, 18 L.Ed.2d 527 (1967).

Kent v. United States, 383 U.S. 541 (1966).

People ex rel. O'Connell v. Turner, 55 Ill. 280, 8 Am.Rep. 645 (1870).

Stanford v. Kentucky, 492 U.S. 361 (1989).

Wilkins v. Missouri, 492 U.S. 361 (1989).

The Juvenile Court in Action

There is evidence in fact, that there may be grounds
for concern that the child receives the worst of two
possible worlds; that he gets neither the protections
accorded adults nor the solicitous care and
regenerative treatment postulated for children.

—Justice Abe Fortas, *In re Gault*

Do You Know?

- Who is included in the juvenile court team?
- What rights children involved in the juvenile justice system have?
- What three phases occur when filing a petition?
- How Supreme Court decisions have changed juvenile court procedure?
- What the trend in the disposition of juvenile cases is?
- What the four basic types of juvenile sentences are?
- What factors are usually considered in a juvenile sentencing law?
- What dispositions are available to juvenile judges?
- What the features of a good graduated sanctions system are?
- What the three most common types of restitution are?
- What dilemma juvenile courts face?
- What social and legal issues the juvenile court has become involved in?
- What confidentiality issues the juvenile court faces?
- How states are responding to these confidentiality issues?
- What two changes might be made to improve the juvenile court?

Can You Define?

adjudicate
adjudicatory hearing
bifurcated hearings
blended sentence
CASA
conference
determinate sentence
detention center
discretionary sentence
disposition
dispositional hearing

graduated sanctions
guardian *ad litum*
hearing
incarceration
indeterminate sentence
limited discretionary
   sentence
mandatory sentence
mechanical
   jurisprudence

nondiscretionary
   sentence
petition
preliminary hearing
presumptive sentence
referee
rehabilitation
respite care
restitution
summons

INTRODUCTION

"Historically juvenile courts are informal, private, nonadversary systems that stress **rehabilitation** [restoring to a condition of constructive activity] rather than punishment of youths. Juvenile courts try to secure care and guidance for each minor under the court's jurisdiction. Laws relating to juveniles try to preserve and strengthen family ties whenever possible, removing minors from parental custody only when the minor's welfare or safety or protection of the public cannot be adequately safeguarded without such removal" (Wrobleski and Hess, 2003, p.422).

This chapter begins with a discussion of the youths being served by juvenile court and the processing of their cases. Next the juvenile court team is described, followed by a look at the rights of those being adjudicated. Then the hearings conducted in the juvenile court are explained: the conference, the adjudication hearing and the disposition hearing. Types of sentences and juvenile sentencing laws are included in that discussion as are the dispositions available to juvenile judges. The chapter concludes with a discussion of the issues facing juvenile courts.

Youths Brought before the Juvenile Court

As discussed in Chapter 9 nonviolent first-time offenders may be diverted from the juvenile court, and many chronic violent juvenile offenders may be referred to the adult criminal court. The majority of juvenile offenders referred to juvenile court are status offenders.

Status Offenders

Children and their families brought before the court for status offenses occupy a great share of the court's workload. Status offenders can try the court's patience because such children often are considered to simply be "in need of supervision," resulting in a group of acronyms: CHINS (children in need of supervision), FINS (families in need of supervision), JINS (juveniles in need of supervision) and PINS (persons in need of supervision).

The juvenile courts in some states have dispensed harsher justice for status offenders than for criminal law violators because status offenses are annoyances. There has always been a need to distinguish status offenses from delinquent acts. Often status offenses fall into a separate classification for the court to consider in dispensing justice. According to the American Bar Association, juvenile delinquency liability should include only such conduct as would be designated a crime if committed by an adult.

The referral of status offenses to juvenile court has been viewed by many as ineffective and a waste of valuable court resources. Critics believe that resources would best be used for the more serious recidivist delinquents the court has to deal with. Whether the court is dealing with status offenders or youths who have committed violent crimes or protecting abused or neglected children, it no longer has free reign. The juvenile court must grant many aspects of due process to the youths who come under its jurisdiction.

Delinquents

The juvenile court also hears cases involving more serious offenses, including violent crimes against persons. Although some of these cases are referred to adult

Table 10.1
Delinquency Cases by Most Serious Offense, 1998

Most Serious Offense	Number of Cases	Percent Change 1989–98	Percent Change 1994–98	Percent Change 1997–98
Total	1,757,400	44%	5%	–3%
Person Offenses	403,800	88	12	1
Criminal homicide	2,000	6	–36	–2
Forcible rape	6,000	26	–9	–7
Robbery	29,600	29	–23	–12
Aggravated assault	65,100	36	–22	–6
Simple assault	262,400	128	33	3
Other violent sex offense	10,500	53	2	–1
Other person offense	28,200	87	35	26
Property Offenses	797,600	11	–8	–8
Burglary	125,800	–7	–14	–9
Larceny	370,500	13	–5	–10
Motor vehicle theft	44,200	–34	–28	–11
Arson	8,400	27	–13	–9
Vandalism	118,700	40	–9	0
Trespassing	64,000	26	–3	–5
Stolen party offense	34,000	35	0	3
Other party offense	32,100	37	13	–3
Drug Law Violations	192,500	148	47	1
Public Order Offenses	363,500	73	19	0
Obstruction of justice	152,000	102	38	–2
Disorderly conduct	92,100	100	10	–4
Weapons offense	40,700	61	–20	4
Liquor law violation	19,600	29	32	59
Nonviolent sex offense	10,900	–13	2	–3
Other public order	48,100	36	34	–10
Violent Crime Index*	102,600	33	–22	–8
Property Crime Index**	548,800	3	–10	–10

Note: Detail may not add to totals because of rounding. Percentage change calculations are based on unrounded numbers.

* Includes criminal homicide, forcible rape, robbery and aggravated assault.

** Includes burglary, larceny, motor vehicle theft and arson.

Source Anne L. Stahl. *Delinquency Cases in Juvenile Courts 1998*. Washington, DC: OJJDP Fact Sheet #31, August 2001, p.1. (FS 200131)

criminal court, many find their way to the juvenile court. According to Stahl (2001, p.1): "In 1998, U.S. juvenile courts processed an estimated 1,757,400 delinquency cases." According to Griffin and Torbet (2002, p.33), the overwhelming majority of cases (84 percent in 1998) were referred by the police. Table 10.1 depicts the delinquency cases in juvenile courts in 1998.

Processing of Juvenile Cases

State laws usually spell out how juvenile proceedings are to be conducted from start to finish—from the filing of a petition (who may file it, what it must contain, etc.), through the various intermediate hearings (when they must be held, who is entitled to notice of them, who may and who must attend, what evidence may be considered, what decisions must be made, etc.), to the adjudication (or trial) and disposition (or sentencing) of the delinquent (Griffin and Torbet, 2002, p.12).

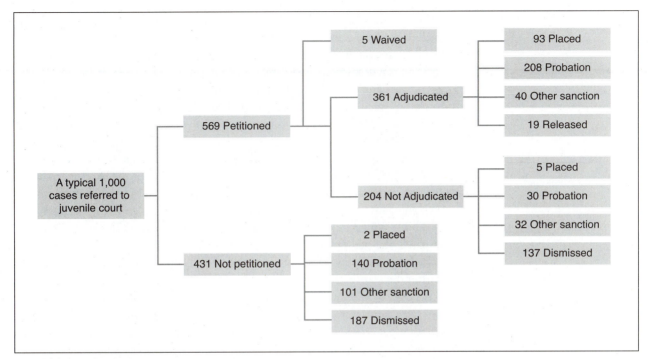

Source: C. Puzzanchera, A. Stahl, T. Tierney Finnegan and H. Snyder, *Juvenile Court Statistics 1998.* Washington, DC: Office of Juvenile Justice and Delinquency Prevention, 2002.

Figure 10.1
**Delinquency Case
Processing Overview**

Of every 1,000 delinquency cases handled in 1998, 569 were petitioned, 431 were not petitioned. Figure 10.1 presents the typical handling of 1,000 delinquency cases.

If at the intake hearing a case is referred to juvenile court, a petition is filed and the case moves from intake through the steps required to place the juvenile within the juvenile court process.

Petition and Summons

The **petition** is a document similar to the complaint in the adult system, alleging that a juvenile is a delinquent, status offender or dependent and asking the court to assume jurisdiction. The petition sets forth:

- The facts that bring the child within the court's jurisdiction, with a statement that it is in the best interest of the child and the public that the proceeding be brought and, if delinquency or unruly conduct is alleged, that the child is in need of treatment or rehabilitation

- The name, age and residence address of the child on whose behalf the petition is brought

- The names and residence addresses, if known to petitioner, of the parents, guardian or custodian of the child and of the child's spouse, if any

- Whether the child is in custody and, if so, the place of detention and the time it occurred

Any person, including a law enforcement officer, may make a petition, but it will not be filed until the court or someone authorized by the court determines and endorses that the filing of the petition is in the best interest of the public and the child.

Several states have separated the procedures for delinquency from those for status offenses and children in need of the court's protection. A delinquency petition may be issued following the same procedure used with children in need of protection or services (CHIPS).

After the petition is filed, the court fixes a time for a **hearing**—an opportunity for the juvenile to tell his or her side of the story before a judge. If the youth is in detention, the hearing must be within 10 days of the filing of the petition. When the hearing date is set, a **summons** is issued to the child, if 14 years or older, the parents, guardians or custodians, and to any other people to appear before the court. This is similar to an arrest warrant in the criminal court. The summons accompanies the petition and clearly states that the person is entitled to a lawyer.

The summons should be served at least 24 hours before the hearing to people within the state at a known address, or sent by registered or certified mail at least five days before the hearing if the address is not known or the person lives out of state. Sometimes the court elects to issue a Notice in Lieu of Summons to send with the petition to the parents or guardians. This is a somewhat less formal, less intimidating process.

Following the filing of a petition and the serving of a summons, the case enters into a series of three hearings. Before looking at these three hearings, consider the individuals involved in the proceedings and the rights of those being adjudicated.

The Juvenile Court Team

 The juvenile court team includes the judge, the prosecutor, the defense attorney, probation services, and often a guardian ad litum, a CASA and a referee.

Judges are the main authority in the juvenile court system, having wide discretion over every phase of adjudication. However, being assigned to juvenile court is not a prime assignment, and judges often seek to obtain different positions to advance their careers. Siegel et al. (2003, p.421) describe the duties of the juvenile court judge:

- Rule on pretrial motions involving such legal issues as arrest, search and seizure, interrogation and lineup identification
- Make decisions about the continued detention of children prior to trial
- Make decisions about plea-bargaining agreements and the informal adjustment of juvenile cases
- Handle trials, rule on the appropriateness of conduct, settle questions of evidence and procedure, and guide the questioning of witnesses
- Assume responsibility for holding dispositional hearings and deciding on the treatment accorded the child
- Handle waiver proceedings
- Handle appeals where allowed by statute

The juvenile prosecutor is charged with representing the state's interests and presenting the case against an accused juvenile. Like police officers and judges, prosecutors have broad discretion. Prosecutors tend to dominate the intake processing stage and their role in juvenile court has increased. The defense attorney represents youths in juvenile court. Defense attorneys often have a secondary role in the juvenile court. Many attorneys, like many judges, would prefer to be working in the criminal court.

Probation services are commonly sought for juveniles who are taken into custody and placed in detention. The Uniform Juvenile Court Act (UJCA) describes how probation officers can be appointed and notes that:

> A competent probation staff is essential to achieving the objectives of the juvenile court system. The staff must be adequately trained, working loads must be limited, and conditions must be provided that permit the giving of the required time and attention called for by each individual case.
>
> A probation service may be established on either a local or a statewide basis. Competent authorities disagree on the relative merits of the two alternatives. The National Council of Juvenile Courts favors a local system, stressing the importance of having these services provided by court personnel responsible to and under the direction of the juvenile court judge, since he is responsible for the successful conduct of the juvenile program. Proponents of the statewide system stress the frequent inadequacy of local resources to provide the needed minimum service required and contend that better probation service is provided by a state system, and that the prospect of the judge successfully achieving the objectives of the court's program is therefore enhanced.

According to guidelines set forth in the UJCA, probation officers should:

- Make investigations, reports and recommendations to the juvenile court

- Receive and examine complaints and charges of delinquency, unruly conduct or deprivation of children

- Supervise and assist children placed on probation

- Make appropriate referrals to other private or public agencies if needed

- Take into custody and detain children who are under their supervision or care as delinquent, unruly or deprived children, if the children's health or safety is in danger

- Arrange to have children removed from the jurisdiction of the court

Probation officers do *not* have the powers of law enforcement officers. The act notes that: "The primary role of the probation officers is the care and protection of the child, and in delinquency cases, his treatment and rehabilitation as well. Incompatible roles such as the power of arrest, conducting the accusatory proceeding in juvenile court and representing the child in court, have been excluded."

A **guardian *ad litem*** (GAL) is a representative of a juvenile, appointed by the juvenile court judge solely for the best interest of the child and to represent that interest on his or her behalf. The Child Abuse Prevention and Treatment Act of 1974 required the provision of a GAL to all youths whose cases were heard in family court. While most often an attorney, the guardian *ad litem* can be anyone the juvenile court judge determines will accept that responsibility and act in the child's best interest. The guardian *ad litem* fulfills this responsibility in all matters involving juveniles, whether they are neglected, abused, dependent or delinquent.

Most states have volunteer guardian *ad litem* programs called **CASA**—Court Appointed Special Advocate for Children. (Casa means *home* in Spanish.). A primary function of a CASA is to conduct investigations and objectively assess each child's needs. They are the safety net that keeps many children from falling through the cracks of the child welfare system by aiding in permanency planning efforts and helping thousands of children to find safe, nurturing homes.

CASAs work primarily in cases of child neglect, physical abuse, psychological abuse, sexual abuse, abandonment or when parents are unwilling or unable to care for their children. CASA volunteers investigate, evaluate, advocate, recommend and monitor to ensure compliance with court orders and to report any changing circumstances.

In many states the law provides for the juvenile judge to appoint a full- or part-time court **referee,** an individual to act as a hearing officer, to reduce testimony to findings of fact and to make recommendations on disposition. The referee's powers are limited by law. In some states that have referees, the referee is not empowered to make a final order, but acts as an advisor to the court. The referee's recommendation may be approved, modified or rejected by the juvenile judge, but when approved or modified it becomes a court order.

Juvenile court referees are a valuable asset to the court, particularly when a judge's caseload is more than can be effectively handled, because referees allow judges more time to focus attention on difficult cases. Referees automatically hear specific cases (often routine, simple cases) and follow guidelines. Judges normally would hear cases in which child custody is in question, as well as serious delinquency cases in which violence occurred. Referees also are not involved in matters where the jurisdiction of the court is in question, such as the transfer or certification of a juvenile to a criminal court. The referee's role, therefore, is to assist the juvenile court judge, rather than to replace or become the judge. Before hearing a case, however, the referee must inform the parties involved that they are entitled to have the matter heard by the judge. If they want a judge, they get one.

The Rights of Those Being Adjudicated

Children have specific rights during a hearing. Children are entitled to have a lawyer present at all stages of any proceedings under the UJCA and, if unable to afford private counsel, to have the court provide counsel. The due process requirement of the appointment of counsel for needy children charged with delinquency was established by *Kent v. United States* and *In re Gault,* discussed in Chapter 1.

 Children have the same rights as adults except trial by jury and, in some states, the right to bail. Children have the right to an attorney at all stages of the proceedings, the right to introduce evidence and tell their side of the story, the right to cross-examine witnesses and the right to remain silent during the hearing.

At the conference or preliminary hearing a judge explains charges against the youth as well as his rights.

Children are also entitled to introduce evidence and to tell their side of the story, as well as to cross-examine adverse witnesses. Children charged with delinquency need not be witnesses against themselves. According to Section 27: "A confession validly made by a child out of court is insufficient to support an adjudication."

Hearings in the Juvenile Court

 The three phases that follow the filing of a petition are (1) the conference or preliminary hearing, (2) the adjudicatory hearing or trial and (3) the dispositional hearing or sentencing.

The Conference

The **conference** or **preliminary hearing** satisfies those matters that must be dealt with before the case can proceed further. At this first hearing, the judge informs the parties involved of the charges in the petition and of their rights during the proceeding. The hearing may also be used to determine whether an alleged delinquent should remain in detention or in the custody of juvenile authorities.

In the matter of detention, if the judge, with the assistance of a probation officer, determines that the child's behavior is a threat to the public, is a danger to himself and others or that the child will not return to court voluntarily, the judge can order the child to remain in custody. Dependent, neglected or abused children as well as status offenders may be placed in foster care or a residential shelter. If the case involves an abused, neglected or dependent child, a guardian is usually appointed to act as an advocate for the child. This person is often a representative of a social service or welfare agency.

© Bob Daemmrich/Stock Boston

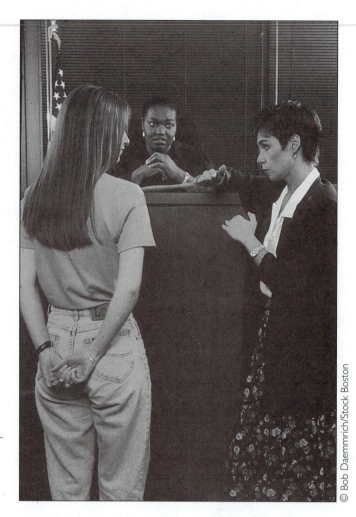

© Bob Daemmrich/Stock Boston

The adjudicatory hearing is similar to an adult trial. Youths are entitled to a lawyer at this stage as well as during all stages of juvenile court proceedings.

The Adjudication Hearing

To **adjudicate** is to judge. The **adjudicatory hearing** is to determine whether the allegations of the petition are supported by a preponderance of evidence (for status offenses) or by evidence that proves beyond a reasonable doubt that a delinquent act occurred. This is comparable to the trial in criminal court. In terms of the juvenile court, adjudication refers to the judge's determination (decision) that a youth is a status offender, a delinquent or neither.

At this stage the child makes a plea, either an admission or denial of the allegations in the petition. If the allegations are sustained, the judge makes a finding of fact (that the child is delinquent, abused, neglected or otherwise in need of supervision), sets a date for a dispositional hearing and orders a social investigation or presentence investigation (PSI) or a predisposition report.

The Predisposition Report

The probation officer who conducts the investigation and completes the report seeks the best available information. The probation officer's report includes the sociocultural and psychodynamic factors that influenced the juvenile's behavior and provides a social history the judge can use to determine a disposition for the case. Judges' decisions can be greatly influenced by such reports.

The reports must be factual and objective—professional statements about a child's family, social and educational history, and any previous involvement with private or public agencies. The report also indicates the child's physical and mental health as reported by a court psychologist or psychiatrist.

A report typically includes (1) interviews with the child; (2) interviews with family members; (3) psychological and psychiatric examinations of the child and family members (usually just parents or custodians) and the results of tests and exams; (4) interviews with employers, youth workers and clergy when appropriate; (5) interviews with the complainant; (6) interviews with the police, their reports and any witnesses; (7) interviews with teachers and school officials; (8) a review of police, school and court records and (9) a recommendation of which treatment alternatives should be available in the case.

The National Advisory Committee (NAC) for Juvenile Justice and Delinquency Prevention recommends that probation departments prepare three-part predisposition reports:

1. Information concerning the nature and circumstances of the offense, and the juvenile's role, age and prior police contacts

2. Summary of information concerning the home environment and family relationships, the juvenile's educational and employment status, the juvenile's interests and activities, the parents' interests and the results of medical or psychiatric evaluations

3. Evaluation of the above, a summary of dispositional alternatives available and the probation officer's recommendation

The probation officer must present the findings with supporting statements about the situation found in the investigation and a recommendation. The recommendation occasionally is not transcribed, but given orally to the judge. The completed report should be comprehensive enough to help the judge make the best disposition available based on the merits of the case and the service needs of the youth.

Nature of the Hearing

According to Section 24 of the UJCA: "Hearings under this Act shall be conducted by the court without a jury, in an informal but orderly manner, and separate from other proceedings." The prosecuting attorney presents the evidence supporting the petition. The hearing may be recorded electronically or minutes may be kept. The child may be excluded from the hearing while the charges are being made.

Traditionally hearings in juvenile court matters have been closed to the public. A Supreme Court ruling, however, has allowed states to open such proceedings on an experimental basis. The practice of open courts in juvenile cases has upset many and raised concerns that the welfare of juvenile court clients is in jeopardy.

Table 10.2
Landmark Juvenile Supreme Court Cases

Case	Year	Holding
Kent v. United States	1966	Established that juvenile transfers to adult court must consider due process and fair play, the child must be represented by an attorney and the attorney must have access to the juvenile records of child.
In re Gault	1967	Required that the due process clause of the Fourteenth Amendment apply to proceedings in state juvenile courts, including the right of notice, the right to counsel, the right against self-incrimination and the right to confront witnesses.
In re Winship	1970	Established proof beyond a reasonable doubt as the standard for juvenile adjudication proceedings, eliminating lesser standards such as a preponderance of the evidence, clear and convincing proof and reasonable proof.
McKeiver v. Pennsylvania	1971	Established that a jury trial is not a required part of due process in the adjudication of a youth as a delinquent by a juvenile court.
Breed v. Jones	1975	Established that a juvenile cannot be adjudicated in juvenile court and then tried for the same offense in an adult court (double jeopardy).
Schall v. Martin	1980	Established that preventive detention fulfills a legitimate state interest of protecting society and juveniles by detaining those who might be dangerous to society or to themselves.

Toward a More Adversarial Court

In 1967 the U.S. Supreme Court decided a landmark juvenile justice case. For the first time in the history of the United States, the basic philosophy and practices of the juvenile court were reviewed. The Court concluded (*In re Gault*):

> While there can be no doubt of the original laudable purpose of the juvenile courts, studies and critiques in recent years raise serious questions as to whether actual performance measures well enough against theoretical purpose to make tolerable the immunity of the process from the constitutional guarantees applicable to adults.

 A series of Supreme Court decisions has changed the juvenile court's procedures into a more adversarial approach.

A brief review of these landmark cases is provided in Table 10.2.

These Supreme Court decisions had a major impact on the adjudication process of the juvenile justice system and the procedural rights afforded juveniles. Some constitutional requirements have been applied to those parts of the states' juvenile proceedings that are adjudicative. In many cases these changes have reflected a move toward a more adversarial system in the juvenile courts. Another result of these decisions was an overall criminalization of the juvenile court. One safeguard, however, against a full adversarial system in juvenile court is the provision of guardian *ad litems* and CASAs.

The Dispositional Hearing

The final phase of the juvenile court process is the disposition. This is comparable to the sentencing stage in criminal court. The **dispositional hearing** is an adjudicated process by the juvenile court, either formal or informal, on the evidence submitted with a guarantee of due process of law for the juvenile in a matter before the court. At the dispositional hearing the judge states what will happen to the youth—what is to be done for or to a child who has been adjudicated by the court.

As Griffin and Torbet (p.64) note: "All standards-setting groups concur in recommending that the hearing to determine whether or not an accused juvenile has committed the delinquent act charged (the adjudication) should be held separately from the hearing to determine what should be done about it (the disposition). There are two good reasons for preferring this bifurcated process: fairness and privacy." **Bifurcated hearings,** however, often allow little or no time to elapse between the adjudication and disposition stages, lessening the fairness and confidentiality of the hearings.

For nearly 30 years the Juvenile Justice and Delinquency Prevention (JJDP) Act of 1974 has guided juvenile courts in the disposition of youthful offenders. During this time the JJDP Act's central mandate has been the deinstitutionalization of status offenders (DSO). During the 1980s, the federal focus shifted from delinquency prevention to criminal justice, emphasizing prosecution of serious juvenile offenders, the plight of missing children, mandatory and tougher sentencing laws and programs to prevent school violence.

 The trend in juvenile dispositions remains the deinstitutionalization of youths.

If the court finds from clear, convincing evidence that a child is deprived or in need of treatment or rehabilitation, the court decides on the proper disposition of the case. *Deprived children* may be permitted to remain with their parents or guardians subject to specific conditions and limitations. Temporary legal custody may be given to any individual the court finds qualified to receive and care for the child. Children may be placed in an agency or other private organization licensed or authorized to receive and provide care for children, such as the Child Welfare Department.

If a court finds from proof beyond a reasonable doubt that the child is delinquent or unruly, it proceeds immediately or at a postponed hearing to hear evidence as to whether the child is in need of treatment or rehabilitation. A child found to be *delinquent* may be placed on probation or placed in an institution, camp or other facility for delinquent children. A child found to be *unruly* may receive any disposition authorized for a delinquent child except placement in the state institution to which commitment of delinquent children is made. The order of disposition that commits a delinquent or unruly child to an institution is in effect for two years or until the child is discharged.

A delinquent or unruly child thought to be suffering from *mental retardation* or *mental illness* may be committed for a period not exceeding 60 days to an appropriate institution, agency or individual for study. If the child is determined to be committable under state laws, the court may order the child detained. If the child is not committable, the court proceeds with the disposition of the child as appropriate.

If a child is or is about to become a *nonresident* of the state, the court may defer hearing on the need for treatment or rehabilitation and ask that the juvenile court of the child's new or prospective residence accept jurisdiction over the child. Likewise the *resident child received from another state* should be accepted by the child's new or prospective residence. These provisions facilitate cooperative action between the courts of the two states involved.

It is important to recognize that an order of disposition or other adjudication in a juvenile court is *not* a conviction of a crime. Section 33 of the UJCA states that: "A child shall not be committed or transferred to a penal institution or other facility used primarily for the execution of sentences of persons convicted of a crime." The comment regarding this section states:

> Although several states permit commitment or transfer of a delinquent child to a penal institution, its constitutionality is in serious doubt since it permits confinement in a penal institution as a product of a non-criminal proceeding. Such legislation has been held invalid in a number of states.

Juvenile Sentencing Laws

Junvenile sentences are of four basic types: indeterminate, determinate, presumptive and mandatory.

- An indeterminate sentence, also called **discretionary sentence,** gives judges and parole authorities a great deal of latitude in determining the length of the sentence. The maximum sentence is often determined by the legislature. Judges can't exceed this but can give a lesser sentence.

- A determinate sentence is one of the two types of **limited discretionary sentences** in which a degree of judicial discretion is removed, but a range of sentence lengths is still allowed.

- A presumptive sentence is the other type of limited discretionary sentence, again involving a degree of judicial discretion but still allowing a range of sentence lengths.

- A mandatory sentence, also known as a **nondiscretionary sentence,** fixes the sentence, eliminating any judicial discretion to suspend the sentence or grant probation.

The state of Washington passed a Juvenile Justice Act in 1977, creating a mandatory sentencing policy that required juveniles ages 8 to 17 adjudicated delinquent to be confined in an institution for a minimum term. As noted in the act:

> It is the intent of the legislature that a system be developed capable of having primary responsibility for being accountable for and responding to the needs of youthful offenders. It is the further intent of the legislature that youth, in turn, be held accountable for their offenses and that both communities and juvenile courts carry out their function consistent with this intent. (Section 13.40.010[2] Supp.1978)

To accomplish its goal, the act includes a formal scoring sheet to determine how long an adjudicated youth must spend in confinement. The mandatory sentencing policy in Washington is based on the juvenile's age, the current offense and the criminal history of the offender. Similar in concept to adult sentencing guideline grids, the score under the Washington system is computed by plotting the type of offense along the vertical axis of a table and the juvenile's age along the horizontal axis. A numeric score is reached, which is then multiplied by a weighting factor based on the youth's prior criminal record. This final number is then plotted on another grid to determine the sentence. Systems such as these help guide judges in their sentencing and tend to make sentencing more equitable from one case to the next.

 Most juvenile sentencing laws are based on the juvenile's age, the offense and the offender's criminal history.

As with adult criminal sentencing, juvenile sentencing has had its share of criticism, reform attempts and alternative remedies. Regarding the trend to toughen up juvenile sentencing, in recent years sentencing reforms in state and federal systems have been driven largely by a desire to "get tough on crime" and to reduce the inconsistency and disparities resulting from judicial discretion.

Some states have attempted legislation making parents responsible for the delinquency of their children. California's legislators resorted to such a parental responsibility law in an effort to prevent gang crime. However while such "punish-the-parent" legislation is not new, it has not proved to be very effective. Furthermore, such laws tend to burden police officers with difficult, subjective decision making regarding what constitutes adequate parenting.

Whatever the sentence and however the court arrives there, it should be individualized. Mechanical jurisprudence should be avoided in the juvenile justice system. Legal philosopher H. L. A. Hart (1965, p.125) expresses an underlying assumption in any government of laws:

> It is a feature of human predicament . . . whenever we seek to regulate, unambiguously and in advance, some sphere of conduct by means of general standards to be used without further official direction on particular occasions. . . . If the world in which we live were characterized only by the finite number of features, and these together with all the modes in which they could be made in advance for every possibility, we could make rules, the applications of which to particular cases never called for a further choice. Everything could be known, and for everything since it could be known, something could be done and specified in advance by rule. This could be a world for "mechanical jurisprudence."

Mechanical jurisprudence suggests that everything is known and that, therefore, laws can be made in advance to cover every situation. Unfortunately the concept of mechanical jurisprudence is often applied to juvenile conduct and behavior. Mechanical jurisprudence is inappropriate in our justice system because everything cannot be known about any offense. Because delinquency includes a wide variety of behaviors, there is no single common problem of delinquency but, instead, a series of separable problems each with its unique psychodynamic and social orientation.

Table 10.3
Common Juvenile Dispositions

Disposition	Action Taken
Informal consent decree	In minor or first offenses, an informal hearing is held, and the judge will ask the youth and his or her guardian to agree to a treatment program, such as counseling. No formal trial or disposition hearing is held.
Probation	A youth is placed under the control of the county probation department and required to obey a set of probation rules and participate in a treatment program.
Home detention	A child is restricted to his or her home in lieu of a secure placement. Rules include regular school attendance, curfew observance, avoidance of alcohol and drugs, and notification of parents and the youth worker of the child's whereabouts.
Court-ordered school attendance	If truancy was the problem that brought the youth to court, a judge may order mandatory school attendance. Some courts have established court-operated day schools and court-based tutorial programs staffed by community volunteers.
Financial restitution	A judge can order the juvenile offender to make financial restitution to the victim. In most jurisdictions, restitution is part of probation, but in a few states, such as Maryland, restitution can be a sole order.
Fines	Some states allow fines to be levied against juveniles 16 and older.
Community service	Courts in many jurisdictions require juveniles to spend time in the community working off their debt to society. Community service orders are usually reserved for victimless crimes, such as possession of drugs, or crimes against public order, such as vandalism of school property. Community service orders are usually carried out in schools, hospitals or nursing homes.
Outpatient psychotherapy	Youths who are diagnosed with psychological disorders may be required to undergo therapy at a local mental health clinic.
Drug and alcohol treatment	Youths with drug- or alcohol-related problems may be allowed to remain in the community if they agree to undergo drug or alcohol therapy.
Commitment to secure treatment	In the most serious cases a judge may order an offender admitted to a long-term treatment center, such as a training school, camp, ranch, or group home. These may be either state- or privately run institutions, usually located in remote regions. Training schools provide educational, vocational, and rehabilitation programs in a secure environment.
Commitment to a residential community program	Youths who commit crimes of a less serious nature but who still need to be removed from their homes can be placed in community-based group homes or halfway houses. They attend school or work during the day and live in a controlled, therapeutic environment at night.
Foster home placement	Foster homes are usually used for dependent or neglected children and status offenders. Judges often place delinquents with insurmountable problems at home in state-licensed foster care homes.

Source: Larry J. Siegel, Brandon C. Welsh and Joseph J. Senna. *Juvenile Delinquency: Theory, Practice and Law,* 8th ed. Belmont, CA: Wadsworth Publishing Company, 2003, p.440.

Dispositions

The **disposition** is the juvenile court's decision that a juvenile be committed to a confinement facility, placed on probation or be given treatment and care; meet certain standards of conduct or be released or a combination of court decrees. Table 10.3 provides an overview of the most common juvenile court dispositions.

Disposition are numerous. Judges can:

- Dismiss the case with no charges at all.
- Refer the youth to a social service agency.
- Order the youth to make restitution.
- Put the youth on probation.
- Sentence the youth to a correctional facility.

Graduated sanctions are receiving much attention in the 21ˢᵗ century—this is a continuum of treatment alternatives that includes immediate intervention, intermediate sanctions, community-based correctional sanctions and secure corrections (Burns et al., 2003, p.10). Griffin and Torbet (p.77) describe the essential features of a good graduated sanctions system.

 A good graduated sanctions system features certainty, speed, consistency, economy, proportionality, progressiveness and neutrality.

- Certainty: It responds to every infraction.
- Speed: The response is swift.
- Consistency: Similar infractions receive similar responses.
- Economy: The response chosen is the minimum likely to produce the desired result.
- Proportionality: The level of response should equal the level of the offense.
- Progressiveness: Continued noncompliance results in increasingly severe responses.
- Neutrality: Responses are an objective, impartial reaction to an offense.

Blended sentences are also receiving attention in the 21ˢᵗ century. A **blended sentence** combines both a juvenile sentence and an adult sentence. In some states if a youth is adjudicated to have committed a violent but not extreme or murderous crime, and if they comply with the terms of the juvenile sentence—which includes longer and more intensive supervision than a typical juvenile sanction—they will be released without the stain of an adult criminal record. If they fail to comply with the terms of the juvenile sentence, they will receive the sentence that would have been incurred in criminal court.

Mendel (2000, p.44) notes: "Blended sentencing options are available to the states to add teeth to the sanctions available in the juvenile courts without incurring the collateral damage associated with transfer to criminal jurisdiction."

Supporters of blended sentences say it gives offenders a choice of avoiding a life of crime, or, if they fail, winding up in prison. Opponents of juvenile-adult sentences say they are a reversion to soft-on-crime methods. About a dozen states, including Connecticut, Kansas, Kentucky, Minnesota and Oregon have instituted blended sentences.

Out-of-Home Placements

According to Puzzanchera (2002, p.1): "In 1998, more than one in four adjudicated delinquency cases resulted in out-of-home placement. . . . Of the 634,000 adjudicated delinquency cases, 26 percent resulted in a judicial disposition of out-of-home placement (for example, placement in a residential treatment center, juvenile corrections facility, foster home or group home); 58 percent resulted in an order of probation; 11 percent resulted in some other disposition, such as restitution, fines, community service or referral to other treatment agencies; and 5 percent were released at disposition without sanctions."

Probation

Probation is one of the most common dispositions. Probation is discussed in the next chapter. Most youths placed on probation also receive other dispositions. A probation order may include additional requirements such as drug counseling, restitution or community service.

Respite Care

Quraishi et al al. (2003) note that a number of jurisdictions throughout the country have established **respite care** programs for runaway youths. Respite care is designed to give runways and their parents a temporary break from each other, followed by intensive counseling. These programs appear to be more successful and much less costly than the alternative—a lengthy stay in a detention center or other juvenile institution. A **detention center** is a government facility that provides temporary care in a closed, locked facility for juveniles pending a court disposition.

Respite care programs give juvenile court judges a way to handle runaways and thrownaways. According to Quraishi et al., some families beg probation officers, family court judges and child welfare workers to take control of their children. Most states have a system to handle such families, but if the child or the parent refuses to participate, judges often have no choice but to remand the youth to a nonsecure detention center, foster care group home or other institution, even when the youth poses no threat to the community. In some cases, however, it becomes clear that family reunification is impossible or is not the best solution. Then the focus shifts to keeping the youth out of juvenile institutions, perhaps finding a relative willing to take the youth in.

Restitution

An increasingly popular disposition of the juvenile court is **restitution,** that is, personally righting a wrong or restoring property or a right to a person unjustly deprived of the property or right. As victims' rights movements gain momentum, more attention is being paid to this group. One way this is happening is through restitution programs.

Closely related to restitution is the victim-offender mediation program, modeled after the Victim Offender Reconciliation Program (VORP) that originated in Canada in the mid-1970s. The purposes of this were to provide an alternative method of dealing with crime, to allow victim and offender an opportunity to reconcile and mutually agree on restitution, to use a third party to mediate and facilitate reconciliation and to deal with crime as a conflict to be resolved.

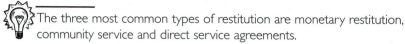

The three most common types of restitution are monetary restitution, community service and direct service agreements.

In *monetary restitution* a specific dollar amount is agreed to that the offender will pay to the victim through scheduled payments. *Community service,* com-

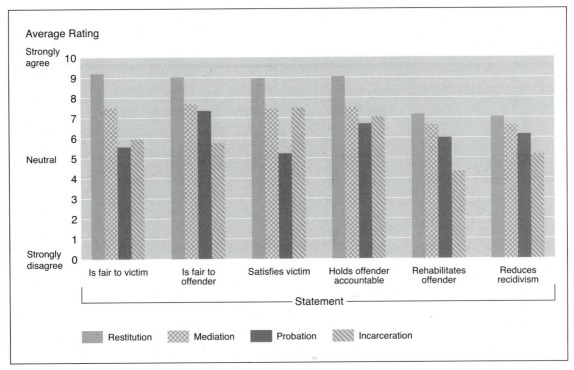

Figure 10.2
Perceived Effectiveness of Dispositional Alternatives

Source: Stella P. Hughes and Anne L. Schneider. *Victim-Offender Mediation in the Juvenile Justice System.* Restitution Education, Specialized Training & Technical Assistance Program (RESTTA), September 1990, p.9.

monly arranged through a probation agency, has a juvenile perform unpaid labor for the community, a specific neighborhood or institution. A hoped-for by-product of community service is that the juvenile develops useful life skills and learns responsibility. *Direct service agreements* hold juveniles accountable by having them work directly with and for their victim(s). For example a 13-year-old boy who admitted to burglarizing the vehicles of elderly mobile home residents was made to mow their lawns, rake their leaves and sweep their driveways.

One noteworthy result was that, although the perceived effectiveness of dispositional alternatives varied, all respondents rated restitution as the most effective way to reduce recidivism, rehabilitate offenders, increase victim satisfaction, hold offenders accountable and be fair to both offenders and victims. Mediation was rated second most effective in most instances. However **incarceration,** being placed in a locked secure facility, was seen as equally effective, if not slightly more so, than mediation in increasing victim satisfaction. (See Figure 10.2.)

Support for mediation programs was highest among juvenile court judges, followed by family members and alternative juvenile program providers. Least supportive were state legislators, although they, too, were on the positive side, as shown in Figure 10.3.

Any restitution program that places youths in paid or unpaid positions also assumes responsibility for their safety and their behavior. Restitution programs

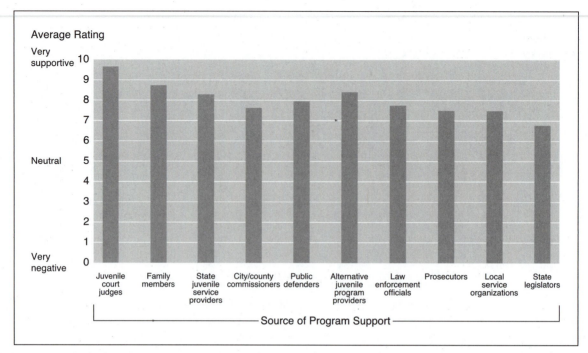

Figure 10.3
Amount of Support from Various Sources

Source: Stella P. Hughes and Anne L. Schneider. *Victim-Offender Mediation in the Juvenile Justice System*. Restitution Education, Specialized Training & Technical Assistance Program (RESTTA), September 1990, p.7.

must consider injuries sustained by the juvenile in a court-ordered placement, injuries or harm done by the juvenile at the worksite and loss or damages caused by the youth as the result of a crime committed at the workplace. Before looking at the issues facing juvenile courts, review Table 10.4 to see how the juvenile process flows and how it compares to the criminal court.

Issues Facing Juvenile Courts— Dilemmas and Criticisms

In the United States, legislators have tremendous interest in the handling of juveniles and their rights. The "child savers" are still present, and those who wish to get tough with juveniles are continually lobbying for severe measures in all phases of the juvenile process. The U.S. Supreme Court is prepared to protect children and their parents against the custom of informality within the system.

 The juvenile court's current dilemma hinges on its dual roles as a court of law and social service agency.

The juvenile court must gain strength in its judicial role and retain and develop only that part of its social service role necessary to administer individualized justice. As a court, even in the administration of individualized justice, it must express and reinforce the values of society.

Table 10.4
An Overview of the Juvenile Court Process Compared with Criminal Court

Adult	Juvenile	
Preliminary hearing	*Conference*: Proceeding during which the suspect is informed of rights and a disposition decision may be reached.	In the vast majority of petitioned cases, the juvenile admits guilt during the conference.
Grand jury	Not applicable.	One percent (12,300) of juvenile cases are transferred to adult court.
Arraignment	Occurs during the conference.	Fifty-five percent of juvenile delinquency cases are handled formally (petitioned).
Evidence	Juveniles have the same constitutional protections as adults involving unreasonable search and seizure and interrogation.	Police gathering of evidence is rarely contested.
Plea bargaining	*Plea bargaining*: Formal and informal discussions resulting in juvenile admitting guilt.	Even more so than adult court, dispositions in juvenile court are the product of negotiations.
Trial	*Adjudicatory hearing*: Hearing to determine whether a youth is guilty or not guilty.	• Fifty-eight percent of petitioned cases are disposed of by adjudication. • Adjudicatory hearings are more informal than adult trials.
Sentencing	*Disposition*: A court decision on what will happen to a youth who has not been found innocent.	• Dispositions are often referred to as treatment plans.
	Placement: Cases in which youths are placed in a residential facility or otherwise removed from their homes.	• More than 150,000 juveniles are placed in residential facilities each year.
	Probation: Cases in which youths are placed on informal/voluntary or formal/court-ordered supervision.	• More than 500,000 juveniles each year receive court supervision.
	Dismissal: Cases dismissed (including those warned, counseled and released) with no further disposition anticipated.	• Even case dismissals may include a treatment plan or restitution.
	Other: Miscellaneous dispositions, including fine, restitution, community service.	• Teen courts are a modern version of other dispositions.
Appeal	*Appeal*: Request that a higher court review the decision of the lower court.	Appeals are rare in juvenile proceedings.

Source: David W. Neubauer. *America's Courts and the Criminal Justice System*, 6th ed. Belmont, CA: Wadsworth Publishing Company, 1999, p.501. Reprinted by permission.

The facts of adjudication and disposition cannot be examined as if they are separate from each other. The juvenile court must be seen as a court—not as an administrative agency—designed in its adjudication to protect children from the traumatic experiences of a criminal trial and to balance the interests of the child and the community. It is not especially equipped to do welfare work. Whenever possible it should be divested of jurisdiction and adjudication over cases in which the child is simply in need of aid. It should be governed by simple, specific rules, so that while children are receiving guidance and protection, their rights and community security are not neglected.

After they had been operating for half a century, criticism of the nation's juvenile courts began surfacing during the 1950s. In 1949 the lawyer-sociologist Paul Tappan published a volume on juvenile delinquency that drew together and raised for the first time a number of problems inherent in the work of the court:

- The persistence in some courts of punitive practices, in contrast to rehabilitative theory
- The abandonment of all semblance of regularized legal procedures or due process

The Fundamental Nature of Juvenile Court

The juvenile court has been criticized for its fundamental system. What most critics or people unfamiliar with the jurisdiction of the court fail to understand is that the scope of the court is varied and that criminal law, or law that refers to antisocial conduct, is only one part of the court's responsibility.

All courts within the juvenile justice jurisdiction exercise the principles of civil procedures, which emphasize notice and opportunity to defend. They also emphasize due process factors that protect juveniles who come under their authority, making dispositions in the child's best interest.

In effect the juvenile court is less a law enforcement agency and more a social agency, handling truants, orphans, runaways and other misguided youths. It is, however, also responsible for youthful gang members, robbers, rapists and murderers. The court is seen as being inadequate to satisfy the community's need to express its disapproval of antisocial conduct. In addition, the juvenile court has broadened its scope, becoming involved in child development, psychological concepts of understanding maturity and public policy for the good of the community. It has become involved with:

- Abortion (*Bellotti v. Baird,* 1979; *City of Akron v. Akron Center for Reproductive Health,* 1983; *H. L. v. Matheson,* 1981; *Thornburgh v. American College of Obstetricians and Gynecologists,* 1986)
- School prayer (*Wallace v. Jaffree,* 1985)
- Search and seizure issues in school lockers or classrooms (*Dow v. Renfrow,* 1981; *New Jersey v. T. L. O.,* 1985)
- Interracial custody and adoption (*In re R. M. G.,* 1982; *Palmore v. Sidoti,* 1984)
- Adolescent judgment and maturity (*Planned Parenthood of Kansas City v. Ashcroft, 1983)*
- Determination that minors are persons entitled to protection under the Bill of Rights (*Parham v. J. R.,* 1979)
- Legal issues in terminating parental rights (*Jewish Child Care Association v. Elaine S. Y.,* 1980; *Nebraska v. Wedige,* 1980)

Juvenile courts have been involved in such social and legal issues as abortion, school prayer, search and seizure, interracial custody and adoption, adolescent judgment and maturity, and legal issues in terminating parental rights.

The involvement of the juvenile court in these social and legal issues has detracted, to a point, from its primary duties of delinquency adjudication and protecting the child. This wide range of issues illustrates the courts' involvement in nondelinquent matters and its tendency to take on matters that many believe should not be legislated, or at least should not be legislated for juveniles any differently than they are for adults—for example abortion and search and seizure.

Current dissatisfaction with the juvenile system is described by Greenwood (p. 2):

> Conservative critics, focusing on public safety, fault the system for giving serious offenders too many chances on diversion or probation and for imposing terms of confinement that are too short. These critics often characterize juvenile facilities as country clubs and argue that some juveniles should be confined in more punitive settings.

> Liberal critics, concerned with the problems of juveniles and anxious to protect them from unwarranted state intrusions, fault the system for being too tough. Where conservative critics use the evidence of "no rehabilitative effect" to argue for more explicitly punitive sanctions, liberals use the same evidence to argue for less state involvement altogether. Liberals generally support the view that subjecting juveniles to confinement only further criminalizes them, no matter how benign the treatment.

Another liberal group, heavily represented by defense attorneys and other youth advocates, deplores the lack of adequate procedural protections for juveniles. This group argues that many young people are railroaded through the system that offers no adequate protection of their rights.

Attacks on the juvenile court's jurisdiction and procedures have been continually repelled, however. While shortcomings have been acknowledged, they have been characterized as the usual shortcomings to be expected in any novel enterprise, which faith, time and money surely would cure. For a century, therefore, the juvenile courts have been permitted to develop and mature, nurtured by judicial support and large doses of faith, if not money.

| *Criminalization of Juvenile Court* | Both the IACP and the National Council of Juvenile Court Judges have expressed concern that the juvenile courts are becoming too formalized and are beginning to resemble adult courts. This concern was expressed by Chief Justice Warren Burger in his dissenting opinion in *In re Winship* (1970): |

> My hope is that today's decision will not spell the end of a generously conceived program of compassionate treatment intended to mitigate the rigors and trauma of exposing youthful offenders to a traditional criminal court; each step we take turns the clock back to the pre-juvenile court era. I cannot regard it as a manifestation of progress to transform juvenile courts into criminal courts, which is what we are well on the way toward accomplishing.

Examples of how the juvenile court is beginning to resemble criminal court include:

- The creation by some states of mandatory minimum sentences for juvenile offenders and blended sentences that combine juvenile and adult sanctions
- Growing pressure to publish the names of juvenile offenders

- Calls to lower the minimum and maximum ages of jurisdiction for the juvenile court
- A push to broaden the scope of offenses for which juveniles can be transferred to adult criminal court

The end result of such changes is that the treatment of youths is becoming more similar to that of adults, with a consequent erosion of the juvenile justice system and its underlying philosophies.

Quality of Representation

A report by the American Bar Association's (ABA) Juvenile Justice Center suggests that juveniles are not receiving adequate legal representation in delinquency proceedings and that juvenile courts are not meeting the requirements established in *In re Gault.* The ABA's assessment report identified high caseloads as the "single most important barrier to effective representation," with the average annual caseloads of some public defenders exceeding 500 cases, more than 300 of which were in juvenile court. Other barriers to adequate legal representation were found to be high turnover rates in juvenile defender positions, a lack of professional support, the unavailability of computerized legal research, lack of bilingual staff and a shortage of client meeting space.

Burruss and Kempf-Leonard (2002) studied the impact of legal representation in juvenile court and found that defense counsel representation was relatively uncommon among juveniles accused of felony offenses and that disparity existed in legal representation across the juvenile courts. In addition, a disposition of out-of-home placement was significantly more likely to occur if a youth had an attorney, even while controlling for other legal and extra-legal explanatory factors. They recommend that public defenders should adopt a team approach with multidisciplinary capabilities. Most defense lawyers are not familiar with the field of child development and other matters critical to defending juveniles. So they must develop contacts with social workers, child psychologists, investigators and others who can help uncover their clients' problems.

Young (2000, p.1) suggests that juveniles transferred to criminal court also do not receive adequate representation: "Defense attorneys, including organized public defenders, are ill-prepared to handle the cases of children who appear in criminal courts. They, like judges, prosecutors and probation officers assigned to criminal courts, are generally untrained and inexperienced in recognizing the needs and characteristics of young defendants. In addition, almost no one involved has thought through the administrative, logistical or case-handling implications of moving children, many of them detained, from juvenile to criminal courthouses." He (p.2) contends: "Representing children prosecuted as adults requires a blend of the services provided in both adult and juvenile courts."

High-quality defender-based programs that deliver first-rate legal services to juveniles usually are able to limit or control caseloads, enter cases early and have the flexibility to represent or refer clients. *Keeping Defender Workloads Manageable* (2001, p.3) recommends that a distinction be made between caseload and workload. Caseload captures only a portion of a defender's full workload: "With the advent of sentencing guidelines and the expanded use of mandatory minimum sentences, the complexity of criminal defense practice has increased dramatically."

Racism and Discrimination

Many have criticized the juvenile justice system for perpetuating the unequal treatment of minority youths. Walker et al.(2000, p.148) note: "There is evidence that defendant race/ethnicity continues to affect decisions regarding bail, charging and plea bargaining. Some evidence suggests that race has a direct and obvious effect on these pretrial decisions; other evidence suggests that the effect of race is indirect and subtle. . . . Discriminatory treatment during the pretrial stage of the criminal justice process can have profound consequences for racial minorities at trial and sentencing." They (p.175) also contend: "There is compelling evidence that racial minorities are treated more harshly than whites at various points in the juvenile justice process. More important, minority youths are substantially more likely than white youths to be detained pending disposition, adjudicated delinquent and waived to adult court. They also are sentenced more harshly than their white counterparts."

Poe-Yamagata and Jones (2000) reached similar conclusions, reporting that minority youths are more likely than whites to be formally processed by the juvenile court, more likely to be detained, more likely to face trial as adults and more likely to go to jail than white youths who commit comparable crimes. Although African-Americans comprised 15 percent of youths under age 18, they experienced 26 percent of juvenile arrests, 31 percent of referrals to juvenile court, 44 percent of the detained population, 34 percent of youths formally processed by the juvenile court, 46 percent of youths judicially waived to criminal court, 32 percent of youths adjudicated delinquent, 40 percent of youths in residential placement and 58 percent of youths in state and adult prisons. Their report shows that the disparity extends to other minority groups as well. National custody rates were five times higher for African-American youths, and two times higher for Latino and Native American youths than for their white counterparts.

A study by the Institute for Children, Youth and Families at Michigan State University found that Latino juvenile offenders get harsher treatment ("Latino Juvenile Offenders Get Harsher Treatment, Study Finds," 2002, pp.2–3). This study found that among youths with no prior admissions to state correctional facilities, Latinos charged with violent offenses were more than five times as likely as whites to be incarcerated (as compared with other forms of sanctions). Latinos charged with property offenses were nearly two times as likely as whites to be incarcerated. For drug offenses, the admission rate for Latinos was 13 times the rate for white youths.

Others agree that racism is a problem but that it is not always against ethnic and racial minorities. In other words, blacks receive harsher treatment at intake and disposition, while whites endure harsher treatment during adjudication.

Other factors contributing to racial discrimination at the various stages of the juvenile justice process, such as court location and family status, have also been documented.

Gender Discrimination

According to Bloom et al. (2002, p.37): "Until recently, girls and young women have been largely overlooked in the development of juvenile justice policy and programs." But as Nicholas (2001) reports: "In ever-increasing numbers, girls are colliding with a juvenile justice system that simply fails to meet their needs for education, counseling and support." MacDonald and Chesney-Lind (2001, p.173) report that female offenders are more likely than male offenders to be handled informally at the early stages of the system, but the court's benevolence declines as trials move into the disposition stage.

Gang Membership—Master Status

It has been theorized that certain types of offenders receive biased treatment by the justice system because of their social affiliations or "master status." Gang members have been identified as one such group that results in a significant effect on both charging and sentencing decisions. Labeling a suspect as a gang member has mixed consequences. It may stimulate greater social control efforts by police (e.g., unfounded arrests, harassment), or the label may hinder prosecution because the stereotypical imagery surrounding these offenders (e.g., dangerous, revenge-seeking, impulsive youth) may heighten victims' and witnesses' fears of retaliation. In many states gang members face increased sanctions for any crimes they might commit.

Confidentiality Issues

 Confidentiality issues involve juvenile hearings, release and publication of juvenile's names and juvenile court records.

Juvenile Hearings

Historically juvenile court hearings were closed to the public, and many still are. In the late 1990s six states enacted laws that opened juvenile court hearings to the public for specified violent or other serious crimes; six states modified existing statutes. States required or permitted open juvenile court hearings of cases involving either juveniles charged with violent or other serious offenses or juveniles who were repeat offenders. Currently, according to Griffin and Torbet (p.14): "A majority of states now have open hearing statutes allowing victims, members of the public and/or the media to attend, at least in cases involving juveniles charged with violent or otherwise serious offenses."

Release or Publication of Juvenile's Names

Just as more states are allowing access to juvenile court hearings, they are allowing the release of publication of a juvenile's name and address. As of 1997, 42 states permitted the release of a juvenile's name, address and/or picture to the media or general public under certain conditions.

Juvenile Court Records

Juvenile records are open to inspection only by the judge, officers and professional staff of the court; the parties to the proceedings and their counsel and representatives; a public or private agency or institution providing supervision or having custody of the youth under court order; a court and its probation and other officials or professional staff; and the attorney for the defendant.

Section 55 of the UJCA states that: "Law enforcement records and files concerning a child shall be kept separate from the records and files of adults. Unless a charge of delinquency is transferred for criminal prosecution, the interest of national security requires, or the court otherwise orders in the interest of the child, the records and files shall not be open to public inspection or their contents disclosed to the public." Juvenile records may be sealed if:

1. Two years have elapsed since the final discharge of the person.
2. After the final discharge the person has not been convicted of a felony, or of a misdemeanor involving moral turpitude, or adjudicated a delinquent or unruly child and no proceeding is pending seeking conviction or adjudication.
3. The person has been rehabilitated. This is to protect a "rehabilitated youth from the harmful effects of a continuing record of the adjudication of delinquency."

State legislatures have made changes to the confidentiality of juvenile court records for violent juvenile offenders, usually in the following areas: access to or disclosure of information, use of record information and sealing or expunging of records.

 States are de-emphasizing traditional confidentiality concerns to emphasize information sharing.

Griffin and Torbet (p.14) contend: "Access to juvenile court records and law enforcement records relating to juveniles is considerably less restricted than it used to be. A court order was once generally required to authorize a disclosure of juvenile record information. But nearly all states now allow at least some categories of disclosures without special court order, and many require them—for example, to officials of schools attended by youths who have been found delinquent."

Merging of Juvenile and Criminal Court Records

In October 1997 the Senate Judiciary Committee approved S.10, essentially a juvenile justice overhaul bill. Among the items covered in the bill was legislation to merge juvenile offense records into the adult criminal records system, ending a system in which juvenile arrest records have been kept secret, even from courts and other criminal justice agencies. According to this bill, juvenile records would have to be retained for the same length of time as adult records and would have to be made available to schools, law enforcement and the courts. Many states have amended their laws to extend adult criminal court jurisdiction and adult system record-keeping to juveniles at a younger age and for a greater range and number of offenses. The two-track justice system, in which a juvenile can have a violent criminal career and then begin again at age 18 or 19 as an adult first offender, is over.

In Favor of One Record A dual system of juvenile and criminal justice that prevents sharing information and permits a serious, chronic violent juvenile to become a first-time offender after he loses his minor status is a strange situation.

Judges faced with the difficult responsibility of deciding whether an offender should be released or detained must be able to make the most informed decision possible. Proponents of one record believe that keeping juvenile fingerprints out of the AFIS database is counterproductive to society and to the interests of juvenile justice.

Opposing One Record Opponents of one record think a single record would make hash of either one or the other systems, and perhaps both of them, because they are founded on different philosophies. The juvenile justice system's goal is to use the records to rehabilitate, treat, supervise and protect children. A single record would hinder this goal. The question is, why are juveniles in a separate system in the first place?

Expunging of Records

According to Griffin and Torbet (p.14): "While 'burying the past' is still common in the juvenile justice system—the sealing or destruction of juvenile offense records after a period of time, either automatically or at the request of the individuals involved—many states have now limited the practice, creating exceptions for certain serious offenses, imposing new restrictions or lengthening the time that records must be retained."

Table 10.5 presents the National School Safety Center's proposed "Model Interagency Juvenile Record Statute."

Proposed Changes to Improve the Juvenile Justice Court System

The saying "desperate times call for desperate measures" has recently been applied to the juvenile court, with some suggesting that the country do away with these distressed forums altogether. In Chicago, where the first juvenile court was created in 1899, judges today preside over assembly-line justice, hearing an average of 60 cases a day, about six minutes per case. In New Orleans, public defenders have to represent their poor clients with no office, no telephone, no court records and little chance to discuss the case before trial. While the juvenile court has withstood much criticism from those who claim it is damaged beyond repair, many believe it can still work.

 Two changes that might improve juvenile courts are to have open hearings and to improve the status of the juvenile court.

Closed hearings have not been particularly successful in shielding youngsters from adverse publicity in high-profile cases. In addition, closed hearings can lead the public to believe the court is overly lenient. When open hearings have been tried there have been few negative consequences.

Table 10.5
**Model Interagency
Juvenile Record Statute**

A. The following records are confidential and shall not be released to the general public except as permitted by this statute:

1. Juvenile court records, which include both legal and social records (legal records include petitions, dockets, motions, findings, orders and other papers filed with the court other than social records. Social records include social studies and medical, psychological, clinical or other treatment reports or studies filed with the court);

2. Juvenile social service, child protective service agency or multidisciplinary team records, whether contained in court files or in agency files (this includes all records made by any public or private agency or institution that now has or has had the child or the child's family under its custody, care or supervision);

3. Juvenile probation agency records, whether contained in court files or in probation agency files;

4. Juvenile parole agency records, whether contained in court files or in parole agency files;

5. Juvenile prosecutor, state attorney, district attorney or county attorney records relating to juvenile cases;

6. Juvenile law enforcement records, including fingerprints and photographs; and

7. School records that are maintained by school employees on all students, including but not limited to, academic, attendance, behavior and discipline records.

B. Access to the records listed in Section A is permitted without court order for official use to the following:

1. All courts;

2. All probation or parole agencies;

3. All attorneys general, prosecutors, state attorneys, district attorneys, county attorneys;

4. All social service or protective service agencies or multidisciplinary teams;

5. All law enforcement agencies;

6. All schools attended by the minor; and

7. All persons, agencies or institutions that have responsibility for the custody, care, control or treatment of the minor.

C. The juvenile court may issue an order releasing juvenile records to any person, agency or institution asserting a legitimate interest in a case or in the proceedings of the juvenile court.

D. Juvenile records may be sent to a central repository, which may be computerized. The central repository may be accessed by all agencies and organizations listed in Section B above.

E. The juvenile, the juvenile's parents and guardians and the juvenile's attorney may have access to the legal records maintained on the juvenile that are in the possession of the juvenile court without court order. The juvenile's attorney may have access to the social records maintained on the juvenile that are in the possession of the juvenile court and to the records listed in Section A for use in the legal representation of the juvenile. The juvenile on whom records are maintained may petition the court to correct any information that is incorrect.

The National School Safety Center [1988] has proposed this model juvenile record-sharing statute for the stated purpose of "foster[ing] the sharing of information among those organizations and agencies that need information from juvenile records to adequately perform their jobs as they work in an official capacity with youths and their families." The focus of the statute is restricted to the sharing of records among child-serving agencies and does not concern itself with the broader issue of public access to juvenile records.

Source: Used with permission from *The Need to Know: Juvenile Record Sharing.* Copyright 1989 by the National School Safety Center.

In addition, in many jurisdictions, assignment to the juvenile court is not a highly sought after appointment by judges or by public defenders. The juvenile court is often viewed as a dead-end for a career.

Summary

The juvenile court team includes the judge, the prosecutor, the defense attorney, probation services, and often a guardian *ad litum,* a CASA and a referee.

Children have the same rights as adults except trial by jury and, in some states, the right to bail. Children have the right to an attorney at all stages of the proceedings, the right to introduce evidence and tell their side of the story, the right to cross-examine witnesses and the right to remain silent during the hearing.

The three phases following the filing of a petition are (1) the conference (or preliminary hearing), (2) the adjudicatory hearing (or trial) and (3) the dispositional hearing (or sentencing). A series of Supreme Court decisions has caused the juvenile courts to make their procedures more adversarial, yet the trend in juvenile dispositions remains the deinstitutionalization of youths.

Sentences are of four basic types: indeterminate, determinate, presumptive and mandatory. Most juvenile sentencing laws are based on the juvenile's age, the offense and the offender's criminal history. Disposition options are numerous. Judges can dismiss the case with no charges at all, refer the youth to a social service agency, order the youth to make restitution, put the youth on probation or sentence the youth to a correctional facility. A good graduated sanctions system features certainty, speed, consistency, economy, proportionality, progressiveness and neutrality. Restitution is a frequently used disposition. The three most common types of restitution are monetary restitution, community service and direct service agreements.

The juvenile court's current dilemma hinges on its dual roles as a court of law and as a social service agency. Juvenile courts have been involved in such social and legal issues as abortion, school prayer, search and seizure, interracial custody and adoption, adolescent judgment and maturity and legal issues in terminating parental rights. Confidentiality issues involve juvenile hearings, release publication of juvenile's names and juvenile court records. States are de-emphasizing traditional confidentiality concerns to emphasize information sharing.

Discussion Questions

1. If to adjudicate is to hear and decide a case, why is this terminology used for criminal matters in juvenile court?
2. What changes to the adjudication process should be considered in your state? What would be the advantages or disadvantages of these changes?
3. Should a guardian *ad litem* be provided in addition to a defense counsel in all juvenile proceedings? Why or why not?
4. Are there inconsistencies in the justice dispensed by the juvenile courts in your area?
5. Should there be a separate justice system for juveniles, or should all juveniles be dealt with in the adult system?
6. What types of behavior should the juvenile court deal with?
7. What criteria are used in determining the disposition of a case in juvenile court in your state?
8. What are the major decision points in the adjudication process in juvenile court in your state? Are these decisions mechanical or determined by individual judges based on specific cases?
9. Does the public have the right to know which juveniles are committing crimes by publishing their names with the offense? Why or why not?
10. Should delinquency proceedings be secret?

InfoTrac College Edition Assignments

- Use InfoTrac College Edition to answer the Discussion Questions as appropriate.
- Read and outline one of the following:
  - "The Common Thread: Diversion in Juvenile Justice" by Franklin E. Zimring.
  - "Planned Respite Care: Hope for Families under Pressure" by Jon O'Brien (respite care)

Internet Assignments

Complete one of the following assignments and be prepared to share your findings with the class:

- Go to www.ojjdp.ncjrs.org and find and outline one of the NCJ publications listed in the references for this chapter.
- Research one of the following key words or phrases: *blended sentences, graduated sanctions, adjudicate, determinate sentence, discretionary sentence, dispositional hearing, guardian ad litum,*

indeterminate sentence, limited discretionary sentence, mandatory sentence, mechanical jurisprudence, nondiscretionary sentence, presumptive sentence, respite care

- Go to the Web site of any reference giving an online address to read and outline the material.

References

Bloom, Barbara; Owen, Barbara; Deschenes, Elizabeth Piper; and Rosenbaum; Jill. "Moving toward Justice for Female Juvenile Offenders in the New Millennium." *Contemporary Criminal Justice,* February 2002, pp.37–56.

Burns, Barbara J.; Howell, James C.; Wiig, Janet K.; Augimeri, Leena K.; Welsh, Brandon C.; Loeber, Rolf; and Petechuk, David. *Treatment, Services and Intervention Programs for Child Delinquents.* Washington, DC: Child Delinquency Bulletin Series, March 2003. (NCJ 193410)

Burruss, George W., Jr. and Kempf-Leonard, Kimberly. "The Questionable Advantage of Defense Counsel in Juvenile Court." *Justice Quarterly,* March 2002, pp.37–68.

Greenwood, Peter. *Juvenile Offenders.* Washington, DC: National Institute of Justice Crime File Study Guide, no date.

Griffin, Patrick and Torbet, Patricia. *Desktop Guide to Good Juvenile Probation Practice.* Washington, DC: National Center for Juvenile Justice, June 2002.

Hart, H. L. A. *The Concept of Law.* Oxford: Oxford University Press, 1965.

Keeping Defender Workloads Manageable. Washington, DC: Bureau of Justice Assistance Monograph, January 2001. (NCJ 185632)

"Latino Juvenile Offenders Get Harsher Treatment, Study Finds." *Criminal Justice Newsletter,* July 26, 2002, pp.2–3. Online: www.buildingblocksforyouth.org

MacDonald, John M. and Chesney-Lind, Meda. "Gender Bias and Juvenile Justice Revisited: A Multiyear Analysis." *Crime & Delinquency,* April 2001, pp.173–195.

Mendal, Richard A. *Less Hype More Help: Reducing Juvenile Crime: What Works—and What Doesn't.* Washington, DC: American Youth Policy Forum, 2000.

Nicholas, Anne. "Girls Ill-Served by Juvenile Justice System: Joint American Bar Association and the National Bar Association Report Highlights Factors Underlying Soaring Crime Rates." Press release, 2001. http://www/abanet.org/media/apr01/juvgirls.html

Poe-Yamagata, Eileen and Jones, Michael. *And Justice for All.* National Council on Crime and Delinquency, 2000.

Puzzanchera, Charles M. *Juvenile Court Placement of Adjudicated Youth, 1989–1998.* Washington, DC: OJJDP Fact Sheet #02, February 2002. (FS 200202)

Quraishi, Fiza; Segal, Heidi J.; and Trone, Jennifer. *Respite Care: A Promising Response to Status Offenders at Risk of Court-Ordered Placements.* New York: Vera Institute, 2003. Online: www.vera.org

Siegel, Larry J.; Welsh, Brandon C.; and Senna, Joseph J. *Juvenile Delinquency: Theory, Practice and Law,* 8th ed. Belmont, CA: Wadsworth Publishing Company, 2003.

Stahl, Anne L. *Delinquency Cases in Juvenile Courts, 1998.* Washington, DC: OJJDP Fact Sheet #31, August 2001. (FS 200131)

Walker, Samuel; Spohn, Cassia; and DeLone, Miriam. *The Color of Justice: Race, Ethnicity and Crime in America,* 2nd ed. Belmont, CA: Wadsworth Publishing Company, 2000.

Wrobleski, Henry M. and Hess, Kären M. *Introduction to Law Enforcement and Criminal Justice,* 7th ed. Belmont, CA: Wadsworth Publishing Company, 2003.

Young, Malcolm C. *Providing Effective Representation for Youths Prosecuted as Adults.* Washington, DC: Bureau of Justice Statistics Bulletin, August 2000. (NCJ 182502)

Cases Cited

In re Gault, 387 U.S. 1 (1967).
Kent v. United States, 383 U.S. 541 (1966).
In re Winship, 397 U.S. 358 (1970).

The Response of Corrections

It is in the juvenile justice system that we will succeed or fail in reducing corrections populations . . . If we do not address juvenile corrections fully, these children will end up as tomorrow's clients in the adult system.

—John J. Wilson

Do You Know?

- What four types of interventions are typically included in a modern, comprehensive graduated sanctions system?
- Whether juveniles have a right to treatment?
- How the conservative and liberal approaches treat juveniles?
- What the most common intermediate sanctions are?
- Who the first probation officer was?
- What the most common disposition from the juvenile court is?
- What the formal goals of probation are?
- What the essence of juvenile probation is?
- What the two main functions of a probation officer traditionally have been?
- What the single greatest pressure on probation officers is?
- What the effect of isolating offenders from the community might be?
- What kinds of nonresidential programs have been implemented?
- What the five major categories of residential community-based corrections are?
- What three justifications are given for putting juveniles in locked facilities?
- How public and private correctional institutions differ?
- Whether juvenile institutions model adult institutions in social organization? Culture?
- What incarcerated groups are over-represented?
- How prison gangs differ from street gangs?
- What the six performance-based standards goals for corrections are?
- What most youthful offender programs include?
- What three principles underlie the National Institute of Corrections training program?
- What the weakest element in the juvenile justice system process often is?
- What institution is often crucial in the transition of an incarcerated juvenile back to the community?

Can You Define?

aftercare
alternative education
boot camp
criminogenic need
   principle

cruel and unusual
   punishment
deterrence
foster group home
foster home

group home
halfway house
immediate sanctions
intensive supervision
intermediate sanctions

nonresidential program   probation   shelter
nonsecure facility   probation officer   shock incarceration
ombuds   responsivity principle training schools
parole   risk principle

INTRODUCTION

Corrections serves several functions, with one of the most obvious being to protect the public by removing juvenile offenders from the community. Corrections has a dual function with these offenders, holding them accountable for their behavior and providing them with the educational, vocational, personal and social skills needed to successfully return to the community. As Matthews and Leffler (2000, p.36) report:

> In most cases, within six to eighteen months, an incarcerated youth is back on the streets. How do we ensure public safety then? Surely, the youth will have made gains that led to his or her release. But is the youth returning to an environment or community that will support those gains? The correctional staff, often isolated from youth-serving systems that previously tried to help, must work diligently to return the youth to his or her family and community. Reconnecting the youth and family with previous support systems can be a discouraging encounter.
>
> It is a daunting task, but the Indiana Department of Corrections (DOC) Division of Juvenile Services has a vision for how this can be accomplished. "Our vision," says the DOC vision statement, "is that every child experience successes in caring families and nurturing communities that cherish children and teach them to value family and community. Our vision is guided by the fact that our decisions and actions affecting children today determine the quality of our life tomorrow."
>
> This vision statement reflects an understanding of who the children are who end up at the door of correctional services. Too many of them have been victims of abuse and neglect. They have lived in households in which alcohol and drugs were abused, or they are substance abusers themselves. They have lived in multiple group homes, foster homes or treatment centers. They struggle to read and are failing in school. They have few friends or positive role models. They may suffer developmental disabilities or mental health problems. Some are dangerous to others and some are dangerous to themselves.

The goal of corrections is to successfully return youths to their family, school and community. Figure 11.1 illustrates opportunities to intervene and provide needed services to accomplish this goal.

This chapter focuses on the correctional portion of the contemporary juvenile justice system beginning with a description of graduated sanctions. Corrections should include an array of choices existing along a continuum, from least restrictive and intensive to most restrictive and intensive supervision. This is followed by a discussion of the right to treatment and the controversy between conservatives and liberals about the course of any treatment. Next intermediate sanctions are described, followed by an in-depth discussion of the most common, least restrictive disposition of the juvenile/family court—probation. Intensive supervision is then explained.

This is followed by a discussion of several community-based correctional alternatives, including day treatment alternatives and residential programs such as shelters, group homes, foster homes and camps. Next, further along the

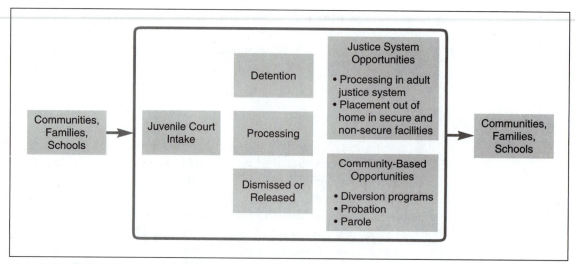

Figure 11.1
From Communities to the Justice System and Back: Opportunities to Intervene and Provide Needed Services to Youths with Disabilities

Addressing the Needs of Youths with Disabilities in the Juvenile Justice System: The Current Status of Evidence-Based Research. Washington, DC: National Council on Disability, May 2003, p.165.

continuum of increasing restriction, intermediate sanctions are explored, including electronic monitoring and boot camps. The chapter then focuses on youths who are institutionalized—who they are and the conditions under which they are confined, including the issue of disproportionate minority confinement (DMC). The chapter concludes with a discussion of parole and aftercare, often the more neglected aspect of the juvenile justice process.

Graduated Sanctions

Graduated sanctions were introduced in Chapter 10. The basic premise underlying a graduated system is **deterrence.** Deterrence theory states that the decision to commit a crime is based on a cost-benefit calculation. If a person believes the legal costs of committing a crime are greater than the benefits, crime will be deterred. When a person believes the benefits outweigh the costs, a crime will be committed. Deterrence theory suggests that sanctions be tailored to be just severe enough to exceed the gain offered by crime. Overly severe sanctions are unjust; sanctions that are not severe enough will not deter.

According to Lipsey et al. (2000): "Unfortunately, most juvenile justice systems have not offered this range of sanctions and instead have relied on confinement for serious offenders and probation for less serious offenders—with little in between despite recent literature reviews and meta-analyses demonstrating that intervention programs can be effective in reducing delinquent behavior."

Promising Sanctioning Programs in a Graduated System (2003, p.2) stresses: "A modern comprehensive juvenile justice system must include programs less restrictive than confinement but more intensive than probation. But such a system should not simply be a hodgepodge of alternative programs. It must embody a correctional philosophy that can deal with youths who commit serious and violent offense, 'one time and you're out youths,' and everyone in between." In other words, a juvenile justice system that offers a continuum of care must include a wide range of sanctions designed to increase offender accountability so a sanction can be matched to the seriousness of the offense.

 The four types of interventions in a modern comprehensive graduated sanctions system are (1) immediate sanctions, (2) intermediate sanctions, (3) secure confinement and (4) aftercare/re-entry.

Immediate sanctions are usually diversion mechanisms that hold youths accountable for their behavior by avoiding formal court processing. They are typically appropriate for most first-time offenders, status offenders and some minor repeat offenders. Such sanctions usually follow restorative justice principles and include community service, informal hearings, family group conferences, mediation, mentoring, special courts and restitution.

Promising Sanctioning Programs (p.3) identified 10 promising immediate sanction programs: Earn It (restitution) in Keene, New Hampshire; UT Juvenile Restitution Program in Salt Lake City, Utah; Dakota County Family Group Conferencing in Hastings, Minnesota; Indianapolis Restorative Justice Conference in Indianapolis, Indiana, www.hudson.org; Barron County Victim Impact Panel in Rice Lake, Wisconsin, www.bcrjp.org; Travis County Dispute Resolution Center in West Austin, Texas, www.realtime.net/drc; Oregon Dispute Resolution Commission in Salem, Oregon, www.odrc.state.or.us; Across Ages Center for Intergenerational Learning (mentoring) in Philadelphia, Pennsylvania, www.temple.edu/cil; Big Brothers/Big Sisters of America of Philadelphia, Pennsylvania, www.bbbsa.org; Colonie Youth Center (youth court) in Latham, New York, www.colonieyouthcourt.org; and Anchorage Youth Court of Anchorage, Alaska.

Immediate sanctions (diversion programs) were discussed in Chapter 10. This chapter focuses on the other three types: intermediate sanctions, secure confinement and aftercare/re-entry. Whichever sanction is imposed, implicit is the youth's right to treatment.

The Right to Treatment

Second Chances: Giving Kids a Chance to Make a Better Choice (2000, p.2) states: "The juvenile justice system still largely promotes the concept that kids should be helped to turn their lives around. This publication describes 25 people who are 'living, breathing testaments' to the importance of simply giving kids repeated chances to turn their lives around and room to grow up, sometimes on their own." Included are Olympic Gold Medalist Bob Beacon, poet Luis Rodriguez, professor and Juvenile Probation Commission President Joe Julian and Columbia University Law Review editor Lawrence Wu, all gang members with multiple contacts with law enforcement before they changed direction. Without appropriate sanctions and treatment their valuable contributions to society doubtless would have been lost, and society would be providing room and board perpetually.

The U.S. Supreme Court has based the right to treatment on the principle that the restriction of fundamental liberties through involuntary confinement must follow the "least restrictive alternative" available. This principle was stated by the Supreme Court in *Shelton v. Tucker* (1960):

> In a series of decisions this Court has held that, even though the governmental purpose be legitimate and substantial, that purpose cannot be pursued by means that broadly stifle fundamental personal liberties when the end can be more narrowly achieved. The breadth of legislative abridgement must be viewed in the light of less drastic means for achieving the same basic purpose.

Under this rationale, the state violates a person's constitutional rights if it fails to confine and provide treatment in the least restrictive setting possible. This is especially important for juveniles with disabilities, including mental health problems. According to a study by the National Council on Disability (NCD), children involved in the juvenile justice system are entitled by the Individuals with Disabilities Act (IDEA) to have their disability-related needs met (*Addressing the Needs of Youths . . .*, 2003).

 The U.S. Supreme Court has never definitively ruled on whether there is a constitutionally based right to treatment. The state violates an individual's rights if it fails to confine and provide treatment in the least restrictive setting possible.

Two opposing views exist as to just what this treatment should consist of.

Conservative and Liberal Philosophies of Corrections

The conservative attitude is to "get tough," "stop babying these kids" and "get them off the streets." Such conservative philosophies accept retribution as grounds for punishment and believe in imprisonment to control crime and anti-social behavior. Rehabilitative programs may be provided during incarceration, but it is imprisonment itself, with its attendant deprivations, that must be primarily relied on to prevent crime, delinquency and recidivism. Correctional treatment is not necessary.

 The conservative philosophy of juvenile justice is to "get tough" on juveniles—to punish and imprison them.

This "law and order" reaction typifies conservatism, a trend that first affected adult offenders and now extends into juvenile justice.

At the opposite end of the spectrum from this conservative philosophy is the liberal view of juvenile justice, which sharply criticizes the "get tough" approach and all its trappings, such as the need to build more prisons to hold the rising number of incarcerated youths. An attorney has commented: "Those who advocate increased prisons as a solution to youth crime are equal to those who advocate increasing the number of grave sites as a treatment for cancer." The liberal

Table 11.1
Respondents' Views on What Is and What Should Be the Main Emphasis in Juvenile Prisons and the Amount of Importance Placed on Each (in percentages)

A. Main Emphasis of Juvenile Prisons

Goals of Imprisonment	Is	Should Be
Rehabilitation: Do you think the main emphasis in juvenile prison is [should be] to try and rehabilitate the adolescent so that he might return to society as a productive citizen?	29.4	63.3
Punishment: Do you think the main emphasis in juvenile prison is [should be] to punish the adolescent convicted of a crime?	16.8	18.7
Protection: Do you think the main emphasis in juvenile prison is [should be] to protect society from future crime he might commit?	17.6	11.2
Not sure	36.1	6.7

B. Importance of Goals of Juvenile Institutions

Goals of Imprisonment	Very Important	Important	A Little Important	Not Very Important
Rehabilitation	64.5	30.0	4.3	1.1
Punishment	42.5	52.1	4.3	1.1
Protection	43.2	47.0	8.4	1.3

Source: Melissa M. Moon, Jody L. Sundt, Francis T. Cullen and John Paul Wright. "Is Child Saving Dead? Public Support for Juvenile Rehabilitation." *Crime & Delinquency*, January 2000, p.26. Reprinted by permission of Sage Publications, Inc.

philosophy of juvenile justice advocates treatment, not punishment, for youths who become involved with the juvenile justice system.

 The liberal philosophy of juvenile justice stresses treatment and rehabilitation, including community-based programs.

Moon et al. (2000) studied public support for juvenile rehabilitation to answer the question: "Is Child Saving Dead?" They (p.38) found that rehabilitation should be an integral goal of the juvenile correctional system. They also endorsed a range of community-based treatment interventions and favored early intervention programs over imprisonment as a response to crime. They conclude: "Taken together, these findings revealed that the public's belief in 'child saving' remains firm, and that citizens do not support an exclusively punitive response to juvenile offenders." Table 11.1 summarizes respondents' views on what the emphasis should be in juvenile prisons.

In addition, research by Fass and Pi (2002, p.363) found: "Harsher sentencing can indeed prevent some offenses. The value of this gain, however, is much less than its cost to produce. As a result, by consuming public resources that might otherwise be invested in more productive purposes within or outside the justice system, the policy of toughness visits substantial opportunity costs on communities that embrace it." They (pp.385–386) conclude: "Our findings, as accurate and as useful as our data and methods allow, are specific to Dallas County [Texas]. But given similarities in economic, demographic and juvenile characteristics across major metropolitan areas of the United States, we can with confidence suggest that other communities that pursue policies of more restrictive sanctions, if curious about relationships between costs and benefits, are likely to discover that material gains to victims and others, though perhaps substantial, do not make up for the added spending needed to produce the gains." Whatever stance one takes, some type of intermediate sanction should be included as part of a graduated sanctioning system.

Intermediate Sanctions

Intermediate sanctions hold youths accountable for their actions through more restrictive and intensive interventions short of secure care. They provide swift, certain punishment while avoiding the expense and the negative effects of institutionalization. Intermediate sanctions are appropriate for youths who fail to respond to immediate sanctions by re-offending or some violent or drug-involved offenders who need supervision, structure and monitoring but not necessarily institutionalization.

 Common forms of intermediate sanctions are probation, intensive supervision, electronic monitoring, house arrest, boot camps and alternative schools/education.

The most common intermediate sanction is probation.

Probation

After the dispositional hearing, if the court orders that a youngster be placed on probation, certain procedures and commitments must be satisfied. An order must give the probation officer authority for controlled supervision of the youth within the community. The terms of the probation are described in the order. **Probation** allows youths adjudicated delinquent to serve their sentences in the community under supervision.

An important responsibility of the probation officer is helping the court to establish the conditions for probation. Two kinds of probationary conditions are usually established: mandatory and discretionary. Most mandatory conditions specify that probationers (1) may not commit a new delinquent act, (2) must report as directed to their probation officer and (3) must obey all court orders. The discretionary conditions are more extensive, as illustrated by the discretionary conditions set forth in New Jersey Juvenile Statutes: pay a fine; make restitution; perform community service; participate in a work program; participate in programs emphasizing self-reliance, such as intensive outdoor programs that teach survival skills, including but not limited to camping, hiking and other appropriate activities; participate in a program of academic or vocational education or counseling, which may require attendance after school, evenings and weekends; be placed in a suitable residential or nonresidential program for the treatment of alcohol or narcotic abuse; be placed in a **nonresidential program** operated by a public or private agency that provides intensive services to juveniles for specified hours, which may include education, counseling to the juvenile and the juvenile's family if appropriate, vocational counseling, work or other services; or be placed with any private group home with which the Department of Correction has entered into a purchase of service contract.

The New Jersey statute also allows the court to set conditions for the probationer's parents and to revoke the juvenile's driving license as a condition of probation. Conditions may include such matters as cooperating with the program of supervision, meeting family responsibilities, maintaining steady employment or engaging in or refraining from engaging in a specific employment or occupation, pursuing prescribed educational or vocational training, undergoing medical or psychiatric treatment, maintaining residence in a prescribed area or in a prescribed facility, refraining from consorting with certain types of people or frequenting certain types of places, making restitution or reparation, paying fines, submitting to search and seizure or submitting to drug tests.

Several constraints govern the setting of probation conditions. The conditions must be do-able, must not unreasonably restrict constitutional rights, must be consistent with law and public policy and must be specific and understandable. If the conditions are *not* met, probation can be revoked. This is normally accomplished by the probation officer reporting the violation of conditions to the juvenile court. A violation of probation starts the judicial process over, beginning with a revocation hearing, where evidence and supportive information are presented to a juvenile judge. (Such hearings are also called *surrender hearings* or *violation hearings*.) If the court decides to revoke the probation, the youth can be institutionalized.

Probation originated with John Augustus (1784–1859), a prosperous Boston shoemaker. One August morning in 1841 he was in court when a wretched-looking man was brought into court and charged with being a drunkard. Augustus spoke briefly with the man and then provided the man's bail on the provision he sign a pledge to never drink spirits again and to return to court at a set time as a reformed man.

For the next 18 years, Augustus spent much time visiting the courts, showing an interest in prisoners and bailing out misdemeanants who could not pay the fines themselves. He would help offenders find work or a place to live. His own home was filled with people he had bailed out. When Augustus and a defendant returned to court, he would report on the progress of the defendant's rehabilitation and recommend a disposition in the case. These recommendations usually were accepted by the court.

 John Augustus was the first probation officer.

During the first year of his work, Augustus assisted 10 drunkards, who because of his help received only small fines instead of imprisonment. Augustus later assisted other types of offenders, young and old, men and women. As he continued his work, he was able to report that of 2,000 cases, only 10 offenders failed to appear and jumped bail or probation.

Several aspects of the system used by Augustus remain a basic part of modern probation. He thoroughly investigated each person he considered helping. He considered the character of the person, his or her age and likely future influences. Augustus not only supervised each defendant but also kept careful case records which he submitted to the court.

Probation is the most widely used disposition of the juvenile or family court. During 1998 more than one-third of delinquency cases resulted in probation (Black, 2001, p.1). Property offense cases continued to account for the majority of cases placed on probation, but their share of the probation caseload declined.

 Probation is the most common disposition of the juvenile or family court.

According to Griffin and Torbet (2002, p.1): "We envision the role of juvenile probation as that of a catalyst for developing safe communities and healthy youths and families. We believe we can fulfill this role by:

- Holding offenders accountable.
- Building and maintaining community-based partnerships.
- Implementing results-based and outcome-driven services and practices.
- Advocating for and addressing the needs of victims, offenders, families and communities.
- Obtaining and sustaining sufficient resources.
- Promoting growth and development of all juvenile probation professionals."

The researchers reject the "closed, passive, negative and unsystematic approach that has too often characterized traditional juvenile probation practices." They (p.2) emphasize that protecting the public is one of the primary responsibilities of juvenile probation. In addition, probation is a guidance program to help juveniles overcome problems that may lead to further delinquency and to supervise them. It functions as an alternative to a correctional facility and operates much like adult probation.

 The formal goals of probation are to protect the public, to hold juveniles accountable for their actions and to improve the delinquent's behavior—in short, rehabilitation.

Probation's goal of rehabilitation is sometimes short-circuited by the public's preoccupation with *control*. Probation may reflect public demands that the court "do something" about recurrent misconduct. It may be organized to keep the delinquent in line, to prevent any further trouble, and so the ultimate goal of reforming the delinquent's personality and conduct becomes subordinated to the exigencies of maintaining immediate control. Probationary supervision, consequently, takes on a decidedly short-term and negative character. Probation becomes a disciplinary regime to inhibit troublesome conduct.

Supervision

 Supervision is the essence of probation.

Often, by the time a juvenile is placed on probation, he or she has a record of previous run-ins with the juvenile justice system, usually the police. The police regard probation as something juveniles "get away with" or "get off with." Many juveniles who receive probation instead of being sentenced to a correctional facility view it the same way. Some youths have stated, "I never see my P.O. [probation officer]. It's a joke! Don't ask me to tell you what he looks like, I can't remember. When I get done with this beef, I'll be cool so I don't get hassled again."

The Probation Officer

The role of the probation officer was introduced in Chapter 10. Probation officers are in the unique position of serving both the court and the correctional areas of juvenile justice. While technically considered a correctional employee, a **probation officer** is an officer of the court first and foremost.

 The probation officer has traditionally been responsible for two key functions: (1) personally supervising and counseling youths on probation and (2) serving as a link to other community services.

While counseling skills are considered important, the role of probation officers has shifted to that of social service "brokers." In many jurisdictions, the probation officer links "clients" with available resources within the community, such as vocational rehabilitation centers, vocational schools, mental health centers, employment services, church groups and other community groups, such as Girl Scouts, Boy Scouts and Explorers. This broad use of community resources has some inherent risks. Linking youths to such groups may actually amplify a small problem into a much larger one. Over-attendance by a youth in one or more of these groups may become an attention-getting device. The over-prescription of community group participation may also reinforce the youth's or the community's perception of the problem as serious. In either case further delinquency may well result.

In 1987 the National Center for Juvenile Justice (NCJJ) established the Juvenile Probation Officer Initiative (JPOI) to increase professionalism in juvenile probation. The JPOI has developed *The Desktop Guide to Good Juvenile Probation Practice,* a reference book written by and for juvenile probation officers (Griffin and Torbet).

The Current Role of Probation Officers

In many states probation officers determine whether the juvenile court has jurisdiction, especially at the intake stage of contact with a child. The probation representative also determines, to some degree, whether a formal or an informal hearing is called for.

Informal hearings have critics, because informal processing requires an explicit or tacit admission of guilt. The substantial advantages that accrue from this admission (the avoidance of court action) also act as an incentive to confess. This casts doubt on the voluntary nature and truthfulness of admissions of guilt. The process results in informal probation.

Informal probation can be a crucial time in the life of a juvenile. If it succeeds, the youngster may avoid further juvenile court processing and its potentially serious consequences. If informal probation efforts fail, the usual recourse is for the probation officer to request a petition be filed to make the case official. This could result in the youth being confined in a locked or controlled facility for disciplinary action.

Filing Petitions and Court Hearings

Recall from Chapter 10 the three phases of the juvenile court system that youths usually go through after a petition is filed. The probation officer may play an important role in each phase.

During the first phase, the conference or preliminary hearing, the judge may determine with the assistance of a probation officer whether a child's behavior is a threat to the public or to himself. If so, the judge will order preventive detention of the youth.

During the second phase, the adjudication hearing or trial, the judge will usually order a social investigation, presentence investigation (PSI) or predisposition report. The probation officer is responsible for investigating and assessing the child's home, school, physical and psychological situation. The *predisposition* or *presentence investigation report* has the objective of satisfying the goal of the juvenile court, which is to provide services.

Other Services

In addition to assessing the needs of probationers, devising a case plan or contract and supervising compliance with that contract, probation officers can also serve as mature role models. They can provide family counseling, crisis intervention and mediation. Mediation can be used to divert cases at intake, settle cases by community groups or by the probation officer and settle disputes between a juvenile and the school or family. The demanding, challenging, multifaceted role of the juvenile probation officer is illustrated in Table 11.2.

Spriggs (2003, p.65) describes the Special Needs Diversionary Project for Texas juvenile offenders with mental health needs. This project's concept is to create a caseload of juveniles with mental health issues assigned to probation to be supervised by juvenile probation officers trained to work with this population. The specialized probation officers work closely with mental health practitioners to provide delivery of necessary mental health services.

Problems with Probation   Courts often attribute juveniles' troubles to something that is wrong with the youths or with their social milieu. The courts seldom sense that a juvenile's problems may be due to the court's program for guidance and control. In many cases probation officers simply do not have the training, skills or resources to provide probationers with the kinds of assistance they might require. A problem commonly encountered at the dispositional stage is a lack of options to help or treat a youngster. Inexperienced or uninformed probation officers may recommend treatment that is simply not available. Often a youngster is placed on or continued on probation because of a lack of viable alternatives.

Table 11.2
The Multifaceted Role of the Juvenile Probation Officer

Role	Description
Cop	Enforces judge's orders
Prosecutor	Assists D.A., conducts revocations
Father confessor	Establishes helpful, trustful relationship with juvenile
Rat	Informs court of juvenile's behavior/circumstances
Teacher	Develops skills in juvenile
Friend	Develops positive relations with juvenile
Surrogate parent	Admonishes, scolds juvenile
Counselor	Addresses needs
Ambassador	Intervenes on behalf of juvenile
Problem solver	Helps juvenile deal with court and community issues
Crisis manager	Deals with juvenile's precipitated crises (usually at 2 A.M.)
Hand holder	Consoles juvenile
Public speaker	Educates public re: tasks
P.R. person	Wins friends, influences people on behalf of probation
Community resource specialist	Service broker
Transportation officer	Gets juvenile to where he has to go in a pinch
Recreational therapist	Gets juvenile to use leisure time well
Employment counselor	Gets youth a job
Judge's advisor	Court service officer
Financial advisor	Monitors payment, sets pay plan
Paper pusher	Fills out myriad forms
Sounding board	Listens to irate parents, youths, police, teachers, etc.
Punching bag	Person to blame when anything goes wrong, youth commits new crime
Expert clinician	Offers or refers to appropriate treatment
Family counselor/marriage therapist	Keeps peace in juvenile's family
Psychiatrist	Answers question: Why does the juvenile do it?
Banker	Juvenile needs car fare money
Tracker	Finds youth
Truant officer	Gets youth to school
Lawyer	Tells defense lawyer/prosecutor what juvenile law says
Sex educator	Facts of life, AIDS and child support
Emergency foster parent	In a pinch
Family wrecker	Files petitions for abuse/neglect
Bureaucrat	Helps juvenile justice system function
Lobbyist	For juvenile, for department
Program developer	For youth, for department
Grant writer	For youth, for department
Board member	Serves on myriad committees
Agency liaison	With community groups
Trainer	For volunteer, students
Public information officer	"Tell me what you know about probation"
Court officer/bailiff	In a pinch
Custodian	Keeps office clean
Victim advocate	Deals with juvenile's victim

Source: Adapted from Juvenile Probation Officer Initiative (JPOI) Working Group, *Desktop Guide to Good Juvenile Probation Practice.* Washington, DC: Office of Juvenile Justice and Delinquency Prevention, May 1993, pp. 119–120.

Another factor is time. Even if probation officers possessed the skills necessary to offer psychotherapy, vocational guidance and school counseling with diverse types of youths, caseloads dictate that they would not have the time to exercise these skills.

 Excessive caseloads are probably the single greatest pressure on probation officers.

In most probation offices, especially in large urban areas, certain characteristics pervade the personality of the office. Juveniles are viewed by their records, in terms of the trouble they have caused or gotten into. Records are not regarded as formulations assembled by various people in the juvenile justice system. That is to say, a juvenile's record is treated as a set of relevant facts instead of as a social product created by an organization.

Privatizing Juvenile Probation Services

Problems such as illegal drug use, street gangs, school violence and abused, homeless and runaway youths have strained the resources of the juvenile justice system. Given that probation departments are the single largest component of juvenile corrections, these departments especially feel the strain. One proposed solution is privatization.

Community Corrections Model for Probation

As Townsend (2003, p.41) suggests, four strategies used by community corrections agencies that serve juveniles seem to have the greatest impact:

1. Placing public safety first
2. Providing for strong enforcement of probation conditions and a quick response to violations
3. Supervising probationers in the neighborhood, not the office
4. Developing partners in the community

Engaging Families

One of the most important partners in the community is the family. As Evans (2002, p.116) notes: "The benefits of engaging the family to help supervise offenders is clear: Families are there when probation and parole officers are not. . . . Families can provide around-the-clock supervision and support, provide long-term involvement and sometimes have special insight into offender's problems."

Evans (p.117) suggests: "Probation officers should consider family involvement in supervision because it (1) provides an opportunity for families and government agencies to work together; (2) provides a way of avoiding learned helplessness on the part of families and, thus, helps to break the cycle of dependency; (3) assists in treatment by providing for a better match between the intervention and context of the offender; and (4) enhances public safety and public health."

School-Based Probation

According to the Juvenile Sanctions Center (JSC), *School-Based Probation: An Approach Worth Considering* (2003), placing juvenile probation officers in schools rather than in central offices goes a long way toward increasing the contacts between officers and the youths they are monitoring, leading to more immediate and effective responses to problems: "School-based probation (SBP) changes the very nature of probation by physically moving probation officers from the 'fortress' of traditional central or district offices into middle, junior and high school buildings where youths on probation spend the majority of their day."

According to the JSC document: "School-based probation represents an important shift in the delivery of probation services for in-school probations, and departments across the country are embracing this approach. More importantly, two evaluations of Pennsylvania's SBP program have documented several important benefits, including more contact, better monitoring, a focus on school success and a fit with balanced and restorative justice framework."

Torbet et al. (2001) report on a statewide process evaluation of SBP in Pennsylvania conducted by the NCJJ, in which school-based probation officers, probation administrators and school administrators all reported high levels of satisfaction with the SBP. This included high marks given for the overall impact of the program on probationers, the services the program provided youths and families, the effect on school climate and communication facilitated between schools and courts. *Promising Sanctioning Programs* (p.6) identified the National Center for Juvenile Justice's school-based probation program as a promising intermediate sanction.

Drug Testing and Probation

Drug testing is frequently a condition of probation (and parole). Haapanen and Britton (2002) studied drug testing of youthful offenders and found that the level of drug testing does not affect recidivism among youthful parolees. They also found, however, that drug testing may serve as a relatively straightforward risk assessment procedure for future criminal behavior. Moon et al. (2000, p.49) report that 80.3 percent of their respondents fully support drug testing, and 11.8 percent moderately support it. Only 2.5 percent did not support drug testing.

Intensive Supervision

Intensive supervision is like highly structured probation. As described in *Promising Sanctioning Programs* (p.4): "Intensive Supervision Programs (ISPs) are community-based, postadjudication, nonresidential programs designed to provide restraints on offenders in the community. The basic premise of an ISP is to provide a high level of control over an offender for public safety, but without the additional costs associated with incarceration. ISPs are characterized by high levels of contact and intervention by the probation officer or caseworker, small caseloads and strict conditions of compliance."

ISPs usually include:

- Greater reliance placed on unannounced spot checks; these may occur in a variety of settings including home, school, known hangouts and job sites.
- Considerable attention directed at increasing the number and kinds of collateral contacts made by corrections staff with family members, friends, staff from other agencies and concerned residents in the community.

- Greater use of curfew, including both more rigid enforcement and lowering the hour at which curfew goes into effect. Other measures for imposing control include home detention and electronic monitoring.
- Surveillance expanded to ensure 24/7 coverage.

Other components of intensive supervision are clear, graduated sanctions with immediate consequences for violations; restitution and community service; parent involvement; youth skill development; and individualized and offense-specific treatment.

To determine whether a probationer needs intensive supervision, the probation officer should have a classification procedure. Because intensive supervision is extremely time-consuming, it should be reserved for those probationers at greatest risk of violating their probation.

The National Institute of Corrections (NIC) Classification Project has been adopted by many juvenile court jurisdictions. NIC research suggests that an assessment of the following variables appears to be universally predictive of future delinquent behavior:

- Age at first adjudication
- Prior delinquent behavior (combined measure of number and severity of priors)
- Number of prior commitments to juvenile facilities
- Drug/chemical abuse
- Alcohol abuse
- Family relationships problems
- School problems
- Peer relationships problems

The NIC calls for a reassessment every six months. After the assessment is completed, a case plan must arrange services so the youth, the family and the community all are served. The National Council on Crime and Delinquency (NCCD) has a case planning strategy that involves two main components:

1. Analysis, including identification of problems, strengths and resources.
2. Problem prioritization based upon:
    - Strength—Is the problem an important force in the delinquent's behavior?
    - Alterability—Can the problem be modified or circumvented?
    - Speed—Can the changes be achieved rapidly?
    - Interdependence—Will solving the problem help resolve other problems?

This case plan is next reduced to a contract between the probation department, the juvenile offender and the family. The probation officer then presents this contract to the juvenile and the parents and reaches agreement to it. The probation officer then monitors compliance with the contract. *Promising Sanctioning Programs* identifies the Community Intensive Supervision Project in Pittsburgh, Pennsylvania, as a promising intermediate sanction program.

Community-Based Corrections Programs

The community corrections philosophy follows the juvenile justice rhetoric of treatment and restoration instead of punishment and decay. Probation and intensive supervision may also be thought of as community-based corrections programs if the family and/or the public are involved. According to Borum (2003, p.114): "More than a half-million juveniles are under community supervision as a result of violent or delinquent behavior." As Gondles (2002, p.6) stresses: "Our responsibility for youthful offenders cannot begin once a juvenile enters the criminal justice system. It must begin in the community, even before a youth comes into contact with the criminal justice system. . . . Our goal cannot simply be returning youthful offenders to society, but it must also include helping to ensure that there are not others to take their place within our facilities."

 Isolating offenders from their normal social environments may encourage the development of a delinquent orientation and, thus, further delinquent behavior.

Community-based correctional programs, such as foster care and group homes, try to normalize social contacts, reduce the stigma of being institutionalized and provide opportunities for jobs and schooling. Community-based programs might include involving young people in community activities; training and employing youths as subprofessional aides; establishing Youth Services Bureaus to provide programs for young people; increasing the involvement of religious institutions, private social agencies, fraternal groups and other community organizations in youth programs; and providing community residential centers.

Programs such as work release allow delinquents to leave institutions to work in the community. Similar programs may provide release to delinquents for education. Under these programs youths receive conditional releases to a **halfway house,** a prerelease center or a residential treatment facility. Living within the community, youths go to work or school under some supervision and counseling.

Feldman and Kubrin (2002) describe Philadelphia's Detention Diversion Advocacy Program (DDAP), a community-based alternative to staying in a secure detention facility while awaiting adjudication. This program provides case management to ensure delinquent youths will attend their scheduled court hearings and to reduce the likelihood that they will re-offend while awaiting case deposition. The executive director of the Center on Juvenile and Criminal Justice has stated: "The multiple successes of DDAP add further support to the mounting evidence that community-based programs are truly viable and invaluable alternatives to the locked detention of youth" (Feldman and Kubrin, p.1).

Nonresidential corrections programs include community supervision, family crisis counseling, proctor programs and service-oriented programs, including recreational programs, counseling, alternative schools, employment training programs, and homemaking and financial planning classes.

Community Service

Community service is usually part of a graduated sanctions program and may be used alone or in combination with other sanctions, especially probation. It is an important component of most restorative justice approaches. Etter and Hammond (2001, p.114) point out that community service in corrections is not new, beginning in 1966 in Alameda County, California. They (p.115) suggest: "In order to establish a successful community service work program, it is essential to determine three things: what type of work will be performed, who will be the recipients and which offenders will be required to perform, or be eligible for and capable of performing the requested work."

In addition to performing work, community service sometimes requires offenders to speak to various community groups about their offenses and what it has cost them financially and emotionally. According to Moon et al. (p.49) 77.9 percent of those in their study fully supported community service; 14.7 moderately supported it. Only 2.1 percent did not support it.

Nonresidential Day Treatment Alternatives

As described by *Promising Sanctioning Programs* (p.4): "Day treatment facilities (also known as day reporting centers) are highly structured, community-based, postadjudication, nonresidential programs for serious juvenile offenders. The goal of day treatment is to provide both intensive supervision to ensure community safety and a wide range of services to the offender to prevent future delinquent behavior."

Many state and local governments are turning to day treatment for delinquent juveniles because it appears to be effective and is less costly than residential care. Alternatives might include evening and weekend reporting centers, school programs and specialized treatment facilities. Such programs can provide education, tutoring, counseling, community service, vocational training and social/recreational events.

Day treatment programs tend to succeed because they can focus on the family unit and the youth's behavior in the family and the community. They are also effective from a legal standpoint in states that require that youths be treated in the least restrictive environment possible.

Community-based corrections has supplemented, not replaced, institutionalization. *Promising Sanctioning Programs* (p.6) lists three intensive nonresidential day programs: The Multidimensional Treatment Foster Care program in Eugene, Oregon, www.oslc.org; the Multisystemic Therapy Family Services Research Center at the University of South Carolina; and the Functional Family Therapy program at the University of Utah, www.fftinc.com. Communities also sometimes provide residential, nonsecure facilities with accompanying programs.

Alternative Schools/Education

Addressing the Needs of Youths with Disabilities in the Juvenile Justice System: The Current Status of Evidence-Based Research (p.80) describes alternative schools/education:

A variety of **alternative education** programs have been developed to serve vulnerable youth, including children with disabilities, who drop out or are "pushed" out of traditional K-12 schools (or are at risk of doing so). The term *alternative education* refers to all educational programs that fall outside the traditional K-12 school system. The programs can be physically located in many different places, and sometimes the location is what makes the program "alternative" (e.g., in a juvenile justice center).

Alternative education program settings include (in order of distance from traditional classrooms in regular K-12 schools): resource rooms (separate room/teacher provides additional services like study skills, guidance, anger management, small group/individual instruction); a school-within-a-school; and, finally, pull-out programs, which can be run from a storefront, community center or former school and can include schools/programs within the juvenile justice system (detention, corrections, etc.) or a homeless services system (emergency and transitional shelters). These programs may be administered by any one of a variety of organizations including community-based organizations (CBOs), school districts, adult education divisions, state departments of juvenile justice, charter schools and, in the case of Job Corps, contractors to the U.S. Department of Labor.

The National Governors Association's Center for Best Practices (2001) notes that existing alternative education programs vary by type and quality. Most offer high school or General Educational Development (GED) diplomas. However, they can differ from traditional schools by having flexible hours and schedules, as well as open admission and exit policies and instruction tailored to the individual needs of the student, often with connections to employment. Alternative schools serve the dual purpose of reinforcing the message that students are accountable for their offenses and removing disruptive students from the mainstream.

Nonsecure Residential Programs

Residential programs are divided into five major categories.

 The five major categories of residential programs are shelters, group homes, foster homes, foster group homes and other types of nonsecure facilities.

Shelters

A **shelter** is a nonsecure residential facility where juveniles may be temporarily assigned, often in place of detention or returning home, after they are taken into custody or after adjudication while they await more permanent placement. Shelters usually house status offenders and are not intended for treatment or punishment.

Group Homes

The **group home** is a **nonsecure facility** with a professional corrections staff that provides counseling, education, job training and family-style living. The staff is small because the residence generally holds a maximum of 12 to 15 youths. Group home living provides support and some structure in a basically nonrestric-tive setting, with the opportunity for a close but controlled interaction with the staff. The youths in the home attend school in the community and participate in community activities. The objective of the home is to facilitate reintegrating young offenders into society.

Group homes are used extensively in almost all states. Some are operated by private agencies under contract to the juvenile court. Others are operated directly by probation departments or some other governmental unit.

Some, called boarding homes, deserve special mention. Since these homes often accommodate as few as three or four youths, they can be found in an apartment or flat in an urban setting. They are sometimes called "Mom and Pop" operations because the adults serve as parent substitutes. The adults are usually paraprofessionals whose strengths are personal warmth and an ability to relate to young people.

Foster Homes

A **foster home** is intended to be family-like, as much as possible a substitute for a natural family setting. Small and nonsecure, foster homes are used at any of several stages in the juvenile justice process. In jurisdictions where a juvenile shelter is not available, foster homes may be used when law enforcement authorities take a juvenile into custody.

Foster care is used less for misbehaving and delinquent children than it is for children whose parents have neglected, abused or abandoned them. Social service agencies usually handle the placement in and funding of foster care programs. The police and courts coordinate their efforts through these agencies.

Foster Group Homes

A **foster group home** is a blend of group home and foster home. Foster group homes provide a real family concept and are run by single families, not professional staffs. They are nonsecure facilities usually acceptable to neighborhood environments that can give troubled youths a family-neighborhood type relationship. Foster group homes can be found in various parts of the United States.

Other Nonsecure Facilities

Correctional farms, ranches and camps for youths are usually located in rural areas. These facilities are alternatives to confinement or regimented programs. The programs with an outdoor or rural setting encourage self-development, provide opportunities for reform and secure classification and placement of juveniles according to their capabilities. Close contact with staff and residents instills good work habits.

The Dilemma of Community Programs

Court dispositions are often compromises among deterrence, incapacitation, retribution and rehabilitation. Community-based programs do not permit the freedom of dismissal or of suspended judgments, but neither do they isolate offenders from the community as institutions do. Community programs are sometimes perceived as being easy on youngsters and thus as not providing enough supervision to ensure deterrence, incapacitation and retribution. Nonetheless commitment to such programs represents a considerable degree of restriction and punishment when compared to dismissal, suspended judgment or informal processing out of the system at an early stage.

After this look at nonsecure facilities such as ranches, shelters and camps, focus now on the facilities that serve most youths who are not placed on probation or diverted from the system.

Detention Facilities

The nation's original training and industrial reform schools have survived to the present under new names—detention centers. They still function, however, under the same regimented format. Detention centers, unlike group homes and

© AP/Wide World Photos

Students at Texas Youth Commission's state school correctional facility in San Saba, Texas, play basketball behind the fences and razor wire that surround the facility. The San Saba unit, which specifically houses violent offenders, is one of thirteen TYC facilities in the state.

shelters, are secure, locked facilities. They hold juveniles prior to and following adjudication. (Detention was discussed from a law enforcement perspective in Chapter 8 and again as part of the court process in Chapter 10.)

In 1989 the National Juvenile Detention Association (NJDA) developed and ratified a comprehensive national definition of juvenile detention: "Juvenile detention is the temporary and secure custody of children, accused or adjudicated of conduct subject to the jurisdiction of the family/juvenile court, who require a physically restricting environment for their own or the community's protection while pending legal action."

 Formally only three purposes justify putting juveniles in a locked facility: (1) to secure their presence at court proceedings, (2) to hold those who cannot be sent home and (3) to prevent juveniles from harming themselves or others, or from disrupting juvenile court processes.

Two youths share a sparse cell in a detention center. Does it appear that rehabilitation is occurring here?

© Joel Gordon

The NJDA clearly states that juvenile detention is to be reserved for juveniles who are violent and/or who pose a serious threat to community safety. Even with such restrictions, detention centers throughout the country are overflowing. Juvenile victimization, however, may also occur in detention centers where the offender populations consist entirely of youths. In some areas a detention center is incorporated in a jail.

The National Advisory Commission on Corrections referred to the jailing of juveniles as a "disconcerting phenomenon." Because they are intended to be temporary holding facilities, jails and detention centers offer little or nothing in the way of correctional treatment.

Before adjudication juveniles may be detained for periods that range from a day to several weeks. This raises the question of whether detention is appropriate before a juvenile is adjudicated delinquent. One rationale for detention prior to adjudication is that it serves as an informal punishment, advocated by those who believe in "getting tough on juveniles."

Training Schools

Training schools exist in every state except Massachusetts, which abolished them in the 1970s. They vary greatly in size, staff, service programs, ages and types of residents. Some training schools resemble adult prisons, with the same distinguishing problems of gang-oriented activity, homosexual terrorism and victimization, which often lead to progressive difficulties or suicide.

Most legislation requires training schools to provide both safe custody and rehabilitative treatment. A 1983 federal court case, however, rejected the idea of a constitutional right to treatment and training: "We therefore agree . . . that, although rehabilitative training is no doubt desirable and sound as policy and perhaps of state law, plaintiffs have no constitutional right to rehabilitative training" (*Santana v. Collazo,* 1983).

Electronic Monitoring and Home Detention

Moon et al. (p.50) explain that electronic monitoring requires a juvenile to wear a bracelet that tells the probation officer where the juvenile is. In their study, 49.2 percent of the respondents fully supported electronic monitoring; 24.3 percent moderately supported it. Ten percent did not support it.

Electronic monitoring (EM) has been tried with some success in several jurisdictions. In fact it is sometimes a key component in intensive probation and parole programs. Electronic monitoring can be used to impose curfew, home detention (more restrictive than curfew, the offender must be home except when at work or at treatment) or home incarceration (the offender must be at home at almost all times). The use of EM has grown considerably. Electronic monitoring is a supervision tool that can satisfy punishment, public safety and treatment objectives. It can provide cost-effective community supervision for offenders selected according to specific program criteria; promote public safety by providing surveillance; and increase the confidence of legislative, judicial and releasing authorities in intensive supervision probation or parole program designs as a viable sentencing option. Figure 11.2 illustrates the key decision points where EM can be used.

Electronic monitoring is frequently used in home incarceration, that is having juveniles stay in their homes rather than in prison. Such youths are allowed to leave their homes for specific reasons, such as meeting with their probation officer, attending a treatment program or going to the doctor or dentist. According to Moon et al (p. 50), only 22.7 percent of their respondents fully support home incarceration; 23.2 percent support it moderately; and 23 percent do not support it.

There are generally two types of home confinement: pretrial and postadjudication. Pretrial programs use home confinement as an alternative to detention to ensure that juveniles appear in court. Postadjudication programs use it as a sanction that is more severe than intensive supervision but less restrictive than incarceration.

Boot Camps

Juvenile boot camps are fundamentally the same as those for adults, and their use as an intermediate sanction is growing. More than half the states and the federal system currently operate at least one boot camp. Also known as **shock incarceration,** a **boot camp** stresses military discipline, physical fitness and strict obedience to orders, as well as educational and vocational training and drug treatment when appropriate. Most boot camps are designed for young, nonviolent, first-time offenders as a means

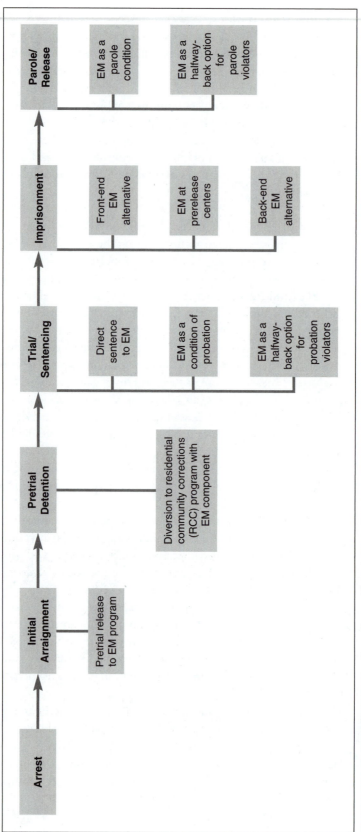

Figure 11.2
Key Decision Points Where Electronic Monitoring (EM) Is Being Used

Source: Bureau of Justice Assistance. *Electronic Monitoring in Intensive Probation and Parole Programs.* Washington, DC: February 1989, p.2.

Boot camp inmates display their utensils after eating. The Massachusetts "Boot Camp" Facility is an alternative to incarceration for nonviolent offenders.

of punishment and rehabilitation without long-term incarceration. Furthermore, offender consent is required for placement in shock incarceration.

Boot camps should be thought of as providing a foundation rather than offering a cure. Most offenders entering a boot camp lack basic life skills, are in poor physical condition, have quit school and have had frequent encounters with the justice system. Their self-esteem is low, and they are seen as losers. Young offenders' false sense of pride must be stripped away before positive changes can be made. This is one of the primary functions of the prison boot camp, just as it is in a military boot camp. The camps are intended to provide a foundation of discipline, responsibility and self-esteem to be built on. Several examples of successful boot camp operations have been noted nationwide. A relatively new site for boot camps is the jail.

Dale (2000, pp.91–92) describes the boot camp in Martin County, Florida, the Juvenile Offender Training Center (JOTC). This boot camp is a moderate risk facility with a maximum capacity of 90 juvenile offenders ages 14 to 18 who have committed nonviolent felonies. The JOTC is a three-phase, 24-hour live-in facility. JOTC's academy "builds character, self-esteem, mental discipline, coping skills, responsibility, accountability, educational goals and healthy living practices." The process begins in juvenile court when the judge sentences a juvenile felon to a secure facility. Phase One consists of a 4-month shock incarceration, during which an extensive training program begins based on a thorough needs assessment profile. At the same time, the drill instructors begin the process of tearing down and reframing negative attitudes to build self-esteem, confidence and a sense of self-responsibility. Each juvenile formulates 15 goals they need to accomplish to graduate to the next level.

Students graduating into phase two—the Academy—move from a secure individual environment to a group barracks with 30 peers. During this phase juveniles learn to respect and trust authority and build basic skills.

The third phase is Day Treatment. During this phase juveniles continue their education and counseling between 8:30 am and 3:00 pm and are then allowed to return home in the evening or hold a part-time job. It is probably this third phase which accounts for the success of the program. According to Dale: "February 2000 statistics reflect that the program has one of the lowest recidivism rates in Florida. Compared to similar Level 6, moderate risk boot camps and drill academies in the state, Martin County's recommitment rate was 11.1 percent versus 35.3 percent."

According to Stinchcomb and Terry (2001, p.221): "Because boot camps have emerged from such a wellspring of varied motivations and intentions, it is not surprising that their goals have been multiple and wide ranging, often resulting in inconsistency and ambiguity. Boot camp goals most often stressed are reducing recidivism, providing general education and drug education, protecting the public, saving money, reducing prison crowding, deterring future crime and developing good work skills (rehabilitation). Most successful programs also have an aftercare component. Boot camps for juvenile offenders have received mixed reviews on how well they achieve their intended goals.

Tyler et al. (2001) reviewed the literature on boot camps and report that the number of juvenile boot camps has continued to increase despite a steady stream of studies indicating that they do not reduce recidivism. They found, in fact, some evidence that these programs may have harmful effects, especially for younger juveniles or those with histories of abuse. They conclude: "At best, juvenile boot camps have some potential to be effective if they include proven strategies for inducing change. At worst, these programs are expensive sentencing options whose objective is punishment rather than rehabilitation."

Stinchcomb and Terry note: "Despite their public popularity, research thus far has cast doubt on the practical ability of such interventions [boot camps] to fulfill their expectations." Their study of a 90-day, jail-based shock incarceration program adds to the mounting empirical evidence suggesting that boot camps may not be producing the desired results. They (pp.240–241) conclude: "It takes more than 90 days of regimentation followed by a crisp salute, a firm handshake and heartfelt wishes for good luck to divert felons from future criminal involvement. . . . In the U.S. military itself, recruits are not expected to succeed on the basis of boot camp alone. Rather, their initial military experience is followed by further specialized training and career planning. Moreover, those who remain in military service are sequestered in a cloistered setting that provides everything from housing to hospitalization. Without such protective insulation, boot camp graduates are directly exposed to the detrimental environments from which they came. Armed only with the flimsy insulation of feeling better about themselves, cadets are ill equipped to face the realities of life back on the streets."

Stinchcomb and Terry (p.237) conclude: "The results of the jail-based program reported here indicate that the lure of the street corner prevailed in the competition for capturing the affiliations of boot camp graduates. Compared with others who received either jail time, probation or community control, former cadets were statistically no more likely to be arrested, although they were arrested more frequently."

Parent (2003) reports on a National Institute of Justice sponsored 10-year study of boot camps that concluded:

- Boot camps generally had positive effects on the attitudes, perceptions, behavior and skills of inmates during their confinement.
- With limited exceptions, these positive changes did not translate into reduced recidivism. He (p.1) notes that one factor responsible for the failure of the boot camps to reach goals related to recidivism was insufficient focus on offenders' reentry into the community.

Shelden et al. (2001, p.211) comment on the effect of boot camps on gang members: "The punitive model for dealing with gangs enjoys widespread support. However, it is evident that within this model there is not only little rehabilitation occurring but also no significant positive change. This is particularly true in one of the most recent fads within the correctional industry—boot camps. As some camp directors have themselves commented, 'The effectiveness of the boot camp lasts about as long as the haircut.'"

Nonetheless, boot camps are popular with taxpayers because of their "get tough" stance. Moon et al. report that 54.8 percent of respondents fully support boot camps and that 24.1 percent moderately support them. Only 6.6 percent did not support them.

Institutionalization

Juvenile offenders are placed in a variety of correctional institutions, often alongside adult offenders. Some of the most secure institutions are merely storage facilities for juvenile offenders. Here juvenile delinquents often simply "do their time," with release based on conditions of overcrowding and, amazingly, the inability of the system to rehabilitate the offender. Such nonconstructive time, when juveniles should be developing their values and planning their futures, can be devastating. Although lockups may be needed for a portion of the chronic, violent offenders, they serve as criminal training schools for other juveniles.

According to Sickmund (2002b, p.2), in 2000 the first Juvenile Residential Facility Census (JRFC) collected data from 3,690 facilities, 3,061 of which held a total of 110,284 offenders younger than 21 on the census date. Four in ten juvenile facilities were publicly operated and held 70 percent of juvenile offenders in custody, as shown in Table 11.3.

Juveniles in Public Institutions

The number of youths detained in or committed to both short-term and long-term public facilities is increasing. An investigation of the characteristics of inmates of public long-term juvenile institutions shows a pattern not unlike that of America's jails and prisons. The disadvantaged and the poor make up a large percentage of the population. In addition, disproportionate minority confinement (DMC) is common, as discussed later in the chapter.

Juveniles in Private Institutions

Whereas the private institutions of an earlier period were products of philanthropic or religious impulse, the newer ones result from a more economic, entrepreneurial drive. From the earliest days, private institutions attracted more youths

Table 11.3 Juvenile Public and Private Institutions Correctional Facilities in 2000

State	Juvenile facilities			Offenders younger than 21		
	All facilities	Public	Private	All facilities	Public	Private
U.S. Total*	3,061	1,203	1,848	110,284	77,662	32,464
Alabama	46	12	34	1,583	926	657
Alaska	19	5	14	339	261	78
Arizona	51	16	35	2,248	1,752	398
Arkansas	45	11	34	639	295	344
California	285	116	169	19,286	17,551	1,735
Colorado	73	12	61	2,054	1,112	940
Connecticut	26	5	21	1,360	900	460
Delaware	7	3	4	295	246	49
Dist. of Columbia	17	3	14	272	159	113
Florida	166	53	113	7,278	3,269	4,009
Georgia	50	29	21	3,270	2,593	677
Hawaii	7	3	4	122	107	15
Idaho	22	14	8	580	470	110
Illinois	46	26	20	3,402	3,074	328
Indiana	97	41	56	3,334	2,239	1,095
Iowa	76	16	60	1,166	395	771
Kansas	51	17	34	1,185	831	354
Kentucky	58	31	27	950	757	193
Louisiana	64	20	44	2,663	2,105	558
Maine	17	3	14	300	248	52
Maryland	43	11	32	1,492	690	802
Massachusetts	71	18	53	1,431	567	914
Michigan	108	42	66	3,896	1,782	2,114
Minnesota	121	22	99	1,922	986	936
Mississippi	20	19	1	787	785	2
Missouri	65	57	8	1,540	1,290	250
Montana	18	8	10	260	173	65
Nebraska	23	6	17	789	577	212
Nevada	15	10	5	1,176	750	426
New Hampshire	8	2	6	193	123	70
New Jersey	57	45	12	2,274	2,171	103
New Mexico	27	19	8	885	838	47
New York	210	59	151	5,081	2,883	2,198
North Carolina	67	27	40	1,555	1,237	318
North Dakota	13	4	9	203	105	98
Ohio	106	71	35	4,890	4,342	548
Oklahoma	52	14	38	1,034	535	479
Oregon	48	27	21	1,637	1,415	222
Pennsylvania	163	29	134	5,085	1,241	3,844
Rhode Island	11	1	10	360	211	149
South Carolina	42	16	26	1,592	1,072	520
South Dakota	22	9	13	646	365	265
Tennessee	63	28	35	1,824	1,041	783
Texas	138	77	61	8,354	6,475	1,879
Utah	51	17	34	1,135	453	682
Vermont	5	1	4	158	26	132
Virginia	74	62	12	2,868	2,616	252
Washington	42	31	11	2,064	1,938	126
West Virginia	27	6	21	381	241	140
Wisconsin	94	27	67	2,017	1,271	746
Wyoming	24	2	22	379	173	206

Note: State is the state where the facility is located. Offenders sent to out-of-state facilities are counted in the state where the facility is located, not the state where their offense occurred.

*U.S. total includes 158 offenders in 10 tribal facilities. These offenders were located in Arizona, Colorado, Montana, Oklahoma and South Dakota.

Source: Melissa Sickmund, *Juvenile Residential Facility Census, 2000: Selected Findings*. Washington, DC: Juvenile Offenders and Victims National Report Series Bulletin, December 2002, p.2. (NCJ 196595)

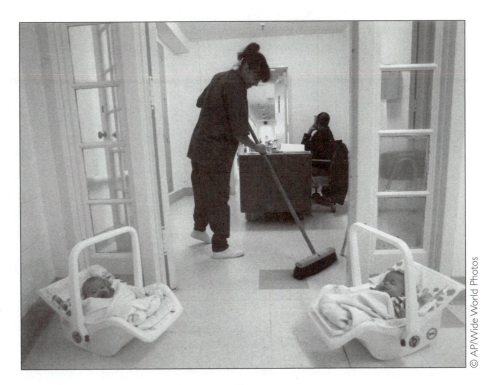

A 19-year-old inmate sweeps the nursery playroom floor at New York's maximum-security women's prison in Bedford Hills with her twin daughters nearby.

from affluent backgrounds than did public institutions. Many of the newer private institutions have chosen to emphasize their mental health and drug treatment programs. In this way they can capitalize on young people from families who have medical insurance or who can pay the costs of their children's confinement and treatment.

Private juvenile facilities include detention centers, shelters, reception centers, training schools, ranches, camps and halfway houses.

 Compared with public correctional institutions, private correctional institutions confine more whites, more girls, more status offenders and more dependent and neglected youths. The inmates are younger, and their stay is usually much longer.

Several reasons may account for this disparity. First the population of private institutions probably includes a larger proportion of dependent and neglected children who have few family resources. For these youths the institution becomes a surrogate home placement, which may last for several years. Second, because confinement is a profit-making activity, private institutions are reluctant to discharge youths as long as their families can pay the bills. As a final proposition, private institutions are not forced to discharge to make room for new admissions, as is often the case in the public institutions. Public institutions often consider bed space as a criterion for release.

Private institutions may offer greater diversity in programs and structures than public institutions. They also may have very strict rules. For example a private institution promoting itself as a placement option for girls describes in its brochure the following requirements:

1. No coffee, tea, magazines, TV, radios, cigarettes or newspapers will be brought in.

2. No dresses or skirts above the knee. No pants or pants suits allowed.

3. No eye shadow.

4. Only two letters are written out, and those only to relatives or guardians.

5. All bags and boxes will be inspected on entering and leaving.

6. All money sent will be kept by the Home and given as needed. No girl will be allowed to have money in her room.

7. If while at the Home any girl should run away, her bags, clothes, etc., will not be sent home—they will be the property of the Home.

8. If anyone brings pants, eye make-up or any of the items listed as not allowed, they will be taken and destroyed.

9. No telephone calls will be made except in an emergency or of great importance.

10. Phone calls are permitted once a month from parents or guardians.

11. During June, July and August, all phone calls will be received only between 9:30 A.M. and 4:00 P.M. Monday through Friday.

12. Calls will be limited to five minutes unless an emergency.

13. No visiting in the girl's room—all visiting must be in a reception room or one of the visiting rooms.

14. Any girl who leaves the dorm with parents must have permission from staff when she leaves and report in when returning.

15. The Home will not be responsible for the girls' actions when they are with parents.

16. All medical, dental and other personal bills will be mailed to the parent or guardian for payment.

Sickmund (2002a, p.1) reports that private facilities experienced greater growth in their population of juvenile offenders than did public facilities, as shown in Table 11.4.

Social Structure within Correctional Institutions

Correctional institutions—whether high or low security, locked or unlocked facilities, public or private, sexually integrated or segregated—often have an elaborate informal social organization and culture. The social organization includes a prestige hierarchy among inmates and a variety of inmate social roles. The inmate culture includes a complex of norms that indicate how inmates should relate to one another, to staff members and to the institutional regimen.

 The sociopolitical events in juvenile correctional institutions are the same as those found in adult institutions.

Table 11.4
Growth in Private Juvenile Correctional Facilities

Private facilities experienced greater growth in their population of juvenile offenders than did public facilities

Facility operation	Juvenile offenders in residential placement		Percent change 1997–99
	1997	1999	
All facilities	105,790	108,931	3
Public	76,335	77,158	1
Private	29,455	31,599	7
Tribal*	–	174	–

*Tribal facilities were not included in the CJRP in 1997.

Source: Melissa Sickmund. *Juvenile Offenders in Residential Placement:*
1997–1999. Washington, DC: Juvenile Offenders and Victims National Report
Series Fact Sheet #07, March 2002, p.1. (FS 200207)

A logbook listing of cases of in-house violence serious enough to be taken to court reveals another glimpse of how brutal the world of young inmates can be:

> 1/9—Danny attacks Jeffrey while he is watching TV, causing multiple fractures of the jaw which require a number of surgical procedures.
>
> 2/15—Jorge assaults Henry outside Evergreen Lodge with a sharpened flat metal bar with one end cut to be sharp. Henry had never had any problems with Jorge but became an enemy when he got in an argument with the head of Jorge's Southern Chicano Gang. The victim suffered lacerations on the skull and neck.
>
> 12/28—Stuart and Lee assault and injure Michael, an American Indian inmate, with an X-Acto knife, repeatedly slashing him and causing lacerations to his back, arms, thumbs, scalp and chest. Michael had allegedly made some racially derogatory remark.

Disproportionate Minority Confinement (DMC)

Walker et al. (2000, pp.280–281) report: "Generally, nonwhite youths (the majority of whom are African-American) are over-represented at every stage of decision making [of juveniles under correctional supervision]. They are also at greater risk of receiving harsher sanctions than white youths. . . . Specifically, 26 percent of nonwhite youths were detained, whereas 17 percent of whites were in custody. . . . Whites are more likely to receive the benevolent sanction of probation, and nonwhites are at greater risk of receiving the harsher sanction of confinement. . . . More than half of the juveniles in public facilities are minorities, with the largest category of these juveniles identified as African-Americans. . . . The private populations are predominately white. . . . Private facilities may not be an option for parents of African-American and Hispanic youths, given the over-representation of these groups under the poverty level."

Males and Macallair (2000) studied juvenile adult court transfers in California and found that minority youths are sentenced more harshly by adult courts for equivalent offenses, as shown in Table 11.5. Males and Macallair (p.10) report: "First, minority youths are 2.7 times more likely than white youths to be arrested for a violent felony (the crimes most likely to result in transfer to adult court). Second, once in the system, minority juvenile violent crime arrestees are 3.1 times more likely than white juvenile violent crime

Table 11.5
Minority Youth Are Sentenced More Harshly by Adult Courts for Equivalent Offenses than Are White Youth, California, 1996–98 (Arrests) and 1997–99 (Sentencings)

Percent of	White	Hispanic	Black	Asian/Other	3-Year Totals
Pop. 10–17	44.6%	35.4%	7.8%	12.2%	11,012,000
Arrests for					
Violent crime	23.0%	42.1%	26.8%	8.1%	62,726
Homicide	11.8	52.2	21.1	14.9	1,047
Rape	24.6	40.6	29.6	5.1	1,340
Robbery	14.9	40.9	36.7	7.5	23,654
Ag. assault	28.5	42.7	20.4	8.4	36,685
Property crime	30.1	40.6	18.5	10.8	123,778
Drug felonies	26.3	44.8	24.0	4.9	23,791
All felonies	27.9%	42.4%	20.6%	9.1%	244,492
Sentencings to CYA by Adult Court					
	8.9	51.5	28.6	11.0	639
Sentencings to CYA by Juvenile Court					
	15.5	50.1	26.4	8.1	5,938

Source: California Youth Authority, Research Division, data provision by request, January 2000. California Criminal Justice Statistic Center. *California Criminal Justice Profiles,* Los Angeles County, 1996, Table 22. Sacramento: California Department of Justice.

arrestees to be transferred to adult court and sentenced to confinement in a CYA [California Youth Authority] prison." They note: "While it is debatable whether the disproportionate minority youth arrests are a reflection of race-based violent crime differentials or racially biased policing and charging policies, the discriminatory treatment of minority youth arrestees accumulates within the justice system and accelerates measurably if the youth is transferred to adult court."

According to Mendel (2000, p.62): "The facts are unavoidable: at every stage of the juvenile justice process, minority youth—and African-Americans in particular—are treated more harshly than white youth." Research by Yamagata and Jones (2000) also found a disproportionate number of African-American youths throughout the juvenile justice process, as shown in Figure 11.3.

From previous chapters, underlying reasons for this over-representation of minority youths in public custody facilities should come to mind. Several are illustrated in Figure 11.4.

The percentage of minorities and males in juvenile institutions far exceeds their proportions in the general population.

Most studies of DMC have focused on African-American juveniles. However, as Kehoe (2001, p.6) cautions: "There are serious risk indicators, and they are sounding the alarm that unless juvenile justice systems act responsibly now, they will be seeing a 'second generation' of minority over-representation, but this time it will involve Hispanic youths. The juvenile justice system did not proactively watch the increasing trend of African-American youths in juvenile correctional facilities until it was too late. It cannot afford to make that mistake again."

Figure 11.3
**Minority Youths
Disparate Sentencing**

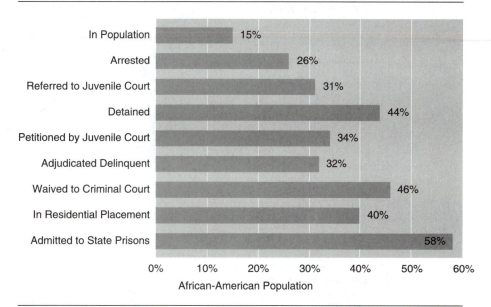

African-American Proportion of Youth, 1998

Category	African-American Population
In Population	15%
Arrested	26%
Referred to Juvenile Court	31%
Detained	44%
Petitioned by Juvenile Court	34%
Adjudicated Delinquent	32%
Waived to Criminal Court	46%
In Residential Placement	40%
Admitted to State Prisons	58%

African-American Population

Source: E. Poe-Yamagata and M.A. Jones: "And Justice for Some: Differential Treatment of Minority Youth in the Justice System." *Building Blocks for Youth*, 2000.

One project of an OJJDP and ACA partnership is a training curriculum on cultural differences for law enforcement and juvenile justice officials. The training curriculum is designed to reduce the over-representation of minority youths in the juvenile justice system. In addition, a study reported by Jamison (2002, p.1) shows that Portland, Oregon, leads the nation in successfully reducing racial disparity in juvenile detention. The Multnomah County Juvenile Detention Alternatives Initiative (JDAI) began in 1994 with 42 percent of minority youths referred to detention detained while 32 percent of white youths were detained. In 2000 an identical 22 percent of minority and white youths were detained. As use of detention became more equitable, the number of youths entering detention each year decreased as did juvenile crime rates.

Says Jamison (p.2): "To promote better outcomes for African-American, Hispanic and Asian and Native American youths, Multnomah County brought in a series of juvenile detention reforms, including reducing the time youths have to wait to have their cases processed; more objective risk assessment instruments; hiring a more diverse workforce; developing alternatives to detention programs in communities of color; racial and cultural sensitivity training for staff; and resources for monitoring over-representation in the juvenile justice system."

Prison Gangs

Prison gangs are quite different from the street gangs described in Chapter 6.

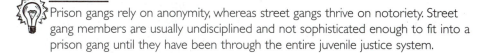

Prison gangs rely on anonymity, whereas street gangs thrive on notoriety. Street gang members are usually undisciplined and not sophisticated enough to fit into a prison gang until they have been through the entire juvenile justice system.

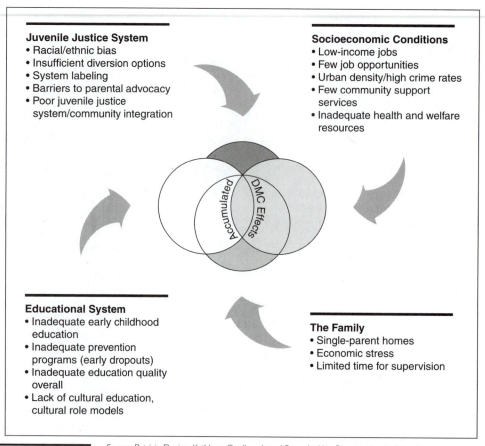

Juvenile Justice System
- Racial/ethnic bias
- Insufficient diversion options
- System labeling
- Barriers to parental advocacy
- Poor juvenile justice system/community integration

Socioeconomic Conditions
- Low-income jobs
- Few job opportunities
- Urban density/high crime rates
- Few community support services
- Inadequate health and welfare resources

Educational System
- Inadequate early childhood education
- Inadequate prevention programs (early dropouts)
- Inadequate education quality overall
- Lack of cultural education, cultural role models

The Family
- Single-parent homes
- Economic stress
- Limited time for supervision

Accumulated   DMC Effects

Figure 11.4
Underlying Factors That Contribute to Minority Overrepresentation

Source: Patricia Devine, Kathleen Coolbaugh and Susan Jenkins. *Disproportionate Minority Confinement: Lessons Learned from Five States.* OJJDP Juvenile Justice Bulletin, December 1998, p.8.

Table 11.6 outlines reported gang activity during 2000 in the Adobe Mountain Facility (Arizona). Youth-on-youth assaults were the most frequent "activity," followed by use of force and gang-related verbal offenses. Promoting gang affiliation through clothing occurred infrequently, but gang affiliation was promoted through gang signs, tattoos, and gang drawing and writing.

Conditions of Confinement

The frequently cited *Conditions of Confinement: Juvenile Detention and Corrections Facilities* (Parent, 1994) was a comprehensive, nationwide study of juvenile detention and corrections commissioned by the OJJDP in 1988. The study included all 984 public and private juvenile detention centers, reception centers, training schools and ranches, camps and farms in the United States. Excluded were youth halfway houses, shelters and group homes, police lockups, adult jails and prisons and psychiatric and drug treatment programs.

The study identified four areas with substantial deficiencies: living space, security, control of suicidal behavior and health care. Forty-seven percent of con-

Table 11.6
All Reported Gang Activity in the Adobe Mountain Facility for 2000

	January	February	March	April	May	June	July	August	September	October	November	December	Total
Number of incidents	440	334	331	223	112	113	116	110	99	111	88	112	2,219
Staff assaults	66	33	33	33	30	00	00	22	11	00	00	11	119
Youth/youth assaults	227	226	221	112	26	24	26	11	24	00	33	55	1,115
Gang-related verbal conflicts	44	88	55	44	00	22	11	00	33	77	55	11	441
Destruction state property/graffiti	00	22	22	00	22	00	22	11	00	22	00	22	113
Promoting gang affiliation w/clothing	00	00	00	00	30	11	00	22	00	00	00	00	13
Gang signs	00	00	44	11	33	22	00	11	22	11	22	10	116
Tattoos	00	11	11	33	30	23	33	00	00	00	00	11	112
Gang paraphernalia (drawing/writing)	11	00	00	22	22	11	22	55	00	11	22	33	119
Use of force	88	110	112	44	11	11	44	11	33	00	33	00	445
Other	11	00	00	00	44	33	22	66	22	00	00	22	220
Total	447	554	448	229	118	117	220	229	115	111	115	115	3,314

Source: *2000–2001 Prison and Street Gangs in Arizona.* Arizona Criminal Justice Commission Statistical Analysis Center Publication, May 2002, p.36.

fined juveniles lived in crowded facilities (p.7). The study also estimated that there were 18,000 incidents of suicidal behavior and 10 suicides. Further, juvenile and staff injury rates were higher in crowded facilities, and juvenile-on-juvenile violence rates were highest for youths housed in large dormitories.

According to the OJJDP study, three areas in which conditions of confinement appeared adequate were (1) food, clothing and hygiene, (2) recreation and (3) living accommodations.

Some of the conditions noted a decade ago still exist. According to Sickmund (2002b, p.3): "Nationwide, 39 percent of juvenile facilities reporting bed information held more residents than they had standard beds," as shown in Table 11.7.

Sickmund (p.4) reports: "Deaths of juveniles in custody are relatively rare. The death rate was lower for youths in custody than for youths in the general population." In 1994, 45 juveniles died while in custody, but in 2000, 30 youths died in custody. More than half of the deaths reported occurred outside the facility (17 of 30). Table 11.8 shows that accidents were the most commonly reported cause of death in custody in 2000.

Improving Conditions

In 1980 Congress enacted the Civil Rights of Institutionalized Persons Act (CRIPA) to help eradicate unlawful conditions of confinement for juveniles held in correctional facilities. Through CRIPA the Department of Justice is authorized to bring action against state or local governments for violating the civil rights of any person institutionalized in a publicly operated facility.

Table 11.7
Overcrowding in Juvenile Facilities

State	Facilities Reporting Bed Information			Percent of Facilities with More Residents Than Standard Beds		
	All Facilities	Public	Private	All Facilities	Public	Private
U.S. Total*	2,875	1,164	1,704	39%	37%	40%
Alabama	45	11	34	38	73	26
Alaska	15	4	11	27	25	27
Arizona	51	15	32	39	47	41
Arkansas	36	11	25	33	27	36
California	258	115	143	56	37	71
Colorado	70	12	57	31	67	25
Connecticut	23	5	18	30	20	33
Delaware	7	3	4	57	100	25
Dist. of Columbia	11	3	8	18	0	25
Florida	147	53	94	52	47	55
Georgia	50	29	21	42	59	19
Hawaii	7	3	4	43	33	50
Idaho	21	13	8	52	62	38
Illinois	42	25	17	19	16	24
Indiana	95	41	54	23	29	19
Iowa	74	16	58	43	13	52
Kansas	47	16	31	28	25	29
Kentucky	57	30	27	28	30	26
Louisiana	62	20	42	35	30	38
Maine	17	3	14	41	0	50
Maryland	43	11	32	30	36	28
Massachusetts	69	18	51	77	89	73
Michigan	104	39	65	34	21	42
Minnesota	114	22	92	29	45	25
Mississippi	14	13	1	29	23	100
Missouri	63	55	8	25%	27%	13%
Montana	19	8	10	26	25	20
Nebraska	21	6	15	33	50	27
Nevada	15	10	5	33	40	20
New Hampshire	8	2	6	50	50	50
New Jersey	54	45	9	35	38	22
New Mexico	27	19	8	33	37	25
New York	208	59	149	53	37	59
North Carolina	62	24	38	37	33	37
North Dakota	13	4	9	0	0	0
Ohio	106	71	35	35	38	29
Oklahoma	43	14	29	53	57	52
Oregon	44	24	20	30	25	35
Pennsylvania	149	28	121	33	36	32
Rhode Island	10	1	9	80	100	78
South Carolina	37	13	24	38	38	38
South Dakota	21	7	13	24	0	31
Tennessee	58	27	31	52	48	55
Texas	125	73	52	33	37	27
Utah	51	17	34	39	29	44
Vermont	5	1	4	20	0	25
Virginia	74	62	12	41	44	25
Washington	42	31	11	21	19	27
West Virginia	27	6	21	52	67	48
Wisconsin	91	24	67	14	13	15
Wyoming	23	2	21	17	0	19

Note: A single bed is counted as one standard bed, and a bunk bed is counted as two standard beds. Makeshift beds (e.g., cots, rollout beds, mattresses and sofas) are not counted as standard beds. Percents are based on facilities reporting bed information. State is the state where the facility is located. Offenders sent to out-of-state facilities are counted in the state where the facility is located, not the state where their offense occurred.

*U.S. total includes seven tribal facilities that reported bed information. These tribal facilities were located in Arizona, Colorado, Montana and South Dakota.

Source: Melissa Sickmund, Juvenile Residential Facility Census, 2000: Selected Findings. Washington, DC: Juvenile Offenders and Victims National Report Series Bulletin, December 2002, p.3. (NCJ 196595)

Table 11.8
Causes of Death of Juveniles in Correctional Custody in 2000

Cause of death	Total	Inside the facility			Outside the Facility		
		All	Public	Private	All	Public	Private
Total	30	13	9	4	17	5	12
Accident	9	2	0	2	7	2	5
Illness/natural	8	5	4	1	3	2	1
Suicide	7	6	5	1	1	0	1
Homicide by nonresident	4	0	0	0	4	1	3
Other	2	0	0	0	2	0	2

Accidents were also the leading cause of death for youth ages 13 to 17 in the general population, followed by homicide and suicide.

Note: Data are reported deaths of youth in custody from 10/1/1999 through 9/30/2000. Death information was reported by 94% of facilities that held 96% of all residents.

Source: Melissa Sickmund. *Juvenile Residential Facility Census, 2000: Selected Findings.* Washington, DC: Juvenile Offenders and Victims National Report Series Bulletin, December 2002, p.4. (NCJ 197595)

Another way to improve confinement conditions and to protect the rights of youths in custody is to establish **ombuds** programs. Ombuds can monitor conditions, investigate complaints, report findings, propose changes, advocate for improvements, and help expose and reduce deficiencies in juvenile detention and correctional facilities.

Perhaps most important is setting standards. In 1995, the OJJDP launched the Performance-based Standards (PbS) project, largely in response to its landmark *Conditions of Confinement* study (*OJJDP Research 2000 Report,* 2001).

 The performance-based standards goals for corrections cover security, order, safety, programming, justice and health/mental health.

- *Security:* To protect public safety and provide a safe environment for youths and staff. Security is essential for effective learning and treatment.

- *Order:* To establish clear expectations of behavior and an accompanying system of accountability for youths and staff that promotes mutual respect, self-discipline and order.

- *Safety:* To engage in management practices that promote the safety and well being of staff and youths.

- *Programming:* To provide meaningful opportunities for youths to improve their educational and vocational competence, address underlying behavioral problems and prepare for responsible lives in the community.

- *Justice:* To operate the facility in a manner that is consistent with principles of fairness and that provides ways to ensure and protect the legal rights of youths and their families.

- *Health/Mental Health:* To identify and effectively respond to youths' physical and mental health problems and related behavioral problems throughout the course of confinement by using professionally appropriate diagnostic, treatment and prevention methods.

OJJDP Research 2000 (p.13) reports: "Standards appear to be making a difference in the quality of service. Since beginning implementation of PbS, several facilities have reported measurable improvements, such as reduction of youth injuries and decline in staff turnover." This report (p.14) also notes: "Interest in and adoption of PbS are growing. In fall 2000, the 32 facilities originally engaged in PbS activities were joined by 25 new facilities." The PbS Web site is www.performance-standards.org.

Youthful Offender Programs

LeBlanc (2002, p.107) notes: "In order to develop a youthful offender program that meets an individual state's needs, it has to have the flexibility to change, as well as a very dedicated and professional staff."

 Most effective youthful offender programs include in-depth evaluation, screening and assessment; daily scheduling; point system discipline; positive behavioral support therapy; and education, including literacy, GED preparation and computer literacy.

In-Depth Evaluation, Screening and Assessment

Underwood and Falwell (2002, p.22) stress: "There is an urgent need for proper guidelines, testing and interview materials and acceptable procedures for youth's treatment upon entering the juvenile justice system. Often, adolescent offenders are quickly shuffled through court proceedings and into the juvenile justice system, where others before them are either awaiting proper screening and assessment or receiving improper treatment."

They also contend: "In addition to the need for guidelines and testing procedures, there is a lack of psychological tests for screening and assessing co-occurring mental health and substance abuse disorders." Underwood and Falwell (p.23) suggest: "Screening and assessment tests should measure emotional, behavioral, chemical and criminal characteristics linked to problems in an individual's or family's overall functioning."

Daily Scheduling

LeBlanc (p.108) describes the daily schedule used at the Dixon Correctional Institute in Jackson, Louisiana:

5:00 A.M.	Wake up
5:45	Inspection
6:00	Breakfast and the morning news
7:00	Work, therapy or school
10:30	Lunch
11:30	Major count
12:00 P.M.	Work, therapy or school
3:00	Dress-out for physical training

3:30	Physical training
4:30	Major count
4:45	Dinner
6:00 to 8:00	Structured activities such as guest speakers, letter writing, study hall and individual recreation (television and recreation room)
10:30	Lights out

Point System Discipline

Many youthful offender programs use a point system of rewards and consequences operating on four levels and in four areas: security, school, work and therapy. LeBlanc (p.110) explains: "A point average of 85–89 for Level 2, 90–94 for Level 3 or 95–100 for Level 4 must be maintained to remain at each level and to proceed to the next. Youthful offenders must maintain these scores for the first three levels for at least two months and for a minimum of six months once they reach Level 4. Certificates are presented at a special ceremony for successful completion of each level."

Positive Behavioral Support Therapy

Addressing the Needs of Youths (p.78) explains that positive behavioral support is a general term referring to applying behavior analysis to achieve socially important behavior changes. They say: "Positive behavioral interventions and support (PBIS), which are often based on functional behavioral assessments (FBA), are long-term problem-solving strategies designed to reduce inappropriate behavior, teach more appropriate behavior and provide supports necessary for successful outcomes."

According to the U.S. Department of Education (2000), PBIS emerged 12 years ago as an alternative to traditional behavior approaches for students with severe disabilities who engaged in extreme forms of self-injury and aggression. Since then it has evolved into an approach used with a wide range of students, with and without disabilities.

Education

Burrell and Warboys (2000, p.9) contend: "Education may be the single most important service the juvenile justice system can offer young offenders in its efforts to rehabilitate them and equip them for success. School success alone may not stop delinquency, but without it, troubled youths have a much harder time."

A study by the National Council on Disability (*Addressing the Needs of Youths . . .,*) cautions: "Alternative education programs, detention and correction facilities and other juvenile justice programs are all legally mandated to provide individualized education programs (IEPs) to youths who need them."

"When it comes to the education of youths under the care of the juvenile justice system, you had better set your camera on panoramic if you want to get the full picture. In large measure, youths' placements (into either state-operated, locally operated or contracted programs) may determine who provides educational

Table 11.9
Characteristics of Successful Education Programs in Secure Facilities

- Administrators regard education as a vital part of the rehabilitation process.
- Programs help students develop competencies in basic reading, writing and math skills, along with thinking and decision-making skills and character development traits, such as responsibility and honesty.
- Student/teacher ratios reflect the needs of the students.
- Academic achievement is reinforced through incremental incentives.
- Teachers are competent, committed and trained in current research and teaching methods, rather than relying on old model drill and workbook exercises.
- Instruction involves multiple strategies appropriate to each learner's interests and needs.
- Youths are assessed for learning disabilities and provided with special education in full compliance with federal law.
- When appropriate parents, community organizations and volunteers are involved in the academic program.
- Opportunities exist for on-the-job training, work experience and mentorships.
- Partnerships are developed with potential employers.
- Students are scheduled for jobs and further education prior to re-entry into the community.

Source: *Abandoned in the Back Row: New Lessons in Education and Delinquency Prevention.* Washington, DC: Coalition for Juvenile Justice, 2001, pp. 30–31.

services, the level of funding for education and even if the academic credit earned while in the justice system is transferable" (Wolford, 2000b, p.128).

Wolford conducted a national survey using 20 states to determine who was responsible for education within the juvenile justice system. He (2000a, p.i) found that: "In many jurisdictions in the United States the choice of placement of a delinquent offender is a primary determinate of both the provider and level of education that is available to the youth. Although state level juvenile justice agencies were found to be the primary provider of educational services to youths in state operated programs, the public schools were responsible for educating the majority of the youths in the juvenile justice system." In all surveyed states the teachers were required to hold a teaching certificate. Table 11.9 outlines characteristics of successful education programs in secure facilities.

Drug Testing of Juvenile Detainees

The Arrestee Drug Abuse Monitoring (ADAM) program was fully implemented in 2000, replacing the NIJ's Drug Forecasting (DUF) program established in 1988. *Annual Report 2000: Arrestee Drug Abuse Monitoring* (2003, p.134) notes: "As with adult arrestees, drug use and related behavior among juvenile detainees are measured by means of a questionnaire and urinalysis. And as with adult arrestees, participation is both voluntary and anonymous."

The data revealed that marijuana was the most commonly used drug, with at least 41 percent of those tested showing positive for marijuana. These findings are consistent with the findings of the National Household Survey on Drug Abuse, which revealed marijuana as the drug of choice among young people. Cocaine (undistinguished between crack and powder) came in a distant second in 2000, except in San Diego, California, and Portland, Oregon.

Incarcerated Juvenile Females

"Girls are the fastest growing segment of the juvenile justice population, despite the overall drop in juvenile crime. Over the past two decades we have witnessed an exponential rise in the number of girls in detention facilities, jails and prisons" (*Justice by Gender,* 2001, p.1). Girls are more likely than boys to be detained for minor offenses such as running away from home. Communities need to look at alternatives to locking up chronic runaways, many with valid reasons not to return home.

LeMaster and Maniglia (2003, p.100) note: "Juvenile female offenders have unique needs and require differentiated programs and services from those offered to male juvenile offenders in the same system. *Justice by Gender* (p.22) also notes: "Of the limited programs that currently exist for girls, most are modeled after programs that serve males. Consequently, girls, and especially minority girls, increasingly are being placed in programs that fail to meet their unique developmental, physiological and emotional needs."

Mental Health and Adolescent Girls in the Justice System (2003, p.1) notes: "Females bring with them into the juvenile justice system complex health and mental health issues related to sexual behavior, substance abuse, trauma and violence. In many cases, involvement in the juvenile justice system exacerbates the difficulties they face as adolescent girls." This report (pp.1–2) lists the following treatment needs of girls in the juvenile justice system:

- Adolescent female offenders exhibit high rates of mental health problems. Girls have higher rates of depression than boys throughout adolescence and are more likely to attempt suicide.

- The substance-abuse treatment needs of females involved in the juvenile justice system are particularly acute.

- Adolescent girls who come into contact with the juvenile justice system report extraordinarily high levels of abuse and trauma.

- Adolescent female offenders face significant challenges with parenting and other interpersonal relationships.

This report (p.2) recommends: "Juvenile justice systems need to develop specific programs for girls that focus on building relationships and addressing victimization and improving self-esteem. Adolescent girls have multiple and unique programming needs, including health care, education, mental health treatment, mutual support and mentoring opportunities, prenatal care and parenting skills, substance abuse prevention and treatment, job training and family support-strengthening services." *Justice by Gender* (p.26) concludes: "As the number of girls in the justice system continues to climb, it is imperative that the organized bar, policymakers and others ensure that in our quest to provide better services and programs for girls we do not inadvertently cast the net wider. The vast majority of girls in the justice system can and should be diverted from formal juvenile court processing. The re-criminalization of status offenses . . . has had a particularly devastating impact on girls. We must, therefore, ensure that communities and courts support an array of gender-specific community-based services and alternatives for girls."

Juveniles Sentenced to Adult Institutions

Austin et al. (2000) studied selected prisons and jails to assess their handling of juveniles in their custody. They (p.x) report that approximately 14,500 juveniles are housed in adult facilities. The largest proportion, approximately 9,100 youths, are housed in local jails, and some 5,400 youths are housed in adult prisons. The vast majority of these youths are age 17 (79 percent) or age 16 (18 percent). Gaarder and Belknap (2002) studied girls in the adult criminal justice system and found, consistent with previous research on female offenders, the girls in this study reported experiencing much violence, victimization, racism, sexism and economic hardship.

"Compared with youth confined in juvenile institutions, youthful offenders housed in adult jails and prisons are eight times more likely to commit suicide, five times more likely to be sexually assaulted, twice as likely to be beaten by staff, and 50 percent more likely to be attacked with a weapon" (Mendel, p.41).

Many correctional agencies are trying to successfully integrate young offenders into their adult prison populations, but the obstacles can be hard to overcome. Bryant-Thompson et al. (2002, p.75) point out: "This population [youthful offenders] has its own characteristics, some of which were foreign to adult corrections. In addition, these offenders are immature, impulsive, unskilled and undereducated. They did not have a real grasp on the meaning of time and lacked the ability to understand that there were consequences for their behavior. Although these offenders are adjudicated as adults, they are still adolescents."

Austin et al. (p.xi) recommend developing specialized programs responsive to the developmental needs of youthful offenders, including educational and vocational programs, sex offender and violent offender programs and substance-abuse programs that take into account the roles these issues play in adolescent development. They also recommend expanding the array of nonviolent incident management techniques effective in de-escalating volatile incidents involving youthful offenders.

Shomaker and Gornik (2002) describe a National Institute of Corrections (NIC) training program called *Youthful Offenders in Adult Corrections: A Systemic Approach Using Effective Interventions.* The program is based on three primary principles that have emerged from research: risk, need and responsivity. They (p.123) say: "The **risk principle** embodies the assumption that criminal behavior can be predicted for individual offenders on the basis of certain factors. Some factors, such as criminal history, are static and unchangeable. Others, such as substance abuse, anti-social attitudes and anti-social associates, are dynamic and changeable. With proper assessment of these factors, researchers and practitioners have demonstrated that it is possible to classify offenders according to their relative likelihood of committing new offenses with as much as 80 percent accuracy."

They also explain the **criminogenic need principle:** "Most offenders have myriad needs. However, certain needs are directly linked to crime. Criminogenic needs constitute dynamic risk factors or attributes that, when changed, influence the probability of recidivism. Non-criminogenic needs also may be dynamic and changeable, but they are not directly associated with new offense behavior."

Finally, according to Shomaker and Gornik: "The **responsivity principle** refers to the delivery of treatment programs in a manner that is consistent with the ability and learning style of an offender."

 In the National Institute of Corrections (NIC) training program, applying the risk principle helps identify who should receive treatment, the criminogenic need principle focuses on what should be treated, and the responsivity principle underscores the importance of how treatment should be delivered.

A critical shortage of detention space for violent juvenile offenders has led to fervent debate between those who support and those who oppose housing juveniles in adult facilities. Advocates of juveniles in adult facilities include U.S. Congressman Lamar Smith (R-Texas) (2003, p.20): "I strongly believe that we can no longer tolerate young people who commit violent crimes simply because of their age. Young people have the ability to decide between right and wrong, as the vast majority do every day. But those youths who choose to prey on other juveniles, senior citizens, merchants or homeowners will be held responsible. If that choice results in confinement in an adult prison system, perhaps youths who have a propensity to commit violent crimes will think twice before acting."

On the opposite side of the debate is Shay Bilchik, president and CEO of the Child Welfare League of America (2003, p.21): " This country's laws recognize that juveniles are too young to drink alcohol, vote, engage in legal contracts and enter into marriage, all because they are still developing mentally and emotionally. Legislators created the juvenile justice system based on the belief that youths have much to learn, with the hope that early interventions might alter the path that youths pursue. . . . Too many communities are failing to determine which offenders are beyond the reach of the juvenile justice system and failing to provide programs to hold those youths accountable in a timely manner, for the duration and intensity needed. As we increasingly transfer juveniles blindly, we are failing both our youths and our communities."

Schiraldi (2000, p.122) provides some statistics to add to the debate: "Youths tried as adults were rearrested more quickly, more frequently and for more serious offenses than youths with similar offense backgrounds who were retained in the juvenile justice systems. The states that try more youths as adults than any other—New York and Florida—continue to have the highest and second highest rates of youth violence in the country, respectively. Apparently, if a teenager is locked up with an adult offender, he or she gets more than just a cell mate. The teen gets a role model." He concludes: "It is only by intervening now and helping to develop mature, responsible, caring, empathetic children, that we can assure a safer society. What we sow today, we will reap in the future."

The Impact of Incarceration

Despite the diverse ideologies and strategies pursued by correctional institutions, to a great extent they all generate an underlife that includes an informal social organization and an inmate code. While they are confined, youths are immersed in a culture that defines the institution, its staff and many of its programs in negative terms. This perspective does not lend itself to seeing the institution as benefiting the "best interests" of the youths.

Confinement that subjects inmates to assaults and threats of violence is considered cruel and unusual punishment by some states. **Cruel and unusual punishment** is physical punishment or punishment far in excess of that given to a person under similar circumstances and, therefore, banned by the Eighth Amendment. Juveniles who are victims of assaults by other inmates may sue for violation of their right to be reasonably protected from violence in the facility.

Further if juveniles are kept in isolation (segregation) to protect them from assault, they may nevertheless suffer such sensory deprivation and psychological damage as to violate their constitutional rights. Confinement often leads to the ultimate self-destruction—suicide.

The impact of incarceration on juveniles often conflicts with the purpose of the juvenile justice system, which was created to remove children from the punitive forces of the criminal justice system. Exposing juveniles to coercive institutional conditions may jeopardize their emotional and physical well being.

Recall that one provision of the JJDP Act was that status offenders and nonoffenders (youths who are abused or neglected) should be removed from juvenile detention and correctional facilities. It further mandated that when youths were detained in the same facilities as adults they were to be completely segregated.

Parole

Parole is a planned, supervised early release from institutionalization that is authorized by the correctional facility. Parole is unlike probation in authority and concept. Probation can be granted only by the juvenile court subject to the court's stipulations. It provides the individual with freedom and continuity within the community. Parole is a release from confinement issued by the correctional facility or a board upon a recommendation by the correctional facility. Each state has its own procedures for parole, as do federal corrections.

In Minnesota the Department of Corrections parole agents supervise juveniles who have been sentenced to a correctional facility. The release of a juvenile from a correctional institution is the responsibility of a juvenile hearing officer. The juvenile hearing officer uses a scale that incorporates the severity of the offense and the delinquent's history.

After returning to the community, the youth is supervised by a parole officer or by a probation officer given that responsibility. The youth is required to abide by a set of rules, which, if violated, can return the youngster to a locked or secure facility. The conditions under which a typical juvenile parole agreement is granted include obeying all federal, state and local laws and ordinances; obtaining approval before purchasing or using any motor vehicle, borrowing money, going into debt, doing any credit or installment buying, changing residence, changing employment, changing vocational or school programs or getting married; obtaining permission before leaving the state for any reason; keeping in close contact with the supervising agent; not possessing or using narcotics or other drugs except those prescribed by a physician; and not purchasing or otherwise obtaining any type of firearm or dangerous weapon.

The parole officer makes regular contacts and visits to the youth's residence, school or place of employment. One objective is to involve the family, school and community in helping the youth to rehabilitate and integrate back into the community. This is also the goal of probation officers.

Aftercare

Aftercare is the supervision of youths for a limited time after they are released from a correctional facility but while they are still under the control of the facility or the juvenile court.

 Aftercare is often the weakest element in the juvenile justice process.

Many juveniles being released from confinement and requiring aftercare come from dysfunctional or abusive homes and must be provided with alternative living arrangements. The types of aftercare that can help youths to transition back into the community include home visits prior to release, a continuation of the treatment program and services within the community, identification of community support systems, availability of 24-hour supervision, and a gradual phasing-out of services and supervision based on the youth's response, not on a predetermined schedule.

Unfortunately, in many jurisdictions, aftercare is an afterthought. Byrnes et al. (2002) report on a study commissioned by the California State Senate and conducted by the Center on Juvenile and Criminal Justice. The major conclusion of the report is that aftercare services for youths discharged from the California Youth Authority are inadequate or non-existent and the situation is expected to worsen with recent budget cuts.

This landmark report examines the current barriers to effective aftercare services for youths discharged from the California Youth Authority. According to Byrnes et al. (p.iii): "It costs society more than $1.7 million for each youth that drops out of school to become involved in a life of crime and drug abuse." They note: "Although each individual faces unique barriers, common challenges face all youthful offenders re-entering their communities, many of whom are 21 and no longer eligible for many services. The following barriers to successful re-entry have been identified by researchers and were repeatedly cited in interviews with parole agents, service providers, researchers and former wards:

- Lack of educational options
- Lack of housing options
- Limited skills and education. In 2001, only 11.5 percent of CYA students passed the California High School Exit Exam.
- Gang affiliations and attendant racial tensions
- Institutional identity. Institutional policies, constant structure and external discipline do not prepare wards for independent living.
- Substance abuse problems for more than 65 percent of wards

- Mental health problems for an estimated 45 percent of male wards and 65 percent of female wards
- Lack of community support and role models
- Legislative barriers that limit access to education, cash assistance and public housing."

Mendel (p.57) asserts: "Of all the weakness in the arsenal of local juvenile justice systems nationwide, perhaps the most self-defeating is the lack of support and supervision for youths returning home from juvenile correctional institutions." Byrnes et al. (p.14) note: "Given the staggering cost of failure, it is hard to imagine any justifiable argument against providing education and services to this population."

 The school is a crucial institution in aftercare for most offenders.

As Stephens and Arnette (2000, p.1) note: "The successful reintroduction of juvenile offenders from correctional facilities into the communities in which they live is fraught with challenges. It is, however, an essential process in which schools play a key role in ensuring the offender's chances for success and the classroom's status as a safe environment of learning. In fact, the transition that a juvenile offender makes from secure confinement to school will likely shape the youth's transition to the community. Schools need to provide a coordination and support structure for promoting the success of young people who have had contact with the juvenile justice system."

Stephens and Arnette (p.15) conclude: "Youths re-entering public school systems from custodial settings frequently are alienated from the formal education process. Without help, they may drop out of school or be expelled for exhibiting inappropriate behaviors. These high-risk youths cannot be expected to succeed in a vacuum. Young people, particularly troubled young people, need structure, supervision and support." Table 11.10 describes promising transition practices for youths in custody.

Examples of Effective Aftercare

Wraparound Milwaukee is frequently cited as an exemplary aftercare program. The program has been described as a best practice by the OJJDP for working with youths with serious mental health needs in the juvenile justice system (Milwaukee County Mental Health Division, 2001). Wraparound Milwaukee began as a successful pilot for returning youths in residential treatment centers to the community, and it has developed into a Medicaid managed care program. In 2001 Wraparound had contracts with eight lead agencies to provide care coordination services and a network of 230 agencies offering 80 different services. At the heart of this provider network are 80 care coordinators who work with small caseloads (typically eight families) arranging services from a variety of agencies.

Kamradt (2000) reports that since its inception, the use of residential treatment has decreased 60 percent from an average daily census of 364 youths in treatment to fewer than 140. Inpatient psychiatric hospitalization has dropped by 80 percent. In addition, data collected one year before enrollment and one year

Table 11.10
Best and Promising Transition Practices for Youths in Custody

- Staff awareness of and familiarity with all county, state, local and private programs that receive and/or send youths to/from jail, detention centers or long-term correctional facilities.

- To the extent possible, individualized pre-placement planning prior to the transfer of youths from jails, detention centers to the community or long-term correctional facilities.

- Immediate transfer of youth's educational records from public and private educational programs to detention centers or other programs to detention or long-term correctional facilities.

- In short-term detention centers, an extensive diagnostic system for the educational, vocational and social, emotional and behavioral assessment of youths.

- In long-term correctional facilities, a range of specific educational programs (e.g., vocational and job related skills, social skills, independent living skills, and law-related education); support services (e.g., work experience and placement, alcohol and drug abuse counseling, anger management, vocational counseling, health education and training for parenthood); and external resources (e.g., speakers, tutors, mentors, vocational trainers and counselors, drug abuse counselors, employers and volunteers).

- Access to a resource center, which contains a variety of materials related to transition and support.

- Special funds earmarked for transition and support services.

- Regular interagency meetings, cooperative in-service training activities and crossover correctional and community school visits to ensure awareness of youths and agency transition needs.

- A process for the immediate identification, evaluation and placement of youths with disabilities.

- Individualized education program developed for each student with disabilities.

- Individual transition plan developed for all students, which includes the student's educational and vocational interests, abilities and preferences.

- A transition planning team formed immediately upon student entry into a long-term correctional facility to design and implement the individual transition plan.

- Community-based transition system for maintaining student placement and communication after release from a long-term correctional facility.

- Immediate transfer of youth's educational records from detention centers and long-term correctional facilities to community schools or other programs.

- Coordination with probation or parole to ensure a continuum of services and care is provided in the community.

- Coordination between educational program and justice system personnel to ensure that they advocate for youths with disabilities, cultivate family involvement, maintain communications with other agencies and place students in supportive classroom settings.

- A system for periodic evaluations of the transition program and all its components.

Source: National Center on Education, Disability and Juvenile Justice, 2002, pp.179–180.

after enrollment shows that Wraparound youths had lower recidivism rates for a variety of offenses. Further, Wraparound is cost-effective. The average monthly cost per enrolled youth in Wraparound is $4,350, whereas care for a child in residential treatment or a juvenile facility would have cost more than $7,000 (Milwaukee County Mental Health Division).

Another exemplary aftercare program is the Pathfinder Project, a transitional educational placement for troubled youths in Arizona. After seven years of intensive reform efforts, Arizona established a research-based and accredited alternative school emphasizing performance-based accountability. As Stephens and Arnette (p.9) note: "In the Pathfinder model, the purpose of Success School is to recognize and serve system-involved youths who have little or no hope for the future and who do not believe they can achieve personal success within the traditional educational system." A key component of the Pathfinder model is transition to a mainstream school environment.

Summary

The four types of interventions in a modern comprehensive graduated sanctions system are (1) immediate sanctions, (2) intermediate sanctions, (3) secure confinement and (4) aftercare/re-entry. Although the U.S. Supreme Court has never definitively ruled on whether there is a constitutionally based right to treatment, the state does violate the individual's constitutional rights if it fails to confine and provide treatment in the least restrictive setting possible. What this treatment consists of is a subject of controversy. The conservative philosophy of juvenile justice is to "get tough on juveniles"—to punish and imprison them. The liberal philosophy of juvenile justice stresses treatment and rehabilitation, including community-based programs.

John Augustus was the first probation officer, and today probation is the most common disposition of the juvenile court. Supervision is the essence of probation, and the formal goal of probation is to improve the delinquent's behavior—in short, rehabilitation. Other common goals of probation are (1) to protect the community from delinquency, (2) to impose accountability for offenses committed and (3) to equip juvenile offenders with the abilities they need to live productively and responsibly in the community. The probation officer has traditionally been responsible for two key functions: (1) personally counseling youths who are on probation and (2) serving as a link to other community services. Excessive caseloads are probably the single greatest pressure on probation officers.

Isolating offenders from their normal social environments may encourage the development of a delinquent orientation and, thus, further delinquent behavior. Community-based corrections, therefore, should be considered seriously for juvenile offenders.

Nonresidential corrections programs include community supervision, family crisis counseling, proctor programs and service-oriented programs, including recreational programs, counseling, alternative schools, employment training programs and homemaking and financial planning classes.

The five major categories of residential programs are shelters, group homes, foster homes, foster group homes and other types of nonsecure facilities. The National Advisory Committee for Juvenile Justice and Delinquency Prevention recommended foster homes for neglected juveniles and those charged with status offenses. Three common forms of intermediate sanctions are intensive supervision, electronic monitoring and boot camps.

Formally only three purposes justify putting juveniles in a locked facility: (1) to secure their presence at court proceedings, (2) to hold those who cannot be sent home and (3) to prevent juveniles from harming themselves or others, or from disrupting juvenile court processes. Compared with public correctional institutions, private correctional institutions confine more whites, more girls, more status offenders and more dependent and neglected youths. The inmates are younger, and their stays are usually much longer.

The sociopolitical events that occur in correctional institutions for youths are the same as those found in adult institutions. The percentages of minorities and males in juvenile institutions far exceed their proportions in the general population. Prison gangs are better disciplined, more calculating and more sophisticated than street gangs. They also rely on anonymity.

The performance-based standards goals for corrections cover security, order, safety, programming, justice and health/mental health. In the National Institute of Corrections (NIC) training program, applying the risk principle helps identify who should receive treatment, the criminogenic need principle focuses on what should be treated, and the responsivity principle underscores the importance of how treatment should be delivered. Aftercare is often the weakest element in the juvenile justice process. The school is a crucial institution in aftercare for most offenders.

Discussion Questions

1. How effective is probation in juvenile justice? What, if any, changes should be made in the juvenile probation process?
2. Should a juvenile have close supervision while on probation? If not, describe how you would supervise a youth who had committed a violent crime and was placed on probation or one who was a status offender.
3. Should parents, custodians or guardians of youths be actively involved in a youth's probation? Why or why not?
4. Do you favor a system of state or local probation? What does your state have?
5. Is community corrections worthwhile? Does it work? What would you do to improve it?
6. Is there a difference in attitude between a youth who has been confined and one who has been directed by programs in community corrections? What makes the difference?
7. Do community corrections give judges more options in sentencing youths? Is this an advantage or disadvantage?
8. Should violent offenders be subject to community corrections or directed to a secure facility? Why?
9. What are some potential alternatives to secure detention? What problems may be involved in expanding alternative programs?
10. Do you support a conservative or a liberal approach to treating juveniles? Why? Why do you think society is inclined to a "get tough on juveniles" attitude?

InfoTrac College Edition Assignments

- Use InfoTrac College Edition to help answer the Discussion Questions as appropriate.
- Use InfoTrac College Edition to read and outline one of the following articles to share with the class:
  - "Parents to Pay Bigger Chunk of Juvenile Incarceration Costs" by Jennifer Sullivan and Timothy O'Hara (key words: *juvenile incarceration*)
  - "Correlates of Suicide Risk in Juvenile Detainees and Adolescent Inpatients" by Charles A. Sanislow et al. (key words: *detention center*)
  - "Children's Services Pose Tough Challenges, Including Integration, Wraparound Aftercare"—no author (*aftercare*)
  - "Probation Foster Care as an Outcome for Children Exiting Child Welfare Foster Care" by Melissa Jonsen-Reid and Richard P. Barth (*juvenile probation*)

Internet Assignments

Complete one of the following assignments and be prepared to share your findings with the class:

- Go to www.ojjdp.ncjrs.org and find and outline one of the NCJ publications listed in the references for this chapter. (Of special interest might be *Second Chances* NCJ 181680)

- Research one of the following key words or phrases: *alternative education, juvenile boot camp, criminogenic need*

principle, cruel and unusual punishment, deterrence, foster group home, foster home, group home, intensive supervision, juvenile parole, juvenile probation officer, responsivity principle, risk principle, juvenile shock incarceration.

- Go to the Web site of any reference in this chapter giving an online address. Read and outline the material.

References

Addressing the Needs of Youths with Disabilities in the Juvenile Justice System: The Current Status of Evidence-Based Research. Washington, DC: National Council on Disability, May 2003. Online www.ncd.gov

Annual Report 2000: Arrestee Drug Abuse Monitoring. Washington, DC: National Institute of Justice, April 2003. (NCJ 193013)

Austin, James; Johnson, Kelly Dedel; and Gregoriou, Maria. *Juveniles in Adult Prisons and Jails: A National Assessment.* Washington, DC: Institute on Crime, Justice and Corrections at The George Washington University and the National Council on Crime and Delinquency Monograph, October 2000. (NCJ 182503)

Bilchik, Shay. "Sentencing Juveniles to Adult Facilities Fails Youths and Society." *Corrections Today,* April 2003, p.21.

Black, Meghan C. *Juvenile Delinquency Probation Caseload, 1989–1998.* Washington, DC: OJJDP Fact Sheet #34, September 2001. (FS 200134)

Borum, Randy. "Managing At-Risk Juvenile Offenders in the Community." *Journal of Contemporary Criminal Justice,* January 2003, pp.114–137.

Burrell, Sue and Warboys, Loren. *Special Education and the Juvenile Justice System.* Washington, DC: OJJDP Juvenile Justice Bulletin, July 2000. (NCJ 179359)

Bryant-Thompson, Kathy; Glymph, Deloris; and Sturgeon, Wm. "Bill." "Youthful Offenders: Today's Challenges, Tomorrow's Leaders?" *Corrections Today,* October 2002, pp.74–76.

Byrnes, Michele; Macallair, Daniel; and Shorter, Andrea D. *Aftercare as Afterthought: Re-Entry and the California Youth Authority.* San Francisco, CA: California State Senate Joint Committee on Prison and Construction Operations, August 2002. Online http://www.cjcj.org/pubs/aftercare/aftercarepr.html

Dale, Nancy. "Boot Camp: The Last Stop for Juvenile Offenders." *Law and Order,* December 2000, pp.91–94.

Etter, Gregg W. and Hammond, Judy. "Community Service Work as Part of Offender Rehabilitation." *Corrections Today,* December 2001, pp.114–125.

Evans, Donald G. "Enhancing Supervision by Engaging Families." *Corrections Today,* June 2002, pp.116–118.

Fass, Simon M. and Pi, Chung-Ron. "Getting Tough on Juvenile Crime: An Analysis of Costs and Benefits." *Journal of Research in Crime and Delinquency,* November 2002, pp.363–366.

Feldman, Lisa B. and Kubrin, Charis E. *Evaluation Findings: The Detention Diversion Advocacy Program, Philadelphia, Pennsylvania.* Washington, DC: Center on Juvenile and Criminal Justice, August 7, 2002.

Gaarder, Emily and Belknap, Joanne. "Tenuous Borders: Girls Transferred to Adult Court." *Criminology,* Vol. 40, No. 3, 2002, p.481.

Gondles, James A. "A Changing Society." *Corrections Today,* October 2002, p.6.

Griffin, Patrick and Torbet, Patricia. *Desktop Guide to Good Juvenile Probation Practice.* Washington, DC: National Center for Juvenile Justice, June 2002.

Haapanen, Rudy and Britton, Lee. "Drug Testing for Youthful Offenders on Parole: An Experimental Evaluation." *Criminology and Public Policy,* March 2002, pp.217–244.

Janison, Ross. *Reducing Disproportionate Minority Confinement: The Multnomah County Oregon Success Story and its Implications.* Press release. January 23, 2002. Online http://www.cjcj.org/pubs/Portland/portlandpr.html

Justice by Gender: The Lack of Appropriate Prevention, Diversion and Treatment Alternatives for Girls in the Juvenile System. A Report jointly issued by the American Bar Association and the National Bar Association, May 1, 2001.

Kamradt, Bruce. "Wraparound Milwaukee: Aiding Youths with Mental Health Needs." *Juvenile Justice,* August 2000, pp.14–23.

Kehoe, Charles J. "Juvenile Corrections in a Changing American Landscape." *Corrections Today,* December 2001, p.6.

LeBlanc, James M. "How to Successfully Develop a Youthful Offender Program." *Corrections Today,* October 2002, pp.107–111,140.

LeMaster, Leslie S. and Maniglia, Rebecca. "Meeting the Needs of Juvenile Female Offenders." *Corrections Today,* June 2003, pp.100–101.

Lipsey, M.; Wilson, D.; and Cothern, L. *Effective Interventions for Serious Juvenile Offenders.* Washington, DC: U.S. Department of Justice, Office of Justice Programs, National Institute of Justice, 2000.

Males, Mike and Macallair, Dan. *The Color of Justice: An Analysis of Juvenile Adult Court Transfers in California.* Los Angeles, CA: California Youth Authority, January 2000.

Matthews, Brent and Leffler, Ron. "Juvenile Corrections in Indiana: The Dawning of a New Era." *Corrections Today,* February 2000, pp.36–40.

Mendal, Richard A. *Less Hype More Help: Reducing Juvenile Crime: What Works — and What Doesn't.* Washington, DC: American Youth Policy Forum, 2000.

Mental Health and Adolescent Girls in the Justice System. Fact Sheet from the National Mental Health Association. Online http://www.nmha.org/children/justjuv/girlsjj.cfm

Milwaukee County Mental Health Division. *Wraparound Milwaukee 2001 Annual Report.* Milwaukee, WI: Milwaukee County Mental Health Division, Child and Adolescent Services Branch, 2001.

Moon, Melissa M.; Sundt, Jody L.; Cullen, Francis T.; and Wright, John Paul. "Is Child Saving Dead? Public Support for Juvenile Rehabilitation." *Crime & Delinquency,* January 2000, pp.38–60.

National Governors Association's Center for Best Practices. *Setting High Academic Standards in Alternative Education.* Washington, DC: National Governors Association's Center for Best Practices, 2001.

OJJDP Research 2000 Report. Washington, DC: Office of Juvenile Justice and Delinquency Prevention, May 2001.

Parent, Dale G. *Conditions of Confinement: Juvenile Detention and Corrections Facilities: Research Summary.* Washington, DC: Office of Juvenile Justice and Delinquency Prevention, February 1994.

Parent, Dale G. *Correctional Boot Camps: Lessons from a Decade of Research.* Washington, DC: National Institute of Justice, June 2003. (NCJ 197018)

Poe-Yamagata, E. and Jones, M.A. "And Justice for Some: Different Treatment of Minority Youths in the Justice System." *Building Blocks for Youth,* 2000.

Promising Sanctioning Programs in a Graduated System. Reno, NV: Juvenile Sanctioning Center, 2003.

Schiraldi, Vincent. "Lessons Can Be Learned." *Corrections Today,* June 2000, pp.122–123.

School-Based Probation: An Approach Worth Considering. Juvenile Sanctions Center, 2003. Online 222.ncjfcj.unr.edu/juvenile_sanctions_center.htm

Second Chances: Giving Kids a Chance to Make a Better Choice. Washington, DC: OJJDP Juvenile Justice Bulletin, May 2000. (NCJ 181680)

Shelden, Randall G.; Tracy, Sharon K.; and Brown, William B. *Youth Gangs in American Society,* 2nd ed. Belmont, CA: Wadsworth Publishing Company, 2001.

Shomaker, Nancy and Gornik, Mark. "Youthful Offenders in Adult Corrections: A Systemic Approach Using Effective Interventions." *Corrections Today,* October 2002, pp.112–123.

Sickmund, Melissa. *Juvenile Offenders in Residential Placement: 1997–1999.* Washington, DC: Juvenile Offenders and Victims National Report Series Fact Sheet #07, March 2002a. (FS 200207)

Sickmund, Melissa. *Juvenile Residential Facility Census, 2000: Selected Findings.* Washington, DC: Juvenile Offenders and Victims National Report Series Bulletin, December 2002b. (NCJ 196595)

Smith, Lamar. "Sentencing Youths to Adult Correctional Facilities Increases Public Safety." *Corrections Today,* April 2003, pp.20–21.

Spriggs, Vicki. "Identifying and Providing Services to Texas' Juvenile Offenders with Mental Health Needs." *Corrections Today,* February 2003, pp.64–66.

Stephens, Ronald D. and Arnette, June Lane. *From the Courthouse to the Schoolhouse: Making Successful Transitions.* Washington, DC: OJJDP Juvenile Justice Bulletin, February 2000. (NCJ 178900)

Stinchcomb, Jeanne B. and Terry, W. Clinton, III. "Predicting the Likelihood of Rearrest among Shock Incarceration Graduates: Moving beyond Another Nail in the Boot Camp Coffin." *Crime & Delinquency,* 2001, pp.221–242.

Torbet, Patricia, et al. *Evaluation of Pennsylvania's School-Based Probation Program.* Washington, DC: National Center for Juvenile Justice, September 2001.

Townsend, Cheryln K. "Cherle." "Juvenile Justice Practitioners Add Value to Communities." *Corrections Today,* February 2003, pp.40–43.

Tyler, Jerry; Darville, Ray; and Stalnaker, Kathi. "Juvenile Boot Camps: A Descriptive Analysis of Program Diversity and Effectiveness." *Social Science Journal,* Vol. 38, No. 3, 2001, p.445.

Underwood, Lee A. and Falwell, Sally H. "Screening and Assessing Co-Occurring Disorders." *Corrections Today,* June 2002, pp.22–23.

Walker, Samuel; Spohn, Cassia; and DeLone, Miriam. *The Color of Justice,* 2nd ed. Belmont, CA: Wadsworth Publishing Company, 2000.

Wolford, Bruce I. *Juvenile Justice Educating: "Who Is Educating the Youth?"* Richmond, KY: Council for Educators of At-Risk and Delinquent Youth (CEARDY), May 2000a.

Wolford, Bruce I. "Youth Education in the Juvenile Justice System." *Corrections Today,* August 2000b, pp.128–130.

Cases Cited

Santana v. Collazo, 714 F.2d 1172, 1177 (1st Cir. 1983).

Shelton v. Tucker, 364 U.S. 479, (1960).

The Juvenile Justice System's Reliance on the Broader Community

Violence and crime have grown to an intolerable level that detrimentally impacts the lives of all citizens. This condition will continue unless, and until, all segments of our society assume their responsibilities and respond in a coordinated fashion.

—IACP Summit on Violent Crime

Do You Know?

- How to define community?
- What the broken-window phenomenon refers to?
- What community policing is?
- How social work has influenced juvenile justice policy?
- What parts of the juvenile justice system social work is involved in?
- What the current emphasis in social services for youths is?
- What type of intervention appears to hold the greatest promise?
- What a key to building safe schools and communities is?
- What basic skills should be taught in schools in addition to reading, writing and mathematics?
- What the key elements of a successful career academy are?
- What benefits are derived from using volunteers in community-based corrections?
- Why jobs are important to youths?
- What three areas can be combined in a community's efforts to reduce and prevent delinquency and juvenile crime?

Can You Define?

broken-window phenomenon	community community justice	community policing integrated community

INTRODUCTION

The importance of family and schools in the development of youths was stressed in the second part of this book. The importance of the community in the form of community corrections was described in Chapter 11. Unfortunately for today's youths, many parents are too stressed, many schools are too impersonal and many communities are too disorganized to fill children's basic need to belong. When children are estranged from family, friends, school and productive work, the seeds of discouragement and alienation are sown. The result, all too often, is antisocial behavior. Alienated youths often become angry, antisocial offenders.

To prevent and control youth delinquency and violence, efforts must be built into the fabric of community life. This can happen only if the community accepts its share of responsibility for generating and perpetuating paths of socialization that lead to brief status or criminal offenses for some youths and careers in crime for others.

This chapter focuses on the broader community and the role it plays in the juvenile justice system. It begins with defining community and looking at perceptions of the community and how it can be a positive or negative influence on those growing up. Next the current trend toward a justice system that seeks to align itself more closely with the community is examined as a way to promote community justice. The most common evidence of this trend is the implementation of community policing, community prosecution, community courts and community corrections throughout the country.

This is followed by an in-depth look at the role of social workers and social services. Just as probation officers are officers of the court as well as practitioners in corrections, so social workers may be an integral part of every aspect of the juvenile justice system, while at the same time being a part of the broader community.

Following that discussion is a description of the federal agencies, programs and organizations that assist community efforts, with a focus on the Office of Juvenile Justice and Delinquency Prevention (OJJDP). Then partnerships in schools are considered, especially as they relate to dealing with the problems of violence. The chapter concludes with a discussion of how citizens, civic organizations and the community as a whole can contribute to solving the problems of crime and violence associated with youths and a look at three areas that can be combined in a community's efforts to reduce and prevent delinquency and juvenile crime.

Community Defined

Community can have several meanings. It can refer to a specific geographic area, such as a small town or a suburb. It can be thought of as a group of people with common interests, such as a community of worshippers in a congregation. In the legal sense, it refers to the area over which the police and courts have jurisdiction.

Miller and Hess (2002, p.55) note: "To many people it [community] conjures up images of their hometown. To others it may bring images of a specific block, a neighborhood or an idyllic small town where everyone knows everyone and they all get along. Community has also been defined as a group of people living in an area under the same government. In addition, community can refer

Youths from Detroit and the city's Grosse Pointe suburbs work together to paint a mural on the wall of a building near the dividing line between their communities. The Detroit side of the border—economically devastated, mostly African-American—contrasts sharply to the Grosse Pointe side, which is wealthy and mostly white.

to a social group or class having common interests. Community may even refer to society as a whole—the public." Klockars (1991, pp.247–248) suggests a sociological definition of community: "Sociologically, the concept of community implies a group of people with a common history, common beliefs and understandings, a sense of themselves as 'us' and outsiders as 'them' and often, but not always, a shared territory."

In this chapter **community** will be used in both the legal, geographic sense and the philosophical, sociological sense.

> Community is not only a geographic area over which local agencies within the juvenile justice system have jurisdiction; it also refers to a sense of integration, of shared values and a sense of "we-ness" of individuals, organizations and agencies.

In an **integrated community** people take ownership and pride in what is right as well as responsibility for what is wrong. They also share values and agree on what is acceptable and unacceptable behavior, and they expect conformity to those values. Without such integration, the justice system is greatly hindered.

Perceptions of Community

Children are very aware of their communities and how they feel about them. The positive outward appearance of the community is important to children and youths, as are the friendliness and caring of the people in the neighborhood. Unfortunately, not all communities generate such positive feelings. In a classic article, "Broken Windows," Wilson and Kelling (1982, p.31) describe how a run-down neighborhood can promote crime:

> Social psychologists and police officers tend to agree that if a window in a building is broken *and is left unrepaired,* all the rest of the windows will soon be broken. This is as true in nice neighborhoods as in run-down ones. Window-breaking does not necessarily occur on a large scale because some areas are inhabited by determined window-breakers whereas others are populated by window-lovers; rather, one unrepaired broken window is a signal that no one cares, and so breaking more windows costs nothing. (It has always been fun.)

 The **broken-window phenomenon** states that if it appears "no one cares," disorder and crime will thrive.

Many communities are facing challenges. Residents of different races, cultures and languages are coming into closer contact. Class divisions are widening, broken families and homelessness are on the rise, and anger is growing on the part of the disadvantaged. On the other hand, many communities are mobilizing to reduce or prevent delinquency and to promote positive community values. It is this sense of community values and the power of the community that has resulted in the awareness that the juvenile justice system cannot function alone, that it needs the support and assistance of the broader community.

Community Justice

Chapter 3 described the community's influence on youths' development. The community also plays a vital role in the juvenile justice system, helping to prevent crime and violence and rehabilitate youths involved in crime and violence. **Community justice** is about "creating new relationships both within the justice system and with stakeholders in the community such as residents, merchants, churches and schools, and testing new, aggressive approaches to public safety rather than merely responding to crime" (Feinblatt et al., 2001, p.1). Community justice has at its core partnerships and problem-solving, as evidenced by six central goals:

- Restoring the community
- Bridging the gap between communities and courts
- Knitting together a fractured justice system
- Helping offenders deal with problems that lead to crime
- Providing the courts with better information
- Building a courthouse that fosters these ambitions (Feinblatt et al.)

Community justice initiatives often develop because citizens are dissatisfied with the criminal justice system, viewing it as slow, formal and unable to cope with matters, especially low-level offenses that need rapid and informal attention. "If community justice is to be created, two things must happen: The justice system's relation to the community must be realigned, and community members must work to create civility" (*Community Justice in Rural America . . .*, 2001, pp.9–12).

Whether it is called a village, a neighborhood or a community, the trend is for the juvenile justice system to seek the support and assistance of the broader community. One way in which this is being done is through involvement in community policing.

Community Policing

 Community policing is a philosophy that embraces a proactive, problem-oriented approach to working with the community to make it safe.

Community policing takes many forms throughout the country. As noted by Miller and Hess (p.xix): "Community policing offers one avenue for making neighborhoods safer. Community policing is not a program or a series of programs. It is a philosophy, a belief that working together, the police and the community can accomplish what neither can accomplish alone. The *synergy* that results from community policing can be powerful. It is like the power of a finely tuned athletic team, with each member contributing to the total effort. Occasionally heroes may emerge, but victory depends on a team effort."

Wilson and Kelling (1989, p.49) describe the types of changes that occur in a police department that institutes community policing: "Community-oriented policing means changing the daily work of the police to include investigating problems as well as incidents. It means defining as a problem whatever a significant body of public opinion regards as a threat to community order. It means working with the good guys and not just against the bad guys." In other words community policing is proactive rather than reactive, and it is problem driven rather than incident driven.

Although community policing makes sense to many within the justice system, it is sometimes difficult for law enforcement administrators to make such a change. As noted by Wilson and Kelling (1989, p.49): "While the phrase 'community-oriented policing' comes easily to the lips of police administration, redefining the police mission is more difficult. To help the police become accustomed to fixing broken windows as well as arresting window breakers requires doing things that are very hard for many administrators to do."

Wilson and Kelling (1989, p.52) note that implementing community policing may also cause dissention within the ranks. Officers with opposing views of the nature of police work face off in what has been described as the conflict between the crime fighter function and the social service function: "In every department we visited, some of the incident-oriented officers spoke disparagingly of the problem-oriented officers as 'social workers,' and some of the latter responded by calling the former 'ghetto blasters.'" Yet another obstacle facing community policing, according to Wilson and Kelling (1989, p.52), is lack of interagency cooperation:

> The problem of interagency cooperation may, in the long run, be the most difficult of all. The police can bring problems to the attention of other city agencies, but the system is not always organized to respond. In his book

Neighborhood Services, John Mudd calls it the "rat problem": If a rat is found in an apartment, it is a housing inspection responsibility; if it runs into a restaurant, the health department has jurisdiction; if it goes outside and dies in an alley, public works takes over.

Kanable (2000, p.36) notes: "You can't truly solve problems long-term if everybody isn't involved. The police department shouldn't set the priorities—the community sets the priorities." She suggests that police departments should be more youth oriented. Children and teenagers are an important segment of the community often overlooked when implementing the community policing philosophy. Kanable notes: "I think where some police departments fall a little short is that the youths of today will be either the good citizen or the criminal element of tomorrow."

Community Prosecution

Some prosecutors are teaming up with citizens in the overall community justice movement. As with community policing, community prosecution is not a program but rather a process dedicated to generating flexible solutions and responses to the various needs and problems faced by individual neighborhoods. Swope (2000, p.11) suggests: "Community prosecution recognizes differences in neighborhoods and provides customized service." Swope (2001, p.11) has referred to community prosecution as the "missing link" and states: "The police are only the gatekeepers [to the justice system], and the law enforcement effort really has no teeth without the support of the prosecutor. . . . Community policing can never reach its full potential without the inclusion of the prosecutor as a full partner, joining the police and neighborhood residents."

Community prosecution is also supported by Boland (2001, p.38): "Because effective crime control is a joint effort, prosecutors need to ask other key actors, most importantly citizens and police, what they think they are getting from community prosecution. The best answers to these questions lie not in citywide random surveys, but in the police beats where the crime issue is defined in terms that are specific and concrete."

Community Courts

One alternative to the traditional courtroom is the community court. As Feinblatt et al. (p.81) state: "Community courts are neighborhood-based courts that use the power of the justice system to solve local problems. These courts seek to play an active role in the life of their neighborhoods, galvanizing local resources and creating new partnerships with community groups, government agencies and social service providers." According to Feinblatt et al. (p.7):

> To be effective a community court must address the needs of the court system's most important constituency: the people who live and work in neighborhoods affected by crime. To address these needs, a community court must ask a new set of questions. What can a court do to solve neighborhood problems? What can courts bring to the table beyond their coercive power and symbolic presence? And what roles can community residents, businesses and service providers play in improving justice?

Chapter 10 described several types of specialized community courts designed specifically for juveniles.

Community Corrections

Several instances of community corrections were described in Chapter 11. As Wrobleski and Hess (2003, pp.461–462) point out: "A community approach to corrections has three significant advantages: humanitarian, restorative and managerial. The humanitarian aspect is obvious because no one should be subjected to custodial control unnecessarily. Second, restorative measures should help offenders achieve positions in the community in which they do not violate the law. Third, the managerial goal of cost effectiveness can often be achieved because any shift from custodial control saves money."

Wrobleski and Hess (p.462) stress: "Community correctional programs cannot succeed without the understanding and cooperation of the police because those within these programs *will* come in contact with the police, and the nature of that contact will directly affect the offender's adjustment. The police can make affirmative contributions to community-based corrections programs. They know the resources available and the pitfalls to be avoided. In essence the police are an integral part of any successful corrections program, from using good judgment in making arrests to helping those on parole or probation to re-enter the community."

Because aftercare is so crucial to helping incarcerated individuals re-enter the community, individuals and organizations in the community must also be supportive.

The Role of Social Workers and Social Services

Social workers are involved in community supervision programs for troubled youths and their families, in juvenile court-sponsored, community-based diversion programs and in school-based counseling programs. These programs are designed to help youths in conflict with their families as well as youths in conflict with the law.

The public interest in preventing delinquency and controlling youths and the interest in youth crime and rehabilitating youthful offenders are topics constantly discussed in communities and state legislatures across the country. Referral programs range from diversionary actions to socially designed programs in the "best interest of the child" and the best interest of the public safety.

Referring youths to adjustment and corrective programs under the guise of treatment is an issue of growing concern due to the increased demands for public and private services and the limited available resources. As a result legislators, policy makers and juvenile justice professionals are taking a hard look at the social services available and how they are invested in youth referral programs. They also are asking whether better ways exist to serve youths and protect the public.

There is great interest in assessing and treating youths with emotional and behavioral problems. Many families experience child management problems at one time or another: incorrigibility, defiance, waywardness, temper tantrums, school disruptiveness, truancy and related problems. And many children experience neglect and abuse, which, as already discussed, are often the prelude to delinquency.

Treatment philosophies are regularly debated. Many think that juvenile courts are too lenient. They advocate a "get tough" attitude, emphasizing responsibility of actions and a system of accountability rather than rehabilitation and treatment, which are hallmarks of most existing state codes. Treatment is the focus of Chapter 14.

The public is also concerned about the inability of social services to properly investigate and treat cases of child physical and sexual abuse.

 Social workers have greatly influenced trends in juvenile justice policy in the areas of diversion, victim restitution, the decriminalization of status offenses and deinstitutionalization.

Social workers are among the few involved in the juvenile justice system who are willing to disregard the jargon of treatment, control or punishment. They work with both adjudicated and nonadjudicated juveniles to find the best ways to prevent recurrence of mischievous or antisocial behavior. By teaming up with law enforcement and the courts, social workers can operate in all areas of juvenile justice. As a result innovative programs and relationships have been developed, enhancing social work's role in the justice system and extending the reach of social justice, especially to minority and low-income youths.

 Social work functions in all aspects of the juvenile justice system.

Usually a combination of approaches is most effective. Social work can provide a range of services that may include, but by no means be limited to, direct counseling with the juvenile. The broader role of social work within the context of juvenile facilities may include advocacy and brokerage on behalf of juveniles in their relations with family members, social agencies, school officials and potential employers. Social work tries by a variety of means to ease juveniles' passage through the most difficult stage of life and to prevent institutionalized youths from becoming brutal, embittered adults.

Social work also addresses the needs of nondelinquent children and families. Since the passage of the Social Security Act in 1935, the federal government has supported many services for children and families, from programs commonly called "welfare" to foster care maintenance and a range of adoption services.

In 1961 Congress amended part of the Social Security Act to provide states with substantial federal reimbursement for the cost of providing foster care to poor children. State child welfare departments, in association with the court, assigned more and more children to foster care and group homes.

In 1975 parents and advocates pressed Congress to adopt the Education for All Handicapped Children Act, which grants all children the right to free and appropriate education in the least restrictive environment possible. This law discouraged removing handicapped children from public schools, and offered fiscal incentives to states in exchange for meeting federal standards.

In 1978 Congress passed the Indian Child Welfare Act, giving tribes greater control over the adoption and foster placement of their children and encouraging alternatives to placement by providing limited funds for services to Native American children and families.

After five years of testimony on foster care and adoption, in 1980 Congress passed the Adoption Assistance and Child Welfare Act, an important achievement for families at risk of extended or permanent separation. The act requires that reasonable efforts be made to bring children who have been taken from their families for more than 12 months back to the juvenile court. The court then reviews each case and makes a disposition for the best interests of the children and their families. Thus children are no longer placed in limbo with no further review. The purpose of the act is to assure that children and their families no longer suffer extended separation from each other without at least an annual review.

Current Emphasis

The federal emphasis on diverting status and minor offenders from the juvenile justice system stimulated the development of services for delinquent and troubled youths. This philosophy emphasized the importance of a wide range of activities and programs, commonly referred to as community-based services.

 The current emphasis in social services for youths is diversion to a wide range of community-based services and programs.

These services include residential treatment centers, youth service bureaus, group or foster homes, halfway houses and adolescent units in psychiatric hospitals. These facilities vary in such important considerations as the degree of security provided, whether they are residential or nonresidential, the extent and nature of treatment provided and size.

 Studies suggest that family therapy is more effective in dealing with the problems of youths than is traditional juvenile justice intervention.

Social workers often use behavioral and structural techniques in intrafamilial communication. This positive attention paid to the child is generally more effective than probation.

Federal Agencies and Programs to Assist Communities

Several federal agencies can provide resources to communities as they become involved in community justice. Perhaps the most comprehensive resource is the Office of Juvenile Justice and Delinquency Prevention (OJJDP). Other agencies include the Office of Justice Programs, the Department of Health and Human Services and the National Children's Advocacy Center.

The Office of Juvenile Justice and Delinquency Prevention (OJJDP)

A primary purpose of the OJJDP is to protect children from violence, abuse, neglect and other forms of victimization as mandated by the Juvenile Justice and Delinquency Prevention Act of 1974 and other legislation since that time. To carry out this mandate, OJJDP created the Child Protection Division (CPD) in

2000. As Cullen (2001, p.1) notes: "The Child Protection Division administers projects, programs and initiatives related to crimes against children and children's exposure to violence. It provides leadership and funding in the areas of prevention, intervention, treatment and enforcement."

Another OJJDP initiative is the National Center for Missing and Exploited Children (NCMEC). As Girouard (2001b, p.1) explains: "In partnership with the OJJDP, NCMEC continues to enhance and expand its ability to offer critical intervention and prevention services to families and support law enforcement agencies at the federal, state and local levels in cases involving missing or exploited children." According to Girouard (2001a, p.1): "The Missing and Exploited Children's Program helps locate and recover missing children and prevents the abduction, molestation, sexual exploitation and victimization of children. NCMEC operates a 24-hour toll-free telephone hotline for callers to report the location of missing children or obtain assistance when a child is missing."

Yet another OJJDP initiative is its program of research for tribal youths, described by Fung and Wyrick (2001, p.1): "Since 1999, OJJDP's Tribal Youth Program (TYP) has funded tribal programs, training and technical assistance, and research and evaluation projects to help improve juvenile justice systems and delinquency prevention efforts among federally recognized American Indian tribes."

The OJJDP also has numerous programs and grant opportunities for communities wanting to engage in community justice efforts. Two of the better known are *Blueprints for Violence Prevention* and *Building Blocks for Youths,* discussed in the next chapter. Their mentoring program, JUMP, was discussed in Chapter 7. Other efforts include the Targeted Community Action Planning (TCAP) Technical Assistance Program; the National Youth Network; the Safe Kids/Safe Streets, Safe Start and Safe Futures initiatives; the Internet Crimes against Children (ICAC) Task Force; and the Functional Family Therapy program.

Targeted Community Action Planning (TCAP) Technical Assistance Program

Since 1995 the OJJDP has supported local comprehensive strategic planning through a four-phase results-oriented process: (1) diagnostic awareness, (2) interviews of key community leaders, (3) a summit of key community leaders and (4) a targeted response. The "buy in" of key community leaders is a vital element of OJJDP's new approach. Stakeholders and leaders who have the resources must be committed to making the change.

The National Youth Network

The National Youth Network consists of diverse youth leaders from across the nation who are sponsored by youth serving organizations. The goal of the network is to recognize and build on the power and importance of youth leadership by uniting young people and adults, through communication and action, to enable youth organizations and nonaffiliated youths to have a positive, formidable impact in our communities and throughout our nation.

Safe Kids/Safe Streets, Safe Start and Safe Future Programs

Safe Kids/Safe Streets is a major community initiative begun in 1996 and intended to help break the cycle of abused or neglected children resorting to delinquent or violent behavior later in life. Each year five communities are awarded funds to improve their response to abused and neglected children and their families. Each community works to coordinate the management of abuse and neglect cases by improving the policies and practices of the criminal and juvenile justice, child welfare, family services and related systems.

The Safe Start initiative is a joint project of the OJJDP, DOJ and the Department of Health and Human Services. According to Kracke (2001, p.1), the purpose of this initiative is to prevent and reduce the impact of family and community violence on young children (primarily from birth to age 6) and their families. The goal of the Safe Start demonstration project is to expand existing partnerships among service providers in key areas such as early childhood education/development, health, mental health, child welfare, family support, substance abuse prevention/intervention, domestic violence/crisis intervention, law enforcement, courts and legal services. The project seeks to create a comprehensive service delivery system that will meet the needs of children and their families at any point of entry into the system.

The Safe Futures project is an OJJDP program that awards demonstration grants to six communities annually (four urban, one rural and one tribal government) to assist with existing efforts to reduce youth violence and delinquency.

Internet Crimes against Children (ICAC) Task Force

As Medaris and Girouard (2002, p.1) note: "Although apprehending sex offenders who use the Internet to facilitate their crimes presents significant challenges, the ICAC program can help state and local law enforcement agencies develop an effective response to online enticement and child pornography cases. Included in this response are community education, forensic, investigative and victim service components." Figure 12.1 depicts law enforcement agencies participating in the program as of September 2001.

From July 1998 to June 2001, 44,303 cybercrime tips were reported, with the majority involving child pornography, as shown in Figure 12.2. During the first two years of this program, participating agencies arrested more than 550 individuals for child sexual exploitation offenses; seized approximately 850 computers; served 627 search warrants and 1,338 subpoenas; conducted forensic examinations of more than 1,500 computers for task force investigations and other law enforcement agencies; provided training for more than 1,433 prosecutors and 12,500 law enforcement officers; and reached thousands of children, teenagers, parents, educators and other individuals through publications, presentations and public service announcements about safe Internet practices for young people.

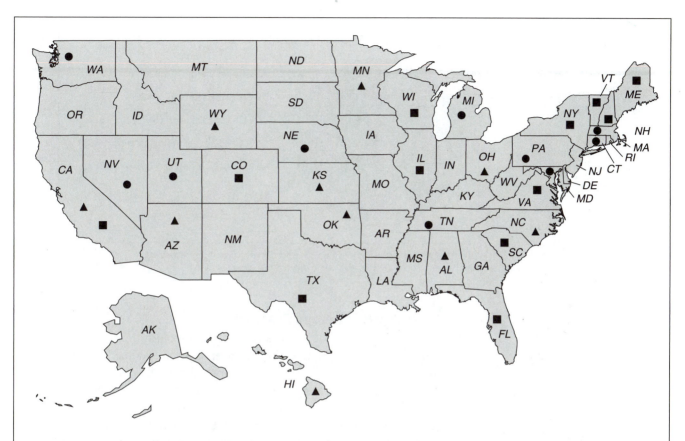

■ Starting operations in spring 1999 were the Bedford County (VA) Sheriff's Department; Broward County (FL) Sheriff's Department; Colorado Springs (CO) Police Department; Dallas (TX) Police Department; Illinois State Police; New York State Division of Criminal Justice Services; Portsmouth (NH) Police Department (including Maine State Police, New Hampshire State Police and Chittendon County, VT); Sacramento County (CA) Sheriff's Office; South Carolina Office of the Attorney General; and the Wisconsin Department of Justice.

● Starting operations in spring 2000 were the Delaware County (PA) District Attorney; Michigan State Police; Seattle (WA) Police Department; Utah Office of the Attorney General; Nebraska State Patrol; Connecticut State Police; Massachusetts Department of Public Safety; Las Vegas (NV) Metropolitan Police Department; Maryland State Police; and the Knoxville (TN) Police Department.

▲ Starting operations in summer 2000 were the Alabama Department of Public Safety; Cuyahoga County (OH) District Attorney; Hawaii Office of the Attorney General; North Carolina Division of Criminal Investigation; Oklahoma State Bureau of Investigation; Phoenix (AZ) Police Department; Saint Paul (MN) Police Department; San Diego (CA) Police Department; Sedgwick County (KS) Sheriff's Office; and the Wyoming Division of Criminal Investigation.

Figure 12.1
Law Enforcement Agencies Participating in the ICAC Task Force Program

Note: The agencies shown are those participating in the program as of September 2001.

Source: Michael Medaris and Cathy Girouard. *Protecting Children in Cyberspace: The ICAC Task Force Program.* Washington, DC: OJJDP Juvenile Justice Bulletin, January 2002, p.4. (NCJ 191213)

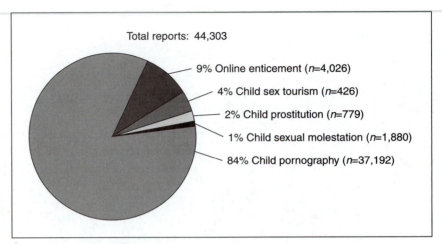

Total reports: 44,303

9% Online enticement (*n*=4,026)

4% Child sex tourism (*n*=426)

2% Child prostitution (*n*=779)

1% Child sexual molestation (*n*=1,880)

84% Child pornography (*n*=37,192)

Figure 12.2
CyberTipline Citizen Reports July 1, 1998, to June 30, 2001

Source: Michael Medaris and Cathy Girouard. *Protecting Children in Cyberspace: The ICAC Task Force Program.* Washington, DC: OJJDP Juvenile Justice Bulletin, January 2002, p.5. (NCJ 191213)

Functional Family Therapy Program

As Sexton and Alexander (2000, p.1) suggest: "Until recently, most communities were left on their own to determine how to address juvenile crime, and many communities turned to exclusively punitive approaches such as incarceration. Mounting evidence, however, indicates that such approaches are ineffective and costly. By removing adolescents from their families and communities, punitive programs inadvertently make adolescents' problems more difficult to solve in the long run. Regardless of how adolescents' problems manifest themselves, they are complex behavioral problems embedded in adolescents' psychosocial systems (primarily family and community). Thus, family-based interventions that adopt a multisystemic perspective are well suited to treating the broad range of problems found in juveniles who engage in delinquent and criminal behavior."

The Functional Family Therapy (FFT) program is a family-based prevention and intervention initiative that has been applied successfully in a variety of contexts to treat a range of high-risk youths and their families. Table 12.1 presents the Functional Family Therapy clinical model's intervention phases across time.

The National Council on Crime and Delinquency (NCCD)

The National Council on Crime and Delinquency (NCCD) has issued a 19-page report, *Preventing Delinquency through Improved Child Protection Service,* which describes a program in Michigan that has proved successful in sorting through cases of child maltreatment to accurately identify the cases that pose the highest risk of continued maltreatment. As the report states: "A large proportion of children involved in the child welfare system subsequently become involved in the juvenile justice system." Many federally funded programs to help youths are summarized in Appendix C on the book companion Web site (cj.wadsworth.com/hess_drowns_jj4e).

Coordinating Council on Juvenile Justice and Delinquency Prevention

The Juvenile and Justice Delinquency Prevention (JJDP) Act establishes the Coordinating Council on Juvenile Justice and Delinquency Prevention as an independent body within the executive branch of the federal government. The council's primary functions are to coordinate all federal juvenile delinquency

Table 12.1
Functional Family Therapy Clinical Model: Intervention Phases across Time

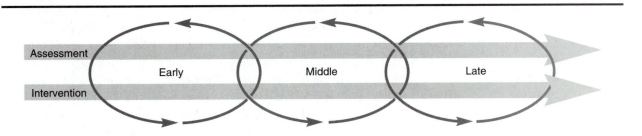

	Engagement and Motivation	Behavior Change	Generalization
Phase goals	Develop alliances.	Develop and implement individualized change plans.	Maintain/generalize change.
	Reduce negativity, resistance.	Change presenting delinquency behavior.	Prevent relapses.
	Improve communication.	Build relational skills (e.g., communication and parenting).	Provide community resources necessary to support change.
	Minimize hopelessness.		
	Reduce dropout potential.		
	Develop family focus.		
	Increase motivation for change.		
Risk and protective factors addressed	Negativity and blaming (risk).	Poor parenting skills (risk).	Poor relationships with school/community (risk).
	Hopelessness (risk).	Negativity and blaming (risk).	Low level of social support (risk).
	Lack of motivation (risk).	Poor communication (risk).	Positive relationships with school/community (protective).
	Credibility (protective).	Positive parenting skills (protective). Supportive communication (protective).	
	Alliance (protective).	Interpersonal needs (depends on context).	
	Treatment availability (protective).	Parental pathology (depends on context).	
		Developmental level (depends on context).	
Assessment focus	Behavior (e.g., presenting problem and risk and protective factors).	Quality of relational skills (communication, parenting).	Identification of community resources needed.
	Relational problems sequence (e.g., needs/functions).	Compliance with behavior change plan.	Maintenance of change.
	Context (risk and protective factors).	Relational problem sequence.	
Therapist/ Interventionist skills	Interpersonal skills (validation, positive interpretation, reattribution, reframing and sequencing).	Structure (session focusing).	Family case manager.
		Change plan implementation.	Resource help.
	High availability to provide services.	Modeling/focusing/directing/training.	Relapse prevention interventions.

Source: T. L. Sexton and J. F. Alexander. *Functional Family Therapy: Principles of Clinical Intervention, Assessment, and Implementation.*
Henderson, NV: RCH Enterprises, 1999. Reprinted by permission.

programs, all federal programs and activities that detain or care for unaccompanied juveniles, and all federal programs relating to missing and exploited children. Its Web site is http://ojjdp.ncjrs.org/council/index.html.

The International Association of Chiefs of Police, the Child Welfare League of America and the National Children's Alliance Summit	The International Association of Chiefs of Police (IACP) has taken an active interest in supporting community justice for juveniles. According to Glasscock (2001, p.6): "Information regarding incidents of child abuse, when available at all, is often fragmented. This fragmentation frequently leads to an uncoordinated response to abuse and neglect situations, with numerous agencies working at cross-purposes to address the same case. In response to this situation, IACP, in conjunction with the Child Welfare League of America (CWLA) and the National Children's Alliance (NCA), held a Child Protection Summit to explore family-centered, community-based concepts to strengthen child protection nationwide, sponsored by the OJJDP. The theme of the summit was *Building Partnerships that Protect Our Children: Child Welfare, Law Enforcement and Communities Working Together.*"

Koepfler-Sontos (2001, p.67) describes the seven areas considered crucial: responding to child abuse reports, building a community response to child maltreatment, enhancing the professionalism of child abuse and neglect responders, leveraging and sharing resources, shaping legislation and public policy, building strong interdisciplinary working relationships and partnering in the prevention of child maltreatment.

The National Children's Advocacy Center	The National Children's Advocacy Center (NCAC), located in Huntsville, Alabama, is a non-profit agency providing prevention, intervention and treatment services to physically and sexually abused children and their families using a child-focused team approach.

Building Blocks for Youth	Building Blocks for Youth is an alliance of children's advocates, researchers, law enforcement professionals and community organizers that seeks to protect minority youths in the justice system and promote rational and effective justice policies. Specifically, partners in the initiative are the Youth Law Center, American Bar Association, Juvenile Justice Center, Justice Policy Institute, Juvenile Law Center, Minorities in Law Enforcement, National Council on Crime and Delinquency, and Pretrial Services Resource Center. Their Web site is http://www/buildingblocksforyouth.org.

Partnerships between Child Welfare and Juvenile Justice Services	McCoy and Higdon (2003, p.142) describe how Clark County, Nevada, has developed a program named Family TRACS to integrate the services provided by the Department of Juvenile Justice Services and the Department of Family Services. Each of these agencies was operating independently, providing services typical of such agencies. Project 2000 was initially conceived to study the departments and develop ideas to improve and streamline service delivery. A new model conceived for an improved way to provide services became the blueprint against which all future work was measured.

Leadership decided on four key factors to guide the re-engineering of the new case management system: family focus, process driven, teamwork and a focus on results. The resulting new case management system was comprehensive and automated to improve procedures, stimulate knowledge-sharing through information exchange and support staff and management in determining what works and what does not. In 1998 the new system, Family TRACS (Family Tracking, Reporting and Automated Case Support) was launched. The system included the two departments and was linked to the District Attorney's Office, Family Court, the County Clerk's Office, the Public Defender's Office and Family Mediation. According to McCoy and Higdon (p.144): "Nearly five years later, more than 700 staff from both departments use Family TRACS daily. Its data repository contains more than 25 years of historical data. Periodic management and ad hoc reports provide supportive statistics used in successful grant award applications and assist the management teams of both departments in programming and workload decision making."

Partnerships with the Schools

The role of schools in juvenile justice was discussed in Chapter 3. Some students are worried about their physical safety. You cannot be concerned with the issues of learning if you have to worry about your safety. Recall the statistics given in Chapter 3 regarding violence in schools. School crime and violence are community issues—not just school problems. For the vast majority of children on probation or in aftercare, educational success is crucial to preventing recidivism and further involvement in the juvenile and criminal justice systems, as discussed in Chapter 11.

Pollack and Sundermann (2001, p.13) note: "More than anything else, the school shootings of recent years have taught us that school safety is not about any one method of control: metal detectors, surveillance systems or swift punishment. Nor is it about any single risk factor such as dysfunctional homes and inadequate schools. We have learned that we cannot identify with certainty those students who, for reasons clear only to themselves, will assault their teachers and peers. We now understand that safe schools require broad-based efforts on the part of the entire community, including educators, students, parents, law enforcement agencies, businesses and faith-based organizations."

They (p.15) stress: "School/community partnerships are the key to building safe schools and communities. Students, teachers, parents, law enforcement officials, and civic and business leaders have important roles to play in reducing school violence and improving the learning environment. The ways in which schools and communities can collaborate are limitless, and they should be tailored to respond to the needs of each partner."

School/community partnerships are a key to building safe schools and communities.

According to Small and Tetrick (2001, p.12): "Most of the indicators (except for serious violent crimes and classroom disruption) suggest that progress is being made in reducing crime and violence in the schools. However, these indicators represent a wide range of events and behaviors that are not always easily interpreted. For example, although school-associated violent deaths are extremely tragic, they are also rare. Classroom disruption, on the other hand, although significantly less serious, is prevalent and erodes the educational opportunities of many students."

Research supports the finding that students who have positive school experiences not only learn better but also have higher self-esteem and are better socialized. They are much more likely to become contributing members of society. Because of this, in 1984 President Ronald Reagan directed the Departments of Justice and Education to form the National School Safety Center (NSSC). This center is structured in five specialized sections: law enforcement, education, legal, research and communications. The goal of the five sections is to provide a comprehensive approach to school safety.

Another organization heavily involved in school safety is the National Crime Prevention Council (NCPC). This organization, in conjunction with the National Institute for Citizen Education in the Law, has developed a program called Teens, Crime and the Community (TCC), which combines education and student action to reduce crime and at the same time develop students' sense of mutual responsibility. Funded by the OJJDP, the TCC curriculum includes information on how and why crimes occur, how community is defined and how individual and group action can help protect the community against crime. According to Calhoun and O'Neil (2001, p.93): "TCC reaches students in more than 1,000 schools, community settings and juvenile justice facilities around the nation, using both a textbook and a newly developed set of lessons designed for less structured settings such as youth clubs." TCC also includes information on 10 ways students can make their schools safer:

1. School crime watches apply Neighborhood Watch concepts to the school.
2. Cross-age teaching provides a chance for middle and high school students to present prevention information to younger students.
3. Mediation programs, in which trained students act as a neutral third party, help resolve conflicts without violence.
4. Plays and prevention performances present information to the student body in appealing ways.
5. Student forums and discussions promote the use of research and resource persons to develop student insight into problems and possible solutions.
6. Surveys on crime and other issues collect facts, engage student interest and spread word of impending projects.
7. Crime prevention clubs teach students to watch out for and help overcome crime.
8. School crime prevention fairs or special observance days give students an opportunity to participate in workshops on prevention and safety.
9. Community service activities build students' self-esteem and school pride.
10. Student courts consider and dispose of student infractions.

Promoting Safety in Schools (2001, p.27) lists seven steps for developing and implementing a comprehensive school safety plan: (1) create partnerships, (2) identify and measure, (3) set goals, (4) research programs and strategies, (5) implement, (6) evaluate and (7) revise plans. It (p.31) also outlines pitfalls to be aware of when implementing a school safety plan:

- Raising awareness about school safety and the risks of violence can increase fears and insecurity among students, staff and families.
- Better reporting and data collection may result in apparent increases in incidents, so there must be careful monitoring and evaluation of other indicators.
- The media can inflame anxieties, leading to exaggerated and rigid responses.
- Projects must be appropriate to the culture of their school communities.
- The challenge of developing partnerships and engaging the local community can be compounded when a school is not located in the community from which it derives most of its students.
- Schools that are receptive to developing projects often are not those with the most problems.
- Schools need financial support from national, regional and local governments for policy development.

Some of the most persistent and serious behaviors occurring in schools are bullying, intimidation and harassment. McMahon (2003, p.24) describes a partnership formed by students, members of the New York State Police, a school psychologist, a teacher and members of the administration to develop the School-Based Partnership (SBP) project. The COPS office offered the SARA problem-solving model to be used with its four components of scanning, analysis, response and assessment. Says McMahon (p.26): "In response to the empirical evidence, the project team adopted a prevention response that includes a series of instructional videos focused on various levels of school violence. The videos were developed with the assistance of community members who have expertise in film making along with local experts in school violence and the New York State Police."

In response to the number of school shootings, the U.S. Secret Service conducted a survey for the Safe Schools initiative. Their report, *Preventing School Shootings* (2002, p.11) stresses: "The findings clearly emphasize the importance of paying attention and listening to America's young people. More than a handful of adults—parents, teachers, school administrators and counselors, coaches and law enforcement—can make an important contribution to and play a key role in preventing violence on school grounds." The report (p.14) notes: "A significant problem in preventing targeted violence is determining how best to respond to students who are already known to be in trouble. This study indicates the importance of giving attention to students who are having difficulty coping with the major losses of perceived failures, particularly when feelings of desperation and hopelessness are involved."

Table 12.2 **Traditional Policing Compared with Community Policing in Schools**	Traditional Policing in Schools	Community Policing in Schools
	Reactive response to 911 calls	Law enforcement officer assigned to the school "community"
	Incident driven	Problem oriented
	Minimal school-law enforcement interaction, often characterized by an "us vs. them" mentality	Ongoing school-law enforcement partnership to address problems of concern to educators, students, and parents
	Police role limited to law enforcement	Police role extended beyond law enforcement to include prevention and early intervention activities
	Police viewed as source of the solution	Educators, students and parents are active partners in developing solutions
	Educators and law enforcement officers reluctant to share information	Partners value information sharing as an important problem-solving tool
	Criminal incidents subject to inadequate response; criminal consequences imposed only when incidents reported to police	Consistent responses to incidents is ensured—administrative *and* criminal as appropriate
	Law enforcement presence viewed as indicator of failure	Law enforcement presence viewed as taking a positive, proactive step to create orderly, safe and secure schools
	Police effectiveness measured by arrest rates, response times, calls for service, etc.	Policing effectiveness measured by the absence of crime and disorder

Source: Anne J. Atkinson. *Fostering School-Law Enforcement Partnerships.* Northwest Regional Educational Laboratory, September 2002, p.7. Reprinted by permission.

The School/Law Enforcement Partnership

The presence of law enforcement in schools was discussed in Chapter 7. Table 12.2 compares traditional policing and community policing in schools.

Atkinson (2002, p.1) asserts: "Schools and law enforcement agencies share responsibility for the safety of schools and the communities they serve. Schools function as communities within broader communities and are affected by crime, victimization and fear." Atkinson notes commonality in the roles of schools and law enforcement agencies, including being responsible for the safety and well-being of students and their important responsibility to help youths to become productive, law-abiding citizens. Table 12.3 summarizes the characteristics of effective schools and how law enforcement partnerships can contribute.

Teaching Conflict Resolution and Mediation Skills

The traditional subjects taught in our schools have been expanded by including interpersonal skills in mediation and conflict resolution. Crawford and Bodine (2001, p.21) suggest: "Conflict resolution education should be taught to all students, not just those with disruptive behavior." They (p.24) explain: "Conflict resolution is based on a structured problem-solving process that uses the following steps: (1) set the stage, (2) gather perspectives, (3) identify interests, (4) create options, (5) evaluate options and (6) generate agreement. Each of the following strategies is amenable to this process. Negotiation occurs when two disputing parties work together, unassisted, to resolve their dispute; mediation occurs when two disputing parties work together, assisted by a third party called the mediator, to resolve their dispute; and consensus decision-making uses a group

Table 12.3
Characteristics of Effective Schools and How School-Law Enforcement Partnerships Contribute

Characteristics of Effective Schools	How School-Law Enforcement Partnerships Contribute
Safe and Orderly Environment A safe and orderly environment is often referred to as "the number-one correlate of effective schools." In such schools there is an orderly, purposeful, atmosphere free from the threat of physical harm. School climate is not oppressive but is conducive to teaching and learning. Teachers and students interact in a positive, cooperative manner.	SROs bring to the school setting the expertise of a public safety specialist. They provide an immediate response to life-threatening situations, ensure that laws are enforced when illegal activities occur and work collaboratively with schools to resolve problems that threaten the safety of schools. Their presence has a deterrent effect on illegal and disruptive behavior and communicates that the school and larger community have made school safety a priority.
High Expectations for Success In the effective school, there is a climate of expectation in which staff members believe and demonstrate that all students can master the essential content and school skills, and also believe that they have the capability to help all students achieve that mastery.	SROs reinforce clear expectations for appropriate behavior through enforcement of laws, law-related education and involvement of students in crime prevention activities.
Clear School Mission In the effective school, there is a clearly articulated school mission through which the staff shares an understanding of and commitment to instructional goals, priorities, assessment procedures and accountability.	The school-law enforcement partnership helps schools to focus on their central mission—educating—by reducing the amount of time the staff must spend on disciplinary matters.
Instructional Leadership In an effective school, the principal and other staff members take an active role in instructional leadership with the principal becoming a "leader of leaders" (rather than a leader of followers), functioning as a coach or partner.	When crime and other disruptive behaviors are reduced, school leaders can focus more effectively on their central instructional leadership role.
Frequent Monitoring of Student Progress In the effective school, student academic progress is measured frequently using a variety of assessment procedures. The assessment results are used to improve individual student performance and the instructional program.	The school-law enforcement partnership uses data on crime and discipline to assess and improve school safety.
Opportunity To Learn and Student Time on Task In the effective school, teachers allocate a significant amount of classroom time to instruction in the essential skills.	Opportunity to learn and student time on task are increased when disruptive behavior is reduced.
Home-School Relations Effective schools have formed partnerships with parents who are given the opportunity to play important roles in the school. These schools have built trust and communicated with parents who understand and support the school's basic mission.	Partnership, characterized by trust and communication, is a central component of community policing. Law enforcement adds a public safety specialist to home-school partnerships.

Source: Anne J. Atkinson. *Fostering School-Law Enforcement Partnerships.* Northwest Regional Educational Laboratory, September 2002, pp. 10–11. Reprinted by permission.

problem-solving strategy in which all parties affected by the conflict collaborate to craft a plan of action, with or without the assistance of a neutral party."

 Conflict resolution and mediation are important basic skills that schools now teach.

Project ACHIEVE

Project ACHIEVE is a school reform and school effectiveness program developed for use in preschool, elementary and middle schools that want to implement school-wide positive behavioral prevention programs (www.coed.usf.edu/ projectachieve). It was designed with a particular emphasis on increasing student performance in the areas of social skills and conflict resolution, improving student achievement and academic progress, facilitating positive school climates and increasing parental involvement and support.

The Jesse Keen Elementary School was the first Project ACHIEVE school when the program's School-Wide Positive Behavioral Self-Management System was implemented during the 1990–1991 school year. After implementation of Project ACHIEVE at Jesse Keen, positive outcomes included a 61 percent decrease in special education referrals, a 57 percent decrease in special education placements, a 16 percent decrease in overall discipline referrals, a 29 percent decrease in out-of-school suspensions and a 47 percent decrease in grade retention. The Substance Abuse and Mental Health Services Administration (SAMHSA) (2002) named Project ACHIEVE a model program. The White House Conference on School Safety called it an "exemplary program," and the Center for Effective Collaboration and Practice, American Institutes for Research called it an "Effective School Reform Program."

This national model program through the Center for Substance Abuse Prevention and the U.S. Department of Health and Human Services helps schools and school districts to maximize students' academic achievement, create safe school environments and positive school climates, build effective teaching and problem-solving teams that speed successful interventions to challenging students, increase and sustain effective classroom instruction as well as strong parent involvement, develop and implement effective strategic plans, organize building committees and student learning clusters, and develop effective data management systems for outcome evaluation.

Among Project ACHIEVE's innovative components are the Stop and Think Social Skills Program and the special situations analysis of school and peer group hot spots.

The Career Academy Concept

According to Coffee and Pestridge (2001, p.1): "Career academies are schools within schools that link students with peers, teachers and community partners in a disciplined environment, fostering academic success and mental and emotional health." They suggest: "Career academies allow youths who may have trouble fitting into the larger school environment to belong to a smaller educational community and to connect what they learn in school with their career aspirations and goals. Career academies provide at-risk youths with an alternative to joining gangs and offer these youths an opportunity to become assets to their communities." Coffee and Pestridge suggest three key elements of a successful career academy:

 The key elements of a successful career academy are a small learning community with a core group of teachers over three or four years; college preparatory curriculum with a career theme; and partnerships with employers, community and higher education.

A five-year evaluation of career academies, covering nine academies and 1,900 students conducted by Manpower Demonstration Research Corporation, documents the following findings (Kemple and Snipes, 2000):

- Career academies reduced dropout rates by nearly one-third for at-risk students.

- Students enrolled in career academies attended high school more consistently, completed more academic and vocational courses and were more likely to apply to college than their counterparts who were not enrolled in academies.

- Career academics provide at-risk youths opportunities to set goals and reach academic and professional objectives that may have otherwise been unobtainable.

YouthBuild U.S.A.   Hernandez (2001, p.1) notes: "For almost 25 years, YouthBuild has harnessed the positive energy of unemployed young adults to rebuild their communities and their own lives through a commitment to work, education, responsibility and family." At YouthBuild alternative schools, students earn their GEDs or high school diplomas, participate in counseling, perform community service and belong to a positive community of peers and adults who are committed to their success. Community-based, independent organizations operate local YouthBuild programs, which are kept small to create supportive minicommunities for the students.

YouthBuild prepares young people for the work world in diverse ways. At construction sites, youths receive close supervision and training in building homes. In addition, YouthBuild provides an academic program that integrates reading, writing and mathematics with life skills training, social studies and other subjects. It also provides leadership development opportunities.

According to Hernandez: "Nationwide, about 6,000 young people, ages 16 to 24, participate in YouthBuild each year. Approximately 70 percent are male. They are racially diverse with 55 percent African-American, 20 percent Latino, 1.5 percent Asian-American and 1 percent Native American. Ninety percent are from very low-income families." She (p.2) also reports: "Since 1993, YouthBuild students have built more than 7,000 low-income housing units. Finished buildings are either owned and managed by community-based organizations as permanent low-income rental housing or are sold to low-income homeowners. As a result, gutted shells and abandoned buildings become attractive homes in communities that have a critical need for housing." Of the 60 percent of YouthBuild students who complete the program, 85 percent go on to college or construction-related jobs with

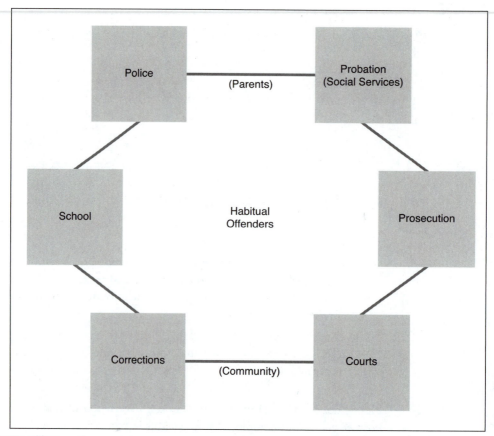

Figure 12.3
A Community Model for Controlling Habitual Offenders

Source: Timothy D. Crowe. *Habitual Juvenile Offenders: Guidelines for Citizen Action and Public Responses.* Serious Habitual Offender Comprehensive Action Program (SHOCAP). Washington, DC: Office of Juvenile Justice and Delinquency Prevention, October 1991, p.44.

good salaries. Alumni receive postprogram counseling and have continued opportunities to play leadership roles in the local YouthBuild chapter and in the community.

Partnerships of Community Agencies, Businesses and Volunteers

Schechter and Edleson (2000, p.12) stress: "Every community should build teams—linking public and private resources and using formal institutions and informal supports such as neighbors and family members—to protect victims, to ensure family stability and monitor and rehabilitate those who commit family violence." In addition, they (p.13) recommend: "Communities and their institutions should create a network of early intervention and prevention responses." Intervention and prevention responses are the focus of the next two chapters.

In addition to institutions within a community many government agencies and officials have provided services for years, but most are totally unaware of their ignorance of how other operations work or of the problems and needs of other components within the system. The OJJDP has devised a community model for controlling habitual offenders and a functional model for a community habitual offender program, as shown in Figures 12.3 and 12.4.

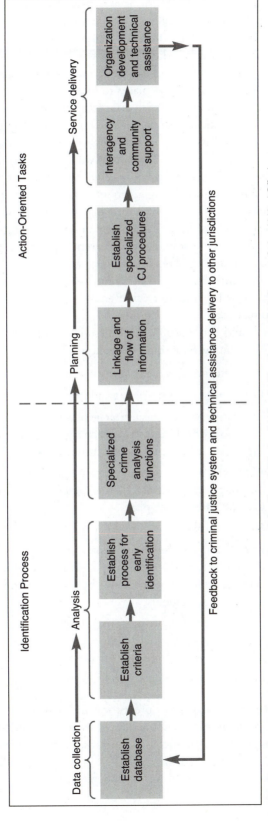

**Figure 12.4
Functional Model of a
Community Habitual
Offender Program**

Source: Timothy D. Crowe. *Habitual Juvenile Offenders: Guidelines for Citizen Action and Public Responses. Serious Habitual Offenders Comprehensive Action Program* (SHOCAP). Washington, DC: Office of Juvenile Justice and Delinquency Prevention, October 1991, p.45.

Successful efforts do not have to be so formalized. They can be as informal as the mayor of a city calling for the removal of graffiti, as Minneapolis Mayor Sayles-Belton did in her "Don't Deface My Space" campaign. Another practical, grass-roots approach is the Neighborhood Tool Kit series of stories about things that citizens are doing and can do to make their neighborhoods friendlier, safer, more vital, more attractive places to live, for example, by removing eyesores, creating jobs, cleaning up alleys, combating crime, starting block clubs and the like.

Fawcett et al. (2000) contend: "Building healthy communities is the process of people working together to address what matters most to them, including prevention of violence among youths as well as promoting youth health and development." Francisco and Bremby (2001, p.64) believe: "Effective collaborative partnerships focus on bringing about community change, an intermediate outcome in the long process of improving community health. Community changes may be defined as those that are new or have been modified, including programs such as after-school activities and prevention services; policies such as increased fines for selling illegal tobacco products to minors and family-friendly policies in businesses; and practices such as improved access to health services and increased opportunities for academic achievement in schools and relate to community-determined goals."

Kelly and Settle (2001, p.59) describe Kentucky's Delinquency Prevention Council: "The purpose of the council is to:

- Pinpoint problem areas in the community.

- Develop a three-year plan to address these needs.

- Enter into written local interagency agreements that specify the nature and extent of contributions that each signatory agency will make in achieving the goals of the local juvenile justice plan.

- Apply and receive public or private grants to be administered by a local unit of government or DJJ that support one or more components of the local juvenile justice plan.

- Share information.

- Provide a forum for the presentation of interagency recommendations and the resolution of disagreements relating to the contents of the interagency agreement or the performance by the parties of their respective obligations under the agreements.

- Assist the efforts of local community support organizations and volunteer groups in providing enrichment programs and other support services for clients of the local juvenile justice system.

- Provide an annual report and recommendations to DJJ."

The key principles for preventing and reducing juvenile delinquency according to the Kentucky Delinquency Prevention Council (p.60) are to strengthen families, support core social institutions, promote prevention strategies and programs, intervene immediately and effectively when delinquent behavior occurs and identify and control the small percentages of serious, violent and chronic juvenile offenders.

Francisco and Bremby (p.66) have identified seven factors found to lead to successful community-change incentives:

1. Targeted mission. Having a targeted mission is especially important to making a difference for the entire population of the community.

2. Leadership. Having charismatic leaders may be necessary to mobilize community members to help accomplish especially difficult goals. Additionally, having leaders who demonstrate distributed leadership behavior, i.e., creating niches of opportunity for other community members to make a contribution, also is required.

3. Action planning. Action planning is the identification of all the new or modified policies, programs and practices that, when taken together, will result in resolution of the mission.

4. Community organizers. Without community members, there can be no community coalition.

5. Technical assistance. There are many core competencies necessary to make a difference in community and systems change efforts. Not everyone affiliated with the community partnership will be equally competent in all areas.

6. Documentation and feedback. Tracking community and systems change accomplished over time can be achieved simply by having coalition members report the number of new or modified programs, policies and practices facilitated by the organization and related to its mission.

7. Making outcomes matter. Although the other six factors are important, if the outcome does not really matter to the community or if the means to achieve the outcome are not in keeping with local norms, little will result from the effort.

Community Partnerships and Volunteers

The success of most community-based justice programs is heightened by citizen involvement. Such community participation plays a crucial role in "normalizing" the environment and developing offenders' ties to the community, as well as in changing community attitudes toward offenders.

 Community participation through volunteerism improves programs, breaks down isolation and helps youthful offenders explore possibilities for adjustment to the community.

Volunteers are encouraged to assess needs and review all activities, programs and facilities to ensure their suitability in light of community standards and offender needs. Volunteers are used in some institutions and as aides to adjunct institutional programs, such as work release, that are carried out within the community. In some jurisdictions volunteers serve as assistants in probation, parole and other community-based alternatives to incarceration.

Volunteers have been an integral part of justice for centuries. Traditionally the role of volunteers in private endeavors has been to fill gaps between governmental social services and actual needs. In 1912 volunteers rallied for the child labor laws that were the result of the first White House Conference on Children in 1910. During the 1930s volunteers filled the gap in welfare and mental health programs until President Franklin D. Roosevelt made vast social changes. The rehabilitative powers of the local community and its volunteers were popularized during the late 1960s and the 1970s, and today volunteerism continues to increase. Some programs today use senior citizens as volunteers to work with high-risk juveniles.

School Activities, Community Service and Delinquency

Hoffmann and Xu (2002, p.568) note: "A common observation is that lack of involvement in communities is linked to a host of social problems, including delinquency. In response to this observation, youths are increasingly encouraged to volunteer for community service projects. Involvement in school activities is also seen as a way to attenuate delinquency." Using linked individual-level and school-level data, Hoffmann and Xu investigated the impact of school and community activities on delinquency. Their results indicate that community activities are related negatively to delinquency, especially in schools that are perceived as unsafe. However, race/ethnicity and percentage of minority students in the school condition the impact of school activities on delinquent behavior. In high-minority schools, African-American students who participate in school activities are involved in more delinquent behavior, yet those in low-minority schools are less involved in delinquent behavior.

Youth Service America

Youth Service America (YSA) is a resource center and premier alliance of more than 300 organizations committed to increasing the quantity and quality of opportunities for young Americans to serve locally, nationally or globally. This powerful network of organizations is committed to making service the common

Youths assigned to community service or youths who volunteer may engage in graffiti removal projects.

© Phil McCarten

A group of teens watches the Step Up program graduation ceremony at the Boys and Girls Club of Fullerton, CA.

expectation and common experience of all young Americans. YSA believes a strong youth service network will create healthy communities and foster citizenship, knowledge and the personal development of young people.

Each year project grants are awarded to young people who participate in public service on an ongoing basis. State Farm Companies Foundation provides a Good Neighbor Service-Learning Award, AT&T provides The AT&T CARES™ Youth Service Action Learning Award, and the National Education Association provides a Youth Leaders for Literacy Award.

According to the YSA Web site (http://www.ysa.org), students who volunteer are more likely to do well in school, graduate, vote and volunteer during the rest of their lives. They are less likely to abuse drugs and alcohol and engage in other destructive behaviors. The Web site also notes that youth volunteers contribute more than 2.4 billion hours each year worth more than $34.3 million to the U.S. economy.

YSA sponsors an annual National Youth Service Day which, according to its Web site, brought together millions of young people from all 50 states and the District of Columbia. The three primary goals of the National Youth Service Day are to *mobilize* youths to identify and address the needs of their communities through service, *recruit* the next generation of volunteers and *educate* the public about the year-round contributions of young people as community leaders.

Jobs and Restitution

Some community efforts focus on creating jobs for youths. Some dispositions of the juvenile court include restitution in the form of work or pay. Providing jobs for youths who are required to make restitution helps them fulfill their obligations.

Work is an important part of a balanced approach to juvenile justice.

Jobs are important to youths not only for the money generated but for the feeling of self-worth that may accompany a job.

Suppression

Enforce zero-tolerance sanctions for probation violations.

- Juvenile court sets enforceable conditions of probation for Eigers.
- Police-probation teams monitor Eiger compliance with court-ordered conditions of probation.
- Police Department's Operation Takedown identifies and reports Eiger probation violations.

Intervention

Provide intensive intervention services for Eiger youth and families.

- Juvenile court refers probationers to Eiger program.
- Police-probation teams assess Eiger service needs and family situation.
- Eiger case coordinator develops and oversees a case plan for each Eiger.
- Life Skills Academy offers mentoring, anger management educational/ employment and family strengthening programs.

Prevention

Build resiliency in the community by addressing risk factors.

- Eiger and Probation Department staff work with the community to identify Eiger siblings and other youth at risk.
- School- and community-based programs and Life Skills Academy address needs of at-risk youth.
- Community-strengthening initiatives reduce neighborhood deterioration, promote community cohesion and address economic factors.

Source: Alan Lizotte and David Sheppard. *Gun Use by Male Juveniles: Research and Prevention.* Washington, DC: OJJDP Juvenile Justice Bulletin, July 2001, p.9. (NCJ 188992)

Figure 12.5
Baton Rouge Operation Eiger's Linked Strategies

Job Corps

Job Corps Centers throughout the country offer education and training opportunities to economically disadvantaged young adults ages 16 through 24. The national office is in Washington, DC, with centers in Alaska, Arkansas, California, Georgia, Indiana, Maryland, Montana, Tennessee and Washington state.

Linked Strategies

Baton Rouge's Operation Eiger's Linked Strategies, a program to reduce gun use by male juveniles, provides an example of combining suppression, intervention and prevention to build a safer community. The strategies used in each area are illustrated in Figure 12.5.

 Suppression, intervention and prevention efforts can be linked by communities in their efforts to reduce or prevent delinquency and juvenile crime.

Lizotte and Sheppard (2001, p.9) conclude: "Effective efforts are as dependent on community participation as on actions taken by police and other criminal and juvenile justice agencies. Law enforcement agencies can do their job more effectively when community priorities shape their actions." As Skogan et al. (2000) report: "Evidence suggests that the buildup of trust engendered by such an approach enhances the partnership between police and the communities they serve, resulting in greater police-community cooperation and mutual cooperation and support."

Summary

The role of the broader community in assisting the juvenile justice system cannot be ignored. Community is not only the geographical area over which the justice system has jurisdiction; it is also a sense of integration, of shared values and a sense of "we-ness." Without such "we-ness," areas may experience the broken-window phenomenon—if it appears no one cares, disorder and crime will thrive.

The importance of community is recognized in areas that have implemented community justice, including community policing, which embraces a proactive, problem-oriented approach to working with the community to make it safe.

Another important community resource is social services. Social workers have greatly influenced trends in juvenile justice policy in the areas of diversion, victim restitution, decriminalization of status offenses and deinstitutionalization. Social workers operate in all aspects of the juvenile justice system, although in the first juvenile courts social workers were probation officers. The current emphasis in social services for youths is diversion to a wide range of community-based services and programs.

Other emphases include family therapy and teaching conflict resolution and mediation skills. Studies suggest that family therapy is more effective in dealing with the problems of youths than is traditional juvenile justice intervention. School/community partnerships are a key to building safe schools and communities. Important basic skills that schools now teach are conflict resolution and mediation. The key elements of a successful career academy are a small learning community with a core group of teachers over three or four years; college preparatory curriculum with a career theme; and partnerships with employers, community and higher education.

Community participation through volunteerism helps to improve programs, breaks down isolation and helps youthful offenders explore possibilities for adjustment to the community. In addition, jobs are important to youths not only for the money they generate but for the feelings of self-worth that accompany a job. Suppression, intervention and prevention efforts can be linked by communities in their efforts to reduce or prevent delinquency and juvenile crime.

Discussion Questions

1. Is there a sense of community where you live? Are there any instances of the broken-window phenomenon?
2. What are the advantages and disadvantages of community policing? Is it used in your community?
3. Why is there a need for social workers? How extensively should social workers be involved in juvenile justice?
4. Should social workers or probation officers handle youths directly from courts? Why or why not?
5. Do social workers seek the best ways to prevent recurrences of mischievous or antisocial juvenile behavior? What do they do?
6. Should social services provide education for disruptive youths who do not want to go to school? Why or why not?

7. A 15-year-old boy is caught shoplifting food from a large supermarket. Security personnel call the police. While waiting for the police, the youth tells them he has not eaten anything for a week. There is no food at his home. The police are advised of the youth's situation. The police investigate, find the youth was telling the truth and advise the supermarket. The supermarket manager does not want to make a formal complaint. Should this matter be handled by social services or the juvenile court? What would happen in your area?

8. What social service programs operate in your state? Do these programs serve the purpose for which they were designed, or do they add to the array of referral programs in existence?

9. Should all juvenile incidents be referred to the juvenile court, or is there justification for referral to other agencies when the offense is not serious? Which do you support? What criteria would you use?

10. Should schools be able to refer a disruptive juvenile to an agency that might help the juvenile rather than involve the police? Why or why not?

InfoTrac College Edition Assignments

- Use InfoTrac College Edition to help answer the Discussion Questions as appropriate.
- Use InfoTrac College Edition to read and outline one of the following articles to share with the class:
  - "Schools Career Academy Aims for Practical Training" by Dan Eaton (*career academy*)

  - "Theorizing Community Justice through Community Courts" by Jeffrey Fagan and Victoria Malkin (*community justice*)
  - "Reconstituting Community: Social Justice, Social Order and the Politics of Community" by Christine Everingham

Internet Assignments

Complete one of the following assignments and be prepared to share your findings with the class:

- Go to www.ojjdp.ncjrs.org and find and outline one of the NCJ publications listed in the references for this chapter.
- Research one of the following key words or phrases: *broken-window phenomenon, career academy, community justice, integrated community.*

- Go to the Web site of any reference in this chapter giving an online address. Read and outline the material.
- Research using *child advocacy center* and look for your state.

References

Atkinson, Anne J. *Fostering School-Law Enforcement Partnerships.* Northwest Regional Laboratory, September 2002.

Boland, Barbara. "The Manhattan Experiment: Community Prosecution." In *Crime and Place: Plenary Papers of the 1997 Conference on Criminal Justice Research and Evaluation.* Washington, DC: National Institute of Justice Research Report, April 2001.

Calhoun, John A. and O'Neil, Jean. "Making a Connection: The National Crime Prevention Council Joins Youthful Offenders with their Communities." *Corrections Today,* December 2001, pp.91–94.

Coffee, Joseph N. and Pestridge, Scott. *The Career Academy Concept.* Washington, DC: OJJDP Fact Sheet #15, May 2001. (FS 200115)

Community Justice in Rural America: Four Examples and Four Futures. *Washington, DC: Bureau of Justice Assistance Monograph, February 2001. (NCJ 182437)*

Crawford, Donna K. and Bodine, Richard J. "Conflict Resolution Education: Preparing Youths for the Future." *Juvenile Justice,* June 2001, pp.21–29.

Cullen, Thomas. *Keeping Children Safe: OJJDP's Child Protection Division.* Washington, DC: OJJDP Juvenile Justice Bulletin, March 2001. (NCJ 186158)

Fawcett, S.G.; Francisco, V.T.; Hyra, D.; Paine-Andrews, A.; Schultz, J.A.; Russos, J.; Fisher, J.L.; and Evensen, P. "Building Healthy Communities." In *The Society and Population Health Reader: A State and Community Perspective.* A. Tarlov and R. St. Peter, editors. New York: New Press, 2000, pp.75–93.

Feinblatt, John; Berman, Greg; and Sviridoff, Michele. "Neighborhood Justice at the Midtown Community Court." In *Crime and Place: Plenary Papers of the 1997 Conference on Criminal Justice Research and Evaluation.* Washington, DC: National Institute of Justice, July 1998, pp.81–92. (NCJ 168618)

Francisco, Vincent T. and Brembly, Roderick. "Promoting Community Change for Juvenile Justice: Collaborative Change and Community Partnerships." *Corrections Today,* December 2001, pp.64–66.

Fung, Cynthia and Wyrick, Phelan A. *OJJDP's Program of Research for Tribal Youth.* Washington, DC: OJJDP Fact Sheet #10, April 2001. (FS 200110)

Girouard, Cathy. *The Missing and Exploited Children's Program (Update).* Washington, DC: OJJDP Fact Sheet #16, May 2001a. (FS 200116)

Girouard, Cathy. *The National Center for Missing and Exploited Children.* Washington, DC: OJJDP Fact Sheet #28, July 2001b. (FS 200128)

Glasscock, Bruce D. "The Child Protection Summit: Exploring Innovative Partnerships." *The Police Chief,* August 2001, p.6.

Hernandez, Rudy. *Youth in Action: YouthBuild U.S.A.* Washington, DC: OJJDP Fact Sheet #5, May 2001. (YFS 00106)

Hoffman, John P. and Xu, Jiangmin. "School Activities, Community Service and Delinquency." *Crime & Delinquency,* October 2002, pp.568–591.

Kanable, Rebecca. "Community Policing at Its Best: Award Winners Share Ideas Worth Replicating." *Law Enforcement Technology,* October 2000, pp.34–40.

Kelly, Ralph E. and Settle, Leah M. "Innovative Community Partnerships: Kentucky's Statewide Delinquency Prevention Councils." *Corrections Today,* December 2001, pp.59–62.

Kemple, J.J. and Snipes, J.C. *Career Academies: Impacts on Students' Engagement and Performance in High School.* San Francisco, CA: Manpower Demonstration Research Corporation, 2000.

Klockars, Carl B. "The Rhetoric of Community Policing." In *Community Policing: Rhetoric or Reality,* edited by Jack R. Greene and Stephen D. Mastrofski. New York: Praeger, 1991, pp.239–258.

Koepfler-Sontos, Theresa. "Building Welfare Partnerships that Protect Our Children: Child Welfare, Law Enforcement and Communities Working Together." *The Police Chief,* September 2001, pp.66–67.

Kracke, Kristen. *Children's Exposure to Violence: The Safe Start Initiative.* Washington, DC: OJJDP Fact Sheet #13, April 2001. (FS 200113)

Lizotte, Alan and Sheppard, Daniel. *Gun Use by Male Juveniles: Research and Prevention.* Washington, DC: OJJDP Juvenile Justice Bulletin, July 2001. (NCJ 188992)

McCoy, Jeffrey and Higdon, Lori. "FamilyTRACS Revolutionizes Child Welfare and Juvenile Justice Services." *Corrections Today,* April 2003, pp.142–144.

McMahon, James W. "Partnership Program Targets Bullying, Intimidation and Harassment." *The Police Chief,* April 2003, pp.24–26.

Medaris, Michael and Girouard, Cathy. *Protecting Children in Cyberspace: The ICAC Task Force Program.* Washington, DC: OJJDP Juvenile Justice Bulletin, January 2002. (NCJ 191213)

Mendel, Richard A. *Less Hype, More Help: Reducing Juvenile Crime, What Works and What Doesn't.* Washington, DC: American Policy Forum, 2000.

Miller, Linda S. and Hess, Kären M. *The Police in the Community: Strategies for the 21ˢᵗ Century,* 3ʳᵈ ed. Belmont, CA: Wadsworth Publishing Company, 2002.

Pollack, Ira and Sundermann, Carlos. "Creating Safe Schools: A Comprehensive Aproach." *Juvenile Justice,* June 2001, pp.13–20.

Preventing Delinquency through Improved Child Protection Services. Washington, DC: National Council on Crime and Delinquency, 2001.

Preventing School Shootings. A Summary of a U.S. Secret Service Safe Schools Initiative Report. *NIJ Journal,* No. 248, 2002, pp.10–15.

Promoting Safety in Schools: International Experience and Action. Washington, DC: Bureau of Justice Assistance Monograph, August 2001. (NCJ 186937)

Schechter, Susan and Edleson, Jeffrey L. *Domestic Violence & Children: Creating a Public Response.* Center on Crime, Communities & Culture for the Open Society Institute, 2000.

Sexton, Thomas L. and Alexander, James F. *Functional Family Therapy.* Washington, DC: OJJDP Juvenile Justice Bulletin, December 2000. (NCJ 184743)

Skogan, W.G.; Hartnett, S.M.; DuBois, J.; Comley, J.T.; Kaiser, M.; and Lovig, J.H. *Problem Solving in Practice: Implementing Community Policing in Chicago.* Research Report. Washington, DC: U.S. Department of Justice, Office of Justice Programs, National Institute of Justice, 2000.

Small, Margaret and Tetrick, Kellie Dressler. "School Violence: An Overview." *Juvenile Justice,* June 2001, pp.3–20.

Substance Abuse and Mental Health Services Administration (SAMHSA). *Project ACHIEVE: SAMHSA Model Program Fact Sheet.* Rockville, MD, 2002.

Swope, Ross E. "Community Prosecution." *Police Quarterly,* March 2000, pp.105–115.

Swope, Ross E. "Community Prosecution: The Real Deal." *Law Enforcement News,* January 15/31, 2001, pp.11,14.

Wilson, James Q. and Kelling, George L. "Broken Windows." *Atlantic Monthly,* March 1982, pp.29–38.

Wilson, James Q. and Kelling, George L. "Making Neighborhoods Safe." *Atlantic Monthly,* February 1989, pp.46–52.

Wrobleski, Henry M. and Hess, Kären M. *Introduction to Law Enforcement and Criminal Justice,* 7th ed. Belmont, CA: Wadsworth Publishing Company, 2003.

CHAPTER 13

Approaches to Juvenile Crime Prevention

The truism that an ounce of prevention is worth a pound of cure surely applies to delinquency. If we are to check . . . violent crime by juveniles, we must go beyond treating symptoms, however diligently, to examine causes. Nor must we be so preoccupied with what is wrong with a minority of our youth that our tunnel vision blinds us to what is right with the majority.

—OJJDP

Do You Know?

- What approach to the delinquency problem emerged during the late 1960s?
- What three approaches to juvenile crime prevention are?
- What the three general levels of prevention are?
- How the numerator and denominator approaches to prevention differ?
- What the two-pronged public health model for prevention consists of?
- What an effective prevention approach must address?
- What the Blueprints for Violence Prevention Initiative is?
- What kinds of programs are recommended by the Metropolitan Court Judges Committee to help prevent child abuse and neglect?
- What the committee recommends for disabled families?
- What the committee recommends for children at risk?
- What two strategies have proved effective in reducing gun violence? What strategy has proved ineffective?
- What the TARAD program does?
- What the purpose of drug testing in the school is?
- What antigang programs can be implemented?

Can You Define?

corrective prevention
denominator approach
gateway drugs
Gould-Wysinger Award
mechanical prevention

numerator approach
polydrug use
primary prevention
protective factors

punitive prevention
risk factors
secondary prevention
tertiary prevention

INTRODUCTION

Common sense says it is better to prevent a problem than to react to it once it arises. This is true for juvenile delinquency as well as for child neglect and abuse. Traditionally our society's approach to youthful crime has been reactive. Juvenile courts and diversion programs have responded to crimes by juveniles with a wide range of services focused on punishment, control or rehabilitation.

In 1967 the President's Commission on Law Enforcement and the Administration of Justice advocated: "In the last analysis, the most promising and so the most important method of dealing with crime is by preventing it—by ameliorating the conditions of life that drive people to commit crime and that undermine the restraining rules and institutions erected by society against anti-social conduct."

During the late 1960s a new approach for dealing with delinquency emerged—a focus on the prevention of crime.

Subsequently this prevention emphasis was written into federal law in the Juvenile Delinquency Prevention Acts of 1972 and 1974 and the Juvenile Justice Amendments of 1977. As Mendel (2000) observes: "Attempting to reduce crime by focusing only on law enforcement and corrections is like providing expensive ambulances at the bottom of a cliff to pick up the youngster who falls off, rather than building a fence at the top of the cliff to keep them from falling in the first place."

Each municipality, county and state is unique in its particular crime problems. Each is also unique in how it approaches crime and how it disposes of those who engage in crime. What constitutes delinquency is subject to varied interpretations across places, times and social groupings. A youth's behavior may be viewed as "delinquent" by police, as "acting out" by mental health professionals, as "sin" by members of the clergy and as "just plain mischief" by those who view some misbehavior as a normal part of growing up.

The National Crime Prevention Council (NCPC) Web site states: "Many adults do not think well of teenagers. In individual teenagers, they see rebellion, mood swings and tempers. In groups of young people, they see threats (even when none are made), malice (even when they're just talking outside the local convenience store) and gangs (even in kids just walking around the mall). But the great majority of teens are sources of strength, not trouble, to their communities. They are, by and large, intensely interested in the adult world and eager to help. Even among those who get into trouble, the first brush with the juvenile justice system is usually the last."

This chapter begins with a definition of prevention and some ways it has been classified, including prevention compared with control and its three levels. This is followed by a discussion of preventing delinquency through improved child protection services and through councils. Next which youths should be targeted in prevention programs are described, followed by a discussion of prevention as an attack on causes. Then the Blueprints for Violence Prevention Initiative is introduced. After that discussion, strategies to preserve families to prevent delinquency is explored followed by a look at strategies to prevent child neglect and abuse. The next major discussion is on prevention programs in the schools. Then general delinquency prevention programs and violence prevention programs are described. This is followed by discussions of drug prevention programs and gang prevention programs. The chapter concludes with an exploration of what works to prevent delinquency and violence and a caution regarding net widening.

Prevention Defined

The Department of Juvenile Justice (DJJ) defines prevention to use its limited resources appropriately: "Prevention is a measure taken before delinquent behavior has occurred and is directed toward preventing such occurrences. Addressing pre-delinquent behavior is a process of identifying problems related to delinquency, developing needed resources and building a strategy directed toward lowering the levels of pre-delinquent behavior through the provision of services to individuals or groups with specific needs."

Classification of Prevention Approaches

Several approaches to classify prevention efforts have been set forth. Following are two ways to look at and classify prevention efforts.

Prevention vs. Control

Technically prevention is a measure taken *before* a delinquent act occurs to forestall the act; control is a measure taken *after* a delinquent act occurs. In this context, three kinds of prevention are relevant for juvenile justice.

 Prevention can be corrective, punitive or mechanical.

- **Corrective prevention** focuses on eliminating conditions that lead to or cause criminal behavior.
- **Punitive prevention** relies on the threat of punishment to forestall criminal acts.
- **Mechanical prevention** is directed toward "target hardening," making it difficult or impossible to commit particular offenses. Locks on doors, bars on windows, alarms, security guards and many other options are available to protect possible targets of criminal acts.

Another way to classify prevention efforts is by level. These levels encompass the three methods just discussed.

Three Levels of Delinquency Prevention

The first line of defense against all forms of juvenile crime is prevention, whether *primary* (directed at the population as a whole), *secondary* (aimed at a specific at-risk population), or *tertiary* (targeted at an offending population to prevent repetition of the behaviors).

 Prevention may be primary, secondary or tertiary.

Primary Prevention

Primary prevention is directed at modifying and changing crime-causing conditions in the overall physical and social conditions that lead to crime. Corrective and mechanical prevention fit into this level. Primary prevention efforts are usually directed toward **risk factors** with no distinction between those who have committed a crime and those who have not. Shader (2002, p.2) explains: "Risk factors have been broadly defined as those characteristics, variables or hazards that, if present for a given individual, make it more likely that this individual, rather than someone selected from the general population, will develop a disorder." Fitting into the primary prevention category are programs that provide after-school activities and mentoring, including boys and girls clubs, Big Brothers/Big Sisters and youth foundations.

An example of primary prevention is the community crime prevention program in Seattle, Washington. This program focused on preventing residential burglaries, specifically crimes of opportunity by juveniles who entered homes through unlocked doors and windows during the day when residents were away.

Prevention efforts were aimed at contributing environmental factors. Certain neighborhoods and types of housing were identified as being vulnerable to burglaries using demographics, criminal incidents and physical characteristics statistics. The community then gave citizens home security checklists. Citizens in target areas used these checklists to protect their homes against relatively easy entry by burglars.

This program was directed at making crime more difficult rather than at attacking individual motivations to commit crime. Such deterrence programs effectively increase the risks of and decrease the opportunities for burglary.

As noted by the American Psychological Association (APA) (pp.55–56) in its discussion of primary prevention programs: "Prevention programs directed early in life can reduce factors that increase risk for antisocial behavior and clinical dysfunction in childhood and adolescence." Among the most promising primary prevention programs are those that include family counseling for pregnant women and for new mothers in the home, with continued visits during the first few years of the child's life. The American Psychological Association (p.55) reports that in a 20-year follow-up of one home visitor program, positive effects were seen for both the at-risk child and mother.

Preschool programs also hold promise if they include activities that develop intellectual, emotional and social skills and introduce children to responsible decision making. According to the APA (p.56):

> Primary prevention programs of the type that promote social and cognitive skills seem to have the greatest impact on attitudes about violent behavior among children and youth. Skills that aid children in learning alternatives to violent behaviors include social perspective-taking, alternative solution generation, self-esteem enhancement, peer negotiation skills, problem-solving skills training and anger management.

Secondary Prevention

Secondary prevention seeks early identification and intervention into the lives of individuals or groups that are found in crime-causing circumstances. It focuses on changing the behavior of those who are likely to become delinquent. Punitive prevention fits into this level. The APA (p.56) notes:

> Secondary prevention programs that focus on improving individual affective, cognitive and behavioral skills or on modifying the learning conditions for aggression offer promise of interrupting the path toward violence for high-risk or predelinquent youth. . . .
>
> Programs that attempt to work with and modify the family system of a high-risk child have great potential to prevent development of aggressive and violent behavior.

Tertiary Prevention

Tertiary prevention, the third level, is aimed at preventing recidivism—that is, it focuses on preventing further delinquent acts by youths already identified as delinquent. Tertiary prevention, also called treatment or rehabilitation, is the focus of Chapter 14.

Preventing Delinquency through Improved Child Protection Services (CPS)

One of the potentially most powerful prevention efforts, frequently overlooked, is to reduce the incidence of child neglect and abuse. As noted by Wiebush et al. (2001, p.1): "The link between experiencing maltreatment as a child and committing offenses as a juvenile is profound." They (pp.3–4) describe the OJJDP's comprehensive strategy using a risk-focused approach to prevention efforts, that is, it requires careful attention to factors identified through research as precursors to delinquency, violence and other problem behaviors. The strategy divides these risk factors into four categories: community, family, school and individual/peer, as shown in Table 13.1.

By this point, most of these factors should be very recognizable to readers of this text. The other core component of the OJJDP comprehensive strategy is *Structured Decision Making* (SDM). According to Wiebush et al. (pp.5–6):

> The SDM model is based on four primary principles:
>
> First, because decisions can be significantly improved when they are structured appropriately, every worker in every case must consider specific criteria through highly structured assessment procedures. Failure to clearly define decision-making criteria and identify how workers should apply these criteria results in inconsistency and, sometimes, inappropriate case actions.
>
> Second, priorities assigned to cases and service plans (or responses) must correspond directly to results of the assessment process. The assessment process has little meaning unless its results lead directly to an appropriate decision. Decisions should be structured to ensure that the agency's highest priority is given to the most serious and/or the highest risk cases. Moreover, if agencies are to translate priority setting into practice, they must have clearly identified and consistently implemented service standards—differentiated by level of risk—for each type of case. . . .
>
> Third, virtually everything that an agency does—from providing services in an individual case to budgeting for treatment resources—should be a response to the assessment process.
>
> Fourth, a single, rigidly defined model cannot meet the needs of every agency. Not all state and county child welfare agencies are organized to deliver services in the same way. Nor do they always share similar service mandates. As a result, the CRC [Children's Research Center] approach to designing an SDM system is collaborative and engages agencies in a joint developmental effort.

Table 13.1
Risk Factors for Health and Behavior Problems

	Substance Abuse	Delinquency	Teenage Pregnancy	School Dropout	Violence
Community					
Availability of drugs	•				•
Availability of firearms		•			•
Community laws and norms favorable toward drug use, firearms and crime	•	•			•
Media portrayals of violence					•
Transitions and mobility	•	•		•	
Low neighborhood attachment and community organization	•	•		•	
Extreme economic deprivation	•	•	•	•	•
Family					
Family history of the problem behavior	•	•	•	•	•
Family management problems	•	•	•	•	•
Family conflict	•	•	•	•	•
Favorable parental attitudes and involvement in the problem behavior	•	•			•
School					
Academic failure beginning in late elementary school	•	•	•	•	•
Lack of commitment to school	•	•	•	•	•
Peer and Individual					
Early and persistent antisocial behavior	•	•	•	•	•
Rebelliousness	•	•		•	
Friends who engage in the problem behavior	•	•	•	•	•
Gang involvement	•	•			•
Favorable attitudes toward the problem behavior	•	•	•	•	
Early initiation of the problem behavior	•	•	•	•	•
Constitutional factors	•	•			•

Source: R. F. Catalano and J. D. Hawkins. *Risk-Focused Prevention Using the Social Development Strategy.* Seattle, WA: Development Research and Programs, Inc., 2000, p.4. © 2003 Channing Bete Company, Inc. All rights reserved. Reproduced with permission of the publisher.

Wiebush et al. (p.4) stress: "The primary goals of the Structured Decision Making model are to (1) bring a greater degree of consistency, objectivity and validity to child welfare case decisions and (2) help CPS agencies focus their limited resources on cases at the highest level of risk and need." They (p.18) conclude: "Any program that effectively reduces abuse and neglect can serve as a prevention strategy for juvenile delinquency. Given the firmly established relationship between abuse/neglect and subsequent delinquency and criminality, it seems imperative that policymakers embrace emerging technologies that significantly improve decision making and help communities devote resources to children and families most at risk. It is clearly time to resolve age-old conflicts between clinical judgment and structured decision making. In particular, the use of empirically based risk assessment is not a question of replacing professional judgment with statistical inference; it is simply a matter of using the best information available to protect children from harm. . . . By reducing the extent of maltreatment experienced by children, the SDM model can make a significant contribution to breaking the link between abuse and delinquency."

Delinquency Prevention through Councils

One popular effort to address delinquency, crime and violence is through delinquency prevention councils. Kelly and Settle (2001, p.59) describe Kentucky's statewide delinquency prevention councils: "Council members work together to define problem areas in the community and identify community programs that can provide services for these problems and award grants for programs, including community education, community ministries, schools, and boys and girls clubs. Delinquency councils address juvenile justice issues at state and local levels. They provide a forum for the development of a community-based, interagency assessment of the local juvenile justice systems. Council members meet to discuss community juvenile delinquency issues." They describe the purposes of the council as being to:

- Pinpoint problem areas in the community, such as truancy, substance abuse and vandalism.
- Develop a three-year plan to address these needs.
- Enter into written local interagency agreements that specify the nature and extent of contributions that each signatory agency will make in achieving the goals of the local juvenile justice plan.
- Apply and receive public or private grants to be administered by a local unit of government or DJJ that support one or more components of the local juvenile justice plan.
- Share information, as authorized by law, to carry out the interagency agreements.
- Provide a forum for the presentation of interagency recommendations and the resolution of disagreements relating to the contents of the interagency agreement or the performance by the parties of their respective obligations under the agreements.
- Assist the efforts of local community support groups in providing enrichment programs and other support services for clients of the local juvenile justice system.
- Provide an annual report and recommendations to DJJ.

Kelly and Settle (p.60) state: "A unique characteristic of the delinquency prevention councils is the direct involvement of elected officials. School board members, commonwealth attorneys, county attorneys, sheriffs and judges have enabled councils to impact their communities through their direct involvement.

Delinquency prevention councils are most effective in addressing meaningful change at the community level. They are DJJ's direct link to local communities."

They also stress: "Delinquency prevention councils, in partnership with DJJ, are the key to building a strong juvenile justice system. . . . The key principles for preventing and reducing juvenile delinquency are to strengthen families; support core social institutions; promote prevention strategies and programs; intervene immediately and effectively when delinquent behavior occurs; and identify and control the small percentages of serious, violent and chronic juvenile offenders."

Which Youths to Target

Recall that the public health model (Chapter 6) called for focusing the scarce resources of the juvenile justice system on those at greatest risk—young black males living in areas of poverty with high crime rates and drug dealing. Using a mathematical analogy, look at the number of at-risk youths compared to the total number of youths; the at-risk youths would be the *numerator* and the total number of youths would be the *denominator*. Many researchers suggest we deal with the denominator for best results. Focusing efforts on juvenile offenders is unlikely to reduce youth crime, just as focusing on those who are unemployed will not lower unemployment rates. The relative ineffectiveness of the numerator approach and the effectiveness of the denominator approach is seen in medicine. A numerator approach in polio and tuberculosis has had little impact on prevalence; but denominator approaches such as vaccination and screening have almost eradicated these diseases. Denominator approaches are effective in medicine because they deal with general public health as well as specific symptoms. Such an approach can also be effective in delinquency prevention.

One reason the denominator approach is ignored is because it tends to generate turf fights. It is easier to act to improve an existing problem than to focus on a broader approach to prevent problems in the future.

 The **numerator approach** focuses on individuals and symptoms, whereas the **denominator approach** focuses on the entire group and causes.

The denominator approach is consistent with the public health model.

Prevention and the Public Health Model

According to Farrington (2000), in recent years juvenile justice has adopted an approach from the public health arena in an attempt to understand the causes of delinquency and work toward its prevention. Effective crime prevention based on the public health model uses a two-pronged strategy involving risk factors and protective factors.

 The public health model's two-pronged juvenile crime prevention strategy reduces known risk factors and promotes protective factors.

A report from the U.S. Surgeon General defines a risk factor as "anything that increases the probability that a person will suffer harm" (Office of the Surgeon

Table 13.2
Risk and Protective Factors

Category	Risk Factors	Protective Factors
Individual	Alienation, lack of bonding to society	Resilient temperament, positive attitudes
Family	Child abuse, family conflict, parental rejection	Bonding with prosocial family members, provision of clear standards for behavior by the family
School	Early academic failure, lack of commitment to school	Bonding with teachers, commitment to school
Peer Group	Friends involved in crime and violence	Healthy friendships with prosocial peers
Community	Poverty, high rates of drug abuse and crime	Clear standards for behavior and recognition of positive behavior

Source: Daniel McGillis. *Beacons of Hope: New York City's School-Based Community Centers.* National Institute of Justice Program Focus, January 1996, p.3. (NCJ 157667)

General 2001). Applying this strategy to juvenile crime prevention, several risk factors within the community, the family, the school and the individual can increase the probability that a young person will exhibit certain adolescent problem behaviors, including violence (review Table 13.1). In fact, according to Herrenkohl et al.(2000), a 10-year-old exposed to six or more risk factors is 10 times as likely to commit a violent act by age 18 as a 10-year-old exposed to only one risk factor.

Protective factors are those that reduce the impact of negative risk factors by providing positive ways for an individual to respond to risks. Among these are individual characteristics such as having a resilient temperament and positive social orientation; bonding with family and having positive relationships with other adults, teachers and peers; monitoring and supervision; positive discipline methods; and having healthy values and high standards. Alvarado and Kumpfer (2000, p.9) contend: "Parental supervision, attachment to parents and consistency of discipline are the most important protective factors." Table 13.2 presents risk and protective factors by domain and early onset or late onset.

In the mid-1980s, the OJJDP launched its Strengthening America's Families Initiative to provide parents with the critical skills required to enhance family resilience and decrease risk factors. This initiative's Web site is www.strengthening-families.org. In 1999, the OJJDP joined with the Center for Substance Abuse Prevention (CSAP) and the University of Utah to continue and expand the initiative.

Prevention as an Attack on Causes

Of the three levels of prevention, primary and secondary prevention most closely approach the essence of the term *prevention,* in that they seek to preclude delinquent acts *before* they occur. Tertiary prevention is really remediation aimed at forestalling future acts after an initial act has been committed and detected.

Primary and secondary prevention activities do not begin only after juveniles are arrested. These prevention approaches can be effective only if they address the underlying causes of delinquency. To prevent a behavior from occurring, those factors that stimulate the behavior must be removed. Conditions that stimulate delinquent acts and a lack of constraints to inhibit those acts are both potential causes of delinquency; therefore effective prevention must address both the conditions and the lack of constraints.

 Effective prevention approaches must address the causes of delinquency.

Former Minneapolis Chief of Police Tony Bouza once exclaimed: "We have to stop swatting at the mosquitoes and start looking to the swamps that produce them." With crooks as with mosquitoes, it's much harder to get rid of this year's swarm than to prevent next year's from hatching. That takes foresight and patience waiting for the payoff.

Sherman (2000, pp.71–72) relates the parable of the screwworm to illustrate this concept, describing the work of Edward Knipling, whose work led the way to eliminating screwworms in North America. Screwworms sought out wounds on any warmblooded animal and could cause death in a few days.

> Knipling's epidemiological research found that screwworm plagues were fostered by male worms mating many times but female worms mating only once. This finding prodded his imagination. If sterile males used up each female's one-and-only mating opportunity, he reasoned, there would be no offspring. If he could figure out a way to sterilize enough males, he would be able to drive the species into extinction. But when he proposed the idea to his superiors in 1938, they told him his idea was crazy.
>
> Fifteen years later, Knipling procured an old Army x-ray machine and conducted experiments showing he could sterilize male screwworms. He then released large numbers of them on Sanibel Island, Florida. Although the species quickly disappeared on the island, new worms from the mainland soon took their place. When the Dutch government offered the more isolated island of Curacao, Knipling released almost 2 million sterilized male worms over three months. This treatment completely eradicated the pest. At that point the USDA set up full-scale eradication programs in Florida and the Southwest, using giant sterilization factories to engineer the screwworm into extinction. Within 12 years, the pest was eradicated in the United States and most of North and Central America.

This epidemiology approach is expanded on later in the chapter in the discussion on reducing gun violence. Consider the appropriateness of this approach to the National Institute for Juvenile Justice and Delinquency Prevention's 12 strategies to distinguish delinquency prevention approaches. Each strategy addresses a distinct presumed cause of delinquency and an accompanying approach, as summarized in Table 13.3.

Blueprints for Violence Prevention Initiative

 The Blueprints for Violence Prevention Initiative is the OJJDP's comprehensive effort to provide communities with a set of programs whose effectiveness has been scientifically demonstrated.

Launched by the Center for the Study and Prevention of Violence (CSPV) at the University of Colorado at Boulder, the initiative provides the information necessary for communities to begin replicating programs locally.

Table 13.3
Causes of Delinquency and Associated Strategies of Delinquency Prevention

Presumed Cause	Strategy	Goal of Strategy
Physical abnormality/illness	Biological-physiological (health promotion, nutrition, neurological, genetic)	Remove, diminish, control underlying physiological, biological or biopsychiatric conditions
Psychological disturbance or disorder	Psychological/mental health (epidemiological/early intervention, psychotherapeutic, behavioral)	Alter internal psychological states or conditions generating them
Weak attachments to others	Social network development (linkage, influence)	Increase interaction/involvement between youths and nondeviant others; increase influence of nondeviant others on potentially delinquent youths
Criminal influence	Criminal influence reduction (disengagement from criminal influence, redirection from criminal norms)	Reduce the influence of delinquent norms and persons who directly or indirectly encourage youths to commit delinquent acts
Powerlessness	Power enhancement (informal influence, formal power)	Increase ability or power of youths to influence or control their environments, directly or indirectly
Lack of useful, worthwhile roles	Role development/role enhancement (service roles, production roles, student roles)	Create opportunities for youths to be involved in legitimate roles or activities they perceive as useful, successful, competent
Unoccupied time	Activities/recreation	Involve youths in nondelinquent activities
Inadequate skills	Education/skill development (cognitive, affective, moral, informal)	Provide individuals with personal skills that prepare them to find patterns of behavior free from delinquent activities
Conflicting environmental demands	Clear and consistent social expectations	Increase consistency of expectations/messages from institutions, organizations, groups that affect youths
Economic necessity	Economic resources (resource maintenance, resource attainment)	Provide basic resources to preclude the need for delinquency
Low degree of risk/difficulty	Deterrence (target hardening/removal, anticipatory intervention)	Increase cost and decrease benefits of criminal acts
Exclusionary social responses	Abandonment of legal control/social tolerance (explicit jurisdictional abandonment, implicit jurisdictional abandonment, covert jurisdictional abandonment, environmental tolerance)	Remove certain behaviors from control of the juvenile justice system; decrease the degree to which youths' behaviors are perceived, labeled, treated as delinquent

Source: Hawkins et al. Reports of the National Juvenile Justice Assessment Center. *A Topology of Caused-Focused Strategies of Delinquency Prevention.* Washington, DC: National Institute for Juvenile Justice and Delinquency Prevention, U.S. Government Printing Office, 1980.

In 2001, more than 500 programs were reviewed using rigorous selection criteria. From these, 11 model programs, or Blueprints, proved effective in reducing adolescent violent crime, aggression, delinquency, substance abuse, predelinquent childhood aggression and conduct disorders. Another 19 programs were identified as promising. Eight of the exemplary programs will be discussed as they relate to specific areas in this chapter. The remaining three programs are treatment focused and are discussed in Chapter 14. Of the eight exemplary prevention programs, four focus on the family. The program descriptions are adapted from Mihalic et al. (2001). Copies of each description were sent to the program directors. Five directors confirmed and/or modified the information, as will be indicated by a "confirmed" notation at the end of the description.

Preserving Families to Prevent Delinquency

The importance of families has been stressed throughout this text. The fact that four of the eleven OJJDP Blueprints for Violence exemplary programs focus on the family confirms the criticality of family in preventing delinquency and violence. Two of the exemplary programs are primarily prevention programs; two are primarily treatment programs and are discussed in Chapter 14.

Prenatal and Infancy Home Visitation by Nurses

Nurses visit the homes of low-income, first-time mothers to improve their health, parenting skills and chances of giving birth to children free of health and developmental problems.

The most serious and chronic offenders often show signs of antisocial behavior as early as the preschool years. Three risk factors associated with early development of antisocial behavior can be modified: (1) adverse maternal health-related behaviors during pregnancy, (2) child abuse and neglect and (3) troubled maternal life course.

Nurses begin visiting first-time mothers during pregnancy and continue the visits until the child is 2 years old. During home visits, nurses promote the physical, cognitive and social-emotional development of the children and provide general support and instruction in parenting skills. The following components are fundamental to the program's effectiveness:

- Trained and experienced nurses who have strong interpersonal skills and a maximum caseload of 25 families make the home visits.

- Families are visited every one to two weeks.

- Nurses focus simultaneously on the mother's personal health and development, environmental health and quality of caregiving.

Visiting nurses help young parents gain the confidence and skills necessary to set and achieve goals such as completing education, finding work and avoiding unplanned pregnancies.

Nurse home visitation has had positive outcomes on obstetrical health, psychosocial functioning and other health-related behaviors. One study found that women who smoked 10 or more cigarettes per day during pregnancy when they entered the nurse home visitation program reduced their smoking by approximately 3 cigarettes per day and improved their diets. On follow-up, the children of these women showed no intellectual impairments, whereas the children of mothers who smoked 10 or more cigarettes per day during pregnancy and did not receive nurse home visits did have impaired intellectual functioning.

The program also has helped reduce rates of child abuse and neglect by helping young parents learn effective parenting skills and deal with a range of issues such as depression, anger, impulsiveness and substance abuse. One study found that participating in the program was associated with a 79 percent reduction in state-verified cases of child abuse and neglect among mothers who were poor and unmarried. In their second year of life, nurse-visited children had 56 percent fewer visits to emergency rooms for injuries and ingestions than children who were not visited.

During the first 15 years after delivery of their first child, low-income, unmarried women who received nurse home visits had 31 percent fewer subsequent births, longer intervals between births (an average of two years), fewer months on welfare (60 versus 90 months), 44 percent fewer behavioral problems, 69 percent fewer arrests and 81 percent fewer criminal convictions than those in the control group.

Adolescents whose mothers received nurse home visits more than a decade earlier were 60 percent less likely to have run away and 55 percent less likely to have been convicted of a crime than adolescents whose mothers did not receive home visits. They also smoked fewer cigarettes per day, had consumed less alcohol in the past six months and exhibited fewer behavioral problems related to alcohol and drug use.

When the program focuses on low-income women, program costs are recovered by the time the first child reaches age 4. The RAND Corporation estimated that once the child reaches age 15, cost savings are four times the original investment because of reductions in crime, welfare expenditures and health care costs and as a result of taxes paid by working parents.

Contact information: Matthew Buhr-Vogl, Site Development Specialist; National Center for Children, Families and Communities; 1825 Marion Street; Denver, CO 80218; (303) 864-5839; (303) 864-5236 (fax); buhr-vogl. matthew@tchden.org.

The Incredible Years Series

This comprehensive set of curriculum is designed to promote social competence, prevent, reduce and treat conduct problems in young children.

Aggression in young children is escalating—and at younger ages. Young aggressive children may have already established a pattern of social difficulty in preschool that continues and becomes fairly stable by middle school. Many children with conduct problems (defined as high rates of aggression, defiance and oppositional and impulsive behaviors) have been asked to leave four or five schools by age 6, and by the time they enter middle school, their negative reputation and their rejection by peers and parents may be well established. Early intervention is key in reducing aggressive behavior and negative reputations before they develop into permanent patterns.

The program's targets are children ages 2 to 8 who exhibit or are at risk for conduct problems. Trained facilitators use interactive presentations, videotape modeling and role-playing techniques to encourage group discussion, problem solving and sharing of ideas.

The parent training component comprises three series: BASIC, ADVANCE and SCHOOL. BASIC is the core element of program delivery; the other two series in the parent training component—and the teacher and child training components discussed below—are recommended elements of program delivery. BASIC teaches parents interactive play and reinforcement skills, nonviolent discipline techniques, logical and natural consequences, and problem-solving strategies. ADVANCE addresses family risk factors such as depression, marital discord, poor coping skills, poor anger management and lack of support. SCHOOL focuses on ways to further youth's academic and social competence.

The teacher training component focuses on strengthening teachers' classroom management skills. It seeks to help teachers encourage and motivate students, promote students' prosocial behavior and cooperation with peers and teachers, teach anger management and problem-solving skills and reduce classroom aggression.

The child training component, known as the Dina Dinosaur curriculum, emphasizes skills related to developing emotional literacy, having empathy with others or taking their perspective, making and keeping friends, managing anger, solving interpersonal problems, following school rules and succeeding at school. It is designed for use as a "pull out" treatment program for small groups of children who exhibit conduct problems. The classroom-based version of this curriculum is also available as a prevention program for preschool and early school-age teachers.

In six randomized trials, the parent training component of The Incredible Years Series has been shown to reduce conduct problems and improve parenting interactions; these improvements have been sustained up to three years after the intervention. The cycle of aggression appears to have been halted for approximately two-thirds of families whose children have conduct disorders and who have been treated in clinics. In two randomized trials, the teacher training component has been shown to improve children's behavior in the classroom (improvements include less hyperactivity, antisocial behavior and aggression and more social and academic competence) and teachers' classroom management skills. The child training component resulted in significantly improved social skills and positive conflict management strategies with peers, in addition to reduced child behavior problems at home and school. Preliminary results of the classroom-based dinosaur curriculum suggest it is effective in reducing overall classroom aggression and increasing children's social competence.

Several hundred service agencies in the United States, Canada, the United Kingdom, Norway and Australia have adopted at least one of the three components in The Incredible Years parent training series. Funding to purchase the programs may be obtained from local Parent Teacher Associations or from charitable organizations. Once the initial costs of the materials and group leader training have been assumed, these programs can be offered at minimal cost.

Contact information: Carolyn Webster-Stratton; 1411 Eighth Avenue West, Seattle, WA 98119; (206) 285-7565 (phone and fax); (888) 506-3562 (toll-free phone and fax); incredibleyears@seanet.com; www.incredibleyears. com. Confirmed.

Other programs have been identified by the OJJDP in other contexts. One such program, Permanent Families for Abused and Neglected Children, is a training and technical assistance project of the National Council of Juvenile and

© AP/Wide World Photo

High school youths participating in a program sponsored by Student Conservation Association, Inc. work on the Hulls Gulch trail in the foothills near Boise, Idaho. The New Hampshire based non-profit group organizes outings to introduce urban youths to the outdoors.

Family Court Judges (NCJFCJ). A program focus is preservation of families suffering from drug abuse. When a drug-dependent infant is born and placed outside its biological family, the court tries to learn whether the mother is willing and able to undergo drug treatment, with the goal being eventual reunification of the family.

Another program, Targeted Outreach, is a delinquency intervention program sponsored by the Boys and Girls Clubs of America (BGCA). Targeted Outreach provides positive alternatives for at-risk youths through a referral network that links the clubs with schools, courts, police and other community youth-service agencies. The core program activities are designed to promote a sense of belonging, competence, usefulness and power or influence. These goals are very similar to those of the Boy Scouts of America, who also have much to offer high-risk youths.

Another program that emphasizes the family is Des Moines, Iowa's, In-Home Family Support Services, which views delinquency as resulting in some measure from an unstable home and family environment. In such situations family members often are not supportive of each other, and adults are hindered from socializing children positively. The program seeks to improve family communication and stability, bolster self-esteem and teach effective parenting skills.

Preventing Child Neglect and Abuse

As noted at the beginning of the chapter, a disproportionate number of neglected and abused children become delinquents, so preventing child neglect and abuse serves a dual function. According to Graves (2002, p.137): "Child abuse is present

A student at Capital High School in Helena, Montana, holds the school's Baby Think It Over doll. The $250 infant simulator is used in child development classes to teach students how their lives will change if they become parents.

in 30 to 70 percent of families in which there is spousal abuse, and the severity of the child abuse generally parallels the severity of the abuse to the spouse." Ennis (2000, p.95) contends: "If the public remains silent about child neglect and abuse, then the supportive services these children need will not reach them. The children who survive may produce another generation to perpetuate the cycle of violence."

An influential group to consider the problems of children who have been abused, deprived or neglected is the Metropolitan Court Judges Committee, a committee of the National Council of Juvenile and Family Court Judges. The National Council was founded in 1937 to improve the nation's complex juvenile justice system. Its training division at the University of Nevada, Reno, the National College of Juvenile Justice, has reached more than 65,000 juvenile justice professionals, an influence unparalleled by any judicial training organization in the country.

Recommendations of the Metropolitan Court Judges Committee

The Metropolitan Court Judges Committee also stresses the importance of preventive measures (pp.35–40): "The response of society to the tragedy of deprived children has been after-the-fact and ineffective. . . . Prevention of child abuse and neglect requires the awareness and involvement of the entire community. Deprived children are everyone's business. Their social and economic costs affect all Americans now and in the future." Among the committee's recommendations are the following:

- *Priority for prevention.* Prevention and early intervention efforts must receive high priority, with a greater emphasis placed on providing adequate services to prevent child abuse, neglect and family breakups through adequate education, early identification of those at risk, and family-based counseling and homemaker services.

- *Parenting education.* Continuing education in parenting and understanding the physical and emotional needs of children and families should be widely available in schools, health care systems, religious organizations and community centers.

- *Teenage parents.* Communities must provide special parenting education and services for pregnant teenagers as well as teen parents, including counseling on relinquishment and adoption.

- *Child care facilities.* Adequate child care facilities and services with training, licensing and monitoring of the providers should be available to all parents needing such services.

- *Employee assistance programs.* Employer-sponsored assistance and counseling programs for family violence and child abuse or neglect, such as those used for alcoholism and drug abuse, should be established.

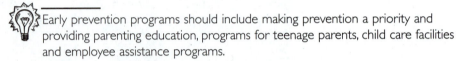

Early prevention programs should include making prevention a priority and providing parenting education, programs for teenage parents, child care facilities and employee assistance programs.

- *Children's disabilities.* Identification and assessment of the physically, mentally or emotionally disabled or learning disabled child must occur as early as possible.

- *Help for disabled.* Services and education must be designed for and provided to mentally ill, emotionally disturbed and physically or developmentally disabled children and parents.

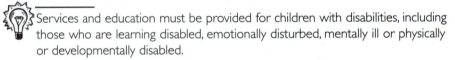

Services and education must be provided for children with disabilities, including those who are learning disabled, emotionally disturbed, mentally ill or physically or developmentally disabled.

- *Child support enforcement.* Judges must assure that child support orders are expedited and vigorously enforced and urge cooperation among all components of the child support enforcement process and all federal and state government agencies, which may affect child support enforcement proceedings.

- *Exploited children.* Persons convicted of exploiting children through pornography, prostitution or drug use or trafficking must be severely punished. High priorities also must be given to national efforts to curtail the availability to children of pornography and excessively violent materials.

- *Runaway and incorrigible children.* Courts and communities must provide services and courts must intervene, when necessary, to assist homeless, truant, runaway and incorrigible children. Parents must be held personally and financially accountable for the conduct of their children.

- *Truancy and school dropouts.* Courts should cooperate with schools and other agencies to substantially reduce truancy and dropouts by coordinating and providing services and assistance to the habitual truant.

- *Security and custody.* The courts should have authority to detain, in a secure facility, for a limited period, a runaway, truant or incorrigible child whose chronic behavior constitutes a clear and present danger to the child's own physical or emotional well-being, when the court determines there is no viable alternative.

 All children at risk, including runaways, habitual truants, the chronically incorrigible and those not receiving any or inadequate child support, must be considered when providing prevention services.

Parents Connecting with their Teenagers

Clinton (2000, p.3) describes the first-ever White House Conference on Teenagers during which a poll commissioned by the YMCA was released. According to this poll, more than three of four teenagers say they still turn to their parents in times of trouble: "In fact, while parents list the threat of drugs and alcohol as their chief worries, teenagers themselves list education and 'not having enough time' with their parents as their top concerns." She (p.4) stresses: "What teens need is a connection. They need a relationship with an adult who cares about them. In the words of psychologist Urie Bronfenbrenner, 'Somebody's got to be crazy about that kid, and vice versa!' "

Programs in the Schools—Blueprints for Violence Prevention

The importance of the schools in preventing delinquency, crime and violence has also been a focus throughout this text. Blueprints for Violence includes five programs, three focused on schools in general and two focused on substance abuse prevention.

Promoting Alternative Thinking Strategies (PATHS)

This school-based intervention includes lessons in self-control, emotional understanding, self-esteem and interpersonal problem-solving skills.

The need for universal, school-based curriculums promoting social and emotional competence and decreasing risk factors associated with maladjustment prompted the creation of Promoting Alternative Thinking Strategies (PATHS). The program, a school-based intervention, is taught by kindergarten through fifth-grade teachers as part of the regular curriculum. PATHS, which is designed to be taught three times per week for at least 20 minutes per session, includes lessons in self-control, emotional understanding, self-esteem, relationships and interpersonal problem-solving skills. Focusing on these protective factors provides youths with tools that enable them to achieve better academically in elementary school. In addition, PATHS helps enhance classroom atmosphere and the learning process.

Lessons are sequenced according to increasing developmental difficulty and include activities such as dialoguing, role-playing, storytelling, modeling by teachers and peers, and social and self-reinforcement. Among other lessons, youths are taught to identify and label their feelings; express, understand and regulate their emotions; understand the difference between feelings and behaviors; control impulses; and read and interpret social cues. Youths are given activities and strategies to use inside and outside the classroom, and parents receive program materials to reinforce behaviors at home.

Studies have compared classrooms receiving the intervention with matched controls using populations of normally adjusted students, behaviorally at-risk students and deaf students. Compared with the control groups, youths in the PATHS program have done significantly better in recognizing and understanding emotions, understanding social problems, developing effective alternative solutions and decreasing frequency of aggressive/violent solutions. Teachers reported significant improvements in children's self-control, emotional understanding, ability to tolerate frustration and use of conflict resolution strategies. Among special-needs youths, teachers reported decreases in internalized symptoms (sadness, anxiety and withdrawal) and externalized symptoms (aggressive and disruptive behavior).

Contact information: Mark T. Greenburg, Ph.D.; Prevention Research Center for Promotion of Human Development; Pennsylvania State University, 110 Henderson Building South, University Park, PA 16802-6504; (814) 863-0112; (814) 865-2530 (fax); prevention@psu.edu; www.prevention.psu.edu. Confirmed.

Bullying Prevention Program

This program attempts to reduce bullying in school children by reducing opportunities and rewards for bullying behavior, improving peer relations, disseminating an anonymous student questionnaire and holding interventions with bullies, victims and their parents.

The Bullying Prevention Program was developed, refined and systematically evaluated in Bergen, Norway, after three young Norwegian boys committed suicide as a result of severe bullying by peers. The original project, which took place from 1983 to 1985, involved 2,500 youths in 42 schools throughout the city. According to more than 150,000 Norwegian and Swedish students ages 7 to 16 who completed a bully/victim questionnaire, 15 percent had been involved in bully/victim problems. Of these, 5 percent had been frequent targets of bullies or had bullied frequently (once a week or more). In a recent U.S. study, 23 percent of more than 6,000 middle school students in rural South Carolina reported that they had been bullied several times or more during the past three months; 20 percent claimed they had bullied others with the same frequency. Because bullying is such a prevalent problem, the program has been replicated throughout Norway and in other countries, including the United States.

The program's major goal is to reduce bullying among elementary, middle and junior high school children by reducing opportunities and rewards for bullying behavior. School staff are largely responsible for introducing and carrying out the program, and their efforts are directed toward improving peer relations and making the school a safe and pleasant environment. Bullying Prevention increases awareness of and knowledge about the problem, actively involves teachers and parents, develops clear rules against bullying behavior and provides support and protection for bullying victims. Core components of the program are at three levels:

- *School.* School personnel disseminate an anonymous student questionnaire to assess the nature and prevalence of bullying, discuss the problem, plan for program implementation, form a school committee to coordinate program delivery and develop a system of supervising students during breaks.

- *Classroom.* Teachers and/or other school personnel introduce and enforce classroom rules against bullying, hold regular classroom meetings with students and meet with parents to encourage their participation.
- *Individual.* Staff hold interventions with bullies, victims and their parents to ensure that the bullying stops.

The use of school, classroom and individual interventions ensures that students are exposed to a consistent, strong message from different people in different contexts regarding the school's views of and attitudes toward bullying.

In Bergen, Norway, the frequency of bullying problems decreased by 50 percent or more in the two years following the original project. These results applied to both boys and girls and to students across all grades studied. In addition, school climate improved and the rate of antisocial behavior in general such as theft, vandalism and truancy dropped during the two-year period. In the South Carolina replication site, the program slowed the rate of increase in youth's engagement in antisocial behavior. In addition, students reported that they bullied other students less after seven months in the program (a 25 percent reduction in the rate of bullying).

Contact information: Dan Olweus, Ph.D., University of Bergen, Research Center for Health Promotion, Christies gt. 13, N-5015, Bergen Norway; 47-55-58-23-27; 47-55-58-84-22 (fax); olweus@psych.uib.no or Susan Limber, Ph.D., Institute on Family and Neighborhood Life, Clemson University, 158 Poole Agricultural Center, Clemson, SC 29364; (864) 656-6320; (864) 656-6281 (fax); slimber@clemson.edu.

Quantum Opportunities Program

This program provides youths with an intensive array of coordinated services and a sustained relationship with peers receiving similar services for the four years they are in high school.

The Quantum Opportunities Program (QOP) was developed and implemented to benefit youths from families receiving public assistance. QOP was designed to help youths overcome their disadvantaged backgrounds by compensating for their perceived and real lack of opportunities, providing them with a prosocial environment conducive to success, enhancing their skills levels to equip them for success and reinforcing their achievements and positive actions. A QOP coordinator, who acts as surrogate parent, role model, advisor and disciplinarian, provides services to a small group (no more than 25) of high-risk youths just entering the ninth grade. The group environment helps youths bond with each other and with a caring adult, and this bonding appears to make the largest difference in student motivation and success. The program includes 250 hours per year of (1) educational opportunities (e.g., peer tutoring, computer-based instruction) to enhance basic academic skills, (2) development opportunities (e.g., family planning, career and college planning, cultural enrichment, personal development) and (3) community service opportunities (e.g., volunteering, working at public events). Financial incentives are offered to increase participation, completion and long-range planning.

Results from the pilot test of this program, which took place from 1989 through 1993, indicated that QOP participants, when compared with a control group, were less likely to be arrested during the juvenile years (19 versus 23 percent), more likely to have graduated from high school (63 versus 42 percent), more likely to be enrolled in higher education or training (42 versus 16 percent), more likely to attend a four-year college (18 versus 5 percent) and less likely to become a teen parent (24 versus 38 percent). Six months after completing the program, 21 percent of QOP youths had taken part in a community project; 28 percent had volunteered as a tutor, counselor or mentor; and 41 percent had volunteered at a nonprofit, charitable school or community group. In comparison, the percentage of control youths were 12, 8 and 11, respectively.

Contact information: C. Benjamin Lattimore, Opportunities Industrialization Centers of America, Inc., 1415 North Broad Street, Philadelphia, PA 19122; (215) 236-4500, ext (251); (215) 236-7480 (fax); oica@aol.com; www.oic-world.org.

Life Skills Training

This drug prevention program focuses on tobacco, alcohol and marijuana and targets the psychosocial factors associated with the onset of drug involvement by providing drug-related resistance skills training in middle schools.

The most common approaches to substance abuse prevention for the past two decades have involved either the presentation of information concerning the dangers of drug use or the use of classroom discussion and classroom activities designed to enrich youths' personal and social development. These approaches do not address the risk factors for substance abuse among youths and therefore are largely ineffective. Life Skills Training (LST), however, is based on an understanding of the causes of tobacco, alcohol and drug use and has been designed to target the psychosocial factors associated with the onset of drug involvement.

The three-year curriculum includes 15 sessions taught in the first year of the program by regular classroom teachers with booster sessions provided in years two and three. The three basic components of the program teach youths: (1) personal self-management skills (e.g., decision making and problem solving, self-control skills for coping with anxiety and self-improvement skills), (2) social skills (e.g., communication and general social skills) and (3) information and skills designed to have an impact on youths' knowledge and attitudes concerning drug use, normative expectations and skills for resisting drug use influences from the media and peers.

LST has been found to cut alcohol, tobacco and marijuana use among young adolescents by 50 to 75 percent. Long-term results of the program reveal a 66 percent reduction in **polydrug use** (use of tobacco, alcohol and marijuana), a 25 percent reduction in pack-a-day smoking and a decrease in the use of inhalants, narcotics and hallucinogens. Long-term follow-up data reveal that reductions can last through twelfth grade.

Contact information: Gilbert Botvin, Ph.D., President, National Health Promotion Associates, Inc., 141 South Central Avenue, Suite 208, Hartsdale, NY 10530; (914) 421-2525; (914) 683-6998 (fax); www.lifeskillstraining.com.

Midwestern Prevention Project

This project targets the factors thought to be responsible for higher levels of drug use; one of the program goals is to decrease the rates of onset and prevalence of gateway and other drug use in youths ages 10 to 15.

Many researchers, policymakers and drug prevention program planners have begun to question whether single-channel programs (i.e., those implemented entirely within one setting) are effective in promoting significant and lasting changes in youths' drug use behavior. To ensure that its drug prevention message is heard throughout the community in many settings, the Midwestern Prevention Project (MPP), also known as Project STAR, integrates a school-based program with parent, community, mass media and local policy components.

MPP's goals are to decrease the rates of onset and prevalence of **gateway drugs** (tobacco, alcohol and marijuana) and other drug use in youths ages 10 to 15 and, secondarily, to decrease drug use among parents and other community residents. To achieve these goals, MPP targets the person-, situation- and environment-level factors thought to be responsible for higher levels of drug use, including prior use, low level of resistance skills, perceived norms for use, peer pressure to use, lack of social support for nonuse, and school and community norms.

The program consists of five components: school program, parent education campaign, mass media, community organization and training, and local policy change. The school program teaches active social learning techniques (e.g., modeling, role-playing, discussion) and assigns homework designed to involve family members. The parent education campaign involves parent-child communication training and a parent-principal committee that reviews the school drug policy. The other three components deliver a consistent message to the community supporting drug-free living. Collectively, the components focus on promoting youths' drug use resistance and counteraction skills (direct skills training), parents' and other adults' prevention practices and support of adolescent prevention practices (indirect skills training) and community's dissemination and support of social norms and expectations against drug use (environmental support).

MPP has been shown to reduce marijuana use and daily cigarette smoking by approximately 40 percent among program participants, with smaller reductions in alcohol use. These reductions were maintained through age 12. Reductions in daily smoking, heavy use of marijuana and use of some hard drugs have been shown through early adulthood (age 23). MPP also has helped decrease parental alcohol and marijuana use and increase positive parent-child discussion about drug use prevention.

Contact information: Mary Ann Pentz, Ph.D., University of Southern California, Institute for Prevention Research, 1000 S. Fremont Ave., Unit 8, Alhambra, CA 91803; (626) 457-6691; (626) 457-6695 (fax); pentz@usc.edu. Confirmed.

Other programs to prevent drug use are discussed later in the chapter.

Other School-Based Programs

Several other school-based programs address delinquency and violence prevention.

Coalition for Juvenile Justice

Abandoned in the Back Row: New Lessons in Education and Delinquency Prevention (2001) is the annual report of the Coalition for Juvenile Justice (CJJ), a nationwide response to juvenile crime and delinquency—"building safe communities one child at a time." The report notes that youths who receive an inadequate education or do not succeed in school often enter the juvenile court system. Consequently, children with learning or emotional disabilities are highly susceptible to delinquency. More than 35 percent of students with learning disabilities drop out of school, twice the rate of students without learning disabilities. Youths who drop out of school are 3.5 times more likely to be arrested than high school graduates. Each year the United States is drained of more than $200 billion in lost earnings and taxes because of the high rate of youths dropping out of school.

This document (p.3) suggests: "In a misguided attempt to increase classroom safety, some schools have adopted policies that all too quickly slam doors in the faces of distressed students. For example, under such policies students may be automatically expelled for drug and weapons violations, as well as infractions like writing graffiti. . . . By removing students with problematic behavior, severely punitive measures send harmful messages to students: You are not worth helping. It also teaches the entire school community that problems, including anger and frustration, are to be avoided, rather than addressed by the whole in a productive, meaningful fashion."

Although not a program itself, the report suggests what helps youths to stay in school, including early childhood education (overall, $7.10 is returned to society for every dollar spent on early education), mentors, activities that enhance self-esteem, counseling services, social and life skill training and service learning—connecting meaningful community service experiences with academic learning.

The report (p.4) also outlines the characteristics of successful education programs:

- Programs that emphasize competency development in reading, writing and math, along with thinking and decision-making skills
- Low student/teacher ratios or ratios that fully reflect the needs of the students
- Parents, families, teachers, community organizations and volunteers involved in the academic program
- Youths assessed for learning disabilities and other special needs and provided with special education in full compliance with federal law

Alternative Schools

Prevention programs in Rhode Island and Oregon schools use alternative education programs to reach at-risk youths. Such programs are based on the belief that failure in school increases the likelihood that youths will commit delinquent acts. The school is considered an appropriate vehicle to help children meet their early developmental needs in six major roles: learner, individual, producer, citizen, consumer and family member. Helping children recognize and prepare for these roles should prevent problems, including delinquency, in later life. Included in other prevention programs are:

- *Job/career programs* that help youths define their career interests, provide vocational training and teach youths how to look for a job and other employment services.
- *Advocacy programs* in which youths, their families and school staff members monitor and pressure for needed changes in youth services.

Communities in Schools (CIS)

The Communities In Schools (CIS) network is a web of local, state and national partnerships working together to bring at-risk youths four basics that every child needs and deserves: a personal one-on-one relationship with a caring adult, a safe place to learn and grow, a marketable skill to use upon graduation and a chance to give back to peers and community. CIS treats the student and his or her family in a holistic manner, bringing together in one place a support system of caring adults who ensure that the student has access to the resources that can help him or her build self-worth and the skills needed to embark on a more productive and constructive life. According to *2001–2002 Network Report: Personal, Accountable and Coordinated* (2003), 98 percent of CIS programs provide a one-on-one loving relationship with caring adults using 49,000 volunteers. CIS is the nation's largest stay-in-school network, coordinating 10,000 agencies and service providers, 2,600 schools, 54,000 individuals and providing services to 2 million students. CIS fills gaps in services and reduces duplications. It seeks to decrease dropout rates, increase promotion and graduation rates, and improve attendance, discipline and academic performance.

The Alternative to Suspension Program (ASP)

The Alternative to Suspension Program (ASP) addresses the problem of suspended students and how, instead of staying home under parental supervision during such suspensions, such students often tend to hang out at the mall, loiter at local convenience stores or engage in criminal activity such as breaking into homes and cars. To counter such unsupervised suspensions, the North Miami Beach, Florida, community created the Alternative to Suspension Program (ASP), bringing together parents, schools and law enforcement in an effort to keep suspended students off the streets and away from criminal activity.

The YouthARTS Development Project

Clawson and Coolbaugh (2001, p.1) note: "The YouthARTS Development Project, initiated in 1995, is a collaborative effort among federal agencies, national arts organizations and a consortium of three local arts agencies in Atlanta, Georgia; Portland, Oregon; and San Antonio, Texas, designed to identify, implement and refine effective arts-based delinquency prevention programs." They explain: "The YouthARTS Development Project was launched with three overarching goals: To enhance program development and capacity-building in local arts agencies, to identify effective arts-based delinquency prevention and intervention programs and to disseminate information about program planning, implementation and evaluation nationally. Figure 13.1 provides an overview of the YouthARTS development project design. Table 13.4 describes the parameters of the program at three of the sites.

Culinary Education and Training Program for At-Risk Youths (CETARY)

According to Brunson and Smith (2001, p.1): "In 1998, with support from the Office of Juvenile Justice and Delinquency Prevention, Johnson & Wales University's (JWU's) North Florida Campus designed and implemented this nine-month, custom designed culinary arts certificate program. The CETARY program offers professional training in one of Miami's high growth industries—food service." Youths referred to the program are 16 to 18 years old with at least a ninth-grade academic capability who have committed a nonviolent crime and

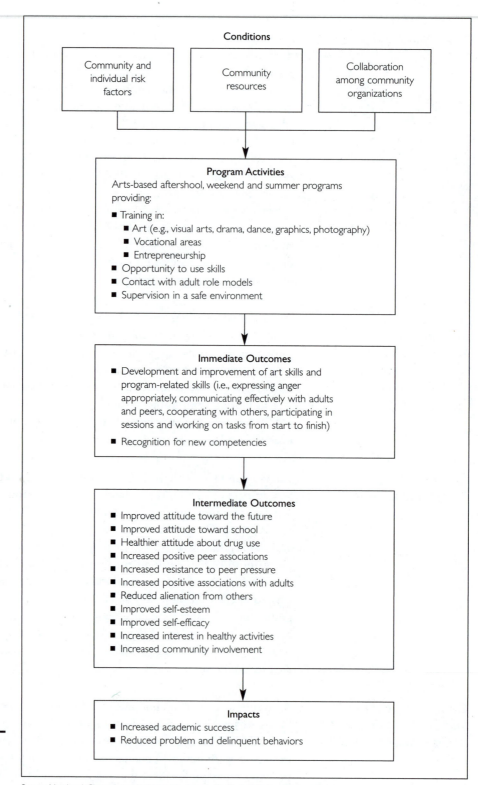

Figure 13.1
**YouthARTS Development
Project Design**

Source: Heather J. Clawson and Kathleen Coolbaugh. *The YouthARTS Development Project.*
Washington, DC: OJJDP Juvenile Justice Bulletin, May 2001, p.2. (NCJ 186668)

Table 13.4
Summary of YouthARTS Programs

Parameter	Art-at-Work Atlanta, GA	Youth Arts Public Art Portland, OR	Urban smARTS San Antonio, TX
Local collaborative partners	Fulton County Arts Council and Fulton County Juvenile Court	Portland Regional Arts and Culture Council and Multnomah County Division of Juvenile Justice Service	City of San Antonio Department of Arts and Cultural Affairs, Department of Community Initiatives and San Antonio Independent School District
Target population	Truant youths ages 14–16 referred by current probation counselors	Adjudicated youths (except those adjudicated for sex offenses) ages 14–16 referred by current probation officers	Nonadjudicated, at-risk youths ages 10–12 referred by teachers, principals, and self-referrals
Capacity	Fifteen youths per program period	Fifteen youths per unit per session (gang reduction unit, North unit and Southeast unit)	60 youths at each of seven schools
Duration	Four sessions (8–12 weeks each) with the same group of participants	One session per unit (12 weeks each)	One session (16 weeks) per school per year
Frequency	8 hours per week during school, 25 hours per week during summer	6 hours per week	9 hours per week
Staffing	Program director, project manager, lead artist/program coordinator, professional artists and probation counselors	Program director, project manager, professional artists and probation officers	Program director, project manager, teacher liaison, professional artists and caseworkers.
Training	Two-day artist training focusing on child development, conflict resolution, problem solving and classroom management	Informal training of artists and probation officers focusing on program design, goals and objectives, background of participants and rules and regulations	Five-day cross-training of artists and caseworkers focusing on working with at-risk youths, child management, curriculum development and school rules and regulations.
Approach	Arts-based afterschool and summer education and job-training program designed to serve one group of youths for 2 years Part of each day is spent learning art skills and producing saleable art. Projects have included furniture design and application, ceramics, mosaics, photography, drama and computer graphics. Part of each day is spent learning entrepreneurship and planning exhibits. Students help organize exhibits at the end of the session. All proceeds support the program.	Arts program designed to involve youths in the production and administration of a public arts project, from design to production and public exhibition Youths work with the artists twice per week during afterschool hours. Probation counselors are present at each session to help artists control problem behaviors. Each session focuses on a different art medium. The media include printmaking, photography, poetry, drama and videography. A final exhibit or presentation designed to provide youths with recognition for their accomplishments is scheduled for the end of each session.	Afterschool arts education program for youths at seven schools Each school is assigned three artists who design and implement the art activities (i.e., dance, visual arts, drama, creative writings and story telling). The program also provides educational field trips. Transportation home from the program and snacks during programs hours are provided. Case management is provided by the Youth Services Division of the Community Initiatives Department. Every youth referred to the program receives a home visit from a caseworker for intake and assessment of the youth and family.
Incentive	Students receive $5 per hour during school year and $100 per week during summer vacation.	Participants from the North and Southeast units receive time off probation or community service hours for successful completion. Gang reduction unit participants are given a $100 incentive and are required to participate.	N/A
Intended outcome	Art skills Vocational/entrepreneurial skills Life skills Prosocial behavior	Art skills Vocational/entrepreneurial skills Life skills Prosocial behavior	Art skills Vocational/entrepreneurial skills Life skills Prosocial behavior

Source: Heather J. Clawson and Kathleen Coolbaugh. *The YouthARTS Development Project.* Washington, DC: OJJDP Juvenile Justice Bulletin, May 2001, pp.4–5.

either dropped out of high school or are at risk of dropping out. Brunson and Smith report: "Since the inception of this program, the president of JWU has deemed the CETARY program one of the Florida campus's top community outreach priorities and, in 1999, the program was highlighted as a model in the University President's Report."

Safe Schools/Healthy Students (SSHS) Program

The Safe Schools/Healthy Students (SSHS) Program supports urban, rural, suburban and tribal school district efforts to link prevention activities with community-based services and thereby strengthen local approaches to violence prevention and child development. Grants totaling more than $80 million are available to communities. Plans are required to address six elements: (1) a safe school environment; (2) violence, alcohol and drug abuse prevention and early intervention programs; (3) school and community mental health prevention and treatment intervention services; (4) early childhood psychosocial and emotional development services; (5) education reform; and (6) safe school policies.

Truancy Reduction: The ACT Now Program

The problems caused by truancy were introduced in Chapter 7. As noted by Baker et al. (2001, p.1): "Left unchecked, truancy is a risk factor for serious juvenile delinquency. Truancy's impact also extends into the adult years where it has been linked to numerous negative outcomes. Consequently, it is critical to identify strategies that intervene effectively with youths who are chronically truant and that interrupt their progress to delinquency and other negative behaviors by addressing the underlying reasons behind their absence from school."

The OJJDP identified ACT (Abolish Chronic Truancy) Now—a prosecutor-led program in Pima County, Arizona, as an exemplary program in truancy prevention. The truancy plan includes three key elements:

- Enforcement of the mandatory attendance law by holding parents accountable
- Provision of a diversion program that offers services to address the root causes of truancy
- Sanctions for parents and youths for continued truancy or failure to complete the diversion program successfully

Figure 13.2 depicts the partners identified as necessary to reducing truancy.

Project H.E.L.P.: High Expectations Learning Program

Project H.E.L.P.'s program mission is to ensure all students have the opportunities they need to work to their full academic and social potentials. This program is a year-round educational program offering an extra 200 hours of supplemental classroom instruction per year to underachieving elementary school students. This supplemental instruction is offered within the context of a five-week Summer Term and a nine-month School Year Extension. To ensure a powerful transition into the regular school year Project H.E.L.P. provides teacher continuity; the student's teacher during the Summer Term is also the student's teacher during the school year.

According to the program's Web site: "The key component in the success of Project H.E.L.P. has always been parental involvement. From the beginning, Pro-

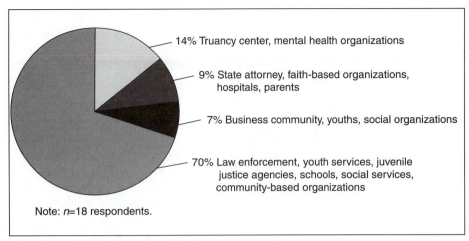

Figure 13.2
Partners Identified as Necessary to Reduce Truancy

Note: *n*=18 respondents.

Source: Myriam L. Baker, Jane Nady Sigmon and Elaine Nugent. *Truancy Reduction: Keeping Students in School.* Washington, DC: OJJDP Juvenile Justice Bulletin, September 2001, p.12. (NCJ 188947)

ject H.E.L.P. has set high standards for parent participation, and the pre-requisite for enrollment in Project H.E.L.P. is a clear understanding of the role parents will need to play if they wish their children to be a part of the project." The parental performance standards include (1) attendance at weekly parent/teachers conferences during the Summer Term and monthly conferences during the School Year Extension, (2) setting aside time each evening to monitor homework and provide assistance and encouragement as needed, (3) attending parent seminars that offer encouragement, support and strategies to implement at home to enhance their child's prospects for academic programs and (4) financial support through tuition, which typically covers 15 to 20 percent of program costs, with financial aid available to parents who demonstrate a need for tuition assistance.

Programs to Raise Minority Academic Achievement

An American Youth Policy Forum (AYPF) report details a two-year effort to find, summarize and evaluate school and youth programs that show gains for minority youths across a broad range of academic achievement indicators. *Raising Minority Academic Achievement: A Compendium of Education Programs and Practices* (James et al., 2001) provides an accessible resource for policymakers and practitioners interested in promoting the academic success of racial and ethnic minorities from early childhood through advanced postsecondary study.

According to this report, evaluations of early childhood programs were particularly strong and positive. When compared with control groups, minority children who attended early childhood development programs were more likely to remain in school, complete more years of education and require less special education. The high school/transition programs studied showed increasing high school graduation, more high school credits earned, higher GPAs earned or increased enrollment in higher-level courses.

All programs used a combination of strategies to improve student performance, not a single intervention. The ten most frequent strategies identified in those programs showing gains for minority youths are (1) quality implementation, leadership, accountability, (2) academically demanding curriculum, (3) family involvement, (4) individualized supports for students, (5) community involvement, (6) scholarships and other financial supports, (7) professional development for teachers and staff, (8) reduced student-to-teacher ratios, (9) extended learning time and (10) long-term (multiple year) programs.

OJJDP Exemplary Programs in the Schools[1]

Many programs that follow have received the **Gould-Wysinger Award,** an award established in 1992 to give national recognition for local achievement in improving the juvenile justice system and helping our nation's youths. These programs are designated GWA in the sections to come.

Anger Management Program, North Dakota

Located in Bismarck, the Anger Management Program works with youths and their parents to help them control outbursts of angry, aggressive behavior. The 10-week training program reduces the frequency of aggressive or violent incidents by developing awareness of anger patterns and teaching new skills for handling anger-provoking situations. The curriculum includes separate groups for parents, junior and high school students, and fifth and sixth graders.

Young people enrolled in the program have reduced their involvement in aggressive and violent incidents. The program draws on the resources of virtually every youth-serving agency, public and private, that maintains a local staff. The state training school and a private residential facility have requested training in anger management so they can incorporate a similar component in their programs. (GWA)

Bright Future Project, Tennessee

This juvenile delinquency prevention project provides academic and social support to African-American youths ages 5 to 15. Bright Future provides study resources to help youths complete their homework assignments. Reading and comprehension testing and prescribed tutoring are available for a limited number of youths. Decision-making rap sessions, discussions and practice sessions are also provided. Supervised opportunities allow youths to contribute to their communities by participating in neighborhood improvement projects.

The program serves 30 children per day. Teachers note that participants' quantity and quality of schoolwork have improved. The program has gained the respect of the community, and Bright Future's Neighborhood Association has become the center of community life largely as a result of this project. (GWA)

McAlester Alternative School Project, Oklahoma

The McAlester Alternative School Project was developed to provide education services to at-risk students in the McAlester Public School District. The school allows students to learn at their own pace in a more relaxed setting. It provides onsite childcare for teen parents and teaches fundamentals of childcare. Class sizes are small, and a counselor is available throughout the day to provide personal, crisis and career counseling. Attendance is voluntary. The school has helped meet the needs of a community experiencing serious socioeconomic problems. (GWA)

---

[2]Program descriptions written by Pam Allen, director of special projects for the Coalition of Juvenile Justice and overseer of administration of the award solicitation process.

Table 13.5
Measures of Hypothetical Predictors of Program Quality

Category and Predictor Scale or Item Name	Number of Items	Alpha Reliability
Organizational capacity		
School amenability to program implementation	11	.81
Turnover in implementing staff	1	-
Organizational support		
Amount of training in activity/program	3	.67
Quality of training in activity/program	6	.87
Supervision or monitoring of implementation of program or activity	3	.55
Principal support for program or activity	1	-
Program Structure		
Standardization	5	.72
Integration into normal school operations		
Local responsibility (school insiders) for program initiation	14	.82
Variety of information sources used to select program or activity	7	.70
Amount of provider's job related to program or activity	1	-
Activity is part of regular school program	1	-
Provider is full-time	1	-
Paid workers deliver program or activity	1	-

Source: Denise C. Gottfredson and Gary D. Gottfredson. "Quality of School-Based Prevention Programs: Results from a National Survey." *Journal of Research in Crime and Delinquency,* February 2002, p.15. Reprinted by permission of Sage Publications.

Griffin Alternative Learning Academy, Florida

Griffin Alternative Learning Academy (GALA) diverts students from failing in school, being suspended, needing court intervention or dropping out of school. The program focuses on disruptive, unsuccessful, disinterested and otherwise problematic students at Griffin Middle School in Leon County. The objective is to mainstream or promote 75 percent of the at-risk students back into regular classes by providing individualized academic assistance and business mentoring.

A project evaluation confirmed overall improvement in participants' grade point averages, a decrease in the number of absences and suspensions, and a reduction in delinquency referrals. All participants were promoted to the next grade. Because of the success of the program, the Governor's JJDP Advisory Committee funded replications of the project in two other schools. (GWA)

Quality of School-Based Prevention Programs

Gottfredson and Gottfredson (2002, p.3) conducted a national survey on the quality of school-based prevention programs and found: "The quality of school-based prevention practices as they are implemented in the typical school is low. The level of implementation of prevention practices can be improved through better integration of these activities into normal school operations; more extensive local planning and involvement in decisions about what to implement; greater organizational support in the form of high-quality training, supervision and principal support; and greater standardization of program materials and methods." Table 13.5 lists the hypothetical predictors of program quality.

Table 13.6
Community Activities to Achieve Crime Prevention Goals

Academic enrichment	Enforcement of weapons laws	Probation and supervised release
After-school activities	Environmental work projects	Public education
Aftercare services	Family support services	Public-private partnerships
Apprenticeships	Gang intervention	Recognition
Building safety and security	Gun safety	Recreation
Child care	Health care access	Safe passages/corridors
Child protective services	Home visits	School antidrug/weapon policies
College scholarships	Housing placement	Self-defense training
Community mobilization	Housing renovation	Service integration
Community policing	Interagency coordination	Shelters
Community schools	Job creation	Sports leagues
Community service	Job placement	Stress management
Computer skills training	Job training	Summer jobs for youth
Conflict resolution	Leadership skills development	Substance abuse education
Counseling	Literacy	Substance abuse treatment
Cultural awareness	Media campaigns	Theater and the arts
Domestic violence awareness	Mental health screening	Transportation
Domestic violence shelters	Mentoring	Tutoring
Drug courts	Nutrition services	Victim restitution
Drug testing	Outreach	Youth involvement
Educational stipends	Parent education and training	Zoning
Employment skills	Parental involvement	
Enforcement of drug laws	Park and neighborhood clean-up	

Source: *Helping Communities Fight Crime: Comprehensive Planning Techniques, Models, Programs and Resources.* Washington, DC: The President's Crime Prevention Council Catalog, 1997, p.4.

General Delinquency Prevention Programs

Prevention and intervention are equally important in any effort to address adult crime. Jane Alexander, Chair for the National Endowment for the Arts, states: "Give a child a paintbrush or a clarinet, and he is much less likely to pick up a gun or a needle. Give a child a chance to explore and express perceptions of the world, and you are encouraging positive behavior. This has everything to do with crime prevention." Table 13.6 lists the myriad activities communities nationwide are using to achieve their crime prevention goals.

Several programs are aimed at the general concept of delinquency prevention, including five OJJDP exemplary projects described by Allen.

Project HELP, North Carolina

Project HELP (Helping Equip Little People) is an early intervention program that concentrates on delinquency prevention. The goals of the program are to promote wholesome values and moral living, impart work-readiness skills, develop social and cultural skills, give youths an opportunity to interact with positive adult role models and involve parents in all phases of the program.

The program serves youths ages 6 to 10 who have exhibited behaviors that make them at-risk of entering the juvenile justice system. Volunteers, who are matched with an appropriate youth, work with program staff, parents and youths to develop individual programs and create opportunities for leadership development.

To date every parent of a child in the program has become involved, and three-quarters of the children have participated in HELP's social and cultural enrichment programs. Everyone has participated in community service activities either through the schools, local civic groups or the housing authority. Not one participant has become involved with the juvenile justice system. (GWA)

Graffiti Street, Virgin Islands

Graffiti Street is a teen talk show designed to prevent juvenile delinquency by improving communication and developing understanding between youths and adults. The format uses a teen panel, guest speakers and guest performers. Participants represent a cross-section of the population. The show is very popular with youths and adults and has received a national public broadcasting award. (GWA)

Hollandale Temporary Holding Facility, Mississippi

The Hollandale Temporary Holding Facility was established to provide a separate facility that meets all federal and state standards for juveniles awaiting further action by a youth authority. Facility staff are on call 24 hours a day. Emergency care and crisis intervention include youth court counselors' services and referrals to a local community health service. The facility also provides supervised educational and recreational activities while youths are awaiting disposition or placement.

The facility holds juveniles who would otherwise have been placed in an adult jail or lockup—decreasing by 90 percent the number of juveniles held in adult jails and lockups in the six counties served. (GWA)

Regional Juvenile Justice Program Development, Washington State

The Regional Juvenile Justice Program Development program is an interagency approach to developing strategies for preventing and reducing juvenile delinquency in Snohomish County. The major goal of the program is to implement the Juvenile Justice and Delinquency Prevention Act. Project staff develops and recommend procedures for the coordination of local juvenile justice activities and works to ensure that duplication and conflict between agencies are minimized, service gaps are identified and systemwide problems are addressed. The program serves as a resource for the State Advisory Group (SAG) in identifying technical assistance and training needs, providing information and assistance to local agencies to help them develop proposals responsive to SAG priorities, and reviewing and prioritizing proposals for SAG funding.

Other program activities include collecting data for a needs assessment to identify local juvenile justice needs.

Rites of Passage, Iowa

Rites of Passage was developed to address minority overrepresentation by reducing the delinquency rate among middle school African-American males from high-risk situations. The project involves tutoring, mentoring, crisis intervention, individual and family counseling, and recreational activities. Development of participants' self-esteem and personal responsibility are emphasized. The project is so safe and supportive that participants attend even when activities have not been scheduled. The project has built a community of trust among participants and their mentors. As a result participants' family lives and academic performance have significantly improved. (GWA)

Bringing Young People into Civic Life

Bringing Young People into Civic Life is one of the four major initiatives of the National Crime Prevention Council (NCPC). NCPC has consistently advocated for involving young people in bettering their communities. One such program, Teens, Crime and the Community (TCC), is a nationwide effort sponsored by NCPC and Street Law, Inc. implemented at the local level to reduce the incidence of teen victimization and engage teens as crime prevention resources in their schools and communities. Participating teens tackle critical issues facing American society today, including violent crime, shoplifting, child abuse, rape, hate crime and substance abuse. More importantly, TCC empowers youths with the skills and knowledge to make a difference in addressing these problems. Its 2001 annual report describes several other programs.

Youth as Resources (YAR) programs, governed by boards composed of youths and adults and supported by local funders, provides grants for youth-initiated and youth-led community projects. In 2001, YAR youths helped feed the homeless, made holiday gifts for elderly shut-ins and nursing home residents, organized intergenerational oral history activities, held freedom rallies to commemorate the victims of September 11, designed a program befriending children with autism, rebuilt used or damaged computers and donated them to low-income families, organized games for children in the hospital, served as mentors to new Americans and turned abandoned lots into playgrounds.

The Center for Youths as Resources (CYAR) was founded by the NCPC in 1995 to serve as a separate nonprofit organization for YAR. The growing network of YAR programs expanded in 2001 to 80 communities in 23 states. International YAR programs also operate in Poland, New Zealand and England.

Another program, Youth Vision is a collaboration of NCPE, the CYAR and Street Law, Inc. Youth Vision offers young people and their adult partners a comprehensive tool for planning and evaluating youth-initiated violence prevention school and community projects. The Youth Vision Roadmap and Action Guide assists young people to identify problems, develop action strategies, identify needed resources and measure success. Youth leaders 8 to 23 years old from more than 400 communities throughout the United States have successfully used the Roadmap and Action Guide to design, implement and evaluate their projects.

After-School Programs

After-school programs are one popular strategy to address delinquency prevention. According to Gottfredson et al. (2001a, p.62): "Criminologists have been aware of a peak in juvenile crime rates after school hours for half a century." They (p.63) suggest: "The most common understanding of the reason for higher rates of crime during the after-school hours is that youths experience lower levels of adult supervision during these hours." These researchers used self-reports to examine when students commit delinquent acts and whether this behavior is related to the degree of parental supervision the students receive after school. Their results showed that although much delinquency occurs during the hours after school, this trend was much more modest than that observed in official police reports. They (p.61) also found: "Children who are unsupervised during the after-school hours—the primary target population for after-school programs—are found to be more delinquent at all times, not only after school."

Their results suggest that factors (including social competencies and social bonding) in addition to inadequate supervision produce delinquency during the after-school hours and that the effectiveness of after-school programs for reducing delinquency will depend on their ability to address these other factors. They suggest that after-school programs are not likely to reduce delinquency during the after-school hours simply by providing "safe havens."

After-school programs do have promise if they can attract youths who are at risk for engaging in delinquency by teaching them important social skills for resisting peer pressure, by establishing bonds with prosocial others and by increasing commitments to conventional pursuits. They (p.81) comment: "After-school programs are perhaps better suited to meet this challenge than are school programs, because academic teaching and learning must remain the priority during the school day. After-school programs can provide the kind of structured programming that has proven effective in other contexts for reducing problem behavior." Gottfredson et al. (2001b) summarize effective models for prevention that may be adapted to an after-school setting.

Violence Prevention

The OJJDP identifies six principles for preventing delinquent conduct and reducing serious, violent and chronic delinquency:

- Strengthen families to instill moral values and provide guidance and support to children
- Support core social institutions such as schools, religious institutions and other community organizations to alleviate risk factors for youths
- Promote delinquency prevention strategies that reduce the impact of risk factors and enhance the influence of protective factors for youths at the greatest risk of delinquency
- Intervene immediately when delinquent behavior occurs
- Institute a broad spectrum of graduated sanctions that provide accountability and a continuum of services to respond appropriately to the individual needs of an offender
- Identify and control the small segment of serious, violent and chronic juvenile offenders

Many delinquency prevention efforts are unsuccessful because of their negative approach—attempting to keep juveniles from misbehaving. What has proved to work more effectively are positive approaches that emphasize opportunities for

	Education	Legal/Regulatory Change	Environmental Modification
Table 13.7 **Strategies to Prevent** **Youth Violence**	Adult mentoring Conflict resolution Training in social skills Firearm safety Parenting centers Peer education Public information and education campaigns	Regulate use of and access to weapons: 　Weaponless schools 　Control of concealed weapons 　Restrictive licensing 　Appropriate sale of guns Regulate use of and access to alcohol: 　Appropriate sale of alcohol 　Prohibition or control of alcohol sales at events. . . .Training of servers Other types of regulations: 　Appropriate punishment in schools 　Dress codes	Modify the social environment: 　Home visitation 　Preschool programs such as Head Start 　Therapeutic activities 　Recreational activities 　Work/academic experiences Modify the physical environment: 　Make risk areas visible 　Increase use of an area 　Limit building entrances and exits

Source: National Center for Injury Prevention and Control.

healthy social, physical and mental development. Table 13.7 presents several education, legal/regulatory change and environmental modification strategies to prevent youth violence.

Bell (2002, p.66) presents two basic premises of violence prevention: "The first premise of violence prevention, often overlooked by practitioners when they design violence prevention programs across age and ethnic/racial groups, is that there are different types of violence and each type requires different prevention, intervention and follow-up strategies." Table 13.8 shows these different types of violence.

A second premise, similarly neglected, is that different racial/ethnic groups experience different types of violence at different rates, and each calls for different prevention strategies.

Bell (pp.68–69) also presents seven violence prevention principles: (1) rebuilding the village; (2) providing access to health care; (3) improving bonding, attachment and connectedness dynamics, (4) improving self-esteem; (5) increasing social skills; (6) re-establishing the adult protective shield; and (7) minimizing the residual effects of trauma. According to Bell (p.69): "Social disorganization theories of deviance suggest that poverty, lack of job opportunities, single-head households, isolation from neighbors and weakened community networks and institutions leads to reduced informal and formal social control, which, in turn, promotes violence." One nationally acclaimed program that seeks to address several of these factors is the Big Brothers Big Sisters of America program.

Reducing Gun Violence

Sherman (p.69) notes the controversy regarding gun control: "Opposition to gun control comes largely from the political right, which resists any new legislation as unnecessary. It frames the alternative as more enforcement of existing laws, which would be so effective as to make any new laws unnecessary. Almost buried in the debate is the opposition from the left, which advocates the policies of all other nations with advanced economies; virtual bans on the possession of handguns, with tight registration and control of a limited number of long guns."

Table 13.8
Types of Violence

- Group or mob violence
- Individual violence
- Systematic violence, such as war, racism and sexism
- Institutional violence, such as preventing inmates from getting the benefit of prophylactic medications to prevent hepatitis
- Hate-crime violence, such as terrorism
- Multicide (e.g., mass murder, murder sprees and serial killing)
- Psychopathic violence
- Predatory violence, also known as instrumental or secondary violence
- Interpersonal altercation violence, also known as expressive or primary violence (e.g., domestic violence, child abuse, elder abuse and peer violence)
- Drug-related violence, such as systemic drug-related violence (whereby drug dealers kill to sell drugs), pharmacological drug-related violence (whereby an individual perpetrates violence because of drug intoxication), economic-compulsive drug-related violence (whereby a drug addict uses violence to obtain drugs), and negligent drug-related violence (such as a drunk driver who kills a pedestrian)
- Gang-related violence
- Violence by mentally ill individuals
- Lethal violence directed toward self (suicide)
- Lethal violence directed toward others (homicide)
- Violence by organically brain damaged individuals
- Legitimate/illegitimate violence
- Nonlethal violence

Source: F. M. Baker and Carl C. Bell, "Issues in the Psychiatric Treatment of African Americans," *Psychiatric Services* 50 (1999): 362–368. Copyright © 1999, the American Psychiatric Association; http://ps.psychiatryonline.org. Reprinted by permission.

Sherman (p.72) notes: "Public health successes have always linked the policy intervention to the epidemiology of the problem. Polio vaccines have been given to children, not adults. Typhoid prevention was aimed at the water supply, not beer. Any effort to assess what works in gun policy must begin with the epidemiology of the problem." He (p.74) also notes: "The key epidemiological fact is that most gun crimes would still occur even if every convicted felon in the United States were shipped to Australia (not just barred from legal gun ownership)." According to Sherman (p.75): "The most important epidemiological fact is that gun violence is geographically concentrated in the areas of greatest inequality in the nation—the hyper-segregated poverty areas of inner cities. Half of all homicides occur in the 63 largest cities, which house only 16 percent of the population."

Sherman (p.77) contends: "The two programs known to work are epidemiological focused on the high risks of gun violence."

 Two programs known to work to reduce gun violence are uniformed police patrols in gun crime hot spots and background checks for criminal history to restrict gun sales in stores. Gun buyback programs do not appear to work.

Sherman suggests that promising programs are virtual bans on private handgun possession and bans on the sale and manufacture of new assault weapons.

Drug Prevention Programs

Because of the known link between drug abuse and delinquency, many programs focus on drug abuse prevention.

DARE

DARE is perhaps the best known and most recognized drug prevention program in the country. DARE and its spin-off project, the National DARE Parent Program, were discussed in detail in Chapter 8.

The National Commission on Drug-Free Schools

A comprehensive drug education and prevention program should have eight key elements:

- Student survey, school needs assessment and resource identification

- Leadership training of key school officials and staff with authority to develop policies and programs

- School policies that are clear, consistent and fair, with responses to violations that include alternatives to suspension

- Training for the entire staff on the school's alcohol and drug policies and policy implementation throughout

- Assistance programs/support for students from preschool through grade 12, including tutoring, mentoring and other academic activities; support groups (e.g., Alcoholics Anonymous and Children of Alcoholics); peer counseling; extracurricular activities (e.g., sports, drama, journalism); vocational programs (e.g., work-study and apprenticeship); social activities (including drug-free proms and graduation activities); alternative programs (e.g., Upward Bound and Outward Bound); and community service projects

- Training for parents, including the effects of drug use, abuse and dependency on users, their families and other people; ways to identify drug problems and refer people for treatment; available resources to diagnose and treat people with drug problems; laws and school policies on drugs, including alcohol and tobacco; the influence of parents' attitudes and behavior toward drugs including alcohol and tobacco, and of parents' expectations of graduation and academic performance of their children; the importance of establishing appropriate family rules, monitoring behavior of children, imposing appropriate punishments and reinforcing positive behavior; ways to improve skills in communication and conflict management; the importance of networking with other parents and knowing their children's friends and their families

- Curriculum for preschool through grade 12, including information about all types of drugs, including medicines; the relationship of drugs to suicide, AIDS, drug-affected babies, pregnancy, violence and other health and safety issues; the social consequences of drug abuse; respect for the laws and values of society, including discussions of right and wrong; the importance of honesty, hard work, achievement, citizenship, compassion, patriotism and other civic and personal values; promotion of healthy, safe and responsible attitudes and behavior; ways to build resistance to influences that encourage drug use, such as peer pressure, advertising and other media appeals (refusal skills); ways to develop critical thinking, problem-solving, decision-making, persuasion and interpersonal skills; strategies to get parents, family members and the community involved in preventing drug use; information on contacting responsible adults when young people need help and on intervention and referral services

- Collaboration with community services to provide student assistance programs; employee assistance programs for school staff; latchkey child care; medical care, including treatment for alcohol and other drug abuse; nutrition information and counseling; mental health care; social welfare services; probation services; and continuing education for dropouts and pushouts

Curriculum should be developmentally oriented, age-appropriate, up-to-date and accurate. Individual components work best as part of a comprehensive curriculum program. When presented in isolation, components such as information about drugs can exacerbate the problem.

National Crime Prevention Council Programs

The National Crime Prevention Council (NCPC) has also focused efforts on drug abuse prevention. They identified three communities and highlighted their success in reducing drug abuse by using the talents of youths within the community.

> Too many of us, when we look at young people, see problems or potential problems. What we could and should be seeing are enormous resources—talented, enthusiastic, able people who want to do good and want to be part of the community.

One program the NCPC supports is arts-related drug prevention, a strategy that offers an alternative path to youths who may not respond to other antidrug programs. According to the NCPC Web site: "Arts-related drug prevention programs offer a wide variety of fine arts projects that attract young people with visual, musical or theatrical talent. Youths participate in designing a program or performance, constructing the stage props, creating promotional flyers, talking with the press to publicize the event, serving refreshments or arranging for concessions stands, collecting tickets and cleaning up after the event. The projects or events offer at-risk youth an alternative to drug use. They may also educate the public about alcohol and other drugs through their content." The Learning Systems Group, in partnership with the U.S. Department of Education, initiated a national "Murals Reflecting Prevention" project to prevent youth involvement with alcohol, tobacco and other drugs. To date the program has involved more than 10,000 students nationwide in expressing prevention themes. The student-designed murals have been displayed at exhibitions in several states and provide a novel approach to uniting youths and their communities around the issue of drug abuse.

Another program, called Teens as Resources Against Drugs (TARAD), is funded by the Bureau of Justice Statistics. TARAD was piloted at three sites: New York City (Teens Go after Worms in the Big Apple), Evansville, Indiana, (Drugs Are Out in Evansville) and communities in South Carolina (Kids in the Know Say No in South Carolina).

The TARAD program of the National Crime Prevention Council uses youths to take on the community drug prevention challenge.

The concept is based on two premises: (1) teens are deeply concerned about the effects of drug abuse on their peers and on the community at large, and (2) as young people go through adolescence, they need to develop independence and a sense that their skills and accomplishments are needed and valued by their community.

Community support for TARAD is strong, as evidenced by the following project sponsors: high schools, middle schools, elementary schools, special education programs, alternative schools, youth membership organizations, nonprofit organizations, community centers, neighborhood organizations and groups, churches, colleges, hospitals, group homes, support groups, youth councils, mental health centers and police athletic leagues. In addition, a wide variety of projects have been undertaken, including peer helping and mentoring, puppet troupes, awareness campaigns, drug patrols, lock-ins, establishing drug/alcohol-free organizations, drop-in or teen centers, beautification of drug infested areas, murals, newspapers, contests, videos, products, conferences, events and health fairs. The NCPC reports the following results:

- For the communities: drug dealers moved out; communities more frequently turned to youths for assistance in policy making; a school changed its curriculum to acknowledge the value of community service, and annual abuse prevention activities are becoming part of local calendars.

- For the youths: youths found a safer, drug-free environment; they had an opportunity to be themselves, "warts and all"; they came to believe they could make a difference; they received assistance with jobs and scholarships; and they learned new life skills.

According to the *National Drug Control Strategy* (2002, p.10): "The newly reauthorized Drug-Free Communities Support Program will provide critical resources to expand prevention programs across America, including small towns, rural areas and Native American communities, all of which have been hit hard in recent years by drug problems that have historically plagues big cities." This report (p.9) also notes: "Prevention programs involve schools and faith-based organizations, civic groups and the mass media. But the single indispensable element of an effective prevention program is not a program at all. Parents and other caregivers have a tremendous influence on whether their kids use drugs."

Parents: The Anti-Drug

The Office of National Drug Control Policy (ONDCP) through its National Youth Anti-Drug Media Campaign launched new national advertising targeting parents and other adult caregivers, reminding them that they are an important influence in their children's lives and that they can make a difference in their children's decision making ("Parents: The Anti-Drug," 2000, p.25).

The advertising focuses on five basic values: truth, love, honesty, communication and trust. The advertising sends consistent messages in all media—print, billboards, radio and television—to reassure parents that they can positively affect their children's decisions regarding drugs by spending time with them; listening to them genuinely; asking them what they think; giving them clear, consistent rules to follow; praising and rewarding them for good behavior; telling them they are loved; encouraging them to participate in extracurricular activities; and being involved in their lives. The National Youth Anti-Drug Media Campaign's Web site is www.mediacampaign.org/. Information can also be found on the Partnership for a Drug-Free America's Web site at www.drugfreeamerica.org/.

A Reality-Based Approach to Drug Education

Rosenbaum (1999, p.1) notes: "Despite expenditures of more than $2.1 billion on prevention, government surveys indicate that many teenagers experiment with drugs." She (p.6) contends: "The foundations of conventional school-based drug education are fundamentally flawed." The first flaw is that many programs are based on the idea that any use of illegal drugs is inherently pathological, dangerous behavior when, in reality, experimentation with mind-altering substances, legal or illegal, might instead be defined as normal, given our culture.

A second flaw in drug education according to Rosenbaum (p.7) is that the programs assume drug use is the same as drug abuse, often using the terms interchangeably: "But teenagers know the difference. . . . Programs that blur the distinctions between use and abuse are ineffective because students' own experiences tell them the information presented to them is not believable."

Rosenbaum (p.9) suggests: "The consistent mischaracterization of marijuana may be the Achilles Heel of conventional approaches to drug education because these false messages are inconsistent with students' actual observations and experience." She further suggests: "While the abstinence-only mandate is well meaning, it is misguided." What is needed as a reality-based alternative she (p.10) calls Safety First: "A safety-first strategy for drug education requires reality-based assumptions about drug use." This approach is based on three assumptions:

1. Teenagers can make responsible decisions if given honest, science-based drug education.
2. Total abstinence may not be a realistic alternative for all teenagers.
3. The use of mind-altering substances does not necessarily constitute abuse.

Rosenbaum (p.14) concludes: "Reality-based drug education will equip students with information they trust, the basics for making responsible decisions."

Promising Practices: Drug-Free Communities Support Program

According to Simonson and Maher (2001, p.1): "The Drug-Free Communities Support Program (DFCSP) helps strengthen community antidrug coalitions working to reduce substance abuse among youths. The White House Office of National Drug Control Policy (ONDCP), in partnership with OJJDP, awards grants of up to $100,000 to community coalitions that support prevention of youth alcohol and drug abuse." Strategies used by communities receiving funding include educational support, public relations/outreach campaigns, enforcement efforts, coalition building and other community efforts.

Simonson and Maher (p.2) describe one exemplary program, TOGETHER!: Youth Violence, Alcohol and Drug Prevention of Lacey, Washington: "The Neighborhood Center's project of TOGETHER! provides a targeted drug abuse

Table 13.9
Cultural Interventions in American Indian Prevention Programs

Ceremonies and Rituals

- Participating in sweatlodge ceremonies
- Smudging
- Attending social dances
- Learning scared dances
- Attending a Sundance
- Fasting

- Going on a vision quest
- Paying attention to dreams
- Attending powwows and other sober community activities
- Storytelling and listening to stories
- Participating in a Talking Circle

Tribal Crafts

- Making traditional attire for powwows and other ceremonies
- Tanning hides
- Making ribbon shirts
- Sewing quilts
- Learning the native language

- Cooking traditional foods
- Picking and drying herbs
- Making jewelry and moccasins
- Making cradle boards

Traditional Forms of Living

- Hunting
- Fishing
- Shepherding
- Participating in tribal sports

- Horsemanship
- Camping and participating in survival retreats
- Picking berries and harvesting crop

Source: Ruth Sanchez-Way and Sandie Johnson. "Cultural Practices in American Indian Prevention Programs." *Juvenile Justice*, December 2000, p.21.

prevention program to children and families living in low-income apartment complexes. TOGETHER! rents an apartment in each complex and offers after school and summer programs that promote a drug-free climate for children. Activities range from homework assistance and computer availability to skills building, conflict resolution and peer pressure resistance training. Girl Scout meetings, arts and crafts, and field trips are offered. Drug abuse information, in addition to information about employment and community resources, is disseminated to parents at family potluck dinners and informal coffee hours. Programs for preschool children are also sponsored at the neighborhood centers.

Substance Abuse Prevention Programs for American Indians

Sanchez-Way and Johnson (2000) describe how cultural practices can be used in American Indian prevention programs. Table 13.9 lists some cultural interventions that American Indian prevention programs have used. All the activities assume the participation of elders and include transmission of tribal history, values and beliefs. In addition, music, drumming and singing are integral parts of most activities.

The Center for Substance Abuse Prevention (CSAP) believes primary prevention should be implemented from within the community rather than from the top down by federal agencies. Over the years CSAP has developed prevention materials adaptable to different tribes and tribal groups. A good example is *The Gathering of Native Americans* (GONA). Community healing of historical and

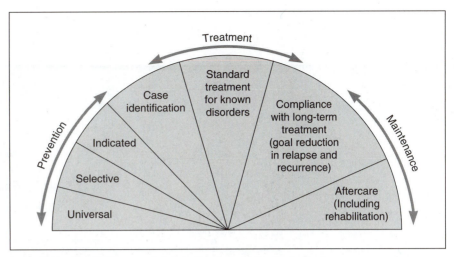

Figure 13.3
Continuum of Health Care

Source: P. J. Mrazek and R. J. Haggerty, eds. *Reducing Risks for Mental Disorders: Frontiers for Preventive Intervention Research.* 1994. Reprinted with permission of the National Academy of Sciences, courtesy of the National Academics Press, Washington, DC.

cultural trauma is the central theme of the GONA approach. The GONA manual is a culturally specific prevention tool that can provide structure to communities addressing the effects of alcohol and other substance abuse. According to Sanchez-Way and Johnson (p.28): "Because so many tribal communities have been traumatized by substance abuse, poverty, unemployment and historical grief, tribal leaders have found this model useful in beginning community healing by gathering the people together to develop a community response to the problems they are facing."

Sanchez-Way and Johnson point out: "One factor to consider is that American Indian substance abuse programs treat the link between prevention and treatment differently than non-Indian programs. Non-Indian practitioners tend to see prevention as one step on a continuum that progresses from primary prevention through intervention to treatment and aftercare/rehabilitation" as shown in Figure 13.3. They note: "In contrast, American Indian practitioners see primary prevention as part of a cycle that moves through intervention, treatment, aftercare/ rehabilitation and back to primary prevention" as shown in Figure 13.4

Sanchez-Way and Johnson (p.30) conclude: "Just as there is no single American Indian drinking pattern, there is no single American Indian prevention strategy. It is not a matter of choosing between culturally based prevention strategies and other prevention strategies. Rather, American Indians can create more effective substance abuse prevention programs by combining ethnic and cultural components with other proven prevention strategies. Taking this action as a matter of course will make prevention programs more effective in the long run by enhancing protective factors and mitigating risk factors in the lives of American Indian youths."

Drug Testing in Schools   In June 2002, the U.S. Supreme Court broadened the authority of public schools to test students for illegal drugs. Voting 5 to 4, the Court ruled to allow random

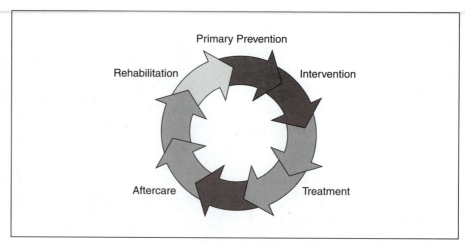

Figure 13.4
Tribal View of Substance Abuse Cycle

Source: Ruth Sanchez-Way and Sandie Johnson. "Cultural Practices in American Indian Prevention Programs." *Juvenile Justice*, December 2000, p.30.

drug tests for all middle and high school students participating in competitive extracurricular activities (*Board of Education of Independent School District No. 92 of Pottawatomie County et al. v. Earls et al.*). Justice Clarence Thomas commented: "We find that testing students who participate in extracurricular activities is a reasonably effective means of addressing the school district's legitimate concerns in preventing, deterring and detecting drug use. This ruling expands the scope of school drug testing, which previously was allowed only for student athletes."

According to *What You Need to Know about Drug Testing in Schools* (2002, p.1): "It is up to communities and schools to decide if drugs are a significant threat, and if testing is an appropriate response." This publication (p.4) notes: "The expectation that they may be randomly tested is enough to make some students stop using drugs—or never start in the first place." The publication (p.16) also notes: "For those who worry about the 'Big Brother' dimension of drug testing, it is worth pointing out that test results are generally required by law to remain confidential, and in no case are they turned over to the police."

The publication (p.16) stresses: "The aim of drug testing is not to trap and punish students who use drugs. It is, in fact, counterproductive simply to punish them without trying to alter their behavior. If drug-using students are suspended or expelled without any attempt to change their ways, the community will be faced with drug-using dropouts, an even bigger problem in the long run."

 The purpose of drug testing is to prevent drug dependence and to help drug-dependent students become drug free.

At Hunterdon Central Regional High School in Flemington, New Jersey, teachers and administrators found that testing for drugs did make a difference, with drug use declining in 20 of 28 categories. Cocaine use among seniors dropped from 13 percent to 4 percent. The number of tenth graders reporting little or no use of drugs or alcohol increased from 41.8 percent to 47.3 percent. However, in September 2000, the school suspended all random testing when the American Civil Liberties Union filed a lawsuit in New Jersey state court on behalf of students who claimed their Fourth Amendment rights were violated. That suit is pending.

Of interest is the report by Winder (2003, p.A15) stating: "Drug testing in schools does not deter student drug use any more than doing no screening at all. . . . A new federally financed study of 76,000 students nationwide, by far the largest to date, found that drug use is just as common in schools with testing as in those without it."

Mentoring

The mentoring movement began at the end of the nineteenth century, when adults called the Friendly Visitors served as role models for poor children. During the 1970s, mentoring found its way into corporate America as a means for the ambitious employee to find success on the corporate ladder. Most recently mentoring has returned to its roots, focusing on disadvantaged youths and providing support and advocacy to children in need. Under the Juvenile Justice and Delinquency Prevention (JJDP) Act, the OJJDP is authorized to fund mentoring efforts. In fiscal 1998, Congress appropriated $12 million to support the Juvenile Mentoring Program (JUMP), including associated programs such as Big Brothers Big Sisters.

Juvenile Mentoring Program (JUMP)

JUMP was introduced in Chapter 12. According to the JUMP Web site, this program supports one-to-one mentoring projects for youths at risk of failing in school, dropping out of school or becoming involved in delinquent behavior, including gang activity and substance abuse.

Since 1994, the OJJDP has funded 203 JUMP sites in 47 states and 2 territories. The three principle goals of JUMP are (1) to reduce juvenile delinquency and gang participation by at-risk youths, (2) to improve the academic performance of at-risk youths and (3) to reduce the school dropout rate for at-risk youths.

Big Brothers Big Sisters of America (BBBSA)

Volunteer mentors are screened and trained and then matched with youths ages 6 to 18.

Big Brothers Big Sisters of America is an exemplary program in the Blueprints for Violence Prevention initiative. BBBSA began in the early 20th century as a means to reach youths in need of socialization, firm guidance and connection with positive adult role models. BBBSA, with a network of more than 500 local programs throughout the nation, continues to operate as the largest and best-known mentoring organization in the United States, maintaining more than 250,000 one-to-one relationships between youths and volunteer adults.

Volunteer mentors are screened and trained, and matches are made carefully using established procedures and criteria. Individual BBBSA agencies adhere to national guidelines but customize their programs to fit local circumstances. The program serves youths ages 6 to 18, a significant number of whom are from disadvantaged single-parent households.

In the community-based program, a mentor meets with his or her youth partner at least three times a month for three to five hours, participating in activities that enhance communication skills, develop relationship skills and support positive decision making. Such activities are determined by the interests of the child and the volunteer and could include taking walks, attending school activities or sporting events, playing catch, visiting the library or just sharing thoughts and ideas about life.

In the past five years, a second core program has been added to the BBBSA service options: Big Brothers Big Sisters in Schools includes volunteers whose lifestyle, family commitments or work schedule preclude becoming a Big Brother or Big Sister in the community-based program meet with a child weekly at school for one hour. The same goals and relationship-building activities characterize these in-school matches. Many children whose parents would not have entered them in the program are referred by teachers or guidance counselors. Providing this additional program has increased the number of volunteers and provided access to previously unserviced children in need. Both programs provide a fun and rewarding experience for volunteers and positive youth development for their "Littles."

Communities may run into two obstacles when setting up a mentoring program: the limited number of adults available to serve as mentors and the scarcity of organizational resources necessary to carry out a successful program. Although BBBSA maintains more than 250,000 matches between volunteers and youths, estimates reveal that between 5 and 15 million children could benefit from a mentoring program. An 18-month study of eight BBBSA affiliates found that when compared with a control group on a waiting list for a match, youths in the mentoring program were 46 percent less likely to start using drugs, 27 percent less likely to start drinking and 32 percent less likely to hit someone. Mentored youths skipped half as many days of school as control youths, had better attitudes toward and performance in school and had improved peer and family relationships.

Contact information: Joyce Corlett, Director, Program Development, Big Brothers Big Sisters of America National Office, 230 North 13th Street, Philadelphia, PA 19107-1538; (215) 567-7000; (215) 567-0394 (fax); www.bbbsa.org.

Gang Prevention

Several approaches to gang prevention were discussed in Chapter 8. This chapter goes into more depth on the topic. The Bureau of Justice Assistance (*Addressing Community . . .*, 1998, p.xxii) states: "Communities with emerging or existing gang problems must plan, develop and implement comprehensive, harm-specific responses that include a broad range of community-based components." Three suggested approaches are:

- Developing strategies to discourage gang involvement and membership
- Providing ways for youths to drop out of gangs
- Empowering communities to solve gang-associated problems through collaboration with law enforcement, parents, schools, businesses, religious and social service organizations, local government officials and youths themselves in a comprehensive, systematic approach

In emphasizing the importance of cooperation and collaboration, the BJA (p.118) claims: "Approaches to local gang problems that emphasize sharing resources and forming community coalitions are based on the premise that no single organization or individual can prevent the development of gangs or their harmful activities." Furthermore (p.119): "Team building as well as training in cultural and ethnic diversity and conflict resolution may be necessary to facilitate progress toward collaboration."

Antigang Programs

The National School Safety Center's (1988, p.35) classic publication, *Gangs in Schools: Breaking Up Is Hard to Do,* notes: "We do a lot of work helping separate gang members from gangs. We want to give them a shot at making something of themselves. It's not easy." The center suggests that "a positive, consistent approach to discipline and conflict prevention can achieve long-term and far-reaching results and improve the overall school climate" (p.25). The center suggests several prevention and intervention strategies.

Behavior codes should be established and enforced firmly and consistently. Such behavior codes may include a dress code, a ban on the showing of gang colors and a ban on using gang hand signals. Friendliness and cooperation should be promoted and rewarded.

Graffiti removal should be done immediately. Graffiti is not only unattractive, it allows gangs to advertise turf and authority. A Los Angeles school administrator suggests that graffiti be photographed before removal so the police can better investigate the vandalism. Evidence, such as paint cans and paint brushes, should be turned over to the police. In addition students might design and paint their own murals in locations where graffiti is likely to appear.

Conflict prevention strategies can also be effective. Teachers should be trained to recognize gang members and to deal with them in a nonconfrontational way. All gang members should be made known to staff. Teachers should try to build self-esteem and promote academic success for all students, including gang members. School-based programs can combine gang and drug prevention efforts.

Crisis management should be an integral part of the administration's plan for dealing with any gang activity that might occur. A working relationship should be established with the police department, and a plan for managing a crisis should be developed. The plan should include procedures for communicating with the authorities, parents and the public.

Community involvement can also be extremely effective in reducing or even preventing gang activity. Parents and the general public can be made aware of gangs operating in the community, as well as heavy metal and punk bands that promote violence or inappropriate behavior. They can be encouraged to apply pressure to radio and television stations and bookstores to ban material that promotes the use of alcohol or drugs, promiscuity or devil worship.

Antigang programs include establishing behavior codes, removing graffiti, implementing conflict prevention strategies, developing a plan for crisis management and fostering community involvement.

The National League of Cities (2001, p.1) provides another proven strategy: curfews. The overwhelming majority of cities with curfews say they are effective in improving safety in several areas: combating juvenile crime (effectiveness reported by 97 percent of respondents), fighting truancy (96 percent of respondents), making streets safer (95 percent) and reducing gang violence (88 percent.)

The National Crime Prevention Council's (NCPC's) *Effective Strategy: Provide Positive Alternative to Gang Activity* (2003) suggests: "By providing positive alternatives to violent gang activities and tracking interacting with gang members, community groups can combat gang violence successfully." According to the NCPC: "The key components of this strategy include community groups' recognition that gang activities involve violence and dangers to the individual members and to their communities; group resolve to identify, monitor and reduce gang membership and activities; and a community-based effort to discourage young people from joining gangs. Strategies to deter youth gang membership include education, counseling and alternative activities, such as recreation and job training."

The NCPC also stresses: "The key partnerships must exist among community groups providing services and must include community members who can identify the services most needed by youths involved in gang activity. The service providers, cooperating through a community organization, should include local schools, youth programs, recreation centers, religious groups, citizen patrols and the police. Young people who are former gang members and staff of community organizations can form a variety of partnerships targeted to referring gang members to the program for support and services."

One challenge to this approach is to reduce the fear of gang activity, which can make some individuals and groups reluctant to get involved. Another challenge is to gain the trust of gang members by listening to them and designing services that respond to their needs.

Respondents to surveys in several major cities with serious youth gang violence reported that providing positive alternatives for gang members was the most effective strategy, with community organization being next most effective. Suppression strategies were considered to be less effective except in conjunction with other approaches.

The NCPC has applied the strategy of providing alternatives to gang activity in its Teens on Target program. This program helps youths become advocates for violence prevention. In collaboration with a school district, hospital and rehabilitation center, Teens on Target trains urban youths who are at risk of participating in violent or gang activities to become advocates for violence prevention. As the NCPC states: "Established in 1989, the Teens on Target program provides peer education on violence and violence prevention at schools and conferences, educates professionals, informs the media on the causes of and solutions to violence, provides good role models and urges policy makers to take action. Teenagers in the program serve as catalysts for more comprehensive community involvement with youths at risk and gang members and for mobilizing community resources to provide youths with opportunities that will reduce gang membership, violence and victimization." Appendix D (found on the book companion Web site) contains descriptions of several antigang problems.

In an after-school program in New Haven, Connecticut, teenages volunteer to work with neighborhood youths, keeping all involved off the streets and out of trouble.

What Works in Preventing Delinquency and Violence?

With many programs now having several decades of experience behind them, and the road ahead appearing more challenging than ever for those involved in handling juvenile crime, the question being asked is: "What works?" The reviews, thus far, are mixed.

According to a study, "many favorite anti-crime programs simply don't work" ("Getting Your Money's Worth," 1998, p.1). A research team of criminologists at the University of Maryland, led by Lawrence W. Sherman, reviewed more than 500 scientific evaluations of crime-prevention programs funded by the Justice Department, with a special focus on factors relating to juvenile crime and program effects on youth violence. The study showed that large amounts of money are spent on programs that do not demonstrate any positive impacts on juvenile delinquency and violence. Among the programs identified in the study that don't work (p.8): gun buyback programs, military-style correctional boot camps, "scared straight" programs, shock probation/parole, home detention with electronic monitoring, neighborhood watch programs, the DARE program and arrests of juveniles for minor offenses.

The news was not all bad, however. Programs considered promising: gang offender monitoring by community workers and probation and police officers, community-based after-school recreation programs, drug courts and community policing with meetings to set priorities. Several programs found to be working: family therapy and parent training for delinquent and at-risk pre-adolescents, school-based coaching of high-risk youths in "thinking skills" and special police units that focus on high-risk repeat offenders.

Despite the harsh evaluation of some of the more popular programs for youths, the National Criminal Justice Association (pp.10–11) states: "More and more research indicates that juvenile crime and delinquency prevention programs not only have a positive impact on troubled youths, but are a good investment when compared with the costs associated with the behavior of serious, violent and chronic juvenile offenders." Programs that consistently demonstrated positive effects on youths at risk of developing delinquent behavior include those that strengthen the institutions of school and family in the life of the youth, such as smaller class sizes during early years of education; tutoring and cooperative learning; classroom behavior management, behavioral monitoring and reinforcement of school attendance, progress and behavior; parent training and family counseling; and youth employment and vocational training programs. In addition programs identified as holding promise included mentoring relationships, peer mediation, conflict resolution and violence prevention curricula in schools, community services for delinquent youths, restrictions on the purchase or possession of guns and enhanced motorized patrol and community policing.

A Caution Regarding Net Widening

The issue of net widening has been introduced in previous chapters, but it bears consideration at the conclusion of this chapter on prevention strategies. As Jamison (p.2) notes: "The issue of net widening was first recognized in the 1970s with the advent of diversion programs and other policies intended to reduce exposure to traditional justice system processing. . . . Diversion advocates underestimated the capacity of established systems to adapt to new initiatives without changing established practices."

Net widening is a serious issue because the process depletes the system's resources and impairs its ability to properly intervene with appropriate youths. Instead of improving public safety, some early intervention and prevention strategies promote net widening by shifting resources from youths most in need to youths least in need.

Summary

In the late 1960s, a new approach for dealing with delinquency emerged: the prevention of crime before youths engage in delinquent acts. Prevention can be corrective, punitive or mechanical. It can also be classified as primary, secondary or tertiary.

Yet another way to look at prevention is the mathematical analogy of numerator/denominator. The numerator approach focuses on individuals and symptoms, whereas the denominator approach focuses on the entire group and causes. The public health model's two-pronged strategy reduces known risk factors and promotes protective factors. Effective prevention approaches must address the causes of delinquency.

The Blueprints for Violence Prevention Initiative is the OJJDP's comprehensive effort to provide communities with a set of programs whose effectiveness has been scientifically demonstrated. Other crucial programs are aimed at preventing child neglect and abuse. Such early prevention programs should include making prevention a priority, and providing parenting education, programs for teenage parents, childcare facilities and employee assistance programs. Services and education also must be provided for children with disabilities, such as the learning disabled, emotionally disturbed, mentally ill or physically or developmentally disabled. All children at risk, including runaways, habitual truants, the chronically incorrigible and those not receiving any or receiving inadequate child support, must be considered when providing prevention services.

Two programs known to work to reduce gun violence are uniformed police patrols in gun crime hot spots and background checks for criminal history to restrict gun sales in stores. Gun buyback programs do not appear to work. Some prevention programs are aimed at the drug problem and the gang problem. The TARAD program of the National Crime Prevention Council enlists youths to take on the community drug prevention challenge. The purpose of drug testing in schools is to prevent drug dependence and to help drug-dependent students become drug free.

Antigang strategies include establishing behavior codes, removing graffiti, implementing conflict prevention strategies, developing a plan for crisis management and fostering community involvement.

Discussion Questions

1. Do you support the numerator or the denominator approach to juvenile crime prevention? Be prepared to defend your choice.
2. Do delinquency prevention programs succeed? Do the programs deter delinquency?
3. What prevention programs are available in your area? Is there a specific target area?
4. Are all three levels of delinquency prevention applied in your area? Which one best suits your area? Why?
5. If social responses treat youths' behavior as delinquent in prevention strategies, does this cause a labeling effect? How would you handle a program so that labeling was not a factor?
6. At what types of delinquency should programs be directed? Violent youths? Status offenders? Antisocial and criminal activity in general? Gang activity?
7. List the assumptions that you think are basic to effective delinquency prevention programs. To what extent do you think each assumption is justified?
8. What are some contemporary attempts to prevent delinquency? Why are they effective or ineffective?
9. What kinds of programs exist in your area to prevent child neglect and abuse?
10. What kinds of programs to prevent child neglect and abuse do you think have the most promise?

InfoTrac College Edition Assignments

- Use InfoTrac College Edition to help answer the Discussion Questions as appropriate.
- Use InfoTrac to read and outline one of the following articles to share with the class:
  - "Source of Firearms Used by Students in School Associated Violent Deaths—United States 1991–1999" (no author; *gun violence*)
  - "Tattoos and Body Piercing as Indicators of Adolescent Risk Taking" by Sean T. Carroll et al. (*gateway drugs*)
  - "An Early Community-Based Intervention for the Prevention of Substance Abuse and Other Delinquent Behavior" by Thomas E. Hanlon et al.

Internet Assignments

Complete one of the following assignments and be prepared to share your findings with the class:

- Go to www.ojjdp.ncjrs.org and find and outline one of the NCJ publications listed in the references for this chapter.

- Research one of the following key words or phrases: *corrective prevention, denominator approach, gateway drugs, Gould-Wysinger Award, polydrug use, delinquency primary prevention, protective factors, delinquency punitive prevention, delinquency risk factors, delinquency secondary prevention, delinquency tertiary prevention.*

- Go to the Web site of any reference in this chapter giving an online address. Read and outline the material.

References

Abandoned in the Back Row: New Lessons in Education and Delinquency Prevention. Washington, DC: Coalition for Juvenile Justice 2001 Annual Report.

Addressing Community Gang Problems: A Practical Guide. Washington, DC: Bureau of Justice Statistics Monograph, May 1998.

Allen, Pam. "The Gould-Wysinger Awards: A Tradition of Excellence." *Juvenile Justice,* Fall/Winter 1993, pp. 23–28.

Alvarado, Rose and Kumpfer, Karol. "Strengthening American Families." *Juvenile Justice,* December 2000, pp.8–18.

American Psychological Association. *Violence & Youth: Psychology's Response,* Vol. 1. Summary Report of the American Psychological Association Commission on Violence and Youth. No date.

Baker, Myriam L.; Sigmon, Jane Nady; and Nugent, M. Elaine. *Truancy Reduction: Keeping Students in School.* Washington, DC: OJJDP Juvenile Justice Bulletin, September 2001. (NCJ 188947)

Bell, Carl C. "Violence Prevention 101: Implications for Policy Development." In *Perspectives on Crime and Justice: 2000–2001 Lecture Series.* Washington, DC: National Institute of Justice, March 2002, pp.65–93. (NCJ 187100)

Brunson, Sandra Susan and Smith, E. Wilburn. *Culinary Education and Training Program for At-Risk Youths.* Washington, DC: OJJDP Fact Sheet #07, April 2001. (FS 200107)

Clawson, Heather J. and Coolbaugh, Kathleen. *The YouthARTS Development Project,* Washington, DC: OJJDP Juvenile Justice Bulletin, May 2001.

Clinton, Hillary Rodham. "Talking It Over." *Juvenile Justice,* December 2000, pp.3–7.

Effective Strategy: Provide Positive Alternative to Gang Activity. Washington, DC: National Crime Prevention Council. Web site: www.ncpc.org

Ennis, Charles. "Twelve Clues that Could Save a Child." *Law and Order,* June 2000, pp.92–95.

Farrington, D.P. "Explaining and Preventing Crime: The Globalization of Knowledge—The 1999 American Society of Criminology Presidential Address." *Criminology,* Vol. 38, No. 1, 2000, pp.1–24.

"Getting Your Money's Worth." *Law Enforcement News,* September 30, 1998, pp. 1, 8.

Gottfredson, Denise C.; Gottfredson, Gary D.; and Weisman, Stephani A. "The Timing of Delinquent Behavior and Its Implications for After-School Programs." *Criminology and Public Policy,* November 2001a, pp.61–86.

Gottfredson, Denise C.; Wilson, David; and Najaka, Stacy Skroban. "School-Based Crime Prevention." In *Evidence-Based Crime Prevention* edited by David P. Farrington, Lawrence W. Sherman and Brandon Welsh. United Kingdom: Harwood Academic Publishers, 2001b.

Gottfredson, Denise C. and Gottfredson, Gary D. "Quality of School-Based Prevention Programs: Results from a National Survey." *Journal of Research in Crime and Delinquency,* February 2002, pp.3–35.

Graves, Alexander. "Child Abuse and Domestic Violence." *Law and Order,* July 2002, pp.137–141.

Herrenkohl, T. L.; Hawkins, J. D.; Hill, Chung I.; Hill, K. G.; and Battin-Pearson, S. "School and Community Risk Factors and Interventions." In *Child Delinquents: Development, Intervention and Service Needs* edited by R. Loeber and D. P. Farrington. Thousand Oaks, CA: Sage Publications, 2001, pp.211–246.

Herrenkohl, T. L.; Maguin, E.; Hill, K. G.; Hawkins, J. D.; Abbott, R. D.; and Catalano, R. F. "Developmental Risk Factors for Youth Violence." *Journal of Adolescent Health,* Vol. 26, No. 7, 2000, pp.176–186.

James, Donna Walker; Jurich, Sonia; and Estes, Steve. *Raising Minority Academic Achievement: A Compendium of Education Programs and Practices.* Washington, DC: American Youth Policy Forum, 2001.

Kelly, Ralph E. and Settle, Leah M. "Innovative Community Partnerships: Kentucky's Statewide Delinquency Prevention Councils." *Corrections Today,* December 2001, pp.59–62.

Mendel, Richard A. *Less Hype, More Help: Reducing Juvenile Crime, What Works and What Doesn't.* Washington, DC: American Policy Forum, 2000.

Metropolitan Court Judges Committee Report. *Deprived Children: A Judicial Response.* Washington, DC: U.S. Government Printing Office, 1986.

Mihalic, Sharon; Irwind, Katherine; Elliott, Delbert; Fagan, Abigail; and Hansen, Diane. *Blueprints for Violence Prevention.* Washington, DC: OJJDP Juvenile Justice Bulletin, July 2001. (NCJ 187079)

National Criminal Justice Association. *Juvenile Justice Reform Initiatives in the States: 1994–1996.* Washington, DC: OJJDP Program Report, October 1997.

National Drug Control Strategy. Washington, DC: The White House, February 2002.

Office of the Surgeon General. *Youth Violence: A Report of the Surgeon General.* Washington, DC: 2001. Online: www.surgeongeneral.gov/library/youthviolence

"Parents: The Anti-Drug." *Juvenile Justice,* December 2000, pp.25–26.

Sanchez-Way, Ruth and Johnson, Sandie. "Cultural Practices in American Indian Prevention Programs." *Juvenile Justice,* December 2000, pp.20–30.

Shader, Michael. *Risk Factors for Delinquency: An Overview,* 2002. Online: http://ojjdp.ncjrs.org/ccd/pubsrfd.html

Sherman, Lawrence W. "Reducing Gun Violence: What Works, What Doesn't, What's Promising." In *Perspectives on Crime and Justice: 1999-2000 Lecture Series,* March 2001, pp.69–96. (NCJ 184245)

Simonson, James M. and Maher, Pat M. *Promising Practices: Drug-Free Communities Support Program.* Washington, DC: OJJDP Fact Sheet #11, April 2001. (FS 200111)

2001–2002 Network Report: Personal, Accountable and Coordinated. Washington, DC: Communities in Schools, 2003.

What You Need to Know about Drug Testing in Schools. Washington, DC: Office of National Drug Control Policy, 2002. (NCJ 195522)

Wiebush, Richard; Freitag, Raelene; and Baird, Christopher. *Preventing Delinquency through Improved Child Protection Services.* Washington, DC: OJJDP Juvenile Justice Bulletin, July 2001. (NCJ 187759)

Winter, Greg. "Drug Tests in Schools No Deterrent to Use, Federal Study Finds." *New York Times* as reported in (Minneapolis/St. Paul) *Star Tribune,* May 17, 2003. p.A15.

Approaches to Treatment

In practice, treatment programs are still offered, but
no one really believes that they will work, unless the
young person wants to change. The truth is that no
one really knows what works in treatment.

—Timothy D. Crowe

Do You Know?

- What two primary characteristics of effective intervention programs are?
- What one thing effective treatment programs often take advantage of?
- What crisis intervention capitalizes on?
- What treatment requirements are recommended by the Metropolitan Court Judges Committee?
- What service requirements are recommended by this committee?
- What the committee's recommendations for establishing permanency for a child are?
- What the key to managing delinquency cases in the community is?
- What the four key elements of a Community Assessment Center are?
- What dual functions a management information system should serve?
- What three concerns related to assessment centers are?
- What three-pronged approach to treatment is needed?
- What two agencies might form a partnership to effectively prevent further delinquency?
- What constitutes effective supervision?
- What guidelines the OJJDP provides for a comprehensive strategy for use with serious, violent and chronic juvenile offenders?
- Whether the 8% problem offenders can be readily identified and what should happen to them?
- How juvenile justice might be reoriented when responding to needs of youths with mental problems?
- What dual functions the juvenile justice system is called upon to fulfill when dealing with youths who are mentally ill?
- How gang-related harms might be treated?
- Whether punitive treatments are effective?
- What seven clusters of strength are included in a resiliency model?

Can You Define?

abatement	the 8% problem	recidivism
crimogenic factors	holistic approach	relapse prevention
crisis intervention	nuisance	resiliency
desistance	paraphilias	static risk factors
dynamic risk factors	permanency	tort

INTRODUCTION

The correctional portion of the juvenile justice system is most intimately concerned with treatment options, as discussed in Chapter 11. Unfortunately as stated in the opening quotation from Crowe, research is lacking or inconclusive in this area.

Although prevention and treatment are discussed in separate chapters, they are integrally related. When prevention efforts fail, if youths are found breaking the law, some intervention should be provided to prevent future offenses. However, what often follows is a cycle of crime, with the treatment failing to prevent future offenses—or recidivism. This cycle is illustrated in Figure 14.1.

Most children get into trouble while growing up, urban, suburban or rural, poor or wealthy. Most grow up to be law-abiding, productive citizens through the maturation process and a process called desistance. **Desistance** refers to a process commonly occurring during the transition between late adolescence and early adulthood that discourages youths from a life of crime.

One question for the juvenile justice system is: Where should resources be focused? Some think resources should be focused on first-time offenders to make certain that the cycle of crime is broken for those most likely to be rehabilitated.

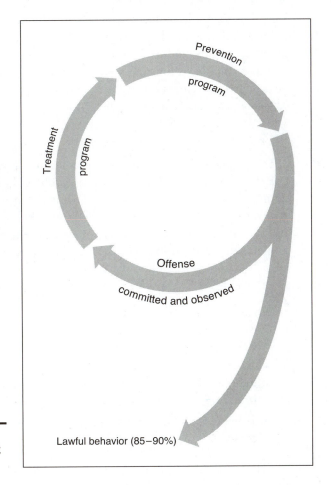

Figure 14.1
The Prevention/Treatment Cycle

Others think that youths who commit violent crimes and those who commit numerous crimes should be the top priority because most youths will "mature" out of unlawful behavior. This issue remains unresolved.

A second question is: What treatment is most effective.? This chapter presents a wide variety of treatments, but those that are most successful use a **holistic approach.** This approach treats not only the youth's symptoms but also the causes and in context, that is, in relation to family, peers, classmates and others with whom they interact.

This chapter expands on the information from Chapter 11, looking first at some theoretical concepts about treatment as tertiary prevention and some general characteristics of effective interventions. It then looks at treatments suggested for abused and neglected children. This is followed by a description of delinquent youths needing treatment in the juvenile justice system and the importance of thorough assessment, perhaps through a community assessment center. Next several diversion alternatives or community-based treatment programs as well as collaborative efforts are described. Then exemplary programs are discussed, including those that have received the OJJDP's Gould-Wysinger Award and the OJJDP's guiding principles for comprehensive services for serious, violent and chronic juvenile offenders. Next three exemplary programs from the Blueprints for Violence Prevention Initiative are described. This is followed by a discussion of targeting high-risk youths, including young children, serious repeat offenders, truants, youths with mental illness, youths who abuse drugs and sex offenders. Treatment for gang members and one approach to treating gangs also are explored. The chapter concludes with descriptions of punitive treatments and resiliency as a treatment approach.

Treatment as Tertiary Prevention

Chapter 13 described three levels of prevention—primary, secondary and tertiary. The tertiary level focuses on preventing further delinquent acts by youths who are already identified as delinquents. That is the focus of this chapter and the challenge of the entire juvenile justice system. As has been stressed throughout this text, not any part of the system nor the system as a whole can solve the problems that come from child abuse and neglect, delinquency, crime and violence. It takes a total community effort.

One example of this prevention process is the informal adjustment program authorized by the Texas Family Code. The objectives of this program are:

- To meet the court's needs in fulfilling the intent of the family code as it relates to informal adjustment
- To provide a coordinated, comprehensive service delivery system aimed at self-rehabilitation and short-term supervision, diversion and prevention from further involvement in the judicial system
- To provide quality service to children through an informal adjustment contract

The informal adjustment contract is a 6-month informal probationary period, during which a child is supervised by a probation officer or counselor.

The child and family members must meet certain criteria, such as good school attendance, positive attitudes toward change, a demonstrated willingness to see and use resources that can help change behavior, good attitudes toward authority figures and a willingness to cooperate with the juvenile probation department. Through this agreement, children are given a second chance.

Under this program the probation officer, the parent and the child have clearly defined roles. The probation officer supervises and monitors the child's behavior during the 6-month contract. Cooperation is essential for both parents and child. The parents provide emotional and financial support to the child, seek assistance from the probation officer as needed, advise the probation officer of any problems that arise, monitor the child's activities, report violations to the probation officer and provide supervision. The child must obey rules set by the parents, attend school every day as required by law, keep parents informed of his or her whereabouts, have full-time employment if not in school and follow all rules agreed on in the contract.

The contract ends exactly 6 months after it is signed. The case is then closed and the file is returned to the probation department. A letter is sent to the parents advising them that the case has been closed and that they may ask the court to seal the record.

A child can terminate the contract at any time. If this occurs, however, the probation officer returns the case for a court hearing. Should the child or parent decide not to enter into an informal adjustment contract or should the child not meet the criteria established, the case is docketed for a court hearing.

Another example of tertiary prevention is a program in Lansing, Michigan. The School Youth Advocacy Program includes youths who have been institutionalized and then returned to school. It places these youths in a structured peer support group to improve their attitudes about themselves and school and to improve their academic performance, thereby reducing the likelihood that they will commit further delinquent acts.

Youths are recommended for program participation by faculty, administration, other youths and parents. They are selected for their leadership qualities, both negative and positive. Nine to twelve students participate in a group. The program has found that junior high youths are more comfortable talking about problems with peers of their own gender; thus groups are segregated by sex.

The group can decide on sanctions for any infractions by members. For example if someone in the group is caught smoking marijuana, group members decide what the consequences should be, and that decision is enforced. The groups do not get involved in the daily functions and decision-making powers of the school administration or in school government or policy formation.

A third tertiary prevention program is Denver's Junior Partners with Senior Partners. This program links youths and adult community volunteers in a relationship that seeks mutual honesty, open communication and value sharing. It targets youths 10 to 18 who may or may not be in trouble but who have been in trouble in the past and who might get in trouble again without immediate intervention.

Yet another approach uses parental involvement in court, making parents responsible for their children's actions and, in some instances, fining parents for

This anti-drug rally for junior high students is sponsored by DARE. Educational programs to keep youths off drugs are crucial because the link between drug abuse and delinquency has been clearly established.

© Gale Zuckert/Stock Boston

delinquent acts committed by their children. This approach is gaining momentum in some areas.

Of course the challenge for any prevention effort remains identifying those youths at greatest risk and focusing resources on them. The American Psychological Association (p.58) notes:

> Several promising techniques have been identified for treating children who already have adopted aggressive patterns of behavior. These include problem-solving skills training for the child, child management training for the parents (e.g., anger control, negotiation and positive reinforcement), family therapy and interventions at school or in the community.

Characteristics of Effective Intervention Programs

Two primary characteristics of effective intervention programs are: (1) they draw on an understanding of the developmental and sociocultural risk factors that lead to antisocial behavior and (2) they use theory-based intervention strategies known to change behavior, tested program designs and validated, objective measurement techniques to assess outcomes (American Psychological Association, pp.53–54).

Other key intervention program criteria identified by the American Psychological Association (pp.54–55) include the following:

- Programs begin as early as possible to interrupt the "trajectory toward violence."
- They address aggression as part of a constellation of antisocial behaviors in the child or youth.
- They include multiple components that reinforce each other across the child's everyday social contexts: family, school, peer groups, media and community.
- They take advantage of developmental "windows of opportunity": points at which interventions are especially needed or especially likely to make a difference. Such windows of opportunity include transitions in children's lives: birth, entry into preschool, the beginning of elementary school and adolescence.

 Effective treatment programs often take advantage of windows of opportunity, times when treatment is especially needed (in crises) or likely to make a difference (during transition periods).

The Association (p.54) suggests that adolescence is an important window of opportunity "because the limits-testing and other age-appropriate behaviors of adolescents tend to challenge even a functional family's well-developed patterns of interaction." In addition (pp.54–55):

Antisocial behaviors tend to peak during adolescence, and many adolescents engage in sporadic aggression or antisocial behavior. Programs that prepare children to navigate the developmental crises of adolescence may help prevent violence by and toward the adolescent.

Although many adult criminals were antisocial children, not every antisocial child is destined for a life of crime. In fact, relatively few delinquent children become adult criminals. The process of desistance occurs when offenders are diverted from serious to more minor violations, the individual offending rate is significantly reduced or the time between offenses is significantly increased. Research has yet to show why most delinquent teenagers turn from criminal activity while a few continue to commit offenses through adulthood. Some researchers suggest that desistance of delinquency behaviors during adolescence and young adulthood is associated with a discontinuation of substance use over time. The link between drug use and delinquency is well established. Table 14.1 contains the results of an analysis of more than 200 types of delinquency intervention programs, categorized according to their effectiveness.

It is of interest that wilderness/challenge programs, often publicized, appear to have weak or no effect for either institutionalized or noninstitutionalized youths. It is hoped that such an analysis of the treatments will help juvenile justice practitioners select effective dispositions that reduce **recidivism** or repeat offending.

According to Borum (2003, p.127), a review of the literature finds that most effective programs use (1) social learning approaches, (2) family therapy and

Table 14.1
Summary of Effectiveness of Types of Treatment for Reducing Recidivism Rates among Juvenile Offenders

Treatment Type	Offender Status	Treatment/Control Recidivism Contrast (a)	Median Effect Sizes	Consistency Rating
Positive Effects				
Individual counseling	noninstitutional	.28/.50	.46	consistent
Interpersonal skills	noninstitutional	.29/.50	.44	consistent
Behavioral programs	noninstitutional	.30/.50	.42	consistent
Interpersonal skills	institutional	.31/.50	.39	consistent
Teaching family home	institutional	.33/.50	.34	consistent
Multiple services	noninstitutional	.36/.50	.29	less consistent
Restitution, probation/parole	noninstitutional	.43/.50	.15	less consistent
Behavioral programs	institutional	.34/.50	.33	less consistent
Community residential	institutional	.36/.50	.28	less consistent
Multiple services	institutional	.40/.50	.20	less consistent
Mixed Positive Effects				
Employment-related	noninstitutional	.39/.50	.22	inconsistent
Academic programs	noninstitutional	.40/.50	.20	inconsistent
Advocacy/casework	noninstitutional	.41/.50	.19	inconsistent
Family counseling	noninstitutional	.41/.50	.19	inconsistent
Group counseling	noninstitutional	.45/.50	.10	inconsistent
Individual counseling	institutional	.43/.50	.15	inconsistent
Group counseling	institutional	.46/.50	.07	inconsistent
Weak or No Effect				
Wilderness/challenge	noninstitutional	.44/.50	.12	consistent
Early release, prob./parole	noninstitutional	.48/.50	.03	consistent
Deterrence programs	noninstitutional	.53/.50	−.06	consistent
Vocational programs	noninstitutional	.59/.50	−.18	consistent
Employment-related	institutional	.43/.50	.15	inconsistent
Drug abstinence	institutional	.46/.50	.08	inconsistent
Wilderness/challenge	institutional	.46/.50	.07	inconsistent
Milieu therapy	institutional	.46/.50	.08	consistent

(a) Recidivism of treatment group in comparison to assumed control group recidivism of .50. (From Lipsey & Wilson, 1998)

Source: Ken D. Winters. "Kids and Drugs: Treatment Recognizes Link between Delinquency and Substance Abuse." *Corrections Today*, October 1998, p. 120. Reprinted with permission of the American Correctional Association, Lanham, MD.

Table 14.2
**Treatment Targets
and Their Effect on
Reducing Recidivism**

Description	Effect Size (r)
Criminogenic	
Family supervision	.35
Family affection	.33
Barriers to treatment	.30
Self-control	.29
Anger/antisocial feelings	.28
Vocational skills and job	.26
Academic	.23
Prosocial model	.19
Antisocial attitudes	.13
Reduce antisocial peers	.11
Noncriminogenic	
Increase conventional ambition	.00
Physical activity	−.03
Respect antisocial thinking	−.05
Vague emotional/personal problems	−.06
Target self-esteem	−.09
Family, other	−.11
Increase cohesive antisocial peers	−.12
Fear of official punishment	−.18

Source: Randy Borum. "Managing At-Risk Juvenile Offenders in the
Community." *Journal of Contemporary Criminal Justice,* February 2003, p.125.
Reprinted by permission of Sage Publications, Inc.

(3) cognitive approaches. He notes: "There is additional evidence that focusing on thinking and behavior is a critical combination." Pearson et al. (2002), likewise, suggest that cognitive-behavioral programs generally showed stronger effects in reducing recidivism than pure behavior modification strategies. Table 14.2 presents the most frequent **criminogenic factors** (offense enhancing) and noncriminogenic factors targeted in juvenile offender programs and their effect on reducing recidivism.

Programs focusing primarily on criminogenic factors showed much larger effects in reducing re-offending than those that did not. In fact, some factors such as improving self-esteem or inducing fear of official punishment have negative correlations, that is, targeting these factors tends to increase, rather than decrease, reoffending. Before looking at specific treatment programs, consider the approaches being taken to those who come into the juvenile justice system because they have been neglected or abused.

Treatment Programs for Children and Juveniles Who Have Been Abused

As has been noted throughout this text, the one-pot character of the juvenile justice system includes children and juveniles who have been neglected and/or abused. Their needs are often quite different from those of delinquent youths, but often the same personnel are called upon to deal with both. Figure 14.2 presents a model of child abuse.

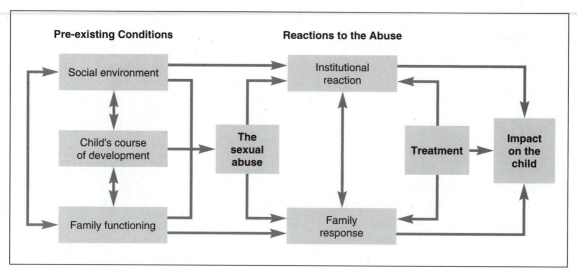

Figure 14.2
A Model of Child Abuse

Source: Beverly Gomes-Schwartz and Jonathan Horowitz. *Child Sexual Abuse Victims and Their Treatment.* Washington, DC: U.S. Department of Justice, National Institute for Juvenile Justice and Delinquency Prevention, July 1988, p.1.

Note that the child's development and the treatment provided are influenced by the family's and institution's reaction to the abuse.

The treatment in this case is the Family Crisis Program (FCP), Division of Child Psychiatry at Tufts New England Medical Center in Boston. The treatment approach is based on crisis theory, which begins with the assumption that at certain times in people's lives they are faced with insurmountable obstacles requiring more than the ordinary coping mechanisms.

Crisis intervention capitalizes on windows of opportunity when the individual may be especially receptive to treatment and establishes new approaches to problem-solving.

FCP, drawing upon crisis theory, incorporates rapid intervention, outreach and focal treatment involving 12 intensive sessions and liaison with other agencies. The Metropolitan Court Judges Committee (1986, p.29) states in its introduction to the recommendations for treatment and planning for deprived children:

> Although child victims frequently require help to alleviate the guilt they are experiencing about their family's problems, they are often placed into foster care without additional supports or necessary therapeutic intervention. The lack of immediate and effective treatment and coordinated planning and resources represents serious problems. Providing an adequate number of foster homes, trained foster parents, special homes for special needs children, emergency shelter care facilities and other alternatives prior to termination of parental rights are also critical. After termination, providing resources for the treatment and subsequent adoption of deprived children is the wisest investment society can make. An abused or neglected child, whether removed from the home or remaining in the home, needs assistance, which is often not provided.

Although 80 percent of all substantiated cases of abuse or neglect receive "casework counseling," given the excessive caseloads, this response must be seen as more paperwork than counseling. (The ratio of cases to workers in some large jurisdictions has exceeded an unrealistic 150:1, allowing less than an hour per month for each deprived child.)

Treatment Recommendations of the Metropolitan Court Judges Committee

The committee made the following recommendations (pp.30–34):

- *Immediate treatment.* Treatment of abused and neglected children must be immediate, thorough and coordinated among responsible agencies.
- *Family focus.* Treatment provided to children through court or agency intervention should involve the entire family or focus on family relationships and should stress the primary responsibility of the parents for their children's welfare and protection. Family involvement, where at all possible, should be stabilized rather than disrupted as a result of intervention and treatment.
- *Parental responsibility.* Child protection agencies and the courts should require parental responsibility for children's well being.
- *Positive parental behavior.* Judges must have authority to order treatment for the parents, to require other positive conduct and to impose sanctions for willful failure or refusal to comply.
- *Substance abuse.* Substance abuse treatment, if appropriate, should be mandated for parents and their children.
- *Mandated treatment.* Judges must have the authority to order the treatment determined necessary and should regularly review the efficacy of such treatment.
- *Youthful sex offenders.* Judges must require appropriate treatment for youthful sexual offenders, many of whom have been victims of sexual abuse. The cycle of young victims of sexual abuse later becoming perpetrators of sexual abuse must be broken. Unless intensive intervention and effective treatment of such youthful sexual offenders is provided, the cycle will continue.

Treatment requirements recommended by the Metropolitan Court Judges Committee include immediate treatment, family focus, parental responsibility, positive parental behavior, treatment for substance abuse, mandated treatment and treatment for youthful sexual offenders.

Service Recommendations

The committee also made recommendations for the provision of services to juveniles (pp.30–34):

- *Qualified treatment personnel.* Child protection caseworkers must be screened, trained and certified to improve child protection services and treatment. People who work with deprived children should undergo detailed background investigations.

- *Volunteer assistance.* Screened, qualified and trained volunteers should be used to enhance the quality of services.

- *Foster homes.* A sufficient number of foster homes, adequately reimbursed and provided access to treatment and support services, should be established. Strict screening, improved recruiting, professional training, licensing requirements and adequate compensation will encourage quality foster care.

- *Foster care drift.* Frequently moving children from foster home to foster home is detrimental to children's physical and emotional well being and must be reduced.

- *Children with special needs.* Specialized foster homes and foster parents should be available for children with special needs. Older, minority, disabled or seriously abused children require particular care, with specialized foster homes, trained foster parents and continuing agency assistance tailored to their needs.

- *Homeless children.* Homeless and runaway children must be provided proper emergency shelter facilities as well as necessary services. Much of the problem of at-risk or exploited children could be alleviated by improved and expanded emergency shelter facilities, with necessary services and counseling. Children who are "broke and on the streets" are particularly vulnerable.

In providing services, the Metropolitan Court Judges Committee recommends that treatment personnel be well qualified, that volunteer assistance be used, that quality foster homes be available, that foster care drift be reduced, that children with special needs be provided special foster homes and that shelters be established for homeless children.

One of the greatest challenges in providing services to youths who have been neglected or abused is to assure that none of them "fall through the cracks." Michigan has developed contact standards for Child Protection Service workers that are based on the risk level of the child, as shown in Table 14.3.

Permanency Recommendations

The final set of recommendations made by the committee dealt with planning for **permanency** for children, that is, assuring the most lasting placement or solution possible: "The Court must find a way to provide a permanent and loving home for the child" (pp.33–34).

- *Termination of parental rights.* When there is clear, convincing evidence that the parents' conduct would legally permit termination of parental rights and it is in the child's best interests to do so, termination should proceed expeditiously. The immediate availability of adoptive parents should not be required to terminate parental rights.

- *Alternative permanent plans.* When reunification is not possible or termination of parental rights is not in the child's best interests, courts

Table 14.3
Michigan Contact Standards for CPS Workers by Risk Level

Case Type	Number of Required Face-to-Face Contacts Per Month	Contact Level	Collateral Contacts
Low risk	1	Face-to-face with child and/or parent/caretaker	1
Moderate risk	2	Face-to-face with child and/or parent/caretaker	2
High risk	3	Face-to-face with child and/or parent/caretaker	3
Intensive risk	4	Face-to-face with child and/or parent/caretaker	4
Purchase of service (POS) through private agency	Varies, but minimum once per month	Worker contacts can be replaced on one-for-one basis by POS agency worker	2 phone calls per month with agency worker
Families First/FTBS*	1	1 contact per month with Families First or FTBS worker	None required
Pending adjudication	None required	Contacts as needed	None required

* Families Together Building Solutions.

Source: Michigan Family Independence Agency. *CPS Policy and Procedures Manual.* Lansing, MI: Family Independence Agency, 1996.

In Richard Wiebush, Raelene Freitag and Christopher Baird. *Preventing Delinquency through Improved Child Protection Services.* Washington, DC: OJJDP Juvenile Justice Bulletin, July 2001, p.12. (NCJ 187759)

should consider other permanent plans. In some cases, terminating a parent's rights is inappropriate and the court should examine such alternatives as:

º Long-term custody in a homelike setting, such as placement with relatives, substitute or extended families, and foster grandparents;

º Permanent or temporary guardianship after a finding of dependency and removal; or

º Any other solution short of termination leading to permanency for the child.

■ *Expedited adoption process.* When needed, adoption should proceed as quickly as possible. Foster parents should be able to adopt their foster child.

■ *Subsidized adoptions.* Subsidized adoption programs should be more widely available and used for special needs and hard-to-place children.

In planning for permanency, the committee recommends that when necessary, parental rights may be terminated, that alternative plans should be made if parental rights are not terminated and that the adoption process be expedited, including providing subsidized adoption programs for hard-to-place children.

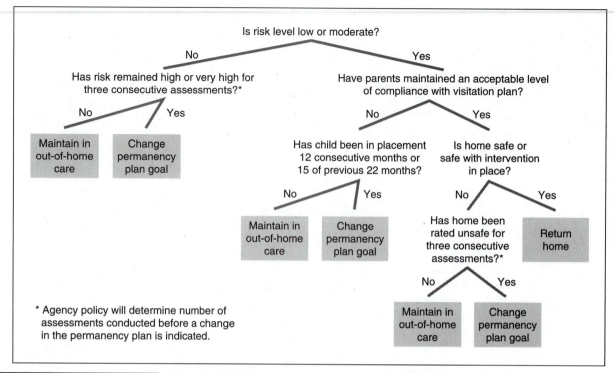

Figure 14.3
Placement/
Permanency Plan
Guidelines Example

* Agency policy will determine number of assessments conducted before a change in the permanency plan is indicated.

Children's Research Center. *Structured Decision Making in CPS: Generic Policy and Procedures Manual.* Madison, WI: National Council on Crime and Delinquency, Children's Research Center, 2001.

Source: Richard Wiebush, Raelene Freitag and Christopher Baird. *Preventing Delinquency through Improved Child Protection Services.* Washington, DC: OJJDP Juvenile Justice Bulletin, July 2001, p.13. (NCJ 187759)

Figure 14.3 presents guidelines for placement/permanency.

As has been frequently noted, youths who are neglected or abused have a much greater chance of ending up in the juvenile justice system because of delinquent behavior.

Delinquent Youths Needing Treatment in the Juvenile Justice System

According to Hamilton et al. (2002) and Stouthamer-Loeber et al. (2001), the majority of youths being treated within the juvenile justice system have experienced severe physical abuse or neglect by parents or caregivers. In addition to those who have been neglected or abused, the juvenile justice system also must respond to the needs of juvenile perpetrators who have also been victims of crime and violence (Finkelhor and Hashima, 2001). Because the juvenile justice system is responsible for such a diverse population, effective assessment is vital.

As noted by Borum (p.130): "Serious, chronic juvenile offenders, almost by definition, have very high rates of recidivism; typically about two thirds re-offend over the course of a year. It is possible, though, to manage most of these cases in the community with success rates that are at least as good—probably better—than with institutional confinement. The key is to adequately assess the offender's risks, needs and strengths; to choose treatment targets that are related to offense risk; and apply proven interventions—especially those that are theoretically grounded and that use cognitive behavioral methods—to address those problems. And if we reserve intensive interventions—both monitoring and treatment—for the highest risk cases but apply it there with rigor and fidelity, we will prevent much more overall crime and violence."

 The key to managing cases in the community is to adequately assess offenders' risk and apply proven interventions using cognitive behavioral methods to address the problems.

The Community Assessment Center Concept

Oldenettel and Wordes (2000) report on the OJJDP's Community Assessment Center (CAC) initiative. Four communities were selected to be part of the CAC demonstration efforts: Denver, Colorado; Lee County, Florida; Jefferson County, Colorado; and Orlando, Florida.

Key Elements of the Community Assessment Center

The CAC model has four key elements.

 The four key elements of the Community Assessment Center are (1) a single point of entry, (2) immediate and comprehensive assessments, (3) management information system and (4) integrated case management.

Single Point of Entry

Oldenettel and Wordes (p.4) note: "Youths often enter the same system repeatedly, but through different doors, such as child welfare organizations, juvenile justice agencies or various treatment programs. For these youths and their families accessing appropriate services requires navigating a maze of case workers, intake workers and counselors. The idea of providing a 24-hour centralized point of intake and assessment for juveniles who have come or are likely to come into contact with the juvenile justice system is consistent with OJJDP's Comprehensive Strategy." As a key leader said in an interview: "Create a one-stop shop, a single point of entry where cops and other community points could access; where all kinds of resources that were needed would be there; and kids would get hooked up with those resources before going back into the community."

Immediate and Comprehensive Assessments

Assessment includes all aspects of a youth's situation, including known risk factors and protective factors. Table 14.4 presents a list of items from a violence risk inventory.

Risk factors can be either static or dynamic. **Static risk factors** are historical (for example, early onset of violence) or dispositional and are unlikely to change over time. **Dynamic risk factors,** in contrast, are individual, social or situational factors that often do change, for example, associates, attitudes and stress levels. These might be amenable to modification and are sometimes referred to as *needs* (Hoge, 2002). Hirth (2001, p.81) reports that programs targeting youths at highest risk of reoffending or of violence select their population based on those

Table 14.4
Items from the Structured Assessment of Violence Risk in Youth (SAVRY)

Historical Risk Factors
- History of violence
- History of nonviolent offending
- Early initiation of violence
- Past supervision/intervention failures
- History of self-harm or suicide attempts
- Exposure to violence in the home
- Childhood history of maltreatment
- Parental/caregiver criminality
- Early caregiver disruption
- Poor school achievement

Social/Contextual Risk Factors
- Peer delinquency
- Peer rejection
- Stress and poor coping
- Poor parental management
- Lack of personal/social support
- Community disorganization

Individual/Clinical Risk Factors
- Negative attitudes
- Risk taking/impulsivity
- Substance-use difficulties
- Anger management problems
- Psychopathic traits
- Attention deficit/hyperactivity difficulties
- Poor compliance
- Low interest/commitment to school

Protective Factors
- Prosocial involvement
- Strong social support
- Strong attachments and bonds
- Positive attitude toward intervention and authority
- Strong commitment to school
- Resilient personality traits

Source: Randy Borum. "Managing At-Risk Juvenile Offenders in the Community." *Journal of Contemporary Criminal Justice,* February 2003, p.119. Reprinted by permission.

who were first arrested at age 15 or younger and who have at least three of four high-risk characteristics:

- Academic failure, school suspensions and truancy
- Lack of family stability and supervision, including single-parent households, poor parenting skills, parents or siblings in the criminal justice system or domestic violence
- Mental health or substance abuse problems
- Predelinquent behaviors, including running away, gang affiliation, stealing and disruptive behavior

Protective factors are not simply the absence of risk factors. They are the positive presence of some person, characteristic or circumstance that can reduce the negative impact of one or more risk factors. Borum (p.117) stresses: "To develop an effective plan for managing a juvenile's risk for reoffending, it is critical to conduct a systematic assessment of risk, need and protective factors."

Management Information System (MIS)

Oldenettel and Wordes (p.7) suggest: "At a minimum, a CAC must have an internal database to manage information on the youths it serves. The CAC should also have some level of access to the information systems of related agencies, if not directly, then through an intermediary employed by the related organization."

 A management information system (MIS) should perform two tasks: (1) link data from multiple agencies and (2) monitor trends.

Integrated Case Management (ICM)

According to Oldenettel and Wordes (p.9): "The case manager (or case team) is the critical link between comprehensive assessments and effective integrated service delivery. Case managers should . . . develop individualized, flexible and responsible treatment plans and should define criteria to determine levels of case management."

Reasons to Develop an Assessment Center

There are several reasons to develop an assessment center, including gaps in services, lack of communication among agencies, poor mental health services because of Medicaid cuts, confusion about how the system works, inadequate funding to serve the needs of juveniles and their families, public concern for increasing incidents of violent juvenile crime and increases in violent juvenile crime in the late 1980s and early 1990s. Based on these perceived needs, assessment centers developed numerous goals.

Goals of an Assessment Center

The following list of goals is taken from the four demonstration sites highlighting objectives in the areas of law enforcement, services and treatment and case processing:

- Reduce law enforcement time devoted to juveniles
- Create a central booking and receiving facility for juvenile offenders
- Collect good, clear information about juveniles' needs
- Accelerate juvenile access to treatment
- Pool resources from different agencies
- Provide referrals to parents and children
- Develop a facility to hold dependency juveniles awaiting placement
- Expedite court proceedings by providing better information to defense attorneys and prosecutors
- Provide early intervention services for troubled juveniles
- Develop a single point of entry for assessing and referring juveniles
- Facilitate cooperation and coordination among the agencies
- Expedite processing of juveniles through the system
- Streamline the current fragmented service delivery system
- Provide courts with better tools and information

Potential Problems

 Three concerns related to assessment centers are (1) violating due process rights, (2) stigmatizing youths and (3) net widening.

Due Process Concerns

Although youths must sign a consent form before being assessed, some question a young person's ability to understand the form or possible negative consequences of consenting. Information on youths entered into the MIS is shared with other agencies/organizations involved on a right-to-know and need-to-know basis.

Oldenettel and Wordes (pp.9–10) suggest: "Communities establishing CAC's can take a variety of steps to avoid infringing on juvenile's due process rights. First, defense counsel should play an active role in the assessment center from the very beginning. . . . Next, communities should educate themselves about their state statutes and case law regarding youth's ability to provide consent, especially in cases where parents are not present. . . . Communities must also be fully cognizant of the laws governing youth's ability to waive their right to counsel."

Stigmatizing Youths

The creation of a nonsecure processing system and protocol can help address the concern of stigmatizing youths. Youths not accused of delinquent acts can be brought to the center in a way that protects them from negative labeling and avoids contact with delinquent offenders. This nonsecure process can be used for status offenders, dependent youths and high-risk youths demonstrating inappropriate behavior. In addition, controlling access to and use of the records in the MIS is an important component of controlling for possible stigmatization. If youths are prosecuted on delinquent charges, CAC records of prior nondelinquent incidents must not be used against them.

Net Widening

The CAC model intends that only youths appropriate for juvenile justice system intervention or referral to services become involved. High-risk (nondelinquent) youths should receive services or referrals from the CAC, but should not be brought under the jurisdiction of the juvenile justice system. OJJDP does not view bringing appropriate youths in for preventive services as widening the net of the justice system but rather as keeping children in need from "falling through the cracks" of the service delivery system. In addition, if more youths are brought in on delinquency charges because patrol officers have more time to enforce the law, then the net has not been widened, just strengthened (p.10). As noted in Chapters 9 and 13, when possible the preference has been to divert nonviolent, first-time offenders from the formal juvenile justice process.

 A recommended three-pronged approach to treatment includes prevention, intervention and enforcement.

Offenders taking part in a mock job-interview at the Work Ethics Camp in McCook, Nebraska. Here, the word offender is used instead of inmate, and it is all about learning.

Diversion Alternatives— Community-Based Treatment Programs

"More than a half-million juveniles are under community supervision as a result of violent or delinquent behavior" (Borum, p.114). Borum reports: "Research has shown that treatment can reduce their risk of reoffending." Hirt (p.80) suggests that the goal of diversion is "to address negative issues and offer children a way to avoid failure. Mental health counseling, substance abuse treatment, stress and anger management, tutoring, mentoring and parenting classes—whatever resources can be applied to the individual child's situation—fit within the framework of this program. Parents must agree to participate and be part of the solution."

Common diversion alternatives include intensive community supervision, home detention and electronic monitoring, day treatment, evening and weekend programs (providing tutoring, recreation, alternative schools, work and treatment services), work and apprenticeship (to develop a work ethic, a sense of responsibility and a feeling of accomplishment), restitution (in services or in cash) and community service (cleaning up parks).

Second Chance Camps

Second Chance camps are community-based alternatives to placing delinquents in training schools. Such camps usually emphasize positive relationships, challenging activities, structure and discipline and the development of self-esteem and a sense of responsibility. Programs are geared to improve self-esteem and behavior by focusing on challenges specifically designed to improve interpersonal and living skills. These experiential, action-oriented programs include canoe trips, hikes, a ropes course and community service projects.

Leverette-Sanderlin (2001, pp.123–124) describes one such camp, Camp Turning Point, held at the Lake Darpo recreation area near Society Hill, South

Carolina. At this camp young men ages 13 to 16 are taught to make the right choices for their futures and participate in courses about anger and conflict management. She notes: "While Camp Turning Point has the typical camp activities of swimming and fishing, it is not a fun camp. . . . The campers also learn about working as a team in a ropes course and with horses provided by Carolina Family Ministries." Leverette-Sanderlin also notes: "By the time Camp Turning Point entered into its third year, the non-repeater success rate has remained close to 90 percent." She reports that one of the founders of the camp strongly believes that juvenile offenders are a community problem that demands a community solution: "Juvenile crime is a breeding ground for the beginning of criminal careers that last a lifetime."

Collaborative Efforts

As stressed throughout this text, success in reducing juvenile crime and delinquency often rests on the innovative, collaborative efforts of those closest to the issue. Following are some successful efforts between law enforcement officers and probation officers.

Operation Night Light

A collaboration between police and probation agencies is Boston's Operation Night Light, begun in 1992. This effort teams police and probation officers to ensure that gang members and other high-risk offenders adhere to the conditions of their probation. Police officers start practicing community corrections; probation officers begin doing community crime control. Night Light is a catalyst to get the relevant players onto the same field to better address youth violence. Statistics indicate that Night Light has made a tremendous impact on crime in Boston. Since implementation of the overall Boston strategy in 1996, of which Night Light is a primary component, the city has experienced a 70 percent decrease in the number of people age 24 and younger killed by guns.

 Partnerships between police and probation departments are having success in preventing further delinquency by youths who have been adjudicated delinquent in the past.

The Coordinated Agency Network

On the West Coast, police and probation collaboration has also met with success. The Coordinated Agency Network (CAN) is a collaboration between the San Diego Police Department and the San Diego County Probation Department that targets low-risk juvenile probationers for intensive and systematic supervision. The program also includes mentoring by police officers and referrals to a wide array of participating individual and family services. CAN joins local criminal justice, community-based organizations and human service agencies in an alliance to combat juvenile delinquency.

 Effective supervision is active, local and community based.

Visitors gather for an open house at the new Rogue Valley Youth Correctional Facility in Grants Pass, Oregon. The prison is one of five in Oregon to handle increasing numbers of young offenders.

AP/Wide World Photo

Exemplary Programs

The following treatment programs or research projects received the OJJDP's Gould-Wysinger Award (GWA), described in Chapter 13.[2]

Juvenile Intervention Project, Colorado

The goals of the Juvenile Intervention Project are jail removal and deinstitutionalization of status offenders. A training program for sheriff's officers explains screening criteria and procedures. Officers who perform intake screening are trained to provide status offenders with appropriate services. The program contracts with a host home to ensure a bed is available for status offenders. Crisis intervention, temporary holding or attendant care, and volunteer tracking and mentoring are also provided. The program resulted in an immediate decrease in juvenile arrests and detention, and new patrol officers now participate in a special four-hour field-training program. (GWA)

Juvenile Detention Center, Western Nebraska Juvenile Services

The Juvenile Detention Center was established to provide programming, intervention and rehabilitation services for juveniles. A 20-bed facility serving Scotts Bluff County and the surrounding area, it is the only secure juvenile detention center in western Nebraska.

The center has a transitional living program designed to provide juveniles with the knowledge, skills and experience to live independently. A family preservation component encourages the family to cooperate in the reconciliation of the

---

[1]Program descriptions provided by Pam Allen.

offender to the family unit. A substance abuse program provides intervention and treatment. An educational program offers four types of programs: class continuation, credit work, GED programs and college. The center also offers a 4-H program, a craft program and instruction in creative writing. Opportunities to attend church services are available.

As a result of the center's programs, recidivism has been reduced by 50 percent. Acceptance of the center has grown as other communities and counties increase their use of the facility. (GWA)

Partnership for Learning, Inc., Maryland

Partnership for Learning (PFL) was established in 1991 to screen first-time juvenile offenders appearing before juvenile court in Baltimore City and to identify and assist offenders diagnosed as learning disabled. After first-time offenders have been identified, tested and interviewed, the requirements for participating in PFL are presented. After an agreement has been executed the child's case is postponed, and the child is matched with a tutor trained in a special reading and spelling program. Of the children matched with tutors, more than 80 percent have successfully completed or are actively involved in the program and have not re-offended.

PFL is a joint project of the Office of the State's Attorney for Baltimore City, the Office of the Public Defender, the Department of Juvenile Services, the Maryland State Department of Education, the Baltimore City Department of Education and the Maryland Association for Dyslexic Adults and Youth. It has gained national and international attention as a cost-effective program that reduces the rate of recidivism among youthful offenders. (GWA)

Fremont County Youth Services, Wyoming

This program's goals are to improve the efficiency and the effective use of the juvenile justice system and existing services in Fremont County, to develop programs to serve county youths, to assist the county in developing policies for secure detention of juveniles as well as alternatives to detention in the county jail, and to reduce the liability of the board of commissioners and sheriff regarding detention of juveniles prior to a court hearing. The program provides report/intake for law enforcement and the county attorney, a deferred prosecution program, a youth council coordinator, a work alternatives program, a sentencing alternatives program, pre-sentence investigation for county courts, formal probation supervision, limited pre-dispositional reports for juvenile court, home detention program supervision, 24-hour intake at county jails, youth advocacy, a cooperative agreement to provide staff-secure shelter care and a jail removal transportation subsidy program.

Serving hundreds of children a year in a county of more than 9,000 square miles, the program has enabled the county to address the mandates of the Juvenile Justice and Delinquency Prevention Act. (GWA)

Earn-It Project, New Hampshire

Earn-It is a victim restitution program that serves as a sentencing alternative for juvenile court and the Juvenile Conference Committee. Juvenile offenders are referred to the program for monetary and community service work placements. Earn-It arranges the work placement at an area business, nonprofit agency or municipality by matching the offender's strengths with the needs of the worksite and monitors the youth's performance.

Earn-It has worked with juvenile offenders in 17 towns within the jurisdiction of the Keene District Court. More than 80 percent of offenders have completed their court-ordered community service obligations and restitution to their victims. Participants have performed hundreds of hours of community service work and have repaid thousands of dollars to victims. The recidivism rate for youths completing the program is below 30 percent. (GWA)

Juvenile Work Restitution, Alabama

Located in Tuscaloosa, this program instills a sense of personal accountability, improves behavior and reduces recidivism. Jobs are created in the public and private sectors, and juvenile offenders are matched to an appropriate job. Offenders work to reimburse victims and provide community service.

The program has helped reduce minority over-representation in the state school for juvenile offenders and has developed greater confidence in the juvenile justice system. Recidivism has been reduced by 10 percent. (GWA)

Prosocial Gang, New York

This unique intervention program implements Aggression Replacement Training (ART) with gang members involved in delinquent behavior. The program is conducted at two Brooklyn sites—the Brownsville Community Neighborhood Action Center and Youth DARES. ART improves prosocial skills, moral reasoning and anger control by channeling aggressive behavior into a positive force so gang members become a constructive influence in the community.

Four evaluations found that the ART program significantly improves the quality of youths' interpersonal skills; enhances their ability to reduce and control anger; decreases the level of egocentricity and increases concern for the needs of others; substantially decreases antisocial behaviors; substantially increases prosocial behaviors; improves community functioning, especially with peers; and decreases criminal recidivism. (GWA)

Sex Offender Assessment, Ohio

The Sex Offender Assessment research project was created to improve the assessment and treatment of juvenile sex offenders and enhance understanding of the victimization process. The project evaluates how offenders attempt to gain a victim's trust; what types of nonsexual behaviors are engaged in prior to the abuse; and how enticements, bribes, threats and coercion are used to obtain cooperation in sexual activity. The last part of the project is to disseminate the study findings to practitioners during a daylong, statewide workshop.

Prior to the project, little research was available to guide the assessment and treatment of adolescent offenders. The results provide professionals with crucial information and improve caretakers' ability to treat offenders and victims. (GWA)

Study of Serious Juvenile Offenders, Virginia

This comprehensive study of serious juvenile offenders defines the population of juveniles who have been convicted in circuit court by offense and service history; compares transferred and convicted juveniles with those retained in the juvenile justice system and committed to learning centers; identifies jurisdictional variation in the transfer option; evaluates which factors influence the decision-making process for transfer-eligible juveniles; and develops recommendations for policy-makers. Study findings are available in a detailed report.

The project makes a substantial contribution toward developing an informational base from which legislators can draw in deciding juvenile justice issues. There is a commitment to continue this important research. (GWA)

The OJJDP's Guiding Principles for a Comprehensive Strategy

The OJJDP guiding principles were developed for use with serious, violent and chronic juvenile offenders but, in actuality, can apply to any treatment program. The following guidelines can assist communities' efforts to prevent delinquent conduct and reduce juvenile involvement in delinquency:

- *Strengthen the family* in its primary responsibility to instill moral values and provide guidance and support to children.

- *Support core social institutions* such as schools, religious institutions and community organizations in their efforts to develop capable, mature and responsible youths.

- *Promote delinquency prevention* as the most cost-effective approach to dealing with juvenile delinquency. When children engage in acting out behavior such as status offenses, the family and community, in concert with child welfare agencies, must respond with appropriate treatment and support services.

- *Intervene immediately and effectively when delinquent behavior occurs* to successfully prevent delinquent offenders from becoming chronic offenders or committing progressively more serious and violent crimes.

- *Establish a system of graduated sanctions* that holds each juvenile offender accountable, protects public safety and provides programs and services that meet identified treatment needs.

- *Identify and control the small group of serious, violent and chronic juvenile offenders* who have committed felony offenses or who have failed to respond to intervention and nonsecure community-based treatment and rehabilitation services.

 The OJJDP guiding principles for a comprehensive strategy for serious, violent and chronic juvenile offenders recommend (1) strengthen the family, (2) support core social institutions, (3) promote delinquency prevention, (4) intervene immediately and effectively when delinquent behavior occurs, (5) establish a system of graduated sanctions and (6) identify and control the small group of serious, violent and chronic juvenile offenders.

Blueprints for Violence Prevention Initiatives Focused on Treatment

The Blueprints for Violence Prevention Initiative focuses three of its eleven programs on treatment. The descriptions are provided by Mihalic et al. (2001), adapted with information provided from the programs.

Multidimensional Treatment Foster Care

This program recruits, trains and supervises foster families to provide youths with close supervision, fair and consistent limits and consequences and a supportive relationship with an adult.

Incarceration of youths is costly and may have negative long-term effects on the youths involved. Alternatives to incarceration typically involve placement in a group care setting. However, association with delinquent peers has been shown to be a strong predictor of future aggressive and delinquent behaviors. Placing youths in group care with other juvenile delinquents may facilitate further bonding and social identification among group members.

A viable and cost-effective alternative to group care is Multidimensional Treatment Foster Care (MTFC), where youths' contact with delinquent peers is minimized. The youths are supervised closely at home, in the community and at school and are disciplined for rule violations and mentored by their MTFC parents. MTFC parent training emphasizes behavior management methods to provide youths with a structured and therapeutic living environment.

After they complete a preservice training, MTFC parents are matched with participating youths. A program supervisor, with the help of the MTFC parents, develops an individualized daily program for each youth that specifies the youth's schedule of activities and behavioral expectations and sets the number of points he or she can earn for satisfactory performance. The intervention is a gradual process based on youth's compliance with each level of program treatment. Three levels of supervision are defined in MTFC: Level 1 requires adult supervision at all times; Level 2 grants youths limited free time in the community, and Level 3 allows for some peer activities that require less structure.

Routine consultation with and ongoing supervision of MTFC parents is a cornerstone of the program; parents are called daily to check on youth's progress, and they also attend weekly group meetings. Family therapy is provided for the youth's biological or adoptive families, who are taught to use the structured system of the MTFC home to increase the likelihood of parenting success when the youths return home.

One of the most significant problems in implementing an MTFC program is recruiting and training a group of competent MTFC parents. Another implementation problem is developing effective methods of communication for treatment staff and MTFC parents. The quality of teamwork is crucial to the success of MTFC cases.

Evaluations of MTFC youths show they had significantly fewer arrests during a 12-month follow up than a control group of youths who participated in residential group care programs (an average of 2.6 versus 6.4 offenses). During the first two years after treatment and program completion, youths who participated in the MTFC program spent significantly fewer days in lockup than youths who were placed in other community-based programs, resulting in a savings of $122,000 for the program in incarceration costs. In addition, significantly fewer MTFC youths were ever incarcerated following treatment. MTFC also has been shown to be effective for youths ages 9 to 18 leaving state mental hospital settings. Results showed that MTFC youths were placed out of the hospital at a significantly higher rate. During a seven-month follow up, 33 percent of the control group remained in the hospital because no appropriate aftercare services could be found.

Contact information: Patricia Chamberlain, Ph.D., Oregon Social Learning Center Community Programs, 160 East Fourth Avenue, Eugene, OR 97401; (541) 485-2711; (541) 485-7087 (fax); pattic@oslc.org; www.oslc.org. Confirmed.

Functional Family Therapy

This program has been applied successfully to a wide range of problem youths and their families in various contexts and treatment systems. Participating youths attend on average 12 one-hour sessions spread over three months. Treatment includes three phases: (1) engagement and motivation, (2) behavior change and (3) generalization.

Many communities turn to punitive measures to deal with juvenile crime. Mounting evidence suggests, however, that removing youths from their homes and families is costly and ineffective. Punitive programs that separate youths and their families can be detrimental to a youth's long-term progress. Youth's behavioral problems are deeply embedded in their psychosocial systems (e.g., family and community); to be effective, therefore, interventions should treat youths while addressing their complex multidimensional problems.

Functional Family Therapy (FFT) is a short-term, well-documented program that has been applied successfully to a wide range of problem youths and their families in various contexts (e.g., rural, urban, multicultural, international) and treatment systems (e.g., clinics, home-based programs, juvenile courts, independent providers). Researchers designed this multisystemic program to help diverse populations of underserved and at-risk youths and their families who often enter the system angry, hopeless and/or resistant to treatment.

On average, participating youths attend 12 one-hour sessions spread over three months; more difficult cases require 26 to 30 hours of direct service. FFT clearly identifies three treatment phases, each of which includes descriptions of goals, requisite therapist characteristics and techniques.

Phase 1: Engagement and motivation. Phase 1 applies reattribution and related techniques to address maladaptive perceptions, beliefs and emotions. Use of such techniques serves to help targeted youths and their families increase hope and their expectations of change, respect for individual differences and values, and trust between family and therapist; reduce resistance; and overcome the intense negativity within the family and between the family and community that can prevent change.

Phase 2: Behavior change. FFT clinicians develop and implement intermediate and long-term behavior change plans that are culturally appropriate, context sensitive and tailored to the unique characteristics of each family member.

Phase 3: Generalization. FFT clinicians help families apply positive family change to other problem areas and/or situations, maintain changes and prevent relapse. To ensure long-term support of changes, FFT links families with available community resources.

Success has been demonstrated and replicated for more than 25 years with a wide-range of interventionists, including paraprofessionals and trainees representing the various professional degrees. Controlled comparison studies with follow-up periods of one, three and five years have demonstrated significant and long-term reductions in youths re-offending and in sibling entry into high-risk behaviors. Comparative cost figures demonstrate very large reductions in daily program costs compared with other treatment programs.

In the nation's largest FFT research and practice site, 80 percent of the families receiving FFT services completed the treatment, a high completion rate compared with the rate for standard interventions. Of those who completed the program, 19.8 percent committed an offense in the year following completion, compared with 36 percent of youths in the control group.

On average, FFT treatment in this practice site cost between $700 and $1,000 per family for a two-year study period. By contrast, the average cost of detention was at least $6,000 per youth, and the average cost of a county residential program was at least $13,500 per youth for the same time.

Contact information: James F. Alexander, Ph.D., Department of Psychology, University of Utah, 390 South 1530 East, Room 502, Salt Lake City, UT 84112; (801) 585-1807; jfafft@psych.utah.edu; www.fftinc.com.

Multisystemic Therapy

This treatment program was developed to provide cost-effective, community-based treatment to youths with serious behavior disorders who are at high risk of out-of-home placement.

Before Multisystemic Therapy (MST), scientifically validated, cost-effective, community-based treatment was generally unavailable, and youths often were placed out-of-home in expensive treatment or psychiatric facilities or were incarcerated. MST views individuals as living within a complex social network encompassing individual, family and extrafamilial (peer, school, neighborhood) factors. Behavioral problems can stem from problematic interactions within the social network, and MST specifically targets the multiple factors that can contribute to antisocial behavior. MST uses the strengths in each youth's social network to promote positive change in his or her behavior. The overriding purpose of MST is to help parents deal effectively with their youth's behavior problems; help youths cope with family, peer, school and neighborhood problems, and reduce or eliminate the need for out-of-home placements. To empower families, MST also addresses identified barriers to effective parenting (e.g,. parental drug abuse, parental mental health problems) and helps family members build an indigenous social support network involving friends, extended family, neighborhoods and church members.

To increase family collaboration and enhance generalization, MST is typically provided in home, school and community locations. Treatment is designed with input from the family being served, and this approach encourages collaboration and participation. Therapists with low caseloads—available 24/7—provide the treatment, placing developmentally appropriate demands for responsible behavior on youths and their families. Intervention plans include strategic family therapy, structural family therapy, behavioral parent training and cognitive behavior therapies.

To address the known causes of delinquency, MST focuses on the individual youth and his or her family, peer context, school/vocational performance and neighborhood/community supports. Family interventions seek to promote the parents' capacity to monitor and discipline their children, peer interventions remove offenders from deviant peer groups and help them develop relationships with prosocial peers, and school/vocational interventions enhance the youth's capacity for future employment and financial success. The average duration of treatment is approximately four months, which includes approximately 60 hours of face-to-face therapist-family contact.

Program evaluations have revealed 25 to 70 percent reductions in long-term rates of re-arrest and 47 to 64 percent reductions in out-of-home placements. Moreover, families receiving MST reported extensive improvements in family functioning and decreases in youths' mental health problems. Positive results were maintained after almost four years.

Despite its intensity, MST has been demonstrated as a cost-effective treatment for decreasing the antisocial behavior of violent and chronic juvenile offenders. MST costs approximately $3,500 per youth in one replication site in South Carolina, which compared favorably with the average cost of the state's institutional placement of approximately $18,000 per youth for a time period of about 59 weeks post referral.

Contact information: Marshall E. Swenson, Manager of Program Development, MST Services, Inc., 710 J. Dodds Blvd., Suite 2E, Mt. Pleasant, SC 29464; (843) 284-2215; (843) 856-8227 (fax); marshall.Swenson@mstservices.com; www.mstservices.com. Confirmed.

Targeting Youths at High Risk

Those at high risk of becoming delinquent or of re-offending include young children, serious repeat offenders, truants, youths with mental illness, youths who abuse drugs and sex offenders. Often youths fall into two or more of these categories.

Treatment for Child Delinquents

Burns et al. (2003) note: "Youths who start offending early in childhood—ages 12 or younger—are far more likely (two to three times more) to become serious, violent and chronic offenders later in life than are teenagers who begin to offend during adolescence." The Study Group on Very Young Offenders, 39 experts on child delinquency, has concluded that juveniles who commit serious and violent offenses most often have shown persistent disruptive behavior in early childhood and committed minor delinquent acts when quite young (Burns, et al).

A study that compared inpatient treatment with multisystemic therapy (MST) found that this community-based alternative treatment was more effective at the four-month follow up (Schoenwald et al., 2000). A series of controlled studies (Burns et al., 2000) with older delinquents involved in MST found multiple positive outcomes, for example, lower arrests and less time in incarceration.

Burns et al. (2000, p.6) note: "Research shows that school interventions that change the social context of schools and the school experiences of children can reduce and prevent the delinquent behavior of children younger than 13." In addition, these results clearly document the important role that schools can play in the prevention of child delinquency. This role is particularly important in light of research findings that indicate that children whose academic performance is poor face a greater risk of becoming involved in child delinquency than other children (Herrenkohl et al., 2001).

Burns et al. (2000, pp.8–9) report on four exemplary programs for child delinquents: the Michigan Early Offender Program, the Minnesota Delinquents under 10 Program, the Sacramento County Community Intervention Program and the Toronto under 12 Project.

Michigan Early Offender Program

Established in 1985 by a Michigan probate court, the Early Offender Program (EOP) provides specialized, intensive, in-home interventions for children 13 or younger at the time of their first adjudication and who have had two or more prior police contacts. Interventions include individualized treatment plans, therapy groups, school preparation assistance and short-term detention of up to 10 days. Comparisons with a control group showed that EOP participants had lower recidivism rates, fewer new adjudications per recidivist and fewer and briefer out-of-home placements. In general, both parents and children reported positive changes in family situations, peer relations and school performance and conduct after participating in EOP.

Minnesota Delinquents under 10 Program

The Delinquents under 10 Program in Hennepin County, Minnesota, involves several county departments (Children and Family Services, Economic Assistance, Community Health and County Attorney's Office). A screening team reviews police reports and determines appropriate dispositions for children. Interventions include an admonishment letter to parents from the county attorney, referrals to child protection services and other agencies, diversion programs and targeted early interventions for children deemed to be at the highest risk for future delinquency. For each targeted child, a specific wraparound network is created. Networks include the following elements:

- A community-based organization to conduct in-depth assessments, improve behavior and school attendance and provide extracurricular activities
- An integrated service delivery team made up of county staff who coordinate service delivery and help children and family members access services
- A crucial support person or mentor
- A corporate sponsor that funds extracurricular activities

Sacramento County Community Intervention Program

Sacramento County, California, welfare authorities found that families of most young (ages 9 to 12) children arrested in the county had been investigated for both neglect and physical abuse. In addition, children who were reported as abused or neglected were 6 to 7 times more likely than other children to be arrested for delinquent behavior. Based on this data, the Community Intervention Program (CIP) for child delinquents was developed. The intervention begins when law enforcement officers notify the probation department that a child between 9 and 12 has been arrested. The court intake screeners then refer the children who have instances of family abuse or neglect to CIP. Next, a community intervention specialist conducts a crisis assessment and provides initial crisis intervention services to the child and family. The intervention specialist then conducts an in-depth assessment, which includes physical and mental health, substance abuse, school functioning, economic strengths/needs, vocational strengths/needs, family functioning and social functioning. The intervention specialist coordinates all services, which are community-based and family-focused and may vary in intensity over time to match the needs of the child and family. Intervention services include individual and family counseling, and abuse and neglect risk monitoring.

Toronto under 12 Outreach Project

The Under 12 Outreach Project in Toronto, Canada, is a fully developed intervention program that combines social learning and behavioral system approaches. The multisystemic approach uses interventions that target children, parents, schools and communities as required. Interventions include skills training, cognitive problem solving, self-control strategies, cognitive self-instruction, family management skills training and parent training. These interventions are organized in eight major program components, such as a 12-week after-school structured group session, a 12-week parent training group, in-home academic tutoring, school advocacy, teacher consultations and individual befriending, which connects juveniles with volunteers who help them use recreational facilities in their community.

As has been noted, child delinquents are also at high risk to become serious, repeat juvenile offenders.

Treatment for Serious, Repeat Juvenile Offenders

According to *The 8% Solution* (2001, p.1): "The prevalence of serious juvenile delinquency could be reduced significantly by identifying and treating the small percentage of juveniles who are at risk of becoming chronic offenders when they first come into contact with the juvenile justice system."

The Orange County (California) Probation Department tracked two groups of first-time offenders for three years and found that a small percentage of the juveniles were arrested repeatedly (a minimum of four times within a three-year period) and were responsible for 55 percent of repeat cases. This group of repeat offenders is referred to as **the 8% problem.**

According to *The 8% Solution:* "The characteristics of this group of repeat offenders were dramatically different from those who were arrested only once. These differences did not develop after exposure to the juvenile justice system, as some might expect; they were evident at first arrest and referral to juvenile court, and they worsened if nothing was done to alleviate the youth's problems. Unfortunately, in wanting to 'give a break' to first-time offenders, the juvenile justice system often pays scant attention to those at greatest risk of becoming chronic offenders until they have established a record of repeated serious offending."

The 8% offenders can be reliably identified at first contact with the juvenile justice system. They should be treated, not given a "second chance."

The 8% offenders enter the system with complex problems or risk factors identified as (1) involvement in crime at an early age and (2) a multiproblem profile including significant family problems (abuse, neglect, criminal family members, and/or a lack of parental supervision and control), problems at school (truancy, failing more than one course or a recent suspension or expulsion), drug and alcohol abuse, and behaviors such as gang involvement, running away and stealing.

The 8% Solution

Based on their research, Orange County created its 8% Early Intervention Program to serve first-time offenders who were no older than 15½ and who exhibited at least three of the four risk factors in the multiproblem profiles. The program focuses on these problem youths and their entire families. The program's goals are to increase structure, supervision and support for families; make potential "8-percenters" accountable; ensure that youths and families understand the importance of school; and promote prosocial values, behavior and relationships (*The 8% Solution*, p.1).

Probation officers identify youths appropriate for the program and refer them to the Youth and Family Resource Centers where agencies collaborate as a team to assess a youth's needs and devise a case planning strategy. Services include an onsite school for students in junior and senior high school; transportation to and from home; counseling for drug and alcohol abuse; mental health evaluation and follow-up services; health screening and health education; employment preparation and job placement services; afternoon programs, including recreation, life-skills classes, study hall and community service projects; at-home, intensive family counseling for families that can benefit from it; intermittent evening classes for the whole family, such as parenting classes; and Saturday community service activities twice a month (*The 8% Solution*, pp.1–2).

The article "Community-Based Treatment Plans Said to Cut Recidivism and Costs" (2001, pp.5–6) identifies the 8% solution of Orange County as a model program and reports that since 1997 it has been undergoing rigorous evaluation. Among the 71 youths who completed the 8% program by mid-1999,

34 percent committed two or more new offenses in the 12 months after program entry, compared with 49 percent of those in the control group. *The 8% Solution* (p.2) concludes: "Even a modest reduction in recidivism rates for the 8% problem group could result in major, long-term savings."

Treatment for Truants

The link between truancy and delinquency has been clearly established. White et al. (2001) note that truancy reduction programs can be an effective means of improving school performance and keeping students in school. According to *Youth Out of School: Linking Absence to Delinquency* (2002, p.5) statistics from the Colorado Division of Criminal Justice for 2002 showed that more than 90 percent of youths in detention for delinquent acts had a history of truancy; 70 percent of suspended youths were chronically truant in the preceding six months; nearly half of expelled students had been chronically truant the previous year; and 20 percent of youths were suspended for truant behavior. Suspending youths for truancy seems entirely illogical for a school with a program to reduce truancy.

According to *Youth Out of School,* although communities have established unique programs, communities are encouraged to maintain the following common elements:

- A continuum of services provided to identified truants and their families
- A community-based collaboration including members from multiple agencies
- Community-wide public awareness campaigns
- Demonstration of system reform and accountability

This publication (p.12) notes that when youths are identified as chronically truant, the program case manager determines the course of action. Community resources to address the problem might include linking them to mental health agencies, drug or alcohol treatment, after-school tutors, Boys and Girls Clubs or mentoring programs. Local merchants can further the cause by refusing to serve youths during school hours or informing police officers when they see youths out of school.

Most programs use a combination of "carrots," incentives to improve attendance and "sticks," deep-end sanctions to enforce compliance. Students report that having someone checking up on them at school motivates them, so a case management model is often effective. Another promising strategy is a Student Attendance Review Board (SARB), a multidisciplinary team that reviews the records of chronic truants at risk of failing which meets with the youth and family to determine what should be done to rectify the truancy problem. Another intervention is use of a teen court where youths are judged by a jury of peers for first-time minor offenses such as chronic truancy. Consequences such as community service, jury duty or apologies are given.

The National School Safety Center has identified five primary elements of a comprehensive community and educational strategy to combat truancy: (1) involve parents/guardians in all truancy prevention activities, (2) ensure students face firm sanctions for truancy, (3) create meaningful incentives for parental responsibility, (4) establish ongoing truancy prevention programs in school and (5) schools should address the unique needs of each child and consider developing initiatives to combat the root causes of truancy. Such initiatives include tutoring programs, drug prevention initiatives, campaigns for involving parents/guardians in school attendance and referrals to social service agencies.

The Colorado Foundation has a Web site "Re-Engaging Youths in School" (http://www.coloradofoundation.org/nationaltruancyproject), which is the source of the information on truancy that follows. It posts a list of crucial elements for an effective truancy program quite similar to that of the National School Safety Center:

- Parent/guardian involvement
- A continuum of services, including meaningful incentives, consequences and supports
- Collaboration with community resources, such as law enforcement, mental health, mentoring and social services
- School building-level administrative support and commitment to maintaining youths in the educational mainstream
- Ongoing evaluation, including meaningful and relevant outcome data geared toward increasing protective factors and reducing risk

The Web site describes several model truancy prevention programs, including one in Los Angeles County, California, which has been adapted by several school districts throughout the country. Table 14.5 lists collaborative efforts at the state level and with law enforcement, juvenile courts and the Department of Juvenile Justice.

Abolish Chronic Truancy (ACT)

ACT targets K-sixth grade students and uses a series of progressively intrusive steps to hold children and parents/guardians accountable for truancy. The steps are: (1) a letter is sent home to parents/guardians whose children have school attendance problems; (2) parents/guardians and children are invited to a meeting with the deputy district attorney, along with community-based organizations and school personnel who offer parenting classes, counseling and other needed services: (3) parents/guardians whose children continue to have attendance problems are invited to a School Attendance Review Team (SART); (4) students who continue to have attendance problems are referred to School Attendance Review Board (SARB); and (5) if all the preceding steps fail, a case is filed against the parent/guardian and/or child.

OJJDP Demonstration Sites

The Colorado Foundation is also the site to oversee the OJJDP demonstration sites on truancy prevention. Its Web site notes that thousands of youths have had contact with these demonstration sites. In 2001–2002, 214 students were served, with an equal number of males and females. Figure 14.4 shows the ethnicity and grade of the students.

Table 14.5
Joint Efforts to Improve School Attendance

State Level

- Build and maintain the health and productivity of a School Attendance Task Force.
- Clarify and share information at the state level among schools, courts, probation, social services, mental health, faith, business and law enforcement regarding school attendance law, system flow among agencies, services, supports and gaps.
- Develop a Memorandum of Understanding among agency partners to commit to the improvement of school attendance.
- Develop a public education and awareness campaign targeting parents/guardians, youths and the general community about state law, consequences for non-attendance and importance of staying in school.
- Form a group to target key legislators for support in passing statutes that will support the goals of the coalition.
- Educate and empower community members to write their legislative representatives about the need for supporting prevention programs.

Law Enforcement

- Provide outreach to the community about the importance of school attendance. Show an interest in youths who are out of school during the day; let them know you are aware.
- Make routine visits to schools to inform school personnel and students about attendance law and consequences.
- Establish procedures and protocols for reporting nonattendance by the community and escorting students to school or to a community center.
- Law enforcement should be integrally involved in the community-level programs that improve school attendance. Several community policing models are in existence nationally that use the cooperation of law enforcement to significant advantage, including documented reductions of daytime crime.

Juvenile Courts

- The court should consider a variety of sanctions for non-attending youths, such as community service, denied driving privileges, required school attendance of parents/guardians and other consequences prior to detention.
- Judges and magistrates need to be made aware of existing community programs to positively engage youths in school.
- The juvenile court needs to be represented in any state or local-level efforts targeting re-engaging youths in school.

Department of Juvenile Justice

- Develop standard protocols for intake and processing of cases of violation of attendance law. Train staff on the proper procedures and use of these protocols.
- Forge an information sharing agreement among agencies to reduce duplication of services for multiple-issue youths and their families.
- Access local universities for assistance in data collection and interns to assist with direct services in local pilot communities.

Source: Colorado Foundation for Families and Children. Reprinted by permission.

Of the students involved in the programs, 58.4 percent had fewer unexcused absences from the time of intake to the first update (3 months later). Students had an average of 18 fewer unexcused absences. In overall academic achievement, 49.6 percent improved, 28.2 percent stayed the same, 6.8 percent worsened and 15.4 percent had no data collected.

The Web site provides program descriptions for each demonstration site and evaluation data. Several innovations are described. The program in Jacksonville, Florida, conducts an annual Truancy Awareness Month and presents gift certificates to students who have perfect attendance. The program in Yaphank, New York, houses a probation officer in the school to act as a truancy case manager. In addition, two school-wide interventions are in place. The first is BEST (Be Educated Stop Truancy), which uses rewards and positive peer reinforcement rather

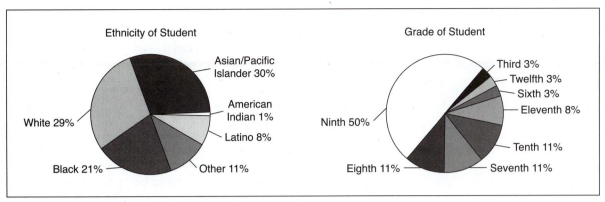

Figure 14.4
OJJDP Demonstration Sites Aggregate Data

Source: OJJDP Data Fact Sheet Academic Year 2001-2002

than sanctions to improve attendance. Teams of five in each homeroom compete monthly for incentives as the group with best attendance. Students with marked improvement are recognized along with their parents at an informal breakfast with school staff. In addition, a V.I.P. lunchroom has been established for students with perfect attendance the previous month. Youths are able to listen to music and receive additional incentives. The second school-wide program is the Truancy Homeroom, where students with five absences are placed for two weeks. During that time an informational letter is sent to parents, and students attend a truancy workshop and view a video about truancy. If attendance improves, the student returns to a traditional homeroom. If not, the student stays with the probation officer and an intervention plan is created. Of the 31 students placed in truancy homeroom, only 3 returned.

Treatment for Youths with Mental Illness

Mears (2002, p.1) notes: "The Andrea Yates trial taught us that earlier identification and treatment of mental illness might have prevented a tragedy of unspeakable horror—that of a mother murdering her own children." He suggests that many mentally ill youths walk in and out of juvenile courts without ever being noticed or treated. Mears reports: "The use of extended isolation, excessive or deadly bodily restraints and punishment for behaviors resulting from specific disorders has been documented. A preoccupation with punishment helps explain attitudes and policies toward youths with mental illness. This preoccupation is odd, given that more than 100 years ago the juvenile courts founders envisioned a system that would promote the best interests of youthful offenders. Then, as now, the overwhelming majority of youths brought to court committed minor offenses. Few, if any, are the 'super predator' offenders whose specter drove the past decade's 'get tough' efforts."

According to Mears (p.2) as many as 70 percent of youths referred to the courts suffer from mental disorders, a much greater rate than for the general youth population. More than half suffer from conduct disorders, attention-deficit/ hyperactivity disorder or from both a mental disorder and a substance abuse problem.

Mears contends that youths should be made a priority so the courts do not become the last resort for help. A judge from Dallas noted: "It's tragic if you are a young person and mentally ill, you have to get arrested to receive treatment."

 Juvenile justice should be reoriented from punishment toward treatment and rehabilitation of youths with mental illness reflecting the philosophy of the early courts.

Mears does not advocate forgetting about punishment. He believes youths should be held accountable for their actions. However, he argues: "To focus only on punishment is to miss the forest for the trees—most youths entering the juvenile system are there for minor offenses and most suffer from mental health problems that can and should be addressed."

Rosenblatt et al. (2000) compared the characteristics of youths receiving only mental health services with those receiving mental health services who also are involved in the juvenile justice system. They found that mental health and juvenile justice caseloads overlapped, highlighting the need for collaboration of services. Most communities have services available to assist youths with mental health problems. The key is to identify the youths and get them the help they need. Frequently such youths also are substance abusers.

Treatment for Drug and Alcohol Abusers

Breaking the Juvenile Drug-Crime Cycle: A Guide for Practitioners and Policymakers (Vander-Waal et al. (2001, p.1) note: "For more than two decades, researchers, clinicians and juvenile justice program administrators have known of the link between drug use (including alcohol) and juvenile crime. In many communities, the majority of juveniles entering the system are drug users. Other research indicates that juvenile drug use is related to recurring chronic and violent delinquency that continues well into adulthood. Juvenile drug use is also strongly related to poor health, deteriorating family relationships, worsening school performance and other social and psychological problems."

Vander-Waal et al. summarize existing knowledge about efforts to intervene in the juvenile drug-crime cycle and propose interventions and programmatic changes to successfully address that cycle. One of the key approaches recommended is the coordination of case management strategies to meet the diverse needs of juveniles from their entry into the juvenile justice system until they no longer require supervision. Other key strategies include using a balanced and restorative justice approach, graduated sanctions, system collaborations and integrated case management. Major elements of a comprehensive model include a single point of entry and immediate and comprehensive assessment. Figure 14.5 depicts the elements of a model intervention system.

According to Vander-Waal et al. (p.8), *noninstitutional interventions* showing consistent evidence of being *effective* were (1) individual counseling (including multisystemic therapy and reality training), (2) interpersonal skills training and (3) behavior programs (including family counseling and contingency contracting). These interventions reduced recidivism by about 40 percent. Weak or *ineffective*

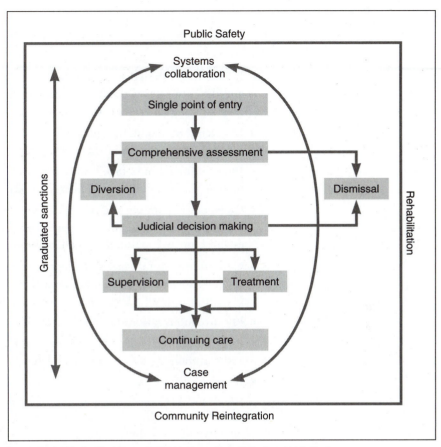

Figure 14.5
Elements of a Model
Intervention System

Source: Curtis J. Vander-Waal, Duane C. McBride, Yvonne Terry-McElrath and Holly Van Buren. *Breaking the Juvenile Drug-Crime Cycle: A Guide for Practioners and Policymakers.* Washington, DC: National Institute of Justice, May 2001, p.5. (NCJ 186156)

programs, based on the evidence, were (1) wilderness and challenge programs, (2) early release from probation or parole, (3) deterrence programs (e.g., shock incarceration such as boot camps) and (4) vocational programs (vocational training, career counseling, job search and interview skills and the like." Programs *requiring more research* are academic programs, advocacy/casework, family counseling, group counseling and employment-related programs.

Vander-Waal et al. report that *institutional interventions* showing consistent evidence of being effective were interpersonal skills training (such as social skills, aggression replacement and cognitive restructuring) and supervised family homes (including small behavior modification group homes with teaching parents and token economies). Weak or *ineffective* programs, based on the evidence, included milieu therapy programs (in which the environment is structured with generalized behavioral targets applied to the entire group in the institution). Inconsistent evidence suggested that employment-related and wilderness and challenge programs, short-term residential facilities and state training schools also were weak or ineffective. *Needing more research* were individual counseling, guided groups and group counseling.

Several principles to consider when designing a comprehensive intervention system to break the juvenile drug-crime cycle are provided by Vander-Waal et al. (pp.12–13):

- Interventions should strike a balance among accountability to the victim and the community, the need to protect the public and the goal of rehabilitating and reintegrating juveniles.

- Interventions should recognize the central role and importance of the juvenile justice system in the treatment process.

- Interventions should take place early, when they have the best chance of reversing or ameliorating problem behaviors.

- Collaboration among and across systems relevant to juveniles should be established and maintained. An agent or agency should be accountable for establishing and maintaining collaboration.

- Consistent with principles of client confidentiality and juvenile justice system responsibility, a management information system should be in place to supply all relevant information to those who provide services.

- Effective interventions need to be related to school, peer and family systems.

- Program interventions and staff training need to be sensitive to the unique and culturally specific needs of adolescents.

- Because juvenile delinquency occurs within specific national and local community, educational and economic structures, a successful intervention should include efforts to ensure high-quality education and job opportunities for those at risk.

- Given the general lack of experimental evidence that supports more restrictive services, treatment dollars should be targeted toward less restrictive programs that are more likely to address juvenile problems in the context in which they occur and are reinforced: the family, school and peer groups of the adolescent.

Vander-Waal et al. (p.13) note the core role of the juvenile justice and treatment systems: "As the party responsible for the safety of the community, the juvenile justice system should be the final authority in treatment and supervision decisions for drug-using juvenile offenders. However, within a BARJ framework, key players in the justice system (including judges, prosecutors and defense attorneys) change from adversaries to problem solvers as part of a collaborative team, even while continuing to perform traditional functions of protecting the community, applying the law and pursuing due process."

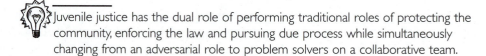
Juvenile justice has the dual role of performing traditional roles of protecting the community, enforcing the law and pursuing due process while simultaneously changing from an adversarial role to problem solvers on a collaborative team.

"Family Justice: A Program Taps the Family as a Resource in Reducing Drug Abuse and Recidivism" (2003, p.8) describes an innovative program of the Vera

Institute, La Bodega de la Familia, that uses the family as a largely untapped and free resource: "Vera's research bears out the promise upon which La Bodega was founded. The family-support model is opening doors to fundamental changes in community supervision policies and practices for the future." The article notes: "La Bodega's signature service is called Family Case Management (FCM), through which a case manager brings together the offender under supervision, family members, the supervision officer and treatment providers to identify the family's strengths and needs, and to build a healthy network of support around the user. Case managers provide information, encouragement and crisis intervention to the family. They also act as advocates for family members, helping them navigate government agencies to access medical care, housing and placement in drug treatment." The article (p.13) also notes: "The success of the La Bodega program is also attributable to its extensive relationships with local police, parole and probation departments, tenant associations, the public housing authority, health providers and other community groups." As La Bodega's relationship with the criminal justice system grew stronger, referrals from that system increased to account for about two-thirds of its clients. Findings of an evaluation of the program include the following:

- La Bodega family members were significantly more likely than the comparison family members to receive needed medical and social services, housing, food and job training over the study period.

- La Bodega family members had a stronger sense of being supported, both emotionally and materially, in their social relationships.

- La Bodega participants were less likely to be arrested and convicted of a new offense. Researchers attribute this, in part, to case managers' ability to persuade authorities to deal with relapse as part of the process of recovery.

Another program of the Vera Institute is its Adolescent Portable Therapy (APT) program. According to the Institute's Web site, one out of every five juveniles entering detention centers in New York and in cities across the country has been using drugs nearly every day for the past month. Mostly these young teens have been smoking marijuana and drinking alcohol. Although they may not be chemically dependent on these substances, using them so frequently is a clear sign of a serious problem. To treat these young offenders, rather than delivering treatment from a fixed location, APT works with youths inside New York City detention centers and upstate institutions and then continues treating them in their home communities. By providing therapists who travel with adolescents as they move through the justice system, APT helps government fulfill its responsibility to provide and coordinate treatment services for the juveniles under its care.

The importance of the quality of treatment is stressed by Mears and Kelly (2002, p.111) who report: "Once appropriate (e.g., high-need and high-risk) youths are selected for treatment, it seems that individual characteristics (e.g., demographic, risk or performance) matter less than organizational and site-specific factors in reducing recidivism." They stress: "Much greater attention should be given to ensuring that significant resources are used to systematically

	Domain	Characteristic
Table 14.6 **Sex Offense** **Characteristics**	Victim characteristics	■ Female children are targeted most frequently.[a,b,c,d,e,f,g,h]
		■ Male victims represent up to 25 percent of some samples.[e,h,i]
	Relationship characteristics	■ Victims are more often substantially younger than the offender, rather than peer age.[a,b,c,d,e,f,g,h,i]
		■ Victims are usually relatives or acquaintances; rarely are they strangers.[a,e,f,g,h,i]
		■ Babysitting frequently provides the opportunity to offend.[b,h]
	Use of aggression	■ Although juvenile sex offenders usually are less physically violent than adult offenders, they may secure the victim's compliance via intimidation, threats of violence, physical force or extreme violence.[a,j]
		■ Approximately 40 percent of the juveniles from a sample of 91 displayed expressive aggression in their sex offense(s).[d]
		■ Juveniles who victimized peers or adults tended to use more force than those who victimized younger children.[k]
	Triggers	■ Some of the triggers that have been described as related to sex offending include anger, boredom and family problems.[g]

Notes: [a]Davis and Leitenberg, 1987; [b]Fehrenbach et al., 1986; [c]Hunter and Figueredo, 1999; [d]Miner, Siekert and Ackland, 1997; [e]Rasmussen, 1999; [f]Righthand, Hennings and Wigley, 1989; [g]Ryan et al., 1996; [h]Smith and Monastersky, 1986; [i]Wieckowski et al., 1998; [j]Knight and Prentky, 1993; [k]Becker, 1998.

Source: Sue Righthand and Carlann Welch. *Juveniles Who Have Sexually Offended: A Review of the Professional Literature.* Washington, DC: Office of Juvenile Justice and Delinquency Prevention, March 2001, p.4. (NCJ 184739)

monitor the implementation and delivery of treatment. The failure to do so is to miss a cost-effective opportunity to improve substantially the efficacy of treatment programming. Indeed, without such monitoring, there is a significant risk of investing considerable resources to little effect."

Treatment for Juvenile Sex Offenders

Righthand and Welch (2001, p.1) stress: "The importance of early intervention with juveniles who evidence sexual behavior problems cannot be overstated." They (p.3) report that juveniles who commit sex offenses are a heterogeneous mix. Table 14.6 presents the most common sex offender characteristics. They (p.31) note that most juvenile sex offenders (JSOs) rarely were charged with subsequent sex crimes, as shown in Table 14.7.

Miner (2002) researched factors associated with recidivism in juvenile sex offenders and found that increased risk for re-offense was associated with impulsivity, involvement with significantly younger children, younger age at first offense and shorter treatment stays. Decreased risk for re-offense was associated with having a male victim, having been a sexual abuse victim and multiple **paraphilias** (*paraphilias* is the sum of three variables: the presence of fetishism, transvestitism and promiscuity).

Righthand and Welch (p.37) list several assumptions reflecting the current thinking related to a comprehensive systems response to juveniles who have sexually offended:

■ After a full assessment of the juvenile's risk factors and needs, individualized and developmentally sensitive interventions are required.

Table 14.7
Sexual and Nonsexual Recidivism by Juvenile Offenders

Study	Follow-up Period	Sexual Recidivism		Nonsexual Recidivism	
		Sex Offenders	Other Offenders	Sex Offenders	Other Offenders
Kahn and Chambers, 1991	M: 20 months[a]	8%[b][c] (N=221)			
Miner, Siekert and Ackland, 1997	M: 19 months[a]	8% (N=96)		38% (N=96)	
Rasmussen, 1999	M: 5 years[d]	14% (N=170)		54% (N=170)	
Rubinstein et al., as cited in Sipe, Jensen and Everett, 1998	M: 8 years[d]	37% (N=19)	10% (N=58)		
Schram, Milloy and Rowe, 1991	R: 2–7 years[e]	12% (N=197)		15% (violent felonies), 40% (nonviolent felonies), 53% (misdemeanors)[f] (N=197)	
Sipe, Jensen and Everett, 1998	M: 6 years[d] R: 1–14 years[e]	10% (N=124)	3% (N=132)	16% (N=124)	33% (N=132)
Smith and Monastersky, 1986	M: 17 months[a]	14% (N=112)		35% (N=112)	

Notes: [a]M=mean time at risk in the community. [b]Percentages have been rounded off to the nearest whole number. [c]N=the total number of subjects in the group sample. [d]M=mean number of months or years followed by the study. [e]R=range. [f]Offense categories were not mutually exclusive, and the juveniles may have been rearrested for more than one type of offense.

Source: Sue Righthand and Carlann Welch. *Juveniles Who Have Sexually Offended: A Review of the Professional Literature.* Washington, DC: Office of Juvenile Justice and Delinquency Prevention, March 2001, p.32. (NCJ 184739)

- Individualized treatment plans should be designed and periodically reassessed and revised. Plans should specify treatment needs, treatment objectives and required interventions.

- Treatment should be provided in the least restrictive environment necessary for community protection. Treatment efforts also should involve the least intrusive methods that can be expected to accomplish treatment objectives.

- Written progress reports should be issued to the agency that has mandated treatment and should be discussed with the juvenile and parents. Progress must be based on specific measurable objectives, observable changes and demonstrated ability to apply changes in current situations.

The National Task Force on Juvenile Sexual Offenders suggests that satisfactory treatment will require a minimum of 12 to 24 months. To adequately address both the needs of individual juveniles and the demands of the community, a continuum of care model is usually most appropriate. This continuum might include short-term, specialized psychoeducational programs; community-based outpatient sex offender treatment programs for juveniles remaining at home or in foster care; day treatment programs; residential group homes or residential facilities; training schools for short-term placements providing assessments and facilitating readiness

Table 14.8
Treatment To Reduce Offending Behaviors

Modes of Treatment	Target Areas of Treatment						
	Impaired Social Relationships	Empathy Deficits	Cognitive Distortions	Deviant Sexual Arousal	Problematic Management of Emotions	Impulsive/ Antisocial Behaviors	Consequences of Personal History of Child Maltreatment
Anger Management	X		X		X		
Assertiveness Training	X				X		
Aversion Therapy				X			
Childhood Victim Survivors' Group	X	X	X		X		X
Cognitive Restructuring	X	X	X		X	X	X
Covert Sensitization				X			
Expressive Therapy		X			X		X
Family Interventions	X	X	X		X	X	X
Group and Individual Therapy	X	X	X	X	X	X	X
Multisystem Interventions (e.g., MST and MTFC)	X	X	X		X	X	X
Pharmacotherapy				X	X	X	
Positive Identification Development	X		X				X
Relapse Prevention and Offense Cycles			X	X	X	X	
Self-Control and Impulse Management				X	X	X	
Self-Help Groups	X					X	X
Sex Education and Dating Skills	X						
Social Skills Training	X						
Stress and Anxiety Management	X				X	X	
Substance Abuse Education and Treatment					X	X	
Systematic Desensitization	X			X			
Vicarious Sensitization				X			
Victim Empathy Training	X	X	X			X	

Source: Sue Righthand and Carlann Welch. *Juveniles Who Have Sexually Offended: A Review of the Professional Literature.* Washington, DC: Office of Juvenile Justice and Delinquency Prevention, March 2001, p.43. (NCJ 184739)

for community-based treatment; and secure units providing comprehensive, intensive treatment, including daily unit groups; two to three small daily groups focusing on interpersonal skills; weekly sessions on a variety of topics such as sex offending issues, stress cycles, anger management and social skills; parent groups; family therapy; individual treatment; and substance abuse therapy if needed.

Righthand and Welch (p.39) say that recommended treatment content areas for juvenile sex offenders typically include sex education, correction of cognitive distortion, empathy training, clarification of values concerning abusive versus nonabusive sexual behavior, anger management, strategies to enhance impulse control and facilitate good judgment, social skills training, reduction of deviant arousal and relapse prevention. Table 14.8 presents modes of treatment and areas they target.

Family support can help reduce recidivism and improve treatment. Right-hand and Welch (pp.41–42) recommend using a relapse prevention model. **Relapse prevention** requires juveniles to learn to identify factors associated with an increased risk of sex offending and use strategies to avoid high-risk situations or effectively manage them when they occur.

Treatment for Gang Members

Gang members who come to the attention of the juvenile justice system frequently have many of the same problems as nongang members: a history of neglect and abuse, mental problems and drug and/or alcohol abuse. In most cases, gang members should receive the same treatment as nongang members. The challenge for the juvenile justice system is to reduce the influence of gangs. Efforts may shift from tertiary (treatment) prevention to primary or secondary prevention. One such option is using civil remedies to lessen a gang's influence on its members.

Civil Remedies to Lessen a Gang's Influence

Because criminal law focuses on wrongs against the state, it is frequently overlooked that virtually every crime is also a **tort,** or a civil wrong against a person or persons for which the perpetrator is civilly liable. Gang activity is likely to violate several civil ordinances, and gang members can be held responsible for the harm they create by these violations.

 Gang-related harm may be treated by civil remedies.

Table 14.9 lists the types of harm caused by gangs, including civil matters and ordinance violations.

One way to attack the gang problem is to redirect the focus from the offenders themselves toward other contributing aspects. Figure 14.6 illustrates the gang problem by separating it into three components: the offender, the victim and the place where the harm occurs.

This model proposes that by removing one element of the triangle, we can break the cycle of gang violence and prevent future harm. Traditionally law enforcement has concentrated on gang members, the offender side of the triangle. However a community-policing, problem-oriented approach focuses on the *place* and on the third parties who control those places. Concentrating on problem places accomplishes two things: (1) places can be changed so gang members no longer see them as good places for gang activity, and (2) actions can be taken to keep gang members and potential victims from being together at particular places when the victims are especially vulnerable.

One civil remedy involving property dates back to the Middle Ages. The legal concept of **nuisance** pertains to the use of property and requires landowners to use their property so as not to injure their neighbors' use of their properties. The concept applies to physically damaging neighboring property, reducing its value or reducing its enjoyment. Typically defined by local ordinance or state statute, public nuisances encroach on public rights and offend public order and standards of decency. Examples might include prostitution and crack houses.

Table 14.9
Types of Harm Caused by Gangs

Criminal Offenses	Ordinance Violations	Juvenile Offenses	Civil Matters
Felonies	Traffic	Truancy	Code violations
Murder	Parking	Runaway	Fire
Aggravated assault	Littering	Beyond control of parents	Safety
Rape	Vandalism	Curfew	Health
Robbery	Malicious mischief		Torts
Armed	Graffiti		Trespass
Strong-arm	Noise		Nuisance
Arson	Disorderly conduct		Waste
Burglary	Public drunkenness		
Larceny or theft	Obstruction of public passageway		
Auto theft			
Criminal intimidation			
Witnesses			
Victims			
Jurors			
Misdemeanors			
Simple assault			
Reckless endangerment			
Petit larceny			
Criminal trespass			
Criminal mischief			
Harassment			

Source: *Addressing Community Gang Problems: A Practical Guide*. Bureau of Justice Assistance Monograph, May 1998.

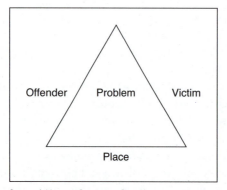

Figure 14.6
Gang-Problem Triangle

Source: *Addressing Community Gang Problems: A Practical Guide*. Bureau of Justice Assistance Monograph, May 1998, p.154.

Nuisance statutes commonly refer to "nuisance abatement." **Abatement** basically means doing whatever is necessary to get rid of the nuisance and bring the problem to an end. Abatement might consist of boarding up vacant dwellings used as crack houses or demolishing entire city blocks to remove sites commonly used for drug transactions and gang activities. Additionally, personal property may be seized and sold; hotels, restaurants and other businesses may be closed; and certain named individuals may be barred from designated properties. Abatement orders can impose specific conditions for continuing to operate a property, including establishing a system for screening tenants and installing security systems to keep gang members off a property. Abatement can be an invaluable remedy to gang-related harms.

Punitive Treatments

Since the 1950s the emphasis in many residential facilities for juvenile delinquents has followed a custody/clinical model, treating delinquent youths as deviant or abnormal. According to Grisso and Schwartz (2000): "In the mid-1980s a surge of youth violence fueled public fear of juveniles and steered juvenile justice policy toward a punitive rather than a rehabilitative approach."

One highly publicized approach using punitive prevention is the scared straight approach. Using this strategy, boys and girls identified as being delinquency-prone are taken to an adult prison where hard-core adult lifers verbally confront them with the reality of prison life, the brutality, degradation, homosexual rapes and lack of freedom. The adult criminals yell at the youths, bullying and threatening them.

The original scared straight program occurred at New Jersey's Rahway maximum-security prison and was initially telecast in 1979. A DVD, Scared Straight—20 Years Later, was released in August 2003, hosted by Danny Glover. Although the now-grown delinquents praise the program and the difference it made in their lives, Petrosino et al. (2003, p.1) report: "The analysis shows the intervention to be more harmful than doing nothing."

 The punitive treatment approach has met with limited success. A different model, a sociological model—one that stresses a positive environment—might be more effective.

Scaring the pants off youths as a way to prevent juvenile delinquency does not appear to work. Studies have shown that youths participating in such programs have more subsequent arrests than the control groups. Most juvenile justice practioners advocate using a more positive approach and building on the resiliency of most juveniles.

Resiliency as a Treatment Approach

Resiliency is the ability to bounce back from adversity. According to Vasquez (2000, p.107), the resiliency concept as a treatment approach reframes a client's life based on his or her strengths. These strengths develop by surviving painful childhood experiences and emerging as a "survivor who battled adversity." The resiliency approach includes seven clusters of strength (p.107):

1. *Insight.* The habit of asking tough questions that pierce the denial and confusion in troubled families.
2. *Independence.* Emotional and physical distancing from a troubled family that keeps survivors out of harm's way.
3. *Relationships.* Fulfilling ties to others that provide the stability, nurturing and love that troubled families do not.
4. *Initiative.* A push for mastery that combats the feelings of helplessness that troubled families produce in their offspring.
5. *Creativity.* Representing one's inner pain and hurtful experience in art forms; "building a new world on the ruins of the old."

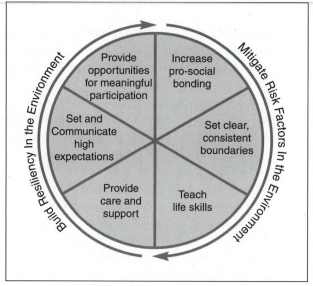

Figure 14.7
The Resiliency Wheel

Source: Nan Henderson and Mike Milstein. *Resiliency in Schools: Making It Happen for Students and Educators*, Thousand Oaks, CA: Corwin Press, 1996. Reprinted by permission of Sage Publications.

6. *Humor.* The ability to minimize pain and troubles by laughing at oneself.

7. *Morality.* An informed conscience that imbues the survivor, surrounded by "badness" with a sense of his or her own "goodness."

 The resiliency model's seven clusters of strength build on insight, independence, relationships, initiative, creativity, humor and morality.

The resiliency model focuses on enhancing protective factors and reducing risk factors. Vasquez (p.107) asserts: "Resilience research documents the powerful role protective factors play in helping individuals overcome risks, stress and adversity and lead healthy and successful lives." Figure 14.7 illustrates the resiliency wheel containing components that can be incorporated into most treatment programs.

Resilience and Second Chances

Second Chances: Giving Kids a Chance to Make a Better Choice (2000) contains profiles of youths who were able to turn their lives around and become contributing members of society. According to this OJJDP bulletin (p.1): "The 12 randomly chosen profiles . . . are inspiring examples of individuals whose lives reflect the juvenile court's purpose and achievements." The profiles that follow are graphic examples of resilience.

Scott Filippi fatally shot a parent who had been abusing him for several years. According to court records, Filippi and his sister were abused so badly that his sister lost her hearing and sight. Filippi was sexually abused by a stranger, learned of his sister's sexual abuse at the hands of his stepfather and walked in on his mother being unfaithful to his stepfather on several occasions. Filippi was beaten with a two-by-four and belts, was punched and kicked and thrown down the stairs and across rooms. This period of abuse spanned from before Filippi entered kindergarten until the time of his arrest. According to juvenile hall court records, "He was in a serious state of shock and for several days was unable to do anything but shake and cry. . . . He is very sad and tearful when questioned about this offense."

As noted in the profile (p.10): "Throughout Filippi's life, he had tried desperately to please his mother by doing his chores and cleaning his room to perfection so as to avoid abuse. Filippi's perfectionism now began to serve him well. He excelled in the regimen of juvenile hall." He also thrived in the Oakendell residential treatment facility where he spent the next 21 months undergoing a strict regimen of psychological treatment. After he was released from custody, Filippi served honorably in the U.S. Army and was a member of the U.S. Army's Presidential Honor Guard under President George H. Bush.

Another success story is that of Ronald C. Laney, who was adjudicated delinquent for larceny, disorderly conduct (fighting) and drinking as a minor. Laney was on a first-name basis with judges and police officers. He served a handful of sentences in juvenile detention and spent almost a year at a state training school in Marianna, Florida, where he studied hard at the old-style reform school, complete with corporal punishment. He was planning to pull his life together when he got out, but when he returned to his hometown, he quickly fell back in with the same crowd and was arrested for drinking on the beach. Because of his age, he was tried in criminal court. His former juvenile judge and a police officer he knew well interceded for him, pleading with the criminal court judge to give Laney the option of joining the Marines rather than going to prison. Laney chose the Marines and had a stellar seven-year career. He was drawn toward criminology when he resumed academic life at a junior college, interested in helping others like himself. He is now the director of the Child Protection Division of the Office of Juvenile Justice and Delinquency Prevention, U.S. Department of Justice. In Laney's words: "They [the Marines] don't take bad kids like me anymore. I met a lot of people in the military with similar backgrounds, and we've lost an opportunity to give youths a chance at a different life. . . . The adult system is a failure at rehabilitation, with high recidivism. Why would we want to put a troubled kid into a system that doesn't give him a chance to succeed? It doesn't make any sense."

Appendix F (located on the book companion Web site at cj.wadsworth.com/hess_drowns_jj4e) describes numerous prevention and treatment programs, their focus, key components and findings.

Summary

Two primary characteristics of effective intervention programs are: (1) they draw on an understanding of the developmental and sociocultural risk factors that lead to antisocial behavior and (2) they use theory-based intervention strategies known to change behavior, tested program designs, and validated, objective measurement techniques to assess outcomes. Effective treatment programs often take advantage of windows of opportunity—times when treatment is especially needed (in crises) or likely to make a difference (during youth transition periods). Crisis intervention capitalizes on windows of opportunity when a person may be especially receptive to treatment that establishes new approaches to problem-solving.

Treatment requirements recommended by the Metropolitan Court Judges Committee include immediate treatment, family focus, parental responsibility, positive parental behavior, treatment for substance abuse, mandated treatment and treatment for youthful sexual offenders.

The committee recommended that treatment personnel be well qualified, that volunteer assistance be used, that quality foster homes be available, that foster care drift be reduced, that children with special needs be provided special foster homes and that shelters be established for homeless children.

In planning for permanency, the committee recommended that when necessary, parental rights may be terminated, that alternative plans should be made if parental rights are not terminated and that the adoption process be expedited, including providing subsidized adoption programs for hard-to-place children.

The key to manage cases in the community is to adequately assess offenders' risks and apply proved interventions using cognitive behavioral methods to address the problems. The four key elements of the Community Assessment Center are (1) a single point of entry, (2) immediate and comprehensive assessment, (3) a management information system and (4) integrated case management. The management information system (MIS) should perform two tasks: (1) link data from multiple agencies and (2) monitor trends. Three concerns related to assessment centers are (1) violating due process rights, (2) stigmatizing youths and (3) net widening.

A recommended three-pronged approach to treatment includes prevention, intervention and enforcement. Partnerships between police departments and probation departments are successfully preventing further delinquency by some youths who have been adjudicated delinquent in the past. These partnerships enhance the level of supervision given to juvenile offenders. To be effective supervision must be active, local and community based.

The OJJDP guiding principles for a comprehensive strategy for serious, violent and chronic juvenile offenders recommend that the strategy: (1) strengthen the family, (2) support core social institutions, (3) promote delinquency prevention, (4) intervene immediately and effectively when delinquent behavior occurs, (5) establish a system of graduated sanctions and (6) identify and control the small group of serious, violent and chronic juvenile offenders.

The 8% offenders can be reliably identified at first contact with the juvenile justice system. They should be treated, not given a second chance. In addition to taking a hard line on the easily identified 8% offenders, the juvenile justice system should be reoriented from punishment toward treatment and rehabilitation of youths with mental illness reflecting the philosophy of the early courts. When treating youths with mental problems, juvenile justice has the dual duty of performing the traditional roles of protecting the community, enforcing the law and pursuing due process while simultaneously changing from an adversarial role to problem solvers on a collaborative team.

Another challenge facing the juvenile justice system is treating gangs and gang members. Gang-related harm may be treated by civil remedies. In dealing with gang or nongang members, the punitive treatment approach has met with limited success. A different model, a sociological model—one that stresses a positive environment—might be more effective. The resiliency model's seven clusters of strength build on insight, independence, relationships, initiative, creativity, humor and morality.

Discussion Questions

1. Which recommendations of the Metropolitan Court Judges Committee do you think are most important? Do you disagree with any of the committee's recommendations? If so, which ones and why?

2. What kind of training should foster care providers receive?

3. What diversionary alternatives are available in your community?

4. Does your state have any "second chance" camps for juvenile offenders? If so, have you heard anything about them?

5. How involved is your local police department in collaborative efforts with other agencies?

6. Are there any special collaborations in your area to deal with gang violence?

7. If you were a juvenile and were adjudicated delinquent because you stole a car, what type of treatment program do you think would be most effective?

8. Of all the treatment programs discussed in this chapter, which do you think offers the best chance for success? The least chance for success? Can you think of other treatment programs that might be tried?

9. Do you think the 8% offenders should be denied a second chance? If so, why?

10. Have you seen examples of individuals exhibiting resiliency, either in public or private life? If so, explain.

InfoTrac College Edition Assignments

- Use InfoTrac College Edition to help answer the Discussion Questions as appropriate.

- Use InfoTrac to read and outline one of the following articles to share with the class:

  - Mental Health Assessment in Juvenile Justice: Report on the Consensus Conference" by Gail A. Wasserman et al. (*juvenile justice system*)

  - "Retention of Court Referred Youths in Residential Treatment Programs: Client Characteristics and Treatment Process Effects" by Maria Orlando et al. (*juvenile justice system*)

Internet Assignments

Complete one of the following assignments and be prepared to share your findings with the class:

- Go to the NCJRS Web site and find *Second Chances: Giving Kids a Chance to Make a Better Choice.* Select one profile to outline.

  - Go to www.ojjdp.ncjrs.org and find and outline one of the NCJ publications listed in the references for this chapter.

Research one of the following key words or phrases: *criminogenic factors, desistance, dynamic risk factors, 8% problem, permanency, recidivism, youthful resiliency.*

- Go to the Web site of any reference in this chapter giving an online address. Read and outline the material.

References

Allen, Pam. "The Gould-Wysinger Awards: A Tradition of Excellence." *Juvenile Justice,* Fall/Winter 1993, pp.23–28.

American Psychological Association. *Violence & Youth: Psychology's Response,* Vol. 1. Summary Report of the American Psychological Association Commission on Violence and Youth, Vol. 1. no date.

Borum, Randy. "Managing At-Risk Juvenile Offenders in the Community." *Journal of Contemporary Criminal Justice,* February 2003, pp.114–137.

Burns, B. J.; Schoenwald, S. K.; Burchard, J. D.; Faw, L.; and Santos, A. B. "Comprehensive Community-Based Interventions for Youths with Severe Emotional Disorders: Multisystemic Therapy and the Wraparound Process." *Journal of Child and Youth Studies,* Vol. 9, 2000, pp.283–314.

Burns, Barbara J.; Howell, James C.; Wiig, Janet K.; Augimeri, Leena K.; Welsh, Brandon C.; Loeber, Rolf; and Petechuk, David. *Treatment, Services and Intervention Programs for Child Delinquents.* Washington, DC: Child Delinquency Bulletin Series, March 2003. (NCJ 193410)

"Community-Based Treatment Plans Said to Cut Recidivism and Costs." *Criminal Justice Newsletter,* June 18, 2001, pp.5–7.

The 8% Solution. Washington, DC: OJJDP Fact Sheet #39, November 2001. (FS 200139)

"Family Justice: A Program Taps the Family as a Resource in Reducing Drug Abuse and Recidivism." *NCJA Justice Bulletin,* May 2003, pp.8, 13.

Finkelhor, D. and Hashima, P. "The Victimization of Children and Youth: A Comprehensive Overview." In *Handbook of Youth and Justice* edited by S. White. Newell, MA: Kluwer Plenum, 2001, pp.49–78.

Grisso, T. and Schwartz, R, editors. *Youth on Trial: A Developmental Perspective on Juvenile Justice.* Chicago: University of Chicago Press, 2000.

Hamilton, C.; Falshaw, L.; and Browne, K. "The Link between Recurrent Maltreatment and Offending Behaviour." *International Journal of Offender Therapy and Comparative Criminology,* Vol. 46, 2002, pp.75–94.

Herrenkohl, T. I.; Hawkins, J. D.; Chung, I.; Hill, K. G.; and Battin-Pearson, S. "School and Community Risk Factors and Interventions." In *Child Delinquency: Development, Intervention and Service Needs,* edited by R. Loeber and D. P. Farrington. Thousand Oaks, CA: Sage Publications, Inc., 2001, pp.217–218.

Hirth, Diane. "Early Intensive Help for High-Risk Juveniles." *Corrections Today,* December 2001, pp.80–83.

Hoge, R. "Standardized Instruments for Assessing Risk and Need in Youthful Offenders." *Criminal Justice and Behavior,* Vol. 29, 2002, pp.380–396.

Leverette-Sanderlin, Anne. "Camp Turning Point." *Law and Order,* October 2001, pp.122–124.

Mears, Daniel P. "Treat Mental Illness of Juvenile Offenders." April 22, 2002. http://www.urban.org/url.cfm?1D=900503

Mears, Daniel P. and Kelly, William R. "Linking Process and Outcomes in Evaluating a Statewide Drug Treatment Program for Youthful Offenders." *Crime & Delinquency,* January 2002, pp.99–115.

Mendel, Richard A. *Less Cost, More Safety: Guiding Lights for Reform in Juvenile Justice.* Washington, DC: American Youth Policy Forum, 2001. www.aypf.org

Metropolitan Court Judges Committee Report. *Deprived Children: A Judicial Response.* Washington, DC: U.S. Government Printing Office, 1986.

Mihalic, Sharon; Irwin, Katherine; Elliott, Delbert; Fagan, Abigail; and Hansen, Diane. *Blueprints for Violence Prevention.* Washington, DC: OJJDP Juvenile Justice Bulletin, July 2001. (NCJ 187079)

Miner, Michael H. "Factors Associated with Redicivism in Juveniles: An Analysis of Serious Juvenile Sex Offenders." *Journal of Research in Crime and Delinquency,* November 2002, pp.421–436.

Oldenettel, Debra and Wordes, Madeline. *The Community Assessment Center Concept.* Washington, DC: OJJDP Juvenile Justice Bulletin, March 2000. (NCJ 178942)

Pearson, F.; Lipton, D.; Cleland, C.; and Yee, D. "The Effects of Behavioral/Cognitive-Behavioral Programs on Recidivism." *Crime & Delinquency,* Vol. 48, 2002, pp.476–496.

Petrosino, A.; Turpin-Petrosino, C.; and Buehler, J. *"Scared Straight" and Other Juvenile Awareness Programs for Preventing Juvenile Delinquency.* 2003. http://www.update-software.com/abstracts/ab002796.htm

Righthand, Sue and Welch, Carlann. *Juveniles Who Have Sexually Offended: A Review of the Professional Literature.* Washington, DC: Office of Juvenile Justice and Delinquency Prevention, March 2001. (NCJ 184739)

Rosenblatt, Jennifer A.; Rosenblatt, Abram; and Biggs, Edward E. "Criminal Behavior and Emotional Disorder: Comparing Youths Served by the Mental Health and Juvenile Justice Systems." *Journal of Behavioral Health Services and Research,* Vol. 27, No. 2, 2000, p.227.

Schoenwald, S.; Ward, D.; Henggeler, S.; Rowland, M.; and Brondino, M. "Multisystemic Therapy versus Hospitalization for Crisis Stabilization of Youths: Placement Outcomes 4 Months Post-Referral." *Mental Health Services Research,* Vol. 2, No. 1, 2000, pp.3–12.

Second Chances: Giving Kids a Chance to Make a Better Choice. Washington, DC: OJJDP Juvenile Justice Bulletin, May 2000. (NCJ 181680)

Stouthamer-Loeber, M.; Loeber, R.; Homish, L.; and Wei, E. "Maltreatment of Boys and the Development of Disruptive and Delinquent Behavior." *Development and Psychopathology,* Vol. 13, 2001, pp.941–955.

Vander-Waal, Curtis J.; McBride, Duane C.; Terry-McElrath, Yvonne, M; and Van Buren, Holly. *Breaking the Juvenile Drug-Crime Cycle: A Guide for Practitioners and Policymakers.* Washington, DC: National Institute of Justice, May 2001. (NCJ 186156)

Vasquez, Gloria. "Resiliency: Juvenile Offenders Recognize Their Strengths to Change Their Lives." *Corrections Today,* June 2000, pp.106–110, 125.

White, Michael D.; Fyfe, James J.; Campbell, Suzanne P.; and Goldkamp, John S. "The School-Police Partnership: Identifying At-Risk Youths through a Truant Recovery Program." *Evaluation Review,* Vol. 25, No. 5, 2001, p.507.

Wiebush, Richard; Freitag, Raelene; and Baird, Christopher. *Preventing Delinquency through Improved Child Protection Services.* Washington, DC: OJJDP Juvenile Justice Bulletin, July 2001. (NCJ 187759)

Youth Out of School: Linking Absence to Delinquency, 2nd ed. Denver, CO: Colorado Foundation for Families and Children, September 2002.

Juvenile Justice at the Crossroads—
100 Years Later

More than 100 years have passed since the first juvenile court ushered in a separate justice system for juveniles. Many researchers and practitioners contend that the juvenile justice system is at a crossroads. According to Mendel (2003): "After a dramatic lurch toward punishment in the 1990s and little effort to solve underlying problems in delinquency courts and corrections systems, American juvenile justice stands at a crossroads. Glaring weaknesses remain. The very notion of a separate justice system for youths is under siege, yet the evidence suggests that far better results are possible if states and local court systems reaffirm their commitment to youth-focused justice reform."

Mendel asserts that the juvenile justice system has four crucial choices facing it in the 21st century. Choice 1: Rhyme or Reason? He notes that a simple rhyme "adult time for adult crime" turned America's juvenile justice debate on its head in the 1990s. Forty-nine states and the District of Columbia changed laws that resulted in an increase in the number of minors tried in adult courts. Each year some 210,000 minors are tried in criminal court.

Choice 2: Confinement or Commitment? Mendel suggests that community programs cost less than one-third as much as confinement, which could result in an $8.8 million in savings for U.S. taxpayers. America's training schools should be reconsidered. These large, congregate facilities in the correctional system have been extensively evaluated, and they are clearly an ineffective treatment for delinquency.

Choice 3: Rights or Wrongs? Are we protecting the rights of court-involved youths? In 1967, *In re Gault,* the U.S. Supreme Court clearly stated: "Under our Constitution, the condition of being a boy does not justify a kangaroo court." What of the racial imbalance? According to *For Juvenile Justice: Serious Concerns,* (2003), 25 new studies from 1989 to 2001 document racial disparities in the way youths are treated in the nation's juvenile justice system. This source also questions whether youths are receiving "assembly line justice." For example, a juvenile judge in Cook County, Illinois, makes 110 rulings on a typical day.

Choice 4: Run-of-the-Mill or Research-Based Programming? Juvenile justice needs to pay attention to what works and to researching what works. Nelson (2003) contends that it is time to end "fad justice": "The trend toward tough-sounding action in juvenile justice is pervasive, with little regard to costs or consequences." He cites boot camps, scared straight programs and supporting "adult time for adult crime" as among the fads that have demonstrated they usually cause more harm than good.

Juvenile Justice at the Crossroads: Literature-Based Seminars for Judges, Court Personnel and Community Leaders Final Report (2003) details the conclusions and recommendations of a varied group of educators, law enforcement professionals, judges and court personnel, and social and youth service agencies participating in a federally funded seminar. This group focused on three major areas: racial and ethnic disparities in treatment of juvenile crime, female juvenile delinquency and efforts at restorative justice, and reintegration of juvenile offenders within the community.

Among the recommendations of the group (p.6) were: (1) celebrate always those children who are overcoming obstacles, (2) watch for at-risk children who are not acting out but may be deeply depressed or angry and (3) look to mentor every child and not let some get lost in the system. The theme of societal and individual disconnection resonated through participants' remarks. They cited the need for interpersonal and organizational change in schools, agencies and courtrooms, not just systemic change. They also expressed concern about focusing always on the negative. All agreed that attitudinal change from oppression and sometimes patriarchy involving children, with minorities and girls as prime examples, can come best from reflective and one-on-one seminars.

The report described the crucial issues related to adolescents in the juvenile justice system as the need for them to be seen and heard, victimization, bearing witness and the difficulty of working across differences (race, ethnicity, gender, even language).

According to the report (p.7): "There was wide consensus that as the legal system becomes more and more punitive for children, there is even greater need for community involvement. This could and should occur before the court involvement and could become part of the actual process through community policing efforts."

A general theme of the seminar was to promote systemic change with an emphasis on creating problem solving in courts through agencies such as the Department of Social Services and schools, which often involve a "daily rush to judgment" without time and resources and sometimes without options to attend to individual cases. The juvenile justice system is often overburdened. There is often either a vacuum of information or else information overload, either of which can result in the individual child or family getting lost in the judicial system. This is true whether it be the juvenile court, the probate/family court, the superior court or the probation system.

A second theme reverberating throughout the seminar was communication, especially listening and the difficulty of both listening and hearing, especially by those in power. The report (p.8) also notes: "The complex issues of compassion and accountability for juvenile offenders surfaced again and again, especially in renewed efforts to look at the whole child and his/her family, not just the offender or the offense. Despite recognition of limited resources and options, the participants vowed to avoid preconceptions and predispositions to label children, judging them upon superficial evidence. This shared recognition of differences among and between ethnic groups, gender and socio-economic groups must be acknowledged. . . . All agreed that the idea and, indeed, the ideal of law should match the developmental stages of children, should focus on care and protection of children and on education of children and their parents to prevent juvenile crime before it occurs."

This focus on a developmental perspective is also stressed by Beyer (2003, pp.1-2): "Holding juveniles accountable for acts that have harmed others must be approached in a developmental context because young people think differently than adults, are emotionally immature and do not have fully formed moral values. Young offenders must be taught to view their victims as people and to view themselves as being more in control of their choices. They must also become successful at something other than crime. Neither treatment nor punishment repairs the damage done to victims and the community by delinquent acts. Juvenile accountability requires a combination of skills building, reparation to victims and citizen protection in an approach that encourages the development of young people so they become contributors to the community." Beyer (p.2) describes three interdependent areas of accountability:

1. For *young offenders,* recognizing what they have done and taking action to make amends to victims and the community.

2. For the *community,* reinforcing young offenders' efforts to make amends by teaching them and volunteering in restitution and mediation programs rather than sending adjudicated offenders out of the community.

3. For the *juvenile justice system,* restructuring to hold itself responsible for outcomes and to devise a carefully calibrated continuum of responses to juvenile crime.

The need for education of children and youths is stressed by Nessel (2001, p.1) who describes "Youth for Justice," a unique initiative in law-related education (LRE) supported by the OJJDP. Nessel states: "Youths often think of the law as something that is imposed on them rather than as something that allows society to function and that makes their lives more secure. Law-related education teaches children that they have both rights and responsibilities under the law and that a democracy depends on its citizens to actively exercise those rights and responsibilities. . . . Law-related education inculcates protective factors in the youths it educates, thus buffering them from the problems and circumstances that might lead to their involvement in delinquency and other negative behaviors. In so doing, it protects the rights and liberties of Americans to ensure a better future for all."

Juvenile justice is, indeed, at a crossroads. Will it continue the trend toward being more punitive and increasingly sending minors to criminal court? Is a separate juvenile justice system even needed in the twenty-first century? Table E.1 presents a review and summary of the main features of the juvenile justice system and the criminal justice system.

Table E.1
Comparison of the Juvenile and the Criminal System

Although the juvenile and criminal justice systems are more alike in some jurisdictions than in others, generalizations can be made about the distinctions between the two systems and about their common ground.

Juvenile Justice System	Common Ground	Criminal Justice System
Operating Assumptions		
■ Youth behavior is malleable. ■ Rehabilitation is usually a viable goal. ■ Youths are in families and not independent.	■ Community protection is a primary goal. ■ Law violators must be held accountable. ■ Constitutional rights apply.	■ Sanctions should be proportionate to the offense. ■ General deterrence works. ■ Rehabilitation is not a primary goal.
Prevention		
■ Many specific delinquency prevention activities (e.g., school, church, recreation) are used. ■ Prevention is intended to change individual behavior and is often focused on reducing risk factors and increasing protective factors in the individual, family and community.	■ Educational approaches are taken to specific behaviors (drunken driving, drug use).	■ Prevention activities are generalized and are aimed at deterrence (e.g., Crime Watch).
Law Enforcement		
■ Specialized juvenile units are used. ■ Some additional behaviors are prohibited (truancy, running away, curfew violations). ■ Some limitations are placed on public access to information. ■ A significant number of youths are diverted from the juvenile justice system, often into alternative programs.	■ Jurisdiction involves the full range of criminal behavior. ■ Constitutional and procedural safeguards exist. ■ Both reactive and proactive approaches (targeted at offense types, neighborhoods, etc.) are used. ■ Community policing strategies are employed.	■ Open public access to all information is required. ■ Law enforcement exercises discretion to divert offenders out of the criminal justice system.
Intake—Prosecution		
■ In many instances, juvenile court intake, not the prosecutor, decides which cases to file. ■ The decision to file a petition for court action is based on both social and legal factors. ■ A significant portion of cases are diverted from formal case processing. ■ Intake or the prosecutor diverts cases from formal processing to services operated by the juvenile court prosecutor's office or outside agencies.	■ Probable cause must be established. ■ The prosecutor acts on behalf of the state.	■ Plea bargaining is common. ■ The prosecution decision is based largely on legal facts. ■ Prosecution is valuable in building history for subsequent offenses. ■ Prosecution exercises discretion to withhold charges or divert offenders out of the criminal justice system.
Detention—Jail/Lockup		
■ Juveniles may be detained for their own protection or the community's protection. ■ Juveniles may not be confined with adults unless there is "sight and sound separation."	■ Accused offenders may be held in custody to ensure their appearance in court. ■ Detention alternatives of home or electronic detention are used.	■ Accused individuals have the right to apply for bond/bail release.

Table E.1
Continued

Juvenile Justice System	Common Ground	Criminal Justice System
	Adjudication—Conviction	
■ Juvenile court proceedings are "quasi-civil" (not criminal) and may be confidential. ■ If guilt is established the youth is adjudicated delinquent regardless of offense. ■ Right to jury trial is not afforded in all states.	■ Standard of "proof beyond a reasonable doubt" is required. ■ Rights to be represented by an attorney, to confront witnesses and to remain silent are afforded. ■ Appeals to a higher court are allowed. ■ Experimentation with specialized courts (e.g., drug courts, gun courts) is under way.	■ Defendants have a constitutional right to a jury trial. ■ Guilt must be established on individual offenses charged to conviction. ■ All proceedings are open.
	Disposition—Sentencing	
■ Disposition decisions are based on individual and social factors, offense severity and youth's offense history. ■ Dispositional philosophy includes a significant rehabilitation component. ■ Many dispositional alternatives are operated by the juvenile court. ■ Dispositions cover a wide range of community-based and residential services. ■ Disposition orders may be directed to people other than the offender (e.g., parents). ■ Disposition may be indeterminate, based on progress demonstrated by the youth.	■ Decisions are influenced by current offense, offending history and social factors. ■ Decisions hold offenders accountable. ■ Decisions may give consideration to victims (e.g., restitution and "no contact" orders). ■ Decisions may not be cruel or unusual.	■ Sentencing decisions are bound primarily by the severity of the current offense and by the offender's criminal history. ■ Sentencing philosophy is based largely on proportionality and punishment. ■ Sentence is often determinate, based on offense.
	Aftercare—Parole	
■ Function combines surveillance and reintegration activities (e.g., family, school, work).	■ The behavior of individuals released from correctional settings is monitored. ■ Violation of conditions can result in reincarceration.	■ Function is primarily surveillance and reporting to monitor illicit behavior.

Source: *Juvenile Justice: A Century of Change.* Washington, DC: National
Report Series. Juvenile Justice Bulletin, December 1999, pp. 10–12.

References

Beyer, Marty. *Best Practices in Juvenile Accountability: Overview.* Washington, DC: JAIBG (Juvenile Accountability Incentive Block Grants Program) Bulletin, April 2003. (NCJ 184745)

For Juvenile Justice: Serious Concerns, 2003. Web site: http://www.aect.org/publications/advocasey/spring2003/advocasey_index.htm

Juvenile Justice at the Crossroads: Literature-Based Seminars for Judges, Court Personnel and Community Leaders. Waltham, MA: The International Center for Ethics, Justice and Public Life, Brandeis University, June 2002. Online: http://www.brandeis.edu/ethics/seminars

Mendel, Dick. *A Matter of Choice-Forks in the Road for Juvenile Justice,* 2003. Advocacy Web site: http://www.aect.org/publications/advocasey/spring2003/choice/choice1.htm

Nelson, Douglas. *On Adolescent Crime: Time to End Fad Justice.* Advocacy Web site: http://www.aect.org/publications/advocasey/spring2003/choice/choice1.htm

Nessel, Paula A. *Youth for Justice.* Washington, DC: OJJDP Juvenile Justice Bulletin, April 2001. (NCJ 186161)

Glossary

The number following the definition refers to the chapter(s) in which the term is defined.

abatement—doing whatever is necessary to get rid of a nuisance and bring the problem to an end. 14

abuse—see *child abuse*. 4

acting out—the free, deliberate, often malicious indulgence of impulse that frequently leads to aggression as well as other manifestations of delinquency, such as vandalism, cruelty to animals and sometimes even murder. 5

adjudicate—to judge. 9

adjudicated—having been the subject of completed criminal or juvenile proceedings and having been cleared or declared a delinquent, status offender or dependent. 9

adjudication—a juvenile court decision ending a hearing, affirming that the juvenile is a delinquent, a status offender or a dependent, or that the allegations in a petition are not sustained. 9

adjudicatory hearing—the fact-finding process of the juvenile justice system in which the juvenile court determines whether evidence is sufficient to sustain the allegations in a petition. 10

admit—to plead guilty in a juvenile delinquency proceeding. 9

adolescence—the period from age 12 to 18 or 19; children go through puberty, experiencing hormonal changes. 3

adult supremacy—subordination of children to the absolute and arbitrary authority of parents and, in many instances, teachers. 3

adversary procedure—a means to determine guilt or innocence that pits the defense against the prosecution in court proceedings with a judge acting as arbiter of the legal rules. Under the adversary system, the burden is on the state to prove the charges beyond a reasonable doubt. 10

adversary process—in adult court, pitting prosecution and defense attorneys against each other. Demands for due process for children in the juvenile court, including the introduction of defense counsel, developed as a result of the *Gault* decision. "Adversary" versus "best interests" are shorthand ways of referring to these conflicting philosophies of the juvenile court. 10

aftercare—supervision given children and youths for a limited time after they are released from confinement but are still under the control of the institution or of the juvenile court. 11

alternative education—refers to all educational programs that fall outside the traditional K-12 school system. 11

Amber Alert—voluntary partnerships between law enforcement agencies and public broadcasters to notify the public when a child has been abducted. 7

American Dream—the belief that through hard work anyone can become successful and rich. 2

anomie—normlessness. 2, 5

anomie theory—states that the motivations for crime do not result simply from the flaws, failures or free choices of individuals. The American Dream contributes to crime directly by encouraging people to use illegal means to achieve culturally approved goals. 2

anticipated strain—an individual's expectation that current stresses will continue into the future or that new stresses will be experienced. 4

antisocial personality disorder—exists in persons at least age 18 who show evidence of a conduct disorder before age 15 as well as a pattern of irresponsible and antisocial behavior since the age of 15. 6

arrest—taking people into custody to restrain them until they can be held accountable for an offense at a court proceeding. The legal requirement for an arrest is probable cause; see also *take into custody*. 7

at-risk youths—young people with the potential and willingness to take unnecessary risks or chances outside of socially accepted norms and mores for the purpose of self-gratification, aggrandizement and peer acceptance. Youths who engage in at-risk behavior, including habitual truancy, incorrigibility, gang activity, drug abuse, alcoholism, suicide, promiscuity, criminal activity, tattooing or self-mutilating behaviors, vandalism, possession and use of weapons. 5

attention deficit hyperactivity disorder (ADHD)—a common childhood disruptive behavior disorder characterized by heightened motor activity, short attention span, distractibility, impulsiveness and lack of self-control. 3

behavioral activation—refers to novelty and sensation seeking, impulsivity, hyperactivity and predatory aggression. 3

behavioral inhibition—refers to fearfulness, anxiety, timidity and shyness in response to new stimulus or punishment. 3

beyond a reasonable doubt—degree of proof required for guilt in a juvenile court proceeding. It is less than absolute certainty, but more than high probability. If there is doubt based on reason, the accused is entitled to the benefit of that doubt by acquittal. 6

bifurcated hearings—the delinquent act charged is held separately from the hearing to determine the disposition. 10

binge drinking—men who had five or more (or women who had four or more) drinks in a row at least once during the two weeks before they completed a survey questionnaire. 5

biotic balance—an ecological term describing what occurs when the relations between the different species of plants and their necessary conditions for survival (e.g., climate, soil condition) maintain an equilibrium. All the organisms are thus able to survive and prosper. 2

blended sentence—combines both a juvenile sentence and an adult sentence. In some states if a youth complies with the terms of the juvenile

sentence—which includes longer and more intensive supervision than a typical juvenile sanction—they will be released without the stain of an adult criminal record. If the youth fails to comply with the terms of the juvenile sentence, they will receive the sentence that would have been incurred in criminal court. 10

boot camp—a correctional facility that stresses military discipline, physical fitness, strict obedience to orders, and education and vocational training; designed for young, nonviolent, first-time offenders. Also called *shock incarceration*. 11

Bridewell—the first correctional institution, which confined both children and adults considered to be idle and disorderly. 1

broken-window phenomenon/theory—the theory that states that if it appears no one cares, disorder and crime will thrive. 5, 12

bullying—involves intentional, repeated hurtful acts, words or other behavior. 6

burden of proof—the duty of proving disputed facts in the trial of a case. The duty commonly lies with the person who affirms an issue and is sometimes said to shift when sufficient evidence is furnished to raise a presumption that what is alleged is true.

caring environment—one in which individuals and institutions protect young people and invest in their ongoing development. 4

CASA—Court-Appointed Special Advocate for children; a volunteer guardian *ad litem* program. 10

certification—a procedure whereby a juvenile court waives jurisdiction and transfers the case to the adult criminal court. Also called a *waiver*. 9

child—in most states, a person younger than 18 years of age. 1

child abuse—any physical, emotional or sexual trauma to a child for which no reasonable explanation, such as an accident, can be found. Child abuse includes neglecting to give proper care and attention to a young child. 4

child savers—groups who promoted the rights of minors in the late 1800's and helped create a separate juvenile court. Their motives have been questioned by modern writers, who see their efforts as a form of social and class control. 1

child welfare agency—an agency licensed by the state to provide care and supervision for children. An agency that provides service to the juvenile court and which may accept legal custody. It may be licensed to accept guardianship, to accept children for adoption and to license foster homes. 9

chronic juvenile offender—a youth who has a record of five or more separate charges of delinquency, regardless of the gravity of the offenses. 6

civil injunction—a legal tool for addressing the hold that entrenched gangs have on urban neighborhoods; a spatially based, neighborhood-level intervention intended to disrupt a gang's routine activities. 8

civil law—all law that is not criminal, including torts (personal wrongs), contract law, property law, maritime law and commercial law. The juvenile court functions under a blend of civil and criminal law. 9

classical view of criminality—holds that delinquents are responsible for their own behavior, as individuals with free will. 2

classical world view—holds that humans have free will and are responsible for their own actions. 2

coercive intervention—out-of-home placement, detainment or mandated therapy or counseling. 9

collective abuse—attitudes held as a group in a society that impede the psychological and physical development of children. 4

collective efficacy—explains how communities exert control and provide support; parallels parental efficacy but on a much larger scale. 3

common law—law of custom and usage. 1

community—refers not only to the geographic area over which the justice system has jurisdiction but also to a sense of integration, of shared values and a sense of "we-ness." 12

community justice—a justice system that aligns itself more closely with the community; reflected in community policing, community prosecution, community courts and community corrections. 12

community policing—a philosophy that embraces a proactive, problem-oriented approach to working in partnerships with the community to make it safe. 7, 12

community relations—projecting and maintaining a police image of serving the community, rather than simply enforcing laws. 7

competence—a specific, functional ability. 9

competent—properly qualified, adequate. 9

concordance—a high degree of similarity, as in heredity studies where identical twins were more likely to both have criminal records than were fraternal twins. 2

concurrent jurisdiction—something happens at the same time, or a case may be heard in either juvenile or adult court. 9

conditional threat—warns that a violent act will occur unless certain demands are met; for example, "If you don't pay me $100,000, I will blow up this school." 8

conduct disorder—a behavioral disorder characterized by prolonged antisocial behavior ranging from truancy to fistfights. 6

conflict theory—suggests that laws are established to keep the dominant class in power. 2

consensus theory—contends that individuals within a society agree on basic values, on what is inherently right and wrong. 2

contagion—a way to explain the spread of violence, equating it with the spread of infectious diseases. 6

coproducers of justice—the role of citizens as responsible for the prevalence and severity of the crime within their communities. 14

corporal punishment—inflicting bodily harm. 1

corporate gang—a highly structured, disciplined gang with a strong leader; its main focus is participating in illegal money-making ventures. Also called an *organized gang*. 6

corrections institution—a confinement facility with custodial authority over delinquents and status offenders committed to confinement after a dispositional hearing. 11

corrective prevention—a strategy that focuses on eliminating conditions that lead to or cause criminal behavior. Also called *primary prevention.* 13

court, juvenile—an agency of the judicial branch of government established by statute and consisting of one or more judicial officers with the authority to decide controversies in law and disputed matters concerned with intake, custody, confinement, supervision or treatment of alleged or adjudicated delinquents, status offenders and children in need of care. 9

Court-Appointed Special Advocate for Children (CASA)—a volunteer guardian *ad litem* program. 10

crack children—children exposed to crack cocaine while in the womb; may exhibit social, emotional and cognitive problems. 3

crew—a group of taggers. 6

crime—an offense against the state; behavior in violation of law for which a penalty is prescribed. 2, 6

criminogenic factors—offense enhancing. 14

criminogenic need principle—certain needs are directly linked to crime; criminogenic needs constitute dynamic risk factors or attributes that, when changed, influence the probability of recidivism. 11

crisis intervention—capitalizes on windows of opportunity when the individual may be especially receptive to treatment and establishes new approaches to problem-solving. 14

critical theory—combines the classical free will and positivist determinism views of crime, suggesting that humans are both self-determined and society-determined; assumes humans create the institutions and structures that ultimately dominate and constrain them; includes labeling theory, conflict theory and radical theory. 2

cruel and unusual punishment—physical punishment or punishment far in excess of that given to a person under similar circumstances and, therefore, banned by the Eighth Amendment. 11

custodian—a person other than a parent, guardian or agency to whom legal custody of a child has been transferred by a court, but not a person who has only physical custody. A person other than a parent or

legal guardian who stands *in loco parentis* to the child or a person to whom legal custody of the child has been given by court order. 1

custody—a legal status created by court order that vests in a person the right to have physical custody of a child; the right to determine where and with whom the child will live; the right and duty to protect, train and discipline the child, to provide food, shelter, legal services, education, ordinary medical and dental care. Such rights are subject to the rights and duties, responsibilities and provisions of any court order. 1

custody, discharge from—legal release from custody. State statutes specify that a child shall be released to a parent, guardian or legal custodian unless it is impractical, undesirable or otherwise ordered by the court. The legal custodian serves as a guarantor that the child will appear in court and may be asked to sign a promise to that effect. This takes the place of bail in adult court. 7

custody, taking into—the term used in place of *arrest* when a child is taken by a law enforcement officer. State codes and laws prescribe that a child may be taken into custody only under the following conditions: (1) when ordered by a judge for failure to obey a summons (petition); (2) when a law enforcement officer observes or has reasonable grounds to believe the child has broken a federal, state or local law and deems it in the public interest; (3) when the officer removes the child from conditions that threaten his or her welfare; (4) when the child is believed to be a runaway from parents or legal custody; and (5) when the child has violated the conditions of probation. 7

decriminalization—legislation to make status offenses noncriminal acts. 1

deep end strategy—targets youths with the highest likelihood of continuing their delinquent careers without comprehensive interventions. 9

deinstitutionalization—providing programs in a community-based setting instead of in an institution. 1

delinquency—actions or conduct by a juvenile in violation of criminal law or constituting a status offense. An error or failure by a child or adolescent to conform to society's expectations of social order where the child either resides or visits. 1

delinquent—see *delinquent child*. 5

delinquent act—an act committed by a juvenile for which an adult could be prosecuted in a criminal court. 1

delinquent child—a child adjudicated to have violated a federal, state or local law; a minor who has done an illegal act or who has been proved in court to have misbehaved seriously. A child may be found delinquent for a variety of behaviors not criminal for adults (status offenses). 1, 5

denominator approach—placing the focus of efforts on the whole population of youths, not just on the delinquents. 13

deny—a plea of "not guilty" in juvenile proceedings. 10

dependency—the legal status of children over whom a juvenile court has assumed jurisdiction because the court has found their care to fall short of legal standards of proper care by parents, guardians or custodians. 4

dependent—a child judged by the juvenile court to be without parent, guardian or custodian. The child needs special care and treatment because the parent, guardian or custodian is unable to provide for his or her physical or mental condition; or the parents, guardian or custodian, for good cause, desire to be relieved of legal custody; or the child is without necessary care or support through no fault of the parents, guardian or custodian. 1

deprived child—one who is without proper parental care or control, subsistence and education as required by law or other care or control necessary for his or her physical, mental or emotional health or morals, and the deprivation is not due primarily to the lack of financial means of the parents, guardians or other custodians. 1

deserts—punishment as a kind of justified revenge; the offending individual gets what is coming. 1

desistance—a process commonly occurring during the transition between late adolescence and early adulthood that discourages youths from a life of crime. 14

detention—temporary care of a child alleged to be delinquent who is physically restricted pending court disposition, transfer to another jurisdiction or execution of a court order. 7

detention center—a government facility that provides temporary care in a closed, locked facility for juveniles pending a court disposition. 10

detention hearing—a hearing in juvenile court to determine whether a child held in custody shall remain in custody for the best interests of the child and the public. 10

determinate sentence—one of the two types of limited discretionary sentences in which a degree of judicial discretion is removed but a range of sentence lengths is still allowed. 10

determinism—a philosophy that maintains that human behavior is the product of a multitude of environmental and cultural influences. 2

deterrence—punishment as a means to prevent future lawbreaking. 1, 2, 11

developmental pathways—development of disruptive and delinquent behavior in boys that typically occurs in an orderly, progressive manner. 5

deviance—behavior that departs from the social norm. 6

differential association theory—states that a person becomes delinquent because of an excess of definitions favorable to violation of law over definitions unfavorable to violation of law. 2

direct threat—identifies a specific act against a specific target and is delivered in a straightforward manner, clearly and explicitly; for example, "I am going to put a bomb in a locker." 8

discretionary sentence—gives judges and parole authorities a great deal of latitude in determining the length of the sentence. The maximum sentence is often determined by the legislature. Judges cannot exceed this but can give a lesser sentence. 10

disposition—a juvenile court decision that a juvenile be committed to a confinement facility; placed on probation or given treatment and care; meet certain standards of conduct or be released; or a combination of court decrees. 10

dispositional hearing—an adjudicated process by the juvenile court, either formal or informal, on the evidence submitted with a guarantee of due process of law for the child in a matter before the court, as specified in the Fifth, Sixth and Fourteenth Amendments to the Constitution (*In re Gault*). 10

distributive justice—providing an equal share of what is valued in a society to each member of that society. This includes power, prestige and possessions. Also called *social justice.* 2

diversion—the official halting of formal juvenile proceedings against an alleged offender and the referral of the juvenile to a treatment or care program by a private or public service agency. 1, 2, 9

double jeopardy—being tried for the same offense twice. 1

due process—a difficult-to-define term; the due process clause of the U.S. Constitution requires that no person shall be deprived of life, liberty or property without due process of law *or,* the course of formal legal proceedings carried out regularly and in accordance with established rules and principles, as provided for by the Fourteenth Amendment, with the result that no person is deprived of life, liberty of property unjustly. 1

dynamic risk factors—individual, social or situational factors that often change; for example, associates, attitudes and stress levels. In contrast to static risk factors. 14

EBD—emotionally/behaviorally disturbed. Usually emotionally/behaviorally disturbed youths have one or more of the following behavior patterns: severely aggressive or impulsive behavior; severely withdrawn or anxious behaviors, pervasive unhappiness, depression or wide mood swings; severely disordered thought processes that show up in unusual behavior patterns, atypical communication styles and distorted interpersonal relationships. Such children may have limited coping skills and may be easily traumatized. 3

ecological model—a sociological model used to compare the growth of a city and its attendant crime problems to growth in nature. 2

ecology—the study of the relationships between organisms and their environment. 2

educare—safe, constructive child care for all children. 4

the 8% problem—a small group of repeat offenders. 14

emotional abuse—the chronic failure of a child's caretaker to provide affection and support. 4

expressive violence—an acting out of extreme hostility, in contrast to instrumental violence. 6

extrafamilial sexual abuse—sexual abuse of a child by a friend or stranger, a non-family member. 4

family courts—courts with broad jurisdiction over family matters, such as neglect, delinquency, paternity, support and noncriminal matters and behavior. 9

fetal alcohol syndrome (FAS)—a condition in which children exposed to excessive amounts of alcohol while in the womb may exhibit impulsivity and poor communication skills, be unable to predict consequences or use appropriate judgment in daily life; the leading cause of mental retardation in the Western world. 3

folkways—how people are expected to dress, eat and show respect for one another. They encourage certain behaviors. 2

foster group home—a blend of group home and foster home initiatives; provides a "real family" concept and is run by a single family, not professional staff. 11

foster home—an unlocked facility licensed by the state or local jurisdiction and operated by a person or couple to provide care and maintenance for children, usually one to four such children. See *group home.* 11

functionalism—the view that crime is a necessary part of society, providing the need for laws and courts and jobs for lawyers, police officers, judges and jailers. 2

funnel effect—the phenomenon that, at each point in the juvenile justice system, fewer and fewer youths pass through. 2

gang—a group of youths who form an allegiance for a common purpose and engage in unlawful or criminal activity; any group gathered together on a continuing basis to commit antisocial behavior. 6

gateway drugs—tobacco, alcohol and marijuana. 13

geographic integrity—to concentrate intervention efforts in an identified section of a city. 8

Gould-Wysinger Award—established in 1992 to give national recognition for local achievement in improving the juvenile justice system and helping our nation's youths. 13

graduated sanctions—a continuum of treatment alternatives that includes immediate intervention, intermediate sanctions, community-based correctional sanctions and secure corrections. 10

graffiti—wall writing, indoors or outdoors. Outdoors it is sometimes referred to as the "newspaper of the street." 8

group home—a nonconfining residential facility for adjudicated juveniles intended to reproduce as closely as possible the circumstances of family life and at a minimum to provide access to community activities and resources. 11

guardian *ad litem*—an individual appointed by the court to protect the best interests of a child or an incompetent during the juvenile justice process. In some states this can only be an attorney. The appointed individual is a surrogate parent, guardian or custodian and can be replaced in the best interests of the child at any point in a juvenile proceeding. 10

guardianship—a legal status created by court order giving an adult the right and duty to protect, provide food and shelter, train and discipline a child.

halfway house—a nonconfining residential facility for adjudicated juveniles to provide an alternative to confinement; also used to house juveniles on probation or in need of a period of readjustment to the community after confinement. 11

hearing—the presentation of evidence to a juvenile court judge for consideration and disposition. 10

hedonistic gang—one that focuses on having a good time, usually by smoking pot, drinking beer and sometimes engaging in minor property crimes. 6

holistic approach—treating the whole person; examining all facets of a child's life and coordinating all treatment services ensures the greatest benefit for the youth. 14

horizontal prosecution—an organizational structure strategy whereby individual assistant prosecutors or a small group of assistant prosecutors are responsible for certain phases of the adjudication of criminal complaints. In contrast to vertical prosecution. 8

immediate sanctions—usually diversion mechanisms that hold youths accountable for their behavior by avoiding formal court processing. 11

in loco parentis—in place of the parent. Gives certain social and legal institutions the authority to act as a parent might in situations requiring discipline or need. Schools have this authority. 3

incapacitation—making incapable by incarcerating. 2

incarceration—placing a person in a locked facility or a secure confinement for punishment, deterrence, rehabilitation or reintegration into the community. 10

indeterminate sentence—gives judges and parole authorities a great deal of latitude in determining the length of the sentence. The maximum sentence is often determined by the legislature. Judges cannot exceed this but can give a lesser sentence. Also called *discretionary sentence*. 10

Index crimes—Part I and Part II crimes of the Uniform Crime Report (UCR), including homicide, non-negligent manslaughter, forcible rape, robbery, aggravated assault, burglary, larceny, arson and motor vehicle theft. 5

indirect threat—is vague and ambiguous; for example, "If I wanted to, I could blow up this school." 8

individual abuse—physical or emotional abuse by parents or others as individuals. 4

institutional abuse—the approved use of force and violence against children in the schools and in the denial of children's due process rights in institutions. 4

instrumental gang—focuses on obtaining money, committing property crimes for economic reasons rather than for the "thrill." 6

instrumental violence—violence used for some type of gain, such as robbery; in contrast to expressive violence. 6

intake—the point in the juvenile justice process that reviews referrals to the juvenile court and decides the action to be taken based on the best interests of the child and the public good. 6

intake unit—the office that receives referrals to the juvenile court and screens them, either to divert them from the system to a social services agency or to file a petition. 6

integrated community—a geographic/political area where people take ownership and pride in what is right and responsibility for what is wrong. 12

intensive supervision—a highly structured form of observation provided by probation. 11

intermediate sanctions—hold youths accountable for their actions through more restrictive and intensive interventions short of secure care. 11

intrafamilial sexual abuse—sexual abuse of a child by a parent or other family member. 4

jurisdiction—the authority of courts and judicial officers to decide a case. 9

just deserts—see *deserts*. 1

justice—fairness in treatment by the law. 1

justice model—the judicial process wherein young people who come into conflict with the law are held responsible and accountable for their behavior. 1, 9

juvenile court—a court having jurisdiction over individuals defined as juveniles and alleged to be delinquents, status offenders, dependents or in need of decisions by the court regarding their health, safety or welfare. 9

juvenile justice—a system that provides a legal setting in which youths can account for their wrongs or receive official protection. 1

Juvenile Justice and Delinquency Prevention Act of 1974—a federal law establishing an office of juvenile justice within the Law Enforcement Assistance Act to provide funds to control juvenile crime. 1

juvenile justice process—a proceeding for juveniles that differs from the adult criminal process. The philosophy and procedures are informal and nonadversarial, invoked in the best interests of the child rather than as punishment. A petition is filed rather than a complaint; the matter is often not public and the purpose is rehabilitation rather than retribution. 1

juvenile record—a confidential document kept separate from adult records and not open to public inspection; it contains an account of behavior and antisocial activity of juveniles who appeared before a juvenile court. 10

labeling—giving names to things; labels may become self-fulfilling. 3

labeling theory—views society as creating deviance through a system of social control agencies that designate certain people as deviants. This stigmatizes people; they are made to feel unwanted in the normal social order. Eventually they begin to believe the label is accurate and begin to act to fit the label. 2

laws—rules of action to which people obligate themselves to conform. 1

learning disability—one or more significant deficits in the essential learning processes. 3

least restrictive means—a phrase referring to the use of dispositional alternatives for children. 9

lex talionis—a legal principle establishing the concept of retaliation, that is, an eye for an eye. 1

limited discretionary sentence—a degree of judicial discretion is removed, but a range of sentence lengths is still allowed. 10

lock down—high school students are detained in classrooms while police and dogs scour the campus, searching for contraband or any danger to a safe educational environment. 8

mala in se—acts considered immoral or wrong in themselves, such as murder and rape. 2

mala prohibita—acts prohibited because they infringe on others' rights, not because they are necessarily considered evil by nature, such as having more than one wife. 2

maltreatment—includes neglect, medical neglect, physical abuse, sexual abuse and psychological abuse. 4

mandatory sentence—fixes the sentence, eliminating any judicial discretion to suspend the sentence or grant probation. Also known as *nondiscretionary sentence*. 10

maximalist alarmist perspective—the view that the time has come to reject the reluctance of earlier generations to face the facts and to recognize the enormity of the developing crisis. Parents are abusing and neglecting their children in record numbers, and exploitive adolescents, pedophiles (child molesters) and other abusers are preying on youngsters with impunity. 4

mechanical jurisprudence—the view that everything is known and that, therefore, laws can be made in advance to cover every situation. 10

mechanical prevention—prevention efforts directed toward "target hardening" to make it difficult or impossible to commit particular offenses. 13

medical model—the view that offenders are victims of their environment and thus are curable. 1

minimalist skeptical perspective—the view that huge numbers of honestly mistaken and maliciously false allegations are mixed in with true disclosures, making the problem seem worse than it really is and fueling the impression that it is spiraling out of control. 4

minors—persons under the age of legal consent. 1

moniker—a name adopted by a gang member to be used in place of his or her given name. 8

mores—the critical norms vital to a society's safety and survival; often referred to as *natural law.* 2

National Council on Crime and Delinquency (NCCD)—a private national agency promoting efforts at crime control through research, citizen involvement and public information efforts. 13

natural law—the rules of conduct that are the same everywhere because they are basic to human behavior; also called *mores.* 2

neglect—a child is adjudged to be neglected if the child is abandoned, without proper care; without education or health care because of the refusal of a parent, guardian or custodian to provide them; in need of supervision as a result of the neglect. 4

net widening—diverting youths to other programs and agencies rather than away from the system. 1, 9

nondiscretionary sentence—fixes the sentence, eliminating any judicial discretion to suspend the sentence or grant probation; also called *mandatory sentence.* 10

nonjudicial disposition—a decision in a juvenile case by an authority other than a judge or court of law. This is usually an informal method that determines the most appropriate disposition in handling a juvenile. 9

nonresidential program—a program allowing youths to remain in their homes or foster homes while receiving services. 11

nonsecure facility—a facility that emphasizes the care and treatment of youths without the need to place constraints or be concerned about public protection. 11

Norman Rockwell family—a working father, a housewife mother and two children of school age (6 percent of U.S. households in the 1990s). 3

norms—rules or laws governing the actions and interactions of people, usually of two types: folkways and mores. 2

nuisance—a legal concept pertaining to the use of property and requiring landowners to use their property so as not to injure their neighbors' use of their properties; typically defined by local ordinance or state statute, the concept applies to physically damaging neighboring property, reducing its value or reducing its enjoyment. 14

numerator approach—the view that the focus of prevention efforts should be on those youths who are at greatest risk. 13

ombuds—a person whose role is to improve conditions of confinement for juveniles and protect the rights of youths in custody; responsibilities include monitoring conditions, servicing delivery systems, investigating complaints, reporting findings, proposing changes, advocating for improvements, accessing appropriate care, and helping to expose and reduce unlawful deficiencies in juvenile detention and correctional facilities. 11

one-pot approach—lumps children and youths who are abused and neglected, those who commit minor offenses and those who commit vicious, violent crimes into the same judicial "pot." 3

paradigm—a pattern, a way of looking at an entire concept or field. 8, 14

paraphilias—the sum of three variables: the presence of fetishism, transvestitism and promiscuity. 14

parens patriae—literally "parent of the country." The legal provision through which the state may assume ultimate parental responsibility for the custody, care and protection of children within its jurisdiction. The right of the government to take care of minors and others who cannot legally take care of themselves. 1

parental efficacy—examines how parental support and control are interrelated. 3

parole—supervised early release from institutionalization. 11

particular justice—that which is fair and equal. 2

permanency—with regard to treatments, the idea that they will endure. 14

person in need of supervision (PINS)—a youth usually characterized as ungovernable, incorrigible, truant or habitually disobedient. 1

petition—the formal process for bringing a matter before the juvenile court; a document alleging that a juvenile is a delinquent, status offender or dependent, and asking the court to assume jurisdiction; the same as a formal complaint in the adult criminal process. 7, 10

phrenology—studying the shape of the skull to predict intelligence and character. 2

physical abuse—the nonaccidental, or intentional, physical injury of a child caused by the child's caretaker. 4

physiognomy—judging character from physical features, especially facial features. 2

PINS—see *person in need of supervision.* 1

police-school liaison program—places law enforcement officers within schools to help prevent juvenile delinquency and improve community relations. 7

polydrug use—tobacco, alcohol and marijuana. 13

poor laws—established the appointment of overseers to indenture poor and neglected children into servitude. 1

positivist view of criminality—the belief that delinquents are victims of society. 2

positivist world view—the belief that humans are shaped by society and are the product of environmental and cultural influences. 2

predatory gang—commits violent crimes against persons, including robberies and street muggings;

members are likely to use hard drugs, which contribute to their volatile, aggressive behavior. 6

preliminary hearing—the initial conference that satisfies those matters that must be dealt with before a juvenile case can proceed further. At this first hearing, the judge informs the parties involved of the charges in the petition and of their rights during the proceeding. The hearing may also be used to determine whether an alleged delinquent should remain in detention or in the custody of juvenile authorities. 10

presumptive sentence—a form of limited discretionary sentences involving a degree of judicial discretion but still allowing a range of sentence lengths. 10

preventive detention—the confinement of youths who might pose a danger to themselves or to others or who might not appear at their trial. 1

primary deviance—the original act defined as deviant by others. 2

primary prevention—seeks to change conditions that cause crime. Also called *corrective prevention.* 13

probable cause—grounds that a reasonable and prudent person would believe an offense was committed and that the accused committed the crime. 10

probation—a sentence that entails the release of an individual into the community under the supervision of the court, subject to certain conditions for a specific time. Only the court can provide probation. 11

probation officer—a correctional officer under the principal direction of the court; in juvenile matters handles intake and presentence investigations for dispositional hearings and assists the court in determining the proper treatment and care for juveniles. 11

proof beyond a reasonable doubt—the standard of proof needed to convict in a criminal case; the amount of absolute certainty that the defendant committed the alleged offense (*In re Winship*). 10

protective factors—elements that reduce the impact of negative risk factors by providing positive ways for a person to respond to such risks. 13

psychopathic behavior—chronic asocial behavior rooted in severe deficiencies in the development of a conscience; virtually lacking in conscience; unable to distinguish right from wrong. 6

psychopaths—virtually lacking in conscience; do not know right from wrong. 6

public defender—a lawyer who works for the defense of indigent offenders and is reimbursed for services by a public agency. 9

pulling levers—a strategy involving arresting targeted gang members for the slightest infraction, even jaywalking. 8

punitive prevention—relies on the threat of punishment to forestall criminal acts. 13

radial concept—the view that growth and development do not occur in isolation but instead involve a complex interaction of family, school and community, with the family being the first and most vital influence. As children grow the school becomes a more important influence, and as youths approach adolescence, the influence of parents and teachers becomes less and that of peers more influential. All of this occurs within the broader community in which children live. 3

radical theory—the belief that crime is a product of the political economy that, in capitalist societies, encourages an individualistic competition among and between wealthy people and poor people, (the intra- and interclass struggle) and the practice of taking advantage of other people (exploitation). 2

Rave—an all-night party with loud techno music, dancing, drinking and doing drugs. 5

recidivism—repetition of criminal behavior; habitual criminality. 14

referee—a lawyer who serves part-time or full-time to handle simple, routine juvenile cases. 10

reform school—a juvenile facility designed to improve the conduct of those forcibly detained within. 11

rehabilitation—restoring to a condition of constructive activity. 10

relapse prevention—requires juveniles to learn to identify factors associated with an increased risk of sex offending and use strategies to avoid high-risk situations or effectively manage them when they occur. 14

representing—a manner of dressing that uses an imaginary line drawn vertically through the body and shows allegiance or opposition. 8

residential childcare facility—a dwelling other than a detention or shelter facility that provides care, treatment and maintenance for children. Such facilities include foster family homes, group homes and halfway houses. 11

resiliency—the ability to bounce back from adversity. 14

respite care—facility designed to give youths and their parents a temporary break from each other, followed by intensive counseling. 10

responsivity principle—the delivery of treatment programs in a manner consistent with the offender's ability and learning style. 11

restitution—making right; restoring property or a right to a person who has been unjustly deprived of it. 10

restorative justice—the view that justice involves not two, but four parties: offender and victim, government and community—all are injured by the crime. 2

retaliation—personal revenge; the accepted way to deal with members of the tribe who break the rules. 1

retributive justice—justice served by some sort of punishment for wrongdoing *(lex talionis)*. 2

reverse certification—when the criminal court has exclusive jurisdiction, the transfer of a case to the juvenile court. 9

risk factors—elements existing within the community, family, school and the individual that increase the probability a young person will exhibit certain adolescent problem behaviors, including violence. 13

risk principle—embodies the assumption that criminal behavior can be predicted for individual offenders on the basis of certain factors. 11

runaway—a youth who commits the status offense of leaving the custody and home of parents, guardians or custodians without permission and fails to return within a reasonable time. 4

scavenger gang—urban survivors who prey on the weak of the inner city; crimes are usually petty, senseless and spontaneous; has no particular goals, no purpose. 6

school resource officer (SRO)—a law enforcement officer assigned by the employing police department to a school. 3, 7

secondary deviance—an act that results because society has labeled the offender a deviant. 2

secondary prevention—focuses on changing the behavior of juveniles likely to become delinquent. Includes punitive prevention. 13

seesaw model—demonstrates the functional family, where stresses and resources are balanced, and the nonfunctional family, where stresses are greater than the resources to cope with them, resulting in an unbalanced family. 4

self-fulfilling prophecy—occurs when people live up to the labels they are given. 3

serious child delinquent—youth between the ages of 7 and 12 who has committed one or more homicide, aggravated assault, robbery, rape or serious arson. 6

Serious Habitual Offender Comprehensive Action Program (SHOCAP)—a federally funded program of the OJJDP that provides guidelines to various components of the juvenile justice system and the community in dealing with serious habitual offenders. 8

serious juvenile offender—a juvenile who has been convicted of a Part I offense as defined by the FBI Uniform Crime Reports, excluding auto theft or distribution of a controlled dangerous substance, and who was between 14 and 17 years of age at the time the offense was committed. 6

shelter—a nonsecure or unlocked place of care and custody for children awaiting court appearances and for those who have already been adjudicated and are awaiting disposition. 11

SHOCAP—see *Serious Habitual Offender Comprehensive Action Program.*

shock incarceration—a correctional facility stressing military discipline, physical fitness, strict obedience to orders and education and vocational training; designed for young, nonviolent, first-time offenders. Also called *boot camp.* 11

social contract—a philosophy that entails free, independent individuals agreeing to form a community and to give up a portion of their individual freedom to benefit the group's security. 2

social disorganization theory—states that urban areas produce delinquency directly by weakening community controls and generating a subculture of delinquency passed on from one generation to the next. 2

social ecology theory—states that ecological conditions predict delinquency and that gang membership is a normal response to social conditions. 2

social justice—providing an equal share of what is valued in a society to each member of that society, including power, prestige and status. Also called *distributive justice.* 2

socialized delinquency—youthful behavior that violates the expectations of society but conforms to the expectations of other youths. 6

sociopathic behavior—see *psychopathic behavior.* 6

SRO (school resource officer)—a law enforcement officer assigned by the employing police department or agency to a school. 3, 7

static risk factors—historical (for example, early onset of violence) or dispositional factors that are unlikely to change over time; in contrast to dynamic risk factors. 4

station adjustment—occurs when a juvenile offender is handled by the police within the department and released. 7

status offenders—juveniles who have committed a status offense; usually not placed in a correctional institution. 1

status offense—an offense by a juvenile that would not be a crime if committed by an adult, e.g., truancy, running away, curfew violation, incorrigibility or endangering health and morals. 1

strain theory—see *anomie theory.* 2

streaming—bands of juveniles race through store aisles, grab what they can and then tear out of the stores before they can be apprehended. 5

street gang—a group of individuals who meet over time, have identifiable leadership, claim control over a specific territory in the community and engage in criminal behavior. 6

street justice—a decision by police to deal with a status offense in their own way, usually by ignoring it. 7

summons—a legal document ordering a person to appear in court at a certain time on a certain date. 10

symbiosis—an ecological term describing the condition of two different organisms living together in a mutually beneficial relationship. 2

tagging—a form of visual vandalism whose dominant impression includes words, as compared to graffiti, which leaves only a hint of words; often added to existing graffiti. 8

take into custody—the physical apprehension by a police action of a child engaged in delinquency. See also *arrest.* 6

temporary custody without hearing—usually for 48 hours. 7

termination of parental rights—ending by the court, upon petition, of all rights to a minor by his or her parents. Parents may be judged incapable and their rights terminated because of the following: debauchery, use of drugs and alcohol, conviction of a felony, lewd or lascivious behavior or mental illness. 10

territorial gang—designates something, someplace or someone as belonging exclusively to the gang. 6

tertiary prevention—the third level of prevention, aimed at preventing recidivism; focuses on preventing further delinquent acts by youths already identified as delinquents. 13

therapeutic intervention—recommendation of an appropriate treatment program. 9

thrownaway—a child whose family has kicked him or her out. 3, 4

tort—a civil wrong against an individual or individuals for which the perpetrator is civilly liable. 14

training schools—correctional institutions for juveniles adjudicated delinquent by a judicial officer. 11

transfer hearing—a hearing to determine whether a juvenile alleged to be delinquent will be tried in juvenile court or waived to adult criminal court. The juvenile usually must be 16 or older to be considered for the waiver or transfer to adult court. 9

turf—the area claimed by a gang. 6

Uniform Crime Report (UCR)—the FBI's annual statistical summary titled *Crime in the United States.* 5

universal justice—that which is lawful. 2

veiled threat—strongly implies but does not explicitly threaten violence; for example, "We would be better off if this school were destroyed." 8

venue—the geographic location of a trial, established by constitutional or statutory provisions. 9

vertical prosecution—one assistant prosecutor or small group of assistant prosecutors handling one criminal complaint from start to finish through the entire court process; in contrast to horizontal prosecution. 8

vicarious strain—stress experienced by others around an individual experiencing stress. 4

violent juvenile offender—a youth who has been convicted of a violent Part I offense, one against a person rather than property, and who has a prior adjudication of such an offense; a youth convicted of murder. 6

waiver—a procedure whereby juvenile court waives jurisdiction and transfers the case to the adult criminal court. Also called *certification.* 9

window of opportunity—a time when treatment is especially needed (in crimes) or likely to make a difference (during transition periods). 7

youth gang—a self-formed association of youths distinguished from other types of youth groups by their routine participation in illegal activities. 6

youth service bureau—a neighborhood youth service agency that coordinates all community services for young people, especially designed for the predelinquent or early delinquent. 1

youthful offenders—persons adjudicated in a criminal court who may be above the statutory age limit for juveniles but below a specified upper age limit for special correctional commitment. 1

zero-tolerance policies—mandate predetermined consequences or punishments for specific choices and have become a popular disciplinary choice. 3

Index

Credits

This page constitutes an extension of the copyright page. We have made every effort to trace the ownership of all copyrighted material and to secure permission from copyright holders. In the event of any question arising as to the use of any material, we will be pleased to make the necessary corrections in future printings. Thanks are due to the following authors, publishers, and agents for permission to use the material indicated.

Chapter 1. 5: © Stock Montage **10:** © 1995 Stock Montage **12:** The Bettmann Archive/CORBIS **19:** Courtesy of The Colorado Historical Society

Chapter 2. 47: © 1997 North Wind Pictures **54:** © Stephen Shames/Polaris **67:** © Eugene Richards/ Magnum Photos Inc.

Chapter 3. 79: © Michael Weisbrot/Stock Boston **88:** © Jose Luis Pelaez, Inc./Corbis **93:** © Ariel Skelley/CORBIS

Chapter 4. 115: © Joel Gordon/Joel Gordon Photography **121:** © Reuters News Media Inc./CORBIS **130:** © David Woods/CORBIS

Chapter 5. 144: © Cleo Photography/PhotoEdit **153:** © Farnsworth/The Image Works **155:** © Michael Kagan

Chapter 6. 177: © Shawn Thew/Polaris Images **193:** © Katherine McGlynn

Chapter 7. 218: © David Young-Wolff/PhotoEdit **219:** © David Woo/Stock Boston **232:** © Joel Gordon/ Joel Gordon Photography **237:** © Tom Carter/ PhotoEdit

Chapter 8. 256: © 1996 George White Jr. **271:** © Joel Gordon **273:** © Sven Martson/ The Image Works

Chapter 9. 304: © James L. Shaffer

Chapter 10. 339: © Bob Daemmrich/Stock Boston **340:** © Bob Daemmrich/Stock Boston

Chapter 11. 381: © AP/Wide World Photos **382:** © Joel Gordon **385:** © Joel Stettenheim/CORBIS **389:** © AP/Wide World Photos

Chapter 12. 414: © Jim West **438:** © Phil McCarten **439:** © Tony Freeman/PhotoEdit

Chapter 13. 458: © Gale Zucker/Stock Boston **459:** © AP/Wide World Photos **491:** © AP/Wide World Photo

Chapter 14. 500: © Gale Zucker/ Stock Boston **513:** © Mikael Karlsson/Arresting Images **515:** © AP/Wide World Photos